**BISHOP GROSSETESTE
COLLEGE, LINCOLN**

MUE

FAY, C. R.

Great Britain from
Adam Smith to the
resent day 2110

D1436686

BISHOP GROSSETESTE COLLEGE

30101   011520301

GREAT BRITAIN
FROM ADAM SMITH
TO THE PRESENT DAY
AN ECONOMIC AND SOCIAL
SURVEY

GREAT BRITAIN FROM ADAM SMITH TO THE PRESENT DAY

AN ECONOMIC AND SOCIAL SURVEY

BY

C. R. FAY

READER IN ECONOMIC HISTORY AT THE UNIVERSITY OF
CAMBRIDGE, LATE PROFESSOR OF ECONOMIC HISTORY
AT THE UNIVERSITY OF TORONTO

' England cannot afford to be little. She must
be what she is, or nothing.' — HUSKISSON,
Speech on the Civil Government of Canada,
May 2, 1828 (*Speeches*, III. 287)

LONGMANS, GREEN AND CO.
LONDON ◆ NEW YORK ◆ TORONTO

LONGMANS, GREEN AND CO. LTD.
6 & 7 CLIFFORD STREET, LONDON, W.I
NICOL ROAD, BOMBAY I
17 CHITTARANJAN AVENUE, CALCUTTA 13
36A MOUNT ROAD, MADRAS 2

LONGMANS, GREEN AND CO. INC.
55 FIFTH AVENUE, NEW YORK 3

LONGMANS, GREEN AND CO.
215 VICTORIA STREET, TORONTO I

WITHDRAWN

MUE

BISHOP GROSSETESTE COLLEGE
SIBTHORP
LIBRARY
2110
LINCOLN

First Edition	. .	*May 1928*
Second Edition	.	*August 1929*
Third Edition	.	*November 1932*
New Impression	.	*December 1935*
Fourth Edition	.	*September 1937*
New Impression	. .	*April 1940*
New Impression	.	*February 1943*
New Impression	.	*February 1944*
New Impression	.	*December 1944*
New Impression	.	*October 1945*
New Impression	.	*July 1946*
New Impression	. .	*May 1947*
New Impression	. .	*February 1948*

Printed in England
SPOTTISWOODE, BALLANTYNE & CO. LTD.
London & Colchester

TO
MY FRIEND
MRS. ALFRED MARSHALL

PREFACE

I THANK my old Cambridge friend, F. W. Lawe, for the chart and statistical argument on pages 396–400. For assistance in the preparation of this book for the press I am indebted to colleagues at the University of Toronto as well as to friends in what I now call the Old Country, though I think of it still as did the young Virginian. I first learned to respect Canadians in a country that to them and me was overseas ; and six years of university life in Canada have enlarged that respect into affectionate regard. If I have an economic ambition it is that by my writings I shall cause Canada and Great Britain to know each other more intimately. May the sure growth of Canada never obstruct, but on the contrary promote, the welfare of the Motherland from which so many of her sons have come. And furthermore, may Great Britain, through Canada, see steadfastly the essential friendliness of the U.S.A. towards the rest of the English-speaking world.

I owe the Index to my colleague in Economic History, H. A. Innis. The Introduction has already appeared as a Bicentenary Appreciation in Volume III. of the *Dalhousie Review*. As for myself, I am Lancashire-born. My grandfather, as a boy, was employed on the construction of the first coaches used on the Liverpool and Manchester Railway, and later invented the through chain brake in the service of the Lancashire and Yorkshire Railway. Some will say that my pride in the North amounts to an obsession ; and certainly to me there is no place in the world so beautiful as the English Lakes. That industrial Lancashire is unsightly I know full well, but it is precisely when I have been in Dorsetshire, walking the Wessex country with a novel of Hardy in my pocket, that I have felt a great longing to explain and rejoice in the county of my birth. Progress comes by specialisation. Here are docks, mills and mines : there, two hours away, are Coniston and the Furness Fells, and these too are in Lancashire. But how can I enjoy them unless I believe, and try to show, that the throbbing life of industrialism will yet win through to happiness and beauty ?

C. R. F.

TORONTO : *Jan.* 1928.

vii

CONTENTS

INTRODUCTION

PART I

FISCAL POLICY AND FINANCE

PART III

AGRICULTURE AND INDUSTRY

PART IV

LIFE AND LABOUR

MAPS

INTRODUCTION
THE WEALTH OF NATIONS

INTRODUCTION

The Wealth of Nations

1. *Adam Smith and his Environment*

In the year 1776, the darkest year in the annals of the British Empire, one of the world's great books was published. Its author was Adam Smith (born on June 5, 1723) and its title *An Inquiry into the Nature and Causes of the Wealth of Nations*.[1] The writer was a Scotsman, with the national sense and original humour of Scotland at its best. This Scotsman was in policy a liberal imperialist. Because he hated tyranny and was disgusted by shams, he was eager to see ' the project of an empire ' (for as he saw it, it was nothing more) converted into a reality so free that it would endure. This imperialist was a man of cosmopolitan vision ; and his appreciation of differences in national characteristics did not shake his faith in the universal application of those economic principles which would, he argued, benefit the nation that practised them not less than the world at large.

The age, the country, and the experience of the writer were alike favourable to the creation of an economic masterpiece conceived in this mood.

The age was favourable, for the spirit of a new freedom was already in the air. In religion men were turning from the rigid gloom of Calvinism to the light of nature by which the Deity of the 18th century was rationalised and reduced to benevolence. The mediæval conception of an essential clash between private interest and public policy was all but dead. At every turn local regulations were collapsing before nation-wide enterprise, and the economics of Elizabethan England were remembered chiefly for their irritating survivals. Even as Adam Smith wrote, Britain was crossing the threshold of the Industrial Revolution, and Glasgow, Adam Smith's University, assisted the crossing by providing James Watt with a sanctuary where he could experiment in peace upon his steam-engine. In the text of the *Wealth of Nations* there is a reference to fire engines in which ' boy ' is comically confused with ' buoy ' (I. 11), but the word ' steam ' does not occur. The division of labour

---

[1] All references are to the edition by Edwin Cannan. Methuen, 1904, 2 vols.

which Adam Smith observed in pin factories (I. 6) and elsewhere was still a division of hand-processes. But his analysis is altogether on the line of modern development, for the reason that the revolution in mechanical technique was preceded by changes of a commercial and financial order with which he was fully conversant. Indeed his constant emphasis on the cost of bringing a commodity to market puts him closer to us of the 20th century than are his successors, who, dominated by the marvels of factory production, studied too little the economics of marketing and transport.

The country, too, was favourable. The Scotland of 1750, like the Canada of to-day, was a country in the making, poor by comparison with its neighbour to the south, but growing and conscious of growth. As we read the subtle pages of the Third Book, in which Smith sketches out a dynamics of society with his eye on the centuries and on all the continents, we can feel him to be aware that *his* society is not ' one that is standing still,' and that *his* country at any rate had not yet received its ' full complement of riches.' Though Scotland was still ' much poorer' than England, it was ' evidently advancing ' (I. 92). For the Act of Union had brought opportunities and markets. No longer did the Lowlands produce ' scarce anything but some miserable pasture, just sufficient to keep alive a few straggling, half-starved cattle ' (I. 220). But in the biggest things of life, in church and school and university, Scotland—as Adam Smith could fairly claim—was richer than England. His master, the ' never to be forgotten Hutcheson,' had lectured to him and his fellow students at Glasgow in the mother tongue, and had held them spellbound. But ' in the university of Oxford the greater part of the public professors have for these many years, given up altogether even the pretence of teaching ' (II. 251).[1]

Equally favourable was the experience of the man. He studied widely before he taught, and he taught and travelled before he wrote. Born at Kirkcaldy, a small town on the north side of the Firth of Forth, he attended as a lad its excellent Burgh School. Thence he proceeded to Glasgow University, and from Glasgow with a Snell Exhibition to Balliol College, Oxford, where he taught himself much in its rich college library, residing continuously for six years 1740–6, term time and vacation. Returning to a lectureship in Edinburgh, he removed to Glasgow

---

[1] Note, however, that in 1758 the great Blackstone became first Professor of English law at Oxford, to deliver ' those bravura passages . . . which Blackstone so brilliantly executed before crowded and admiring audiences ' (F. W Maitland, *Collected Papers*, II. 162).

to become Professor of Logic in 1751, and of Moral Philosophy in 1752, published in 1759 his *Theory of Moral Sentiments*, and delivered for a number of years lectures on ' Justice, Police, Revenue and Arms,' a copy of which as taken down by a student has by rare good fortune come down to us (edited by Edwin Cannan, 1896). In 1763 he left at such short notice that he felt it incumbent upon him to return the lecture fees. The pupils were loth, but the professor insisted. ' You must not refuse me this satisfaction ; nay by heavens, gentlemen, you shall not,' he said ; and seizing by the coat the young man who stood next to him, he thrust the money into his pocket and then pushed him away.

The occasion of his going was the offer of a travelling tutor-ship to the young Duke of Buccleuch. He gained thereby an increase of income, and that which his catholic soul craved far more, the illuminating experiences of the Grand Tour—a visit to the great Voltaire at Geneva, conversations at Paris with Turgot the financier, the Abbé Morellet, Quesnay, that ' very in-genious and profound author ' (II. 171) of the *Tableau Economique* —a copy of the jigsaw puzzle which goes by this name is repro-duced in Cannan's edition of the *Wealth of Nations*, Editor's Introduction, xxxii—and others of the Physiocratic School. On this tour he began his great book ' in order to while away the time,' and returning from the Continent in 1766, he worked at his manuscript for the next ten years. Standing to dictate it with his back to the fireplace in his study at Kirkcaldy, he would rub his head on the wall above, to which there adhered for many years to come this greasy proof of the absent-minded agony of authorship (John Rae, *Life of Adam Smith*, p. 260). The book was instantly acclaimed by the public, and ran through five editions before his death in 1790.[1] It has been given to few men to achieve a world reputation by a single book, and to fewer still to prepare that work with such deliberation that, though it breaks much new theoretical ground and is intimately concerned with current policy, the author with a few strengthening addi-tions is saying in the last edition essentially what he said in the first.

Adam Smith is the father of political economy. There is indeed a long roll of economic literature before his time, but where it was not Utopian or statistical, it was partial and unsystematised, and usually little more than a party pamphlet for or against a particular economic policy. A great part of it was occupied with the Doctrine of a Favourable Balance of Trade. This doctrine,

---

[1] He was buried in the churchyard of Canongate Parish Church, Edinburgh The headstone touches the wall of the Tolbooth of the Burgh of Canongate.

together with the policy known as the Mercantile System which it was employed to prop up, was ruthlessly attacked by Adam Smith, and the attack supplies the driving force of the *Wealth of Nations*. But the book is more than a polemic. For in smashing a policy he founded a science. He was the first to analyse in a comprehensive fashion the play of economic motive and the interaction of economic forces as these were actually at work in society. As Cunningham well says, ' Adam Smith's great achievement lay in isolating the conception of national wealth, while previous writers had treated it in conscious subordination to the idea of national power. By isolating wealth as a subject he introduced an immense simplification.' [1] That simplification had its dangers, but it is significant that the man who introduced it was also a philosopher and an historian.

2. *His Debt to Others*

Adam Smith did not evolve his theories out of an inner consciousness, or support them by imaginary examples. He made the thoughts and records of others his own, and used them to his purpose. But three British writers exercised a decisive influence on him—his master, Francis Hutcheson ; Dr. Mandeville ; and David Hume. From Hutcheson he got his philosophy and his first introduction to economics. Mandeville's *Fable of the Bees* (1714) encouraged his own inclination to satire. With David Hume, his life-long friend, he shared the give and take of intellectual friendship. If priority of publication is to decide, then it was Hume's Essay on the Balance of Trade in 1752 which first exposed the essential fallacies in the balance of trade argument ; as similarly there are anticipations of Hume's conclusions in the writings of Sir William Petty, Sir Dudley North, and John Locke. But this is priority only in the sense in which all knowledge is a restatement of what has gone before.

The nature of Adam Smith's indebtedness to French writers has been greatly misunderstood. It is a matter of history that after being a Professor of Moral Philosophy in Scotland he went to France, and returned to write the *Wealth of Nations*. Hence it has been argued that he left Scotland an idealist and after three years of contact with the French economists returned a materialist. Less grotesque, but nevertheless misleading, is the view of William Pitt's biographer : ' It was by residence in France and contact with the economists, Quesnay and Turgot, that Adam Smith was able to formulate the ideas soon to be embodied

---

[1] ' Progress of Economic Doctrine in the 18th Century,' W. Cunningham, *Economic Journal*, Vol. I. 1891, p. 86.

in the *Wealth of Nations*. . . . The more nimble-witted people gave to its trading rivals the fiscal principles (neglected at home) which furthered the expansion of its commerce.'[1]

The discovery of the Lectures, which were compiled before ever he set foot in France, took the bottom out of these and similar insinuations. What a man can say in his lectures is enormously less than what he will write in a book, and what a student can take down in notes is also very much less than the whole. Nevertheless, the scheme and leading notions of the lecture course are those of the *Wealth of Nations*. There are indeed important additions. One of them, the lengthy and famous chapter on Colonies (Book IV. chap. vii.), was inspired by the imminence of the American crisis ; for through his friend Benjamin Franklin, to whom, it is said, he read chapters in manuscript, he had intimate access to current opinion and events in the colonies. Other additions are not less clearly due to his contact with France, for example the account of the Agricultural Systems of Political Economy (Book IV. chap. ix.) ; the distinction between Productive and Unproductive Labour (Book II. chap. iii.), which, even as qualified by Adam Smith, is untenable ; and above all the conception of an annual produce and its division into Wages of Labour, Profits of Stock, and Rent of Land—an addition which, though not essential to the scheme of the work, was of fundamental importance to subsequent economics, settling the form of economic treatises for a century at least. (Cf. *Wealth of Nations*, Editor's Introduction, xxx.) If we pushed back to those who in their turn influenced the French economists of Adam Smith's acquaintance, we should reach among others a compatriot of his, Richard Cantillon, whose essay on the ' Nature of Commerce at Large,' written 1730-4 and first published in 1755, was pronounced by Stanley Jevons to be the first systematic treatise of political economy. Cantillon was a banker in Paris at the time of John Law and paper money, and he found in land a standard of value less mutable than the money which within a short space he had seen cried up and down, inflated, depreciated, privileged and proscribed. The elder Mirabeau possessed himself of Cantillon's manuscript and borrowed from it. It was at Mirabeau's house that Adam Smith listened to the French economists and filled out his conception of an economic system, probably little dreaming that but for his compatriot those gatherings might never have been held. The ultimate problem, however, for the historian is not the interplay of mind on mind, but the impress of events on human thought ; the determination of individual priority in opinion is always less

[1] J. H. Rose, *William Pitt and National Revival* (1911), p. 323.

important than the analysis of the soil in which the body of opinion grows. But if priority is being argued, let us not part lightly from the verdict of one who was to Adam Smith what McCulloch was to Ricardo :—' The leading opinions, which the French Economists embodied and systematized, were, in fact, all of British origin.' [1]

3. *Characteristics of the Book*

It is rash to dissect a work of genius. Nevertheless, at the risk of coming miserably short, we shall try to say why the *Wealth of Nations* has made an appeal so universal and abiding.

First of all, it has an inspiring philosophy. The note of liberty rumbles through the book, and the author keeps at hand a standard thunder for denouncing particular violations of it,— ' Evident violation of natural liberty and justice.' Now it is the Statute of Apprentices (I. 123) which causes the thunder to be launched, now the English Law of Settlement of the Poor (I. 142). Now it is a regulation so prosaic as the restriction of private note issue (I. 307), and now a high concern of empire— ' To prohibit a great people, however, from making all that they can of every part of their own produce, or from employing their stock and industry in the way that they judge most advantageous to themselves, is a manifest violation of the most sacred rights of mankind ' (II. 83). He hates, as heartily as Doctor Johnson, ' the odious visits and examination of the tax-gatherers ' (II. 421) ; and, himself in his closing years a Commissioner of Customs, he has a sly sympathy for the smuggler, ' a person who, though no doubt highly blameable for violating the laws of his country, is frequently incapable of violating those of natural justice, and would have been, in every respect, an excellent citizen, had not the laws of his country made that a crime which nature never meant to be so ' (II. 381). Adam Smith denounced ' the impertinent badges of slavery ' imposed by the mother country on the American colonies, and would perhaps have applied the moral of the smuggler to that new prohibition which the American people have seen fit to impose upon themselves.

Secondly, his fellow-feeling makes him see both sides. The balance of his sentences, which lingers so in the reader's mind, accords with the superb balance of his thought. No man had stronger views than he ; yet few men have been fairer. In his strength he could afford it. Thus the declamation against restraint of private note issue concludes, ' Such regulations may,

---

[1] Dugald Stewart (1753–1828), *Life and Writings of Adam Smith,* Collected Works, X. 97.

no doubt, be considered as in some respect a violation of natural liberty. But those exertions of the natural liberty of a few individuals, which might endanger the security of the whole society, are, and ought to be, restrained by the laws of all governments ; of the most free as well as of the most despotical ' (I. 307).

The *Wealth of Nations* opens with a statement of the advantages obtained from the division of labour ; and it is only within the last decade that economists and psychologists have joined forces to study its human disadvantages. But they might well take as their text the following passage from Book V. :

The man whose whole life is spent in performing a few simple operations, of which the effects too are, perhaps, always the same, or very nearly the same, has no occasion to exert his understanding, or to exercise his invention in finding out expedients for removing difficulties which never occur. He naturally loses, therefore, the habit of such exertion and generally becomes as stupid and ignorant as it is possible for a human creature to become. . . . Of the great and extensive interests of his country he is altogether incapable of judging ; and unless very particular pains have been taken to render him otherwise, he is equally incapable of defending his country in war (II. 267).

The passage occurs in the chapter on ' Education,' because these results would occur unless by education they were prevented. Therefore he would have schools for the young and old supported by the State.

In some countries of the New World the conflict of economic interests between town and country is the leading political issue, and the peasants of Russia within recent years have shown the passive but deadly revenge which the grower of produce can take on the townsman who does him violence. Adam Smith did justice to both. He saw that while agriculture was always the most essential industry, yet commerce had been, as a matter of history, the stimulus to agricultural improvement. ' It is thus that through the greater part of Europe the commerce and manufactures of cities, instead of being the effect, have been the cause and occasion of the improvement and cultivation of the country ' (I. 390). Admiring the country gentleman and farmer, ' to their great honour, of all people the least subject to the wretched spirit of monopoly ' (I. 426), he nevertheless found in the merchant turned farmer ' the best of all improvers ' (I. 382) ; and he reminded both that ' landlords, like all other men, love to reap where they never sowed ' (I. 51).

In Adam Smith's day the struggle between capital and labour was young. To combination he was naturally averse, as abridging the scope for individual initiative, and at a later date he would probably have shared with Francis Place, the Westminster tailor, the hope that with education and the removal of persecution the desire of the working classes for combination would disappear. But he was as tolerant as Nassau Senior 65 years later was savage. 'We believe that if the manufacturer is to employ his capital only under the dictation of his short-sighted and rapacious workmen, we shall not retain the industry, the skill, or the capital on which our manufacturing superiority, and with that superiority our power and almost our existence, depends.' [1] So wrote Senior and his colleagues concerning the feeble combinations of starving weavers. Contrast with this the language of the *Wealth of Nations* :

We rarely hear, it has been said, of the combinations of masters ; though frequently of those of workmen. But whoever imagines, upon this account, that masters rarely combine, is as ignorant of the world as of the subject. Masters are always and everywhere in a sort of tacit, but constant and uniform combination, not to raise the wages of labour above their actual rate (I. 68).

Both men love liberty, but one is neutral and the other is partisan. Writing twenty-four years before the prohibiting Act of 1800, Adam Smith supplied in advance the most telling argument for its repeal—its inevitable one-sidedness. Writing sixteen years after the enfranchising legislation of 1824–5, Nassau Senior had learnt nothing, and had not even remembered his Adam Smith. 'They are desperate, and act with the folly and extravagance of desperate men' (I. 69).

Thirdly, he blends history and theory with delicate skill. In what may be considered the artistic climax of the whole work, namely the famous set-piece attack on the Mercantile System, history is his most powerful weapon. Book IV is an historical bombardment, a history of tariffs and bounties and monopolies, concentrated for the delivery of a smashing blow at the economic policy behind which they were entrenched. Two ways of attack were open to him : he might attack mercantilism either as a doctrine or as a policy, and in the end he did both. The first was the more illuminating from the standpoint of theory, because it allowed him to set forth the function of money in the commerce of nations :

To attempt to increase the wealth of any country, either by introducing or by detaining in it an unnecessary quantity of gold and silver, is as absurd as it would be to attempt to increase the good cheer of private families by obliging them to keep an unnecessary number of kitchen utensils (I. 406).

[1] *Final Report of the Handloom Weavers Commission*, 1841, p. 117.

But the second line of attack was more fundamental. For when he wrote, few people of any account could have believed that wealth consisted in money and money alone ; and in earlier times, when ready money was scarce, there was a very real justification for the desire to procure the precious metals, as the Jews in many countries of Europe proved to their profit. And Adam Smith seems to have felt this ; for in the ' Conclusion of the Mercantile System,' which first appears in the third edition, he does not revert to the doctrine of the trade balance, but concentrates upon a critical examination of the fiscal devices which, with the ostensible object of enriching the country, had sacrificed the interests of the consumer to those of the manufacturer and merchant.

Essentially fertile, he always gave to his criticism a constructive turn. He set out the case for free trade with a moderation which strengthened the chances of its adoption. Tariff retaliation might be good policy, as policy was understood by ' that insidious and crafty animal, vulgarly called a statesman or politician ' (I. 432), but ' it seems a bad method of compensating the injury done to certain classes of our people, to do another injury ourselves, not only to those classes, but to almost all the other classes of them ' (I. 433). It might be desirable to introduce freedom of trade ' only by slow gradations, and with a good deal of reserve and circumspection ' (I. 433), but—for reasons which he gives in detail —the disorders occasioned by its sudden introduction would prob- ably be less than was commonly imagined. But Adam Smith's vision reached beyond the coast line of Great Britain. There were things more important than national opulence, and one of these was the settlement of the trouble with America. He pleaded with passion for an imperial union and representation of the colonies in the British parliament : ' That this union could be easily effectuated, or that difficulties and great difficulties might not occur in the execution, I do not pretend. I have yet heard of none, however, which appear insurmountable ' (II. 124). In the closing words of the last book, after he has discoursed on religious instruction and the education of youth and has examined with a technique that is startlingly modern the theoretical incid- ence of actual taxes, he recurs again to the imperial burden : ' either carry it worthily or drop it ' is the substance of his charge. And if an England that was accustomed to dream of fortunes beyond imagination in the South Seas and to celebrate victories almost every month in the year, could by no other means be stung into doing the right thing, surely she would pause before the bleak alternative, which was ' to accommodate her future views and designs to the real mediocrity of her circumstances '

(II. 433) : ' I am a slow, a very slow workman,' he wrote to his publisher Cadell [1]—but he knew how to finish the course.

Fourthly, his mind is a storehouse of information gathered from reading, conversation, and travel. Quotations from the classics jostle by the side of strange customs reported by travellers and of homely details observed by himself. He quotes, as his editor observes, ' by their own name or that of their authors, almost one hundred books. . . . Usually but little, sometimes only a single fact, phrase or opinion is taken from each, so that few authors are less open than Adam Smith to the reproach of having rifled another man's work.' [2] He must have possessed a prodigious memory, which enabled him to deposit a thousand curiosities in the appropriate mental pigeon-holes, and to take each one out years afterwards exactly at the point at which the argument demanded it. Indeed, one may always say of the *Wealth of Nations* two things—there is hardly any remark which may not occur in it ; and no remark, when it does occur, is irrelevant.

In 1776 Arkwright had only just patented his rollers, and so we hear nothing about Lancashire's cotton industry. But between the diet of the north and that of the south there were then well-established differences :

In some parts of Lancashire it is pretended, I have been told, that bread of oatmeal is a heartier food for labouring people than wheaten bread, and I have frequently heard the same doctrine held in Scotland. I am, however, somewhat doubtful of the truth of it. The common people in Scotland, who are fed with oatmeal, are in general neither so strong nor so handsome as the same rank of people in England, who are fed with wheaten bread (I. 161).

Surely a solitary instance of such a confession in the annals of Scottish literature ! And who but Adam Smith could add this ?

But it seems to be otherwise with potatoes. The chairmen, porters, and coal heavers in London, and those unfortunate women who live by prostitution, the strongest men and the most beautiful women perhaps in the British dominions, are said to be, the greater part of them, from the lowest rank of people in Ireland, who are generally fed with this root (I. 161–2).

And similarly a score and more of towns or districts are mentioned, each with its particular incident,—Manchester, Birmingham and Wolverhampton, whose manufactures were outside the Statute of Apprentices, ' not having been exercised in England before the 5th of Elizabeth ' (I. 123) ; Newcastle, whose coal trade with the metropolis employed ' more shipping than all

---

[1] From ' An unpublished letter of Adam Smith,' *Economic Journal*, Sept. 1923. p. 427.
[2] Editor's Introduction to *Wealth of Nations*, p. xlvii.

the carrying trade of England' (I. 351) ; a certain village of Scotland 'where it is not uncommon, I am told, for a workman to carry nails instead of money to the baker's shop or the ale house' (I. 25) ; Edinburgh, which—being situated on the sea-board—found it cheaper to import its timber, so that 'in the New Town of Edinburgh, built within these few years, there is not, perhaps, a single stick of Scotch timber' (I. 167) ; Glasgow, whose trade had doubled in about fifteen years after the erection of the first banks (I. 280) ; the Highlands, where 'a half-starved Highland woman frequently bears more than twenty children' (I. 81)—and so on. His keen eye to local and professional differences makes the sections on wages and working class con-ditions (in which many of these allusions occur) one of the strongest parts of his work. Studying the labourer in different conditions and different trades, he saw that while there was a fundamental connection between the price of labour and the price of subsist-ence, wages were nevertheless in many cases above the level of subsistence. 'The liberal reward of labour, therefore, as it is the necessary effect, so it is the natural symptom of increasing national wealth. . . . There are many plain symptoms that the wages of labour are nowhere in this country regulated by this lowest rate which is consistent with common humanity' (I. 75). This practical knowledge saved him from the crudities of an Iron Law of Wages.

Fifthly, he has a perfect style—nervous, racy and finished In him truly the style is the man. His is the pen of one who has weighed realities and read the balance. He illumines with humour, and when he is minded he can pungently chastise. And over all rides an air of philosophic calm as he contemplates the vanities of men, 'their absurd presumption in their own good fortune' (I. 109), their overweening conceit in their own abilities ; but that which most of all compels the reader is his power of supplying an arresting phrase which once remarked is never forgotten. With a single metaphor he can laugh a heresy out of court. With a simile he can make dry bones live.

4. Defects

There are, however, two respects in which the book is open to definite criticism.

First of all, on the historical side. Adam Smith is not always impartial. His denunciations of the East India Company are more frequent than proofs of their wickedness. He says in his First Book, 'The difference between the genius of the British Constitu-tion which protects and governs North America, and that of the

mercantile company which oppresses and domineers in the East
Indies, cannot perhaps be better illustrated than by the different
state of those countries' (I. 75). Later on, indeed, he makes
amends for his commendation by exposing the evil nature of that
genius, as it was manifested in the old colonial policy ; but his
silence upon the honourable service rendered by the directors and
officials of 'John Company' to the cause of empire is, to say the
least, unhandsome. The joint stock company was associated so
closely in his mind with a repressive monopoly that he underrated the part that joint stock enterprise had played in the
development of British industry and commerce. He condemned
the slackness of joint stock management, but as the learned author
of the *History of Joint Stock Companies* [1] is able to prove by
chapter and verse, the directors' policy was often marked by
enterprise, public spirit and devotion to their company's service.
Adam Smith pronounced them fit only for routine ; but as
again the same critic shows, the ability to handle risks
was often their strongest feature, and they succeeded in
foreign trade in an age when foreign trade was literally a
venture, in banking when banking was full of surprises, and in
insurance before its operations were reduced to a science. It is a
lame excuse to say that he knew much more than he said, for in
that case he must have drawn very unequally on his stock of
knowledge. Rather we must plead that if he had been confronted
with the fruits of modern research he might have seen and
corrected his bias.

Secondly, on the philosophical side. At times he came peril-
ously close to an anti-social exaltation of self-interest :

The natural effort of every individual to better his own conditions,
when suffered to exert itself with freedom and security, is so powerful
a principle, that it is alone, and without any assistance, not only
capable of carrying on the society to wealth and prosperity, but of
surmounting a hundred impertinent obstructions with which the folly
of human laws too often encumbers its operations (II. 43). . . .

By directing that industry in such a manner as its produce may be
of the greater value, he intends only his own gain, and he is in this,
as in many other cases, led by an invisible hand to promote an end
which was no part of his intention (I. 421).

Adam Smith had certainly a powerful principle to enunciate
—the automatic regulation of industry by reference to market
price. Fiscal regulation cramped enterprise and brought evil
consequences which were no part of the national intention, as
patently in his day as war-time price control did in our own ;
and if we confine these passages to their context, their limitation

[1] W. R. Scott, *Joint Stock Companies to 1720*, I. 448 *sqq.*

makes them socially innocuous.   In the one he is exposing the
ineptitudes of the corn bounty : in the other he is exalting
individual enterprise above paternalism and trading companies
privileged by law.   Similarly when the entry in the index (his
own index) ' self-love, the governing principle in the intercourse
of human society ' is referred to the text, all we find is the following : ' It is not from the benevolence of the butcher, the brewer,
or the baker, that we expect our dinner, but from their regard
to their own interest.   We address ourselves not to their humanity
but to their self-love, and never talk to them of our own necessities,
but of their advantages.   Nobody but a beggar chuses to depend
chiefly upon the benevolence of his fellow-citizens ' (I. 16).   This
is hardly more than saying ' Business is business, and must not
be confounded with charity.'

But ' the powerful principle of self-love,' when used to define
social responsibilities, had results which were wholly evil.   Adam
Smith's phrase about ' the invisible hand ' was remembered and
repeated.   In Richard Whately, Archbishop of Dublin, writing in
the middle of the 19th century, it took the form that ' through the
wise and beneficent arrangement of Providence men thus do the
greatest service to the public when they are thinking of nothing
but their own gain.'   But these were days of social stress, when
the industrial machine had run amuck and was doing havoc
among the weaker members of society.   In the name of the
father of political economy, employers and would-be economists
were then denouncing extensions of the Factory Acts, the planning
of towns, and the enforcement of a minimum of sanitation and
safety.

5. *Influence on Economic Policy*

The influence of the *Wealth of Nations* on fiscal policy is difficult to handle only because we are tempted herein to anticipate
the whole story of free trade from 1776 to the close of the 19th
century.   But let us observe, first, that the influence of Adam
Smith was continental.   Through the medium of Mollien he
became the financial guide of Napoleon.   He had put his finger
on the weak spots of French finance before the Revolution,
remarking that the system of taxation yielded ' not the half of
what might have been expected had the people contributed in
the same proportion to their numbers as the people of Great
Britain ' (II. 390), and his recommendations—the substitution
of a heavier land tax for the old *taille* and capitation, uniform
duties throughout the kingdom, and the abolition of the wasteful
plan of farming out the revenue—were adopted by Napoleon
and his successors.   In Germany the doctrines of Adam Smith

were accepted and preached by Stein and Hardenberg ; and the German Zollverein of 1834 secured to those within its boundaries a greater measure of free trade than they had enjoyed before.

In England, William Pitt was Adam Smith's first and greatest disciple, and after the master's death Pitt in his budget speech of 1792 paid tribute to ' the writings of an author of our times, now unfortunately no more (I mean the author of a celebrated treatise on the Wealth of Nations), whose extensive knowledge of detail and philosophical research will, I believe, furnish the best solution to every question connected with the history of commerce or with the systems of political economy.' Adam Smith died in 1790, on the morrow of the Revolution which ushered in the age of European war. But after 1783 there was peace in North America, and therefore between 1783 and 1789 there were years of peace in Europe and America, during which the precepts of the book might be tried in foreign relations.

In 1779 he was consulted by Dundas on the Irish question. Ireland was then in a sorry plight—her goods boycotted, her industries throttled, her cattle under embargo, and her natural market in the colonies closed to her. Adam Smith's reply was as we might expect—' As the wealth and industry of Lancashire does not obstruct but promote that of Yorkshire, so the wealth and industry of Ireland would not obstruct but promote that of England.' [1] In this spirit Pitt's Irish proposals of 1785 were framed, but they foundered on the opposition of British manufacturers and the suspicion of Irish nationalism. The statesman was therefore forced to the unhappy Act of Union in 1800— a solution which the economist, arguing superficially from his own country, had commended in advance : ' Without a union with Great Britain the inhabitants of Ireland are not likely for many ages to consider themselves as one people ' (II. 430). Here we might employ the writer's vein of sarcasm against himself. They became a nation in the 19th century because they learnt to hate with unanimity the shackles of a detested partnership.

Similarly in 1783, when the recognition of American independence called for a modification of the navigation laws, Pitt's inclination to a generous settlement was suppressed by the commercial and shipping interests. It is generally supposed that Adam Smith approved of the navigation laws because of the famous saving sentence, 'As defence, however, is of much more importance than opulence, the act of navigation is, perhaps, the wisest of all the commercial regulations of England ' (I. 429). But once again the context is disturbing. ' Perhaps the wisest ' was not very comforting from one who was engaged in pouring

[1] Rae, op. cit. 352.

scorn and satire on all such manifestations of fiscal wisdom. And so in 1783 he supported Pitt's plan of permitting trade to go on as it did when America was part of the Empire. The West Indies, he argued in a letter [1] to his friend Eden, needed American goods more than America needed theirs.

This friend negotiated the French Treaty of 1786. Pitt's interest in the preliminaries seems to have been lukewarm (perhaps he was disheartened by his failures with America and Ireland), and the result to France was certainly injurious, but it paved the way for success in the less bellicose age of Cobden. Adam Smith in his first edition had stated the case for a freer trade with France, and in the edition of 1784 he added a strengthening paragraph in support of the treaty which was then being advocated from the side of France. Remarking on the obstruction which national animosity was putting in its way, he said, ' The traders of both countries have announced, with all the passionate confidence of interested falsehood, the certain ruin of each in consequence of that unfavorable balance of trade which, they pretend, would be the infallible effect of an unrestrained commerce with the other ' (I. 460).

When a nation is at serious war, the statesman asks of the economist only that he shall show him how to borrow money and find new taxes. Lord North, the predecessor of Pitt, faced with the financing of the American war, pounced on the suggestions in the *Wealth of Nations*, and adopted the taxes on men-servants, property sold by auction, and inhabited houses. On the same authority he increased the tax on malt rather than that on beer. But these were trifles, and for a big war Adam Smith had nothing to offer. Pitt had to feel his way to the income tax alone. Adam Smith disliked the inquisitional nature of such a tax, and, remembering that the merchants by the clamour which they had raised—' so violent, though so unjust ' (II. 370)—had defeated Walpole's much milder scheme of excise, he had good ground for believing that private self-assessment to an income tax would fail, and that public assessment would not be tolerated. ' Merchants engaged in the hazardous projects of trade all tremble at the thoughts of being obliged at all times to expose the real state of their circumstances ' (II. 335). The war drove Pitt to it at long last, eight years after Adam Smith's death. Adam Smith had urged the desirability of paying for the costs of war by taxation during the war, but he did not foresee the only weapon by which this could be done.

The public debt was the legacy of England's victories over Louis XIV of France, and the national conscience was sound

---

[1] Adam Smith to William Eden, Dec. 15, 1783 (*Journal and Correspondence of William, Lord Auckland* I. 64–6).

enough to admit that public debts, like private debts, ought to be discharged. Incidental surpluses, as Adam Smith pointed out, will not do it, because having occurred once they will be anticipated next time by the needy minister of finance, and a new war may break out. ' It would be altogether chimerical, therefore, to expect that the public debt should ever be completely discharged by any savings which are likely to be made from ordinary revenue as it stands at present ' (II. 409). But debt is a cancer which, if not excised, will rot the body politic, for it spreads continuously and at an increasing rate. It must therefore be combated by a plan which itself possesses increasing momentum. This was the psychological basis of Pitt's solemn sinking fund, and indeed it was what Adam Smith expected from a sinking fund supported by increased taxation extending to the whole empire. ' This great sinking fund too might be augmented every year by the interest of the debt which had been discharged the year before, and might in this manner increase so very rapidly, as to be sufficient in a few years to discharge the whole debt, and thus to restore completely the at present debilitated and languishing vigour of the empire ' (II. 423). If Pitt ever believed that a sinking fund had any efficacy apart from increased taxation, he assuredly found no countenance for the delusion in Adam Smith. Pitt, however, proved to the hilt the national habit which Adam Smith had observed with misgiving, ' the ability in the subjects of a commercial state to lend ' (II. 395). For from the proceeds of the industrial revolution and an expanding foreign trade he financed the Napoleonic war. To his honour he also proved that in the crisis of war a commercial nation will submit to heavy taxation.

The return of peace permitted the resumption of the liberal policy begun by Pitt. By three mighty wieldings of the fiscal hammer, Huskisson, Peel and Gladstone gave to Great Britain that freedom of trade which to Adam Smith seemed ' as absurd as to expect that an Oceana or Utopia should ever be established in it ' (I. 435). Between him and Huskisson there was a peculiar affinity of mind. For as a statesman Huskisson was compelled to proceed by degrees ; and at a time when the majority of the commercial community had little familiarity with the arguments for free trade and no faith in its application to themselves, it was a relief to fall back on the trump card of the smuggler, who would have as many citations in an index of Huskisson's Speeches as in that of the *Wealth of Nations*. Moreover, Huskisson had the same large vision of empire ; and when fiscal reform threatened imperial trade or the supremacy of our ocean shipping, that ' nursery of British seamen,' he stayed the fiscal hammer. Peel was the economic child of Ricardo rather than of Adam Smith ; and for Peel's greatest stroke, the repeal of the corn laws, the *Wealth of Nations* was a blunted weapon. At bottom the struggle for repeal was a bourgeois assault on the citadel of the landed aristocracy, and Adam Smith's sympathies were the other way. True, the Anti-Corn Law League answered Ricardo out of Adam Smith, ' wages do not fluctuate with the price of provisions ' (I. 76). True, they shared in his hatred of monopoly, ' the gains of monopolists, whenever they can be come at, being certainly of all subjects the most proper ' (II. 377) ; but their monopoly was landlord's monopoly, and his monopolists were the merchants and manufacturers, for whose supposedly declining profits the Ricardian school had a very tender regard.

On the ground thus cleared by Huskisson and Peel was erected the scheme of Gladstonian finance. With Gladstone the affinity is again clear. Both loved economy, both boggled at the income tax. Adam Smith's conclusion, ' it seems not improbable that a revenue, at least equal to the present neat revenue of the Customs, might be drawn from duties upon the importation of only a few sorts of goods of the most general use and consumption ' (II. 369), stands as a fitting introduction to the principles observed by Gladstone in the selection of articles for indirect taxation. But the age of Gladstone has gone. Between Victorian Liberalism and that which at the outbreak of the Great War was supposed to be the voice of the Liberal party a great gulf is fixed, and across it are written among other warnings ' progressive taxation ' and ' capital levy.' On one bank stand the disciples of Gladstone and John Stuart Mill—' You disapprove, with Mr. Mill, of taxation upon any principle of graduation ? ' ' Entirely and emphatically . . . because it is confiscation.' [1] On the other bank stand the new Liberals—Liberals who court Labour, and Labour men who dislike the courtship.

Can Labour find support in Adam Smith ? Assuredly, for it was to Adam Smith that their predecessors—the early English socialists—also turned. ' In this state of things (namely, ' that early and rude state of society which precedes both the accumulation of stock and the appropriation of land ') the whole produce of labour belongs to the labourer ' (I. 49). Furthermore, ' it is not very unreasonable that the rich should contribute to the public expence, not only in proportion to their revenue, but something more than in that proportion ' (II. 327). The *Wealth of Nations* is cold to ' Taxes on Capital Value,' but the section thereon

---

[1] Evidence of William Newmarch, statistician and joint author of the last 2 vols. of Tooke's *History of Prices*, before Commons Committee on ' Income and Property Tax,' 1861, Q.'s 328 and 748.

contains the encouraging remark, ' There is no art which one Government sooner learns of another, than that of draining money from the pockets of the people ' (II. 346).

The problem of Adam Smith's influence on social policy is elusive. For the scope of the term is indefinite. There are obviously departments of domestic policy which fall outside the range of finance ; but on the other hand it was chiefly through the avenue of fiscal reform that social improvement was expected by Adam Smith and his successors. His direct influence on social policy is therefore only incidental. Adam Smith denounced the forcible removal of the poor, and the restrictions of the Elizabethan Statute of Apprenticeship. The Settlement Act of 1795 forbade removal until a man became actually chargeable ; and the Elizabethan Statute was repealed, the Wages clause in 1813 and the Apprenticeship clause the year following. It is said that Adam Smith's strictures deterred Pitt from supporting Samuel Whitbread's proposal for the regulation of wages in husbandry in 1795; but when Pitt withdrew his Poor Law Bill[1] of November 1796 it was in deference, not to the *Wealth of Nations*, but to the strictures of Jeremy Bentham, which Malthus reinforced two years later in the essay on *The Principle of Population*. The Combination Act of 1800 was passed amid the stress of war and the terror of sedition ; and the blame for it must be divided between the abnormal psychology of war and the general distrust of association, which was as evident in revolutionary France as in reactionary England. During the half century after 1815 the attitude of the country was dominated by individualism, but it derived its inspiration less from the natural rights of Adam Smith than from the utilitarian principles of Bentham. Indeed, during the aftermath of war, Adam Smith was reckoned by the elect to be something of a back-number. ' It was one of my father's main objects,' says the much enduring John Stuart Mill, ' to make me apply to Smith's more superficial view of political economy the superior lights of Ricardo.' [2] But with the turn of the century the mood of pessimism disappeared, and in the seventies the national complacency was at its height. Statisticians gloated over the growth of imports and exports, and worshipped once more at the shrine of the man who had held up ' the electrical illuminations of free trade as applied to the food of the people and to commerce in general.' [3]

[1] The Bill contemplated a parochial pension fund, schools of industry, and ' cow-money ': and was criticised by Bentham in a private pamphlet. *Cf.* Holland Rose, *Pitt and Napoleon*, pp. 84–92.

[2] J. S. Mill, *Autobiography*, p. 28.

[3] C. Walford, *Famines of the World*, p. 123, read before the Statistical Society, 1878–1879. Cornelius Walford, who died in 1885, was the learned author of an incomplete Insurance Cyclopaedia.

PART I
FISCAL POLICY AND FINANCE

CHAPTER I

From Walpole to Pitt

Section 1. Trend of Fiscal Policy, 1700–1850. Section 2. Walpole and Twenty Years of Peace. Section 3. Trade Policy in War Time, 1793–1815. Section 4. The Financial Policy of William Pitt.

Section 1. *Trend of Fiscal Policy, 1700–1850*

CROMWELL brought England and Scotland into one Commonwealth with one Parliament. Though it was the right solution, it was the achievement of a revolutionary soldier and collapsed with him ; and a half-century of mutual trade exclusion followed. To secure an independent foothold in the New World, Scotland embarked in 1695 on the project of a colony in Darien, a project anticipating in its economic purposes the Panama Canal ; but it was a disastrous failure, and the failure forced Scotland to swallow her national pride and enter the precious circle of England's Colonial Empire by the path of political union. By the treaty of 1707 the separate Parliaments of England and Scotland became the Parliament of Great Britain ; and henceforth on the high seas the commercial rights of England and Scotland were equal under the protection of the British Navy.

It was the tragedy of Ireland that she was excluded from a share in the colonial trade by the legislation of 1663 [1] and 1670–1.[2] She was not allowed to send to the colonies anything but provisions or to import directly from them their leading products. These restrictions robbed her of the overseas trade which her favourable situation and coast line would otherwise have secured to her. In the last quarter of the 18th century the boycott was relaxed, and in 1800 by the 6th Article of the Act of Union between Great Britain and Ireland it was entirely removed, but Ireland's economic condition was then too weak to allow her to recover the lost ground.

Thus from 1707 onwards England and Scotland had one trade policy. Ireland and other parts of the Empire were regulated by it, but they were not equal partners. The purpose of this policy was fourfold : (i) to strengthen the mercantile marine, (ii) to develop the colonies and other overseas possessions as

---

[1] 15 Chas. II. c. 7 (The Staple Act).   [2] 22 & 23 Chas. II. c. 26.

sources of supply of raw materials and as markets for British goods, (iii) to promote arable farming at home, especially the cultivation of the staple foodstuff, wheat, (iv) to foster the ancient industries of the country, especially the premier industry of woollens.

These too had been the purposes of 17th-century trade policy, but in the 18th century the emphasis was shifted from colonisation and shipping to productive development at home. Utilising the resources and markets furnished by an aggressive policy of navigation and colonial monopoly, Great Britain turned inward to develop herself—her agriculture, communications, coal mines and manufactures ; in brief, her provincial hinterland. But at no time did she seek self-sufficiency at the expense of foreign trade. She sought to grow rich by exporting the products of her own land and by re-exporting those of her overseas possessions. Carrying for others was a good thing, and still better was the carrying to others of commodities which had been manufactured in Great Britain from native or colonial materials.

The 19th century, with like purpose, aimed to grow rich by foreign trade, but experience showed that the political independence of the United States of America, so far from severing raw supplies, was attended by a remarkable expansion in them ; and therefore merchants and manufacturers, enjoying after the defeat of Napoleon an easy priority in world trade, were converted to the belief that the regulation of trade defeated its own end. They did not, indeed, advocate tariff reduction against themselves, but they fought with enthusiasm for the removal of the chief remaining barrier to their export trade, the monopoly of the East India Company in India and China, and having secured this in 1813 and 1833 respectively,[1] they assailed the protective Corn Laws by which their export trade in manufactures to Europe was indirectly checked. The exigencies of war—the Seven Years War (1756–63), the American War (1776–83) and the long French Wars (1793–1815)—so overburdened and distorted the British tariff that in the interest of simplification statesmen and merchants after 1815 desired freer trade ; but it was only in the course of the Anti-Corn Law campaign (1838–1846) that statesmen and industrialists accepted free trade as an economic faith. Cobden and Bright, the leaders in this campaign, enveloped the fighting trade policy of their predecessors in the halo of international peace. Huskisson was a militant

[1] 53 Geo. III. c. 155 (1813), opened the trade to India to H.M. subjects after April 10, 1814, with the exception of the trade with China and the trade in tea from all parts between the Cape of Good Hope and the Straits of Magellan ; 3 & 4 William IV. c. 93 (1833), repealed these exceptions.

all his life, but Peel in 1846 surrendered to Cobden's spell, and Gladstone, who combined a genius for finance with a peace-loving temperament, carried free trade to completion. The old clash between trade policy and the collection of revenue was ended. The President of the Board of Trade became an administrator without a tariff problem ; the Chancellor of the Exchequer had to consider import duties solely from their desirability as sources of revenue.

Section 2. *Walpole and Twenty Years of Peace*

It chanced that at the opening of three centuries Great Britain was engaged in serious war with a leading European Power. In the first two France was the enemy, in the third Germany. The war with Louis XIV ended in 1713 ; that with Napoleon in 1815 ; the Great War on November 11, 1918. Walpole was a great peace minister. He came into power shortly after the final settlement of the dynastic disturbances and civil upsets which had arrested for a century the internal development of England. He was in supreme power from 1721 to 1742 ; and down to 1739, that is, almost to the end of his term, he kept England at peace with the nations of Europe. To secure for his country internal and external stability was the dual purpose of his life. For the first it was necessary to hold the confidence of the Crown, the City and the landed gentry, and in this he succeeded by constitutional means, laying the foundations of Cabinet government. For the second two things were necessary : naval security and the avoidance of fruitless war. Walpole maintained a strong Navy and increased it. Under its protection British and colonial shipping flourished and great fleets of merchantmen carried British goods to the four corners of the world. Yet the trade greed of the nation forced him to declare war on Spain in 1739, for the avenging of Captain Jenkins' ear, and he fell from office, condemned for the finest action of his life, his resistance to a marauding war. But happily internal peace was not involved. The nation easily survived the escapade of the Pretender in 1745 ; and from that day to this Great Britain enjoyed that greatest of aids to continuous economic development, freedom from war on her own soil.

In trade policy the age is wider than the man. This was the age of mercantilism, and Walpole was a mercantilist. The protection of native industry preceded Walpole, was continued by him and persisted after him. Small regard was paid to the final consumer. But one trade's finished product was sometimes another's raw material ; and inasmuch as the finishing trades

manufactured, they employed more people and therefore possessed a superior claim to the consideration of the State. On
this ground in 1721 the brass-using trades successfully resisted
the demand of the copper and brass smelters for higher duties
on the superior Dutch product. The prohibition of Indian
calicoes from 1720 onwards was intended similarly to protect the
woollen and silk weavers against the loss of their occupation.

In Walpole's time the encouragement of industry was effected
mainly by the encouragement of export and took three forms—
the abolition of prohibitions and prohibitive duties on exports,
export bounties, and the drawback of import duties on re-export.
Since 1660 there had been steady progress in the freeing of exports,
beginning with foreign bullion in 1663 (15 Chas. II, c. 7, s. 12). In
1721 Walpole removed the export restrictions on over one hundred
articles of manufacture and at the same time gave freedom of
import to certain raw materials, such as cochineal, indigo and
undressed flax. Bounties were given on corn, gunpowder, sugar
refined from British plantation sugar, ribbons and silks, and the
products of the herring and whale fisheries. Sometimes the granting of a drawback on re-export hurt the home producer, and
to prevent this Walpole abolished the drawbacks on imported
unwrought hemp and paper. Apparent contradictions in this
complicated policy of regulation can usually be resolved by
remembering that the general purpose was to strengthen the
export power of British producers.

In colonial affairs Walpole showed his shrewdness by declining
to entertain the idea of taxing the colonies and by winking at
the infraction of unenforceable laws. In 1733, under pressure from
the West Indian planters, the Molasses Act (6 Geo. II, c. 13) was
passed, but as the penalties it imposed on sugar from the French
West Indies would have crippled the chief trade of the New England
colonies, it was allowed to remain a dead letter. In 1764, after
the conclusion of the Seven Years War (1756–63), the Molasses
Act was re-enacted and the duty lowered from 6d. to 3d. a gallon,
with a view to its enforcement for revenue ; and the friction
caused by this measure and the Stamp Act of 1765 (5 Geo. III,
c. 12), which also had as its object the raising of revenue from the
colonies, strained their loyalty. In 1773, when the East India
Company was given a monopoly of the American tea trade, it
snapped and Boston had a tea party. Walpole's successors
forgot his ruling motto, ' Let sleeping dogs lie.'

Walpole made his name as a financier by the handling of the
South Sea crisis in 1720.[1] This crisis was the first and greatest

---

[1] *Cf.* the authoritative account in W. R. Scott, *History of Joint Stock
Companies to 1720*, III. 288–360.

of those waves of speculative excitement which are booms while they last and bubbles when they burst. But it had little to do with the South Seas. It was in substance a scheme for funding government debt. However, the credit of the Government was in those days so shaky that it could not obtain permanent loans without attaching to them a durable commercial privilege. It raised loans in this way from the flotation of the Bank of England in 1694 and from the bargaining which preceded the union of the old and new East India Companies in 1709. In 1719 the outstanding liabilities of the Government amounted to £30,000,000 ; and the South Sea Company, in return for a monopoly of trade to the South Seas, agreed to take over the whole of the debt. The boom resulted from the method of conversion. The Government did not fix the cash price at which the South Sea stock was to be exchanged for debt scrip, and it authorised the Company to issue to the public stock equal to the difference between its par value and the price of issue to the debt holders. If the Company had dealt first with the debt holders and realised a genuine premium, the issue of the balance to the public would have been innocuous, but it anticipated the premium and the public bit. The debt holders, observing that the price of the stock was soaring, became eager for conversion and accepted stock at prices which, however fanciful, were less than the estimate of the outside market. All this happened between April and August 1720, but during the same time there were dishonest transactions behind the scenes. The Company gave, or sold at less than market price, blocks of stock to members of the Government and of Parliament. To force up the price it lent money against its own stock, which it then secretly pawned. In fine, it rigged the market by all the devices it knew. But its phenomenal success brought rivals into the field, and when in self-defence it obtained injunctions to restrain the wildest of them, the check recoiled upon itself. The bubble burst, and the ruined public clamoured for vengeance.

At this point Walpole was called upon, with all the more confidence because he was believed to have sold out in time at a profit. The adjustment finally reached was in substance Walpole's proposal. Subscribers who could not meet their calls were released on easy terms and the shrunken stock was supported by a contribution of £6,000,000 from the Sinking Fund. The trading and debt-holding functions of the Company were separated, and, as the former never amounted to anything, the net result was that the original debt holders became holders of South Sea stock on which they received from the Government a somewhat lower interest than before the conversion. After a heated parliamentary inquiry, in which Walpole did his best to hush up scandals, a number of the directors were found guilty and punished by very heavy fines on their estates, but the shock to credit was great. It engendered a long-lasting distrust of joint stock organisation. The one redeeming feature was that the scotching of a South Sea financial trust kept the South American market open for individual enterprise at a later date.

In office Walpole devoted his financial genius to the thankless task of meeting from existing taxes an expenditure loaded with the charges of past wars. In his efforts thereto he laid the foundations of something approaching a system of taxation ; and Adam Smith's analysis of the incidence of taxation owes much of its singular modernity to the fund of experience accumulated by Walpole. The sources of revenue at Walpole's command were threefold : customs, excise, and land tax. Customs duties were the least unpopular ; for British imports were mainly luxuries, and it was believed that their burden fell on the foreigner. But the customs cordon was so lax that any heavy duty on a luxury for which there was a keen demand merely diverted revenue into the pockets of the smuggler. The excise, i.e. the taxes on certain articles of domestic or foreign origin levied inland as they passed into consumption (the idea had been borrowed by Parliament from Holland during the Civil War), was much more satisfactory from the Government's point of view, for it yielded money in war as well as in peace, and being levied internally it was harder to evade. But for that reason and because the articles in most general consumption were necessaries of the poor man, it was intensely unpopular. The list of excises which Walpole inherited included salt, spirits, malt, candles, leather, soap, paper and starch. Most of them had been granted as war taxes and pledged to the interest of particular loans ; and any addition to the list in peace time would have been considered outrageous. There remained the land tax, or tax on rents, which was paid by the landed proprietors. During the Commonwealth Parliament had imposed monthly assessments on its adherents, assigning to each district a quota. In 1692 Parliament granted an aid of four shillings in the pound, and in 1697 returned to the Commonwealth plan of fixing in advance the total to be raised. Personal income was liable, and the balance was to be made up by a pound rate on lands. But when Walpole inherited the tax, personal income had slipped out and the tax was not even a percentage on the true annual value of land. Each so-called shilling in the pound meant a fixed sum of half a million sterling distributed among counties in the proportions fixed by the assessment of 1692. It was varied in rate, according to the needs of different years, between one and four shillings ; and therefore it varied in yield between one-half and two million sterling. Walpole strove hard to keep it down, for he realised that its incidence was unequal and he desired to placate the landed gentry. In 1732, to avoid raising it, he reimposed the intensely unpopular salt excise, which he had repealed in 1730. But when the nation insisted on war in 1739, the tax had to go up to its top rate of four shillings, at which it remained for the next half-century till it became a fixed charge on landed estate, and as such was treated by Pitt in his scheme for redemption in 1798.

There were, however, two possible sources of increased revenue which did not involve the formal imposition of new taxation. The first was the diversion of the surplus on the debt funds. This surplus might arise either through an increase in the yield of taxes specifically pledged to the payment of interest or through a reduction in the rate of interest itself. Walpole's stable government achieved both. It brought increase of trade and therefore of tax yield, and it made possible the reduction of interest from an average of six to an average of five per cent The understanding was that all such surplus should be earmarked for debt redemption and held in a sinking fund. Walpole made a legitimate call on the sinking fund in 1720 when he employed a part to support the South Sea stock, but in 1727 he charged on it an addition to the Civil List for the behoof of the newly ascended sovereign George II, and from 1733 onwards he regularly raided it for current needs.

The second source was the improved administration of the customs. In 1724 he revised the rating of dutiable imports and exports, bringing the old Book of Rates of 1660 up to date. But his main difficulty was the prevalence of smuggling, and he could only arrest this by collecting the bulk of the duty inland through the machinery of the Excise. In 1724 he applied this method to tea, coffee and chocolate, and made compulsory their warehousing until they were taken out for consumption. The tea duty went up by £120,000 ; and the warehousing plan assisted the export trade, since excise was only payable when the article was taken out for internal consumption. In 1733 he tried to do the same with wine and tobacco. In tobacco fraud was peculiarly flagrant. Quantities were stolen from the ships by thieves and still larger quantities were conveyed by a chain of smugglers into the interior with the connivance of merchants. And the Exchequer was further mulcted by fraudulent drawbacks on re-export. Dirt was blended with tobacco to earn a higher drawback. A violent outcry—the outcry of aggrieved law-breakers working through the passions of the mob—greeted his scheme. In vain Walpole

showed that it would assist the export trade and positively reduce
the duty on the domestic consumption. His opponents saw
their chance of overthrowing his long regime. He was trying,
they said, to make the Crown independent of Parliament and to
foist on the people a General Excise. Ballads were published
holding up the author to execration. One of these ' Britannia
Excisa ' is illustrated by a cartoon in which the many-headed
dragon Excise is gulping down every kind of food and drink.

> Grant these and the Glutton
> Will roar out for Mutton,
> Your Bread, Beef and Bacon to boot,
> Your Goose, Pig and Pullet
> He'll thrust down his Gullet
> While the Labourer munches a root.

Walpole had to yield. Lord Scarborough feared for the loyalty
of the Army. ' I'll answer,' he said, ' for my regiment against
the Pretender, but not against opponents of excise.' ' We must
drop it,' said the Queen, Walpole's best friend, and he dropped it.
' This dance will no further go.'

After this Walpole tried no more reforms. To keep down the
land tax he lived on the Sinking Fund and stood aloof from the
attempt to repress the growing evil of dram drinking by the
prohibitive taxation of spirits in 1736 (9 Geo. II, c. 13). This
law was defied. Gin was sold as a medicine in chemists' shops and
hawked through the streets under a variety of disguises and slang
names. Walpole's successors abandoned the unequal contest
The duties on spirits were lowered and the licensing regulations
relaxed ; and Londoners enjoyed a further spell of free trade in
gin, when dram shops advertised their delights with the legend
' Drunk for a Penny, dead drunk for Twopence, clean straw for
nothing.' Happily, however, there were serious wars ahead,
which by compelling a gradual rise in effective taxation restored
the population to comparative sobriety. Our streets are quieter
than Hogarth's Gin Lane, but it is not easy to imagine what
would happen if suddenly, the world over, all interferences with
the sale and price of alcohol were removed.

Section 3.   Trade Policy in War Time, 1793–1815

The continuity of British trade policy over the centuries is
well shown by the determined fashion in which Great Britain
forced her export trade between 1793 and 1815 when she was
at open war with France. She used her naval superiority after
Trafalgar (1805) to flood Europe with British goods. In seasons

when her own harvest was short she took steps to obtain corn from Europe, but owing to the productivity of her own soil her need for foreign food was not more urgent than the need of Napoleon's allies to get rid of their surplus crops. She proclaimed a naval blockade of a large part of Europe—not in order to starve her enemy into submission, as was the purpose of the Allies in the late war—but in order to hold her share in the profits of the export trade to Europe. By making trade with the enemy illegal she provided prize money for her navy and privateers, but at the same time, by issuing freely licences to trade, she promoted the interests of her manufacturers and merchants. Fundamentally her war policy was in accord with the ancient policy of the Navigation Laws as conceived by Cromwell, but France was the enemy in place of Holland and the war was open instead of disguised. In both periods the policy would have been futile if it had not been backed by naval superiority.

Napoleon's reply was the Continental System, and he too was following precedent. From the time of Louis XIV the two nations had been engaged in continuous commercial warfare. The commercial treaty of 1786, the Pitt-Vergennes Treaty (often called the Eden Treaty after its English negotiator), was only an interlude. By it France gave more than she received. For the ban on her silk goods remained ; and in return for lower rates on her wines and spirits she admitted at rates of 10 to 12 per cent. the machine-made manufactures of Great Britain. There was at once an outcry of commercial distress from all the manufacturing centres in France, and shortly before the outbreak of war in 1793 the Government of the Revolution denounced it. Between 1793, when war broke out, and 1802, when the brief Peace of Amiens was concluded, the penalties imposed by France on British goods were as harsh as those imposed by Napoleon under the Continental System which he built up from 1806 onwards. The difference between the two periods of retaliation was that Napoleon was trying to enforce the restrictions upon the whole of Europe.

Napoleon's motto was ' France before all,' and to help French trade he was grandly inconsistent. When the strength of the British Navy prevented him from conveying French goods to America and the West Indies, he found a vent for what he meant to be a one-way traffic with Great Britain in the operations of Dunkirk smugglers. When French agriculturists were suffering, as in 1809, from a plethora of grain, he permitted the export of corn, knowing that its destination would be Britain. But, at once a dreamer and an opportunist, he seems to have comforted himself with the notion that by taking only gold from England he would overthrow the Colossus with feet of Paper Credit. He was also, as the head of a nation in arms, in sore need of funds, and therefore, while Great Britain issued licences in order to keep control over the course of trade, he, as time went on, issued them lavishly in order to replenish his exchequer. ' It is necessary un-doubtedly to injure our enemies, but above all one must live,' he said.[1] The Continental System was a self-blockade against Great Britain, and to succeed it must be complete. By granting exemptions in the interests of French trade and his own treasury he stultified his policy and estranged his allies.

Napoleon acted by Decrees, to which Great Britain replied by Orders in Council. The Berlin Decree of November 1806 prohibiting trade with or from Great Britain was followed by the Orders in Council of November 1807 and others, the effect of which was to make a call at a British port obligatory upon all neutrals, of whom the U.S.A. was the chief. In retaliation Napoleon decreed from Milan, December 1807, that any vessels submitting to British regulations or examination by a British man-of-war were lawful prizes of war. Therefore the neutrals were bound to violate the laws of one or other of the belligerents. By the victory of Jena, October 1806, and the Treaty of Tilsit with the Czar of Russia, 1807, the chain of exclusion was com-pleted. But as Napoleon's allies were unwilling partners—apart from Denmark, who smarted under two recent seizures of her fleet by Great Britain—the Decrees were enforced only to the extent that French officials were present to enforce them. Hamburg became the headquarters of an illicit trade which was so normal that the risk of breaking the French cordon was evaluated exactly and added to the price of the goods.

By the Decree of Fontainebleau, 1810, Napoleon made a final effort to impose his will on the course of trade. Colonial produce which had touched at British ports was confiscated and resold to the profit of his treasury. British-made goods were burned at *autos-da-fé* to the accompaniment of military music. French manufacturers welcomed this drastic elimination of competition, but continental importers, from whom British merchants had exacted cash on delivery, substituted rubbish for genuine articles on the fire-piles as far as they dared. The tightening of the blockade hurt the export trade of Great Britain but did not throttle it.[2] For she found new markets in South America and roundabout routes to her old markets—by the Baltic ports on the

[1] *Cf.* Eli Heckscher, *The Continental System*, p. 253.
[2] Excellent examples of blockade running by the British iron and steel exporters are given in T. S Ashton, *Iron and Steel Industry in the Industrial Revolution*, pp. 148–50.

north and the Danube ports on the south. Gothenburg on the Swedish mainland was the headquarters of the Baltic blockade-running. Salonika was an important base in the Mediterranean. John Galt the novelist, father of Sir A. T. Galt, started life as a blockade-runner in the Levant. Of all Napoleon's allies Russia was the most loth to enforce the blockade ; and when Russia broke loose and Napoleon lost battles his system collapsed like a pack of cards. Contraband goods followed in the wake of the allied armies in their march on Paris, and by 1814 the blockade was no more.

America from the outset of the European conflagration did her best to play a neutral rôle. And for a time Great Britain acquiesced in the very great profits which neutrals were able to earn in war time, but in 1805, disturbed by the loss of some of her colonial trade, she began to interpret strictly the rule of international law under which a neutral was forbidden to convey to enemy ports the produce of ex-enemy colonies. America retaliated, and in 1807, finding it impossible to steer between Napoleon's Decree and the British Orders in Council, introduced an Embargo Act which prohibited American vessels from sailing to foreign ports. But this spiritless policy was not to the liking of American merchants, who freely evaded it by using Canadian ports ; and in 1809 the Embargo Act was replaced by a milder Non-Intercourse Act, which limited non-intercourse to trade with belligerents. But this played into the hands of British shippers by confining American vessels to the short haul to nominally neutral ports in the West Indies, and accordingly the Non-Intercourse Act was renewed in 1810 as a diplomatic weapon : if one of the belligerents rescinded its regulations and the other did not follow suit within three months, the Act was to come into force against the recalcitrant party. Here was Napoleon's chance. Slurring over his brazen confiscation of American shipping in French ports in March 1810, he announced in November the abrogation of his Decrees as against America and called upon her to enforce non-intercourse against Great Britain. This she did, and in June 1812 the British Orders in Council were rescinded in her favour.

But to the dismay of British traders, America declared war on Great Britain a few days previous to this ; for the original quarrel was now overlaid by a sharper difference arising out of the impressment of seamen from American vessels. Great Britain recruited her fleet by the old and barbarous method of the press gang. To escape its severities and better their lot many British seamen had taken service in American ships. With the two nations speaking one language the recovery of deserters inevitably led to mistakes, and though America conceded the right of recovery she resented the insult to which the exercise of the right exposed her. Therefore when her commercial differences with Great Britain were on the eve of settlement, the insult to her flag carried her into war. It was of all wars the most futile. When peace was signed at Ghent in December 1814 the *status quo* was accepted. The Orders in Council, having been already abolished, did not enter into the terms. The right of search was not disavowed, but the exercise of it lapsed with the cessation of war between Great Britain and France : and the press gang, the original cause of the trouble, was not employed any more. In 1815 a commercial treaty was concluded between Great Britain and the U.S.A. Between 1783, when Great Britain recognised American independence, and 1793, when she declared war on France, no formal settlement of trade relations had been reached. Yet some settlement was very necessary. For what had been the main portion of the Empire was now outside it, while its commerce was intimately concerned with the parts of the Empire which remained loyal. In 1794 John Jay secured a treaty, but it granted little and the trade sections expired in 1807. The treaty of 1815 settled one issue, it put an end to the discriminating duties which both nations had imposed on each other's shipping in the direct trade between them. It gave, in Huskisson's words, ' equality of all charges upon the ships belonging to either country in the ports of the other, and a like equality of duty upon all articles the production of the one country, imported into the other, whether such importation be made in the ships of the one or of the other.' [1] But Great Britain was very loth to make any breach in the lucrative triangular trade between herself, the West Indies, and the mainland, and in this theatre an understanding was not reached until 1830, by which time the trading relations between British colonies and foreign countries generally had been radically revised.

Meanwhile, America by her Navigation Act of 1817 had reserved her coastwise shipping ; and having abandoned in 1815 the policy of protecting her overseas shipping by discriminating duties, she turned to a policy of protecting her domestic industries by means of a protective tariff. Just as the forcing of Napoleon's blockade was the prelude to Britain's peaceful penetration of Europe by a policy of free trade, so the natural protection given to American industries by the period of war was the prelude to their consolidation by tariff protection when the war was over. In both countries the manufacturing interests bore down the opposition of the agriculturists. The result in the U.S.A. was

[1] Huskisson, *Speeches*, III. 13, May 12, 1826.

protection for industry during the 19th century, supplemented by protection for agriculture in the 20th, when competition was threatened from the newer lands of the Canadian West. The result in Great Britain was free trade in the 19th century, and between 1914 and 1930 a partial return to protection except for agriculturists, who had the most reason for claiming it.

Section 4. The Financial Policy of William Pitt

Pitt became Prime Minister in December 1783. He was in office from 1783 to 1801 and again from 1804 to the end of 1805. Between 1783 and 1789, when the French Revolution put an end to normal conditions, he introduced important fiscal reforms. In trade policy under the stimulus of Adam Smith he went as far towards free trade as the industrialists would allow him, but that was not far. The breach in the colonial system was not refashioned into a permanent settlement. In 1785 he failed with Ireland, which in 1780 in the stress of war had been admitted to the colonial trade. Anxious in particular to encourage the Irish linen industry, he proposed reciprocal lowering of duties on manufactures between England and Ireland ; but the cotton manufacturers and iron masters feared the competition of Ireland with its low wages and easy taxation, and with the help of Wedgwood and Boulton they defeated the Irish proposals in Parliament. To the Treaty concluded with France in 1786 the big industrialists were favourable, for none of them were vintners and the prohibition on French silks remained. But the Treaty was so one-sided that even if there had been no French Revolution the protests of French manufacturers must have brought it to a speedy end.[1]

As a financier Pitt observed the principle that ' true economy is better than a great revenue.' He reduced waste by abolishing sinecures and rooting out jobbery and corruption. He addressed himself at once to the revenue frauds which had beaten Walpole. By reducing in 1784 the heavy duties on tea (part customs and part excise) to a single *ad valorem* rate of $12\frac{1}{2}\%$ and collecting the whole of it through the agency of the East India Company, he cut the ground from under the smugglers' feet. The City of London supported a change which promised to employ twenty more ships in the China tea trade and to destroy the contraband that the French and Dutch East India Companies had carried on in defiance of the East India Company's monopoly. With the City in a complacent mood Pitt induced Parliament to accept the Budget of 1784, which imposed new excise and licence duties

[1] See above, pp. 17 and 31,

with rigid machinery for collection, and the Manifest Act of 1786 (26 Geo. III, c. 40) which, in brief, required the masters of vessels to produce for the Customs a duly authenticated Manifest of the contents of the cargo and forbade the breaking of bulk within four leagues of the coast. Certain of the excises, however, were very unpopular with the industrialists. The iron masters persuaded Pitt to withdraw the excise on coal before it became law, and next year, 1785, the fustian manufacturers secured modifications in the new cotton excise, the fustian tax as it was called.

Pitt, like Walpole, saw that the key to the smuggling situation lay in the use of the Excise authorities; therefore while he maintained and indeed clarified the distinction between the Customs and Excise Departments, he worked them in close conjunction, collecting through the Excise a part of the Customs When in 1793 war broke out, he relied for his indirect war taxation mainly on increase in the Excise with its special machinery for sure collection. The trade in tea and spirits, home made, foreign and colonial (where the duties of Excise were heavier than those of Customs), was under Excise supervision before Pitt's time. In 1786 he extended this supervision to wines, where the Excise duty had hitherto been relatively small, and in 1789–90 by two drastic Acts [1] to tobacco. Over the tobacco manufacture and the tobacco trade a thorough-going system of supervision by Permit and Survey was established.

While taking these steps for prevention of smuggling and the tightening of indirect taxation, Pitt effected in 1787 by 27 Geo. III, c. 13 a consolidation of the tariff. He substituted for the existing compound duties a single rate for each article and thereby simplified enormously the burden on the trader. The importer of Russian linen, for example, now paid one definite duty instead of a duty under ten different heads built up by the arithmeticians of the Customs House. Other duties, such as the wine duties, had been even more complicated; and their ascertainment had involved legal technicalities and the payment of many fees. In the new Rate Book, i.e. the schedules of the tariff of 1787, the duties as far as possible were made specific, i.e. calculated on weight and size. Specific duties avoided discrepancies between official values and current values in the case of articles enumerated in the Schedules as well as under-valuation in the case of articles not enumerated.

The consolidation of the revenue was in keeping with the consolidation of the tariff. Hitherto the proceeds of particular taxes had been pledged to the service of particular loans. By 27 Geo. III. c. 13 aforesaid, all were paid into one consolidated

---

[1] 29 Geo. III, c. 68, and 30 Geo. III, c. 40.

fund, from which the permanent charges on the revenue were met. The civil list, expenses of justice and the interest on the National Debt did not require to be voted annually, as did supplies for the Army, Navy and Civil Service; and Pitt argued rightly that as the credit of the country was bound to the payment of all its liabilities the separation brought only a meaningless multiplicity of accounts. If in any year the payments into the fund should be insufficient to meet the charges on it, the Treasury was empowered to make good the deficiency out of supply, replacing it as soon as the fund showed a surplus.

These administrative reforms were accompanied by a solemn effort to pay off the National Debt. Wars had raised it from £50,000,000 at the close of Walpole's administration to £273,000,000 in 1783. Of this £238,000,000 was funded debt, i.e. permanent debt which was repayable only at the option of the Government. If this rose above par, the Government was entitled to offer to debt holders the alternative of repayment at par or a lower rate of interest. Reductions on interest had been secured by Walpole. In 1749, at the close of the war of the Austrian Succession, when the credit of the Government was standing high, a big scheme of conversion was carried. The main body of debt, as it then stood, was converted from 4% stock into a new stock, which after 1757 bore interest at 3%. This stock was known as the Reduced Three Per Cents and remained in existence to 1888. In 1752 various 3% annuities were consolidated into one stock. This is the origin of Consols, the $2\frac{1}{2}$% Consols of to-day. At Pitt's accession nearly the whole of the debt was in 3% stock ; and, as the rate at which new money could be borrowed was then between 4% and 5%, the 3% stock was well below par. A scheme of debt redemption, therefore, involved the purchase of 3% stock in the open market.

Pitt announced his plan in 1786. A body of Debt Commissioners was to receive from Parliament a million a year in quarterly instalments. With this they were to buy up stock, to hold it, and to re-invest the interest. Furthermore the payments on certain life annuities and annuities for terms of years, as they fell in, were to be continued to the Commissioners. When the annual sum at the disposal of the Commissioners reached £4,000,000, all stock subsequently purchased was to be cancelled. Pitt's purpose was to surround the scheme with such safeguards that it would be inviolable, and for the first few years of its existence it operated soundly, because the grants came out of current taxation. But the writings of the Rev. Dr. Richard Price fostered a delusion that the re-investment of interest would cause the debt to pay itself off automatically through the mysterious efficacy of compound interest ; and the delusion had injurious results when on the approach of war further borrowing became necessary.

The war which broke out in 1793, and lasted with one short intermission (March 1802 to May 1803) until 1815, affected the national finances in three ways : (i) it necessitated new borrowing, (ii) it necessitated new taxation, (iii) it imposed a strain on currency and credit. Pitt died in 1806, one year after Trafalgar but nine years before Waterloo. Pitt's part, therefore, consisted in launching war measures, which were continued under conditions of increasing strain by mediocre successors.

New Borrowing. The debt of £273,000,000 in 1783 had risen by 1816 to £902,000,000 (£816,000,000 funded, £86,000,000 floating, i.e. short-term, debt). Was the money wisely borrowed ? Most of it was raised in 3% stock at a considerable discount. This meant that posterity was burdened with a larger capital sum of debt stock than if the borrowing had been done in 5% stock at par. Why then did Pitt borrow in this way ? Because, in the words of Hamilton, our authority on the National Debt, ' loans are transacted in the 3%s on easier terms. The lender expects to gain by the rise of stock, and when he gains the public loses at repayment or redemption.' [1] Pitt issued a 5% Loyalty Loan in 1796, but he had to promise the subscribers that it would not be redeemed until two years after the termination of war, and that in that event holders should have the option of repayment at the rate of £133 of 3% stock for every £100 of 5% stock. Sir Henry Parnell, the Corn Law authority and financial reformer, writing in 1829, declared that if Pitt had dealt directly with subscribers instead of with loan contractors he could have combated the preference for 3% stock.[2] But it is always easy to blame the financial middleman ; and it is weak to argue, as Parnell does, that because the much smaller loans of earlier days were subscribed directly at par, therefore the huge calls on the loan market during the French wars could have been met by the same procedure.

Was the money wisely spent ? The greater part, of course, was expenditure on the war—for the Army and Navy and for loans and subsidies to foreign Powers.[3] The loans were rarely repaid. The wisdom of these advances may be questioned, but this is to criticise the policy of supplying silver bullets to impoverished

---

[1] Robert Hamilton, *Enquiry concerning the Rise and Progress, the Redemption and Present State, and the Management of the National Debt of Great Britain and Ireland*, 3rd ed., 1818, p. 251.

[2] Sir Henry Parnell, *Financial Reform*, pp. 289–98.

[3] *Cf.* J. H. Clapham, ' Loans and Subsidies in time of War, 1793–1914,' *Economic Journal*, Dec. 1917.

allies, and Pitt at any rate did not borrow them from another Power. However, a part of the new borrowing was devoted to the maintenance of the Sinking Fund. Between 1786 when the fund was established and 1829 when it was abolished, £320,000,000 cash was paid into the Sinking Fund Account ; and during the war the whole of the contributions were borrowed. As finance this was unwise, because, though the old debt bought and the new debt issued were both mainly in three per cents., the Government by buying with the one hand and selling with the other had to pay the market charges. They could not buy as cheaply as they had to sell, and Hamilton considered that at the end of the war some £16,000,000 of debt stock had been created for which the Government had nothing to show.[1]

It is hard to believe that Pitt, the brilliant student of the *Wealth of Nations*, was deluded by the sophistry of Dr. Price. But the Sinking Fund was his darling, and how could he expect the citizens to support drastic taxation if the Government itself scrapped its solemn decision of 1786 ? In 1792, when war threatened, Pitt reconsecrated the Sinking Fund idea by enacting that a Sinking Fund of one per cent. should be established for all new loans. In 1802 his successor, Addington, amalgamated the new one per cent. Sinking Fund with that of 1786, with a view, he said, to extinguishing the whole debt in a shorter time than by keeping each to its own operation. But this was pretence. He wished to show that he was guarding as jealously as Pitt the financial credit of the nation. In 1813, when the stock held by the Commissioners was nearly £238,000,000—the figure of the funded debt in 1786—it was cancelled in accordance with a modification of Pitt's original scheme introduced by Addington at the time of the amalgamation. But the machinery of the fund was continued beyond the war. After 1815 it should have worked satisfactorily, but the tradition of feeding it with borrowings survived and obscured the real task of post-war finance, the raising of a true surplus through adequate taxation and economy in expenditure. In 1828 the Finance Committee showed that the provision of £5,000,000 annually for the Sinking Fund was being made by avoiding the immediate burden of other charges, such as war pensions. They recommended, therefore, that the Estimates should aim at a surplus of £3,000,000, but ' that in case the eventual annual surplus should not amount to Three Millions, the deficiency ought not to be supplied by borrowing.'[2] In 1829 the Sinking Fund was abolished. Between 1829 and 1875 Governments pursued the informal plan of devoting

---

[1] Hamilton, *op. cit.* p. 198.

[2] *Commons Committee on Finance (1828) Report,* Conclusion of Report.

casual surplus to debt redemption. That such surpluses fre-
quently accrued was due to the able finance of Peel and Gladstone.
This informal plan received in later days the name of Old Sinking
Fund to distinguish it from Stafford Northcote's New Sinking
Fund of 1875.

New Taxation. Here Pitt, after a slow start, achieved exceptional success. A national revenue of £19,000,000 in 1793
was raised to one of £50,000,000 in 1806, the year of his death.
So productive was the war taxation of 1798 onwards that if this
could have been imposed at the outset with equal success the
whole of the war might have been financed from current revenue.
' The great mistake committed by Mr. Pitt,' says Parnell, ' was
postponing till 1798 the plan of war taxes. The paying of the
whole expense of the war had by that time become a much more
difficult task to accomplish than it was in 1793 ; because in
the interval of five years between 1792 and 1798 110 millions
(of principal) had been borrowed, and taxes to the amount of
£5,700,000 had been laid on and permanently mortgaged for
paying the interest on this new debt.'[1]

Pitt misjudged the length of the war ; but he could hardly
have extracted from the pockets of the nation heavy sums in
taxation until he had first put into the circulation of the country
heavier sums through the issue of Army and Navy contracts.
Moreover, he had no machinery at his disposal for the levying
of such taxation. For although in 1799 the yield of the Customs
was double that of 1793, even then it only rose to £7,000,000,
of which £1,000,000, coming from the new Convoy Duties on
exports and imports, was in a sense a charge for service rendered
by the Fleet; while every extension of the Excise involved irritating control. Tradition, including the powerful tradition of
Adam Smith, was against a general income tax. The land tax
was now a fixed charge and so unequal in its incidence that Pitt
made no attempt to restore it to its original purpose. In 1798
(38 Geo. III, c. 60) he gave landowners the right to redeem it by
the payment of a capital sum which would yield to the Exchequer
when invested in consols the amount of the tax plus $\frac{1}{10}$th.[2]

Pitt had to find his way to an income tax along other lines.
He began in 1797 with the ' Triple Assessment ' (levied 1798).
There existed certain small taxes on windows, houses, shops, horses,
carriages and men-servants, by which tax-payers were directly
assessed. Pitt used this as a basis of a tax on spending power,

---

[1] Sir Henry Parnell, *Financial Reform*, p. 288.
[2] In 1853 the stock consideration was reduced by 17½% and in 1896 changed
to 30 years' purchase. Pitt also levied new or increased death duties on probate,
legacy and succession. See Buxton, *Finance and Politics*, I. 117, II. 293.

Lot because he wished to exempt ' hoarding ' but because ' there existed no means of ascertaining the property of individuals except such as were of a nature that could not be resorted to.' [1] The title ' Triple ' arose from the fact that owners of establishments whose assessment the year before was £25 had their assessment *tripled* in 1798. Richer persons paid larger multiples, poorer persons smaller, but the assessment failed through shameful evasion. It yielded only some £4,000,000 instead of the expected £7,000,000, and Pitt was reduced to begging for voluntary subscriptions, which brought in a further £2,000,000. ' The meanness which shrank from fair and voluntary contributions has been compensated by the voluntary exertions of patriotism.' [2]

In 1798 he used the lessons learned in this failure to introduce, as from April 1799, an income tax based on returns furnished by the tax-payer. Under the Triple Assessment of 1798 the person who found that his assessment exceeded 10% of his income was allowed a remission on the excess, if he filed in proof a ' General Declaration of Income.' Under the income tax of 1799 he filed a statement of income and had to accept without demur the amount to which he was assessed, unless he was prepared to disclose full particulars of his income from every source. There were abatements in respect of children and life insurance premiums, a total exemption to £60 and partial exemption between £60 and £200.

The tax was levied at 10% (2s. in the £) and yielded an average of £6,000,000 in 1799, 1800 and 1801. Abolished in 1802 during the brief Peace of Amiens, it was reimposed in 1803 by Addington at the rate of 5%. This was half the former rate, but the yield was nearly as great, because, though the tax-payer was now relieved of the unwelcome liability to disclose the whole of his income, he had his tax deducted at source, where this could be arranged. Thus the tenant of the land or house paid the tax due from the landlord and deducted it from his next payment of rent ; and the public offices paid the tax on the salaries of their employees. This device was of enormous importance in days to come when the majority of commercial profits accrued in the form of dividends from public companies and thus became amenable to stoppage at source.

In 1806 the tax on public funds, an increasingly important item, was deducted at source for the first time. In the same year the limit of total exemption was reduced from £60 to £50, and the deduction allowed all round on children was withdrawn

---

[1] *Parliamentary History of England*, II. 380. Speech of December 14, 1797.
[2] *Ibid*. II. 429. December 3, 1798.

owing to 'an astounding official increase of large families';
and the general rate was raised to 10% again. At this it remained
till 1815, when it was yielding nearly £15,000,000. At last
an income tax had been discovered which could not be evaded,
but it was voted for the duration of the war 'and no longer.'
At the conclusion of peace the Government tried to retain it,
but the Opposition, led by Brougham, held them to their bond.
It was abolished, therefore, in 1816, along with the war duty on
malt (i.e. the addition made to the excise on malt during the
war), which was regarded as the agricultural offset to the contributions of the commercial classes through income tax. In the
handling of taxation the errant parties were neither Pitt nor
Pitt's war-time successors, but an impatient public and the
complaisant Government of peace time. The abolition of the
income tax was not necessary to the restoration of industry, for
the war left Great Britain pre-eminent therein ; and the result
of abolishing it was to prolong the period of borrowing beyond
the war and to overload the revenue system with burdensome
taxes on the course of trade and the necessaries of the poor.

The Strain on Currency and Credit.   In 1797 the Government
authorised the Bank of England to suspend payment of its notes
in cash, and by agreeing to accept them for all payments virtually
made them legal tender. In 1821 cash payments were resumed
in full. Therefore between 1797 and 1821 Great Britain had a
paper pound. We note elsewhere the place of the paper pound
in the history of British currency and the measures taken by the
Bank of England at this time to preserve its independence and
reputation. Here we observe that the inflation of the currency,
which was the outcome of the suspension, served as a third and
final expedient of war finance. For inflation of the currency is
taxation in disguise, giving the Government through the machinery
of the loan market control over resources which it would not
otherwise possess. The inflation, measured by the premium on
gold, was slight down to 1808 : between 1809 and 1814 it was
serious. But at no point did the Government consciously avail
itself of this expedient. It did not turn on the printing press.
While the war lasted the burden of inflation was not felt, except
to the extent that it aggravated the rise in food prices between
1810 and 1813—a rise which would have been serious in any
case owing to the failure of supply. The penalty was paid on
the return of peace, which brought not plenty, as was expected,
but stagnation and unemployment. For as the final stage of
the war was financed in part by a moderate inflation of credit,
so the process of readjustment, when peace came, was rendered
more violent and therefore more damaging to trade. The

creditor class benefited by the fall in prices. In this class the fund holders were the most important element, but they were also the element which had benefited most surely by the abolition of the income tax. The result was a widespread sense of injustice on which Radical politicians like William Cobbett played with effect for the next twenty years.

CHAPTER II

HUSKISSON, 1770-1830

Section 1. Towards Free Trade. Section 2. Huskisson's Career. Section 3. The Corn Laws. Section 4. The Navigation Laws and Commercial Treaties. Section 5. Imperial Preference. Section 6. The Revision of the Tariff. Section 7. Summary.

Section 1. Towards Free Trade

Two great Tory statesmen, trained in the keen school of world war and currency disturbance, resumed the work of fiscal reform which Pitt began and the French wars arrested. These were William Huskisson (1770-1830) and Sir Robert Peel (1788-1850). Huskisson's chief work was done as President of the Board of Trade (1823-7), Peel's during his Premiership (1841-6) : and between them they set the fiscal helm so decisively towards free trade that its completion after 1846 was a matter of detail only.

It was the statesmen who set the pace. In the decade after Waterloo the British Government was in close touch with the problems and requirements of foreign trade. It had just waged a trade war with Napoleon and a war arising out of trade friction with the U.S.A. It was engaged on the restoration of the gold standard and the settlement of the French war indemnity through the house of Baring, and it was bargaining with interested Powers for the suppression of the slave trade. By its diplomacy it furthered the interests of British traders in Central and South America. Castlereagh and Canning saw the value of the markets opened by the detachment of Brazil from Portugal (1808) and the revolt of the Spanish Colonies (1810-16). In 1810 during the Peninsular War Great Britain had secured a commercial treaty with Portugal, giving her entry into the Brazilian market. In 1816 she offered mediation between Spain and its colonies, recommending that the commerce of South America should be opened to all nations upon moderate duties with a reasonable preference to Spain ; for she knew that this was all her merchants needed. But Spain refused, and therefore the British Government pressed for commercial recognition. It made a place for the ex-colonies in its new Navigation Code of 1822 and despatched commercial agents to South American ports. In these different ways the Government showed that it saw the value of a progressive trade policy more clearly than the manufacturers and merchants, who always thought sectionally when particular remissions were proposed. It is customary to date the movement for free trade from 1820, the year in which the merchants of London presented a Petition for Free Trade; and it is true that after that year free trade doctrine made headway in the country. The London Petition went the whole length: ' Free imports without retaliation and no duties except for revenue '; but Thomas Tooke, the statistician and Baltic merchant who drafted the petition, gives the story of its adoption. He found it hard to obtain signatures until a director and an ex-governor of the Bank of England led the way. ' The simple truth is that the Government were at that time far more sincere and resolute free traders than the merchants of London.' [1]

The agriculturists, though their mind was not more sectional than that of the merchants and manufacturers, were impelled by the circumstances to sing a different tune. They stood to lose by free trade. Having saved the country in war time by feeding it, they refused to support in peace time a trade policy in which the manufacturers enjoyed the markets and they the competition. Huskisson's term of office was cut short by the disfavour with which the landed interest viewed his effort to modify the unworkable Corn Law of 1815. Peel abolished the Corn Laws in 1846 at the price of his own downfall and a split in the party which he led. Shippers and manufacturers were never asked to expose themselves to the competition of advanced rivals. Great Britain became a completely free trade country because the interests which risked little by its adoption were strong enough to bring the agriculturists to their knees. And the British Exchequer was able to afford free trade because of the abounding increase in trade and industry which that policy aided but did not create.

Section 2. Huskisson's Career

Huskisson brought to the work of reform a ripe experience and matchless knowledge. A youth spent in Paris at the British Embassy gave him an insight into diplomatic procedure, which stood him in good stead when he came to negotiate commercial treaties. From 1796 to 1830 he sat almost continuously in Parlia-

[1] Tooke and Newmarch, *History of Prices*, VI. 342.

ment, representing from 1823 to 1830 the commercial constituency of Liverpool in succession to his friend and idol, George Canning. He was a member of the Bullion Committee of 1810 and made his financial mark by a brilliant essay on currency depreciation, in which he supported the bullionist case by showing the affinity between free trade and the free movement of gold. In 1814 he became Minister of Woods and Forests under Lord Liverpool, thus coming into contact with agriculture. For a time he was the spokesman of the Government in matters agricultural, but after 1821 he was in opposition to the majority of the Government's agricultural supporters, and the gap widened until in 1828 it caused his fall. Meanwhile, however, he had launched his fiscal reforms. With Robinson at the Exchequer and Canning at the Foreign Office, he achieved a complete revision of the tariff and shipping policy of the country. After the death of Canning in 1827 he passed through a year of uneasy office, becoming finally Colonial Secretary and leader of the House of Commons under the Duke of Wellington. In 1828 he resigned, nominally over a detail of electoral reform, in reality over a fundamental difference concerning protection to agriculture. In September 1830 he met with a fatal accident at the opening of the Liverpool and Manchester Railway. Never popular in high society, he was held in immense respect by the financial and business community. Impatient of interference with business enterprise in any form—tariff restrictions, official wage regulation or trade unions—he nevertheless had a big sympathy for those whose toil made England great : and the champions of the people saw in him their hope.

> Oh Huskisson ! Oh Huskisson !
> Oh Huskisson, in vain our friend !
> Why hast thou left thy work undone,
> Of good begun, is this the end ?
> Thou should'st have lived if they remain
> Who fetter'd us and hated thee ;
> Oh Huskisson, our friend in vain,
> Where now are hope and liberty ?

So sang the Corn Law rhymer, Ebenezer Elliott, and the commendation by the poet who hated the Corn Laws of the statesman who helped to pass the most hated of them (that of 1815) reads strangely. But 1815 and 1830 were far removed. Huskisson's career had occupied the transition from war to peace : and, learning as he went along, he changed his views as the facts changed.

Section 3. The Corn Laws

When peace loomed in 1813, the champions of Ireland with Sir Henry Parnell at their head were the first to become busy, and in 1814 they procured an Act (54 Geo. III, c. 69), which permitted the export of corn and flour from the United Kingdom at all times without payment of duty or receipt of bounty.[1]

In 1814 the problem was re-examined from the standpoint of British farmers, whose interest in free export was negligible. After evidence had been taken from land agents, merchants, farmers, and agricultural experts such as Arthur Young, the opinion was formed that 80s. per quarter was the lowest price which would cover the increased cost of growing wheat. The Government accepted the principle of an 80s. level, but in order to make it secure departed from Corn Law precedent. The earlier Corn Laws—1670, 1773, 1791 and 1804—set high, low and nominal duty points for the importation of foreign corn, but between 1756 and 1815 they were suspended frequently. To ensure now that with the return of peace protection should be effective, the Government substituted for a scale of duties the following hard-and-fast rule. When the home price of wheat was at or under 80s. per quarter, foreign wheat was excluded : when the home price was above that figure, it was allowed in duty free. This was the hated law of 1815. When the terms of the bill were disclosed, there was an outcry in the country and some disorder. One member complained that ' he had been carried above a hundred yards on the shoulders of the mob just like mackerel from Billingsgate Market and he thought they meant to quarter him.'[2] But the bill became law (55 Geo. III, c. 26) because, in addition to the agriculturists' desire for protection, statesmen were haunted by the fear of dependence upon the foreigner for foodstuffs in the event of war.

' That law,' said Huskisson as late as May 1820, ' had answered the purposes for which it was intended.'[3] And yet, in spite of protection amounting to prohibition, agriculture languished. In abundant years the home harvest reduced prices to an unremunerative level and in scarce years the rigid prohibition obstructed the relief of distress. In 1821 Huskisson presided over an inquiry into agricultural distress, and after hearing the evidence of the corn merchants, among them Thomas Tooke, he came to the conclusion that not only was the law failing to help the farmer, but also it was obstructing the course of foreign trade

---

[1] For Corn Laws from 1660 to 1869 see detailed list in Customs Tariffs (C. 8706 of 1897), pp. 229–261.
[2] *Hansard*, New Series, XXX, 35.   [3] *Speeches*, II 47.

and prompting foreign Powers to refuse commercial reciprocity. The Report of the Committee, which he drafted, gives evidence of his change of view. It propounds the daring question, ' whether the only solid foundation of a flourishing state of agriculture is not laid in abstaining as much as possible from interference, either by protection or prohibition, with the application of capital in any branch of industry.' [1] After adverting to the need for caution in applying this principle to the special case of agriculture, the Report strays into a homily in support of the resumption of cash payments, which was then in progress. The agriculturists considered that they had been outwitted and demanded a further inquiry in 1822. A duel then ensued between the liberal and protectionist elements in the Tory party, and the latter won. For whereas Huskisson had proposed to admit foreign corn at a certain scale of duties and thereafter to keep the ports *continuously open*, the Act of 1822 (3 Geo. IV, c. 60) opened the ports to new wheat only when the home price should have reached 80s., and *closed them again* when it should fall below 70s. As the former figure was not reached, the Act never came into effect apart from a clause relating to colonial corn. Thwarted thus in his effort to obtain a general solution, Huskisson secured some relief for the merchants whose corn lay rotting in bond in London and Liverpool. In 1824 permission was given to grind it for re-export. In 1825 a small quantity was admitted by special Act (6 Geo. IV, c. 65) into the general consumption of the country.

In April 1825, therefore, Huskisson expressed complete hostility to the law of 1815, which still held the field. It limited, he argued, the markets from which we drew our supplies, destroyed the vent which we should otherwise have for our produce whenever we were blessed with a superabundant harvest, and exposed us to violent fluctuations of price. Accordingly in 1827, when Canning was Premier, he made a final effort for a general settlement. There was no talk yet of total repeal ; the choice lay between a fixed duty and a sliding scale. The fixed duty avoided reference to those slippery things, ' the averages,' from which the home price was taken, and it had the approval of Ricardo. But the ground on which Ricardo based his plan of ' Protection to Agriculture,' published in 1822, namely the special disabilities suffered by agriculture, made it impossible of acceptance by a Tory Government. For protection grounded on the disabilities of one English industry as compared with another English industry was grounded on quicksand. If the farmer's poor rate declined, so would his claim to protection, and all the while he would play the sorry part of a lame dog whining for exceptional

---

[1] *Report of Committee on Depressed State of Agriculture* (1821), p. 20.

treatment. Huskisson therefore chose a sliding scale, which was in accordance with Corn Law precedent and seemed to meet the worst feature in the law of 1815, its rigidity. A gently descending scale would restore smoothness to the course of trade. But in order to work the scale it was necessary to decide upon a pivot point at which reasonable protection was afforded and from which, as prices rose, the duty would gently descend. The agriculturists declared that the pivot point of 60s. per quarter, with the duty of 20s. set against it, afforded inadequate protection, and threw out Huskisson's bill on a technical point. In its place a one-year Act, confined to bonded corn, was hurried through (1827). Huskisson in handling this bill fell foul of the Duke of Wellington. For they were at cross purposes. Huskisson was trying to restore an open corn trade, such as the country had enjoyed in the palmy days of the 18th century when corn flowed freely in and out. The Duke and his landed friends, without regard to the course of trade, were bent on consolidating the fortress which they had inherited from a generation of war. Relations, therefore, were already strained when Huskisson accepted office under Wellington in 1828, and he was out of office when the law of 1828, sometimes called the ' Duke of Wellington's sliding scale ' (9 Geo. IV, c. 60), was passed. This law held the field to 1841, and how it worked will be seen when we examine Peel's attempt to improve it.

Section 4.   The Navigation Laws and Commercial Treaties.

In 1820 Holland was no longer the merchant carrier of Europe, Ireland was for trade purposes a unit in the fiscal system of the United Kingdom, America was no longer a British possession, the countries of South America were no longer the colonies of Spain and Portugal. Nevertheless the Navigation Laws, which had been framed in an age when all these things held true, survived in cumbersome fullness. From time to time since 1660 exceptions or additions had been introduced until the regulations became so complicated that traders had to take legal advice upon their provisions and even the law officers of the Crown were sometimes unable to fathom them. The part which they played in the trade rivalries in the 17th and 18th centuries is discussed below (p. 134). It is here sufficient to note that the Restoration Parliament, repeating the militant legislation of Cromwell, excluded foreign countries from the fisheries, the trade with the colonies, and the ocean trade from all distant parts to England. Holland, the carrier of Europe, was the object of special animus. In all the Navigation Laws ' English ' covered colonial, though not

Irish, shipping, and under the protection of the British Navy
the American colonies had built up in the 18th century a strong
merchant marine.

Thus the overhauling of the code was already long overdue.
Wallace in 1822 began the revision and Huskisson completed it
in 1825.   From 1818 to 1823 Thomas Wallace (created Baron
Wallace, 1828) was Vice-President of the Board of Trade.   He
presided over the Commons' Committee of Inquiry into the
Foreign Trade of the Country (1820).   This Committee recommended the revision of the Navigation Acts, and in 1822, before
Huskisson came to the Board of Trade, the preliminary revision
was accomplished.   In 1823 Wallace was made Master of the
Mint.   The custody of the pound sterling, Huskisson must have
felt, was in good hands !   The combined work of Wallace and
Huskisson brought the Navigation Law to the following position
at the end of 1825.

1. In the trade with Europe the old penalties on Dutch
shipping disappeared, and the only remaining restriction was
the prohibition of a ' pick-up ' traffic in enumerated goods.
(For example, country X might not bring into England certain
products of country Y from a port in country Y or country Z.)
It is probable that this branch of the code would have been
abolished in Huskisson's time but for the reluctance of Great
Britain to make a breach in the direct trade of import from
Turkey and the Mediterranean ports of Asia and Africa.   In
1838 this class of restrictions was waived by special treaty in
favour of Austria.   In 1845, when the Navigation Law was for
the last time codified, the term ' natural outlet ' was interpreted
so liberally that Navigation Law restrictions on trade originating
in Europe were virtually removed.

2. In the trade with Asia, Africa and America, the long haul
(i.e. the ocean carriage from the country of origin to a British
port) was still reserved to British ships as against other European
carriers.   But since there now were independent countries in
North and South America, the shipping of these new countries
was allowed to share in the trade.   All such traffic, however,
whether in British or foreign ships, must be direct.   For example,
it was illegal to import Java sugar from Rotterdam in an
unmanufactured condition in anybody's ships.   The ban on
Holland's entrepot trade remained absolute.

3. In the colonial trade inter-imperial trade was still reserved
to British and colonial shipping.   ' All intercourse between the
mother country and the colonies, whether direct or circuitous,
and all intercourse of the colonies with each other, will be considered as a coasting trade to be reserved entirely and absolutely

to ourselves.' [1] But the colonies might send their produce to foreign countries in anybody's ships, and foreign countries might send their produce to the colonies through specified ports of import, provided that such foreign countries gave Great Britain similar facilities in their own colonies. Here the U.S.A. had forced Great Britain's hand owing to the dependence of the West Indies on them for lumber and flour ; and it was Huskisson's policy to extend to all foreign countries in 1825 the concessions which had been granted to the U.S.A. in 1822. For, as he truly observed, if the primary object of the Navigation Laws was to maintain a great commercial marine, ' the next great principle of these laws was to prevent a share of the foreign carrying trade from being engrossed by any one particular country.' [2] And that country now was not Holland, but the U.S.A.

The survivals died hard, outliving Peel. In 1849, under protest from shipowners, they were repealed. Only the home coasting trade was reserved ; and this was thrown open in 1853 in the hope that America would reciprocate, but America said ' thank you ' and did nothing. Already before 1849 commercial treaties had deprived the European clauses of all significance. By 1849 the monopoly of the long haul was seen to be hurting British manufacturers, because, though raw Java sugar might not be imported, this same sugar, if refined in Holland, might be imported as a Dutch manufactured product. Furthermore, the colonies had no longer any enthusiasm for them. Canadian shipping had enjoyed up to 1830 a privileged position in the West Indian trade, but in 1830 the U.S.A. were admitted on equal terms to this ; and in 1846 the repeal of the corn laws destroyed the preference under which a considerable export trade in wheat and wheat flour had been built up from Canada to Great Britain. Therefore after 1846 Canadian merchants were hostile towards any restriction on the nationality of the shipping which handled their wheat.

No ill effects attended the repeal of the Navigation Laws. The Navy did not suffer, because, as the result of Sir James Graham's admiralty reforms of 1830–4, it was now manned by men of its own training. The mercantile marine did not suffer, because competition was stimulating and fortune was kind. The repeal of the Navigation Acts coincided with the substitution of iron for wood as a material for ships, and of steam for sail as a means of propulsion ; and in the new material and the new power Great Britain at that time held the lead.

The Navigation Laws proper gave no tariff preference ; they

[1] Huskisson, *Speeches*, II. 317. [2] *Ibid.* III. 112.

merely prescribed the course of trade. But British shippers were further assisted by the imposition of extra duties and dues on their foreign rivals. Such were the alien duties payable when the goods were imported in foreign ships and the surplus charges for light and pilotage exacted from foreign ships using British harbours. Foreign countries retaliated when they were strong enough ; and these discriminating charges had been abolished by treaty between Great Britain and the United States in 1815. Huskisson saw that it was to Great Britain's advantage to make similar treaties with the countries of Europe, because, given equal treatment, British ships would get the lion's share of the trade. He therefore obtained from Parliament in 1823 a Reciprocity of Duties Act (4 Geo. IV (1823), c. 77) empowering the Government to conclude treaties on condition of reciprocity. Between 1823 and 1830 such treaties were concluded with most of the European Powers, but Holland refused reciprocity, and Canning therefore, in January 1826, ordered retaliation.

> In matters of commerce the fault of the Dutch
> Is offering too little and asking too much.
> The French are with equal advantage content,
> So we clap on Dutch bottoms just twenty per cent.

So ran Canning's rhyming dispatch to the ambassador at The Hague.

The policy of reciprocity inaugurated by Huskisson was employed by his successors to secure reductions in foreign tariffs on British manufactures. The most famous of these was the French Treaty of 1860, when Great Britain, on the highway to complete free trade, modified her tariff in a way that offered advantage to France, and France in return gave equivalent reductions. Richard Cobden acted for Great Britain, and the treaty, which lasted till 1881, was largely his work. It contained a clause whereby the two nations promised to treat each other as favourably as the most favoured nation with whom they were associated by commercial treaty, and in later treaties Great Britain carried the ' most favoured nation ' treatment so far that she barred herself from accepting preferential treatment by her own colonies. These, therefore, had to be denounced before she could avail herself of the preference offered by Canada in 1897. The zeal for most favoured nation treatment had, however, its seamy side. For, though it created a network of commercial liberalism when applied among equals for their mutual advantage, it was an incident in the policy of exploitation as applied by Europe to China. Article VIII of the Chinese Treaty of 1843 prescribed that any additional privileges or immunities granted to other countries should be extended to British subjects ; and other Powers in subsequent treaties exacted a similar guarantee. But for the goods and people of China the European Powers offered no reciprocity of favours in their own countries.

Section 5. *Imperial Preference*

Huskisson retained and liberalised the system of preference by the colonies in favour of the Mother Country, and by the Mother Country in favour of the colonies.

The former replaced the old compulsion under the Staple Act of 1663 to receive manufactures from the Mother Country only. When by the legislation of 1822–5 the ports of the colonies were freely opened to foreign goods, such goods were subjected to duties ' sufficient for the fair protection of our own productions of the like nature.' [1] America, being no longer a part of the empire, had to pay them, and was at first very indignant, scenting a renewal of the shipping discriminations abolished by the treaty of 1815 ; but Huskisson insisted on the difference between them. ' It is just as unreasonable,' he said of America's attitude, ' as it would be, on our part, to require that sugar and rum from our West India Islands should be admitted at New York upon the same terms and duties as the like articles, the growth and production of Louisiana or any other of the twenty-four separate States which now constitute the Federal Union.' [2] Huskisson met retaliation by retaliation. In 1830 the differences were at last adjusted. The U.S.A. acquiesced in Great Britain's claim to give and take preference within the Empire, and, subject to this, they were admitted to full equality in the West Indian trade. Meanwhile in 1828 the U.S.A. had introduced a severely protective tariff, and, though it was aimed at Great Britain, they had as much right to this course as had Great Britain to her preferences.

The preferences from the colonies, ' differentials ' as they were commonly called, were dictated by the Mother Country and therefore displeasing to the colonies. For though Huskisson liberated the trade of the colonies and abolished the fees payable to the Government, naval officers and others, ' which frequently amounted to more than the public duties both on the ship and the cargo,' [3] he did not give them fiscal autonomy. By the Declaratory Act of 1778 (18 Geo. III, c. 12) the Mother Country, in abjuring the power of taxing the colonies, had excepted ' such duties as it may be expedient to impose for the regulation of commerce.' Therefore the position which Huskisson found and

[1] *Speeches*, II. 317.   [2] *Ibid*. II. 315.   [3] *Ibid*. II. 323.

left was that the colonial legislatures levied certain duties for revenue, while the Imperial Parliament levied further ' Imperial ' duties (the proceeds of which went to the colony concerned) in the interest of British trade.   The ' differentials ' were prescribed in the British Possessions Acts. The last of these, that of 1842 (5 & 6 Vict. c. 49), in conformity with Peel's tariff reductions, reduced or repealed the ' differentials ' in favour of British goods or goods from other colonies.   The Enabling Act of 1846 (9 & 10 Vict. c. 94), hurried through Parliament during the last days of the Corn Law crisis, enabled, nay invited, the colonies to reduce or repeal the differentials which remained.   Canada (i.e. Ontario and Quebec) promptly complied, but New Brunswick in 1848 had not yet availed itself of the power.   However, there was still no thought of allowing a colony to frame a tariff which favoured itself at the expense of the Mother Country.   And Canada after gaining self-government had to fight for this further power in 1859 : which she won in the face of protests from the Sheffield manufacturers, strongly backed by the Colonial Office.   It was urged against her that the tariff of 1859 was really a ' differential ' in favour of the U.S.A. owing to the ease of smuggling across the border.   But the British Government had to give way, and having yielded over the main issue confined its efforts henceforward towards keeping the tariffs of the self-governing colonies free of ' differentials ' which would interfere with uniform treatment of all commerce, British or foreign.   This led to a conflict with Tasmania in 1867 ; for the Australian Constitutions Act of 1850, unlike that of 1852 for New Zealand, forbade ' differentials,' and therefore the Home Government disallowed the agreement which Tasmania proposed for reciprocal trading with the Australian colonies and New Zealand.   It gave way in 1873 in consideration of the fact that the ' differentials ' desired were inter-colonial, but it was not till 1895 that the Australian colonies had power to arrange with foreign countries reciprocal tariffs which involved ' differentials.'

Throughout this protracted fight for fiscal autonomy the influence of America was apparent.   The growth of American protectionism reacted on Canada, and the success of the closer trade relations between Canada and the U.S.A. under the Reciprocity Treaty of 1854 inclined Australia and New Zealand to a similar arrangement.   Thus it came about that the policy of ' differentials,' which Huskisson had supported as part of a liberal imperialism, became first a stumbling-block in the way of colonial autonomy and later a pattern for closer relations with other countries to the possible exclusion of the Motherland.

On her side, too, Great Britain gave preferences, which, as they involved no subordination and were valuable commercially, were very acceptable to the colonies. Such preferences were as old as the Empire, but they assumed a new importance at the beginning of the 19th century, when Great Britain was short of timber and corn and seeking to replace the gap made in her scheme of imperial supply by the revolt of America. The oldest of them was on West Indian sugar. Down to 1841, however, this was almost a monopoly, since the duties on foreign sugar were prohibitive ; and therefore Huskisson had little scope here. He lamented the dependence of the West Indies on a single crop, and he extended to West Indian ports the privilege of the British Bonding System in the hope of diversifying their commerce. Sugar, having become a necessary of life in England, yielded a large revenue : in Huskisson's time it was almost one-third of the whole Customs revenue. Hence the West Indian planters demanded lower duties rather than higher protection.

Spirits, tobacco, and wine were also big revenue yielders and the duty of Customs was tied up with that of Excise. Here, therefore, Huskisson exerted his influence through Robinson, the Chancellor of the Exchequer. Rum, the leading colonial spirit and natural drink of the sailors who fetched it, had long enjoyed a preference, which during the French wars was curtailed in the interest of revenue. But in 1826, while the duty of Customs and Excise on brandy and gin was left at £1 2s. 6d. the gallon, which was approximately the rate of 1814 to 1823, that on West Indian rum was lowered from 12s. 7d. to 8s. 6d. This reduction, however, was far outweighed by the fact that the duty of Excise on home-made spirits was lower still, so much lower, indeed, in Scotland and Ireland that the use of rum greatly declined. In this way ' Scotch ' was lifted into alcoholic fame.

Tobacco, i.e. unmanufactured tobacco, was in a curious position. America, the chief source of supply, did not lose her preference over Spain and Portugal till 1826. ' British Plantation or American ' paid a lower rate. After 1826 the U.S.A. was included in ' other parts ' paying 3s. per lb. (Customs plus Excise) against 2s. 9d. by ' British Plantations in America.' But the preference was secured by bringing the rates for other parts down to the former rate for America and giving British Plantations a 3d. preference on that. Otherwise a higher duty than before would have been imposed on the raw material of an important British manufacture. Cape Wine, a comparatively new product, had enjoyed a big preference in the combined duty of Customs and Excise since 1813. In 1825, when the whole of the wine duty was restored to the Customs, the margin was maintained and stood out clearly after 1831, when the differential rate against French wines was abolished. Cape Wine then paid 2s. 9d. a gallon against 5s. 6d. from all other countries.

During the Napoleonic Wars stiff duties were imposed on Baltic timber with a view to aiding the lumbering industry in the Maritime Provinces of Canada. After 1815 these duties were raised. But since the best quality of shipbuilding timber came from the Baltic, the powerful Baltic interest demanded a reduction ; and since the duties yielded a substantial revenue, the Chancellor could not afford a lower rate without compensation elsewhere. Therefore in 1821, when the duty on Baltic timber was reduced by ten shillings a load, the colonial rate was raised from half a crown to ten shillings a load. Huskisson was urged in 1825 to carry the reduction further, but he refused, stressing the imperial argument. ' Canadian timber, considering that it grew in one of our own colonies and was transported in our own ships, was a most valuable trade to Great Britain.' [1] But it was a precarious trade for the crews. Ships so unseaworthy that they would not float if loaded with anything but timber ended their days in the North Atlantic timber trade, and such was the scandal of these ' coffin ships ' that an Act was passed in 1839 (2 & 3 Vict. c. 44) to regulate them. Moreover, even after 1821 the preference was so substantial that there was profit in carrying Norwegian timber to Canada, taking out certificates of origin there and thus fraudulently obtaining the benefit of the preference. Under every Corn Law since 1791 a preference had been granted to the colonies : and to Ireland down to 1806, when bounties and duties on corn passing between Great Britain and Ireland were abolished. During the Corn Law discussions of 1814 and 1815 Huskisson applied for and received a widening of the preferential margin. In 1825 he asked for a special concession to Canada, by which Canadian corn should be admitted at all times into the consumption of the country upon payment of a fixed and moderate duty. Parliament granted this for a period of two years, and under the Sliding Scale Act of 1828 the colonial range of duties ran from 5s. 6d. to 6d. per quarter against the foreign range of 20s. 8d. to 1s.

In corn and timber Huskisson was thinking in terms of North America and in sugar in terms of the West Indies. But sugar was grown also in the East, in East India and Mauritius, which became British in 1810. Since 1814 these other sugars had enjoyed a preference nearly equal to that of the West Indies, and Huskisson continued it, raising Mauritius in 1825 to the West Indian level. India received special preference in silks. When

---
[1] *Speeches*, II. 362.

Huskisson opened the silk trade in 1825 he gave India a preference, which remained at various rates down to 1860 : 20% against the foreign 30% in 1829, 5% against 20% in 1842, and 5% against 15% in 1846. Similarly, when imposing 6*d.* per lb. on foreign wool, he made the Australian rate 1*d.*, and in 1825, when the foreign rate was reduced to 1*d.* (to be abolished finally by Peel in 1844), he admitted colonial wool free.

Taken in the sum Huskisson's preferences were very comprehensive, and they were applied with a balanced regard for every part of the Empire, including that part which had its home in ships. For the reservation of imperial shipping to ships of the Empire was in Huskisson's view the corner-stone of imperial preference. After his death the cause of imperial preference fell into disrepute. As the memory of war faded, the appeal to imperial sufficiency, which had attracted imperialists like Huskisson, lost its force. Peel, under pressure, made one final extension in 1843, when he admitted Canadian wheat and wheat flour at a nominal duty of 1*s.* per quarter—Canada in return imposing a 3*s.* duty on American wheat ; but it excited such opposition among his Tory supporters, the hereditary patrons of Empire, that a request from Australia and New Zealand for similar treatment was refused. In 1846 the repeal of the Corn Laws ended the corn preference ; for Great Britain would not waive on behalf of Canada the 1*s.* registration duty which remained on wheat. In 1854 the duties on colonial and foreign sugar were equalised : in 1860 those on wine and spirits : in 1863 those on tobacco. In 1860 the preferences on timber and silk disappeared, silk goods being placed on the free list. Thereafter for more than thirty years a once great imperial cause lay entombed in the leaden shell of Gladstonian finance.

Section 6.   *The Revision of the Tariff*

1822–1828 were years of prosperous trade, which was checked but not dispelled by the financial crisis of December 1825. The Chancellor of the Exchequer, F. J. Robinson (created Viscount Goderich in 1827), was therefore able to gratify the taxpayer with justifiable remissions of taxation ; and the flourishing reports which he presented in his budget speeches year by year won him the sobriquet of ' Prosperity Robinson.'

Some of these remissions had no direct connection with trade policy. 1823 saw the abolition or reduction of the assessed taxes on windows, shops, horses, carriages and servants ; 1824–5 the reduction and abolition of the transit duties on coals carried coastwise into the port of London or other ports or entering

London by land (London down to 1824 paid as much as 7s. 6d.
a ton) ; 1825 the abolition of the salt excise, which had always
been a burden on the poor consumer and now in addition was a
handicap on the manufacture of soda for bleaching purposes.
Other of the remissions were in the interest of the revenue itself,
being intended to repress smuggling and illicit manufacture.
Thus in 1823 Robinson reduced the duties on Irish and Scotch
spirits with such success that two years later the revenue from
them was greater than before. In 1825 he reduced that on
English spirits, finding it impossible to prevent smuggling across
the Scotch Border and the Irish Channel, when the rates of duty
were widely different. Incidentally, the sale of whiskey, now
the chief drink of Scotland, was legalised in England, where it
had hitherto been illegal to sell it until it had been rectified into
gin. In 1826 he reduced the tobacco duty from 4s. to 3s. per
pound as the result of a ' strange mischance ' in the Customs
Consolidation Act of 1825, but he found the reduction so effective
in bringing illicit tobacco under duty that he continued it.

The remaining remissions were pursuant to the trade policy
of which Huskisson, as President of the Board of Trade, had
charge. The Chancellor of the Exchequer was only interested in
them to the extent that they involved loss of revenue ; and as
Great Britain supplied from her own factories nearly the whole
of her industrial consumption and excluded foreign manufacture
by prohibitions or prohibitive duties, it was only on raw or semi-
finished materials that the loss was important. Huskisson replaced prohibitions and prohibitive duties by moderately protective rates and set 30 % as the upper limit beyond which protection
would be thwarted by smuggling. Silks, hitherto protected by
prohibition (see below, p. 284), were allowed the full 30 % ;
linens, threatened with the loss of their old bounty, 20 % ;
woollens 15 % ; cottons, the strongest of the textiles, 10 %,
which was no more than an offset to the duty on raw cotton.
To strengthen the manufacturer against foreign competition
the duties on many raw materials of the textile and metal
industries were lowered. In line with these reductions on
imports, the remaining export prohibitions and bounties on export
were withdrawn. The Corn Law of 1814 had made the export of
corn free at all times and abolished the corn bounty. Huskisson
applied the principle elsewhere. In 1824 he repealed the law
against the emigration of artisans (5 Geo. IV, c. 97) and in wool
he substituted for prohibition of export an export duty of 1d.
a lb. (5 Geo. IV, c. 47). He would have liked to repeal the prohibition on the export of machinery, but ' considering the great
alarm which pervaded the manufacturing districts on this

subject,' [1] he had to be content with authorisations under licence from the Board of Trade. He abolished the bounty on exported silks, reduced those on Irish linens and the herring and whale fisheries, earmarking them for destruction later.

All these changes in the import and export tariff were effected in 1824-5 ; and in 1825, with the assistance of J. Deacon Hume, the head of the Customs Department, he crowned the work of tariff revision by a codification of the Customs. A thousand and more separate Customs Acts were repealed, and the statutes which remained were codified under eight heads : (1) Management of Customs, (2) General Regulations, (3) Smuggling, (4) Navigation Law, (5) Registration of British Vessels, (6) The actual duties in the Tariff, (7) Warehousing, (8) Bounties and Allowances. The consolidated tariff which came into effect in January 1826 was a single tariff for the whole United Kingdom. For though Great Britain and Ireland were united politically in 1800, their public revenues were not united till 1816, and they had different Customs duties until 1823. But in that year they were equalised as a prelude to the inclusion of Ireland in the British tariff scheme.

Section 7. Summary

Huskisson prepared the way for Peel, as Peel for Gladstone. Free trade, like factory reform, was accomplished by stages. Huskisson's work touched every phase of fiscal policy, national and imperial, agricultural, commercial and industrial, and he combined a mastery of economic facts with a genius for lucid exposition of economic principles. He failed when he met the stone wall of agricultural protectionism, but he carried the commercial and industrial community over an initial nervousness into confident progress along the new way. He liked a fight, a chase after the smuggler or a breeze with America when America in his judgment was arrogant. He desired the British merchant marine to be supreme, but he declined to take the shadow for the substance. Therefore he dismantled the ancient framework of the Navigation Laws and erected in the gaps a structure of reciprocity which would carry British shipping into foreign harbours. He brought order and simplicity into the administration of the Customs, and killed fiscal prohibitions. But in one thing he stood almost alone. He had a vision of empire which his Tory friends could not understand and to which his Whig opponents were cold. Like his intellectual master, Adam Smith, he was a liberal imperialist.

[1] *Speeches*, II. 425.

CHAPTER III

PEEL, 1788–1850

Section 1. Peel's Career. Section 2. Reform of the Excise by the Whigs. Section 3. Tariff Reductions and the Income Tax. Section 4. The Corn Laws (1828–1846) and the Anti-Corn Law League. Section 5. The Multiplicity of Economic Problems in the Forties.

Section 1. Peel's Career

SIR ROBERT PEEL, the son of a wealthy cotton manufacturer, educated at Harrow and Christ Church, Oxford, carried Great Britain safely through a period of acute social stress. Haughty and reserved by nature, he spent himself in the public service, giving to duty what he denied to enthusiasm. Like Huskisson, he was for ever learning—in his study, in the committee room, in his office, in the House. Though he compelled his party to be the instrument of a great popular reform, he did not court the popularity of the crowd, nor did he make supporters and rally waverers by the gift of honours. In the five years of his great ministry (1841–6) he recommended the creation of five peerages only, all for pre-eminent public service, and he did not make a single baronet. He had a middle-class mind in the sense that he sought always to steer a middle way and to see eye to eye with the reasonable business man, but there was not in him a trace of mediocrity. Moderate at all times, he was a strong man in a crisis. He might have spared himself party hatred and the charge of inconsistency by resigning rather than repeal the Corn Laws ; but believing that repeal was necessary to the public safety and knowing that he alone could carry it, he declined this easy way of escape. The Duke of Wellington, who knew a man when he saw one, stood by him ; and so did Queen Victoria. Once she had loved the Whigs and mistrusted Peel, but when it was a choice of Peel or Lord John Russell in December 1845, she wrote to Peel, ' Whatever should be the cause of these differences (sc. in the Cabinet), the Queen feels certain that Sir Robert Peel will *not leave her* at a moment of such difficulty, and when a crisis is impending.' [1]

The prestige with which Peel entered office in 1841 was well earned. At the age of 24 he became Chief Secretary for Ireland, and for six years, 1812–18, handled that turbulent country with the firmness of Mr. Balfour in 1887–91. To restore order he established the Royal Irish Constabulary, which were therefore

[1] C. S. Parker, *Sir Robert Peel*, III. 239.

named 'Peelers' or 'Bobbies'; but his final judgment on Ireland was that 'mere force, however necessary the application of it, will do nothing as a permanent remedy for the social evils of Ireland.'[1] From 1818 to 1822 he was a private member of Parliament, and as plain Mr. Peel (for his father did not die till 1830) he presided over the Committee which recommended the Resumption of Cash Payments. The Act of Resumption was therefore sometimes called Peel's Act. As Home Secretary, 1823–7 and again 1828–30, he took part in the reform of the criminal law and gave to London the Roberts of which it is so justly proud. ' I have been again busy all the morning about my police. I think it is going on very well, the men look very smart and a strong contrast to the old watchmen.'[2]

Thus Peel to his wife, October 10, 1829. But in this period of his life there was one action of ill-omen to agricultural protection. After leading the opposition to Catholic Emancipation, he changed face and carried it in 1829, believing that this alone would save Ireland from rebellion.

In the thirties he was in opposition, slowly rebuilding the discredited Tory party. In 1834, when the Sovereign for the last time dismissed a Government with a majority in the House of Commons, Peel took office and retired a few months later, in Lord Rosebery's words, ' the foremost statesman of the country.' For he showed consummate skill in the difficult situation of a minister in a minority and introduced measures of religious enfranchisement and tithe reform which the Whigs carried on returning to office. He might have come back in 1839 but for a disagreement with the young Queen over the appointment of Ladies to the Bedchamber, but two more years of Whig rule strengthened his position by exposing the essential barrenness of Whig finance. Not daring to reimpose the income tax, Sir F. T. Baring in 1840 crudely added 5 % to all articles in the Customs and Excise, but the revenue showed little resilience and the deficits in the budget continued.

Peel became Prime Minister in 1841 at the head of a united party and a cabinet of exceptional strength. In it, in addition to himself, were five premiers, past or future : Wellington, Goderich (' Prosperity Robinson '), Stanley (Lord Derby), Aberdeen and Gladstone. At the Home Office was his friend and economic ally, Sir James Graham, once a Whig.

---

[1] C. S. Parker, *op. cit.* III. 65. Peel to Graham, Oct. 19, 1843.
[2] Geo. Peel, *Private Letters of Sir Robert Peel*, p. 117.

Section 2.   Reform of the Excise by the Whigs

Between 1830 and 1841, when the Tories were out of office,
the tariff remissions were nominal, but useful changes were made
in the Department of the Excise and in the method of keeping
the public accounts.   In securing these the leading spirit was
Sir Henry Parnell, once the champion of agricultural Ireland
and now a free trader and financial reformer.   In his treatise
on ' Financial Reform ' (1829) he showed that there were three
interconnecting roads to that goal—increased consumption (to
be obtained by repealing all duties on the raw materials of
manufacture and that part of the duty on luxuries which was
excessive) : retrenchment : and an income tax.   In 1832 he was
appointed one of three Commissioners of Inquiry into the Excise,
and the twenty reports published by them between 1832 and
1836 reinforced with a mass of detail the strictures of his earlier
treatise.   In 1836 he was made Paymaster-General, a new office
created with a view to the better control and co-ordination of
expenditure, and, holding that office to his death in 1842, he
introduced changes in administration which on committee or
commission he had previously recommended.

As we have seen (pp. 29 and 36), Walpole and Pitt relied as
much as possible on the Excise Department for the collection of
duties on imported goods which were easily smuggled—tea, wine,
spirits and tobacco.   The Department had also its proper work
of collecting the excise duty on beer, spirits and certain other
articles.   The combined tasks necessitated a great army of excise-
men and irksome restrictions on traders.   At the head of the
army were the Collectors, fifty-five in all in 1835 ; under them the
County Supervisors ; under them the Ride Officers for country
districts, the Footwalk Officers for towns, the Special London
Officers for London.   Every dealer in an excisable article had to
take out a licence for it and to enter every sale in books provided by the Department.   No articles subject to excise could
be removed, except in very small quantities, from one place to
another without a written permit.   Once a month the office
took an account of the stock of every retailer.   By 1832-6, the
years of the Excise Inquiry, the time was ripe for relaxation.
For the building of docks with bonded warehouses, the patrolling
of the coast line by an efficient peace-time Navy, and the general
stabilisation of the country through the commercial reforms of
the 20's had diminished both the opportunity and the desire to
smuggle.   Moreover, certain of the surveys were now unnecessary.   For the wine duty was removed altogether from the
Excise in 1825 and the tea duty in 1833.   And the beer tax was

abolished in 1830, in order to encourage the national beverage
of England against the vile upstart from Scotland : which left
only a duty on the ingredients of malt and hops, that could be
collected from maltsters and brewers without the machinery of
the surveys. These surveys, therefore, were abolished on the
recommendation of the Excise Commissioners. Tobacco was a
more difficult proposition, because here smuggling was still
rampant. Nevertheless the Whig Government took the risk,
and by the Act of 3 & 4 Vict. (1840), c. 18, brought to a conclusion
the exacting system of Survey and Permit devised fifty years
ago by the masterful Pitt.

But if this side of the unreformed Excise was bad, there was
another which was worse. In 1830 duties were still levied on a
number of goods which were neither luxuries nor necessaries of
direct consumption, but ' articles of useful manufacture.' In
1830–2 the excises on leather, printed calicoes, candles and slates
were abolished ; in 1833–4 those on tiles, starch, stone and
earthen bottles and sweets. There remained glass, soap, bricks
and paper. Peel abolished the glass [1] excise in 1845 ; Wood
(Lord John Russell's Chancellor) the brick excise in 1850 ;
Gladstone the soap and paper excises in 1853 and 1861 respectively. All four taxes were admittedly bad and they only
survived thus long because of the revenue which they yielded.
As Parnell showed in his treatise, the taxes on articles of manufacture paralysed technique. Glass was made in a certain way,
not because it was the best way but because it was the stereo-
typed way which the excise officer could understand. Moreover,
processes conducted under excise regulations could not be kept
secret. The result, the Excise Commissioners claimed, was that
' our chemists are for many purposes obliged to have recourse to
vessels of green glass made in other countries ' ; while the manufacture of superior telescope lenses, ' of which at one time England
had the supply of all Europe, has in these few years been transferred to France and Italy.' [2] Only once was a new tax on a single
article of direct consumption ever again proposed. ' Bob Lowe,'
an old Oxford don, Gladstone's Chancellor of the Exchequer, in
vain tried in 1871 to joke the House of Commons into accepting
a match tax of $\frac{1}{2}d.$ per box. *Ex luce lucellum*—out of light a
little profit. John Bull, mindful of the days when almost every
act of his birth, life, and death had been subjected to separate

---

[1] The vicious, lucrative window tax—imposed first in 1696 and doubled by
Pitt in 1784—was not abolished till 1851, when Sir Charles Wood, Lord John
Russell's Chancellor, fulfilling the teaching of the *Wealth of Nations* (II. 327, 331),
replaced it by an extension of the Inhabited House duty, which Lord North had
introduced in 1778.

[2] *Sixth Report of Excise Commissioners*, 1836, Condensed Statement, p. 20.

and individual taxation, declined now when reduction was the order of the day to submit to an imposition on the innocent act of striking a match.

Incidentally in 1840 the Whigs accepted Rowland Hill's Penny Post ; and as the post had hitherto been shamelessly employed as an instrument of taxation, the Chancellor of the Exchequer had to face an immediate loss of over £1,000,000 a year. The Penny Post aided the commerce of the country and likewise the discussion of fiscal reform by correspondence. Without the Penny Post the publicity campaign of the Anti-Corn Law League would have been impossible. If to these two boons, Excise reform and the Penny Post, we add the throwing open of the China trade in 1833, then the contribution of the Whigs to free trade is seen to be substantial.

Section 3.   Tariff Reductions and the Income Tax

Peel was neither Chancellor of the Exchequer nor President of the Board of Trade ; but as First Lord of the Treasury he took charge of the first budget in the 1842–6 series and he was responsible for the policy of the remainder. Determined not to cut the sorry figure of his predecessor, ' seated on an empty chest by the pool of bottomless deficiency, fishing for a budget,' he demanded at once the reimposition of the income tax. Parliament granted it at the rate of 7d. for three years ; and the budgets of 1842, 1843 and 1844 are thus parts of a single plan. The income tax brought in over £5,000,000 a year, and with this and a tax of 4s. per ton on exported coal Peel not only made both ends meet, but also realised a surplus, which he devoted to reducing the tariff and the cost of living. The tariff had the first call. In 1842 the duties on raw materials for manufacture were reduced to very low and in some cases nominal duties, in none exceeding 5% of the value of the article ; those on part-manufactured goods to a maximum of 12%, those on fully manu-factured goods to a maximum of 20%—in place of Huskisson's 30%. In 1843 the export of machinery was freed ; in 1844 the export and import duties on raw wool were abolished : while sugar, not the produce of slave labour, was admitted at a rate somewhat higher than the British preferential rate, but much lower than that on other foreign sugar. Peel refrained from lowering the duties on wine, brandy and fruits, in order to have the wherewithal to bargain with foreign Powers (as was done eventually in the Treaty of 1860 with France), but he relaxed the restrictions on the importation of meat and live stock.

In 1845 he had to decide whether to stay his reforming hand

or ask for a renewal of the income tax.   He asked for a renewal
for three years in order that he might ' repeal other taxes pressing
on industrial and commercial enterprise.'   At the end of this
period, he hoped, the revenue would have recovered to such an
extent that they might dispense with the income tax altogether
if they thought proper.   Having secured the tax, he continued
the downward revision of the tariff in his last two budgets of
1845 and 1846.   In 1845 most raw materials were placed on the
free list :   cotton wool, at a cost of three quarters of a million :
dye stuffs and dyes :   oil, lard and grease.   At the same time the
glass excise and the coal export tax of 1842 were abolished.   In
1846 the programme was completed.   All raw materials, except
timber and tallow, and many semi-manufactured goods reached
the free list.   The rate on fully manufactured goods was reduced
to 10%, silks exceptionally being allowed 15%.   The consumer
received direct relief in 1845 and again in 1846 by the reduction
of the sugar duties and in 1846 by the reduction of the duties
on cheese and butter and the abolition of those on live stock,
meat and potatoes.   The remissions of 1846 were supplementary
to the grand measure of relief to the consumer (which, however,
was outside the general scheme of the tariff), the repeal of the
Corn Laws.

Peel did not take his policy from the Opposition, Whig or
Radical.   In 1829 Parnell had declared that financial reformers
of all creeds ' in suggesting remedies have made an income tax
a part of them.' [1]   When J. C. Herries was Chancellor of the
Exchequer in Goderich's brief ministry of 1827, he planned a
Property Tax with the concurrence of Huskisson.[2]   In 1830 in his
last great speech Huskisson suggested a tax on income from property.   Fund holders, mortgagees, annuitants and landlords, he
argued, paid less than their due.   ' In no other country . . . is
there so large a mass of income, belonging to those classes who
do not directly employ it in bringing forth the produce of labour.' [3]
But on considerations of equity alone Peel could not have
obtained an income tax.   The *Liverpool Journal*, speaking for
the industrial North, denounced it as ' the very wickedest and
most vexatious of taxes which the ingenuity of man could devise.' [4]
The tax, it was held, penalised the business man for his virtues,
of which the chief was the accumulation of capital.   In 1798
the nation had swallowed Pitt's income tax in order to beat
France ;   in 1842 and 1845 it submitted to fresh doses of the same

[1] *Financial Reform*, p. 267.
[2] *Cf.* C. S. Parker, *Life and Letters of Sir James Graham*, I. 308.
[3] *Speeches*, III. 544.
[4] Quoted in *Anti-Bread Tax Circular* (1842), No. 86.

medicine only because they were sweetened by remissions of taxes which it detested even more.

Nor did Peel base his fiscal programme on the disclosures of that much advertised body, the Import Duties Committee of 1840. This Committee, which had been appointed on the motion of Joseph Hume, the apostle of retrenchment, reported in August 1840. Peel wrote to his Chancellor, Goulburn, on December 18, 1841: 'I have not read a particle of the Report on Import Duties.'[1] The Report showed that a very few articles produced nearly the whole of the Customs revenue and that 350 articles produced less than £100 each. But figures of the same order had been presented by the Finance Committee of 1828 and used by Parnell in his treatise. The distinctive feature of the inquiry of 1840 was the evidence given against the Corn Laws and the dogmatic calculation of the tax burden which these laws imposed.[2]

Section 4. The Corn Laws (1828-1846) and the Anti-Corn Law League

The Duke of Wellington's sliding scale of 1828 was Huskisson's scale of 1827 spoiled. For in order to combine a greater measure of protection with a show of equal concern for a hungry public, the point of free import was left at nearly the same figure, 73s. instead of 72s. per quarter, but the pivot point of ' reasonable ' protection was raised. Instead of even drops of 2s., there were big jumps at the lower end of the scale ; and this played into the hands of the speculators. It encouraged the withholding of corn from the market because by raising thus the home price a few shillings it was possible to escape many shillings of duty. Under any sliding scale there would have been some inducement to speculate in English wheat for the rise, inasmuch as foreign wheat could not compete on equal terms until the price rose to free duty point ; but the Act of 1828 aggravated this defect.

Between 1828 and 1841 the rival merits of a fixed duty were canvassed with academic vigour. A few agriculturists favoured it as the one device which had not yet been tried. The Radicals supported it unanimously. In 1841, on the eve of losing office, Lord John Russell committed the Whigs to it, and the economist J. R. McCulloch published a powerful pamphlet in its support. McCulloch showed that the Corn Laws disturbed the export trade in manufactures, and the money market. ' Corn is the principal means which the Poles have of paying for English goods ;

---

[1] C. S. Parker, *Sir Robert Peel*, II. 509.
[2] Cf. *Economic Journal*, March 1921, C. R. Fay, ' Corn Prices and the Corn Laws.'

and, as we frequently shut it wholly out, their imports from England are unavoidably below the average amount of their exports ; so that, when we have an extraordinary demand for corn, the greater part of the excess must be paid for in bullion.' [1] To this he attributed the pressure on the London money market in 1839.

But McCulloch was as little helpful to Peel as Ricardo to Huskisson. He offered it as a sop to farmers' disabilities and ' not because we think it is required to protect agriculture or that it will be of any material service to agriculturists.' [2] The sop, moreover, was insecure. For the corn merchants examined by the Agricultural Committees of 1833 and 1836 were agreed that a duty of 15s., 10s. or even 5s. per quarter would lead to popular disturbances in dear seasons and have to be dropped. This, too, was Peel's view in 1842 ; and furthermore there was a constitutional objection to a suspension of the law by the executive. Peel, therefore, made one last effort to improve the Corn Laws in accordance with the ancient tradition of protection in seasons of plenty and free import in seasons of scarcity. As a sliding scale, Peel's Corn Law of 1842 was perfect ; for as the duties throughout were very much lower, they declined no faster than the price rose—a shilling fall of duty for a shilling rise of price —and at the point where free import approached there was a halt in the scale instead of a sudden jump. But the real merit of Peel's scale was that it concealed in ancient clothing a considerable reduction of protection all along the line.

Meanwhile the Anti-Corn Law League had been founded, demanding neither fixed duty nor sliding scale, but total and unconditional repeal. Originating at Manchester in January 1839, it was a national organisation by the end of that year. By lectures, pamphlets, journals and great public meetings it kept the country for seven years in lively agitation. In 1838 Charles Villiers, the member for Wolverhampton, made the first of his annual motions for inquiry with a view to repeal, and after him Richard Cobden and John Bright championed the cause in Parliament. The League had its moments of fear and despair, of fear when its shrill protests were drowned in the Chartist rage of 1842, of despair when in 1844 Parliament and the country became engrossed in railways, banking and ,of all aberrations the most foolish) factory reform. But the purses of the manufacturers were long, the leaders of the League were able men and dauntless, and Peel their enemy, while he hated clamour, was not

---

[1] J. R. McCulloch, *Statements illustrative of Policy and Probable Consequences of the Proposed Repeal of the Corn Laws*, etc., 1841.
[2] *Ibid.* p. 12

insensible to argument and experience. Bright was a sublime master of the English language : Cobden had figures at his fingers' ends and supported them with compelling logic. Both were careful to eschew the argument that the manufacturers desired cheap bread as a means to cheap labour. They concentrated on landlords' monopoly, on the disturbance which the laws caused to the natural course of commerce and on the hardships which they imposed upon the poor. Down to the summer of 1845 Peel showed no signs of surrender. His policy was to associate the reduction of protection to agriculture with general tariff revision and to press for an uncontroversial solution through a gradual approach to free trade. Convinced of the intrinsic strength of English agriculture, he tried to make his friends see that they had other sources of revenue than wheat and that improved communications by road and railway were extending their markets. The low price which they had to fear, he contended, was the low price which comes from inability to purchase. But in October 1845 the failure of the Irish potato crop compelled Peel to open the Irish ports to wheat and to purchase American maize for the famine-stricken population of Ireland. In the state of public feeling the remission of duties for Ireland meant their remission for England ; and once remitted, Peel was convinced they could not be reimposed. Therefore, in November 1845 he asked his Cabinet to consider repeal. Failing to carry the Cabinet with him he resigned, but Lord John Russell, who had declared for free trade in corn on November 22, 1845,[1] was unable to form a government ; and Peel came back (December 20) to carry repeal, supported by the leading members of his former Cabinet with the exception of Lord Stanley. The bill was introduced forthwith, and in the face of a running fire from Disraeli and Lord Bentinck, the leaders of the Tory revolt, it reached the Statute Book on June 26, 1846. The Act specified that from the date of its passing to February 1, 1849, small duties varying with the home price should be paid on imported grains and that on and after February 1, 1849, there should be a uniform registration duty of 1s. per quarter. The registration duty lasted till 1869.

Repeal having been carried, the League dissolved in a chorus of self-congratulation. But Peel had to pay the penalty. In Ireland famine was followed by disorder, which called for a Coercion Bill. On this he was defeated by a combination of Irish, Whigs and Protectionist Tories—' some for the love of Ireland, more for hatred of Peel.' From 1846 to 1850 he was in

---

[1] ' Edinburgh Letter to the Electors of the City of London ' (*Sir Robert Peel's Memoirs*, II. 175-179).

opposition, supported by some of his former colleagues and lending a friendly support to the free trade measures carried by his successor Lord John Russell. On June 29, 1850, he was killed by a fall from his horse on Constitution Hill.

All parties, including those who supported repeal, while regretting the occasion of it (' Rotten potatoes,' said the Duke of Wellington, ' have done it all : they put Peel in his d—d fright '), were agreed that Peel alone could have carried it.[1] In the opinion of Charles Villiers ' half the commercial men in the City would have been against it had it been attempted by Lord John or anyone else.'[2] Thus once again the strong Tory saved his country. ' By and by, as I believe,' wrote Carlyle from Chelsea, ' all England will say what already many a one begins to feel, that whatever were the spoken unveracities in Parliament—and they are many on all hands, lamentable to gods and men—here has a great veracity been *done* in Parliament, considerably our greatest for many years past, a strenuous, courageous and manful thing, to which all of us that so see it are bound to give our loyal recognition, and such furtherance as we can.'[3]

Repeal did not bring to British agriculture the disaster that was anticipated by many. For in the fifties and sixties the Crimean War and the American Civil War obstructed foreign supply. The Franco-Prussian War of 1870 stimulated a trade boom in which all British industry, including agriculture, shared. But in the late seventies the deluge descended. The bogey of 1815 was a Polish bogey which never materialised. The bogey of the seventies was a real bogey from across the ocean. Its feet were ships of British steel, its arms railroads stretching across the prairies, and in its belly was Chicago wheat. Other countries of Europe protected their farmers against the American invasion by tariff walls, but Great Britain remained faithful to free trade and for this there were three reasons. (1) She had free trade in all other things. (2) She depended on foreign food more than any other country. (3) She had no peasant proprietary. The people considered that wealthy landlords and substantial farmers had backs broad enough to bear the shock.

Section 5. *The Multiplicity of Economic Problems in the Forties*

The tariff and the Corn Laws supplied the fighting part of Peel's great ministry, but it was not of these only that he was

[1] C. C. F. Greville, *The Greville Memoirs*, 2nd Part, II. 351.
[2] C. S. Parker, *Sir Robert Peel*, III. 352.
[3] *Ibid*. III. 378. Carlyle to Peel, June 19, 1846.

thinking when he welcomed his escape from 'the intolerable burden of office.'

In the forties Great Britain was engrossed in the promotion and building of railways ; and the procedure which Parliament adopted to authorise and control this economic novelty was such as to consume an inordinate share of the time of responsible ministers. Peel spent endless hours on railway committees. We cannot say that he left any distinctive mark on railway policy ; but just as he improved the Penny Post in 1843 up to the point of one free delivery daily throughout the country, so also he was behind the legislation of 1844 which compelled the railway companies to run one 'parliamentary' train per day with third-class coaches at a charge of one penny a mile. Cheap postage, cheap travel, cheap food—thus Peel pursued the policy of social plenty.

In the forties the factory reformers were pressing for a ten-hour day as energetically, if not with such elaborate unity, as the Anti-Corn Law League pressed for repeal. Factory legislation fell to Graham as Home Secretary, but Peel had once been Home Secretary : and was he not the son of the man who had introduced the Factory Act of 1819 ? Deputations from the Short-time Committees waited on him and Graham. By reason chiefly of the conflict between Churchmen and Nonconformists over the educational clauses, Graham's Act of 1844 (7 & 8 Vict. c. 15) achieved little. The Ten Hours Act was not passed till 1847. Factory reform involved a call on Peel's time altogether disproportionate to the results achieved, while he was in office.

In 1844 the Bank Charter Act was passed separating the Note-issuing Department of the Bank of England from the Banking Department and compelling the Bank to hold gold against notes, pound for pound. Having watched the currency with expert eye since 1819, Peel was convinced that the convertibility of the note issue must be placed beyond doubt. He therefore favoured the 'currency' school, of which S. J. Loyd, later Baron Overstone, was leader, in opposition to the 'banking' school, which held that freedom of competition and immediate convertibility into coin at the will of the holder would prevent the notes of banks from being issued in excess. A modern writer [1] with protectionist leanings sees in this a surrender to high finance, part Jew, part Nonconformist, to whose interest (he argues) it was that the currency should be contracted and the price of money high. But Peel must be allowed to answer for himself. In a Cabinet Memorandum of 1844 he set out the three possible courses : (1) to maintain the *status quo*, as the banking

[1] Bernard Holland, *The Fall of Protection*, ch. v.

school urged ; (2) to abolish note issue by the Bank of England and other banks, leaving the Government to supply notes. as the most advanced advocates of the currency school urged ; (3) to leave the note issue in the hands of the banks but under legal restriction. The third course was adopted in the Act of 1844 ; and Peel favoured it as being midway between the other two. A crisis, he saw, might still occur ; and ' if it does and *if it be necessary* to assume a grave responsibility for the purpose of meeting it, I dare say men will be found willing to assume such a responsibility.' [1]   A crisis occurred in 1847, but having suspended the Corn Laws which were his party's heritage, he was no longer in office to suspend the Bank Act of which he was the sponsor.

CHAPTER IV

GLADSTONE, 1809–1898

Section 1. Gladstone and his Generation.   Section 2. Completion of Free Trade
Section 3. Direct Taxation and the Income Tax.   Section 4. His Method of Indirect Taxation.   Section 5. Conclusion.

Section 1.   *Gladstone and his Generation*

WILLIAM EWART GLADSTONE, 1809–1898, was the son of the Liverpool merchant, Sir John Gladstone.   Elected to Parliament as a Tory in 1832, he served his cabinet apprenticeship under Peel, as President of the Board of Trade (1843–5) and Colonial Secretary (1845–6).   He had two passions in life, finance and the Church of England.   When Peel raised the Government grant to the Roman Catholic College of Maynooth in Ireland, Gladstone resigned because, although he approved of the step, it conflicted with views which he had expressed in print.   Therefore for the greater part of 1845 Peel was without his ablest lieutenant.   But in the crisis of 1845–6 he was again at Peel's side, going out with him in 1846, and after eight years of uneasy exile he returned to office in 1852 in a coalition Government of Whigs and Peelites under the Earl of Aberdeen.   Thenceforward he was the leader of Liberalism, first its financial and then its political leader.   He was four times Chancellor of the Exchequer and four times Prime Minister, Chancellor for the first time 1852–5, Prime Minister for the last time 1892–4.   As a politician he had an opponent of equal calibre in Disraeli ; as a financier he dominated his generation. Outside Gladstone only three men left any mark on the national

[1] C. S. Parker, *Sir Robert Peel*, III. 140.   Peel to the Governor of the Bank June 4, 1844.

finances in this generation : Stafford Northcote, Disraeli's Chancellor, 1874–80 ; G. J. Goschen, Lord Salisbury's Chancellor, 1886–92 ; and Vernon Harcourt, Gladstone's own Chancellor, 1892–95 ; and the combined achievements of the three were far less than his alone. But curiously enough they succeeded in fields where he did nothing or made his few mistakes.

Gladstone, though chiefly responsible for the fact that the Crimean War made no permanent addition to the National Debt, did comparatively little to reduce the debt which he inherited from the past. In 1875 Northcote introduced the New Sinking Fund. The interest on the debt then amounted to £27,200,000. Northcote proposed a debt vote, rising by two stages to £28,000,000 and then remaining constant, so as to afford a surplus of £800,000 for debt redemption the year the fund came into operation and an increasing surplus each subsequent year as stock was bought up and cancelled. The merit of the scheme was that by giving a more regular action to the process of annual debt redemption it caused taxation to be maintained at a higher level than it otherwise would have been. But of course it was not war-proof, and before the end of his term expenditure on a Zulu campaign caused him to raid his own fund.

In 1853 Gladstone launched a conversion scheme which, owing to the outbreak of the Crimean War, was an embarrassing failure. In 1888 Goschen reduced the interest on three per cent. Consols which were then standing above par. Holders received $2\frac{3}{4}\%$ down to 1903 and $2\frac{1}{2}\%$ thereafter, but they had to decide between repayment at par and a lower rate of interest in 1888 when the scheme as a whole was presented to them. They could not exercise that option in 1903 when the second step came into operation and Consols were under par.

In 1853 Gladstone extended the succession duty on real property, but in 1860 found himself short by a million of the yield estimated in 1853. For, as had been discovered by the later date, real property passed in the direct line in a much greater number of cases than personal property ; and therefore ' while the revenue from this source attains its maximum more slowly than we anticipated, that maximum itself will also be lower.' [1]

In 1894 Harcourt consolidated the death duties with success, grouping the various complicated duties and abolishing the privileged status of real property. The result was two duties : the main estate duty, which is calculated on the value of the estate as a whole and in which large estates pay proportionally more than small ; and the legacy and succession duty, which varies with the degree of kinship. The death duties are imperial taxes,

[1] *Speeches*, ed. A. T. Bassett, p. 262.

as contrasted with Canada, where they are provincial. They are a tax on capital and, if carried too far, will be evaded by transfers *inter vivos*.

Section 2.   Completion of Free Trade

In the two great budgets of 1853 and 1860 Gladstone completed the work of Huskisson and Peel. Never had an abler enthusiast entered the Treasury.   Of 1853 John Morley writes :

Thirteen, fourteen, fifteen hours a day he toiled at his desk, Treasury officials and trade experts, soap deputations and post-horse deputations, representatives of tobacco and representatives of the West India interest, flocked to Downing Street day by day all through March. If he went into the City to dine with the Lord Mayor, the lamentable hole thus made in his evening was repaired by working till four in the morning upon customs reform, Australian mints, budget plans of all kinds.[1]

He prepared his own budgets, knew every detail from A to Z, and never forgot them.   A friend, so the story runs, told to Mr. Gladstone in his later days the incident of a deaf old lady who was overheard vehemently protesting to the Customs officials her innocence of contraband articles, the while a musical box was plaintively performing ' Home, Sweet Home' beneath the flounces of her skirt.   Mr. Gladstone heard the story out with compressed lips and flashing eyes.   ' And this occurred, you say, last year ? It is impossible, monstrously impossible.   I myself abolished the duty on musical boxes in the year 1860.' [2]

In 1853 Gladstone halved the duties on a long list of fruits and dairy products and in 1860 abolished them.   Peel had abolished the duty on cotton wool in 1845, Gladstone freed cotton yarn in 1853 and manufactured cottons in 1860.   1860 saw the end of all duties on manufactures—including silks which had continued to enjoy the exceptional rate of 15%.   In the case of commodities on which the colonies still enjoyed a preference, the rule followed was to reduce the foreign duty to the colonial level and leave it there as a revenue duty until both could be reduced or abolished.   Timber remained subject to duty till 1866 ; sugar till 1874 ; the preferences on both meanwhile having disappeared (*cf*. above, p. 56).   In abolishing the shilling timber duty at a sacrifice of £300,000, Gladstone declared it to be ' as bad a duty as it can be.   It is a protective duty on a raw material of which the country stands in great want ; which is of great bulk and

---

[1] Morley, *Life of Gladstone*, I. 464.
[2] Sydney Buxton, *Mr. Gladstone—A Study*, p. 95 *n*.

thus, in any case, made costly by carriage. The imposition of
the duty, which has the effect of greatly increasing the cost,
and which also, as far as it goes, has a protective character, is
the very essence and quintessence of political folly.' [1]

As sugar was not grown at home the consideration of protection to native industry did not arise. But it was a tax on
food and a very lucrative tax. It is probable that the Whigs
would have abolished the sugar preference soon after coming
into office in 1846 had it not been that some of their followers
wished to encourage free-grown sugar (the slaves in the British
West Indies having been emancipated in 1833). In 1853
Gladstone announced that the sugar duties would be equalised
in the year following. This was a further step in the policy
of free food affirmed in the repeal of the Corn Laws in 1846,
and it was in line with the reductions on fruits and dairy products in the budget of 1853. But owing to its lucrativeness the
sugar duty had to be withdrawn by stages, in 1864, 1870, and
1873, in preparation for the final step of abolition which it fell to
Gladstone's successor to take in 1874.

In 1853 and 1861 (cf. above, p. 62) Gladstone abolished the
excise duties on soap and paper respectively, together with the
corresponding customs duties on the imported articles. The one
was a tax on cleanliness, the other a tax on knowledge. Their
repeal was costly to the Exchequer, but it brought to the country
a double gain. In soap, over and above the duty remitted, which
exceeded £1,000,000, ' the consumer of soap would benefit to the
extent of no less than 25% or 30% in consequence of the cheapened
production. Therefore, for every penny of duty we ask you to
remit, we feel that we are giving double that advantage to the
consumer and a great impetus to trade.' [2]

The same reasoning applied to the repeal of the paper duty,
which was itself the last of three steps taken by Gladstone under
pressure from his Radical supporters to establish a ' free ' press.
In the budget of 1853 he provided for a reduction in the advertisement tax, but by a snap division the tax was fixed at £0 0s. 0d.
In 1855, in response to an eloquent appeal from Sir Edward
Bulwer Lytton, he abolished the penny stamp duty on newspapers and the securities for good behaviour which each publisher
had to give. In 1860 he proposed to abolish the paper duty
itself, the raw material of the newspaper industry. But although
a part of the budget proposals of that year, it was submitted in
a separate bill, and the House of Lords, aware that the Premier,
Lord Palmerston, was lukewarm in his support and that it

---

[1] Sydney Buxton, *op. cit.*, p. 60.
[2] *Speeches*, ed. A. T. Bassett, p. 234.

involved the addition of one penny to the income tax, threw it out. Thereupon the Commons drew up a series of Resolutions stating their rights in the matter of taxation, and next year the Government achieved its purpose by including the repeal of the paper duties, excise and customs, in the budget itself, which passed the House of Lords without alteration.

Free trade meant to Gladstone something more than the abolition of protection. He envisaged therein the removal of all undesirable fetters on trade, whatever their nature and whatever the trade. In 1853 he revised the stamp duties on commercial and legal documents. A penny receipt stamp was substituted for a complicated scale of graduated duties, and in 1881, to the great convenience of the public, the ' postage ' and ' revenue ' stamps were assimilated. This was ' penny wisdom ' which was not ' pound folly,' for ' it is not the mere question of charge that measures the burden and annoyance of a tax, but the necessity of dealing in particular papers, stamped with particular amounts, which you have to send and get as occasion requires, with trouble and loss of time : all these are little things but all of them enter very much into the question of inconvenience and create just objection to the tax.' [1]

Gladstone's perspective was right. Viewed over the centuries free trade meant the freeing first of internal and then of external trade, the removal of restrictions, first on exports and then on imports, and by consequence the raising of the necessary revenue of the country with ever less disturbance to the course of business enterprise. Gladstone began life as a Tory and continued it as a Liberal : he joined the fiscal courage of his Tory origin to the Whig concern for economy and reform.

Section 3. *Direct Taxation and the Income Tax*

Between direct and indirect taxation in the abstract Gladstone refused to make a choice. In the budget speech of 1861 he compared them to two attractive sisters whose favours he courted with equal regard, but of the main direct tax, Income Tax, he disapproved so strongly that he made repeated efforts to abolish it. The income tax had been renewed for a third term of three years in 1848, for one year in 1851, and again for one year in 1852. It was still regarded as an emergency tax which ought to be dropped when the emergency passed. In 1853 Gladstone secured its renewal for seven years on a plan which provided for its gradual reduction from 7d. to nil. But the Crimean War intervened, so that at the end of the term it was at 9d. instead of

[1] *Speeches*, ed. A. T. Bassett, p. 236.

at vanishing point. Therefore, in his first premiership, 1869–74, he made a second effort to abolish it. By 1874 it had been reduced to 3*d*., and the budget surplus would just have sufficed for its abolition if the whole of it were employed in this way. Gladstone appealed to the country on this platform, but, as his Government was for other reasons unpopular, the country rejected the tempting offer.

It is not easy to explain Gladstone's life-long hostility to the tax. In securing its renewal in 1853 he exposed the hollowness of the arguments which were then being raised against it. It was complained that it favoured ' permanent ' by comparison with ' precarious ' incomes, and that it penalised the trading community. But Gladstone showed that the iron-hearted fund-holders of popular imagination included many deserving persons, the daughter and the widow, charitable corporations, savings banks and small investors, and that the stipends of the poor clergymen were accounted ' permanent ' and the profits of ' your bankers and brewers ' ' precarious ' : that owners of real property paid extra taxation in local rates and otherwise, and that many traders paid less than their due by making false returns. In fine, in proving the case for its temporary continuation, he proved the case for its incorporation in the financial system, as far as fairplay went ; and he himself removed its minor inequalities by introducing abatements for smaller incomes and deductions for life insurance, and by improving the method of collection.

But he had begun in 1853 by promising its extinction and therefore he considered it henceforth to be ' the payment of a debt of honour and the fulfilment of a solemn duty.' [1] He was a Don Quixote in finance as well as in religion. Furthermore, he feared that its perpetuation would stand in the way of economy in expenditure and carefulness in the framing of budgets. In 1861 he created the Public Accounts Committee to examine annually the audited accounts of public expenditure. In 1866 he passed the Exchequer and Audit Act (29 & 30 Vict. c. 39), which set up for the first time an effective audit control over Government expenditure as a single whole ; and by this practice he strengthened the rule that moneys voted by the House of Commons must be spent exactly in the manner in which the House had intended. War was a real emergency. By extra taxation, direct and indirect, he met more than half the cost of the Crimean War while the war was in operation, and within twelve years of its termination had reduced the National Debt to its pre-war level. But when the revision of the tariff was concluded the emergency to which Peel had successfully appealed was concluded ; and

<hr>

[1] Sydney Buxton, *op. cit.*, p. 130 *n*.

Gladstone saw with regret the gradual mounting of the national expenditure from £55,000,000 in 1853 to £91,000,000 in 1893, his last year of office. Economy was to Gladstone an end in itself, and this end coloured the whole of his policy. As he said in his address to the electors of Midlothian in 1885 :

In a just and peaceful policy, foreign, Indian and colonial, is to be found the surest road to economical administration of the public affairs, and the best security against the panic and excitement which sometimes cause additions to our great services beyond what they really require.[1]

Section 4. *His Method of Indirect Taxation*

In levying indirect taxation Gladstone followed certain rules, which may be summarised thus :

(1) Concentrate on a few great articles in general consumption.

These articles were tea, sugar, beer, spirits, and tobacco. Concentration had these advantages : the cost of collection was reduced to a minimum and the effect of alleviations could be foreseen with great accuracy. When Gladstone had to increase taxation he operated on two or three taxes only. When he had a surplus for tax reduction he concentrated the reduction in the same way. If the reduction enabled him to strike the article off the tax list he gained in addition an economy in collection and a simpler tariff. He never frittered a surplus away.

(2) Tax for revenue only.

This was interpreted strictly. There was no incidental protection, such as is assumed in a 'revenue tariff,' when that phrase is used in Canada. When the article was produced both at home and abroad, e.g. spirits and tobacco, the foreign article paid no more than the home article, apart from a small surtax to cover the extra cost to which the home manufacturer was subjected in manufacturing under Excise supervision. The equalising process involved technical knowledge of the kind in which Gladstone delighted to excel. When equalising the tobacco duties in 1863 he adjusted the duty on raw tobacco to the amount of moisture in it and then calculated to a nicety the cover that should be allowed the home manufacturer, to offset the cost of Excise control and the liability to wastage in the process of manufacture.

(3) Avoid raw materials and necessary foods.

Timber was an essential raw material of many industries, and therefore the timber duties were abolished as soon as this could be afforded. Sugar was a necessary food and also the raw

[1] *Speeches*, ed. H. W. Lucy, p. 156.

material of jam, sweetmeats, and confectionery ; sugar therefore was freed when circumstances permitted. It was impossible to raise a large revenue from rare luxuries or from non-necessaries whose consumption would quickly shrink under taxation. There remained, therefore, only those articles which had once been luxuries and were now conventional necessities. These were alcoholic liquors ' the sheet anchor of British finance,' tobacco and tea. For all of them there was an insistent demand ; and in the case of alcohol and tobacco any check to consumption had its compensation in the improvement of the national health. 1881 may be taken as a sample year of Gladstonian finance in its maturity. The total revenue was £69,000,000 ; direct taxes £21,000,000, stamps £4,000,000, indirect taxes £44,000,000. Of the last alcohol in various forms yielded 31, tobacco 9, and tea 4 millions.

(4) Select the final stage of manufacture as the point at which the tax is imposed.

Gladstone applied this rule to the taxation of beer. Hops and malt are ingredients. In 1862 he converted the duty on hops into an addition to the brewer's licence. In 1880 he shifted the malt duty from the quarter of barley to the barrel of beer. His purpose was twofold—to free the processes of brewing from Excise control and to prevent the pyramiding of the tax. For when the tax was paid at an early stage in production it was handed on with additions by each agent—maltster, brewer, publican—to cover the cost of advancing it ; in this way the consumer paid more than the Exchequer received. Here Gladstone reversed the advice of Adam Smith, because Adam Smith's reason—the greater difficulty of defrauding the revenue if the duty is carried back to the raw material—was no longer important when illicit trade had been stamped out.

(5) To help the wage-earner, free industry first of all, and then as a second step reduce the price of articles in general consumption.

Down to 1860 Gladstone had sometimes to choose between freeing industry from protection and reducing taxation on articles in general consumption. On free trade philosophy the former course was clearly to the interest of employers. It was also, Gladstone argued, in the interest of the labouring class.

I do not hesitate to say that it is a mistake to suppose that the best method of giving benefit to the labouring classes is simply to operate on the articles consumed by them. If you want to do them the *maximum* of good you should rather operate on the articles which give them the maximum of employment.[1]

[1] *Speeches*, ed. A. T. Bassett, p. 273.

(6) Employ specific in preference to *ad valorem* duties.

This was a further step in an improved Customs administration. Pitt took the first step when he consolidated the Customs and introduced specific duties to the extent then practicable; Huskisson the second when with the help of Deacon Hume he classified the tariff. After a parliamentary investigation in 1851–2 Gladstone decided in favour of specific duties levied according to quantity and grade without reference to price. The removal of manufactured articles from the tariff permitted this. It was therefore a device which suited a free trade system. It is worthy of note, however, that in 1880 one of the grounds on which the renewal of the French Commercial Treaty of 1860 broke down was the insistence of France on completing the conversion of *ad valorem* into specific duties. For Great Britain objected that, as the French classification was not minute enough, specific duties worked unfavourably to English exports.

By following these rules Gladstone secured a resilient revenue, i.e. a revenue which bounded up when the loads upon it were lightened. He set out with this objective in 1853 and based his hopes on the experience of the previous twenty years. From 1830 to 1841 ' commercial legislation was on the whole stationary.' Between 1842 and 1853, ' when you remitted a million a year, your Customs and Excise revenue grew faster than when you remitted nothing or next to nothing at all. I ask, is not this a conclusive proof that it is the relaxation and reform of your commercial system which has given to the country the disposition to pay taxes along with the power also which it now possesses to support them ? ' [1]

Gladstone was justified in his hopes of continued resilience through continued reform. As his economic biographer says :

In the thirty years between 1852 and 1882, during which the finances of the country were chiefly under the control of Mr. Gladstone, taxation to an amount of fifty-three millions was imposed, while taxation to an amount of seventy-two and a half millions was remitted. . . . In 1852 the gross ' tax revenue ' . . . amounted to fifty-four millions ; in 1881 it amounted to seventy-one and a half millions. Twenty millions had been remitted [*sc. on balance*], yet the receipts were by seventeen millions greater than before.[2]

Section 5. *Conclusion*

Mr. Gladstone, like Lord Salisbury, was of Eton and Christ Church. Every Liberal Chancellor of the Exchequer between 1853 and 1898, and nearly every Conservative Chancellor of the

---

[1] *Speeches*, ed. A. T. Bassett, p. 272.
[2] Sydney Buxton, *Mr. Gladstone*, p. 170.

Exchequer, was his financial disciple. The Radicals were sometimes restive under him, but they rose no higher than the Board of Trade, and besides they were usually members of no University. Charles Adderley (Lord Norton), President of the Board of Trade 1874–8, was never weaned from Conservatism, but he was a strong churchman and, as Mrs. Gladstone used to say, ' the kindest of dear William's enemies.' Adderley was not of his stature, but he had the constructive instincts which produced a Chamberlain after him. He was a pioneer of town planning at Saltley near Birmingham, he resisted successfully the Whig Government's design of transporting convicts to the Cape, which therefore honoured him by Adderley Street, Cape Town, and he had a feeling for the national aspirations of the Colonies. But the strongest disciples of Gladstone were the permanent heads of the Board of Trade and the Colonial Office : men like Lord Farrer, Permanent Secretary to the Board of Trade 1865–1886, Lord Blatchford, Permanent Under-secretary of State for the Colonies 1860–1871, and after him Sir R. G. W. Herbert, 1871–1892, who, like Northcote, was an ex-private secretary of the Grand Old Man. And all three were of Eton or Oxford or both. That the Empire survived it, is proof surely of the Empire's immortality. Changing as he did from a Conservative of slave-owning origin to a Liberal home-ruler, Gladstone excited great animosity among some of his generation, but in retrospect he stands out above them all as the financial genius who was also a scholar and a high-minded man.

We may believe that the foreign policy of Gladstone was weak and his Irish policy premature and that the Liberal party halted too long at the point to which he brought it. We may poke fun at Gladstone for devoting so much of his time to abolishing the income tax which in the end he improved and settled more securely on the taxpayers' shoulders. We may urge that the man who took so serious a view of debt should have done more to pay it off. We may enlarge, as did Northcote, on his little financial failures. But it is beyond question that when he had to complete the work of others he completed it well : that while he was in power the country not only paid its way but knew how it paid it : that the economies which turn a deficit into a surplus were obtained by his superb administrative skill : that in improving the plan of national finance he did not do it at the expense of business enterprise, but on the contrary left that enterprise healthy and elastic, so that in 1914, twenty years after he retired, it could sustain the stress of an immensely expensive war with a success which far outdistanced the tax-paying capacity of other Great Powers.

CHAPTER V

Towards a New Economic Policy

Section 1. The Resurrection of the Imperial Spirit. Section 2. Joseph Chamberlain and the Empire of To-day. Section 3. Social Reform and the Aftermath of War. Section 4. The Lessons of War Control.

Section 1. *The Resurrection of the Imperial Spirit*

ENGLAND has been described as the country that no one knows. It is even more truly the country that does not know itself. In economic essence England is the Mother Country of an Empire, and yet for nearly half a century, say 1830 to 1870, she thought herself an isolated nation in a free trade world that would shortly come to be. The Colonies instinctively knew better ; as also did those Englishmen who lived outside England. But the colonists rarely visited England ; and when colonial administrators retired they had been absent too long from the country of their youth to carry weight in it. It was the obstinate loyalty of the Colonies and the apprehension of trade rivalry from Germany and the U.S.A. which turned Great Britain back to her old imperial path. The return was part of a restored faith in a constructive statesmanship ; and the success of Britain in the development of her greatest overseas possession, India, strengthened the case for governmental intervention in domestic and colonial development. But the British Empire is a patchwork : and the authorities have frequently approached apparently new problems without reference to the experience acquired by their successful solution elsewhere. After the Mutiny the Indian Government found that government meant development, and development a direct share in the economic enterprise of railways and irrigation. Not otherwise could India be saved from the periodic paralysis of famine. While the Government of India was thus breaking new ground, opinion at home under encouragement from the self-governing Colonies slowly veered to a new valuation of overseas possessions, but very slowly at first. By 1849 the foundations of responsible government had been well laid in Canada, and between that date and about 1870 leading men of all parties believed that the Colonies having acquired self-government would go on to acquire political independence. The Tories mildly regretted it : the Liberals were pained at the incipient protectionism of Canada : the Radicals reminded both that Colonies cost money and brought no profit. All, however, were agreed that it was the duty of the Mother Country to part on friendly and dignified terms

By the 70's this feeling was weakening ; for the triumph of the North in the American Civil War dispelled the hope that an independent South would trade freely with free-trade England, and America's purchase of Alaska from Russia in 1867 was recognised as the first item in a programme of imperial expansion. In 1868 the Royal Colonial Institute was founded. Hitherto colonial reformers had been occupied with plans of colonisation, the political disabilities of the Colonies, and their abuse as receptacles of criminals and paupers. But now their value as outposts of a Greater Britain was appreciated once again ; and the country supported Disraeli in his strategic purchase (through the Rothschilds) of the Suez Canal shares in 1875 and his proclamation of Queen Victoria as Empress of India in 1877. In 1882 the German Colonisation Society was founded. Then began the scramble for the partition of Africa. Hitherto Africa had meant to England two things : a seaboard from which her Navy had stamped out the slave trade, and a port of call on the route to India, either the ocean route by Cape Colony or the Isthmus land route by Suez and Aden. But in the 80's Africa began to reveal her internal values and a rivalry set in between the leading European Powers for the possession of the African interior. Many British statesmen were averse to expansion, but their hand was forced. The Chartered Companies—the British North Borneo, the Royal Niger, the Imperial British East Africa, and the British South Africa—all formed in the 1880's, repeated the record of the East India Company by converting trading concessions into political dominion.

Meanwhile the great self-governing Colonies also were developing their interiors. The last traces of irritating intervention by the Mother Country had disappeared and they looked now with greater friendliness to the old mother who, they knew, would fight for them at a pinch and who was always sending new children. Canada's day dawned in 1885 when the C.P.R. was completed. By 1897 the harvest was at hand, and in this year of Queen Victoria's Diamond Jubilee Sir Wilfrid Laurier set the seal on the changed feeling by offering a tariff preference for which no equivalent or consideration was asked. During the next ten years the other self-governing Dominions followed suit. Broadly speaking, the preferential tariffs of the Dominions were lower than their general tariffs by 4% in 1914 and 9% in 1924 ; and the percentage of British exports consigned to Empire markets other than India and Newfoundland rose from 23·7% of all exports to 26·2% in the decade after 1914. India granted no preference and used the fiscal freedom gained during the Great War to embark on protection, but she is still Britain's best customer, importing from her 65% of all her imports in 1914 and 57·8% in 1924.[1]

Section 2.   *Joseph Chamberlain and the Empire of To-day*

Chamberlain returned to Parliament in 1886 as a Liberal Unionist.   In 1895 he became Colonial Secretary in the Conservative Government of Lord Salisbury.   Surprise was felt that so enterprising a statesman accepted such a subordinate office, but when he resigned it in 1903 it had become one of the key offices in the Cabinet.   We remember Chamberlain by the clever cartoons of F. C. G. in the *Westminster Gazette*—Mr. Facing-Both-Ways, once a Radical and now an Imperialist, once for Free Trade and now for Tariff Reform, with his orchid, monocle and keen, clean-shaven chin.   The last ten years of his active life, 1896–1906, were spent in such a blaze of controversy, first over the South African War which he zealously supported and secondly over the Tariff Reform campaign which was his own creation, that his enduring work as Colonial Secretary has been obscured. This work was important in both spheres of his office, both for the Crown Colonies and Protectorates and for the self-governing Colonies now of the Dominions.   Attuned by nature to the spirit of the Colonies and possessing great business acumen, he was sensible of the importance of their development to the Mother Country.   ' It is only in such developments that I see any solution of the social problem with which we are surrounded. Plenty of employment and a contented people go together, and there is no way of securing plenty of employment except by creating new markets and developing the old ones.' [2]   His political life ended with a failure ; but after 1906 his policy gradually permeated the Empire in the form which the years of war and fiscal controversy had shown him to be the better way—not, as he first hoped, a free trade empire with an external tariff, but an economic federalism with tariff autonomy for the several parts and preferential arrangements between all.

His work for the Crown Colonies and Protectorates may be summarised thus :

(*a*) He infused a new spirit of enterprise into the Colonial Office.   Obstruction ceased.   He answered by telegram and usually in the affirmative ; and he won from Colonial governors and leading citizens of the Colonies a degree of admiration and

---

[1] Cf. *Committee on Industry and Trade Survey of Overseas Markets* (1925), pp. 24 and 545.

[2] *Speeches*, ed. Boyd I, xxi (intro.) : to business deputation, 1895.

respect never given before. They played up, delighted that a man had at last arisen who could switch his office from constitution tinkering to constructive economic development.

(*b*) He realised that the key of Africa was the valorisation of its hinterland by capital expenditure on communications—docks, railways and roads. By the Colonial Loans Act of 1899 (62 & 63 Vict. c. 36) he secured power for the Treasury to make advances to certain Crown Colonies repayable within fifty years. He also put the Crown Colonies into a position to borrow for themselves on the open market and enlarged the functions of the Crown Agents, which were a self-supporting body maintained by contributions from the Colonies and by commissions on loans. As the Crown Agents not only negotiated the loan but also handled the funds, they were the channel by which contracts reached British firms : and thus, as Chamberlain always desired, colonial progress aided domestic employment. The Crown Colony loans did not enjoy the express guarantee of the Imperial Government : and this was wise because it forced on colonial administrations the necessity of maintaining their credit by economy and adequate taxation. But the low borrowing rate which the imperial guarantee would have conferred was provided in 1900 by the inclusion of colonial inscribed stocks on the list of securities in which Trustees might invest (63 & 64 Vict. c. 62).

(*c*) He made war on tropical disease. In October 1897 Sir Patrick Manson urged the need for special training in tropical medicine in view of the fact that over one-fifth of the medical graduates of Great Britain and Ireland practised in the tropics or were in forces which were liable to serve in those parts. In 1898 Chamberlain offered a grant for a School of Tropical Medicine, calling for support from the Medical Schools of the country and from private generosity : and the London School of Tropical Medicine was opened in October 1899. Liverpool as a port was especially interested in the tropics : and the munificence of Sir Alfred Jones, a leader in the West African and West Indian trades, provided the Liverpool School of Tropical Medicine. Investigations in West Africa confirmed the all-important discovery of Sir Ronald Ross that malaria, the scourge of the white man in the tropics, was due to a parasite carried by mosquitoes and living in their tissue. Within five years marvellous headway was made against the scourge in West Africa, Ismailia at the gate of the Suez Canal, and Malaya. The campaign originated with the purpose of improving the health of Government servants and white traders, but it ended by revolutionising the general health of the tropics, native as well as European, animal as well as human. The Gold Coast, which in 1900 had barely emerged from cannibalism, produced in 1922 nearly half the world's cocoa. Railways, roads and beneficent government achieved the marvel, and medicine prevented it from vanishing under disease. With what joy Chamberlain would have viewed the West African exhibits in the Wembley Exhibition of 1924 !

(d) In 1898 Chamberlain contributed a grant in aid, subsequently continued, to the Imperial Department of Agriculture for the West Indies. Britain and along with Britain the rest of the world were now awake to the fact that the fight for food and raw materials was not between the sweat of man and the niggardliness of nature, but between science and ignorance; and Chamberlain's statesmanship consisted in his appreciation of the rich reward that would indirectly accrue to Great Britain from the development of her dormant tropical wealth. The success of the Department for the West Indies led to the establishment of similar departments elsewhere, and in 1923 to the Trinidad College for the training of men in tropical agriculture for service in all parts of the Empire.

(e) When Chamberlain took office, the economic plight of the West Indies, those ' wretched colonies ' over which the youthful Disraeli had groaned, was still parlous. The first big blow had been dealt by the emancipation of the slaves in 1833, because when emancipated the blacks worked poorly. The labour shortage was met by the supervised migration of Indian coolie labour. This began about 1840. It saved the West Indies ; and was of even greater importance in the nearer regions of Malaya, Mauritius and British East Africa. Indeed, by the end of the 19th century the steady movement of Indian and Chinese labour across the southern oceans had produced economic consequences comparable with those produced by white emigration from Europe. But the West Indies, after losing their sugar preference, had to meet the unfair competition of European beet. The Brussels Conference of 1897–8 led to the signing of a Convention in 1902, by which the bounties on exports of beet were abolished. Great Britain was in a strong position here ; for she was the market for the world's surplus. Chamberlain desired to neutralise bounty-giving by countervailing duties, but this raised the fiscal issue and therefore instead Great Britain prohibited bounty-fed sugar. The successful employment of bargaining power on behalf of the West Indies was one of the stepping-stones by which Chamberlain crossed over to Tariff Reform.

To the self-governing Colonies also Chamberlain rendered signal services, which may similarly be summarised.

(a) He presided over the passage of the Australian Commonwealth Act of 1900. This was a non-controversial measure, which any Government would have facilitated, but Chamberlain's enthusiasm and comprehension of colonial feeling minimised hitches and delays.

(*b*) He associated the self-governing Colonies with the privilege of Trustee investment under the Act of 1900. The value of this privilege in reduced interest has been put as high as 2%, but the advantage was not one-sided, for British investors were suffering at the time from a dearth of Trustee investments, and Canada to-day borrows as cheaply in New York as in London.

(*c*) He was the moving spirit on the British side in the Imperial penny post. It had been advocated by Henniker Heaton since 1885, at which time there was a variety of charges between Great Britain and her Colonies, some being actually higher than those charged by continental countries to the same British Colonies. Lord Goschen in the budget of 1890 conceded a uniform $2\frac{1}{2}d$. rate, but the Post Office opposed a further reduction. The question was agitated at the Colonial Conference held in 1897. Canada forced the Home Government's hand by making her domestic rate of 3 cents ($1\frac{1}{2}d$.) the imperial rate, as from January 1898 ; and at the Colonial Postal Conference consequently summoned to London Canada proposed a penny rate for all parts of the Empire willing to accept it. To this the Postmaster-General, the Duke of Norfolk (not Mr. Chamberlain !), agreed ; and on Christmas Day, 1898, the Imperial penny post came into general operation, Australia, New Zealand and Cape Colony adhering very soon.

(*d*) The heaviest task, however, remained. In 1897 Chamberlain had carried the Government with him in securing the treaty modifications which allowed Great Britain to accept the Canadian preference. But he was aware that his country was not prepared for any modification of its fiscal system. Then came the South African War, involving taxes among which in the budget of 1902 was a shilling duty on imported corn. Chamberlain desired to retain it, allowing free entry to Imperial supplies, but in the budget of 1903 it was dropped, and therefore in September 1903 Chamberlain resigned in order to have a free hand for his scheme of tariff revision.

During the three years of fierce controversy, 1903–1906, the Imperial issue was forced into the background because the food taxes which Chamberlain saw that his original scheme involved met with little favour ; and the protection of British industry against the low wages and dumping of European countries became the main feature in the appeal, which, as such, was heavily defeated in the General Election of January 1906.

Chamberlain had spent himself in the fight. In the middle of 1906 he was seized with serious illness, and living henceforward in retirement died a month before the war on July 2, 1914.

During the war temporary duties were imposed on certain luxuries by Mr. McKenna, the Chancellor of the Exchequer, with a view to restricting consumption and economising naval tonnage. Duties were also imposed under the Safeguarding of Industries Act of 1921, which was aimed at countries with depreciated currencies. Under both sets of duties Empire products received preferential treatment ; and at the Imperial Conference of 1923 the Home Government, now a Conservative Government, proposed to stabilise and extend the preferences. New duties were proposed on foreign apples, canned salmon and certain other non-essential food-stuffs. But before the Conference was concluded the Government appealed to the country on the issue of national protection for the relief of unemployment and was defeated ; and during the tenure of the Labour Government the McKenna duties on a free vote of the House were allowed to lapse. In the budget of 1925, when the Conservatives were again in office, the duties on motors, musical instruments and films were reimposed, Empire products paying two-thirds of the general rate of $33\frac{1}{3}\%$; preferences were given on sugar, tobacco and wine ; and instead of the proposed new duties of 1923 a grant of £1 m. per annum was made for Empire Marketing, to be available for the home producer as well as the producer overseas. For revenue purposes a new duty of excise and customs, with a protective element in it, was imposed on natural and artificial silk. Thus, although there has been no overt breach in the fiscal system of the country, and although on the two occasions when the tariff was the main issue, 1906 and 1923, protection was decisively rejected, yet since 1906 there has been a growing sentiment for Imperial preference and since 1918 a considerable departure from free trade.

Section 3. Social Reform and the Aftermath of War

Lord Shaftesbury died in 1885 after sixty years of social service : within ten years of this Gladstone retired. With Gladstone in charge of the national finances and reformers like Shaftesbury fighting the battle of social betterment Great Britain moved out of the age of dear food and exploitation of the young. But reform had cost the Government next to nothing. Therefore Gladstone and Shaftesbury did not conflict. The new Liberalism, however, made social reform a justification for public expenditure and thus for taxation to cover the cost. It was a definite break with the old Liberalism, but its arrival was obscured and delayed, first by the bitter party fights over Home Rule for Ireland in the 80's and 90's, and secondly by the South African War, which loomed up in 1896, the year of the Jameson raid, broke out in 1899 and was concluded in 1902. Therefore the new Liberals did not get their chance till 1906. Some of the new taxation involved fierce controversy, in particular the increase in the death duties and the new land taxes, but it is symptomatic of the general change in social thought that the Opposition offered similar benefits by another route. The programme may be termed the endowment of citizenship. The first steps towards it were Old Age Pensions, 1908, Labour Exchanges, 1909, and National Insurance against Sickness and Unemployment, 1911. Though the last was on a contributory basis, all three required State funds.

The Great War roused the nation to the necessity and value of education, but at the same time sadly diminished the capacity to afford it. Since 1918 the country has been occupied with balancing the budget, remitting the most burdensome forms of war taxation and financing the social problems created or aggravated by the war. In round hundreds of million sterling the war raised the funded debt from 700 to 7,700 in 1922–3, of which 1000 is held in the U.S.A. Of the total net revenue of 762 million sterling (1922–3), 559 were applied to expenditure directly connected with the war (Debt Charge, 325 ; Army, Navy and Air Forces, 110 ; War Pensions, 124 = 559). The balance, 203, was spent on the Civil Services, which included a heavy outlay for housing and unemployment. But this by itself was more than the whole expenditure of 1913–14, 173.

How then has the extra revenue been raised ? The land taxes imposed in Mr. Lloyd George's budget of 1909 proved a failure and were abolished in 1919 with the exception of the tax on mining royalties. The Excess Profits Tax lasted only while Excess Profits were being made. The main increase has been derived from additions to existing taxes, especially the income tax, which rose from 1s. 2d. (earned income 9d.) in 1913–14 to 6s. 1920–1. From this peak it has fallen by stages to 4s. In addition large incomes pay super-tax, which was introduced in 1909. One new tax, the Corporation Profits Tax, has been added to the tax system, and one very old tax, the Inhabited House Duty, was abolished in 1924. In 1923–4 the majority of revenue was raised from three groups of taxes : income tax and super-tax, 379 ; customs and excise, 275 ; estate (death) duties, 57 ; 711 out of 762 million sterling. This was eight times, four times, and twice the respective yields of 1913–14.

The expenditure on housing [1] was inherited from the war. For the war, while it lasted, stopped building; and after the war rent restriction under the Rent Restriction Acts of 1914 onwards checked speculative enterprise. The shortage was most severe in the munition centres, and especially in Glasgow, the storm centre of labour politics, where even before the war overcrowding was very bad. In 1911 $62\frac{1}{2}\%$ of its population lived in one- or two-roomed houses as compared with $8\frac{1}{2}\%$ for the towns of England and Wales. The Government began in 1919 with a straight subsidy to builders, then it gave the subsidy to local authorities, turning it in 1923 into a subsidy over a period of years. In 1924 the Labour Government introduced legislation with a view to a more ambitious programme of building, in which the subsidy to the local authority was conditional upon the letting of the house at the pre-war rent for houses of its type. On the return of the Conservative Government to power at the end of 1924 the housing policy which it had formerly pursued was resumed under the wider powers given by the Labour Party's Act of 1924 (14 & 15 Geo. V, c. 35) and the Consolidating (Housing of Working Classes) Act of 1925 (15 & 16 Geo. V, c. 14). In 1925–7 Glasgow made up leeway remarkably.

Unemployment insurance is wrongly called a dole. It is a scheme to which employers, employees and the State contribute, the original proportions having been 40, 35 and 25. But after 1918 the Treasury, in addition to finding large sums for the re-establishment of soldiers and civilians, had to make a loan to the unemployment scheme over and above its statutory contribution. For unemployment refused to return to its pre-war dimensions. In the first half of 1924 the sky seemed to be clearing. The percentage of unemployment fell to 7%, which was better than the worst pre-war year of 1908–9. But the improvement was not maintained. In 1925 there were about $1\frac{1}{4}$ millions of unemployed or 11% of those insured under the Unemployment Insurance Act, the increase of unemployment in coal mining offsetting a small general improvement elsewhere. In 1926 the country was prostrated from May to the end of the year by a national coal strike, ushered in by a short-lived general strike.

---

[1] Three agents have provided the nation's stock of houses : (1) the speculative builder, whose economic history is so badly wanted ; (2) voluntary association—on the one hand the building societies of old standing, whose stronghold is Yorkshire, on the other the Tenants Copartnership Societies pioneered from London (the latter add the valuable element of community planning); (3) the State, in the persons of the Ministry of Health and the Local Authorities. For the present relation between Building Societies and the State, under the post-war Housing Acts, see 'Report of Chief Registrar of Friendly Societies,' Part V. (1925). Voluntary association has provided the bridge from individualism to collectivism, and its rôle is still very fruitful here.

Under such abnormal conditions the scheme of unemployment insurance was incapable of operating according to its original purpose; and in 1921 ' covenanted benefit ' was supplemented by ' uncovenanted benefit ' given on stricter lines.   No payments are made if the unemployment is caused by a trade dispute, though this only shifts the burden to the local authorities responsible for Poor Relief.   Thus a measure planned for the high purpose of protecting the worker against risks over which he has no control became in the dislocated economic condition of post-war Britain a relief policy which, however necessary, was disturbing to the better feeling of the country.   The Report of an independent inquiry into the operation of unemployment insurance in Great Britain (1925) merits serious study.   It concluded that :

(1) The alleged evil effect of unemployment insurance benefit on the willingness of the worker to accept employment has been greatly exaggerated.

(2) The administration of the scheme is efficient enough to check any possibility of substantial or widespread abuse.

(3) The application of the word ' dole ' to ' standard ' benefit is wholly misleading, and even ' extended ' benefit is very different from Poor Law relief.

And it recommended, *inter alia*, that the respective functions of unemployment insurance and the Poor Law should be more clearly distinguished and more wisely co-ordinated.[1]

Section 4.   The Lessons of War Control

The great struggle with Napoleon cut so little into the life of the nation that during it the numbers of the University of Cambridge increased.   Matriculations rose as follows :   1800, 130 ;   1805, 170 ;   1810, 200 ;   1815, 300.   In the late war the 4000 of 1914 were reduced to a few score by the end of 1917, apart from cadets training in the college precincts.   In the academic year 1925–6 the number of full-time students was 5203, of whom 4728 were men and 475 women.   In the Napoleonic war merchants traded not only as usual but at super-usual.   With the authority of the government they turned privateers and, like Peter Stubs, the Warrington file-maker, made fortunes at a single stroke.[2] In the late war ' business as usual ' was the cry for a while, but it was soon seen that even that part of the export trade which was

---

[1] *Unemployment Insurance in Great Britain : A Critical Examination by the* authors of ' *The Third Winter of Unemployment*,' pp. 67–8.
[2] Cf. *Economic Journal*, December 1923, G. W. Daniels, ' The Trade Accounts of a London Merchant in 1794.'

desirable, namely to North and South America, was at the expense of essential effort in the production of war material or in the fighting line. Before the end of the war every new requirement of the Allies was obtained definitely at the cost of curtailing other production which was hardly less necessary. It has often been remarked of the British that they have a genius for adaptation and reach reform piecemeal. In this way too they approached the war, and although it was not as impressive as the mass unanimity with which the U.S.A. planned its war effort, it reached results more quickly, and mistakes were remedied as they arose. The reluctance of industry to be conscripted was not altogether selfish. For although the war did in fact last four years it might have lasted less : in which event a smaller disturbance to the economic structure would have produced less trouble at its close.

Three stages may be traced in the growth of control. At the outbreak the Treasury through the Bank of England assumed the outstanding liabilities of the Money Market ; and for the first year of the war the Services contracted for supplies by the customary method of placing competitive contracts. But this policy forced up prices, and the War Office found it necessary to ask the wholesale clothiers to organise production, distribute orders among themselves and charge only reasonable prices. This meant a price less than that which competition under the abnormal war conditions would have brought. For supply was limited and demand unlimited. In 1915, when the fighting settled down to trench warfare, there was a sudden and enormous demand for sandbags. Acting under the Defence of the Realm Act the Government commandeered merchants' stocks and requisitioned the future supply of jute manufacturers. This brought war control to its second stage. For requisitioning of the future supply involved price control and thus the determination of reasonable profit and thus the investigation of manufacturers' books. It was found that the best method was for the Government to purchase supplies at the point of origin and hand them over to the manufacturers, who became what the baker had been under the Assize of Bread, a commission agent working on a regulated margin. In the third stage more and more of the nation's activities were brought under strict control in order to check all production and consumption not absolutely essential to the war. The heavy losses of tonnage from submarine attacks dominated the situation.

In the course of these unprecedented events long-established practices—trade connections and trade union customs alike—were overthrown. Competitors acted together : prominent members in each trade gave their services often for nothing. Organised labour consented to dilution. When the war came to an end there was much talk of reconstruction : could not the lessons of war be switched to the service of peace ?   Were there not features of State control worth retaining ?   However, very shortly after the Armistice there was a general and violent recoil from State control and the post-war boom of 1919–20 seemed to justify this temper. It was only when the boom broke that the victorious Allies realised how difficult the return to normalcy was. Just as the peril of inflation is the agony of deflation, so the peril of control is the disillusionment and painfulness of decontrol. But the Government had no alternative, for the simple reason that it could not afford the cost of further control. The success of it during the war was due to the fact that the Government had unlimited spending power and also from patriotic reasons the support of those to whom control brought irritation and restriction. The foreign trade of pre-war Britain was a miscellaneous volume of individual trading chaotic in detail but orderly in the mass. Her manufactures too were distinguished by economies of propinquity and informal association. And it was to these things that her merchants and manufacturers tried to get back, when the war came to an end.

CHAPTER VI

CURRENCY AND BANKING

Section 1. The Gold Standard. Section 2. The Bank of England. Section 3. The London Bankers and the Country Bankers. Section 4. Joint-Stock Banking. Section 5. The Merchant Bankers. Section 6. Summary of Changes in Banking Function. Section 7. Comparison with Canada.

Section 1.   The Gold Standard

THE history of banking is intimately bound up with that of the currency. Considered theoretically, coin, bullion, bank notes and cheques constitute a single fund of purchasing power in the form of money. Similarly in an historical view the development of banking is bound up with the efforts of the Government to furnish the country with a sound currency. In early times rulers made desperate attempts to secure and retain a sufficient stock of precious metals. They imposed heavy penalties on those who were so unpatriotic as to take them out of the realm, but with a view to the encouragement of foreign trade the Restoration Government in 1663 (15 Chas. II, c. 7, s. 12) allowed the export of *foreign* coin or bullion on the theory that such moneys ‘ are carried in greatest abundance (as to a common market) to such places as give free liberty for exporting the same ’ (preamble of the Act) ; and in 1666 (18 Chas. II, c. 5) it ordered all foreign coin and bullion brought to the mint to be ‘ coined with all convenient speed, without any defalcation, diminution or charge for the assaying, coinage or waste in coinage.’ As banking developed, the function of money was more clearly understood, and also the part that those new things called banks could play in safeguarding and reinforcing the stock of precious metal. Led by the Bank of England, which was founded in 1694, the banking world assisted the Government in replacing worn money by good, in repressing counterfeiting and forgery, and in strengthening the commercial position of the country by the circulation of sound notes, which were not merely an economical substitute for coin, but also in the early days of industrial expansion the only alternative to the circulation of unauthorised tokens. Even with the help of the banks the currency of the country was sorely strained to meet the new phenomenon of wage payments in mass ; and the extent to which it fell short is measured by the general growth of the truck system during the first period of the industrial revolution.

Originally the pound of silver reckoned by weight was the equivalent of the pound reckoned by tale, i.e. by enumeration in currency. The weight was troy weight of 12 ounces to the pound (lb.) and the currency was sterling currency of 20 shillings to the pound (£). Sterling is an abbreviation of Easterlings, the German traders lying to the east, whose money because of its excellence was taken as a model for that of England. But by the reign of Elizabeth debasements had brought the currency to the pass that one pound weight of silver was coined not into 20 shillings, but into 62. Therefore at 12 ounces to the pound the mint price of silver was $\frac{62}{12}$ = 5⅙ shillings = 5s. 2d. per oz. After this time there was no more tampering, for new ways were found of meeting the financial necessities from which some rulers had found refuge in debasement. Charles I seized the bullion which the merchants had deposited in the Tower, and paid for the East India Company’s stock of pepper, which he commandeered and sold for £40,000 cash, in Treasury Bonds for £63,000 which he failed to honour. His son, in January 1672, declared a stoppage of the Exchequer. Such actions were unconstitutional. A constitutional solution was found by William III and his ministers under the pressure of the struggle with Louis XIV. In 1694 the Bank of England was chartered and opened business by loaning to the Government the whole of its capital in the form of bank notes

In 1696 Charles Montagu, the Chancellor of the Exchequer, borrowed from the public on exchequer bills, which were widely taken up when in 1697 they were accepted ' in all payments at the exchequer due to the King.' Now between the bank note and the exchequer bill there is a fundamental difference of function and also of development. For the one is part of the currency or circulating medium of the country : the other is a short-term interest-bearing investment. On the bank note and the cheque was erected the business of banking, which is so potent an aid to production to-day : out of the exchequer bill, by the process known as funding, grew the permanent public debt, which hangs like a millstone around the neck of producers to-day and to come. But in their origin in England bank notes and exchequer bills served a common purpose, the exigency of the State, and they were complementary to a third measure of this period, the great recoinage of the silver currency at the cost of the Government in 1696-9.[1] Sound coin was minted to circulate by the side of sound Bank of England notes, and the Government by exchequer bills tided over the scarcity created by the process of calling in worn coin and issuing new. Thus the City and the Government entered the gateway of modern finance side by side.

In early times the currency of England was based on silver. Later it was a mixed currency of gold and silver. Later still, i.e. in the 18th century, partly as a result of undervaluation at the Mint (which caused silver to leave the country—the full-weight silver coins going first in accordance with Gresham's law [2]) and partly as a result of the growth in commerce and commercial values (which made the gold guinea of 21 shillings a more convenient coin for cash transactions), silver was relegated to the position of a subsidiary coin. Guineas were so called because the first came from the Guinea Coast of Africa. The change from silver to gold was registered in the Coinage Act of 1774 (14 Geo. III, c. 70), which provided for the regular recoinage of light gold coin and made silver by tale legal tender for amounts under £25. Finally, the Coinage Act of 1816 provided for the free coinage of gold at the Mint price of £3 17s. 10½d. per ounce (this figure being simply a calculation from the amount of gold contained in the minted guinea) and made silver coin legal tender for amounts up to 40 shillings only. Silver coin thus became mere ' change,'

---

[1] Sir Isaac Newton, Cambridge's immortal mathematician, became Warden of the Mint in 1696 and was its Master from 1699 to his death in 1727.

[2] Sir Thomas Gresham (1519(?)–1579) was the Elizabethan financier who built at his own cost the first Royal Exchange. In 1558 he observed that the debasement of the coinage by Henry VIII was the occasion of good coin leaving the country. Three centuries later the economist, H. D. McLeod, exalted the observation into the law ' bad money drives out good.'

and to prevent it from being melted down for export, on which after 1819 (59 Geo. III, c. 49, s. 11) there was no restriction, the amount of silver contained in the new shillings was slightly diminished. Cobbett denounced them as ' little shillings,' indifferent to the fact that the shilling was now only a token coin. It is true that the Act of 1816 ordered the Mint to buy at the old rate all silver offered to it and to pay for it in silver coin, but only at a date hereafter to be fixed, and such date never was fixed. The Act of 1816 was passed during the period of suspension, and the new gold coin put into circulation when cash payments were resumed was not the guinea worth 21 shillings, but the sovereign piece worth 20 shillings (the value originally intended for the guinea). This was a more convenient unit for trade. As neither gold nor silver was mined in Great Britain, no domestic producing interest was affected by the demonetisation of silver.

Since Gresham's time England's currency record had been very good. She did not debase her coin, she aligned herself with the new commercial values by circulating a more valuable metal, and she avoided the pit of inconvertible paper money into which John Law dragged France in 1720. She speculated in the glitter of the South Seas, but not in her currency, which is the life-blood of trade. And so the rich defrauded one another instead of the Government defrauding all and sundry, as in France. William Paterson, the prudent founder of the Bank of England, was a very different man from his brother Scotsman, Law. He was a vigorous foe of forced paper. As England, led by London, grew in wealth and stability during the 18th century, so also did Paterson's creation, the Bank of England, which was London's great bank. The Bank had to maintain the convertibility of its notes ; and apart from a brief lapse at the outset of its career in 1696 it did so until 1797. In that year, owing to the abnormal political situation, the Government in the interests not only of the Bank but of the whole mercantile community authorised it to suspend the payment of its notes in cash by 37 Geo. III, 1796–7, c. 45. Passed as a temporary measure, it was kept in force by continuing Acts until after the war. Therefore from 1797 to 1821, the year when resumption was completed, Great Britain had a paper pound. Gold coin at once disappeared from circulation ; for other banks followed suit, with this difference, that, while they had still to maintain the convertibility of their notes into Bank of England notes, the latter was absolved from paying out any other money than its own. However, the tradition against a forced currency was so strong that the Government did not make Bank of

England notes legal tender until its hand was forced in 1811 by Lord King's action in demanding payment of his rents in the ' good and lawful money of Great Britain.' Therefore it passed the Act of 51 Geo. III, c. 127 (1811), known as Lord Stanhope's Act, which forbade two prices, a price in notes and a price in coin. Next year the intention of the Act was strengthened by 52 Geo. III, c. 50 (1812), which declared that the tender of Bank of England notes should stay legal proceedings and that they were good payment to the officers of any court. But both Acts were one-year Acts; therefore the latter was renewed in 1813 by 53 Geo. III, c. 5, and in 1814 by 54 Geo. III, c. 52, which continued the Act of 1812 so long as the restriction of cash payments should last.

Lord King's not too patriotic action was occasioned by the serious gap which appeared in 1809 between the value of notes and that of the gold they were supposed to represent. In that year the Bank circulation increased, the foreign exchanges fell, and the premium on gold rose. These coincident facts ' gave occasion to Mr. Ricardo's first pamphlet entitled *The High Price of Bullion : a Proof of the Depreciation of Bank Notes*, and, subsequently, to the appointment of the Bullion Committee of the House of Commons early in the session of 1810.' [1] The Committee accepted Ricardo's reasoning and recommended that the Government should take steps forthwith for the gradual resumption of cash payments ; but their advice was rejected and action was not taken until four years after the termination of the war. The Act of 1819 (59 Geo. III, c. 49) ordered the return to cash payments and gave the Bank four years to resume in full. But the monetary situation righted itself more speedily than was expected, and therefore in 1821, half-way through the period of grace, the Bank was able to announce that cash payment was resumed in full. The Act of 1819 also freed the trade in bullion and coin, and as Great Britain by the Act of 1816 had adopted a gold standard, this meant free trade in the commodity which was henceforth Britain's chief coin. Fiscal reformers such as Huskisson, a member of the Bullion Committee of 1810, and Peel, the Chairman of the Commons Committee of 1819 on the Resumption of Cash Payments, regarded a free trade in gold and a free trade in commodities as complementary parts of a liberal fiscal programme, and from free trade in money advanced to fight the campaign for a free trade tariff.

In 1826, by 7 Geo. IV, c. 6, notes under £5 were suppressed. This was in accordance with the policy determined upon in 1819, but postponed for a period by a temporary Act in April 1822

[1] T. Tooke, *History of Prices*, I. 359–360.

(3 Geo. IV, c. 70). It had been found advisable before the war, in order to restrain the rash issues of certain country banks, to forbid the circulation of small notes, in 1775 of notes under £1, and in 1777 of notes under £5.[1] The Bank of England, as it did not then issue them, was not concerned. Indeed, until 1759 it did not issue notes as low as £10. But in 1797, when cash payments were suspended, the restriction was withdrawn and the £2 and £1 notes, issued both by the country banks and the Bank of England, provided the chief circulating medium of the suspension period. It was an economical medium ; and Ricardo, the great advocate of the return to a gold standard, did not want to return to gold coin, but to notes of £1, £2 and upwards based on gold. His plan, first outlined in an appendix of 1811 to his *High Price of Bullion* and afterwards published as a separate pamphlet *Proposals for an Economical and Secure Currency*, induced the framers of the Act of 1819 to give it a limited trial. By a supplementary measure, passed while resumption was in progress (1 & 2 Geo. IV (1821), c. 26), they allowed the Bank for two years to pay in coin or ingots, i.e. gold bars, of 60 ounces, as it pleased. But nobody demanded ingots, except one or two curious people. The Bank disliked Ricardo's plan as a permanent plan ; because they considered that it threw on them the responsibility of dealing in bullion and taking care of the national currency, whereas they conceived their ' peculiar and appropriate duty ' to be the management of their banking establishment and the National Debt.[2] And the public led by Cobbett was hostile. ' Your project is essentially a perpetual paper project.' ' All that it can do is to make the misery perpetual.'[3] Accordingly in 1826, when all consideration of Ricardo's complete plan had passed away, the small note issue was suppressed. The Government was convinced (and rightly) that if there was a paper currency of the same denomination as coin, ' the paper and the coin could not circulate together : the paper would drive out the coin.'[4] Huskisson considered that since the country banks in time of crisis relied upon the Bank of England, the Bank ought not to be embarrassed by the presence of small paper in the country, and that the suppression was a fair *quid pro quo* for the Bank's surrender of its banking monopoly (below, p. 111). It was intended to apply the Act to Scotland,

---

[1] 15 Geo. III, c. 51 (1774–5) and 17 Geo. III, c. 30 (1776–7). The Preamble of 15 Geo. III professes concern for ' Poorer Manufacturers, Artisans, Labourers and others.'

[2] Cf. *Economic Journal*, Sept. 1923, James Bonar, ' Ricardo's Ingot Plan.' p. 292.

[3] Cobbett's *Political Register*, 1820, p. 699.

[4] Huskisson's *Speeches*, II. 454.

where £1 notes were of old standing, but Sir Walter Scott, writing under the pseudonym of Malachi Malagrowther, satirised the mania for uniformity and thus saved these notes for that thrifty country.   With the return to cash payments Bank of England notes had ceased to be legal tender.   In 1833 (3 & 4 Will. IV, s. 6) they were made so for all purposes except at the Bank itself.   This relieved the Bank from unexpected withdrawals of gold for domestic purposes by provincial bankers fearing a run on their cash.

In 1844 the great banking legislation of the century was passed.   The main Act, the Bank Charter Act (7 & 8 Vict. c. 32), was accompanied by a subordinate Act (7 & 8 Vict. c. 113) dealing with the constitution of joint stock banks.   At that date three classes of bank issued notes—the Bank of England, the private country banks, and the joint stock banks outside the London area.   All alike were liable to redeem their notes in legal tender : but the Government, on the experience of the crisis of 1825 and the stringency of 1836–9, had come to the conclusion that even with this liability the power of the banks to issue notes as they thought fit imperilled the monetary stability of the country.   Hence the Bank Charter Act, while permitting such banks to continue note issue, attached restrictions (s. 13) which tended to confine note issue to the Bank of England. Joint stock banks with rights of issue forfeited these if they opened a London branch, or united with a London private bank or a London joint stock banking company ; as also did any private bank which increased its partners to more than six (s. 11). No new bank of issue, private or joint stock, might be established (s. 10).   When a note issue was voluntarily surrendered (and the Bank of England already had compensation arrangements with certain banks) or was forfeited, the Bank was empowered to issue its own notes to the extent of two-thirds of the lapsed issue (s. 5).

To safeguard the note issue of the Bank of England, the bank was protected against itself.   For by section 1 the note issuing department was separate wholly from the banking department.   Henceforth over and above an uncovered issue of 14 millions (which rose by degrees to 19¾ millions, as other banks surrendered their power of issue) all further issues had to be backed by an equivalent of gold in the vaults of the Bank of England.   Thus the note-issuing department became what one might call a gold-in-the-slot machine with a reversible action— put in gold, take out notes : put in notes, take out gold.

Though, as we have seen already (p. 70), the cautious Peel was aware that in spite of the limitations imposed by the Act a crisis might still occur, the Currency School wrote and spoke as

B

though this would be impossible, forgetting that the country was passing from a note-using to a cheque-using basis. For excessive issues of credit drawn on by cheque will produce the same bad results as excessive note-issues. A financial breakdown being still possible, the Act was technically a clumsy one ; for if and when a crisis occurred it would be necessary to break either the Bank Act or the Bank of England itself, and, along with the Bank, the commercial community. In fact section 2 of the Bank Act had to be suspended in the three crises of 1847, 1857 and 1866. But the Act for all its clumsiness did its work well. It served as a danger signal and slowed up the runaway express of credit, so that, even though the signal had on occasions to be passed, the runaway came to a stop a few yards only beyond the warning point. To quote Lord Goschen in 1865 : ' Why has the suspension of the Bank Charter Act, in both the instances when it has happened, had such an extraordinary effect ? Because the panic which it met arose less from men wanting the notes, than from their *believing* they could not have them. And the restriction of the Act having kept the circulation of the notes within the limits prescribed, a slight temporary addition could be made without danger.' [1]

The gold standard endured until the outbreak of war in August 1914. In that month most of us saw our last sovereign, and we spent the next four years writing cheques for 125 francs out of a small cheque book, marked Holt or Cox (the Army bankers), as the case might be. When peace came and the steps taken for the maintenance of the exchange with America were withdrawn, the country found itself in possession once again of a paper pound depreciated in terms of gold and, what now mattered, dollar exchange. Instinctively the banking and mercantile community set itself to recover that which in the past had been the hall mark of financial stability, a gold standard combined with a free market for gold ; and this was accomplished by the Gold Standard Act of 1925, introduced by the Chancellor of the Exchequer in connection with the Budget.

The relation between gold and the Bank of England remains in principle what it was before the war. The Bank must pay out gold at the rate of £3 17s. 10½d. per oz. of gold $\frac{11}{12}$ fine, as prescribed by the Coinage Act of 1870. This is the Bank's selling price for gold. The Bank must also take in gold at the rate of £3 17s. 9d. per oz. of similar fineness in accordance with the requirement of the Bank Act of 1844, section 4. This is the Bank's buying price for gold. If the Bank is threatened with a shortage of gold, it does not raise its buying price, but uses its

[1] Viscount Goschen, *Essays and Addresses*, p. 43.

discount rate to arrest the shortage and attract gold from abroad. The Bank, however, is no longer compelled to pay its notes in *coin*. It now pays out gold in fine gold bars of approximately 400 ozs. Nor is it under the obligation to cash the £1 and 10s. currency notes in coin. The currency notes, which were issued by the Treasury at the outbreak of the war to replace the sovereigns and half sovereigns, stated on the face that they were convertible into gold coin at the Bank, but the right was value-less, as it was illegal to melt coin during the period of departure from the gold standard. By the Act of 1925 the currency notes (though legal tender, as since 1914), are inconvertible into gold coin. However, this does not impair the gold standard, because they can be converted into Bank of England notes or credits at the Bank of England with which gold for export can be purchased. Thus Ricardo's plan of gold ingots and a circulating paper medium attached to a gold standard has after a century been adopted. The wisdom of the return to the gold standard in the spring of 1925 was hotly contested by currency reformers. They argue that it sacrificed producing industry to metropolitan finance. But the conservative view prevailed.[1]

Section 2.   *The Bank of England*

The Bank of England has always occupied a distinctive position in relation to the Government of the country. Its foundation was the outcome of political necessity. In return for its charter the Bank subscribed the whole of its capital (£1·2 millions) as a loan to the Government at 8%. But how, one asks, can a bank do banking if it lends the whole of its capital forthwith to another? Why did not this reduce the Bank to the position of a loan company with one fat loan yielding a secure interest? The explanation is, the Bank made its loan in part not in the form of cash, but of bills bearing the seal of the Bank, i.e. Bank of England notes. The hard-pressed Government trans-ferred the notes to creditors and contractors, who were able to circulate them in the mercantile world, partly by reason of the prestige which the backing of the Government gave to the new Bank, and partly because the first notes, unlike later notes, bore interest at 3 to 4½%. It took some little time for the shareholders to meet their calls in cash; and when the cash came in, it was available as a basis of banking operations proper. The same thing happened when the Bank's charter was from time to time renewed. In return for renewal the Government took a fresh loan which the Bank raised by a new issue of capital. This was

[1] For the new situation created by the departure from gold in 1931, see p. 450 below.

done in 1697, when Parliament enacted that no other bank should be chartered by Act of Parliament (8 & 9 Will. III, c. 20), and again in 1709, when by 7 Anne, c. 7, it confirmed an Act of the previous year (6 Anne, c. 22, s. 9), which declared that after September 29, 1708, no corporate body, or partnership of persons exceeding six, should undertake banking business in England. As the Bank grew in strength, further capital was more easily raised.   When it doubled its capital in 1709, ' such was the crowd of people that brought their money to that fund that near one million more could have been subscribed that day.' [1]   Similarly in return for the charter of 1742 (15 Geo. II, c. 13), which defined and protected the Bank's monopoly, and for the charter renewals of 1764 and 1781, the Bank made loans to the Government free of interest or at low interest, increasing its capital to the extent thereby required.

Thus the Bank's origin and early growth were conditioned by the Government's necessity ; but it was not and is not a State bank.   The Government very wisely allowed it to develop without hindrance on its own lines ; and for a time it was not clear what those lines would be.   Its outlook was ' national ' in the sense of confined to England, by contrast with the Bank of Amsterdam, which was established to create an international bank-money in place of the disturbing variety of coins that circulated in central and western Europe.   But what part would the Bank of England play in assisting the nation ?   It soon found that its most lucrative business lay in two directions, note issue and the management of the Government's account.   These fitted well, for advances in anticipation of taxes and the flotation of Government loans were avenues for the circulation of the Bank's notes. The Bank had some private accounts, such as that of the East India Company and other great trading establishments, but it made no attempt to draw banking business from private bankers by the offer of interest on deposits.   The most jealously guarded privilege was always the monopoly of note issue.

There was at one time a danger that the Bank would become the tool of the Government, namely in 1793, when, on the outbreak of war, an Act was hurried through Parliament abrogating section 30 of the Foundation Act of 1694, which forbade advances to the Government without parliamentary sanction.   But the Bank considered that it had its own traditions to maintain, and in 1796, when Pitt's demands seemed to it excessive, it protested, saying that ' if any further loan or advance to the Emperor [sc. of Austria] or any other foreign state should in the present state of things take place, it will, in all probability, prove fatal

---

[1] Quoted in W. R. Scott, *Joint Stock Companies to 1720*, III. 227.

to the Bank.'[1] As a consequence the Bank at the time of the
suspension did not have more funds on loan to the Government
than in 1792, a year of peace. The suspension of 1797 was
caused by the coincidence of two unusual drains on the Bank's
gold reserve—an internal drain to the provinces, where a number
of ill-regulated private banks had tumbled down, and an external
drain to Europe, which was due partly to military expenditure
by Britain and her Allies and partly to the action of the French
Republic in re-establishing its currency on a cash basis after the
debauch of paper *assignats*. The effect of the suspension was to
absolve the Bank from the duty of meeting its obligations in
specie, and at this point it might have pursued a policy of gross
inflation without danger to itself, but it did not. And its prudent
attitude strengthened Pitt's hand in 1799 when he imposed the
only alternative to currency depreciation—drastic taxation. As
the result of this taxation and of the instinctive sobriety of the
Bank in restricting its accommodation to high class bills, its
notes depreciated very little before 1809 ; and though between
1809 and 1815 there was serious depreciation (in August 1813 gold
was as high as 110s. per oz.), it is difficult to see how this could
have been avoided, except at the price of weakening the Government in its effort to defeat Napoleon and paralysing the trading
community in its effort to circumvent the Continental blockade.
Depreciation, therefore, there was, but it was kept within such
moderate limits that the return to cash payments was comfortably
accomplished by 1821.

The Bank entered upon the long peace of the 19th century
with undiminished prestige. The Resumption Act of 1819 reimposed the necessity of parliamentary sanction for advances by
the Bank to the Government. But it is very unfair to the Bank
to say that this put ' a stop to a liberty which had rapidly
degenerated to licence.'[2] For as Tooke shows,[3] the charge is
only true of the last two years of the war and the five years
following the peace ; and the guilty party was not the Government nor the Bank but Parliament. For Parliament by refusing
adequate taxation forced the Government to clean up the expense
of the war by bank advances which eventuated in the further
increase of the National Debt.

As a banker the Bank of England continued to do the class
of business which it had done in the 18th century and gradually
found itself in possession of the only important stock of gold in

---

[1] *Journal of House of Lords*, vol. 41, p. 186 ; Report of Committee of Secrecy
on Bank of England.

[2] The language of A. Andreades, *History of the Bank of England*, p. 242.

[3] Tooke, *History of Prices*, I. 287.

the country. For the country bankers in time of emergency
drew on their balances with the London bankers, who held their
reserves in Bank of England notes. The country and London
bankers kept in their coffers only such gold as they needed for
till money. When cheques ousted bank notes as instruments of
commerce, the bankers, instead of holding their balances in
Bank of England notes, came to hold them in the form of a
credit balance with the Bank of England. Thus the Bank of
England became the bankers' bank, not as the result of an Act
of Parliament or definite understanding at any given date between
the Bank and other bankers, but simply in the course of a natural
evolution in which the commercial pre-eminence of London was
the shaping force.

Until 1826 the Bank had a monopoly of joint stock banking
in England. London was not merely its headquarters but its
sole quarters. After 1826 it used the power given to it by
the Bank Act of that year to open branch establishments. But
it opened them only in leading mercantile centres, e.g. Bristol,
Birmingham, Liverpool, Manchester, Newcastle ; and the business it did there illustrates well its progress towards becoming
a central bank on which the other banking institutions of the
country were grafted. Thus in Bristol, when the Bank of
England opened its branch in 1827, the local bankers protested
at ' being required to compete with a great Company, possessing
a monopoly and exclusive privileges ' ; [1] but the opposition died
down when it was seen that the Bank of England assisted them
in the clearing of mutual indebtedness. In 1844 the Old Bank
of Bristol records that, in order to comply with the limitations imposed on country note issue, they had to have daily
clearings, ' paying or receiving as the balance may be in Bank
of England notes.' [2] Similarly, after 1826 the bankers in the
Newcastle district met weekly or fortnightly in Newcastle to
adjust their balances in Bank of England notes, for these were
easily procurable after the Bank had opened a branch there.
Shortly afterwards the settlement was effected in bank notes at
the premises of the Bank of England branch ; and then by an
account kept by the banks of the district at the Bank of England
branch.

In Liverpool and Manchester the situation was peculiar.
For the banks in those towns did not issue notes. Transactions
between manufacturers and dealers were settled by bills of
exchange payable in London, which circulated freely from hand
to hand until they reached maturity. Liverpool, however, re-

[1] C. H. Cave, *History of Banking in Bristol*, p. 27.
[2] *Ibid.* p. 31.

quired large notes for the payment of customs and Manchester small notes for the payment of wages ; and these were supplied by the Bank of England at first from London and then from its branches in Liverpool and Manchester. Finally cheques superseded the circulation of bills of exchange, and adjustments between bank and bank were effected through an account with the Bank of England, as at Newcastle and other provincial centres. In this way the Bank of England became the bankers' bank in the provinces as well as in London.

By the year 1870 the Bank of England had become fully national in one sense and more than national in another. The experience of the last hundred years had taught the Bank that its first duty was to support the financial stability of the nation rather than to make profit for its shareholders. In this sense it was fully national by 1870. But having become the pivot of the London money market, which was the money market of Great Britain, and having learnt how to control by its discount rate the credit policy of that market, it rose thereby into international authority. It became the regulator of the rate of interest on short time commercial loans throughout the world. If the Bank raised its discount rate, i.e. the rate at which it would lend on approved security, the Bourses of the Continent followed suit ; and a sufficient rise in the rate caused gold to flow in from all corners of the world. Gold flowed freely in because it could flow freely out. Nowhere was the market for gold so free as in London.

Like the course of true love, commercial expansion never did run smooth. For credit, though essential to commercial expansion, is by nature an unruly instrument, and the control of credit is distasteful to the merchants and manufacturers whose operations are thereby curtailed. From the birth of the industrial revolution right down to 1870 there was in each decade at least one general collapse of credit, having as its immediate result a commercial crisis and as its further result industrial distress. There were such crises in 1763, 1773, 1783, 1793, 1797, 1810–11, 1825, 1836–9, 1847, 1857, 1866. Most of these crises had an immediate specific cause in the form of either war or the abuse of some new aid to, or outlet for, production. Thus in 1793 it was war and the canal boom ; in 1797 war ; in 1810–11 over-trading in the new markets of South America ; in 1825 speculation in Mexican mines and other overseas enterprises. 1836–9 were years of stringency around the great American crash of 1837, and one speculative element was the promotion of joint-stock banks. The crisis of 1847 was precipitated by the home railway boom ; that of 1857, the one occasion (excepting

1914) when it was necessary not merely to suspend the Bank Act,
but actually to issue notes in excess of the legal limit, was a reflex
of the American railway boom ; that of 1866 followed upon the
abuse of bank credit by limited liability companies established
under the Companies Act of 1862.   On Black Friday, May 11,
1866, the great discount house of Overend and Gurney fell to
the ground.   The almost decennial regularity of these crises led
Jevons and other economists to investigate that most elusive of
problems, the Trade Cycle.   Since 1866 there have been ups and
downs of trade, but the cycle no longer exhibits its former regularity ; and one reason of this is that the City under the leadership of the Bank of England has learnt how to weather the
transition from boom to depression without an interval of insolvency, and by so learning has to some extent smoothed out
the cycle.

Tooke with the evidence of the pre-1850 crises before him
concluded that ' supposing the existence of motives to speculation
and hazardous enterprise, there is one condition which seems most
highly favourable, if not essential, to the development of them
into extensive operation, and that is a low rate of interest of some
continuance.' [1]   By low rate of interest he meant a low rate for
short period commercial accommodation.   It was this rate which
the Bank by its Bank Rate learnt to control.

The Bank, however, only arrived at this control by coping
with crises when they had broken out, and at first it did not
consider itself under obligation to restrain them in advance.
In the crisis of 1825 its liberty of action was hampered by the
old usury laws (cf. pp. 384–5), which prevented it from raising its
discount rate above 5% and thus from checking unnecessary applications for accommodation.   They were therefore abrogated in
the Bank's favour in the Act of 1833, which contained the further
advantageous provision that the Bank should send its accounts
to the Chancellor of the Exchequer for publication.   The Government recognised that for a national bank publicity was the best
inducement to confidence in it and its policy.   But in the events
leading up to the crisis of 1847 the Bank itself was at fault.   For,
acting as though the Act of 1844 had made it immune to crisis,
it entered into competition with other banks, underbidding them
in the discount market ; and during the crisis it limited the
amount and nature of its accommodation in the interests of its
banking business.   These errors it rectified under experience.
It lent freely at high rates in the crises of 1857 and 1866 and
showed its appreciation of the necessity for still further caution
by withdrawing from the ordinary discount business in normal

[1] Tooke, *History of Prices*, IV. 271

periods and by strengthening its reserves. The Bank Reserve (*i.e.* the reserve in the banking department), which between 1880 and 1890 averaged £13 millions with a maximum variation of £10 m. (9 to 19), was raised between 1895 and 1900 to an average of £25 millions with a maximum variation of only £5 m. (23 to 28). Therefore, although in 1878 there were two formidable bank failures, the City of Glasgow and the West of England, and though in 1890 the great house of Baring became momentarily insolvent, in neither year was a general crisis precipitated. In 1890 the Bank of England and the joint stock banks saved the situation by timely intervention ; and the action of the latter was greatly aided by the solid position which they had reached as the result of recent amalgamations. Reviewing the Bank's record as a whole, we may say (1) that in difficult times it nearly always came up to the scratch and justified the confidence reposed in it : (2) that it was always very loth to consider itself under the duty of imposing a credit policy on the banking community, though in effect it did so by the action it took to maintain the convertibility of its own notes into gold. It was always by instinct wiser and broader than it declared itself to be. It was in this respect, some will say, characteristically English.

Section 3. *The London Bankers and the Country Bankers*

The Bank of England left ordinary banking business to the London bankers, the country bankers, and later, when these were allowed by law, to other joint stock banking companies.

The London bankers were goldsmiths in the reign of Charles II. Though there were ample Elizabethan precedents in the foreign field, the domestic trade of ' bankering ' was the object of some suspicion at first. For the goldsmith bankers were transitional between the old and the new, and they did things which are outside the range of the modern banker. They kept a shop in which they sold articles of gold and silver. They exchanged foreign currency after the fashion of exchange shops in a modern European city. They dealt also in English coin, exchanged gold for silver and vice versa. Finally they did a business which ultimately became their sole business, they acted as custodians for the spare cash of their patrons. From this last function deposit banking grew.

The goldsmiths had their shops in Lombard Street, where once the Lombards, Long Beards, had dwelled. To-day over Martin's Bank, No. 68 Lombard Street (since 1918 the Bank of Liverpool and Martins), you may see the sign of the Grasshopper, the property having once belonged to Sir Thomas Gresham whose crest, the grasshopper, swings over the Royal Exchange. Another famous London bank was Hoare's Bank, with the sign of the Golden Bottle, suggesting a good cheer which is denied to the bankers of some countries to-day. Yet a third was Child's Bank with the sign of Ye Marygold, later No. 1 Fleet Street, the first Francis Child having married the daughter of a goldsmith who traded at Ye Marygold, a public house in the reign of Elizabeth. Dickens in the *Tale of Two Cities* satirised this old banking house : 'Tellson's Bank by Temple Bar was an old-fashioned place, even in the year one thousand seven hundred and eighty. It was very small, very dark, very ugly, very incommodious, etc., etc.' [1] A pretty story is told of the opening of the new buildings in 1880. A small newsboy came in with a few pence and demanded to see the Manager. 'What is that for ? ' asked the Manager, eyeing the handful of pence. The boy pointed to the notice on the door, 'Entrance to Child's Bank.' The story has the moral for bankers ; for such small savings trifling in themselves form in the aggregate a substantial part of the vast funds which are at the disposal of Banks to-day.

For the growth of deposit banking three things were necessary. The first was the deposit itself. Under modern conditions deposits may be created by an act of lending on the part of the bank, but historically deposit banking originated in the transfer of previously possessed cash from the merchant to the goldsmith. For in 17th century London there existed substantial merchants who were accustomed to the bill of exchange and whose business necessitated a cash balance ; and the goldsmith had to persuade these merchants that it was more convenient, and just as safe, for them to keep their balances in his shop as in their own strong room. Balances thus lodged were known as 'running cashes' or current accounts. Having secured a London *clientèle* the London bankers pushed out into the country and established connexions with country agents, who in turn kept their balances in London. Thus the deposits of the London bankers grew.

The merchants, however, kept their balances with a banker, not mainly because he afforded them a place of safe custody, but because thereby they could more conveniently settle their accounts with one another, transferring a part of their balance by an instrument called a cheque. The cheque was the second essential in deposit banking. It differs from a bank note in that it depends on the goodness of the man who draws it. Over a note it has the great advantage that it can be drawn for a specific sum, and can be cancelled in the event of loss or suspected fraud. It was, therefore, a particularly suitable instrument for

[1] Book the Second, Ch. I.

merchants who were in frequent contact with one another. There was an old-world courtesy about the early cheque, which is missing in the bald and part-printed documents of to-day. Here is a sample : ' Bolton, 4th March, 1684. At sight hereof pray pay unto Charles Duncombe, Esq., or order the Sum of £400 (Four Hundred Pounds) and place it to the account of your assured friend Winchester '—addressed to Messrs. Child and Company, Ye Marygold, Strand.

The third essential in deposit banking was the clearing house. The cheques drawn on the different banks had to be cashed, so that the banks might meet the cheques drawn on them and receive payment from other banks for cheques drawn in their customers' favour. Each bank, therefore, kept one or more ' Walk Clerks,' whose duty it was to go round and collect cheques promptly, but in time they found it more convenient to meet in a common room and exchange them. In 1770 the Walk Clerks from the City and West End banks met at a public house in Lombard Street.

Here, in the public room, or, according to tradition, on the posts in the court outside, each day after lunch a rough system of exchange of cheques was carried on between the clerks from each bank, the balances being settled in notes and cash. This rough system of clearing grew to such an extent that the bankers became alarmed at the large amount of notes involved and rented a room for their clerks to meet and exchange drafts.[1]

In 1805 new premises were taken, and about the same time a Committee of London Clearing Bankers came into existence to regulate the procedure at the Clearing. In 1833, owing to the growth of business, the Clearing House was transferred to its present quarters off Lombard Street.

At first each bank settled direct with the other banks. In or about 1841 a single payment for the whole day's business was introduced. In 1854, the year in which the first Metropolitan joint stock banks were admitted to membership, the use of notes and cash in the settlement was abandoned in favour of a transfer of balances by means of a clearing account with the Bank of England, and in 1864 the Bank of England, in order to facilitate the working, itself became a member of the Clearing House. In 1858 the London clearing bankers inaugurated a country clearing, being threatened with the possibility that if they did not the country bankers would establish in London a clearing house of their own : in 1907 they inaugurated a metropolitan

---

[1] P. W. Matthews, *The Bankers' Clearing House*, p. 21, quoting Mr. Holland Martin.

clearing to handle the growing business of branch banks in the London suburbs, which had increased from seventy in 1868 to three hundred and fifty in 1907. The provinces following suit established local clearings, with Manchester as the leader in 1872. The part played by the Bank of England branches in the provincial transition from notes to cheques has been already indicated (pp. 102–3).

Thus by the end of the 18th century the three essentials of deposit banking, the deposit, the cheque, and the clearing house, were developed into an organic unity by the London bankers. The 19th century built on the heritage from them. And just as the Bank of England made no attempt to develop deposit banking, so before the end of the 18th century the London bankers had retired from the business of note issue. Each kept to its own task ; and therefore when joint stock banks entered the London field in competition with the London private bankers, it was no hardship to them that they were prevented by law from issuing notes.

Country banker means provincial banker. England has never had land mortgage or rural credit banks. The prevalence of tenant farming removed the necessity for mortgage banks, and the farmers being as a class substantial men were among the most esteemed clients of the ordinary banks. Now just as London banking grew in the late 17th century out of the goldsmith's shop, so also in the first half of the 18th the country banker grew out of the general merchant. One of the earliest country banks, 'the Old Gloucester Bank,' was established by a chandler James Wood by name, and the original Smith of Smith, Payne and Smith, whose name survived till recently in the Union of London and Smiths, was a draper of Nottingham. The British Linen Bank, one of the four chartered banks of Scotland, is the residuum of the British Linen Company, which was incorporated in 1746 to manufacture and deal in linen and also ' to do everything that may conduce to the promoting and carrying on of the said linen manufacture.' [1] The original Lloyd, Sampson Lloyd, was a Birmingham ironmaster, and his partner John Taylor a maker of buttons and snuff-boxes.

From 1750 onwards the growth of the country banks was rapid—a reflex of the opening stages of the industrial revolution in the provinces. The connexion of the iron-masters with banking was very natural, as they in particular had large wage payments to make in districts outside old centres of population. The suppression of small notes by law in 1775 and 1777 (above,

---

[1] Cf. the account in P. W. Matthews and A. W. Tooke, *History of Barclays Bank Limited* (with which it is now affiliated), pp. 273 and 372–6.

p. 96) was more to the interest of London than of the provinces. However, London was essential to the provinces. Every country banker had his eye on London and used it as a settling house. The contact with London was indeed the main factor in the evolution from general merchant to specialised banker. Such a merchant, having a private account with a London banker not only for his own business but also to oblige local customers, easily passed into a country banker who drew by arrangement on a London house. The Welsh cattle trade supplies a quaint example of the orientation on London. The Black Ox Bank of Llandovery was founded by a drover David Jones in 1799 and was called locally the Black Ox Bank because its notes were engraved with a Black Ox. At Aberystwith there was the Bank of the Black Sheep : each sheep on the note represented a pound, each lamb ten shillings. For generations the Welsh drovers had been receiving money from persons who had payments to make in London and elsewhere. This money they left at home and paid the creditors out of the proceeds of their sales in London, thus avoiding the risk of loss through accident or robbery. When this custom was formalised the drover became a country banker.[1]

Just as all important business was settled in London and all public news came from London, so all main roads led to London ; and the opening of a mail coach service between Bristol and London in 1774 was an epoch in Bristol's banking history. ' The custom of opening in the evening was abolished, it being found that public business interfered so much with the material business of answering their London letters and of making up their re-mittances.' [2] By the end of the 18th century the country business had become so important that some London firms made a practice of delegating a junior partner to a provincial town, where he would open a bank business in conjunction with the parent institution in the City. In contrast with the London banker, note issue was important to the country banker ; and the disrepute into which the reckless note issue of mushroom insti-tutions brought country banking during the Napoleonic war has led to the more solid country bankers receiving less than justice from students of banking history. Many of them were Quakers, such as Jonathan Backhouse of Darlington, county Durham. ' Safe as a Jonathan ' was a proverb in the North ; of this house we are told that ' by the successful manner in which Jonathan Backhouse and Company stood the panic of 1825, they rose high in public favour, so much so that for years in

---

[1] Cf. *Transactions of the Royal Historical Society*, 1926, ' The Cattle Trade between Wales and England,' p. 143.
[2] C. H. Cave, *History of Banking in Bristol*, p. 12.

every market or fair in the county of Durham a " Jonathan " was infinitely preferred to a note of the Bank of England.' [1]

The country banks passed away, not because they were rotten as a class, but because a new and more solid banking structure took their place. This structure was the joint stock banking company, by which they were gradually absorbed, or into which, as with Lloyds and Barclays, they themselves grew.

Section 4. Joint-Stock Banking

Unlike the Bank of England, the Bank of Scotland, constituted by Act of Parliament in 1695, had no monopoly of joint-stock banking. By 1800 there were three old-established chartered banks in Scotland, and over and above these a number of banking companies, which at law were extended private partnerships trading with unlimited liability, one of the oldest being the Dundee Banking Company founded in 1764. It was these last whose achievements made new banking history. From Scotland they found their way into England as the result of an enthusiastic campaign waged against the Bank of England's monopoly by Thomas Joplin, a merchant of Newcastle-on-Tyne, which was close to the Scottish Border.

If it be asked why Scotland led the way, the reply is threefold. In the first place the law permitted it. But this is an insufficient explanation ; we must ask further why, when the law permitted, the idea fell on such fertile ground. In the second place Scotland, though inferior to England in commercial wealth, had a long tradition of education and intimate parochial life. The disciples of John Knox were schooled in an inquisitorial kirk, and the supervision they exercised over their neighbour's conscience was readily extended to the contents of his purse. This intimate knowledge facilitated the granting of credit on personal security, backed by the guarantee of one or two substantial neighbours— a favourite form of security in the old bank practice of Scotland.[2] In the third place Scotland was a very poor country, and her poverty forced her into action for its relief. It was the same with Germany in the middle of the 19th century. German peasants were so heavily in debt to money-lenders that they were stung into co-operative banking as a means of escape. Now Scotland had small prospect of profiting by the mechanical innovations of the industrial revolution, unless she collected the capital for financing new industries within her borders. She had therefore to go out

[1] Maberly Phillips, *History of Banking in Northumberland, Durham and N. Yorks*, p. 58.
[2] *Cf.* the account in Adam Smith, I. 281 *et seq*.

and seek deposits by the offer of a decent rate of interest and to secure the confidence of depositors by a subscription of capital from a number of local shareholders. The money thus locally raised was locally employed ; and the Scottish joint-stock banks became in Joplin's words ' at once the great depositories of the money capital of the country and the source from whence the supplies of it are drawn.' [1] The favourite form of credit was a cash account. ' Any person in business by giving two sufficient securities may open an account with them and overdraw them to the extent of the securities given, for which he is charged 5% upon the balance he owes. Very great advances not only to mercantile men, but to all classes of persons are made in this way ; ' [2] 4% was allowed on deposits and 5% charged on loans.

Joplin's campaign ended in triumph in 1826 when the Act was passed which legalised outside the London area joint-stock banks or, as the Act termed them, ' co-partnerships of bankers ' (7 Geo. IV, c. 46). Joint-stock banks accordingly made their appearance in the provinces without delay. Joplin helped to found establishments at Lancaster, Huddersfield, Norwich and Whitehaven, though curiously enough none of those in the Newcastle district were of his foundation. It was not plain sailing at first. When a useful instrument is invented it is not long before some people abuse it. The rashness of certain newly formed provincial joint-stock banks was a considerable factor in the financial stringency of 1836-9. In 1847, on the collapse of the home railway boom, Scottish investors lost heavily by the failure of a number of exchange banks, which had been formed for making advances on railway shares. In 1857 the Northumberland and Durham District Bank failed, among others. ' It was the last joint-stock bank [sc. in the district] to survive, and when it exploded, Newcastle was again left (with the exception of the Bank of England) in the hands of private bankers.' [3] The check to joint-stock banking in this district was severe and prolonged, confidence being slowly rebuilt under the lead of the National Provincial Bank of England, which opened a Newcastle branch in 1865. The lesson of the forty years from 1826 to 1866 was that the small district bank, joint-stock or private, could not withstand the periodic crises which swept over the country ; and a broader base was secured by amalgamation with one another or with the Metropolitan Joint-Stock Banks which had meanwhile made their appearance in London.

[1] T. Joplin, *Essay on Banking*, 7th ed. (1838), p. 19.
[2] *Ibid.* p. 20.
[3] Maberly Phillips, *History of Banking in Northumberland, Durham and N. Yorks*, p. 116.

When the Bank of England's charter was renewed in 1833 it was expressly stipulated that the Bank's monopoly extended only to note issue ; and the effect of this was to permit joint-stock banks in London provided that they did not issue notes. There appeared therefore within six years the London and West-minster, the London Joint Stock, the London and County, and the Union of London. The new banks had to fight for recognition. Led by J. W. Gilbart, Manager of the London and Westminster, they secured in 1844 a more satisfactory legal status (7 & 8 Vict. c. 113). Their right to accept bills drawn at less than six months after date—which had been successfully challenged by the Bank of England in 1836—was conceded : as also the power ' to sue and be sued by their public officers.' Gilbart's great service was his realisation that the key to development was the connexion with the country banks. He fought the Bank of England between 1836 and 1844 by persuading country bankers to draw upon his bank without acceptance.

However, investment in the shares of joint-stock banks, provincial or metropolitan, was a very risky thing so long as liability remained unlimited, as it did down to 1858 for all joint-stock banks other than those established by special act, royal charter or letters patent. The Banking Companies Act of 1857 (20 & 21 Vict. c. 49) forbade banking companies to register as ' limited ' under the new limited liability legislation (see below, p. 317). The Banking Companies Act of 1858 (21 & 22 Vict. c. 91) removed the ban, but kept the liability in respect of note issue unlimited. The general Companies Act of 1862 specified banking companies in two sections. Section 4 (without reference to the question of liability) forbade the formation, *without registration*, of companies or partnerships in the banking business, if they consisted of more than 10 persons : while for other businesses the limit was 20. The informal banking company was thus specially discouraged. Section 182 continued unlimited liability on note issue. Because of the ease with which limited liability, save in this one respect, could now be obtained, the Act of 1862 gave a great fillip to joint-stock banking. It led many private banks in London and the country to amalgamate with joint-stock banks : and in 1865 Lloyds, the greatest of the country banks, converted themselves into a joint-stock limited. Yet the Act of 1862 did not altogether meet the requirements. Limitation of liability to the amount of the share would have weakened the standing of those banks which had built up a big business on a comparatively small capital. Therefore in 1879, a year after the calamitous failure of the City of Glasgow Bank, when there were calls of £2750 on the £100 share, an Act was passed ' to amend the law with respect to the liability of members of banking and other joint-stock companies ' (42 & 43 Vict. c 76). This Act provided for the registration of unlimited companies as limited companies with a reserve liability : and empowered such banks to increase their capital with provision that no part of such increased capital should be called up except in the event of winding up. The liability on note issue remained unlimited, but by 1879 bank notes other than those of the Bank of England were disappearing. The result of the 1879 Act was to attract a more substantial class of investor, who was afraid of unlimited liability, but not of liability limited to three or four times the paid-up share ; and thus the joint-stock banks became better equipped for territorial expansion.

The final result of Joplin's campaign was not, as he had expected, a number of separate banks locally managed and concentrating on local business, but a course of absorption in which the London bankers, the country bankers and isolated country bank companies passed under the control of a few large joint-stock banks, which had their headquarters in London. The latter entered into the heritage of the country bankers. They converted their country connexions into branch establishments, and opened new branches in districts which had hitherto lacked bank facilities, especially the suburbs of large towns. But the centralising process was quite as much an invasion of London by the provinces as of the provinces by London. It was Lloyds, in origin a country bank, which, while still having its head-quarters at Birmingham, embarked upon a policy of intensive territorial expansion. Then, as its business grew, it moved to London, in order to be central to the London money market of which it formed a part, and in which it found the choicest investments for its rapidly increasing funds. As with Lloyds so with others. In every case in securing a foothold in London the big country bankers were anxious to unite with a private London banker, because such union gave them representation on the London clearing house, which the London bankers had established for their own convenience.

Between 1900 and 1924 the policy of centralisation proceeded apace, but the amalgamations before and after 1914 were of a different nature. Those before 1914 continued the trend of previous amalgamations. They involved the absorption of remaining local banks by a larger and more widely spread joint-stock bank or the union of two comparatively large joint-stock banks for the purpose of territorial integration or a more even balance between their City and provincial business. But those after the war went beyond this. They united two already large groups each possessing ample funds and numerous competing branches ; and the enlarged groups carried territorial expansion beyond England by affiliation with prominent Scottish banks and extension into the foreign field. The result to-day is that the banking world is dominated by a big five : The Westminster ; The Midland ; The National Provincial ; Lloyds ; Barclays.

The short titles taken by the first three in 1924 replaced titles which embodied the result of recent amalgamations—London County Westminster and Parr's (London and County + London and Westminster + Parr's) ; London Joint City and Midland (London and Midland + City + London Joint-Stock) ; National Provincial and Union (National Provincial + Union of London and Smiths).

In 1926 an official history of Barclays Bank [1] was published, comparable in scale with the two volumes of The Canadian Bank of Commerce. In 1862 Barclays became a limited company. One disability of the private partnership noted in this Bank's history was the difficulty which partners had in providing for their families, seeing that the public measure a bank's credit by the amount of each partner's fortune passing at death. In 1896 the edifice of modern Barclays was created by the union of nineteen private banks with Barclay, Bevan, Tritton, Ransom, Bouverie and Company of London and Brighton. It was a compact based on religion, marriage and friendship. It included the Gurneys of Norwich, the Backhouses of Darlington, and the Mortlocks of Cambridge. The amalgamation was in line with the growth of large scale industry. The single private bank could no longer finance the larger commercial undertaking, nor without peril to itself refuse illegitimate demands for accommodation. But the figures of 1896 are small compared with those of to-day—current and deposit accounts and other accounts, July 1, 1896, £26·1 m. ; December 31, 1925, £306·2 m.

In the case of Barclays the modern amalgamation movement began in 1916. Successive amalgamations or affiliations converted a regional and mainly agricultural service into a service with a national network and foreign contacts besides. Thus the United Counties Bank brought in Birmingham and Bradford ; the London Provincial and South Western (itself a recent amalgamation) brought in the Metropolitan and Suburban area and South Wales. Affiliation with the Union Bank of Manchester in 1919 gave a footing in the independent stronghold of Manchester. Contact with Manchester meant contact with cotton and led to

[1] Cf. the review article in *Economic Journal*, Sept. 1927, by Prof. H. S. Foxwell.

the absorption of the Anglo-Egyptian Bank, which was interested in the financing of raw cotton from Egypt. The French branch of Cox and Company, the Army agents, was absorbed in 1922 (the other part of Cox's business uniting with Lloyds) ; and the resultant Barclays Bank (Overseas) Limited was enlarged into Barclays Bank (Dominion, Colonial and Overseas) by amalgamation with the Colonial Bank and the National Bank of South Africa Limited.

One district only has resisted the centralising tendency. Lancashire and the West Riding feared that absorption by a giant bank with headquarters in London would mean the loss of contact between borrower and lender and of that special knowledge of textile needs which their local banks possessed. Therefore in 1904 the Manchester and Liverpool District Bank refused Lloyds and in 1910 the Lancashire and Yorkshire Bank refused Parr's. But they could not keep outside the amalgamation process altogether. In 1918 the Bank of Liverpool joined the famous banking house of Martin and Company to form the Bank of Liverpool and Martins. Other Lancashire banks formed local amalgamations ; while exceptionally in 1919 the Union Bank of Manchester affiliated with Barclays. Affiliation in place of the less dignified absorption has also been the method by which several of the big five have joined forces with leading banks in Scotland.

Section 5. *The Merchant Bankers*

The Bankers' Almanac gives a list of about 1000 merchant bankers. These are not deposit bankers, but specialists in the financing of foreign trade, and they are an institution peculiar to London. The merchant bankers began as ordinary merchants dealing with foreign countries. They or their sons or very responsible members of the firm lived abroad. Having on occasion to remit to, or receive from, London money by way of bills of exchange on London houses, they were often asked by mercantile customers and friends in the foreign countries to obtain similar facilities for them. This developed into the acceptance of the bills of foreigners of good credit. Therefore the merchant bankers are commonly called ' accepting houses.' When these accepted bills are endorsed by great London houses, they become first-class ' bank ' bills on London—the international money of the world—always discountable at any time and in any amount by the London bill market. Over £300 millions of sterling bills were afloat when war broke out in 1914, of which one-third were acceptances on foreign account. The merchant bankers found the acceptance business so profitable

that they dropped the mercantile business for the most part.
Yet they often make a big deal from time to time as occasion
offers. The merchant bankers discount their bills with the
deposit banks or with special discount houses of which the
National and the Union Discount Companies are the chief to-day.
Thus the four great parties in the London money market are the
Merchant Banker, the Discount Houses, the Deposit Banks
(including foreign banks with London branches), and, in unwritten
leadership over all, the Bank of England.

Section 6. *Summary of Changes in Banking Function*

The 19th century changes in banking structure were accompanied by changes in banking function, which may be briefly
summarised as follows :

(1) Taught by experience, the joint-stock banks came to
regard the safeguarding of the depositor as their foremost public
duty. Gradually a financial edifice was erected, which is able to
weather any financial storm, however severe. Even the war,
though it caused a momentary embarrassment, was unable to
bring this structure down. Branch extension and the amalgamation of competing banks have in general been approved by the
public because, whatever disadvantage they may bring to local
borrowers, at any rate they make the position of the depositor
more secure. One of the biggest advantages which the joint-
stock banks had over the private banks was their publicity.
They presented to their shareholders statements of their financial
position ; and the compulsory independent audit of bank
accounts prescribed by the Companies Act of 1879 aforesaid (42 &
43 Vict. c. 76, s. 7) gave to the public an additional safeguard.

(2) While, in the 18th and early 19th centuries London was
mainly a settling house for British business, domestic or colonial,
in the last half of the century it become more and more an
international settling house. The disappearance of the domestic
bill of exchange forced the joint-stock banks to look to the
foreign bill as a field for the employment of their funds ; and they
did so very readily because, with the elaborate machinery of
discount houses, accepting houses and foreign banks with
branches in London interposed between them and the foreign
trade in question, they ran next to no risk. Thus it comes about
that the deposits of the English public are often used to finance
the movement of goods which never enter England at all.
Whether, in thus centralising their funds in the London money
market, they have starved the provinces is a moot point.
Barclays, being an amalgamation of private banks chiefly of

the country, retained their old centres in the form of Local Head Offices with the express object of sparing a customer the annoyance which might be involved in the submission of his proposition to a London official to whom he is only a name. The constitution of the other great banks is more centralised, but it must be remembered that in the course of the century the internal trade of England, as the result of cash shops and consumers' co-operation, came closer to a cash basis and to that extent the need for credit was less urgent. Furthermore, whereas in Germany the banks have often assisted new business by the supply of investment capital, in England this has been left to the stock exchanges of London and the provinces. In many cases in which a continental concern borrows from its bankers, an English concern issues debentures and shares on the local stock exchange.

(3) The main service rendered by the banks to the general public is the machinery they supply for the instant transmission of funds without charge from any part of the country to any other part. And in any given locality they supply the machinery by which cash transactions are settled. The smallest shop-keepers and the smallest professional men have a banking account. An ever-increasing part of their receipts reaches them in the form of cheques and an ever-increasing part of their bills is paid by cheques. So general is the habit of payment by cheque that many individuals use their pass-books as a substitute for a domestic balance sheet. Thousands of individuals, too, have small dividends coming in to them from investments in this or that public company at home or abroad, and they avoid all trouble and risk of loss by having their dividends paid into their accounts direct. In these and many other ways the banks serve the public without having to make any advances of money.

Section 7. *Comparison with Canada*

Canada, the oldest of the self-governing Dominions, has a century of banking history behind her. Her banking practice has been largely shaped by men of Scottish descent ; and a comparison of British with Canadian banking is peculiarly illuminating because it shows the growth of the same root ideas on different soils. The comparison is between the British joint-stock banks and the Canadian chartered banks. For Canada has no central bank corresponding to the Bank of England.

As in Great Britain, so also in Canada, the business community has found safety and solidarity in the big bank with numerous branches. The single bank of the American type is *prima facie* attractive. The borrower feels that he can get at his banker.

They are friends, jointly interested in the advancement of their local town. But this ease of borrowing has been purchased in the past at the high price of the total collapse of banking facilities in the event of a general crisis, and while a country so rich as America can forget such losses by making fortunes afresh, this is not possible either for an old country like Britain which has to safeguard its accumulated wealth, or for a new country like Canada, which has to establish itself as a safe country in the eyes of the investing world. As in Britain, so also in Canada, great care is taken for the safeguarding of the note issue. The rigid position reached in Britain, as the result of her peculiar history, is replaced in Canada by a more elastic plan. The limit of note issue to the amount of the unimpaired paid-up capital, the double liability of shareholders and the existence of the Bank Circulation Redemption Fund (a common pool to which all banks contribute), put the redeemability of the note issue of individual chartered banks beyond question. At the same time there are provisions for an extension of note issue beyond the normal limit during the season when the crops must be moved. As in Britain, so also in Canada, the banking community has contributed to the economic unification of the country. Chains of great banks, stretching from coast to coast, have united the Dominion financially, just as the Canadian Pacific Railway united it by links of steel.

But there are also broad differences. Great Britain is an old country. Canada is a new country. Canada, indeed, is very much in the position of Scotland a century or more ago. She needs capital ; and men of the same shrewd stock that turned the lowlands of Scotland into a hive of rich industry are now, in this 20th century, re-doing the work in a new and vaster homeland. Canadian bankers have shown their far-sightedness in looking for business in the West Indies and the East, but their purpose is not so much to find a field for surplus savings as to build up markets for Canadian produce. The development of the Canadian interior, its agriculture, minerals and manufactures, with an eye partly to sales at home and partly to sales abroad, is the first need of Canada to-day. Therefore, the chief function of the Canadian banks is to assist this development by appropriate banking facilities ; and this necessitates *inter alia* an intimate contact with New York, which is the financial centre of the whole North American continent. Working in a new country, the Canadian banker has to take business at which the British banker would turn up his nose or of which he would be scared. Having often to lend on the security of personal character, he must be skilled in the appraisal of character. He must be prepared to cope with new situations and act in a measure as a pioneer. A manager from the Canadian West, after a visit to the Old Country, whither he had repaired to recover from a nervous breakdown brought on by post-war anxieties, remarked to the writer : ' The task of a branch manager in England is as easy as falling off a stool.' But carrying the farmer or trader over bad times is one thing, and reckless speculation at headquarters is another. The Canadian chartered banks, as a body, are the first to condemn the mal-practices which in 1923 brought a junior member (the Home Bank) under discreditable circumstances to the ground.

PART II
TRADE AND TRANSPORT

CHAPTER VII

The Course of Foreign Trade

Section 1. The Active Rôle. Section 2. The Sinews of Economic Growth. Section 3. The Metropolitan Market. Section 4. Trade Rivals. Section 5. Commodities of Export. Section 6. The Trade Balance.

Section 1.   *The Active Rôle*

ENGLAND once was ' traded with.'   In the East until the awakening of Japan it has always been the European trader who sought out the native and developed his overseas trade ; and so for a time it was with England.   Manufacture was the mainstay of the mediaeval Londoner.   He lived by producing and selling objects of demand rather than by financing others or carrying goods. The bulk of his carrying trade was done by foreigners.   Frenchmen, Italians, and Germans all had a hand in the domination, and the last to go were the Hanse merchants of Germany whom Elizabeth expelled from the Steel-yard in London finally in 1598. Their strength had rested on their sea-power and on their control of Flanders, England's export market, and of the Baltic rich in corn and timber.   However, the subordination of England was due to immaturity only and was weakening even before Columbus discovered America.   Then came England's chance.   Favourably situated on the fringe of the Atlantic she jumped within a century from subordination to empire.   In 1588 the young island nation sank the Armada of continental Spain and naval victory prepared the way for the foundation of the East India Company in 1600 and the settlement in 1607 of Virginia, named after England's Virgin Queen.   Thus was a colonial trading empire born.   As an American historian has observed, ' This desire to free England from the necessity of purchasing from foreigners formed the underlying basis of England's commercial and colonial expansion ; it led directly to the formation of the East India Company and to the colonization of America.' [1]

The overseas expansion of England conditioned the life and character of her people, eliciting traits both noble and mean. The noblest was the zest for discovery, whereby the new-found nation satisfied its seafaring sense.   The service of the sea

---

[1] G. L. Beer, *Origins of the British Colonial System, 1578–1660*, p. 57.

brought danger and discipline, variety and wonder, an alternation
of adventurous exposure with the quiet of haven home, and thus
made a people capable at work but loathing routine and very fond
of play. For the really restless peoples are the great continentals.
These too are the uniform peoples, being free of island limits
and so vast that only by uniformity can they function. Very
appropriately, when the American frontier came to an end, the
automobile was invented to take its place. But God made of
England a fair and little land, whose conservation problem is the
safeguarding not of forest or coal, but of her natural and historical
beauties, the freshness of the one and the mellowness of the other.

Expansion also brought greed and shameful traffic. The
early adventurers were seeking a new way to the treasure house
of the East. Stumbling on the islands in the Caribbean Sea they
called them the West Indies. Westward Ho was at first Eastward
Ho, and all Europe rang with its wealth. ' Why, man, all their
dripping pans . . . are of pure gold, and all the chains with
which they chain up their streets are massive gold ; all the
prisoners they take are fettered in gold ; and for rubies and
diamonds they go forth on holiday and gather 'em by the
seashore.' [1]

But piracy led to a crime worse than itself, for which England's
only excuse can be that she did not begin it and was the first
to end it. The African slave trade was well established when
Elizabeth's sea captain, Sir John Hawkins, wrested a share in it
from the Portuguese. During the 17th century Holland struggled
hard to retain her hold on the West African littoral, the source of
supply, but England prevailed in Africa because she was stronger
in the terminal market in which the black ivory was sold. The
Barbadoes served as the distributing centre for the West Indies ;
and by the *asiento* (agreement) with Spain concluded at the
Treaty of Utrecht in 1713 Great Britain wrested from France the
monopoly of slave shipment to Spanish America. The West
Indian planters welcomed the slaves because without their labour
the sugar estates could not be cultivated ; but by the middle of
the 18th century the Quakers on the mainland were in revolt
against the institution, and when the horrors of the middle
passage (*i.e.* the passage across the Atlantic) became known in
England, the national conscience was touched. However, it
needed a great man, William Wilberforce, and a long campaign
to obtain the Act of 1807 by which Great Britain abolished the
traffic. Having ended it for herself she bent herself to end it for
others. She pressed for abolition at the Congress of Vienna in
1814, bound France to it in the peace settlement, and coaxed

[1] *Eastward Ho*, comedy of 1605 : Act III, Scene 2. Captain Seagull speaks.

other interested Powers into it by concessions of territory and money. With the help of her Navy and Customs service she hunted down the slavers on the coasts and rivers of Africa and by her energy saved the world from a recrudescence of the trade on a bigger scale perhaps than ever before.

The traffic in opium was not cruel as a traffic, but it was harmful to the Chinese to whom it was sent. Opium entered China from India at an early date.[1] When the Chinese Government prohibited the drug, the Company prohibited the carriage of it in their vessels but were unable to stop it in vessels which they licensed. Upon the opening of the China trade in 1833 the smuggling of opium increased by leaps and bounds, constituting 53% of the entire imports of China in 1837. For the drug was insistently demanded and furthermore fulfilled a useful rôle in the financial economy of Great Britain and British India. Opium served as spot cash to pay for tea and silk and thus provided the long-sought alternative to the drain of silver to the East; and the big revenue derived from the cultivation of the poppy in Bengal balanced the Indian budget.

In 1837 China embarked on a campaign of prohibition, which led to high-handed treatment of British soldiers and thus to war, ' the opium war ' of 1839-42, in which China was easily defeated and out of which Great Britain obtained an indemnity, trading concessions and the possession of Hongkong. ' China,' says a well-informed Chinese historian, ' was undoubtedly earnest in her desire to stamp out the vice that was poisoning her people ; her sole aim was to suppress the importation and consumption of the drug, regardless of the cost.' [2] But he does not deny that then as formerly China was averse from trade with foreigners or that the diplomatic methods of the Son of Heaven were, to say the least, irritating. As the Emperor of China wrote to George III in 1793, ' I set no value on objects strange or ingenious, and have no use for your country's manufactures.' [3] A second war followed in 1856, and under the Treaty of Tientsin by which it was settled the import of opium at a moderate duty was legalised. For the rest of the century the opium trade was one of the many transactions in which China had to acquiesce as the Powers of Europe proceeded with the forcible opening of the Chinese door and eventually to the economic partition of China. A British Royal Commission of 1893 declared that

---

[1] See for first reference to the traffic in the Records of the East India Company the entry under June 16, 1733—H. B. Morse, *The East India Company Trading to China*, I. 215.

[2] Chong Su See, *Foreign Trade of China*, Columbia Studies No. 199 of 1919, p. 151.

[3] Sir Frederick White, *China and Foreign Powers*, p. 39. What blasphemy !

China was satisfied with the opium situation and glad of the revenue which it yielded, that its abolition would be disastrous to Indian finance and hard to enforce on the Native States of India, and that the agitation against it was ' built on the uninstructed philanthropy of well-meaning stay-at-home Englishmen.' [1] But China persisted in agreeing with the stay-at-home Englishman, and issued an edict abolishing by stages over a ten-year period the cultivation of the poppy and the non-medicinal consumption of opium. The British Government on behalf of the Government of India agreed to reduce Indian exports *pari passu* with reduction of production by China, but before this was completed China had collapsed into civil war. In 1925–6 the Chinese war lords were financing themselves by taxes on home-grown opium. From many provinces came the report that ' the use of the drug is advancing by leaps and bounds among all classes from the wealthiest to the poorest.' [2]

The analogy with the enforcement of Prohibition in the U.S.A. is interesting. In both cases the countries of supply have questioned the sincerity of the enforcing Power and harped on the prevalence of illicit traffic among the subjects of the latter. But China was weak and America is strong ; and America takes measures against rum-runners which at any time between 1837 and 1914 would have involved China in certain war with one or other European Power.

In West Africa Great Britain has made amends for her slave-trading past by instituting a government that is really beneficent ; for the economic improvements of the 20th century have been obtained without recourse to the plantation system and therefore without disturbance to the tribal life of the natives. But her task in China is more difficult. For she has vast interests at stake and her great commercial establishments, such as Jardine Matheson and Company, Butterfield and Swire, and the Hong-kong and Shanghai Banking Corporation have a long record of peaceful and honourable trade with Chinese merchants. But China has been developed against her will ; and Great Britain, as the leading foreign trader, bears the odium for a state of affairs to which all the Powers have contributed, and from which all have benefited in the past.

---

[1] Cf. *Dictionary of Political Economy* (edn. 1908), III. 761, ' Opium,' by Sir Roper Lethbridge, ex-member of the Bengal Educational Service.

[2] *Opium in China*, Investigation in 1925–6 by the International Opium Association, Peking, p. 7.

Section 2.   *The Sinews of Economic Growth*

By foreign trade Great Britain accumulated the capital which provided for the further expansion of that trade, as well as for the building of great houses in town and country, the improvement of the land, and the increase of industry.   The industrial revolution was financed from the profits of foreign trade.

The guild system was not favourable to capital accumulation. In their technique and in the ordering of their life the merchants and craftsmen of the Middle Ages surpassed perhaps the centuries which followed.   But the guild outlook was municipal and its structure inelastic, and therefore it gave way to a system which lent itself to expansion and change.   This we call merchant capitalism with its complement domestic industry.   The merchant capitalist was a middleman who broke down ancient barriers. He defied corporate towns by giving out work to the country and evaded the monopolies of privileged companies by interloping. Furthermore, as the late George Unwin so truly says : ' it was . . . by a flow of capital inwards from commerce, that most of the early industrial enterprises of Lancashire were started, and that the immense expansion of the cotton industry was rendered possible.' [1] This is a big truth.   Endless error creeps into economic history if we imagine the merchant capitalist an intruder upon an ideal blend of town guild and village community.   He committed excesses, but he was the life-blood of economic growth.

Capital accumulation became important in England with the establishment of joint-stock companies towards the end of the 16th century.   It is significant of the early poverty of capital that companies which later became the symbol of commercial wealth passed through decades of slow growth in which the lack of ready money was their main handicap.   The East India Company and the Bank of England were sorely put to it to collect their first subscriptions, and they had to fight hard to prevent the Government from borrowing funds which were essential to the operations of trade.   In 1720, just before the great set-back to joint-stock methods, the nominal capital of joint-stock companies in Great Britain was about £50 m.   At this time the total trade capital of the country, including the instruments of agriculture, was estimated to be in the neighbourhood of £40 m. ; and the contradiction is explained by the large extent to which the capital of the great companies was tied up in Government loans.[2]

The Jews have always been the great providers of ready

---

[1] *Economic History Review*, Jan. 1927, p. 56, ' The Merchant Adventurers' Company in the Reign of Elizabeth.'

[2] *Cf.* W. R. Scott, *Joint Stock Companies to 1720*, I. 439.

money, and Cromwell, by removing the ban under which they had suffered since the time of Edward I, strengthened England. Their expulsion from Spain, Portugal and Italy hastened the transfer of financial power from the Mediterranean to North-West Europe ; and as 18th-century England gained on Holland in colonial power and commercial strength, many Jews came across to London. They were prominent in stock-broking and stock-dealing : Change Alley was so full of them that it was called the Jews' Walk. The Jew brought valuable characteristics with him. He was ubiquitous and enterprising, persistent but not pugnacious ; he ran after customers without regard for his dignity and made a profit out of articles and transactions which other people rejected or despised. For international finance the Jews had a special bent, overcoming by their tribal bonds the boundaries of nations and yet as individuals retaining that mental detachment which is so necessary to financial analysis. Of this Ricardo was a superb example. But England was not dominated by the Jews. For not to mention Scotland, where, if rumour be true, none but Scotsmen make a living, the Quakers of England were as important. They came from the provinces to the capital to found great banking establishments. Peace-loving and honourable, they supplied the counterpoise to aggressive foreign adventure. More than once in the nation's history their stand for right prevented or repaired policies of economic violence against weaker peoples.

However alert a people may be, it is hard for it to grow rich by agriculture or to draw quick profit from new lands unless they contain precious plants or metals. For new lands are only potential assets, which require for their development capital and waiting. Eighteenth-century Britain was short of capital and skilled labour. The great estates of this century were built up in large part from resources accumulated overseas. Until the industrial revolution brought fortunes from mining, they were only to be won by foreign trade or by ownership of property in London, the creature of foreign trade. In ' planter ' and ' nabob ' England gave new words to the dictionary of commerce, but she has no equivalent for bourgeois or bourgeoisie. Her aristocracy, while affecting to despise trade, participated in it and married it ; and the joint-stock company was an admirable device for the association of blood with brains without stain to the one or too great an imposition on the other. The London merchant was respected in proportion as his interests were wide flung, and the wisest among them were ready to learn from Europe.

Sir Josiah Child (1630–99) was a West Indian merchant, a contractor to the Admiralty for American timber, and Chairman of the East India Company ; and he laid before his contemporaries what he believed to be the secrets of Dutch success—their banks and low rate of interest, and their model methods of packing fish.   The first draft of his *Discourse upon Trade*, written in 1665 during the enforced leisure of the Plague, was published in 1668 and republished with large additions in 1692.

With Sir John Barnard (1685–1764) there came into London life the Quaker strain, sober and liberal.   He was the great power in the City in the time of Walpole, supporting his policy of peace and retrenchment and promoting the first considerable scheme of interest reduction on the National Debt.   The reduced ' Threes ' of 1750 was his work, as also the Act of 1734 (7 Geo. II, c. 8) designed to repress the stock-jobbing which was so virulent at the time of the South Sea Bubble.   Section 8 of this Act prohibited the buying or selling of stock of which the parties were not possessed at the time of the contract.   The Act remained on the Statute Book long after it had ceased to be enforced, being repealed only in 1860 by 23 & 24 Vict. c. 28.

During the 18th century London was evolving those financial functions which were to make her pre-eminent in world finance. The chairmanship of the East India Company, the City's commercial plum, compelled the holder to be at once a merchant and a diplomat.   Messrs. Coutts and Co., the bankers of the Royal family in the reign of George III, were originally corn merchants of Edinburgh.   With buyers in every grain-raising country, as well as throughout the Baltic, they knew the things which a metropolitan banker should know.   The House of Hope, the world-renowned merchant bankers of Amsterdam, was founded by a Scotsman of that name in the 17th century.   Henry Hope, to whom Adam Smith was indebted for his account of the Bank of Amsterdam, retired to England in 1794, when France invaded Holland, and died in 1811 a millionaire.   Out of contacts such as these, 19th-century Britain created expert machinery for the financing of foreign trade and the making of loans to foreign countries.

Samuel Gurney (1786–1856), a Norwich Quaker, founded the house of Overend and Gurney, which by 1850 was the greatest discount house in the world.   During the crisis of 1825 it earned the title of the Bankers' Bank by lending when the Bank of England refused.   In 1866, however, the firm, now a limited liability company, failed through entanglement in speculative enterprise.   This was two years after the firm terminated its connexion with Gurneys, the Norwich bankers, who later amalgamated with Barclays (*cf.* above, p. 114).

The founder of the house of Baring, Sir Francis Baring

F

(1740–1810), was of Lutheran Dutch extraction. His father had made and exported cloth, and he, Sir Francis, specialised in finance, especially in the flotation of the loans for which the French war called on a vast scale. His son Alexander (1774–1848), who was trained in the House of Hope, was the contemporary in Parliament of Huskisson and Ricardo. Later the Barings were agents for the Canadian Government and intimately versed in Canadian public affairs. But this firm, too, had its day of trouble. Commitments to the Argentine Government brought them in 1890 to momentary insolvency, from which they were rescued by the Bank of England and other banks.

Most renowned of all, because most international and never once involved beyond its means, is the house of Rothschild, whose red shield once hung in the Jews' quarter of Frankfort-on-Main. Nathan Meyer (1776–1836) came to England at the end of the 18th century, and after a brief and profitable apprenticeship in the bustling atmosphere of Manchester settled in St. Swithin's Lane, which is the firm's place of business to-day. The Rothschilds had family connexions in the leading capitals of Europe, and it is said that they remitted Wellington's army drafts through their house in Paris, the capital of the country which Wellington was fighting. After 1815 they popularised foreign loans on the London market by arranging for the payment of dividends in sterling in London. Nathan Meyer was also the parent of the instantaneous news service. His pigeons brought him advance news of the result of Waterloo, and it is believed that he did not lose by the knowledge.

Section 3. *The Metropolitan Market*

' Because of the greatness of our city the fruits of the whole earth flow in upon us, so that we enjoy the goods of other countries as freely as our own.' So boasted Pericles of Athens, the mother city of civilisation, and his words mark well the course by which London, and after London the rest of England, became an emporium of world trade with a great and ever open mouth, which it is still the world's delight to fill. But it was not always so; 17th- and 18th-century England secured materials and markets by force, pursuing a policy of power. The 19th century held them by free trade, committed by evolution rather than by design to a policy of plenty. For the rôle of the great consumer has its embarrassments. It is gratifying to build docks and warehouses and ship canals, but disconcerting to readjust under external pressure one's scheme of agricultural economy.

At the close of the 16th century England parted from her old ways in order to share in the riches of world trade. London the capital was the starting-point of foreign venture and the returning point as well. The great trading companies were organised and financed in London. Depending on royal charter or parliamentary enactment they found it expedient to be close to the seat of government. The provinces, when they filled out in the 18th century, based their commerce on London, the established centre of a trading empire. All transactions, foreign and domestic, were cleared in London. Thus London grew without pause in reaction to imperial and provincial expansion. It was in the opposite case to an ambitious prairie town : it was always congested, always encroaching, and from time to time it shed its surplus.

Between 1600 and 1750 London was in the first stage of a metropolitan market. It had numerous industries, an extensive foreign trade, and a rich congregation of consumers. But the provinces were ill developed, and especially to the North the connexions with them were bad. Improved communications introduced the second stage. The Metropolis lost to the provinces certain of its staple industries : ribbons to Coventry, hosiery to Leicester, cutlery to Sheffield, shipbuilding to the Clyde. But improved roads and, after 1840, railways linked London with the provinces for wholesale business ; and there was little conflict of interest between London and the North. Lancashire in 1813 broke loose from the domination of London in the important Eastern trade, but there was no general process of escape from a tyranny of mercantile capital. Foreign trade and internal production increased *pari passu*. The specialised merchant (merchant banker, cotton broker, etc.) and the factory-owner were the co-equal outcome of economic advance.

During the second half of the 19th century metropolitan London passed insensibly into its third, and present, stage. Its financial range was widened by the spread of foreign investment in companies with limited liability, as permitted by the Companies Act of 1862. This Act promoted what Lord Goschen called ' the marriage of English capital with foreign demand.' [1] Railway investment abroad followed railway investment at home ; and after railways came docks, harbours, land development, light and power, tea, rubber, mines and all the strange variety of the modern stock exchange. And London itself swelled into greater London. The West End was invaded by giant shops and cosmopolitan hotels. The population straggled out for many miles along the lines of railway radiating in every direction. In these outskirts the banks opened branches and many industrial plants

[1] Viscount Goschen, *Essays and Addresses*, p. 23.

were built. But London is no longer the unchallenged distributor of foreign imports. In this respect it has developed for geographical reasons contrariwise to New York. Southampton and the ports of the North are encroaching. The latter have always handled much of their imported raw material, and they are more central than London to the bulk of the population. Freights are a handicap to the provisioning of the North from London. To this extent the shipping of London is less secure than its finance, but in 1927 it was still in value of traffic handled by far the premier port of the kingdom.

Every age has its *nouveaux riches*. The new rich of the 18th century were imperial profiteers, grown fat on the profits of the high seas, the plantations and the Indies. They were acquisitive and extravagant : intoxicated by the novelties and luxuries which poured into their lap from every corner of the world. By contrast the men of the 19th century were hard-working and stingy : really self-made and re-investing their profits in the family business. If they had a common faith, it was that high wages were disastrous. They travelled abroad to look for markets and found in foreign competition an excuse for opposing expenditure on social well-being. If the God of the 18th century was visible property with broad acres and elegant shrubberies, the God of the 19th was invisible capital, hidden away in a dusty office.

During the 18th century London ruled supreme in trade and manners. Three-quarters of the recorded imports of the century entered the port of London. Country manners and country diet were despised. The poor aped the rich and the provinces aped London. The rural poor came to regard as a right the fine wheaten bread which Londoners consumed. In the 19th century the industrial North made itself felt. After London had abolished the slave trade Manchester abolished the Corn Laws ; and thereafter there was point in the saying that what Lancashire thinks to-day England thinks to-morrow. As the commerce of London outdistanced its manufactures, the Metropolis developed a consumers' psychology. The rich desired foreign luxuries and a large body of shopkeepers was interested in satisfying the demand. There was thus a conflict of interest between the East India Company which imported calicoes and the manufacturers of native products. In 1697 and 1719 the Spitalfields weavers attacked the persons and property of the Company. Sugar and tea, luxuries in 1700, were necessaries in 1850, and both came from abroad, sugar from the West and tea from the East. Tea at first was boiled in a coffee-pot and served in cups no bigger than large thimbles. The earliest English tea-pot, now in the South Kensington Museum, is a silver tea-pot of 1670 presented to the

East India Company by one of its members ; it was the custom of the Directors to refresh thus their deliberations. A minute of 1674 instructs the cashier general of the Company to issue to the housekeeper, Mrs. Harris, ' tea by one pound at a time and sugar proportionable.' [1] The clerks were allowed free tea, but spent so much time in the drinking that the Court in 1757 forbade it after 10 A.M. John Stuart Mill, the last examiner of correspondence at the East India House, used to breakfast at the office on tea, bread and butter and a boiled egg, taking nothing more until his dinner at home at 6 P.M. [2] Perhaps this is why he thought that a demand for commodities was not a demand for labour !

Eighteenth-century London was delivered from dram-drinking by the cheapening of tea, the recorded consumption of which in the country as a whole rose from 2 million lbs. in 1750 to 20 million lbs. in 1800. Thus began the alliance between temperance and tea which so disgusted Cobbett and of which Dickens made such fun. ' Theere's a young 'ooman ' (says Mr. Weller in chapter XXXIII of the *Pickwick Papers*) ' on the next form but two, as has drunk nine breakfast cups and a half ; and she's a swellin' wisibly before my wery eyes.' Tea, temperance, infant negroes and flannel waistcoats : truly Dickens knew his England.

Section 4. *Trade Rivals*

(1) *Spain and Portugal.* By 1600 the claims of Spain and Portugal to monopolise the New World were broken. South America was left to them only because it was unsuited climatically to Northern peoples, who found in North America more land surface than they could fill. The weakness of Spain was exposed at the opening of the 19th century when the Spanish foothold in North America from Florida to California yielded to the advancing tide of Anglo-Saxon settlement with even less resistance than was offered by the native Indians. In the Far East Portugal had established herself at Macao as early as 1557, but by 1700 England had secured a firm foothold in the neighbouring port of Canton, which thereafter was a centre of cosmopolitan trade and more important than Macao. From Canton the East India Company conducted its great China tea trade. In 1913, 48% of the trade of China was with the British Empire and Hongkong ; 19·7% with Japan ; 1·2% with Portugal and Macao.

(2) *Holland.* England's commercial rival from 1600 to 1750 was the little country of Holland, so like her in every respect save that she lacked the wealth of coal by which a colonial trader

---

[1] W. Foster, *The East India House*, p. 94.
[2] *Ibid.* pp. 216, 230.

could be converted into an industrial nation with world markets. England fought Holland by Navigation Acts and war. It is possible that she could have secured more by negotiation, but Holland was at least as aggressive and as determined on monopoly. England committed no violence comparable with the massacre of English traders at Amboyna in the Molucca islands in 1623. Trade in this age and for long after did follow the flag. The high seas were the hunting ground of pirates and privateers. The early colonies of every Power would have been wiped out time and again but for the Home Government's intervention, armed or diplomatic. It was weakness only which induced Holland to acquiesce in the conversion of New Amsterdam into New York in 1664. When more than a century later the protection of the British flag was withdrawn from American shipping, the latter's Mediterranean trade was wiped out by the Barbary pirates and not restored till they built a small fleet to protect it. The pirates were not finally suppressed until Lord Exmouth's expedition of 1816.

The herring was the fish which the Navigation Acts were concerned to protect. Our forefathers being Protestants never ate as many as they should, but fish-eating Catholics devoured them by the shipload, and with mercantile pamphleteers there was no praise too extravagant for the ' puissant red herring.' The Hansards had crept out of the Baltic after them. The Dutch had so improved the methods of curing and packing that they monopolised the trade until Charles I, with the help of ship money, forcibly asserted the right of Englishmen to catch the herrings in their own waters. Cromwell's Navigation Act of 1651 left no loophole. It was thenceforth unlawful even for Englishmen to bring in any fish except those caught by English or Irish fishermen in English or Irish ships. The herrings were partial to their champions. Disturbed, it may be, by the traffic in the Danish Sound they moved west in the 17th century, and towards the end of the 18th were caught in abnormal abundance off the coasts of Ireland and Scotland. ' In 1779 it was estimated that two-thirds of the seamen who manned the shipping of the Clyde, besides the considerable number in the vessels belonging to Liverpool, Bristol, London and a great number in the Navy, had been bred in the herring industry.' [1] Then the herring passed through its industrial revolution. About 1780 a Scotsman named Dempster employed ice as a preservative, thus opening the long chapter of transport under refrigeration, but Dutch competition in the cured product died hard. In the scarcity years of 1795 and 1800 many Dutch prisoners of war were

[1] A. M. Samuel, *The Herring*, p. 143.

invited to take part in the herring industry ; and in 1805 the Society of Arts offered a prize for ' curing herrings by Dutch methods.' It was won by a Scotsman of Leith, aided by six Dutch fishermen, and the industry then established flourishes to-day on the coasts of Norfolk and Scotland. Steam power came at the close of the 19th century in the form of the steam trawler, which with its drifting tackle could take twice the catch of a sailing boat and work the whole year round.

England's claim to regulate the trade with Europe on her own terms was less easy to enforce. One proof of this is that she had to stiffen the Navigation Act of 1660 by a Statute of Frauds, 1662 (14 Chas. II, c. 11, s. 23), under which it was un- lawful even for English ships to import a list of commodities likely to come from or through Holland. The prohibition was freely evaded by smuggling, and there is little evidence that it shook Holland's hold on European trade, which was an increasing hold down to the middle of the 18th century. She dominated the Greenland whale fishery : her grain granaries at Amsterdam were strategically posted for the carrying trade between the Baltic and the Spanish peninsula : and as the timber needs of Western Europe grew, she became a big timber-carrier as well. Towards the end of the 18th century coal and war changed the balance of power. Napoleon's Continental System paralysed Dutch trade, but only served, through the success with which it was circumvented, to increase British trade with Danzig and Riga. The Baltic Exchange, which now handles the foreign grain of London, was founded about 1750. In 1810, to accom- modate the extending Baltic trade, the Surrey Commercial Dock Company, the most constantly successful of the London dock companies, was formed. Before the Great War five out of ten million loads of imported timber came from Russia.

(3) *France and the Smuggling Trade.* Between 1700 and 1800 the commodities in which England and France respectively had an advantage of production were changed about. In 1700 France was at least the manufacturing equal of England, but by 1780 machine-made Manchester goods were beating out hand- made French goods in France. There was a corresponding reversal in agriculture. In the first half of the 18th century the merchants of Havre spoke of England as the granary of Europe. After 1770 she was on the balance an importing country, and during the French war had almost as great a need of the wheat raised by Napoleon's dependent allies as had Napoleon of British cloth for his armies.

But all through the 18th century and on through the French war trade with nearby European countries was dominated by the smuggler—' All in the way of fair trade—Just loaded yonder at Douglas, in the Isle of Man—neat cognac—real hyson and souchong—Mechlin lace, if you want any,' as Captain Dirk Hatteraick says in *Guy Mannering*, chapter 4.[1] The history of the decline of smuggling and adoption of free trade might be written in parallel columns. When duties were high smuggling was rampant. When they were reduced smuggling declined. There were no services more necessary to the stability of Britain than the collection of her revenue and the manning of her Navy, and yet to defraud the customs and to dodge the press-gang were considered very pardonable offences. No sight was more familiar to the east coast than the ' hoverer ' manœuvring for a chance to run her cargo ashore. When the customs officers came out to her, the captain would produce papers to show that he was bound for Bergen, the Scandinavian staple. From far China came silks to Sweden to be run across the North Sea by respectable Baltic traders. A collier from Newcastle to London was accounted spiritless indeed, if she did not on occasion slip across to the Dutch or French coast and stow some illicit produce beneath her bulk of coal. The history of every county with a coast line is packed with smuggling memories. In counties fringing a great port it was a business. In Somersetshire, which flanks the approach to Bristol, wine, brandy and West India produce were concealed in shipments of salt. Trains of a hundred horses moved the cargo inland from warehouses improvised under the floors of barns, in the thickness of farmhouse walls, and in caves and holes along the coast. Smuggling and river piracy compelled the building of docks and bonded warehouses on the Thames in 1800. But neither docks nor coastguards could eradicate the smuggler so long as the excessive duties inherited from the French war remained. Twenty years of officially encouraged privateering and blockade-running, by exalting the secret practice of centuries, had inured the nation to illicit trade. The argument that lower duties defeated the smuggler was the trump card played by every fiscal reformer from Pitt to Gladstone. Parliamentary inquiries in the early 40's revealed much evasion of the laws restricting the export of machinery, as well as wholesale fraud in the importation of French silks, gloves and lace, in which wealthy City merchants and the customs officials themselves were involved. The Cobdenite was a sanctimonious man, but none can gainsay that the system of free trade for which he fought increased the national stock of administrative and commercial honesty.

[1] It is believed that the Captain is drawn after ' one Yawkins,' who in 1789 troubled Adam Smith, Commissioner of Customs.

(4) Germany. For some two centuries, 1600–1800, Germany was the one country with which England could trade with any assurance of friendship and peace. In 1650 the Company of Merchant Adventurers of England was established at Hamburg with a questionable monopoly of the export trade in English woollens ; but before 1700 ' the free traders ' of the provinces had exacted an open trade, and the company degenerated into a clique of London merchants with a factory at Hamburg, which Napoleon abolished in 1808. During the French war and despite it the Bourse of Hamburg was the financial link between London and Europe. The fluctuation of sterling in *marks banco* was the accepted measure of currency depreciation. After 1815 Great Britain directed her efforts to the keeping of an open door into central Europe. She supported the Middle German Tariff Union against Prussia, and after the establishment of the German Zollverein in 1834 cultivated Frankfort as a starting-point for its penetration. When Frankfort became a member, she made friends with outlying countries, Austria and the Baltic States ; and finally, in 1841, concluded a commercial treaty with the Zollverein itself.

In the same year, 1841, Frederic List raised the standard of fiscal revolt in Germany. ' A nation which exchanges agricultural products for foreign manufactured goods is an individual with one arm.' [1] To the cosmopolitan system of Adam Smith with its supposed emphasis on exchange values List opposed the national system with its emphasis on productive powers. This was also the American system, which he had championed during his residence in America and which he desired now that his Fatherland should follow. The competition which Germany had to sustain was indeed severe. The stream of goods which had borne down Napoleon's edicts increased in volume under the peace. London 'slaughterhouses' cut the price of textile products with results which were as embarrassing to the countries on which they were dumped as they were disastrous to the hand-workers who made them. Nassau Senior of Oxford, in elaborating the law of increasing returns in industries, had his eye on foreign competition. ' The more our rivals produce, the cheaper they will be able to produce.' [2] His contention, that the whole net profit of the cotton factory was derived from the last hour's work, commended itself to a generation which lived in a nightmare of being undersold. The extravagances of Senior were as good an argument for protection by Germany as List could have desired.

[1] F. List, *National System of Political Economy,* ed. Nicholson, p. 130.
[2] *Letters on the Factory Act, 1837.*

Until 1870 the German tariff was liberal, but after the German victories of that year Europe assumed more and more the guise of an armed camp and the 20th century opened on a rising tide of armaments and protective tariffs. The saner elements in Germany read the possibilities more truly. In the period from 1870 to 1914 Germany was learning hard of others, who were ahead of her in 1870. She bought steamships from Glasgow and then built her own. She applied the chemical discoveries of an Englishman to the ores of Alsace Lorraine and erected on coal and iron an industrial empire. She sent her young men to London to learn banking and English. She travelled South America to find out from South Americans in their own language what they really desired. She used her neighbourhood to Russia and South-Eastern Europe to direct the technical developments of their resources and to ship their surplus population to America. In her laboratories she joined university research to the practice of the workshop. But for those who ruled her this was not enough. They must have colonies and a great navy as well as the hegemony of Europe, and therefore they had war.

(5) *America and the East.* America and the West Indies on the one side and East India on the other were the twin pillars of Britain's overseas empire. The Western trade was free to all British subjects within the limits prescribed by the Navigation Acts. But the Eastern trade was confined to the ships of a single company or those of merchants in India which the company licensed ; and so it came about that, when the American colonies revolted, British interlopers found a back way into the East through the U.S.A.

The East India Company sent their first ships to the Spice Islands to fetch back the spices which would relieve the monotony of a winter diet of dried food and salted meat. Spices, like furs, were abundant in their place of growth, highly prized in Europe, and easy to transport. Therefore the trade, as Holland soon discovered, was very profitable. But since the Spice Islanders displayed a regrettable reluctance to clothe themselves in solid English broadcloth, the Company established factories, i.e. trading posts, on the coast of India, from which they obtained cotton fabrics suitable for sale in the Islands. Then the Company imported these into England, bringing also raw silk and silk goods, porcelain, carpets and tea, the produce of Persia and China. The result was a continuously unfavourable balance of trade, which had to be met by the export of specie. After the battle of Plassey, 1757, the Company exported no specie for twenty-five years ; for the plunder of Plassey called for no offset. Not until the middle of the 19th century, when Great Britain sent cottons to India, and India in return sent wheat, rice, jute, raw cotton and tea, was the trade balance one of which the mercantile purist could have approved. In China the balance was adjusted by opium.

By contrast with the East, America and the West Indies began with the supply of primary products ; and being colonists with the wants of white men they offered a favourable vent for British wares. The Staple Act of 1663 compelled them to receive all their manufactures from England. With the West Indies and the Southern colonies of the mainland Britain had an affinity of economic interest. But the Northern colonies produced things which she also produced or could obtain cheaply from elsewhere— grain, fish, timber, and the like. Further, they had to pay for their manufactures from England by indirect means through the West Indies, West Africa, and the Mediterranean ; and these triangular operations made London an international settling house (for all such transactions created bills on London). But they imposed on the Northern colonies commercial restraints which, when aggravated by attempted taxation, precipitated their revolt in 1776.

Between 1800 and 1860 Great Britain and the U.S.A. were in keen maritime rivalry. From American shipyards came the sailing clippers, swift as the falcon that ' clips it down to the wind,' and left the clumsy East Indiamen days behind on every voyage. British builders responded ; and year after year the clippers of both nations raced from China to Europe with cargoes of tea. But during and after the Civil War the American merchant marine fell away. Iron and steam replaced wood and sails, and America found a more attractive outlet for her capital and energies in the development of her interior.

Throughout the 19th century the trade contact between Britain and the American South was very intimate. She derived from the Southern States nearly the whole of her raw cotton ; and down to 1860 the exports to Britain accounted for the greater part of America's cotton crop. A railway from Charlestown inland to the cotton fields of Carolina followed within a year the opening of the Liverpool and Manchester railway. But from the British standpoint colonial America had learnt her lesson only too well. Constrained in the 17th and 18th centuries to take her manufactures from the Mother Country only, she devoted the 19th to becoming under protection a mother country to herself. The American colonies had maintained their trade balance through the West Indies and Africa. The U.S.A. to-day sends to Great Britain cotton, wheat and meat ; and for these Great Britain pays in some part by her manufactures and for the rest either by shipping services rendered to America or by goods and services rendered to countries possessing the tropical products which America is anxious to obtain.

Section 5. *Commodities of Export*

(1) *Woollens*. The Romans came to Britain for lead and tin, and 12th-century England was exporting these together with meat, hides, and wool. But by 1400 she had built up a strong woollen industry, which in the 15th century reached the pre-eminence that it maintained till about 1800. The woollen industry furnished traders with ammunition for the capture of foreign markets. In 1700 woollens comprised nearly one-half of English exports; and one reason why the Methuen Treaty of 1703 was ' celebrated as a masterpiece of the commercial policy of England ' [1] was that in return for a preference on the wines of Portugal, England obtained ' for ever hereafter' an open market in Portugal for woollen goods. Ricardo in his *Principles of Political Economy*, chapter 7, enunciated the theory of foreign trade in terms of English cloth and Portuguese wine. Woollen exports of £3 millions in 1700 rose to over £7 millions in 1833, but by that date cotton was easily ahead with £18 millions of exports to its credit. However, the reputation of British woollens on the world's markets has been maintained. Alike in the 18th and 19th centuries, while Paris led London in women's fashions, London led Paris in masculine attire. There are heavy duties to-day on the import of British clothing into Canada and the U.S.A., but every West-bound liner is an exporter of suits and overcoats, one on the person and several in the trunk.

(2) *Shipping and Re-export*. Sixteenth-century England used her good timber for ships and her stoutest oak for the Royal Navy. As her naval power grew she looked to the Baltic and her own colonies for timber and naval stores. The increase of shipping promoted the invisible export of shipping services. She sailed her ships in foreign seas ; and her trading ventures brought back commodities which augmented by re-export the export trade. This was the fighting value of an emporium. In the 17th century tobacco took its place by the side of woollens as the commodity which issued from English ports, although not a stalk could be legally raised on English soil. (For the cultivation of tobacco in England was forbidden by Cromwell and the Stuarts, and the prohibition was drastically enforced.) There was also a re-export trade in foreign manufactures to British possessions and in Indian textiles to America and Europe. When the

[1] *Wealth of Nations*, II. 48.

African market was opened to private traders in 1697, a considerable business at once developed in the supply of Dutch metal goods to the African natives. The carriage and marketing of foreign goods prepared the ground for the home-made products which followed from England shortly after.

(3) *Wheat and National Production.* Within the shell of a commercial empire, to share in which Scotland agreed to union, Great Britain became a great industrial producer, using partly her own materials and partly those of her colonies and other countries. Of the new commodities which round about 1700 became important in outward trade the most important were wheat, cutlery, hardware and pottery. The wheat was home-grown and the pottery was made from native clays, but the hardware trades used both native and imported ores, and the cutlery trade relied largely on Swedish bar iron.

In earlier centuries there had been a fitful export of wheat, alternating with imports in years of scarcity. After 1660 England became a regular exporter and Parliament approved it by the grant of a bounty, given occasionally at first and after 1688 regularly under the Act of 1 William and Mary, c. 12. London, which in Elizabethan days had stored wheat against a domestic shortage in the granaries of the City companies, became the leading port of shipment for an export trade in wheat to France and other parts. Between 1767 and 1792 surpluses for export alternated with deficits ; 1792, the last year of European peace, was also the last year in which Great Britain had an export surplus.

1697–1731 exports   3·5 million quarters ; imports fractional
1732–1766   ,,   11·5   ,.   ,,   ,,   ,,
1767–1801   ,,   3·0   ,,   ,,   ,,   10 million.
    1 quarter = 8 bushels.

The capacity to export wheat was a sign of agricultural progress, but even more remarkable was the record of 1767–1850, when a rapidly growing industrial population was fed mainly from home growth. In 1850, four years after the repeal of the Corn Laws, the imports of wheat were less than a bushel per head in an estimated consumption of 8 bushels per head per annum. In 1914 Great Britain depended for her leading foodstuff to the extent of one-fifth on her own soil and of four-fifths on her Navy and merchant marine.

(4) *Hardware, Cutlery and Pottery.* From 1700 onwards the Birmingham smiths, untrammelled by the restrictions of corporate towns, were working in iron and copper, making swords, guns,

and a great variety of hardware. The brass industry was Birmingham's specialty. In the course of the 18th century the copper mines of Cornwall and Anglesey yielded so abundantly that there was a large export of copper cake and manufactured copper, with the East India Company as the principal buyer. But manufactured brass, the raw material of the brass worker, was not given freedom of export till 1813 (53 Geo. III, c. 45). Down to 1720 Birmingham was engaged in winning, under fiscal protection, the home and colonial market. By 1750 she was exporting goods to all parts of Europe, Africa and America.

Indeed, in the last quarter of the [18th] century the foreign market was by far the most important one for brass and copper goods. Birmingham had the bulk of the trade of Europe in these, and no less than three quarters of the products of Wolverhampton found a market abroad. Buckles, buttons, thimbles, locks, brass door furniture and all kinds of small goods in copper and brass were sent to the continent.[1]

The button was a late 18th-century substitute for the buckle. The profits of the hardware business of Boulton and Fothergill supplied the capital for the engine business of Boulton and Watt.

Even in France, the home of fashion itself, Boulton and Fothergill had correspondents at Marseilles, Lyons, Aix, Montpellier, Paris and Rouen, while so important was the Russian trade that Fothergill spent a whole year travelling in Russia and Sweden.[2]

When Europe was at peace Birmingham was its toy shop : when Europe was at war, Birmingham and Carron, the new iron centre of Scotland, supplied Britain and her allies with ordnance.

Between 1700 and 1770 the Abram Darbys revolutionised the iron industry.

During the 70's the new processes were carried to France by William Wilkinson, who directed the construction and working of blast furnaces at Le Creuzot between 1778 and 1781. In 1789 one of the Wilkinsons introduced the coke-smelting process into Upper Silesia ; while six years earlier, Charles Gascoigne had taken service under Catherine, and had carried skilled workmen from Carron and established the new methods of gun founding in Russia.[3]

In 1775 Soho delivered its first steam engine to John Wilkinson. By 1795 Wilkinson, who supplied the parts for this and other engines, had shipped several to the Continent. But the export of machinery was unwelcome to British manufacturers.

Benjamin Huntsman's process of making steel in small clay

[1] H. Hamilton, *The English Brass and Copper Industries*, p. 292.
[2] J. Lord, *Capital and Steam Power*, p. 90.
[3] T. S. Ashton, *Iron and Steel in the Industrial Revolution*, p. 54.

crucibles or pots (c. 1740) established Sheffield in the international reputation which it still has as a maker of steel. With an improved navigation between Sheffield and the Humber the merchants of Hull built up an export trade with Europe, sending their produce by boat to Dunkirk for distribution inland. When Arthur Young visited Sheffield in 1769, he was struck by the big earnings which manufacturers were making on account of the brisk trade with America.[1] Huntsman found the Sheffield cutlers prejudiced against his steel and therefore looked abroad for a market ; and his son William extended the foreign business.

The distinction quickly acquired and never lost by the pottery industry of Staffordshire was due in particular to Josiah Wedgwood, who opened his first works at Burslem in 1759 and a new works ten years later at Etruria, a village of his own creation. Between 1762 and 1788 his cousin Thomas Wedgwood was his partner in the Useful Branch : in 1708 Thomas Bentley, a merchant of Liverpool, became his partner in the Ornamental Branch and managed the London warehouse. The founder admitted his three sons and a nephew to partnership in 1790, but remained in charge of the business till his death in 1795. From 1810 to 1823 Josiah Wedgwood II managed the business alone. In 1823 he was joined by his son Josiah Wedgwood III, who retired in 1842.

Wedgwood made a ware for which the prosperous colonists evinced a keen demand and he was soon in Liverpool planning with Bentley the extension of his market and promoting among fellow manufacturers and merchants the cutting of a canal between the Potteries and the Mersey. In 1765 he writes to Sir William Meredith, a friend in government circles. ' The bulk of our particular manufactures are exported to foreign markets, for our own consumption is very slight in comparison to what is sent abroad, and the principal of these markets are the continent and islands of North America. To the continent we send an amazing quantity of white stoneware, and some of the finer kinds; but for the Islands we cannot make any too costly.'[2] At the time of the Orders-in-Council (1807–12) there were no stronger opponents of them than the Wedgwoods. Not less than five parts in six of the whole produce of the Potteries were exported to foreign markets, the firm stated in evidence before the Commons' Committee of 1812 on the Petitions against the Orders-in-Council.

(5) *Cottons.* In 1783 when peace was concluded with the American colonies it looked as though Great Britain had made a sad mess of empire. America—a few dye stuffs and naval

[1] Arthur Young, *Northern Tour*, I. 122.
[2] Miss Meteyard, *Life and Works of Josiah Wedgwood*, I. 367.

materials apart—had yielded tobacco and war. It was not until America became independent that Georgia and the Carolinas turned to cotton and thereby presented to Great Britain the wealth of industrial material which she had looked to her Empire to provide. Cotton was a substitute for tobacco that would have delighted King James I. Tobacco brought smuggling, unthriftiness and filth : cotton bred healthy lasses and fleets of steamers sailing with piece goods to foreign ports. It remained only for the Lancashire manufacturers to secure an open market in the East, and this they did on April 10, 1814, when the Indian trade was thrown open. ' The tonnage which cleared out from the port of Liverpool alone in the year 1851 [sc. for the East] was nearly three times as great as the whole amount of tonnage employed in the British commerce with India and China the year before the trade of India was thrown open to private merchants.' [1]

To the outward tonnage the ever-growing cotton industry made the chief contribution. From next to nothing in 1800 the export of cotton piece goods to India rose to £4·3 m. (1851–55) and £14·1 m. (1876–80), after which it was almost stationary. The export trade to China also grew rapidly between 1850 and 1875 : that to Australia and New Zealand rather later. In all these markets cotton piece goods formed the large majority of all cottons (piece goods and yarns).

Cotton Exports from United Kingdom in £ million.[2]

	India	China, Japan and Korea	Rest of Asia	Australia and New Zealand	All Countries
1851–5 . .	5·5	1·0	1·7	0·5	31·8
1896–1900 . .	17·4	6·1	5·3	3·2	67·1

In 1913 Great Britain exported 80% of the cotton piece goods she produced, and of these nearly one-half went to India and China, the ancient home of the manufacture. The Lancashire cotton industry is in essence a re-export trade with the climate, machinery and manual skill of Lancashire incorporated in the raw material during its warehousing in England ; and Lancashire's fidelity to free trade is very intelligible. In 1882 at the prompting of Manchester the British Government procured the removal of the Indian import duty which had been imposed to pay for the cost of the Mutiny of 1857 ; and in 1894, when the decline of the rupee necessitated its re-imposition, insisted on a countervailing excise. Not till the Great War was India in return for her patriotic services permitted to penalise Lancashire's cotton.

[1] T. Baines, *History of Liverpool*, p. 781.
[2] Figures furnished by Board of Trade Statistical Department.

(6) *Machinery and Foreign Contracts.*   Great Britain entered the long peace with three industrial assets : an assured wealth of raw material, domination in the markets of Europe and the East, and priority in the knowledge and use of machinery.   This last she was very loth to develop as an export trade.   Even free trade Manchester boggled at this.

The law against the export of machinery was built up *seriatim* in the 18th century, beginning with knitting frames in 1696. The prohibited list grew as invention grew and was complicated by amendments and exceptions.   When Huskisson came to the Board of Trade in 1823 J. Deacon Hume worked out a scheme of export by Board of Trade licence, which was administered under the Tariff Acts of 1825 and 1833.   Commons Committees examined the question in 1824 (Artisans and Machinery), 1825 (Exportation of Tools and Machinery), 1841 (Exportation of Machinery).   The Reports of 1824 and 1825 favoured free export, but the manufacturers were so nervous that the restrictions were retained till 1843.   In 1825 manufacturers had feared a scarcity of machinery for their own mills if free export were allowed, but the momentous revolution in machine tools between 1825 and 1840 removed this danger and produced a situation which was damaging to British machine manufacturers.   Machine tools and machine parts were allowed out, or, where prohibited, were smuggled out ; but the export of the finished machine was prohibited and its smuggling was difficult.   Restriction thus defeated itself and was removed in 1843 (above, p. 63).

When the engine business was in its infancy, Boulton and Watt lived in fear that Baron Stein and other sneaking foreigners would take the knowledge of their engines abroad.   ' The Baron's conduct,' wrote Boulton to his partner in 1786, ' was not agreeable to Mr. Boulton's notions of honour.' [1]   A generation later locomotive engines were being sent abroad to run on foreign rivers and railways.   Marine engines went first.   Iron steamboats fitted with engines of British design were running in the 1820's on the Seine and other rivers in France.   They were supplied by Manby Wilson and Co., who managed for a time the Le Creuzot Ironworks.   Railway engines followed, to run on British-made rails.   In 1814 the Improvement Commissioners of London found that their dust heaps had acquired an export value for the rebuilding of Moscow.[2]   In 1841, when Thomas Brassey went to France to construct his first foreign railway, he took with him a small army of British and Irish navvies.   For the next twenty years he was building railways with British material in France,

[1] John Lord, *Capital and Steam Power*, p. 217.
[2] S. and B. Webb. *Statutory Authorities*, pp. 334-5.

Belgium, Italy, Austria, Denmark and Canada. In 1852, when preparing for the Grand Trunk Railway of Canada, he erected workshops at Birkenhead for the construction of rolling stock suited to North American conditions. In 1865 for the Delhi railway 'all the ironwork and machinery were imported from England, and had to be carried upwards of a thousand miles from the ports where they were landed. Including rolling stock these materials weighed nearly 100,000 tons.'[1] His successors have done similar work in the Argentine, China and all parts of Africa.[2]

The construction of railways in continental interiors by British capital was complementary to the importation of foodstuffs and raw materials from those parts. The export of capital goods and mechanical ability brought in return over a period of years a flow of imports which constituted the interest on the investments thus made.

(7) *Tin-Plate.* Some products of the iron and steel industry are the fixed capital of other trades, others are the raw material out of which fixed capital is manufactured; others again are the raw material out of which speedily consumed goods are made, and to these belongs tin-plate, which is a thin sheet of iron coated with tin and used to make containers of various sorts. The export trade became important about 1850 and the biggest single user for the next half-century was the oil industry. But tin-plate is employed also for 'packing' the various products of the 'canning' industry, such as meat, fish and fruit, and also for biscuits, tea, tobacco and certain 'dry' goods. The container of tin-plate is the counterpart in metal of the jute sack, and the growth of long-distance transport by sea and land created a new demand for both. Just as jute and flour sacks made 19th-century Dundee, so tin-plate and oil-cans made 19th-century Swansea. The tin-plate industry grew up in attachment to the South Wales iron industry, deriving tin from Cornwall and iron plate from the local iron industry. Down to 1890 South Wales had a virtual monopoly of the tin-plate industry of the world. It was a skilled industry; and its technique was greatly improved by a crucial invention in the tinning process, the Morewood process of 1880, and the substitution of steel for iron plate in the early 80's. Of the two forms of mild steel, Siemens steel was the more suitable for tin-plating; and the tin-plate demand was sufficiently large to call for a specialised Siemens steel industry in South Wales. The export of tin-plate (which was the greater part of the output) rose from £¾ million in 1850 to over £6 million in 1890. Much

---

[1] A. Helps, *Life and Labours of Mr. Brassey*, p. 275.
[2] *Vide* the entertaining *Chronicles of a Contractor*, by G. Pauling (Constable, 1926).

the largest purchaser was the U.S.A., which indeed brought meat packer and canning into the vocabulary of commerce. Whereas the Lancashire cotton industry depended on America for nearly the whole of its raw material, the South Wales tin-plate industry depended on it for its main market. But the imposition of the McKinley tariff in 1890 killed the export trade in seven years, the last section to go being the Pacific trade, which at first was protected by the heavy costs of inland transportation between East and West, until these were reduced and the duty of import further increased in 1897. After this there remained the re-export trade, which enjoyed a rebate. For the American Oil Companies purchased much of their plate for re-export, and having to meet keen competition from Russia in foreign markets threatened to ship oil in bulk and make cans abroad, if the rebate was withdrawn.

The American tin-plate industry is a plain example of the successful employment of protection to hasten the growth of an infant industry. But the South Wales tin-plate industry also proves the power of a free trade country to survive the loss of a single great market by the development of numerous small ones. Tin-plate exports sank to £2¾ millions in 1898, but rose steadily to £6½ millions in 1910, the biggest new markets being in the East. The dumping of foreign steel bars hurt Welsh steel producers, but the tin-plate manufacturers benefited ; and a strong impetus was given to the integration of steel producers and steel users and to the extension into allied uses of tin-plate, such as galvanised sheeting for roofing. The case of tin-plate is that of British trade in miniature—loss of old markets through hostile tariffs : the capture of new ones under the stimulus of necessity : dependence on foreign countries for raw materials in whole or in part : self-sufficiency in fuel, labour and the processes of marketing and finance.

(8) *Coal.* In 1913 the leading British exports in order of value were textiles, iron and steel manufactures, machinery and coal. The export of coal became important only after 1850. Coal exports rose from 5 million tons in 1855 to 97 million tons in 1913, the latter figure including about 20 million for bunkers of foreign-going vessels. Translated into percentage values of total United Kingdom exports, they rose from 2½% to 10½%. In the same interval the percentage quantity of coal exported to coal raised rose from 8% to 34%. Four-fifths of the coal exported in 1913 went to Europe and the Mediterranean, the balance chiefly to South America. The South Wales coalfield owed its growth to the export trade and the Navy. The building of the Glamorgan canal in 1798 from Merthyr to Cardiff opened it up. Then followed the railway and the steamship to make the fortunes of

Cardiff and Swansea. The Bute East Dock of 1859 followed the Bute West Dock of 1839. Between these dates the name of John Nixon stands out as a pioneer of coal export to France. In 1909 a coal port pure and simple arose at Barry, nine miles along the coast from Cardiff.

Meanwhile the coalfields on the East Coast of Britain were increasing their trade with the Baltic and the Mediterranean. What Newcastle was to London in 1800, North-East Britain and South Wales were to the coal-lacking regions of the world in 1914. Strung out along the trade routes of the world were coaling stations, stocked with British coal for the service of British ships.

Is the export of coal a sign of national decline? Is Great Britain after the lapse of centuries returning to a stage in which other nations will take from her only raw materials? The answer is No, because of the part which coal plays in the economy of British shipping. In 1913 coal accounted for 75% of the total *weight* of exports. Coal thus found employment on the outward voyage for three-quarters of British carrying power. The main imports to Britain are foodstuffs and raw materials, which occupy a large space. Coal made up the deficiency of volume on the outward journey, the other exports being mainly manufactures which are small in volume.

> ' Oh, where are you going to, all you Big Steamers,
>   With England's own coal, up and down the salt seas? '
> ' We are going to fetch you your bread and your butter,
>   Your beef, pork, and mutton, eggs, apples, and cheese. '
>
> ' And where will you fetch it from, all you Big Steamers,
>   And where shall I write you when you are away? '
> ' We fetch it from Melbourne, Quebec, and Vancouver.
>   Address us at Hobart, Hong-kong, and Bombay.'
>
> *Kipling.*

Section 6. *The Trade Balance*

Early writers disputed furiously over the balance of trade. It was their approach to the tariff problem, but very unsatisfactory in view of the lack of comprehensive trade statistics and the prevalence of smuggling. The British trade balance was a disquieting paradox. As she grew in commercial power, it became increasingly unfavourable. For other nations had to pay something for the shipping services and capital which Great Britain supplied and therefore British imports normally exceeded British exports; that is to say, the trade balance was normally unfavourable. But it was unfavourable for a reason precisely opposite to that which made Canada's trade balance so until recently. For whereas Canada had a temporary excess of

imports because she was borrowing heavily for capital investment, Great Britain had a permanent excess of imports, which
every decade made more inevitable. The balance sheet of British
foreign trade stood in 1924 thus :

$£$ million

Recorded imports (1280) + unrecorded diamond imports (8) = 1288
Recorded exports including re-exports, (935) + excess ex-
    port of bullion and specie (12)   = 947

(a) Excess of imports of Merchandise and Bullion .   .   . 341
(b) Net national Shipping Income   .   .   . 130
(c) Net Income from Overseas Investments .   . 185
(d) Commissions and other services   .   .   . 55

(e) Total ' Invisible Exports ' on balance   370
(f) Income available for Investment Overseas (e) — (a) . =   29

(a) is obtained from recorded statistics, in contrast with (b) to
(f), which are conjectural estimates after the Board of Trade.[1]

(b) refers, not to shipowners' profits, which are a very much
smaller figure, but to gross earnings of British shipping less
disbursements in foreign ports. *Per contra*, credit is taken for
disbursements by foreign ships in British ports.

(c) is net income. From the gross estimated income are
deducted the sums payable by Great Britain to foreign countries.
In the latter the main item is £35 million in respect of the war
debt to the government of the U.S.A. (d) consists of the earnings
from the financing of foreign trade. (e) is the sum of (b), (c) and
(d). It is easy to see why shipping and financial services fulfil
the same purpose in the balance sheet as the export of goods.
And income from overseas investments does so too, because to
that extent imports arrive from which no compensating export
is required.

A large (f) rather than a small (a) is the true measure of
favourableness. This item was less favourable in 1924 than in
1913, when it stood at £181 million, or in 1923, when it stood at
£102 million. But the trade balance is not everything. Is the
total external trade of import and export growing ? Are both
growing ? Have they recovered from the disturbance of the war ?

Measured in money both have grown ; but since 1913 money
has declined in value, and if in order to arrive at volume the value
is corrected by the general change in the price level, the following
position is disclosed. Imports rose as from 100 in 1913 to 104·1

[1] *Committee on Industry and Trade, Survey of Overseas Markets* (1925),
pp. 665–6. For a revised estimate issued by the Board of Trade in the light of
later information, see *Economic Journal*, March 1927, pp. 140–6. The revision
puts (f) as high as 86 for 1924. (*Cf.* also *Economic Journal*, December 1927).

in 1924 : but exports declined as from 100 in 1913 to 75·5 in 1924. Of itself it is no disadvantage that the pre-war volume of imports should be purchased with three-quarters of the pre-war volume of exports. But in 1924 nearly 10% of the population was unemployed, and since the majority of British employment depends directly or indirectly on foreign trade, the need for extension of exports is imperative. The war and its aftermath caused a shrinkage in the world total of foreign trade ; and of this shrunken total Great Britain retained its pre-war percentage. Therefore to recover the pre-war volume of exports means a bigger slice of the shrunken total ; and to this the obstacles are twofold. The first class of obstacle concerns the productive and marketing efficiency of British enterprise ; and here two weaknesses have been the disturbance of production by repeated labour troubles and a certain backwardness in specialising to the wants of particular markets. The second class of obstacle concerns the decline of purchasing power abroad and the imposition of hostile tariffs ; and both of these have been felt since the war. As Europe slowly recovered, China fell into chaos. Everywhere self-determination has displayed itself in economic Chauvinism ; and Great Britain has been hurt by shipping discriminations as well as by new tariff walls. The shipping legislation by which numerous countries reserve to themselves their coastal trade and emigration traffic has not been applied against Great Britain exclusively, but they hurt her more than others because she is the nation whose ships have in fact been excluded. So too with new tariffs. An island Power with a world market is hurt more than a continental Power by tariff barriers ; and when two island Powers such as Britain and Japan are in competition on other markets, it is difficult for the old Power to neutralise the geographical and racial contacts of the new, especially when these are supplemented by the short period advantage of cheap labour.

CHAPTER VIII

PORTS AND MERCHANT SHIPPING

Section 1. London and Southampton. Section 2. Liverpool and the Manchester Ship Canal. Section 3. Glasgow as a Port and Ship-builder. Section 4. Trade Routes. Section 5. Evolution of the Shipowner. Section 6. Evolution of the Steamship. Section 7. Insurance and Registration.

Section 1. *London and Southampton*

Marshall writes :

At the time of the Restoration England's foreign trade was less than a hundredth part of her present foreign trade in money value, and less than a two-hundredth part in volume. And though it increased five-fold during the next hundred years, yet in 1760, when the establishment of England's supremacy at sea told that the main work of the great trading companies was accomplished, it had not attained to a sixtieth part of its present bulk.[1]

To accommodate this vast increase artificial port facilities were necessary. The port systems of to-day—the landings, docks and channels of approach—are the construction of the 19th century. In 1800 London had practically no docks, Liverpool had a small dock system, and Manchester was not a port. The Clyde, as we of the 20th century see it, is ' nearly as much an artificial navigation as the Suez Canal.' [2]

London lies on that point of the river Thames at which the marshes of Kent and Essex narrow to a convenient crossing. The old harbours of Billingsgate and Queenhithe were packed away within the City limits ; and when London was rebuilt after the Great Fire of 1666 the demand of merchants for a point of discharge close to the City warehouses frustrated the scheme of a beautiful London with a port further down the river. By 1800 the crowds of colliers were converting the Thames into a coalyard and obstructing the passage of ships. Fleets of merchantmen piled up in the Kentish Downs until a favourable wind allowed them to enter and discharge their cargoes, which then for want of accommodation lay on the open wharves or afloat on barges. During the 18th century about three-quarters of the total recorded imports of England and rather less of the exports passed through London ; and in 1800 the congestion was worse than ever before owing to the necessity of sailing in convoys during the Napoleonic war and the great expansion of the West Indian sugar imports, the whole of which arrived inside three months of the year.

The first modern dock, the West India, was sanctioned by Parliament in 1799 and completed in 1802. Then came the London and the East India Docks, opened in 1805 and 1808 respectively. These, with their later extensions, were all on the north or City side. The dock system on the south or Surrey side developed independently, beginning with the Surrey Commercial Dock Company of 1810, which extended the old Howland Great Wet Dock of c. 1700 ; and it was not amalgamated with the system on the north of the river until 1908.

Dock construction and warehousing went together. Some bonding privileges already existed. By the Act of 13 Anne, c. 18 (1713), merchants were allowed to warehouse tobacco on

---

[1] Alfred Marshall, *Industry and Trade* (1919), p. 37.
[2] W. R. Scott, *The Industries of the Clyde Valley during the War*, p. 5.

their own premises, paying a small duty on arrival and the balance when the goods were taken out for consumption. Bonding privileges were given to plantation rum in 1742, rice in 1765, foreign sugar for re-export in 1760, cocoanuts and coffee in 1767. But the Warehousing Act of 1803 (43 Geo. III. c. 132) greatly widened the range. Its purpose was to make London a depot for colonial and tropical produce ; and the value to the mercantile community was at this time all the greater in view of the heavy increases in war taxation, which under the bonding system had not to be advanced by importers. The Dock Companies built warehouses on their premises ; and the contiguity of warehouse and dock permitted effective customs control and the elimination of the old-time heavy leakage between ship and warehouse, which is portrayed *seriatim* in Sir Patrick Colquhoun's treatise on *The Police of the Metropolis*, 1806—night plunderers, light horsemen, heavy horsemen, game watermen, game lightermen, and the rest. The Act of 1803 was confined to London, but similar privileges were ' very quickly extended to most of the principal ports in Great Britain and Ireland, and in the first three decades of the century by a gradual process of development, goods were permitted to be removed in bond, at first for exportation only, and subsequently for all purposes.' [1]

The London Docks were built by joint-stock companies incorporated by Act of Parliament. The first companies were given a twenty-year monopoly in their trade, the West India in West Indian produce, the East India in the trade of the great company of which they were a subsidiary, the London in tobacco, rice, wine and brandy. But in 1823 Parliament refused to renew the monopoly of the West India Dock Company and in 1825 sanctioned a new company, the St. Katharine's, in order to stimulate competition. But this was so damaging that in 1838 the East and the West India Dock Companies amalgamated. The West Indian trade, having passed its zenith, did not fill the space of the West India Docks and the liberated Indian trade found the East India Docks too small ; the amalgamation therefore was a mutual advantage. In 1864 there was an amalgamation between the London, the St. Katharine's and the Victoria Dock Companies, the last having been built by the firm of Brassey in 1855 to handle the new steamship traffic. Thus after 1864 there were two competing groups, together with the independent Millwall Dock Company, formed in 1864 and never a financial success. In 1875 the London and St. Katharine's Dock Company, as the amalgamation of 1864 was styled, built the Royal Albert alongside the Victoria Dock. The East and

[1] *Customs Tariffs of the United Kingdom* (1897), p. 42.

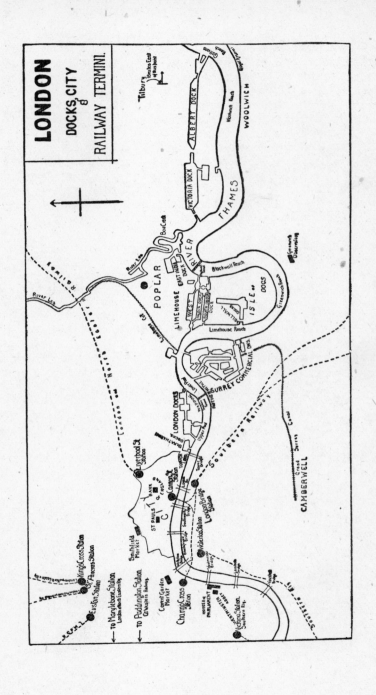

LONDON
DOCKS, CITY
&
RAILWAY TERMINI.

West India Dock Company, determined to go one better, built at Tilbury (1882-6), 24 miles down the river, hoping to obtain a share in the steamship traffic which their rivals threatened to monopolise. But they underestimated the cost of the project and by 1889 were in the receiver's hands—not, however, before their competition had reduced the dividends of their rivals to vanishing point. Therefore a joint committee of operation was formed, and in 1901 the two groups amalgamated. Sir Donald Currie, of Liverpool, when assisting at the inception of the Tilbury Dock in 1882, had invited London to imitate his own city by forming a single dock authority, but it took twenty years for his suggestion to mature. The Royal Commission of 1902, determined to end the long dispute between ship-owners, barge-owners, wharfingers, dock companies and merchants, recommended a single Port of London Authority for the whole port, north and south, from Teddington above Richmond to the isle of Sheppey at the mouth of the Thames estuary. This was brought into existence by 8 Edward VII (1908), c. 68. The only authority remaining outside the scheme was the ancient corporation of Trinity House, chartered in 1514, which continues to exercise the duties of buoying and piloting for the Port of London and is also the lighthouse authority for England and Wales.

The most persistent of the old disputes concerned the ' free water ' clause, which the barge-owners, called lightermen, caused to be inserted in the charters of the dock companies. This gave them the same free movement inside the docks which they had always enjoyed on their own river. They could therefore enter the docks free of charge and convey goods from ships in dock to warehouses outside. The concession was not damaging so long as much of the produce was dutiable and deposited in bonded warehouses, which the dock companies owned. But as free trade put one commodity after another on the free list and the incidence of warehousing for other reasons altered, the dock companies lost most of their warehousing business. In 1898 less than 20% of the goods landed on the dock quays paid warehousing charges. Neither ship-owners nor barge-owners were willing to make extra payment, and the Bill of 1900 promoted by the dock companies for this purpose raised such an outcry that it was dropped in favour of a Royal Commission. The new Port Authority was empowered by the Act of 1908 to levy port rates on a scale sufficient to cover port expenditure. The Port Authority is a public body on which port users and the Government are represented ; but although it has full parliamentary powers to cover its expenditure by sufficient charges, its stock does not rank as a Trustee security. This is an anomaly; for it means, for example, that the Government of New South Wales can borrow for harbour construction more cheaply than the capital of the Empire.[1]

Southampton in the English Channel opposite the Isle of Wight has no industrial area immediately behind it, but the distance by rail from London is only 79 miles by comparison with London–Plymouth 220, and London–Liverpool 200; and railways and motors have so enlarged the distributive range of ports that isolation is no longer an obstacle to its growth. In the middle of the 15th century Southampton was the third port of England, ranking after London and Bristol. About one-eighth of the wine trade of the country passed through it, and it had also a considerable trade with France and the Mediterranean. It was cut off by distance from the first epoch of the industrial revolution, and its first dock was not completed till 1842. But at that point its potentialities as a port for passengers and express freight were appreciated; and in the same year railroad communication was established between the docks and the newly built railway to London. This was also the time when the ocean steamship was passing beyond the experimental stage. The first ocean steamship lines to use the port were the P. and O. and the Royal Mail. In 1856 the Union Steamship Company, since amalgamated with the Castle Line, made Southampton their home port for the arrival and departure of their steamers engaged in the South African trade.

More than any other port in Great Britain, Southampton is favoured by Nature. For the estuary of Southampton Water, 6 miles long and 1 mile wide, is land-locked and safe, and has a minimum tidal depth of 35 feet. As the channel is effectively scoured by the waters of two converging rivers, the Test and the Itchen, very little dredging is required to keep the docks clear of silt. Above all, the port has opposite to it the Isle of Wight, which forms with the mainland the two approaches—the Solent from the west and Spithead from the east—and causes the phenomenon, unique in England, of double tides, with the result that the period of high water lasts about two hours. Finally, Southampton has the good fortune (for it is nothing more) to be the strategic centre of the trade between trans-oceanic countries and North-Western Europe, including the British Isles. This is of special importance in the ever-growing New York passenger traffic, which is pivoted on Southampton and Cherbourg. Passengers and mails outward (the latter by a very large margin) exceed those inward for the reason that North American liners

---

[1] *Cf.* J. M. Keynes in *The Nation*, August 9, 1924.

often land passengers and mails at Plymouth before proceeding to Cherbourg and Southampton.

Modern Southampton began with the acquisition of the dock estate by the London and South Western (now Southern) Railway in 1892, and the landmarks in harbour development since that date are :

1895. Prince of Wales Graving [1] Dock, 745 feet long.
1905. Trafalgar Graving Dock, 912 feet long : each in its day the largest in the world.
1912. The open Ocean Dock, which was intended primarily for vessels of the White Star Line and in which to-day four of the largest vessels in the world are sometimes berthed at the same time.
1924. The Floating Dock, constructed by Armstrong Whitworth, with a length of 960 feet and displacement of 60,000 tons, which is thus capable of holding the *Majestic*, the world's largest vessel. The dock submerges until there is a depth of 33 feet of water over the keel blocks (when lifting a vessel of the *Majestic* type). When it is drained by electric-driven motor pumps, it rises with the vessel high and dry inside it.

Extensions in progress in 1927 will ultimately reclaim 107 acres of mud land between the Royal Pier and Millbrook Point. In front of this area and parallel with it will be built a jetty 5000 feet long and 400 feet wide, on both sides of which vessels will be able to berth. This arrangement, in place of the projecting jetties originally planned, will afford better manœuvring space for ships. With harbour facilities thus always level with demand (in contrast with London), and with Nature and the strategy of trade routes on its side (in contrast with Liverpool), the use of the port since 1892 has grown at the following rate :

	Net inward tonnage in million tons.
1892 .	1·2
1902 .	3·4
1912 .	4·1
1922 .	5·7
1927 .	7·6

Southampton took from London the passenger traffic which London hoped to secure by building the Tilbury Dock. To-day with the increasing industrialisation of the Southern Midlands it bids fair to redress in the sphere of shipping the disparity of

[1] Graving = Cleaning, from Greaves, the melted tallow with which the ship's bottom was cleaned.

economic power which formerly existed between the provincial North and the provincial South.

Section 2.   *Liverpool and the Manchester Ship Canal*

Seventeenth-century Liverpool was a discontented outport of Chester, shipping Cheshire cheese to London and salt from the Cheshire mines to the fishing fleets. In 1690 John Blackburne of Warrington established the first large salt-making plant on the site of the present Salthouse Dock. But the silting up of the river Dee, which was Chester's doom, was Liverpool's opportunity. Liverpool imported potatoes and oats from Ireland and tobacco, no small part of it smuggled, from Virginia. As the textile industry of Manchester grew, Liverpool, the natural port of Manchester, obtained goods with which to force a contraband way into the Spanish Main. And raw cotton was imported. ' In 1770 no more than 6000 bags of it [cotton] entered the Mersey, but by 1800 the imports had reached a quarter of a million bales, and at the end of the century as much as four million bales entered the United Kingdom in a year, of which six out of every seven were discharged at Liverpool.' [1]

The slave trade accompanied the young cotton trade, growing at a great rate after 1730.   Liverpool undercut London and Bristol by stinting its captains and manning its crews from Poor Law apprentices. A profitable triangular trade was developed. The slavers took out provisions and textiles to the Guinea Coast, loaded there with gold-dust, ivory, and slaves for the West Indies, and returned to Liverpool with sugar, cotton and tobacco. For a part of the 18th century Liverpool had a pottery industry, but it was lost to Staffordshire and Liverpool developed as a purely carrier town. Of slaves conveyed from Africa to the West Indies in the eleven years 1783–93 Liverpool had the profit and disgrace of conveying 303,000. By this trade Thomas Leyland, banker and lord mayor, became Liverpool's first millionaire, netting an average profit of £43 per slave. [2] The French wars brought fortunes from privateering, but disturbed the amenity of Liverpool as a bathing place ; for at that time Rochdale, Blackburn and Manchester came to ' bathe and drink salt water.' But ' during the war very few of them durst come down on account of the warmth of the impress.' [3] No living man has voluntarily drunk Mersey water, but as late as the 1890's there

---

[1] *Manchester Guardian Commercial*, July 14, 1927, ' Liverpool,' p. 8.

[2] Gomer Williams, *History of the Privateers and Slave Trade of Liverpool*, p. 607. But according to S. Dumbell, *Profits of the Guinea Trade* (*Economic Journal, Economic History*, II. No. 6), this figure is too high.

[3] *Ibid.* p. 302.

were bathing vans on Seaforth sands ! When the slave trade and privateering were lost, the trade to the East took their place. Sir John Gladstone, father of the statesman and founder of the Liverpool Corn Exchange, led the fight for liberation, and then Liverpool grew quickly to metropolitan stature. ' Liverpool,' wrote Baines in 1853, ' supplies Lancashire, Cheshire and part of Yorkshire and Staffordshire, as well as Ireland and North Wales, with raw materials and tropical produce.' [1] The leading imports were cotton, timber and wheat.

Practically the whole of the modern port front is made ground. When Daniel Defoe visited Liverpool on his tour of 1724, approaching from the Cheshire side, he had to ' ride through the water for some length . . . on the shoulders of some Lancashire clown, who comes knee-deep to the boat's side.' [2] The Pool of Liverpool then stretched inland as far as the modern Church Street ; and across this at its mouth the first dock was built, being sanctioned in 1709 and opened in 1715. It covered 4 acres of ground by comparison with the $55\frac{1}{4}$ acres of water area, the $7\frac{3}{4}$ miles of quayage, and the 57 acres of sheds occupied by the Gladstone Dock of 1927. The big tidal changes of the river made closed docks indispensable for any considerable volume of traffic ; and therefore each great trade extension was followed by the building of new docks. Since 1850 these have been chiefly to the north to secure the deeper draught at the river mouth. The system to-day stretches for seven miles along the river.

Unlike London, Liverpool was undisturbed by the friction of divided authority. The first Dock Act of 1709 (8 Anne, c. 12) empowered the town to impose tonnage rates entering or leaving the port. The port authority was the Corporation of Liverpool, until the Corporation was reformed in 1825 and the management of the dock estate transferred to a body which in 1857 became the Mersey Docks and Harbour Board. This has twenty-eight members, twenty-four of whom are elected by the dock users and four appointed by public authority. The Board derives its revenue from a tonnage rate on ships—which covers the use of the wet docks for two months—and a consolidated dock rate and town dues charge—which covers the use of the quays for seventy-two hours. Vessels passing through to Manchester pay only a small harbour rate. In order to maintain a free flow of traffic through the transit sheds the Board has warehouses in which it stores at owner's charge goods not removed to private warehouses. To-day, as you disembark on the floating landing stage, you see

[1] T. Baines, *History of Liverpool*, p. 745.
[2] Defoe, *Tour through Great Britain* (edition 1742), III. 210.

three great buildings—the Royal Liver, the Cunard, and the Mersey Dock and Harbour Board Offices. These and the docks to north and south in front of the Overhead Railway were a sand flat in Defoe's time. There are no old buildings in Liverpool. In the background rises the new cathedral in red sandstone. The pro-cathedral of St. Peter's in Church Street, itself only two hundred years old, was recently demolished to make way for a Woolworth store.

The Manchester Ship Canal all but broke Manchester. The city felt the stress of competition after 1870 ; and, being restive under the railway freights to Liverpool and the port charges there, determined to bring the sea to its doors as Glasgow had done.

> To bring big ships to Manchester
> Is what we mean to do ;
> You'll sail direct to every port
> On board an ocean screw.

The distance from Liverpool to Manchester by the shortest railway, the original Liverpool and Manchester line, is thirty-one miles ; and a ship canal involved a water length of thirty-six miles from Manchester to Eastham, where the Mersey is deep enough to receive ships. Eastham locks are six miles above the Prince's landing stage, Liverpool, and nineteen miles from the Bar lightship.

In 1882 the project was broached at the house of Daniel Adamson in Didsbury, Manchester. In 1885, after three years of opposition in Parliament, the bill received the Royal assent. In 1887, with Edward Leader Williams as engineer, the first sod was cut. But despite the enthusiastic support of all local interests—individuals, companies, trade unions, co-operative societies—funds fell short. In 1889 the death of the very able contractor Mr. Walker, who had a great hold on the navvies (the navvy after half a century of railroad building was back at his old job), was followed by labour trouble and also by disputes with his executors. In 1890 there were floods and landslips ; and the company had to appeal to the Manchester Corporation, which advanced £5 m. for the completion of the undertaking, protecting itself by a debenture on the canal and part control. On May 21, 1894, the ship canal was opened by Queen Victoria. In December 1925 the expenditure on capital account stood at £18·6 m.

The first ten years were spent in getting business. The company had to fight the shipping lines with their powerful weapon, the deferred rebate : to obtain injunctions against the

railways for refusing to accept traffic : and to advertise the port
abroad.   Lord Rosebery, Foreign Secretary in 1893, replied to
a request for official publicity that it was ' contrary to the
practice of the Office to employ her Majesty's representatives
in calling attention to new industrial enterprises.' [1] But the canal
was an avenue to a superlatively good market ; and very soon
Liverpool ship-owners rather than see traffic pass into other
hands sent their ships up to Manchester to compete with the
new lines which were being organised from the Manchester end.
The canal brought immediate freight reductions and indirectly
great benefit not only to Manchester but also to the whole region
along the canal banks.   Trafford Park, which in 1900 was a park
with a golf course, is now an area of warehouses, flour mills and
industrial plants.   Works have been erected along the canal
between Manchester and Runcorn for the treatment of heavy
by-products, which least of all can afford transhipment by railway or road.   The value of imports into Manchester by the ship
canal rose from £35 m. in 1913 to £56 m. in 1923, thus making
Manchester at that date the fourth port of import in Great
Britain, passed only by London, Liverpool and Hull.   The great
increase of traffic put the canal on a paying basis.   In 1915 its
£10 ordinary shares stood at 16s. 9d. ; by the end of 1923 they
were touching par.   For within a fifty-mile radius of Manchester
there is a consuming population of nine millions, greater, that is,
by a quarter of a million than the population of the Dominion
of Canada at the census of 1921.

Section 3.   Glasgow as a Port and Ship-builder

The population of Liverpool rose from 25,000 in 1750 to
377,000 in 1851.   In 1911, including the Birkenhead district,
it was 668,000.   The population of Glasgow rose from 28,000
in 1768 to 344,000 in 1851.   In 1911, including Govan, which is
now a part of Glasgow, it was 941,000.   The evolution of Glasgow
was that of Liverpool and Manchester rolled into one.   After the
Union the centre of economic gravity in Scotland shifted from
the east coast with an orientation upon Europe to the west coast
with an orientation upon the West Indies and Virginia.   Glasgow
of the pre-industrial revolution throve on shipping, tobacco and
sugar.   In the first stage of the industrial revolution, say from
1770 to 1820, it was the rival of Manchester in the spinning
and weaving of cotton by power.   In this period the iron industry of the Clyde arose.   1820–60 was a transitional period in

---

[1] Sir Bosdin Leach, *History of the Manchester Ship Canal*, II. 163.

which textiles and iron were both prominent. Then came the supremacy of the ship-building and engineering trades.

Every port is a potential ship-builder, but the growth of the steamship caused ship-building to be concentrated in two districts close to coal and iron—the Clyde, with its Ulster offshoot at Belfast, and the Tyne ports with their southern neighbours, Sunderland, the Hartlepools, and Middlesbrough. These two districts in 1913 produced the majority of the ships. The east coast ports were responsible for more cargo boats than the Clyde and in addition undertook a very great amount of repairing and overhauling, but the Clyde led in big ships and Royal Naval units. The pre-eminence of the Clyde in ship-building and engineering is of old standing. It was pronounced in the days of wooden ships, but the advent of the iron steamer brought an irresistible combination of advantages. The Clyde had coal on the spot as well as iron ore, and it could easily import ore when this was necessary. The blast furnaces and steel plants along its banks produced the raw material of the ship-builder. Thus it was that the Clyde led the way in every scientific advance in naval architecture and engineering from the birth of ship-building as a science and of engineering as a profession. In the days of wooden ships designers followed types, aiming at individual grace and securing stability by ballast. With the employment of iron ship-building became a science. Practical experience is still important, but designing is now an exact science based on calculation of stresses, water resistance and economy of engine power.

As a port Glasgow resembles Liverpool in having an excess of exports and is thus in contrast with London and Manchester.

	£ million	
1923[1]	Imports	Exports
London	385	195
Liverpool . . .	244	289
Manchester . . .	56	38
Glasgow . . .	25	52

Many vessels after discharging in London proceed to Glasgow for repairs and coal and thence to the Mersey for their outward cargo of manufactured goods. In 1923 the two ports of London and Liverpool handled 56% of Great Britain's foreign trade of import and export.

[1] See *Chambers of Commerce Atlas* (1925), Plate 71A.

Section 4. Trade Routes

The trunk lines of British ocean commerce are five.   Route 1 is to Egypt, India and the Far East.   It has three sections: the Mediterranean, the Indian, and the Far East.   Some companies, such as the P. and O., serve the whole, others confine themselves to parts of it.   Route 2 is to Australia and New Zealand.   It is a bow with three strings: the Suez, the Cape, and the Panama. Route 3 is to North America, and on this route the imports greatly exceed the exports.   Over it passes one-sixth of the world's tonnage.   Route 4 is the West African route.   Its traffic is distinguished by the variety of the imports.   Route 5 is to South America.   Here, too, the imports exceed the exports ; and though many boats take out coal, in which South America is poor, some during the grain season go out in ballast.

Route 1 was created by the making of the Suez Canal.   The Suez was planned and constructed by a French engineer, de Lesseps, and opened in 1869, the year in which the first trans-continental railway in America, the Union Pacific, was finished. It was stupidly opposed by British interests, by politicians fearing the contact of Europe with Asia, by owners of sailing vessels for which the route was unsuited, and by railway people with interests in the Suez railway, which was then building.   But in 1875 the British Government by purchasing for £4 millions the holding of the debt-burdened Khedive secured 46% of the ordinary shares, and British shippers were not slow to use the new route.   In 1913 60% of the traffic passing through the canal was British.   The canal put a premium on the steamship and especially on large cargo steamers, equipped to collect freight from various Eastern ports and to distribute it at ports of call in the Mediterranean and western Europe.   In this way the old entrepôt trade of Britain—the long haul from overseas with transhipment to the Continent—was adjusted to the geographical changes created by the junction of the Mediterranean with the Indian ocean.

The Panama Canal, begun and abandoned by the de Lesseps Company, was completed by the Government of the United States and opened to commerce in August 1914.   What West Africa owed to Ronald Ross, the Panama owes to General William Gorgas.   By drainage and sanitation, malaria and yellow fever were stamped out.   The canal places the east coast of North America in much closer touch not only with its own west but also with the west coast of South America, with which it is in a direct north to south line ; and it has affected the shipping of the British

G

Empire in three ways. It has opened an alternative route to Australia and New Zealand, shortened the route between Great Britain and British Columbia, and restored the West Indies to a focal point of ocean commerce. In the season 1923–4 over 20 million bushels of Canadian wheat moved to Great Britain from Vancouver via the Panama. Canada and Great Britain should be grateful to President Wilson for upholding the Treaty of 1901 which provided for equal tolls on foreign and American shipping.

Section 5.   *Evolution of the Shipowner*

In the 18th century the trader was his own carrier and ocean trading meant the carrying of a valuable miscellaneous cargo through hostile waters. It was in very truth a venture and all parties took a share in it : the merchant owner, the captain, the crew, and the inhabitants of the port. In 1815 privateering and the press-gang came to an end, and in 1816 the Algerine pirates were bombarded into final silence. There arose, therefore, a shipowning class, which carried for others on regular routes at a regular tariff. The East India Company had led the way by carrying for the merchants of London on the trunk route to India. In 1807 the Society of Shipowners of Great Britain [1] drew attention to the fact that such a personage as a shipowner, pure and simple, existed.

After 1850 the increase in passenger traffic and in the long-distance transportation of foodstuffs and raw materials called for two distinct types of steamship—the passenger liner and the cargo boat, which is either a liner or a tramp. To maintain regularity of sailings cargo steamers engaged on liner business have to be built, manned and maintained on a higher plane than those designated as tramps. But the distinction between the two is not hard and fast. An owner may have some of his boats on regular sailings, others on time-charter with liner companies, and yet others on the tramp. The Departmental Committee of 1918, using the word ' tramp ' in a very wide sense, estimated that vessels of the tramp class accounted for 60% of the steamship tonnage of the British Empire in 1914.[2] Tramp vessels constitute a valuable mass of fluid transportation, which moves freely around the world, accepting bulk freight wherever rates are attractive. The manager of a tramp fleet controls his vessels

[1] *Cf.* E. R. Johnson and Others, *History of the Domestic and Foreign Commerce of the United States*, I. 88.
[2] *Report of Departmental Committee on Shipping and Shipbuilding Industries after the War* (1918), p. 54.

as closely as a chess-player his men.   The cable and wireless have made the freight charter market a sensitive organ, which vibrates instantly to every touch from without.

The history of one old-established shipping firm (Rankin, Gilmour and Co. Ltd., of Liverpool)[1] illustrates excellently the evolution of shipowning and incidentally the interdependence of Liverpool and Glasgow.

In 1812 the Gilmours, a Glasgow partnership of shipowning timber merchants, opened an establishment on the Miramichi in New Brunswick and further establishments later in the Maritime Provinces and on the St. Lawrence.   To these 'foreign houses,' as they were called, the parent firm sent out staffs and supplies.   From them they obtained timber and later, when the foreign house undertook shipbuilding, ships as well.   To handle the provisioning and selling, which involved the selling both of timber and ships, they opened a house at Liverpool ; and when the Glasgow house lost ground through clinging overlong to wooden ships, Liverpool became the firm's headquarters.   Having acquired a fleet of steamships, they imported timber from Canada and cotton from New Orleans, as the season dictated.   When wooden shipbuilding declined, the Canadian offshoots either were disbanded or became independent lumber companies, and the Liverpool house, abandoning everything but the shipping part of the business, became pure shipowners.

A similar thing happened to import merchants generally. The old-time merchants of Liverpool, who had possessed both ships and warehouses, gave way to shipowners who carried anywhere and import brokers who specialised in a single commodity ; and the function of warehousing was shared between the Mersey Dock and Harbour Board and separate warehousing establishments, the latter perhaps belonging to the manufacturers for whom the import was destined.   Wheat was once stored in private warehouses, but now the flour mills, which are chiefly by the riverside, have their own silos.   Importers sell on or before arrival, and steamship arrivals are so continuous and regular that millers can buy their wheat 'to arrive' at more or less regular intervals ; 90% of the wheat imports comes in liners to-day.[2] In the 18th century Liverpool slavers carried slaves on contract and a specified number on private account.   This trade was abolished by law, but its place was taken by passenger liners, which carried at fixed rates ordinary passengers, emigrants and freight.   Shipping firms, such as Rankin, Gilmour and Co. Ltd., followed the same evolution, becoming finally carriers only.

[1] *Cf.* John Rankin, *A History of Our Firm*, Liverpool, H. Young, 1921.
[2] Cf. *Manchester Guardian Commercial,* ' Liverpool,' July 14, 1927, p. 19.

Thus the shipowner in all his forms became a common carrier of persons and things.

British shipping has followed the general economic tendency to an increase in the size of the plant (the ship) and the unit of control (the shipping line or group of lines). The former point is illustrated by the relation between the number of vessels using a port and their tonnage. The port of Liverpool statistics give the number of vessels paying rates for use of the port and their net register tonnage at different dates as follows :

					Vessels	*Net Register Tonnage (in thousands)*
1800	.	.	.	.	4,746	450
1820	.	.	.	.	7,276	805
1840	.	.	.	.	15,998	2,445
1860	.	.	.	.	21,136	4,697
1880	.	.	.	.	20,070	7,524
1900	.	.	.	.	24,870	12,380
1920	.	.	.	.	17,115	16,521
(*1913*	.	.	.	.	*24,982*	*18,433*)

Applied to ships, a ton means 100 cubic feet of carrying capacity : net tonnage means the space available after deducting engine and crew room. It stands to gross tonnage roughly as 5 : 8. The 1920 totals in both columns are affected by submarine losses, and therefore the last pre-war year is added. It is apparent that since 1860 the number of vessels using the port has increased but slowly, whereas between 1860 and 1913 the tonnage grew more than fourfold. 1860 marks the time when the iron steamship prevailed over the wooden sailing vessel.

As the ships increased in size, so did the total tonnage controlled by each line. About 1900 a movement set in towards amalgamation. Thus in 1900 the amalgamation of two South African lines, the Union Line founded in 1853 and the Castle Line founded in 1872, produced the Union-Castle Line. In 1901 the International Mercantile Marine grouped together the White Star, Leyland, American Red Star, Atlantic Transport, Dominion and certain other lines. The pooling of resources during the war hastened the tendency to closer relations, and by 1919 there had appeared a ' Big Five ' in control of the passenger shipping lines :

> Lord Inchcape,
> Sir John Ellerman,
> Sir Owen Philipps,
> Sir Charles Booth,
> Sir Frederick Lewis.

But this did not mean, as in the banking world, a fusion into five great working units. As a recent historian, himself in the shipping business, observes, ' During the last 50 years the leading steamship lines, though they have been controlled by different individuals, from different offices, and even in different cities— Glasgow, or Liverpool, or London—have nevertheless in a large measure kept their identity, their house flags, and the colour of their funnels.' [1]

The high seas are an ideal theatre for the operation of competition ; for there are no artificial tracks, except on the ship canals, and all nations compete. But the competition between each unit became so severe that they agreed together to stabilise rates. This was done in Conferences, the earliest of which was formed for the Calcutta trade in 1875. After this came Conferences in the China trade, 1879 ; the Australian, 1884 ; the South African, 1886 ; the West African and North Brazilian, 1895 ; and the trade to the west coast of South America, 1904. Down to the war there were no Conferences for the North Atlantic trade ; and the reasons were the multiplicity of international competition and the excess of carrying space in the holds of great passenger liners, which enabled them frequently to underbid the tramps.

The hold of the shipping lines on the shipping merchant was secured by the device of the ' Deferred Rebate.' Shippers, using the Conference lines only, were allowed a rebate, which they forfeited if they went outside ; and as the rebate was calculated for the previous six months and paid six months later, the shipping lines had a twelve months' hold on the shipper. The Shipping Conferences were highly unpopular with the exporters of the New World. In 1912 the South African Government prohibited the deferred rebate in lines with which it signed mail contracts. At the end of the war, when there was a shortage of tonnage to move the Australian harvests, the Australian Government instituted its own service—the Commonwealth Line [2]—and friction quickly developed over the rebate. Through the mediation of the Imperial Shipping Committee (a body which began work in 1920) the compromise which was finally reached in the South African trade, an agreement with damages for breach in lieu of the deferred rebate, was applied to the Australian trade. In 1925 the Canadian Government, which since the war had operated a merchant service, launched an attack on the post-war Atlantic Shipping Conference ; but it seems to have acted in ignorance of the extent to which freight rates were controlled,

[1] Clement Jones, *British Merchant Shipping* (1922), pp. 257–8.
[2] Advices from Canberra (November 3, 1927) stated that the ships of this line were to be sold unconditionally.

and the proposed contract for a subsidy to an independent line was not completed.

Section 6. *Evolution of the Steamship*

In industrial production mechanical improvement began in the large firm or factory and later was generalised. In the operation of steamships the reverse was true. The steamer began in the petty traffic of inland waters and took nearly half a century to reach the high seas. Since water offered a smooth bed, and therefore one problem less to the inventor, the steamboat was invented before the steam train. However, the steamboat age was slightly later than the railway age; for whereas by 1850 the railway was supreme over roads and canals, sailing vessels maintained their hold on the high seas until the late 60's. The opening of the Suez Canal in 1869 robbed them of their great preserve—the Eastern trade. It must be remembered, also, that down to the 70's steamships were not pure steamships. To economise fuel they used sail as well as steam.

In 1787 William Symington, a Scottish engineer, took out a patent for a marine steam-engine. In 1789 he experimented on the Forth and Clyde Canal with an engine which was supplied to him by the Carron Company and paid for by Patrick Miller, Esq., of Dalswinton, the price being £363 10s. 10d.[1] In 1801 he was employed by Thomas, Lord Dundas, to erect a boat and construct a steam-engine to propel it; and in 1803 this boat, consequently named the *Charlotte Dundas*, ran on the Forth and Clyde Canal towing two other boats of 70 tons each, well loaded, over a stretch of 19 miles against a strong head wind.

Robert Fulton of America, then resident in England, went with the help of Robert Owen, then of Manchester,[2] to inspect Symington's invention, and after procuring engines from Messrs. Boulton and Watt he returned to New York to launch the *Clermont* on the Hudson in 1807. Henry Bell of Glasgow, working independently, produced in 1812 the *Comet*, a 35-ton boat of 4 h.p. It plied on the Forth and Clyde Canal and, becoming more audacious, crept out along the coast to Leith. Its success led to the establishment of river and cross-channel services. In 1816 steam services were opened between Liverpool and the Cheshire shore, Holyhead and Dublin, Greenock and Belfast; and in 1818 the Dover-Calais service began. By 1829 steamboats were considered safe enough to carry mails; and a public advertisement invited the

---

[1] Cf. *The Carron Company, A Century and a Half of Commercial Enterprise*, p 11.

[2] Cf. *The Life of Robert Owen by Himself* (ed. Bell), pp. 89–97.

citizens of Edinburgh to forsake the coach and travel from Leith to London in a beautiful steamer with accommodation for 100 passengers.

The first boat to use steam on the Atlantic was the American *Savannah*, which arrived in Liverpool on June 20, 1819, after being chased for a day on the Atlantic by an Admiralty cutter, who thought she was on fire. However, she was only under steam for 80 hours out of 29 days. The first boat to cross the Atlantic under steam the whole way was the Canadian *Royal William*, which in August 1833 made the journey from Pictou, Nova Scotia, to London in 20 days. London, Bristol and Liverpool then bestirred themselves, and in 1838 the Atlantic was thrice conquered. On April 4, 1838, the British and American Steam Navigation Company of London dispatched the *Sirius*, which had been built for the London to Cork trade. She reached New York on April 21, one day ahead of the *Great Western*, which left Bristol on April 7 and took only $13\frac{1}{2}$ days. (The first boat to make the run from New York to Queenstown in under 7 days was the *Alaska* of the Guion Line in 1882.) The *Great Western* was the first boat specially built for the Atlantic trade. On July 1838 the Liverpool Atlantic Steamship Company dispatched the *Royal William*—the second of that name. This was the first steamship to cross from Liverpool.

The Great Western Steamship Company, which sent out the *Great Western*, was the creation of Brunel, the engineer of the Great Western Railway. He had in mind a Great Western Ocean Service like that established later on two oceans by the Canadian Pacific Railway. But the scheme failed because the rail haul in Great Britain is too small to make the railway a determining factor either in the selection of a port or in the allocation of traffic, and most unexpectedly the Great Western Steamship Company failed to secure the mail contract which the Admiralty put up to competition in October 1838.

It had been the custom of the Admiralty to charter sailing vessels from private owners for the conveyance of mails. These were known as Admiralty Packets. In 1821 in the person of the Post Office the Government operated its own steamers on certain services, but lost money on all except that between Dover and Calais, and therefore in 1853 retired from the business. Henceforward it paid private companies for the carriage of mails on a commercial basis. But in order to ensure regular and speedy mail services on distant routes and to have the right of use in time of war, the Government offered a contract with a subsidy on certain services ; and in 1839 the North Atlantic contract, with a subsidy of £55,000, was won by Samuel Cunard, a shipowner of Halifax, Nova Scotia. This was the origin of the Cunard Steamship Line.

Similar contracts were awarded in 1837 to the line which later became the Peninsular and Oriental for the conveyance of the East Indian Mails, and in 1840 to the Royal Mail Steam Packet Company for the conveyance of the West Indian Mails. In 1886 the White Star Line divided the North Atlantic subsidy with the Cunard. The White Star Line, organised by Messrs. Ismay, Imrie and Company in 1869, was a reorganisation of an earlier White Star Line which consisted of American-built clippers sailing to Australia. In 1926 it was purchased from the International Mercantile Marine by the Royal Mail Steam Packet Company.

At Halifax Cunard had watched the performance of the first *Royal William*, and, realising its possibilities, came over to England for capital and financial support. He interested David MacIver of Liverpool and George Burns of Glasgow ; and on July 4, 1840, the first Cunarder left Liverpool. At first the line maintained a separate service to Halifax, then it touched at Halifax on the way to New York, and finally after 1867 ceased to call there. Therefore Canada, having given to England Samuel Cunard, had to begin afresh. The Allan Line was founded in 1856 by Sir Hugh Allan to operate between Liverpool and Quebec and was absorbed in 1916 by the Canadian Pacific Railway, which entered the shipping business in 1903.

Whilst steam was replacing sail, iron by a parallel evolution was replacing wood as the material of the hull. Copper, indeed, had been freely employed since 1761 as sheathing for the bottom of ships, but there was no question of using it instead of wood ; it was too expensive.

John Wilkinson in 1787 constructed the first boat of iron, which he named the *Trial*, but it was only a canal barge, as also was the second iron boat of which there is record, the *Vulcan*, built in 1818 for service on the Forth and Clyde Canal. When, however, the passenger steamboat established itself, iron came into use here. In 1821 Mr. Manby, of Messrs. Manby, Wilson and Company, built the *Aaron Manby*, an iron boat, for service on the Seine. Others followed, and in 1824 the River Shannon (Ireland) Steam Packet Company continued the experiment of iron steamboats with success.

In 1832 Macgregor Laird procured from John Laird of Birkenhead an iron steamboat for the Niger river trade—the *Alburkah*. Its behaviour on the ocean encouraged Lairds to build more, and in 1839 they supplied to the East India Company the first iron ship carrying armament. There was great prejudice against the use of the new material, even after the only valid objection—the disturbance of the ship's compass—had been removed in 1839 by a scientific method of compass correction. But the experience of the *Great Britain*, a screw-driven iron ship of 1843, removed the fear that an iron hull would perforate on bumping. For in 1846 she went aground off the coast of Ireland, and after lying there for eleven months was hauled off and resumed service. Notwithstanding this, the Cunard Line did not launch its first iron ship, the *Persia*, till 1865.

The highest class of modern steamship has screw propellers, a steel hull, turbine engines and oil firing.

In 1836 Captain John Ericsson, a Swede, who had established himself in London in partnership with a firm of London engineers, demonstrated the merits of the screw as a method of propulsion, and in 1843 the Admiralty installed its first screw propeller. But at the time of the Crimean War, 1854–5, the screw steamers in the service of the Admiralty were little more than sailing ships with a screw as auxiliary. The first real steam-driven ironclads— the *Warrior*, followed by the *Black Prince*, *Minotaur*, etc.—were laid down in the early 60's. For naval purposes the screw had over the paddlewheel the great advantage of being submerged, and therefore not liable to be shot away like the paddle apparatus above the waterline. The *Great Eastern*, an iron Leviathan constructed by Brunel in 1854, had a combination of screw and paddle, but she was too big (her length, 680 feet, not being appreciably exceeded till the building of the *Mauretania* in 1907) and was a commercial failure. The Cunard Company launched its last paddle ship in 1863. In the 80's a twin screw was added on ocean liners to minimise the risk of a breakdown.

The inventions of Bessemer and Siemens made possible the steel hull. Though Lloyd's Register accepted the new material in 1867, it was not till the early 80's that the price of steel justified its general adoption. In 1887 out of new tonnage launched steel accounted for 257,000 and iron for only 31,000.

The turbine engine is the penultimate phase of the incessant evolution in marine engineering. The early passenger steamers had a one-cylinder engine. In 1854 John Elder, the founder of the Fairfield Shipbuilding and Engineering Company of Govan, Glasgow, designed the compound engine, which effected a great economy in fuel. The difficulty of carrying sufficient coal for a long voyage had caused Dr. Lardner and others to laugh at the notion of crossing the ocean under steam, but the compound engine solved the problem and was first adopted by the Pacific Steam Navigation Company, which traded to South America, a country with no coal. Triple and quadruple expansion engines followed. Then in 1894 Sir Charles Parsons fitted the *Turbinia* with a turbine engine, and ten years later the turbine or rotary engine began to replace the reciprocating engine, but this is by no means the last word. For progress is now being made with the internal combustion engine, which turns the steamship into a motor ship. Such engines are being installed rapidly on cargo and passenger ships now building.

That steam would be raised by any agent other than wood or coal was not contemplated in 1900, but as an American writer of 1921 observes : ' The merchant shipping of the world is rapidly turning to fuel oil as a source of power. The advantages to be derived from liquid oil in place of coal are so outstanding in facilitating bunkering, increasing rates of steaming, and conserving labour in firing that this trend will undoubtedly increase.' [1]

In 1921, out of approximately 55 m. tons gross of merchant shipping in the world, 9 were oil-driven, 8 using fuel for raising steam and 1 the internal combustion engine. The oil consumption in the latter is very much less than when oil is used as liquid fuel, and therefore every further improvement in such engines will increase the superiority of oil over coal ; but limitation of supply stands in the way of total conversion to oil.

During the last fifty years the changes in internal equipment have been as great as those in construction and engineering. The first boat of the White Star—the *Oceanic* of 1869—constructed by Harland and Wolff at Belfast, was in outline and equipment the first of the modern liners, the saloon being placed amidships and steam being applied to all the operations of the ship, and thereafter the Cunard and the White Star strove neck to neck in the race of improvement. In cargo boats there has been development in the direction of special purpose boats, such as oil tankers and vessels fitted with refrigerating plant for the conveyance of perishable meatstuffs and fruits ; and the mast has degenerated into a derrick. Thus lacking masts as well as sails, furnished like an hotel or cold storage plant, and safeguarded by wireless apparatus, the modern steamship has but one contact with the sailing vessel of the past—her dependence on the men who serve her. Wind, fog and ice make seafaring still a free man's job, hard indeed and monotonous, but calling on occasion for those qualities which are the ultimate wealth of a maritime nation.

Section 7.   *Insurance and Registration*

It is not enough that ships should be built and sailed. They and their cargoes must be insured. The passenger takes his

[1] J E. Pogue, *The Economics of Petroleum*, p. 153.

chance with the lifebelt, but commerce puts to sea with an insurance policy.

The history of Lloyd's illustrates well the part which informal group enterprise has played in economic development. Lloyd's is an international service with headquarters in London ; like the Stock Exchange and Money Market, it just grew. Having no corporate name it called itself Lloyd's, after Edward Lloyd, the keeper of a coffee-house at which merchants desiring and offering marine insurance were accustomed to forgather in the latter part of the 17th century. The members of Lloyd's did their business as individuals. ' However these men had common interests : an interest in obtaining information, an interest in exposing fraud and resisting fraudulent claims. There was a subscription : there was a small " trust fund " ; the exclusive use of the " coffee house " was obtained. The *Verein* grew and grew.' [1] In 1774 they settled at the Royal Exchange ; in 1779 they agreed upon a general form of insurance policy ; in 1811 they reorganised with trustees. Finally in 1871 they were incorporated for the threefold purpose of marine insurance, protection of members' interests, and the collection and diffusion of shipping intelligence. But the business of insurance remains individual : the broker desiring insurance takes round his list and the underwriter writes under it his name and the share of the risk which he is willing to assume.

About 1696 Edward Lloyd started a Shipping and Commercial Chronicle, called *Lloyd's News*, which was revived in 1726 as *Lloyd's Shipping List* and is now published as *Lloyd's List and Shipping Gazette*. It records the movements of all vessels afloat and gives in complete and authoritative form the information which a paper such as the *Liverpool Journal of Commerce* supplies, in so far as it affects Liverpool, in addition to its other commercial news.

Some time later the members of Lloyd's started a Shipping Register to aid them in their insurance business. Down to 1834 two rival Registers existed—' The Green Book ' compiled by the underwriters, and ' The Red Book ' compiled by the shipowners. They were then united, and the management was entrusted to a committee of merchant shipowners and underwriters. In 1822 the first steamship was registered : in 1837 the first iron ship. In 1867 steel was accepted as a building material and in 1874 engineering experts were added to the staff of surveyors. In 1913 Lloyd's Register had ten thousand vessels on its list and its

---

[1] F. W. Maitland, *Trust and Corporation*, Collected Papers, III. 372.   For the evolution of the Stock Exchange, see *Royal Commission on Stock Exchange* (XIV. of 1878) ; report and evidence *passim*.

surveying staff of 3 in 1800 was now 300. The repute which its classification carries—'A 1' is a figure of our daily speech—caused it to exercise a silent but all-powerful control over the quality and seaworthiness of merchant vessels. Lloyd's Register of British and Foreign Shipping is, however, a voluntary society only ; and it has rivals, such as the Bureau Veritas established at Paris in 1828, and the more recent British Corporation for the Survey and Register of Shipping.

In 1850 the Marine Department of the Board of Trade was established. Though resented at first by shipowners they came to accept it as an ally, and in any event there were public interests which had to be safeguarded by the State. The seaworthiness of the great majority of cargo ships was already ensured by the classification societies, but the Board of Trade exercises powers which would be improper to a voluntary body. In addition to supervising design, testing appliances, and approving the assignments of the classification societies, it stops unseaworthy vessels from putting to sea, investigates wrecks, issues certificates of seamanship, and makes regulations for the safety of passengers and the treatment of the crew at sea and on land. But for the Marine Department of the Board of Trade the work of the classification societies would have lacked cohesion and authority : but for the classification societies the Marine Department would have had difficulty in enforcing the various Merchant Shipping Acts. The most famous of these, that of 1876, is associated with the name of Samuel Plimsoll. By making a rumpus in Parliament he secured the load-line which is marked on the outside of every British ship. He was suspended for his language, but he gained his line.

Although marine insurance is a very ancient practice, the marine policy of to-day is the opposite of the old-time 'bottomry bond.' Just as the early investors in life insurance paid down a lump sum in return for an annuity, so early investors in marine insurance invested a lump sum on a chance. If the vessel arrived safely, the borrower repaid the loan taken out against the ship's bottom and with it a premium. If it was lost, he paid neither. Until quite recent times the bottomry contract was used by captains in emergencies at foreign ports, but the cable transfer by putting the head office of the shipping company in immediate financial contact with its boats, wherever they may be, has removed the need for this survival of it.

If a ship cannot be insured her owners will not let her put to sea. When war broke out in August 1914 the British Government agreed to underwrite the war risks of the Mercantile Marine ; and in the first days of uncertainty the information most greatly

sought by Canadian bankers and business men was the exact
terms on which the Government insurance could be obtained.
In the last analysis marine insurance determines whether a trade
route shall be used.   It is useless to rail wheat to the Hudson
Bay if no one will insure the ships that are to take it away.

CHAPTER IX

ROADS AND CANALS

Section 1. Communication by Land and Water.   Section 2. Turnpike Trusts and
the Road Builders.   Section 3. The Building of Canals and their Economic
Influence.   Section 4. Causes of Decline.

Section 1.   Communication by Land and Water

TRANSPORT and industry are interdependent : communications
are established to handle traffic, and by their establishment new
traffic is created.   It is not possible to exploit the agricultural
resources of new continents until adequate railroads have been
built across them.   The time lag between the building and the
harvest of traffic is so serious in most new countries that the
Government gives land or money to the builders or operates them
itself.   Though the Canadian Pacific Railway, built with the aid
of valuable land grants, was completed on November 7, 1885, the
Canadian West did not boom till 1900.   But in an old country
with an island seaboard production for a central market may be
far advanced before the building of adequate inland communications.   For the sea serves as a trunk line of commerce, and thus
despite a poorly developed interior the traffic of 17th-century
England attained to imperial dimensions.   As England was a
small country, her navigable rivers were few and she had no chain
of navigable lakes.   Moreover, none of her important rivers were
navigable for any length without improvements ; and in addition to this the merchants who used them for traffic had to contest the right of navigation against landlords who sought privacy
and against industrial users who set up fish traps and water mills
(the mediaeval equivalent of hydro-electric power).
     Seventeenth-century England, lacking civil peace and an
industrial hinterland, had no good trunk roads of inland commerce.   The sea gave her such commercial unity as she had.
The main rivers, the Thames, Severn, Mersey, Yorkshire Ouse,
Trent and Greater Ouse, served to the open sea as retail to wholesale.   London obtained its coal from Newcastle, Dublin from
Whitehaven (Cumberland), Bristol from South Wales.   The

navigable reaches of river were channels of retail distribution to places along their banks. Even when London lived on home-grown wheat, a considerable part of its supply came coastwise, especially the part that was raised in East Anglia ; and similarly the re-exports from London included many coastal shipments of produce brought in bulk on larger ships from overseas. Mrs. Dashwood in Jane Austen's *Sense and Sensibility*, 1797, sends her furniture ' round by water ' from Sussex to Exeter. It would go to-day by motor truck. In 1832 Sir Walter Scott returned from the Continent a dying man. ' On June 13, 1832, he arrived in London, and on 7th July took ship for Leith.' [1] To-day an invalid might go by either motor or train, but certainly not by steamer.

By the end of the 17th century the provinces were alive to the value of making their rivers more navigable, and in the early 18th substantial improvements were effected in the navigations of the Mersey, the Don and the Trent. The navigation of the Mersey streams (the Irwell, Mersey and Weaver) was essential to the growth of Liverpool as a port, and the improvements were made about the time that Liverpool was building its first dock. But investment capital was still very scarce, and when it became more abundant later on, there was a more lucrative outlet for it in the construction of artificial canals which were independent of rivers, though sometimes making junction with them. There-after river navigation was auxiliary to transportation by canal.

At law the king's highway is no more than a right of way from A to B. The Roman roads, straight and well fashioned, were by 1600 a memory, overlaid with centuries of feudal encroach-ment and civil war. But after 1660 the provinces felt a growing need for commercial contact with London, the financial heart of the country, and the nobility sought speedier and more com-fortable travel to their country estates. Moreover for Londoners there were things from which to escape, the Great Plague in 1665 and the Great Fire in 1666. In 1665 the Court and Parliament made a pusillanimous retreat to Oxford : in 1669 the Oxford Fly, the first of the ' flying coaches,' began to run. Therefore at this period the London-Oxford road was heavily travelled and kept in good repair. A century later a foreign professor, who had to make the journey from Cambridge to Oxford, found that the only route was by London. The undergraduate of to-day agrees with the professor.

In 1739 two travellers journeyed from Glasgow to London.[2]

---

[1] John Buchan, *Sir Walter Scott*, p. 210.
[2] *Cf.* S. and B. Webb, *English Local Government, the Story of the King's Highway*, p. 66.

At Grantham, Lincolnshire, they joined the turnpike on the old North Road from London to York. But up to that point they had to travel upon a narrow causeway with a soft unmade road on either side : from time to time they met gangs of pack-horses, whereof the leader carried a bell in order that warning might be given of travellers coming in the opposite direction. The commercial traveller of those days was a bagman with bags slung across his horse.

The stimulus to road improvement came from three quarters : from Government for military and political reasons, from the provinces anxious for industrial outlets and commercial contacts, from landowners and farmers interested in the improvement of their locality and in better access to their markets. The City having forgotten plagues and fires was content with things as they were.

After the rebellion of 1745 the Government built military roads in the Highlands of Scotland as a protection against further Jacobite risings, and at a later date Parliament voted moneys for roads and bridges to connect Scotland with the capital. So, too, when the Union of 1800 compelled the Irish M.P.'s to come to Westminster, they agitated for an improved road from Holyhead to London ; and in 1815 their spokesman, Sir Henry Parnell, secured the appointment of a commission to control the survey of the Holyhead-Shrewsbury-London route and to place the contracts. Furthermore, the Government, owing to the increase in its postal business, was interested in the improvement of through communications and therefore facilitated by legislation the establishment of the turnpike trusts, which had through communications chiefly in mind.

The outlook of the provinces was more local ; and this is the main reason why after some years of improvement the roads of England excited at times the rage of Arthur Young. The roads, like the curate's egg, were only good in parts, and on the evidence of Young the bad parts were especially frequent in the hard-used roads of the industrial North. The main road between Preston and Wigan was ' infernal,' to be avoided by travellers ' as they would the Devil,' and so on.[1] As late as 1817 a writer complains, ' It is in vain that one parish repairs its roads, if its neighbours will not.'[2] Nevertheless every regional improvement was an asset to the industry and agriculture of the provinces. In the Potteries, until about 1760 the roads were in a wretched condition and most of the traffic was carried by packhorses ; after that, by the initiative of

---

[1] A. Young, *Six Months Tour through the North of England*, 1768, published 1770, IV. 580–1.
[2] Quoted in W. T. Jackman, *Transportation in Modern England*, I. 215.

the pottery manufacturers, like Wedgwood and Bentley and other enterprising citizens of the towns in the neighbourhood of the Potteries, turnpikes began to be constructed, roads were widened, and in every way possible the means of communication were brought close to the requirements of an industrial people.[1]

To nobody was the new proximity more welcome than to the farmer, giving him as it did a market at his doors. When the grandfather of George Hope, the Scottish farmer who won the prize essay of the Anti-Corn Law League, began farming in East Lothian in 1773, grain was marketed on horseback, and coals were brought to the farm by a four-wheeled wagon.[2] The men had to take a hedge bill to cut the road and a spade to fill in cavities. Again in Cumberland in 1792 ' the principal part of the corn was conveyed to market on the backs of horses.'[3] The farmers of outlying districts had, of course, to bide their time for good local roads ; but the through roads were at their service if they were raisers of produce that could travel on foot. Highland cattle marched in their thousands to Norfolk, there to be fattened for the London market. The turkeys and geese of Suffolk, ' these devoted feathered legions,' bespread the surface of the roads on their way to the all-devouring Metropolis. Hence the dictum of Adam Smith, who wrote when improvement was in progress, ' Good roads, canals and navigable rivers, by diminishing the expences of carriage, put the remote parts of the country more nearly upon a level with those in the neighbourhood of the town. They are upon that account the greatest of all improvements.' (I. 148.)

Section 2.   Turnpike Trusts and the Road Builders

The instrument of improvement was the turnpike trust and the man of action was the civil engineer. The turnpike trust was a device for piece-meal improvement in an age when local government was inert. The statute labour imposed on the inhabitants by the Statute of 1563 (5 Eliz. c. 13) barely sufficed for the maintenance of roads in their existing condition ; a general highway rate, being new taxation, was unwelcome ; and the parish as such had no security on which to borrow. Therefore in districts anxious for improvement the prominent inhabitants went to Parliament for an Act, authorising them to form a turnpike trust for the improvement of a particular stretch of road and to levy tolls on users other than foot passengers. Each stretch was

---

[1] W. T. Jackman, op. cit. I. 291.
[2] Cf. George Hope of Fenton Barnes, by his Daughter, Edinburgh, 1881.
[3] W. Blamire, Cumberland Pacquet, Feb. 2, 1832, quoted in S. and B. Webb, The King's Highway, p. 6.

protected at either end by turnpikes or toll bars at which the tolls
were taken. Having Parliamentary authority the trust was able
to borrow money for improvement and used the toll receipts to
pay the interest on its bonds and to amortise them. The first
Turnpike Act was secured in 1663, but turnpike trusts did not
become common until after 1700. Between 1730 and 1750 their
erection aroused fierce local opposition, which severe legislation
was enacted to repress. Each trust required a separate Act of
Parliament and most trusts were concerned with a few miles of
road only. They were incorporated in the first instance for
21 years only under the idea that at the end of that period the
improvements would be completed and the roads handed back
to the parish ; but this never happened, and the trusts were
automatically continued. To reduce the cost of procuring an
Act the General Turnpike Act of 1773 (13 Geo. III, c. 84) was
passed, and this was supplemented in 1831 by an Act relieving the
trustees from the heavy charges hitherto incurred on renewal.
Throughout the 18th century there was much laxity of administration and jobbery. When the long stretch of road from Shrewsbury
to Holyhead was improved, the Parliamentary Commission
appointed for the purpose first obtained the assent of the several
trusts along the route, then effected the improvements, and
finally returned the improved road to the care of the trusts.

After 1815 there was a movement towards turnpike consolidation, in the course of which the methods of finance and
administration were revolutionised.   John Loudon McAdam and
his sons rendered national service here ; and in 1827, when the
trusts north of the Thames were consolidated, James McAdam
was made Surveyor-General of Metropolitan Roads.   The larger
trusts led the way in the appointment of salaried surveyors, and
in their hands road maintenance became a profession.   The trusts
were entitled to their share of statute labour, or a money commutation in lieu, and the parishes were naturally anxious that
the money should be spent in the hiring of unemployed parish
labour.   But the salaried surveyors being professional men saw
the advantage of regular labour and set their face against it.
Thus by the instrument of an *ad hoc* authority—the turnpike
trust, employing salaried surveyors and sub-surveyors—the main
roads of the country were extended, rebuilt and kept in good
repair.

However, the mileage under turnpike trusts was only a small
part of the road mileage of the country. Bridges were in the
hands of the county and paid for by a county rate, but roads
were the affair of the parish, which appointed annually an unpaid
parish officer as surveyor. For resources the surveyor of the

parish roads depended on statute labour, or on the money commutation therefor, supplemented by pauper labour. Under this regime no improvements were effected ; and traffic was greatly obstructed by the complicated regulations, the outcome of centuries of chaotic laws, which limited the weight of loads and prescribed the patterns of wheels. In 1835 statute labour was abolished together with the regulations concerning the type of vehicles allowed on the roads (5 & 6 Will. IV, c. 50).

At the opening of Queen Victoria's reign it looked as though the consolidation of the turnpike trusts would eventuate in a system of trunk-line turnpikes, fed by parish roads several times as numerous ; but a new and sensational method of passenger transportation—the railway—captured the national attention and the roads slipped back under parochial control. Eventually between 1865 and 1895 the turnpike trusts were wound up and their powers transferred either to the parishes or to the special highway boards formed in certain districts. The towns, faced with urgent problems of public health, attended to their own roads and streets from the dual standpoint of traffic and sanitation. The county councils, established by the Act of 1888, took over the main county roads. Finally on the arrival of a great new road user, the automobile, a central Road Improvement Board was appointed with powers to make grants for the widening and special improvement of main roads out of money provided by the taxation of motorists and motor spirit under the Finance Act of 1909–10.

The great road builders of Britain in the main period of road construction (1760–1830) were three in number : John Metcalfe (1717–1810), commonly known as 'Blind Jack of Knaresborough' ; Thomas Telford (1757–1834) ; John Loudon McAdam (1756–1836).

Metcalfe, a Yorkshireman, had a long and varied career. He was in turn a soldier, an athlete, a publican, a horse dealer, a stage-coach proprietor, and a road maker. Between 1765, when he took a contract for three miles of turnpike between Harrogate and Boro'bridge, and 1792, when he retired to a farm, he constructed 180 miles of turnpike in the north of England. Old prints show 'Blind Jack' tapping his way along. That a man totally blind from the age of 6 should have been able to engineer roads is truly marvellous.

Telford was a Scotsman, a shepherd boy of Dumfriesshire. His skill in restoring the house of the Member for Shrewsbury caused him to be appointed Surveyor of Roads in Shropshire. Road building, however, was only one of his activities. Like his fellow countryman John Rennie, he built bridges, canals, lighthouses and docks. The professional father of both was John Smeaton, a Yorkshireman, the builder of the third Eddystone Lighthouse (1756–9). Thomas Telford was first President of the Institute of Civil Engineers, which grew out of a dining club founded by Smeaton in London in 1771. Thus the civil engineer found his vocation in the construction of aids to communication by land and water, and henceforth in Britain was more important than the military engineer, who constructed forts and trenches.

To McAdam, also a Scotsman, the building of a model road had been an early passion. His business as a victualling agent to the Admiralty took him to Falmouth in Cornwall, and the reputation he acquired there in the new art of road building led to his appointment as Surveyor-General of the Bristol roads in 1816. By these three men the technique of road building was revolutionised. The old roads were unmade dirt roads with a narrow causeway : all the repairing they received consisted of an occasional levelling with the parish road plough and the dumping of a few loads of stones, which were left to work themselves in under the pressure of traffic. Metcalfe, having to deal with boggy districts in the north of England, made a bed of heather and ling, on which he laid a surface of smooth stones. Telford, who chiefly built new roads, e.g. that from Holyhead to Shrewsbury, had to make a strong road bed and to study gradients and road shape. He adopted a moderate curvature and made the ridge of the road wider than formerly, so that two vehicles could now pass without one of them leaving the made road. For the Holyhead road he constructed the beautiful Menai Straits Suspension Bridge (1819–25) between the island of Anglesea and the mainland of Wales. By means of drainage and bridges he made his roads immune from flooding and therefore usable in all seasons.

McAdam was in agreement with Telford on such points as drainage and curvature, but his work was chiefly the maintenance of old roads, and for this he devised the material which bears his name—a fine network of angular fragments, thinly covered with hardened mud worn from the stone. McAdam proved that on old roads the subsoil, if thoroughly drained and then kept dry by an impervious covering, would carry any weight.

By 1830 the grand period of road building was concluded, but street engineering in large cities was only just beginning. Telford supervised the paving of Hanover Square, London, in 1824. In 1840 Blackfriars Bridge across the Thames was paved with modern sets. Paris invented asphalt, and in 1869 Threadneedle Street, on which the Bank of England fronts, was paved

by the Val de Travers Asphalt Paving Company. Then followed
the various devices for making town roads less slippery, less noisy
and less receptive of dirt. With these problems and the requirements of the new motor traffic for a smooth dustless surface the
road engineer is busy to-day.

Section 3.   *The Building of Canals and their Economic Influence*

The novelty of the canal lay not in the work itself, but in the
purpose which it served. The aqueducts by which at certain
points the canals were taken over rivers and valleys excited the
wonder of the time, for example, that on the Bridgewater Canal
which crossed the River Irwell at Barton (Lancs.) and that on
the Ellesmere Canal by Chirk on the north-west border of Shropshire. But these were paltry pieces of masonry beside the
aqueducts of Imperial Rome. And canals themselves were
ancient things. Before Great Britain had any they were numerous
in Holland (indeed it was a Dutchman, Cornelius Vermuyden,
who with Dutch labour in the days of Cromwell cleared the
English fens by drainage canals) ; and north of the Pyrenees
the Canal du Midi connected the Mediterranean with the Atlantic.
Nevertheless the canals played a revolutionary rôle in the expansion of inland commerce. They were of most value in the
flat country around Birmingham and in the lowlands of Staffordshire, Cheshire and Lancashire. Far more than roads, they
opened and enlarged England's industrial hinterland. They
carried coal cheaply ; and coal was the foodstuff of the industrial
revolution.

The great period of road building was also that of canal
building (1760–1830), and one of the great road builders, Thomas
Telford (1757–1834), was also a canal builder. Telford constructed the Ellesmere (Shropshire) Canal (1793) and other
sections of the Shropshire Union System, also the Macclesfield
Canal between Manchester, Macclesfield and the Potteries (1826).
His biggest work, the Caledonian Ship Canal (1823), was a part
of the Government programme of improved communications for
Scotland and was not a financial success.

But among canal builders there is a greater name than Telford.
James Brindley (1716–72) was the father of canal building in
England and began his first canal when Telford was a boy of two.
He was a Derbyshire lad without any technical education. By
trade he was a wheelwright : in 1752 he was draining coal pits
with a fire engine : in 1755 he was making machinery for a Congle-
ton silk mill. In 1759–61 he built for the Duke of Bridgewater
a canal from Worsley to Manchester ; and this being successful

he proceeded (1763–7) to the larger task of extending it from Manchester to the mouth of the Mersey at Runcorn. The Bridgewater Canal is still in operation, but it was bought ultimately by the Manchester Ship Canal, which reaches Runcorn by a less winding course.

Brindley next worked in the Midlands on the Trent and Mersey Canal, which was authorised by Parliament in 1766 and opened in 1777, five years after his death. The Trent and Mersey Canal was called by Brindley the Grand Trunk Canal, but must not be confused with the Grand Junction Canal built later between London and the Midlands. It left the Bridgewater Canal at Preston Brook and after traversing the salt district [1] of Cheshire and the Staffordshire Potteries turned north-east down the Trent valley past Burton-on-Trent,[2] famous for its ales, to join at Trent Junction the River Trent, which flows into the Humber. The Trent and Mersey was soon connected with Birmingham by the Birmingham Canal and the Birmingham and Fazeley Canal, separate canals which were united in 1784 under the name of the Birmingham Navigations.

The Black Country, however, was nearer to the estuary of the Severn than to that of the Mersey, and Brindley planned the Stafford and Worcester Canal (which was authorised by Parliament in 1768 and opened in 1791) to connect Wolverhampton with the Severn at Stourport. The refusal of the citizens of Bewdley (Worcestershire) to allow the canal to end in their town ruined the fortunes of Bewdley as an iron market and made those of Stourport. However, the navigation of the Severn between Gloucester and Berkeley (on the way to Bristol) was difficult and it was necessary to build the Gloucester-Berkeley Ship Canal, 1792–1827, to overcome this difficulty. This canal was wide enough to take small sea vessels.

Among other canals planned by Brindley were two in the

---

[1] Salt and canals have always been closely associated. The Weaver Navigation (early 18th century) was improved for the transport of rock salt from Northwich (Cheshire) to the Mersey. John Corbett (1817–1901), the founder of the modern salt industry of Worcestershire, was the son of a canal carrier and in the business until it declined. In 1852 he bought up some bankrupt brine works on the Worcester and Birmingham Canal and in 25 years converted an annual output of 25,000 tons to one of 200,000, transforming the technique of production and building canal and railway facilities. In 1889 he sold out to the Salt Union. He was the builder of hydropathic establishments and the new brine works in Droitwich. Vide *Dictionary of National Biography*, Corbett, John.

[2] The great firm of Bass was founded at Burton in 1777. For the first fifty years of its existence its trade in bitter beer was confined to India. About 1830 it turned its attention to the home market and won a great name for itself at the International Exhibition in London, 1851. It specialised in bottled beer and the supply of railway restaurants; and in 1880 turned out in three days a quantity equal to a whole year's supply in 1830. Vide *Dictionary of National Biography*, Bass, M. T.

north, crossing the country from west to east : the Forth and
Clyde Canal, the scene of the early steamboat experiments,
authorised in 1767 and completed from sea to sea in 1790, and
the Leeds and Liverpool Canal, authorised in 1770 and opened
in 1777.   From Leeds there was connection by river navigations
with the Humber.   Neither of these, however, were ship canals.
The first and only canal able to take large steamers was the
Manchester Ship Canal, opened, as narrated (p. 158), in 1894.

In method of financial promotion the canals resembled the
railways which followed them : in the kind of service rendered
they came closer to the turnpike trust.   They were companies
with shareholders, earning profit and distributing dividends.
They offered a speculative investment which was denied to the
holders of turnpike bonds.   But speculative investment was not
the motive to the construction of the first canals.   The projects
of the Duke of Bridgewater cost him £200,000, which he met with
difficulty from his own resources, but thereby he gave a new
value to his coal properties, and Manchester profited greatly from
cheaper coal and improved facilities for the importation of raw
materials from Liverpool.   The Trent and Mersey Canal was the
group effort of Midland manufacturers, headed by Josiah Wedgwood and supported by the hardware men of Birmingham and
the merchants of Liverpool.   The Potteries obtained a vent for
their valuable export trade and were able henceforth to bring
their raw material, the china clay of Devon and Cornwall, the
whole way by boat, coastwise to the Mersey and thence by canal.
The clay came from Fowey by sailing vessel to Runcorn or
Weston Point on the Weaver Canal, where it was transferred to
barges.

' How is the whole face of this country changed in about twenty
years ! ' (exclaims an historian of the Potteries in 1781).   ' Since which,
inhabitants have continually flowed in from every side.   Hence the
wilderness is literally become a fruitful field.   Houses, villages, towns
have sprung up ; and the country is not more improved than the
people.' [1]

And equally remarkable was the result of the canals through
the Black Country north and west of Birmingham.   By the end
of the 18th century the region between Wolverhampton and
Birmingham presented a close network of canals, with numerous
coalpits, foundries and other works clustered along their banks
for convenience of transport.

By the construction (1778) of the Basingstoke Canal in the
south of England,

---

[1] Quoted in W. T. Jackman, *op. cit.* I. 366.

Bagshot Heath, formerly bleak, miserable, uninhabited for miles and scarcely capable of supporting a few sheep during a small part of the year, was transformed into a rich arable country studded with villages within a few years.[1]

Dugdale's *Gazetteer of England* (*circiter* 1840) abounds in references such as these :

Keighley (Yorkshire). Its principal manufactures are woollen cloth . . . the prosperity of which is much increased by the Leeds and Liverpool Canal, which passes within two miles.

Stourport (Worcestershire). The name is derived from its situation near to the Stour, which falls into the Severn on the south side of the town . . . from the Staffordshire and Worcester Canal also adjoining the same river and having extensive basins for the admission of barges which here unload into numerous warehouses. Since the year 1770, this town might be said to have risen out of the fields . . . An extensive trade is carried on in coals from the Staffordshire and Worcestershire Collieries.

Taunton (Somersetshire). Since the construction of the Taunton and Bridgewater Canal, trade has received increased activity, considerable quantities of Welsh coal being brought to the town, and in return the produce of the vale of Taunton being exported to Bristol and other parts of England.

When the early canals proved their success canal building became a local fashion. Merchants, manufacturers and farmers took shares in them. They sometimes lost money as investors, but the trade of their locality was increased. The attitude of the landlords varied. Frequently they opposed them, fearing damage to their estates, but in one prominent instance, the Thames and Severn Canal, they were in support. This canal, opened in 1789, joined the Isis, a tributary of the Thames, with the Stroudwater Canal, which led into the Severn. The final stage was a period of intense building activity accompanied by the consolidation of small canals and a boom in canal shares. Reaching its height in 1792–3 the boom precipitated a general financial collapse. As usual, the loudest wails were raised on behalf of the poor city clerk, the widow and the orphan.

Section 4. *Causes of Decline*

The canals were by no means a uniform financial success. The most profitable were the earlier canals built in the industrial coal-bearing regions or surrounding Birmingham, the centre of the canal system. Such were the Bridgewater, the Trent and Mersey, the Birmingham Navigations, the Coventry, the Erewash,

[1] W. T. Jackman, *op. cit.* I. 414.

the Loughborough, and the River Don Navigation.   But in 1838, before their business was appreciably damaged by railways, at least one-half and possibly two-thirds of the canals were paying less than 5%, whilst a considerable number were paying 1% or nothing.   The canals in the South Midlands were the least successful of all, for passing through agricultural districts they could not find enough remunerative traffic.   The three waterways connecting the Severn with the Thames, the original Thames and Severn, and the later Kennet and Avon, and Wilts and Berks, canals were all financial failures.   When the Kennet and Avon Canal passed into Great Western hands, it was of such little use that it was allowed to become derelict.

The canal companies were not public carriers.   They left that to private parties, such as Pickfords, later of railway fame, who started life as a Birmingham ' fly ' (i.e. an express carrier making 4 miles an hour).   The canals, like the turnpikes, provided a way on which others might go on payment of the tolls authorised by Parliament.   In 1845, in order that they might compete better with the railways, Parliament authorised them to act as carriers and gave facilities for through rates over more than one canal (8 & 9 Vict. c. 42).   But by this date the rot had set in.

Between them, the carriers and canal companies rendered poor service.   The canal carriers, a numerous body, were extortionate and unpunctual : their servants, the ' canal bargees,' were distinguished for intemperance and bad language.   The companies themselves forgot their early traditions of encouraging local industry, as the contact between canal owners and canal users became less intimate.   They charged the maximum tolls, resisted competition, and sometimes added under one pretext or another supplementary charges of doubtful legality.   From 1840 to 1845 the fortunes of the canals were in the balance.   After 1840 ' a creeping paralysis,' in the language of the Commons Committee on Canals (1883), fell upon the canal system.   Great Britain alone among the countries of Europe was failing then to develop her canals.   This failure, the Committee considered, was due partly to their own slackness and partly to the policy of the railways.   There was no consistency in the permanent way. While some canals had walled sides with equal depth from side to side, others had the old weakly constructed sloping ditches. For this reason they were unable to stand the wash of steamboats. There was no uniformity of gauge.   On a journey from London to Liverpool it was necessary to change boats once on account of differences in the width of locks and to alter the weight of cargo three times on account of differences in the depth of bed or sill. There was no unity of management.   Traffic between Liverpool and Hull might go by four routes. Route 1 (the Leeds and Liverpool) involved dealing with 4 companies: route 2 (the Rochdale) with 7: route 3 (the Huddersfield) with 9: route 4 (the Trent and Mersey) with 5.

But the main cause, according to the Committee of 1883, was the absorption of the canals by the railways. The railways owned about one-half, having bought the bulk in 1846 and made additions down to 1873, when further absorption was forbidden without the sanction of the Railway Commission. The railway-owned canals were the central links. The railways therefore had power to starve the outer parts, and it was not to their interest to develop their canals, when they could take traffic the whole way on their own road. For this situation the canal companies had mainly themselves to blame. For the railway companies were forced into buying out the canals, in order to build their lines. In this way in 1846 the Great Northern Railway and the Manchester, Sheffield and Lincolnshire Railway overcame the opposition of the canal proprietors concerned. The canal companies sometimes had valuable way leaves and unused land. The Birmingham Canal Navigations, which served the district between Birmingham and Wolverhampton through which the London and North Western Railway proposed to build, were in this strong position; and they were persuaded to abandon the promotion of a separate railway in return for a 4% guarantee on their canal stock and a substantial holding in the stock of the London and North Western Railway. The railways sometimes acquired with the canals certain legal rights, and they were able to use these against other canals. Such were the ' bar and compensation tolls ' exacted by the first canals for the privilege of making connections with them.

On the whole, the canal companies did very well for themselves by selling out. The public and the independent canals paid the penalty. To these two causes, which impute blame either to the canal companies or to the railway companies, a third cause of a more general nature may be added. The majority of the coal-bearing regions of England are in hilly country. For a sharp ascent or descent very many locks are required; and this makes movement by canal slower and more expensive than in flat country. If all England had been as flat as the country around Birmingham, it would have paid somebody—the canal companies, the railway companies, or the State—to improve the canals and group them into an efficient system.

The success of the Manchester Ship Canal aroused a new interest in the old canals; and with Birmingham to the front, a Royal Commission was appointed, which reported in 1909 in favour of unification of management and a large scheme of improvement to be pivoted on Birmingham and provide trunk line communications with the Severn, the Mersey, the Humber, and the Thames. It was realised, however, that the traffic in sight would not cover for many years the interest on the expenditure. This fact and the general uncertainty created by the arrival of motor transport prevented action both on the general plan and on that part in which Birmingham was most interested, a ship canal to the Severn. If Birmingham had a ship canal, would it still be a stronghold of Tariff Reform ? It is an interesting speculation.

Canals then, like water-power, were an episode. They may, like water-power, reappear in a new form to render modern services, but of this there is little sign. Their services, however, from 1760 to 1846 were very substantial, and may be summarised thus :

(1) They valorised Great Britain's industrial hinterland, doing in particular for the heavy staples—coal, stone, salt, and iron products—what the roads did for passengers and light freight ; and they were complementary to the roads, relieving them of heavy traffic which would have injured them.

(2) They provided a cheaper form of transportation. ' The cost of canal carriage normally did not exceed one-half and in most cases was from one-quarter to one-third the cost of land carriage.' [1] Incidentally they were of service in transporting paupers from southern workhouses to northern factories in pre-railway days.

(3) They helped to distribute population. They provided new factory sites, gave elbow-room for industrial expansion, and brought the factory workers outside the pestilential limits of old overcrowded towns.

(4) They offered a new field for the exercise of engineering talent, in building the canal works themselves—the basins, locks, and aqueducts—in building bridges over them, and in the trial of the first iron barges and steamboats upon them. Their economic tragedy was that they could not make the transition from horse to steam power. They were built when engineering was in its infancy ; and the houses and factories which they attracted to their banks made any scheme of general widening insuperably dear.

[1] W. T. Jackman, *op. cit.* I. 449.

CHAPTER X

RAILWAYS AND MOTOR TRANSPORT

Section 1. The Great Railway Engineers. Section 2. Technical Problems. Section 3. Purpose and Course of Construction. Section 4. Advantages conferred by Railways. Section 5. The Railways and the State. Section 6. The Challenge of Motor Transport.

Section 1. *The Great Railway Engineers*

GEORGE STEPHENSON (1781–1848), the inventor of the railway engine, was the son of a colliery fireman in Northumberland. As a boy he drove the engine horse which wound up the colliery coals. Moving in 1804 to Killingworth, north of Newcastle, he was appointed engine-wright to the colliery in 1812, having meanwhile made himself an expert in the operation and repair of the Watt steam engines employed at the mine-head for pumping and winding. In 1814 he produced a successful locomotive engine for the conveyance of coals to the river Tyne six miles distant ; and when the possibilities of steam locomotion were thus revealed, he devoted himself to the various aspects of it—to the central problem, the improvement of the engine (he patented his locomotive engine with steam blast in 1815) : to engine manufacture at his Newcastle factory, which he owned in partnership with his cousin and Edward Pease of Darlington : to the manufacture of iron rails : and to the surveying and construction of railways. He was engineer to the first two steam-railways, the Stockton and Darlington opened in 1825 and the Liverpool and Manchester opened in 1830 ; and he persuaded the promoters of these projects to adopt the locomotive engine rather than horse traction or fixed engines. After 1830 he worked for the two districts in which his first railways were built. In the Stockton and Darlington area he constructed the line from York to Normanton, which connected the north-east coast with the Midlands, and he surveyed other lines in the service of Mr. Hudson, the railway king and organiser of the North Eastern Railway system. In the Liverpool and Manchester area he was engineer to lines which are now in the London Midland and Scottish system [1]—the Grand Junction, Manchester and Birmingham, North Midland, Birmingham and Derby, Manchester and Leeds.

Robert Stephenson (1803–1859) was a true son of his great father. After serving an apprenticeship with Nicholas Wood, who was coal viewer at Killingworth and the first scientific writer on railways, he went out to South America during the mining

---

[1] The old L. & N.W.; L. & Y.; Midland; and others.

boom of the 20's and returned in 1827 to manage his father's locomotive factory. He was engineer to the London and Birmingham Railway (1833-8), and when this railway was joined with his father's Grand Junction and Manchester and Birmingham Railways under the title of London and North Western Railway (1846) he became their consulting engineer. Euston Square, the London terminus, was thenceforward the headquarters of railway politics. With three noble bridges he crowned his life work—with the Menai Straits tubular bridge, which carried the London and North Western's traffic to Holyhead *en route* for Ireland ; with the Newcastle High-level and Victoria Berwick bridges, which linked England with Scotland along the east coast ; and finally with the Victoria bridge over the St. Lawrence at Montreal, constructed for the Grand Trunk Railway of Canada and opened in 1859, the year of his death.

The Stephensons were native northerners, working safely from coal outwards. Opposed to them were the Brunels, acclimatised foreigners living in the south, who exercised their genius upon railways as one among many outlets for engineering invention. M. I. Brunel, the father (1769-1849), constructed dockyards at Portsmouth (to assist him in which Henry Maudslay the London engineer constructed a complete range of machine tools) [1] : steam tugs : boot machinery for Army boots : Liverpool's floating landing-stage : and, finally (1825-43), the Thames Tunnel between Wapping and Rotherhithe, which became after his death a part of the East London Railway. I. K. Brunel, the son (1806-1859), was engineer to the Great Western Railway and a builder of steamships as well as of the Great Western's broad-gauge railway. It was his ambitious task to bring the West of England into line with the North, to open up the South Wales coal valleys, and to find at Milford Haven a harbour that would rival Liverpool. He also began the beautiful Clifton Suspension bridge which joins Bristol with Clifton. But, like his father, he was too often ahead of his time ; and he is remembered chiefly for his brilliant failures, for the broad gauge, which was finally abandoned, for the harbour which no ships used because it had no Manchester behind it, for the *Great Eastern* steamship, which was a white elephant to its owners, and for his heretical advocacy as late as 1845 of the atmospheric pressure engine in opposition to Stephenson's all-conquering steam locomotive.

[1] *Cf.* Macaulay on the mechanical verses of Mr. Auditor Hoole, ' the ornament of the India House ' (Lamb) : ' poured them forth by thousands and tens of thousands, all as well turned, as smooth and as like each other as the blocks which have passed through Mr. Brunel's mill in the dockyard at Portsmouth.' Essays, *Addison* (ed. Longmans 1877), p. 705.

Two further names deserve special mention on account of the big mark they left on railway construction. Sir John Hawkshaw (1811–1891), for many years consulting engineer of the Lancashire and Yorkshire Railway, was responsible for the Charing Cross and Cannon Street Railways with their bridges and terminal stations on the City side of the Thames, for the great Severn tunnel, 4⅓ miles long (1887) ; and abroad for the Amsterdam ship canal, the first of its kind (1862).

Sir William Cubitt (1785–1861) was engineer of the line which was constructed in 1846 by the firm of Brassey (the contractors to the Grand Trunk Railway of Canada) for the Great Northern Railway of England between London and Peterborough : and also of the two lines which during the war years of 1914–18 were more heavily travelled by men of English speech than any other railways in the world—the South Eastern Railway from London to Folkestone and the Nord Railway from Boulogne to Amiens.

There are two features of general interest in British railroad construction. First, they were made bit by bit. The early railroads in the Midlands and North were built for small companies, which later amalgamated ; and in constructing the longer trunk lines from London outwards it was customary to build the line by sections, the railway company having a single engineer to supervise the whole. The big mileage jobs were those undertaken by British contractors abroad. Secondly, British railroad construction was made expensive by the abundance of tunnels, bridges and embankments. This was due to the hilly nature of many of the industrial districts and the refusal of the public to run risks or allow interference with established communications. In England, therefore, it is not necessary to ' Stop : Look : Listen.'

Section 2. Technical Problems

George Stephenson's technical contribution may be expressed thus : a locomotive engine, running on edged rails laid 4 feet 8½ inches apart.

(1) *The Engine*. Stephenson was not the first man to draw a carriage by steam power. On Christmas Eve, 1801, Richard Trevethick, a Cornishman, took a car load of passengers in a steam carriage along the ordinary highway : and after further experiments a few steam carriages appeared on the roads between 1820 and 1830, but they excited such prejudice that they had to be abandoned. ' Heavy tolls were laid upon them ; country gentlemen, road commissioners, road trustees, farmers, coach proprietors and others who were interested in the continuance of

horse power, opposed the steam coach by every means, even to throwing heaps of stones in the road where it was to pass.'[1]

From Cornwall, the county of tin mines and Watt's first pumping engines, locomotive experiment moved north to Merthyr Tydvil in South Wales, then to Yorkshire, where John Blenkinsop (1811) built a locomotive with a cogged wheel, acting on a rack rail, for a colliery near Leeds : and finally to Northumberland. Early inventors puzzled over the imaginary difficulty of making a smooth wheel bite upon a smooth rail ; and one enthusiast devised an attachment to the engine, which imitated the action of the hind legs of a horse ! But Stephenson in 1814 proved finally what Trevethick had demonstrated some years before, that a locomotive with smooth wheels could draw heavy loads with no other assistance than the force of friction between wheel and rail. He made in his Newcastle factory five out of the first six engines used on the Stockton and Darlington Railway and in October 1829 won the trials which preceded the opening of the Liverpool and Manchester Railway with his famous ' Rocket.' The Newcastle and Carlisle Railway, chartered for horse traction in 1829, changed over to locomotives in 1834, when ' for the last time probably in the history of the early lines, the comparative advantages of animal and steam traction were considered.'[2] But for some years in Northumberland and Durham the weakness of the early engines in drawing heavy loads uphill led to the use of a combination of power, locomotive engines, inclined planes working on gravity, fixed engines, and horses for uphill hauls; and the ' dandy cart ' in the rear of coal trains was to be seen as late as 1850 in these hilly parts. The dandy cart was a crate in which the horse travelled when going down an incline. Arriving at the bottom he obligingly trotted out and helped to haul the train uphill. But the main lines out of London constructed in the late 30's, such as the London and Birmingham, Great Western, London and Southampton, London and Brighton, all had locomotive power alone in view ; and by 1840 the locomotive engine was generally supreme. For half a century it had no rival. Then came electrical power generated from coal : which implied a reversion to fixed generation of power. In 1883, as an experiment, Sir William Siemens applied electric power to a short stretch of light railway between Portrush and the Giant's Causeway in the North of Ireland, two years after the parent firm of Siemens and Halske opened a one-car electric tram line at Lichterfelde near Berlin. In 1890 came the first electric

[1] W. T. Jackman, *Transportation in Modern England*, I. 335 *n*. 2, quoting evidence of Commons Committee on Steam Carriages, 1831.
[2] W. W. Tomlinson, *The North Eastern Railway*, p. 262.

subway railway—the City and South London from Stockwell to King William Street, a distance of three miles. It was followed in 1900 by the Central London Railway (which was popularly known as the Two-Penny Tube because of its then uniform charge of 2d.) and in 1905 by the electrification of the old-established Underground District Railway. Between 1905 and 1925 a number of electric tube railways were built and extended to the surface on the outskirts of London. In 1904 the Lancashire and Yorkshire Railway electrified its suburban service from Liverpool to Southport, an overground route of eighteen miles.

(2) *The Rail.* The colliery railroad preceded by more than a century the application of steam locomotion to it. For in the 17th century on the Newcastle coalfield rails of timber were laid to lead the coals from the colliery head to the river. But wooden rails wore away so quickly that iron plates were nailed on to them at curves and points of heavy traffic. Then the rail itself was made of iron. Except in the north of England the early iron rails were plate rails, shaped like the letter **L**. The projection acted as a guide to the wheel, which ran along the base of it level with the ground. Therefore vehicles could pass from the plate rails to the ordinary highway. In 1811 there were about 150 miles of plate railways in South Wales alone. They used, of course, horse traction. But as early as 1730 the north country colliery owners had invented the raised edge rail, with the guiding flange not on the rail, as in the plate rail, but on the wheel itself, as it is to-day : and soon afterwards they used iron instead of wood in the wheel itself. On the Stockton and Darlington Railway Stephenson employed the edged rail in order to permit of steam locomotion. Trials conducted in 1831 on the Liverpool and Manchester Railway showed that wrought iron rails, though more expensive than cast iron rails, lasted longer and were less liable to split. These, therefore, were generally employed until the 1860's, when Bessemer's steel inventions produced the still better steel rail.

The first sleepers (i.e. ties) were set lengthwise so as to give a fairway along which the horse could trot. On the Stockton and Darlington Railway Stephenson used stone blocks at the Darlington end and wooden blocks at the Stockton end, where cheap ship's timber was to be had. It was not until about 1840, when the comfort of passengers became the foremost consideration, that the railways on the north-east coast replaced the stone blocks by wooden cross sleepers of the type in use to-day.

(3) *The Gauge.* The distance between the rails on all British railways is 4 feet 8½ inches. Most of the old coal railroads had a smaller gauge, but the gauge used by Stephenson on his colliery

road from Killingworth to the Tyne was about 4 feet 8 inches, and he employed the same gauge on the Stockton and Darlington in 1825. The other railways followed suit, with the prominent exception of the Great Western, which adopted the 7-foot gauge. Brunel, thinking of passenger traffic, considered that with a broader gauge travel would be speedier and more commodious and that the difference from that of other railways would make it harder for them to compete in Great Western territory. But when the Great Western and Midland met at Gloucester in 1845, the inconvenience was so obvious that Parliament intervened; and after a parliamentary struggle between the Great Western and the London and North Western, which were promoting rival bills for a line from Oxford to Wolverhampton, the issue was referred to Commissioners, who decided in favour of the narrow gauge. By the Act of 9 & 10 Vict. (1846), c. 57, this gauge was made the standard for Great Britain. But the Great Western was not ordered to change, and it laid some new broad gauge after 1846. However, in the end the Great Western had to conform, and in 1892 converted its system to the narrow gauge at its own cost. It would have been a great saving to Australia if she had adopted a uniform gauge as advised by Gladstone in 1846 during his short tenure of the Colonial Office. But as each State was building to its own interior only, a variety of gauges was used, and though Australia to-day has a connected railway system, she has still to face the great expense of conversion to a uniform gauge. New Zealand was more fortunate. Under her Railway Act of 1870 she obtained a uniform railway policy and as part of it a uniform gauge.

Section 3.   Purpose and Course of Construction

The purpose of the early colliery railroads, as the description signifies, was to carry coal; and in addition to these there were before 1825 a few horse-drawn railways, such as the Surrey Iron Railway constructed between Wandsworth and Croydon in 1801, which carried general freight. Stephenson's success with the locomotive engine determined the future of railway traffic. The railway was henceforth equally fitted to carry both heavy freight and passengers, to do, that is, what the canals and turnpikes had hitherto shared between them. In the North, however, the first steam railways were built with freight in view. Although in 1825, at its opening, the Stockton and Darlington Railway drew a train-load of passengers, the purpose of its promoters was the carriage of coal from the collieries in the vicinity of Darlington to the port of Stockton-on-Tees; and it was extended to Middlesbrough,

which till then was the home of a few fisherfolk only, in order
that the coastal export trade in coal might be more efficiently
handled.   By 1835 there were numerous small steam railways in
Northumberland and Durham, and nearly all were engaged
in the carriage of coal from inland collieries to the coast.
Before long coal export brought in return a traffic of import.
Thus the Hartlepools, opened up by the building of the Hartle-
pool Railway and Dock (1835), began to import timber in 1840 ;
and in 1861 they went on to import Spanish ore for the adjacent
blast furnaces of Ferry Hill.   The Liverpool and Manchester
Railway was the first passenger line, but even here this was not
the purpose which the promoters had in view.   Nobody believed
before 1830 that an engine could move passengers with safety
at several times the speed of a stage coach.   As its prospectus
shows, the railway was built at the instance of Liverpool merchants
in order that they might get a cheaper and better mode of carriage
to Manchester for their cotton, sugar and other foodstuffs.
Similarly the Leeds and Selby Railway opened in 1834 was
designed to connect Leeds with the Humber, to do for the woollen
centre of the West Riding of Yorkshire what the Liverpool and
Manchester had done for the cotton centre of Lancashire.

However, the locomotive engine by its unexpected speed (by
1831 it was running 25–30 miles an hour and by 1850, 50) wrested
from the coaches the passenger traffic along the great arteries
which fed London ; and the projectors of railways in the 30's
and early 40's were thinking mainly of the returns from passenger
traffic.   But freight was always an important item in the North ;
and in 1852 on the railways of England and Wales as a whole
freight receipts exceeded passenger receipts for the first time.

The railways, like the canals, were built by private enterprise ;
and this was possible because England was an old country with
accumulated capital and traffic waiting to be carried.   Furthermore, as with the canals, the promoters of the first railways had
in mind the advancement of their district.   They had the capital
and the business ; and George Stephenson had the engineering
genius.   Edward Pease was a Darlington manufacturer, the friend
of the banker, Jonathan Backhouse ; Joseph Sandars was a
Liverpool corn merchant ; and all three were Quakers.   Pease
took for the motto of his railway *Periculum privatum, utilitas
publica* (at private risk for public service), and the claim was a
just one.

In the 30's railway building made steady progress, in the
late 30's there was a mild boom in railway shares.   As railway
works began to cover the face of the country, the investment net
widened.   Merchants, manufacturers and farmers were anxious

H

to have them and subscribed for shares. The landlords played a waiting game. On aesthetic grounds they detested the ' locomotive monster with a tail of smoke and sulphur ' [1] as heartily as did Charles Dickens, the stage-coachman's champion. But they had land to sell and they secured the agricultural value of their land plus as much again by way of compensation for disturbance.[2] In the 40's the pace became feverish.[3] In 1846 there were huge authorisations for capital expenditure on new railways and the public bit.

> Old men and young, the famished and the full,
> Rich and poor, widow and wife and maid,
> Master and servant, all with one intent
> Rushed on the paper scrip.

The boom broke in 1847, and the ruin of the canal mania of 1793 was repeated on a bigger scale, with this difference, that the bulk of the loss fell upon the broad shoulders of a rapidly growing middle class. The losses were exceptionally severe in Glasgow and some other big towns in Scotland. For a certain Mr. Kinnear of Glasgow had established a new type of investment bank, to lend money on railway shares ; and since these Exchange Banks, as they were called, had transferred their clients' shares to themselves as a measure of precaution, they found themselves, when the break came and their clients' margins vanished, compelled to pay calls upon the shares which frequently exceeded their original loans. All of them went down, the Glasgow Commercial Exchange Company losing £650,000. But the nation got its railways and the working classes a great new employment, railway construction, and when construction came to an end, permanent railway service. The most spectacular figure in the boom was George Hudson, the Railway King. He started as

---

[1] Cf. *The Creevey Papers*, p. 430.

[2] See Lords' Committee on Railway Compensation (1845).

[3] On this point Herbert Spencer, the philosopher (who as a young man was employed as a sub-engineer on the London and Birmingham Railway), makes the following very interesting observation in his Autobiography under the years 1845–46 :

' During the 30's speculative local magnates and farseeing capitalists, having projected railways which would obviously be advantageous, thereupon chose their engineers, and subsequently let portions of their work to contractors ; but as fast as there grew up considerable classes of wealthy contractors and of rich engineers accustomed to co-operate with them, it became the habit for these to join in getting up schemes, forming companies and practically appointing boards —a policy in all ways beneficial to themselves. Thus by 1845 there had arisen many and various interests uniting to urge on railway enterprise ; and anyone who took a broad view of the causes in operation might have seen that great disasters were certain to ensue.'

He extracted his father from a Derby railway investment just before the smash came (*Autobiography*, I. 283-4).

a draper in York, and after founding in 1833 the York Banking Company devoted himself to railway promotion. The object of his attention was the group of railways which were formed in 1854 into the North Eastern. By his energy in Parliament and on the boards which he controlled he advanced considerably the process of unification out of which that system was born, but he was unscrupulous and a chance question at a shareholders' meeting in 1849 exposed a long chapter of irregularities, which included the resale of shares and materials, purchased privately, to the companies of which he was the head. ' His ten per cent. dividends,' say Tooke and Newmarch, ' were obtained by the coarse process of altering the accounts ; or, according to a phrase first employed by one of his confidential subordinates, by " cooking the accounts, in order to make things pleasant." ' [1] Such were the troubles of the early Victorians. They were suffering from nothing worse than financial crisis and an easily overthrown Railway King (for the Chartist demonstration of 1848 was a farce), the while Europe was in the throes of political revolution.

In 1843 the railway mileage of the United Kingdom was 2036 ; in 1855, 8280. [2] At the beginning of 1843, to follow the map from north to south (see map at end), the Newcastle and Carlisle Railway all but connected the North with the Irish Sea. A number of small railways in Northumberland and Durham ran from coalfield to coast : as similarly one from Merthyr to Cardiff in South Wales. From Darlington the Great North of England Railway (Darlington to York, not to be confused with the later Great Northern, London to Doncaster) and the York and North Midland (York to Normanton) connected the North-East with Yorkshire and Lancashire. The Manchester and Leeds with the Leeds, Selby and Hull gave an all-rail route across the industrial North of England from coast to coast. From Lancashire and Yorkshire two routes led to the Midlands : (1) the London and North Western nucleus—the Chester and Birkenhead, the Grand Junction (Newton to Birmingham), the Manchester and Birmingham ; (2) the Midland nucleus—the North Midland (Leeds to Derby), the Birmingham and Derby, the Gloucester and Birmingham and the Midland Counties (Derby to Rugby). From Birmingham through Rugby the London and Birmingham reached the Metropolis. Other trunk lines from London outwards were—the Great Western to Bristol and Taunton : the London and South Western to Southampton and Gosport (Portsmouth) : the London and Brighton to Brighton, from which railway at Reigate (Redhill) the South

---

[1] Tooke and Newmarch, *History of Prices*, V. 361.
[2] *Ibid.* V. 352.

Eastern started towards Folkestone. The future Great Eastern is represented by two stumps, the Northern and Eastern and the Eastern Counties. In Scotland there was railway communication between Edinburgh, Glasgow and Ayr.

In the course of the great building period there was a general process of consolidation. Bradshaw's [1] Railway Guide shows 200 railways in 1846, but in 1848 only 22 large and a few small railways. In the Midlands and North consolidation was commonly effected by amalgamation, in the South by lease. Amalgamation produced the London and North Western (1846) : the Lancashire and Yorkshire (1847) : the North Eastern (1854) : the Great Eastern (1862).

Meanwhile the railway map was rapidly assuming a modern look. By 1850 there was a new trunk line from London—the Great Northern (London to Doncaster) ; and there was through communication with Scotland both by the East and the West coasts. By 1860 the London and North Western had thrown out an arm to Holyhead, the Great Western was in Cornwall and South Wales, and the Midland (originally a N.E. to S.W. line) was planning an independent route from London to Derby and the North.

Section 4. *Advantages conferred by Railways*

The advantages of a new service are most easily appreciated when it is just full grown. Let us therefore halt at this point and review the changes which railways were producing in the economic life of the country.

(i) The railways created new business. This is true both in a general and a special sense. In a general sense railways ushered in an era of mechanical transportation by land. By the application of steam power they completed and extended the work of the turnpikes and the canals. They were to inland transportation and at approximately the same time what the steamship was to the open sea. First came the river and cross-channel services ; then the ocean services. First came the colliery railways and those from one industrial town to another ; then the trunk lines from London outwards—to the West of England and Wales, to the North of England and Scotland. London was a focal point of the railways as it had been of the turnpikes ; but the North meanwhile had advanced to metropolitan stature and the line from Liverpool to Manchester was the base on which the railways of north-western England were built. Railways and steamships in conjunction multiplied industry by enlarging the

---

[1] George Bradshaw was a Manchester Quaker and an engraver of canal maps. His first railway guide bears the date 10th month, 19th, 1839.

area of production and the circle of international trade. The staple manufactures of Great Britain were localised before the advent of railways; and railways assisted local specialisation by improving the communications between one locality and another. But they also exercised a reverse and equally beneficial influence. They helped to distribute population. They enlarged the suburban area of metropolitan centres. They created new towns in their own workshop headquarters, as at Crewe on the London and North Western and at Swindon on the Great Western. They furnished manufacturers with new work sites along their limits.

It is true also in a special sense. For railways rendered joint services. Railways built primarily for traffic business developed also passenger business; and vice versa. And again, as we see clearly from early examples in the North, railways, designed for traffic which offered itself in one direction, developed a return traffic. Thus the Stockton and Darlington Railway and other railways in those parts secured a traffic of import when the coal ports which they supplied began to grow. And after 1850, when the Cleveland iron deposits in the neighbourhood of Middlesbrough began to be worked, the iron ore furnished the Stockton and Darlington with a heavy return traffic for its colliery hinterland. Similarly the Stockton and Darlington pushed into Westmorland to make contact with the district of Cumberland from which hematite iron ore was obtained; and it helped to pay its way with coal, carrying coal from east to west and iron ore from west to east. Finally, although railways were not built as in the Canadian West to haul grain to a terminal market, the railways did traverse agricultural districts and farmers reaped great benefits therefrom, as Peel urged in the days when protection was being withdrawn from agriculture. For the railways brought in coal, fertiliser, farm implements and drainage material, and carried perishable foodstuffs quickly to market, special milk trains, after Peel's day, carrying fresh milk daily to London. These are just examples of traffic growth which are paralleled in the railway history of all countries. Railways, because they rendered joint services, had a direct interest in the all-round development of their district.

(ii) The railways forthwith cheapened considerably the cost of carrying traffic which had formerly gone by canal or road. At numerous points the first effect of the opening of a railway was to reduce the rates on the canals to which they ran parallel. The canals had to meet the cheaper railway rate by immediate reduction of their own or else they lost the traffic. 'As soon as the Liverpool and Manchester Railway was opened, the former insolence of the navigations connecting these two cities was immediately abandoned, and under competition their rates had to be cut down. The rate on light goods carried on the canal was 15s. per ton ; the railway reduced this to 10s.' [1] Similarly on the route from Manchester to Hull, 99 miles by canal, the rates for corn, cotton twist and manufactured goods were reduced nearly 50% after the opening of the railway in 1840. And substantial reductions on the river Thames attended the opening of the Great Western line, which ran along the Thames valley.

(iii) Railways regularised the course of commerce. They did for distribution what standardised machinery did for production. Being able to rely on regular and speedy delivery, merchants carried smaller stocks. Their turnover was accelerated, and they needed less credit to finance it. Business was brought closer to a cash basis.

The peculiar relations subsisting in the north of England between the transport and merchandising of coal were explained to the Royal Commission on Railways of 1865–7. The North Eastern Railway Company maintained at its stations depotagents, who acted as an intermediary between the colliery and the consumer. The railway company would ' send the empty waggons to the colliery, lead the coals to their destination, keep the depots properly stocked, sell the coals at the price he [sc. colliery owner] fixes, keep the sales accounts and remit the funds.' [2] This arrangement, it was claimed, saved unnecessary middlemen and gave the consumer a wide selection. Moreover, it was characteristic of British traffic as a whole : and its *raison d'être* was the short-haul of railway traffic in a small country. In recent times managers returning from foreign parts have tried to improve their system by using bigger waggons. But, as the General Manager of the Great Northern Railway, recently back from the Argentine, admitted to the Royal Commission on Canals of 1906–10, it did not pay. ' The trade of this country is becoming more and more retail. He [sc. the trader] calls for small quantities and expects to have them next day in his place. This enables business to be carried on with a less amount of stock-in-trade, that is of idle capital.' [3] It is for this reason that the challenge of motor transport is more serious in Great Britain than in North America. Transportation in North America is an affair of long hauls and night sleepers. But there is no journey in England which you cannot make by day ; and until recently there were no sleeping cars between England and Scotland for the ordinary man who travels third class.

---

[1] W. T. Jackman, *op cit*. II. 634 *n*.   [2] Evidence, Q. 12,664.
[3] Evidence, Qs. 24,601, 24,788.

(iv) Railways increased the mobility of the population. They made travel more speedy and cheapened its cost. The article on Birmingham in Dugdale's *Gazetteer* exclaims :

Instead of being two or three days on the road the gentlemen manufacturers of Birmingham may, when this railroad is finished, leave their orders and directions at their factories in the morning, and shake hands with their customers in London the same day, perhaps in time to take a dinner and, if necessary, be able to sleep at home the same evening.

Professor Jackman concludes that as the result of improved roads and mail coaches the speed of travel was doubled between 1750 and 1830. ' In 1830 the average rate of speed of the fast mail and other coaches was nine to ten miles per hour.' [1] The railways at once doubled this ; but they were modest and declined to supply the first edition of Bradshaw with times of arrival. ' I believe,' said one director, ' that it would tend to make punctuality a sort of obligation.' However, by 1850 the schedule time for fast trains between important business points exceeded 40 miles an hour. Professor Bowley has brought up to date the famous Chapter III. of Macaulay's *History of England*, in which he compares the England of his day (1848) with Restoration England ; and one is struck by the comparatively small increase in speed between 1848 and 1909, the year of Professor Bowley's comparison. Thus London to Southampton, 79 miles ; best train :

> 1848 : 1 hour 47 minutes = 44 miles per hour.
> 1909 : 1 hour 38 minutes = 48 miles per hour.

In other examples the difference is more substantial ; but the main saving in time since 1860 has accrued from the frequency of fast trains and the organisation of through express services to distant points.

In the 18th century the rich travelled in the family coach or hired a post-chaise ; those of moderate means used the stage coach ; the poor walked or begged a lift from a carter. The nobility at first despised the common railway carriage and mounted their coach on the back of the train. But the custom, it is said, was discontinued after the misfortune to a certain noble lord whose coach took fire in a tunnel from the sparks of the engine, with the result that the occupants were rescued at the other end in a state of suffocation. The railway companies began by catering for the business men of the middle class and awoke slowly to the importance of third-class traffic. At first they provided two classes only. The first class rode in covered,

[1] *Op. cit.* I. 339.

the second in open carriages—corresponding to the insides and outsides of the stage coach. By 1850 second-class passengers were generally conveyed in closed carriages with glass windows and open seats, but the third class long endured the torments of hell in open boxes exposed to wind and rain. The North Eastern only started a third class to keep the generality from walking along the tracks or riding on coal trucks. *Punch* in 1846 issued some ' Rules for Railways,' which included the following : ' No 3rd class carriage is to contain more than a foot deep of water in wet weather ; but, to prevent accidents, corks and swimming belts should always be kept in open carriages.' [1] But the poor man had his charter. For in 1844 (7 & 8 Vict. c. 85) Parliament ordained that every railway company must run at least one third-class train per day at a charge of one penny per mile (hence the word Parl^y on third-class tickets) ; and competition among the railways led gradually to the improvement of third-class accommodation. The ever-enterprising Midland Railway set the pace. In 1875 it abolished its second-class carriages and, making its third class as good as its old second, compelled the other companies to follow suit. Therefore to-day there are two classes only—the third class and the first class ; and these correspond roughly to the day coach and the parlour-car of a Canadian train.

(v) The railways increased the enjoyments and health of the people. Mechanical locomotion was a new joy (and reasonably safe, as soon as you had learnt not to jump out of the train while it was in a tunnel) ; and the locomotive engine, though ugly at first, soon became a beautiful thing, almost the one beautiful thing thrown up by industrialism. To see an express threading its way along the coast or to hear the roar of a train vanishing into the tunnel is very good. The ' melancholy mad ' engines of the factory and the din of the machinery they drove were tyrannical, but railway engines sounded shrill notes of exaltation and escape.

And in a more prosaic way they brought enjoyment and with enjoyment health. A peculiarity of British railway business is the importance of the seaside excursion traffic, resulting from the small distance between any inland point and the sea. Sir Rowland Hill of post office fame introduced excursion trains on the London and Brighton. When it was first proposed to run Sunday excursions from London to Cambridge the University authorities were horrified, and the Vice-Chancellor of the University addressed the following letter to the Directors of the Eastern Counties Railway, the old name of the Great Eastern :

[1] Mr. Punch's *History of Modern England*, I. 67.

The Vice-Chancellor of the University of Cambridge presents his compliments to the Directors of the Eastern Counties Railway and begs to inform them that he has learnt with regret that it is the intention of the Directors of the Eastern Counties Railway to run excursion trains to Cambridge on the Lord's Day, with the object of attracting foreigners and undesirable characters to the University of Cambridge on that sacred day.

The Vice-Chancellor of the University of Cambridge wishes to point out to the Directors of the Eastern Counties Railway that such a proceeding would be as displeasing to Almighty God as it is to the Vice-Chancellor of the University of Cambridge.

The coast is fringed with watering-places which have been made by the railways. Blackpool is Lancashire on holiday, and Scarborough is Yorkshire. The Midlands flow to all points—to North Wales on the west and Norfolk on the east ; and the Midland and Great Northern Railway Companies built a joint line to carry Birmingham to the delights of Yarmouth and Cromer. The sands of Margate are obscured by London's thousands. Bournemouth and Torquay, respectively the preserves of the Southern and Great Western, are at once popular and fashionable. Canada talks of ' trips ' to the Old Country : the Old Country of week-end ' trippers,' who go on ' seaside excursions ' during Easter, Whitsun, and the August Bank Holidays, with an extra day perhaps for a race meeting or the Cup Final.

Section 5. *Railways and the State*

The railway companies were incorporated by Act of Parliament, which prescribed their powers and the maximum charges they might impose. But this did not end the matter ; for Parliament soon found that it was necessary to control them, and the development of this control forms a difficult chapter of economic history, which may be divided for simplicity into two parts, (*a*) problems arising in the course of growth and connected largely with competition and amalgamation, (*b*) problems arising in recent times and connected largely with freight rates and wages.

(*a*) Railways were born in the flush of individualism, when Parliament and the public which it represented believed ardently in competition and abhorred monopoly whether in private or State hands. Parliament had forced the London dock companies into competition and thrown open the trade to the East ; it was engaged in protecting factory workers with the minimum of interference to freedom of contract ; and it attacked the railway problem in the same spirit.

N 2

The first railways gave no sign of monopoly. At the very beginning there was actually some competition between different users of the same road. For example, the Stockton and Darlington let out its unimportant passenger business to hotel proprietors and others, who ran competing services. But as this and other railways in the neighbourhood were built to serve particular mining areas, the competition among users in the main business of coal carrying was necessarily nominal ; and on the passenger lines it was impossible on account of its danger. It is true that the first Railway Acts allowed for different users by prescribing tolls for the use of the way and further charges if carriage was given, but too much must not be made of this. The presumption is that the language of the Acts was copied from the earlier Turnpike and Canal Acts and retained for form's sake after the use of railways by private carriers had ceased to be a possibility. More important was the fact that the first railways broke in many districts the shameless monopoly of the canals. ' It is competition that is wanted,' declared the prospectus of the Liverpool and Manchester Railway. Similarly the merchants of Leeds and Sheffield found a relief from canal domination in the opening of railway communication to the Humber.

Parliament therefore welcomed railways in the name of competition. But it could not sanction every application. It had to make a selection among rival projects ; and to select sound projects with such limitation only as was necessary to prevent fatuous duplication was its concern at first. But by 1840 it scented the inevitable element of monopoly in the railway, and it found reason to believe that competing companies were entering into private agreement for the suppression of excessive competition. The question therefore arose, should it take over the railways and operate them itself ?

In 1844 a parliamentary inquiry was accompanied by legislation dealing with this issue. Belgium was building her railways as a national undertaking on a national plan. But Great Britain lacked the territorial homogeneity of Belgium and military considerations were unimportant. The Act of 1844 (7 & 8 Vict. c. 85), therefore, put off the issue by providing for optional State purchase in twenty-one years' time on terms which made the exercise of the option highly improbable. When the time came, the Royal Commission of 1865–7 reported against it, pointing out that as the option only applied to railways established in and after 1844, further legislation covering railways before that date would be necessary ; for they formed one system and one portion could not be taken over without the other. The Commission further declared itself in favour of ' leaving the construction and management of railways to the free enterprise of the people, under such conditions as Parliament may think fit to impose for the general welfare of the people.' [1] In other words, they commended the *status quo* of 1844 to 1867. And parliamentary control during this period consisted of (i) legislation on special points—the Parliamentary train at 1*d.* a mile (1844) and Gauge Regulation (1846) ; (ii) frequent inquiry into the question of amalgamation ; (iii) general legislation (1854).

The rule which Parliament tried to follow in the matter of amalgamations was to sanction end-on amalgamations, e.g. the Grand Junction and Manchester and Birmingham with the London and Birmingham, and to refuse those between parallel competing lines, but it examined each application on its own merits and steadily refused to transfer its authority to an executive body. The Board of Trade authority appointed in 1844 to report on Railway Bills lapsed through inadequate powers, and a second body, established in 1846, perished in 1851. In thus clinging to authority over railway matters Parliament was reversing its action in the social field, where it entrusted the enforcement of legislation and the shaping of policy to powerful Poor Law and Factory Commissioners.

The system was expensive for the railways in legal fees and promotion costs. But it gave victory to the powerful ; and, once established, the railways, though they could not amalgamate without parliamentary sanction, could and did come to understandings. Of their own volition they established in 1842 the Railway Clearing House, which received legislative sanction in 1850. This body fulfilled the very necessary task of supplying a neutral office in which accounts of through transactions could be kept and the balance due from one company to another adjusted. But this ' end-on ' business contact brought the railways into closer personal touch and contributed to the situation which was revealed by a committee of inquiry in 1853—namely, that the railways were coming to private understandings in the matter of competition and that on the Scottish traffic they were pooling receipts. Therefore in 1854 Parliament placed on the statute book a general measure of protection for the trader. As common carriers the companies had to render reasonable service and accept traffic. Parliament now specified and enlarged on this by statute. It ordered all railway companies to give reasonable facilities to the public, to accept and forward through traffic from and to other companies' lines and to grant no undue preference (17 & 18 Vict. c. 31).

[1] *Final Report*, p. 37.

Under this protection further amalgamations were sanctioned in the 60's, which brought the groupings more or less into the position which they occupied until 1921. As a result, the North Eastern (which the Stockton & Darlington joined, 1863) obtained a compact territorial monopoly, but did not abuse it ; and there was keen competition between lines running from London to the North. In 1873 the Railway Commission was established to report on proposals for the further absorption of canals by railways and to act as a court of appeal for aggrieved traders. In 1888 its powers were strengthened and it was renamed the Railway and Canal Commission, but by this date canal amalgamation was a dead issue. The railways owned more of them than they wanted. The new issue, which made the Railway and Canal Commission a body of the first importance, was the demand for further control of rates.

(b) The Acts of Incorporation specified maximum tolls for the use of the road and maximum total rates for complete service, which were built up by combining the charges for the use of the road, the rolling stock and the locomotive power. But all the companies were now carrying traffic at much less than the original maximum rates, which, therefore, were no present protection. And for such protection traders were calling in view of the trade depression and falling prices of the 80's. Therefore in 1888 an Act (51 & 52 Vict. c. 25) was passed ordering the companies to prepare new classifications and new schedules of maximum charges. The new classification was a great advance, introducing uniformity in place of complications and anomalies. But the compilation of the new schedules had unexpected results. For the railways were hurried in their work, and by January 1, 1893, when the new schedules were to come into force, they were ready with the new maxima, but not with the special rates, lower than these, at which they carried a great part of their traffic. They therefore announced that in certain cases they would charge for the time being the new maxima. This was the opposite of what Parliament and the trading community had intended ; and it led in 1894 to a further Act, 57 & 58 Vict. c. 54, which embodied a big change of principle. For it converted the rates actually in force into the maxima of the future. Beyond these the companies could not go, unless they proved to the Railway Commission that the cost of the service in question had risen ; and this was a difficult thing to prove. Thus the Railway Commission became a powerful rate-controlling body.

Before long the railway companies found that in addition to a rigid limitation of charges they were faced with a persistent increase of expenses. For example, on the North Eastern the ratio of operating expenses to receipts rose from 57·55% in 1894 to 65% in 1901.   And for this increase the coal bill and the labour bill were jointly responsible.   Unable to raise rates and confronted each year with rising costs the companies drew together for the elimination of competitive waste.   In 1908 the London and North Western and the Lancashire and Yorkshire formed a working alliance ;   as also did the Great Northern, the Great Eastern, and the Great Central (the old Manchester, Sheffield and Lincolnshire Railway) ;   and there were other agreements elsewhere.   To all these public opinion was favourable, for it was concerned at the fall in railway stocks and fearful of an increase in rates.   However, the railway labour unions forced the situation.   They had secured recognition in 1907 ; and in 1911 they called a strike, which was only settled after Government intervention.   The railway companies made important wage concessions and to recoup them for these the Government sanctioned in 1913 a limited increase in rates (2 & 3 Geo. V, c. 29).

When the war broke out in August 1914, the railways passed under Government control.   The companies continued to operate them, but the Government took the receipts, met the expenses and made up to the companies each year the net income earned by them in 1913.   After the war the Government returned the railways to the companies together with a sum of £60 millions ' partly as payment for arrears of maintenance for which the Government was responsible, but partly as a free grant to help them over their difficulties during a period of reconstruction.' [1]

But the war had shown the economies of unified management ; and therefore the return was accompanied by the changes of far-reaching importance embodied in the Railways Act of 1921.

(i) The railways of Great Britain were merged into four great groups : the Southern ; the Great Western ; the London Midland and Scottish ; and the London and North Eastern. The last included the Great Eastern, formerly managed by Sir Henry Thornton, the President of the Canadian National Railways.

(ii) A Railway Rates Tribunal was set up with plenary powers to fix and subsequently vary such actual rates, fares and charges as may produce for each group a standard revenue : the standard revenue being defined as the aggregate net revenues in 1913 of all the companies absorbed into the group.   Thus the problem of the future is not to secure power to levy adequate charges, but to raise the standard revenue without losing so much traffic to motor transport that the standard revenue is not earned.

[1] Sir W. M. Acworth, ' Grouping under the Railways Act, 1921,' *Economic Journal*, March 1923, p. 28

(iii) Special machinery was established for determining national wage rates for railway servants and adjusting disputes by conciliation. On this machinery the public is represented.

(iv) In the words of Sir William Acworth, ' the Act provides for the compilation and publication of adequate statistics of operation, in order that the Rates Tribunal and the public may be in a position to judge whether the management of the railways under the new conditions is carried on with that efficiency and economy which it is the expressed object of the Act to secure, and on which the right of each company to the standard revenue is made to depend.' [1]

Section 6.   *The Challenge of Motor Transport*

The British railways before the war were a fair sample of British efficiency. They performed well their long-established rôle in the life of the country ; they were more amenable to change than their biggest customer, the coal trade, and less amenable than the cotton industry, which lived under the challenge of foreign competition. The conquest of the road by the motor car was practically coincident with the peace ; for during the war private motoring was restricted. Soon after the peace came a long depression, which was most persistent in the trades which were most valuable to the railways—namely, the heavy industries of coal and of iron and steel. In the year 1925, which fell between the artificial stimulus given to the coal trade by the Ruhr occupation and the paralysing coal strike of 1926, iron and steel traffic dwindled away and there was a drop of 5 million tons in coal for each railway except the Southern. Out of a total loss of 13,650,000 passengers workmen accounted for 6,200,000. This freight and passenger traffic was not lost to the roads : it was simply not forthcoming. The motor is not responsible for all the trouble. Before 1914 the new railway competitor was the electric tramway ; and tramways too since the war have suffered from the competition of motors. Both are public or semi-public services, and adaptation to new conditions is more difficult for them than for a service which starts *de novo* and is comparatively untrammelled by the regulations of organised labour and public authority. American railways boomed after the war, and, although the example of America is only partly applicable to Great Britain owing to the absence of the long haul, nevertheless even in Great Britain there is reason to believe that the ultimate relationship will be complementary rather than rival. The doomed parties are the horse and, in more senses than one,

[1] *Economic Journal*, March 1923, p. 20.

the pedestrian. The railways have lost to the roads much of their ordinary first-class passenger traffic and some of their express freight traffic, but they have gained from the existence of the motor industry both directly and indirectly. They have gained directly from the heavy traffic in road material and motor spirit—stone for road making, creosote tar and pitch, gravel and sand, and oils. They have gained indirectly from the increased ' catchment ' area created for them by the motor bus and the motor lorry. Bus services feed the suburban railway station : where the horse van could collect from ten miles around, the motor van can collect from thirty.[1]

Moreover, though the number of inhabitants per motor vehicle is much greater in Great Britain than in the U.S.A. or Canada—in May 1926 45·6 against 5·8 and 12·0, yet the total of motor vehicles per road mile (5·1) was almost as high as in the U.S.A. (6·6) and five times as great as in Canada (1·0).[2]

It is not likely that the railways will find financial salvation by general entry into local bus services, where the competition is already cut-throat. But the railways have straight and well-laid routes over which no private cars can ply, and they may find it possible to adapt their trunk line service to the new road users, perhaps by the entrainment of motor lorries in special carrier trains. By this method they could combine bulk carriage with the avoidance of transhipment and delays. Some alleviation may be gained by the adjustment of tax burdens, but this is not fundamental ; and it is by no means proven that as property owners the railway companies are over-taxed or that the motor industry manufacturers and users contribute less than their fair share to the upkeep of the roads.

The motor industry falls logically under industrial production, but like shipbuilding it is more conveniently studied under Trade and Transport. For this emphasises one of the truths of economic history, and of British economic history in particular, the reaction of locomotion on the methods of factory production. Historically the automobile grew out of the bicycle. Coventry turned from silk and watch making to sewing-machines and cycles. For a certain James Stanley of Sussex, a gardener and amateur watchmaker, started in 1857 the Coventry Machinists' Company for the making of sewing machines and in 1868 began to make bicycles after a French model. In 1895 Dr. Lanchester produced his first motor car and in the same year a car designed by Austin was built by the Wolseley Sheep Shearing Machine

---

[1] Cf. E. H. Davenport, *Railways versus Roads* (pamphlet of 1927)
[2] Cf. The Society of Motor Manufacturers and Traders Ltd., *The Motor Industry of Great Britain*, pp. 8 and 17.

Company. Austin was in Birmingham ; and shortly after the Daimler Company began to manufacture in a disused silk mill in Coventry. Thus Birmingham and Coventry became the first centre of the new industry.

The halt between 1868 and 1895 was imposed by the lack of an engine which was sufficiently cheap and light to be used for the propulsion of a small carriage. However in this same period armament firms like Vickers and Armstrong Whitworth, working to the order of the British Admiralty, improved the materials and tools of mechanical engineering. The problem of weight arose in connexion with armour plate. A hard armour plate which was not too heavy was demanded. Similarly the first demand for high-speed cutting tools was due entirely to the need for turning big guns. Both these demands were met by the armament firms before the war ; and the torpedo, which was invented to pierce the armour plate of the battleship, was a self-driven motor car in miniature. When directed to peaceful purposes the new engineering created the automobile industry ; and then during the war the aerial automobile industry called aviation. For without a light and highly reliable engine aviation was impossible.

The automobile industry permeated society in the following order—the private car or cycle for pleasure and business, the taxicab, the motor bus, the motor lorry, the motor char-à-banc. The new industry created feeding and accessory industries. The two new feeders were the aluminium industry, two-thirds of the world output of which is consumed in the motor industry, and the rubber industry for motor tyres. The bicycle reached the pneumatic stage shortly before the birth of the motor car. The accessory industries were fuel and repairing services, and the supply of motor accessories in the narrower sense. The filling station is the public house of 1927 and the receiving stomach is a mechanical tank. It is, therefore, not surprising that Great Britain is more sober than ever before even without Prohibition.

Within the automobile factory itself the new industry has advanced engineering technique beyond the point to which it was carried by the armament firms, and along the same two lines. It called for light engines and therefore for strong alloy steels, which would allow of reduced weight. Such steels were prepared by hardening, which had been used hitherto only for cutting tools and in the special business of naval armament. The metallurgist owes his new importance very largely to the motor industry. Secondly and by consequence it called for machine tools capable of working on these harder substances. This has stimulated a second revolution in the machine tool industry, whose origin in the first half of the 19th century is described below (p. 256). Just as sextants and ships' chronometers were the prelude to Watt, so naval armament and torpedoes were the prelude to the motor engineer. America, a land power, arrived at him through the sewing-machine and Maxim gun. Thus arose the long list of specialised machine tools and interchangeable parts which characterise the motor industry to-day : the multiple-spindle boring machine; the slotting machine for cutting key ways in the solid shaft ; machines for gear cutting and grinding (in which foreign countries have led Great Britain) ; special purpose lathes ; together with the small tool outfit and ball bearings. The bicycle had the ball bearing finally, and the bicycle industry grew to sufficient dimensions to demand some improved machine tools, but machine tool designers were conservative, until the new methods of locomotion were sufficiently established to offer a bulk demand for which it was profitable to design standard machine tools. This point in the British motor industry was reached about 1902, shortly before Henry Ford began his great business at Detroit. It is in the marrow of British manufacturers to consider the export trade indispensable ; and to the motor industry it is indispensable. For temporarily at any rate the threat of a fuel shortage has been removed, and therefore for Great Britain the saturation point of domestic car consumption is set not so much by the purchasing power of the consumer (which, it must be admitted, in all countries of small families or the instalment system is unexpectedly elastic) as by the smallness of her land surface. Hence the surplus of the output which is necessary to bulk production must be exported. The air, however, offers an extra dimension, and perhaps one day the lover of silent beauty will be left only with the hope of an all-electric world.

CHAPTER XI

The Transmission of News

Section 1. Posts and the Post Office. Section 2. Telegraphs, Cables and Wireless. Section 3. The Telephone. Section 4. The Economic Significance of the Electrical Industry.

Section 1. Posts and the Post Office

KING JAMES I gave a monopoly of the Royal Posts to his Postmaster-General. The House of Commons, to whom monopoly was anathema, contested it, but the Commonwealth Parliament of 1657, in an Act for establishing a postal system for England, Ireland, and Scotland, retained the monopoly, and the Restoration Parliament in 1660 re-enacted the Act almost word for word (12 Chas. II, c. 35).

The purpose of the postal monopoly was in part political. Walpole systematically censored letters, and during the Napoleonic war the censorship was used freely for the detection of political conspiracy. After 1815 the continuance of this practice was felt to be intolerable, especially when employed on behalf of foreign Powers against refugees in Great Britain. In 1844 William Lovett, the working-man co-operator and champion of a free press, laid a trap for the Home Secretary, Sir James Graham, by marking the correspondence of the Italian, Mazzini, in such a way that the opening of his letters could be proven.[1] Public feeling ran so high that the Government had to promise to amend its ways ; and though in 1845 a motion forbidding the opening of correspondence was lost, the result of the agitation was to establish the privacy of letters except for the detection of crime, such as burglary.

In early times the enforcement of the royal monopoly was difficult and interlopers were frequent. William Dockwra, a London merchant, in 1680 organised a London Penny Post, which was subsequently incorporated in the General Post, and a Mr. Povey in 1708 started a Half-Penny Post, which was closed by a Government prosecution. The posts, it must be understood, were not operated directly. They were farmed to outsiders ; and to these farmers of the posts or to private enthusiasts the main improvements in the postal services were due.

In 1720 Ralph Allen, the son of an innkeeper, became farmer of the country posts and established a relay service of postboys on horseback, but they were defenceless against the highwaymen who in those days abounded along the routes of travel and especially on the lonely edges of towns, and therefore the postal service between quite important points was desultory as late as 1780. But fast stage coaches were now running on improved turnpikes, and in 1784 John Palmer, a theatre proprietor of Bath, proposed a mail coach service protected by armed guards. The forceful Pitt overcame the opposition of his officials and the mail coach then introduced ' was gradually amplified until its service included all parts of England, both on the main roads and cross roads, and with it there came a new era in both postal and travelling facilities, which lasted until the fourth decade of the nineteenth century, when railways received the preference.' [2]

---

[1] *Life and Letters of William Lovett*, Pop. Ed., II. 303.
[2] W. T. Jackman, *Transportation in Modern England*, I. 327.

The urgency of the Napoleonic wars led the Government to do in 1801 what it had done in 1711 during the war with Louis XIV, namely to use the postal monopoly as an instrument of taxation and that at the very time when the postal wants of the business world were rapidly increasing. Postal charges, therefore, were freely evaded—by circumvention, as when multiple correspondence was sent to one mercantile house for distribution by messengers to the parties indicated ; or by smuggling, as when individual letters were carried by sea captains, coachmen and common carriers, by weavers in their bags or by university students in their ' tuck-boxes.' A Commons Committee of 1837–8 by the offer of pardon in advance obtained evidence which showed that on certain routes the majority of correspondence was illicit. Five-sixths of the correspondence between Manchester and London, for example, was transmitted through private agencies ; while of 122,000 letters sent from Liverpool to America in the course of a year only 69,000 were carried by the Post Office. Furthermore, the privilege of franking enjoyed by Members of Parliament and certain Government officials was greatly abused. To make a man ' free of his Majesty's Post Office ' was an easy and time-honoured act of friendship.[1] At this point Rowland Hill entered the scene. He was an enthusiast with a passion for social and scientific experiment. At school he was famous as ' the calculating boy.' He took as the basis of his postal reforms the Reports of the Excise Commissioners of 1833–6 and calculated that the main cost of the postal service was incurred at either end of the posting, namely in taxing the letter at the starting-point and collecting the postage on delivery. He therefore proposed to disregard distance and to introduce a uniform penny post for the United Kingdom. After the usual opposition from the postal officials, to whom the idea of service to the public was as distasteful as the surrender of a lucrative tax, the Whig Government accepted Hill's scheme and brought him to the Post Office to supervise its operation. The penny post began early in 1840 and prepayment by postage stamps on May 6, 1840. But in 1841 the Tories came into power, and in 1843, to the indignation of Mr. Punch, Britannia presented Rowland Hill with the sack.[2] He then became chairman of the London and Brighton Railway, and in 1867, as a member of the Royal Commission on Railways, raised a solitary voice on behalf of State Purchase. For he had proved at St. Martin's-le-Grand that a public monopoly might be beneficent.

The penny post spread like wildfire over the civilised world :

[1] *Cf.* Scott, *Redgauntlet*, Letter I.
[2] Mr. Punch's *History of Modern England*, I. 37, cartoon.

'Never perhaps,' to use Mr. Gladstone's words, 'was a local invention (for such it was) and improvement applied in the lifetime of its author to the advantage of such multitudes of his fellow creatures.' The penny post, the parliamentary train, the lowered tariff, and free trade in corn were all part of a policy of plenty for the poor consumer. And this policy left its impress on economic theory in the doctrine of Consumers' Surplus, as expounded by Jevons and Marshall.

In course of time the Post Office added to itself numerous services, some of which had no connexion with postal business. For the banks thought in terms of London and the business man, municipal enterprise in the first half of the 19th century was backward, and the Post Office was the one Government organ in constant contact with the people. The money order department, which was started as far back as 1788 by certain postal officials as a private venture, was taken over by the General Post in 1834. In 1848 the book post was instituted ; in 1870 a $\frac{1}{2}d$. rate was given to book post matter (per 2 ozs.) and to newspapers. Newspapers in the early part of the 19th century were subject to a heavy stamp duty, which was reduced to 1d. in 1836. In return for this the Government delivered newspapers free of charge, but in 1855 the 1d. stamp was abolished and therefore in 1870 newspapers were brought under the new $\frac{1}{2}d$. rate. The Continent led the way in the carriage of parcels by post ; and in 1883 Great Britain established an inland parcel post in order that she might be able to accept an invitation from Paris to join an international parcel post. In the U.S.A. there was no parcel post till 1913, the Express Companies having hitherto handled the whole of this matter in conjunction with the railways. In 1898, as described above (p. 85), the Imperial Penny Post was inaugurated during Chamberlain's tenure of the Colonial Office.

All these extensions were a natural outgrowth of the postal business, but in addition to this the British Post Office operates as a receiving centre for small savings, a seller of insurance stamps under the scheme of National Insurance, and a paying authority for old age pensions. The Post Office savings banks were instituted by Gladstone in 1861 (below, p. 409) ; the pension and insurance work accrued under the Acts establishing old age pensions (1908) and national insurance (1911). During the war the Post Office paid out the separation allowances. Thus the Post Office, being a source of benefits as well as of news, plays a much greater part in the life of the community than in Canada or the U.S.A.

Section 2.   *Telegraphs, Cables and Wireless*

The electric telegraph was an invention to which no one nation can lay sole claim. Much of the preliminary research was done in Germany, and in the late 30's practical inventors applied themselves to the construction of telegraphic apparatus for economic purposes. The pioneer in America was Samuel Morse, after whom the Morse code is named. In Great Britain Charles Wheatstone of Gloucester and William Fothergill Cooke patented jointly telegraphic apparatus in 1837 ; and in this year the first practical trial was conducted on the London and North Western Railway. From 1837 to 1850 the use of the telegraph was confined almost entirely to the railways, who used it for signalling purposes. Rowland Hill, who was a postal expert and a railway director, associated himself with Wheatstone in the extension of the telegraph to general business. In November 1851, after the laying of the cable between Dover and Calais, the Stock Exchanges of London and Paris were placed in telegraphic contact ; and immediately thereafter telegraphy boomed.[1] Private telegraph companies laid wires along the railway lines, and those towns which had opposed railways found a second reason for regretting their stupidity. By 1855 two large companies, the Electric and International and the British and Irish Magnetic, had 8500 miles of line and 600 sending stations. Other companies entered the field, and a rate war in the early 60's eventuated in an agreed tariff of one to two shillings per message according to distance.

Public opinion was still strongly individualistic ; nevertheless in 1866 the Associated Chambers of Commerce petitioned for Government ownership, believing that a system similar to that of the post would bring uniformity of charges and services in all districts. In 1868, therefore, Parliament took over the private undertakings at a final cost of £11 m., and gave them to the Post Office to operate. In 1869 the rate for a telegram of 20 words was fixed at one shilling, and reduced in 1885 to 6*d*. for 12 words, at which figure it stood till the war. The Government never made a profit from the telegraphs ; but there seems to be no evidence that this was due to mismanagement. It had paid excessively for the property, and its higher working costs were due to the inadequate staffs and long hours of work under private régime.

---

[1] Reuter's News Service, established in London 1851, made its name in continental politics in 1858. It had representatives with the French and Austrian armies during the campaigns of 1859-60, and in the 60's supplied advance news of the American Civil War from Ireland.

The Government monopoly did not extend to submarine telegraphy, and here a wide field was found for private enterprise. After an initial failure in 1865 the *Great Eastern* steamship completed in 1866 the laying of the Atlantic cable, and by 1887 there were 107,000 miles of submarine cable in use in the world, of which a very large part had been manufactured on the banks of the Thames. Sir John Pender (1815–1896), a textile merchant of Manchester and Glasgow, laid the foundations of this new and profitable business, which accorded so well with Great Britain's far-flung commercial interests. He was director of the first Atlantic Cable Company, joint founder of the Anglo-American Company (1865) and chairman of the Telegraph Construction and Maintenance Company, to which he personally guaranteed £250,000. The importance of the cable as a link of Empire has caused cable communication to occupy a permanent place in the agenda of recent Imperial Conferences. The Dominions Royal Commission, which sat during the war, recommended the nationalisation of private cable companies within the Empire.[1] The position in 1923 was placed before the Imperial Economic Conference of that year in a Post Office memorandum.[2] Two main sets of routes at that date started out from Great Britain, (a) the Transatlantic routes, most of them owned and worked by American companies; (b) the Eastern system owned by the Eastern Telegraph Company (a British Company) and its associated companies, which between them served practically every part of the Empire. With a view to catering for traffic with the Dominions the British Government had acquired and was then operating two Atlantic cables, one an ex-German cable and the other purchased from an American company.

Wireless telegraphy followed the submarine telegraph, not ousting it but providing a rival service. In 1899 Signor Guglielmo Marconi established wireless communication across the English Channel and in 1902 across the Atlantic. The latter was opened as a public service in 1907. Since 1904, the year in which the *Campania* published its first ocean newspaper, the commercial marine of the world has been equipped with wireless. Just as land telegraphy began with railway signalling, so ocean wireless found its first big use in communications between ship and ship and between ship and land for purposes of signalling and safety. The Marconi Company operates under licences from the British Government. In 1922 the British Government

---

[1] *Dominions Royal Commission Final Report*, § 633.
[2] *Imperial Economic Conference Record of Proceedings*, Cmd. 2009, 1924, pp. 404–11.

completed the first link in an Imperial wireless chain by the opening of the stations at Oxford (England) and Cairo (Egypt) ; but the difficulty of adjusting relations with the Marconi Company on the one hand and the Dominion Governments on the other prevented the adoption of the scheme prepared by the Imperial Wireless Telegraphy Committee in 1920.[1]

Section 3.   The Telephone

It is hard to compress into a brief section the story of the telephone. The invention was made in Canada. Born at Edinburgh in 1847 and graduating at London University, Alexander Graham Bell at the age of 23 emigrated with his parents to Brantford, Ontario. His father was an elocutionist, and the son in teaching speech to deaf mutes in Boston, Mass., studied the structure of the human ear. Thus he arrived at the mechanical ear, the telephone. The problem was to make a current of electricity vary in intensity precisely as air varies in density during the production of sound. At Brantford in 1875, at the age of twenty-eight, he found out by experimental chance the secret of the undulating, or never broken but always varying, current ; and in 1876 he patented his invention. He died at his summer home in Baddeck, Cape Breton, in 1922. At the beginning of 1923 there were 22 million telephones in the world, of which the U.S.A. had 14·3 millions, Canada 1 million, Great Britain 1 million. Among great towns Stockholm had per hundred of population 25·4 telephones, Toronto 19·2, New York 18·2, London 5·1, Liverpool 3·4. Toronto in 1926 was making one and a half million calls daily.

For capital Bell went to Boston, as Watt went to Birmingham ; and the result was the Bell Telephone Company of America. In 1880 the Bell Telephone Company of Canada was chartered by the Dominion. Lord Kelvin [2] saw the telephone at the Philadelphia Exhibition in 1876 and pronounced it ' the greatest by far of all the marvels of the electric telegraph.' In 1877 Bell went to England to demonstrate its use. The Post Office, however, advised against it, declaring that its possible use was very limited. On June 14, 1878, The Telephone Company Ltd. (Bell's Patents) was registered. In 1879 a rival appeared in the Edison Telephone Company ; and as the Bell Company had the best receiver and the Edison Company the best transmitter, they found it expedient to amalgamate, under the title of the United Telephone Company, in May 1880. In the 80's the

---

[1] For the situation to April 1927 see Sir Evelyn Murray, *The Post Office*, p. 105 *et seq.*

[2] *Cf.* for the details which follow F. G. C. Baldwin, *The History of the Telephone in the United Kingdom.*

United Telephone Company operated in London, and subsidiary companies, licensed by it, in the provinces. But as the master patents were due to expire in 1890–1 a single new company was formed and named the National Telephone Company after the provincial subsidiary whose shares were nearest to par. The members of the amalgamation had 23,585 lines in all. In 1892 the Post Office acquired the trunk line system. For the Courts had ruled in December 1880 that the telephone was a telegraph within the meaning of the Telegraph Acts. Therefore the private companies operated under licence from the Postmaster-General from this date. The Post Office had installed telephones on its telegraph system and opened exchanges in a few places, but did not try to compete with the private companies, and when it secured the trunk lines in 1892 it left the local services to the National Telephone Company. Between 1900 and 1912, under authority of the Telegraph Act of 1899 (62 & 63 Vict. c. 38), a number of municipalities operated municipal telephone services. With the exception of Hull they were not successful. They were slow in introducing technical improvements, such as the common battery system, and they had not the expert staff of the National Telephone Company. During the same period the Post Office entered into local competition with the National Telephone Company in London, which was divided into three areas, one area being allotted to the Company, a second to the Post Office, while the third and central area was competitive territory. In August 1905 Parliament ratified the agreement made in the previous February between the P.M.G. and the National Telephone Company for taking over its property in 1911 ; and in 1911 the telephone services of the country (trunk and local) became a single State-owned system. The Company received £12 million odd for its property on the award of the Railway and Canal Commissioners.

Although the Post Office obstructed the private companies until its control over them was established at law, it was not after that date the main source of their difficulties. The separation of trunk lines and local services, it is true, impeded standardisation and research on a big scale ; but what was worse for the National Telephone Company was the persistent obstruction from local authorities and the unwillingness of Parliament to grant the essential way leaves. Its enemies were parochialism and public prejudice rather than State bureaucracy. It may be pleaded in partial defence of this conservatism that telephone wires are ugly things and that an old country has amenities to preserve ; and there was also a further reason. Distances were not so great. Communication by post was rapid and frequent, and therefore to the average man, and even to the average business man, the telephone meant much less than to the inhabitants of the New World.

Section 4. *The Economic Significance of the Electrical Industry*

Great Britain entered the age of electricity through the telegraph and submarine cable. She already had cheap power in the form of steam power generated by coal. Towards the end of the 19th century electricity was applied to lighting and local communications. During the last twenty years electricity has risen to be the rival of the steam engine as the motive power of the workshop. In 1905 in engineering workshops there was an electrically driven tool only here and there. Now they are in the majority ; and the trend is towards ever smaller units of electrically driven machines. The electrical industry and the motor industry are close allies, not only because the motor car uses electric light and other electrical accessories but because motor manufacturing is a new branch of engineering and the new factories have naturally installed the newest methods of obtaining their power. In 1927 the general engineering trade was more than 60% electrified and the motor industry still more so. Birmingham and Coventry are in the South-West Midland area. In this area ' 90% of the total electrical energy generated is consumed by industrial undertakings, and, taking the monthly average for 1923–4 as 100%, we find that in the South-West Midlands the production of electricity in 1924 was 111·4%, in 1925, 130·5%, and in the first half of 1926, 138%.' [1]

Great Britain lacks water power ; and hydro-electric power, which is the basis of Canadian industry, is negligible. Electricity in Britain is generated from coal, of which she has plenty. The distinguishing feature of the electrical industry in all its applications—communication, transport, lighting, transmission and utilisation of power—is that from the first it has been in scientific hands. Beginning *de novo* it employed metric units of measurement, which were accepted internationally. The watt, ohm, ampère and volt assemble in their names the contribution of Western Europe. And not only is electric measurement standardised, it is also extraordinarily accurate. By comparison, the steam engine of the 19th century was a guesswork. The Cornish miners, it is said, gave their confidence to the first steam engines in proportion to the noise they made, and it would seem that motor cyclists operate on the same principle. Electric power is the antithesis of this. It is invisible current flowing along a wire, and the work that it does

[1] *Engineering*, July 1, 1927, H. Kerr Thomas, ' The Effect of the Automobile Industry on the Midlands,' p. 27, column 2

cannot be guessed. It must be measured by a scientific instrument, and when so measured is ascertained with high accuracy. The accuracy of electric machinery reacted on the quality of the steam engine. For when a dynamo, for example, had been delivered to a power station to be driven by a steam engine, the users at once desired to know the exact capacity of the steam engine which generated the electric power. In this way electricity exerted some influence on the recent improvements of the steam engine at the hands of Sir Charles Parsons and others.

Apart from the much older and specialised industries of watch and clock making, and the optical trade (both mainly developed owing to nautical needs), the making of scientific instruments is a small and specialised industry within the general electrical group. Here the contact between the University and industry has been exceptionally close, as is well seen, firstly in the work of such men as Lord Kelvin, and again in the rise of firms such as the Cambridge Instrument Company, founded in the early 1890's. It began with students who desired instruments as an aid to teaching and research—in physiology, engineering and the like. The physiologists provided the first demand ; then came c. 1895 the electric thermometer, and since about 1905 the demand for instruments for industrial applications has rapidly extended. Made experimentally for academic purposes the scientific instrument was quickly put to commercial use. Just as the automobile and aircraft reacted on the steel industry by their demand for new steels, so electrical instruments have rendered special service in the measurement of metals at a high temperature. For in metallurgical work to-day the exact control of temperature is indispensable.

In fine, the electrical instrument is a mechanical book-keeper always on the spot. All the plant in a big power station must have a balance sheet of gain and loss of heat : on the debit side so much heat in, on the credit side so much power out. This control over performance is in complete accord with the characteristics of modern finance. It could hardly have occurred to the men of fifty years ago that when farmers combined to sell their wheat or garment-workers combined to insure themselves against unemployment, they would need large central offices filled with calculating machines, but so it is. That helplessness before natural law and so-called economic law, which underlay so much of the social injustice of the past, is now no longer felt. Indeed, it is possible that through new industries such as the electrical industry progress will be made by the force of technical example in clarifying the relations between employer and employee. For inaccuracy is an important secondary cause of industrial friction.

PART III
AGRICULTURE AND INDUSTRY

CHAPTER XII

AGRICULTURE

Section 1.   *The Feeding of the People*

' CONSUMPTION,' said Adam Smith, ' is the sole end and purpose of all production ' (II. 159).   The nations of the world have spent their fiscal energies in defying this rational statement—Great Britain and Holland excepted.   For these two have developed a consumers' psychology as the result of their peculiar position as world carriers.

During the 18th century Great Britain exported about as much foodstuffs as she imported, importing oats and sugar and exporting wheat and provisions.   The object of the Corn Laws was ' to prevent grain from being at any time either so dear that the poor cannot subsist or so cheap that the farmer cannot live by the growing of it.' [1]   Therefore they gave to the farmer a bounty on export in normal years, and in the interest of the consumer the export bounty and duties of import were suspended in years of scarcity.   Between 1815 and 1846 the consumers' battle was fought and won for them by the industrial exporter. Thereupon the workers among them consolidated the victory by forming co-operative stores for the supply of groceries and bread ; and Manchester was the headquarters of the co-operative movement as it had been of the Anti-Corn Law League.

When other nations were able to supply wheat more cheaply, British farmers had to curtail their growth of it and to produce what others could not send.   But foreign meat followed foreign wheat, and therefore to-day there is the anomalous situation that the soil of England, though highly improved and very fertile, is, some of it, patently underworked.   This is the modern form of the age-long conflict between gross produce and net profit.   The landlords of mediaeval England turned themselves into rent receivers because they found the letting of land to sheep

---

[1] C. Smith. *Tracts on the Corn Trade* (1759), p. 72.

farmers more profitable than the raising of crops for the maintenance of tenants and retainers, but throughout the 17th and 18th centuries and indeed down to 1875 the full use of the soil and the advantage of the landlord were in harmony. This was the long period during which arable farming paid, if not always in £. s. d. at any rate in £. s. d. plus social prestige and the gratification of a hobby. Those made money who improved wisely and farmed well. But after 1875 the agriculturist who was kind to his land was unkind to his pocket. As Albert Pell, the progressive Cambridge landlord, wrote in 1887 : ' The rents of these fine soils covered with the best natural pastures have hardly yielded to the pressure of bad times, while rents enhanced by improvements have gone to pieces, and in many cases down to zero.' [1]

The agricultural sky was never brighter than in 1875, and yet a speculator gifted with prescience would have selected none of the great properties with their smiling cornfields, but land suited by soil and location to market gardening, sand hills fitted for golf, and waste land on the edge of suburbs unborn. Perhaps if 19th-century Britain had been cultivated by small owners, the nation would have refused to pay the full price of free trade and insisted, like other European countries, on a fiscal compromise. But latter-day landlords and substantial farmers had to pay the price for the sweeping victory which their forebears obtained over the small man in the days of 18th-century enclosure.

However, it must not be inferred that Great Britain does not raise an important part of her food supply. She imported, it is true, before the war, four-fifths of her wheat and the majority of her meat and dairy produce, but according to an estimate of 1912 the United Kingdom of Great Britain and Ireland raised then £170 millions of foodstuffs and imported only £200 millions, which includes £20 millions for sugar.[2] The products she raised were those which in the last half-century had fallen least in price —milk, vegetables, fresh fruit, prime beef and the like.

It is disputed whether rye was ever a substantial part of the food of mediaeval England, but this much is certain : wheat was always the grain preferred by the South, and London was the first to be able to afford fine wheaten bread. Charles Smith said in 1764 : ' It is certain that bread made of wheat is become much more generally the food of the common people than it was before that time [sc. 1688], but it is still far from being the food of the people in general.' [3] Later writers, such as Sir F. M. Eden in his

[1] T. Mackay, *Albert Pell*, p. 341.
[2] *Cf.* J. H. Venn, *Foundations of Agricultural Economics*, p. 151.
[3] C. Smith, *op. cit.*, Supplement (1764).

State of the Poor, 1797, and Dr. Skene Keith, 1802, commented on the continuation of the process. By 1802 the rivalry of oaten bread in Scotland and of barley bread in England had declined. ' Nearly twice as many persons now eat wheaten bread as formerly consumed this quality of corn,' says the Rev. Dr. Keith.[1] But the scarcity of war time arrested the trend. The Lords Committee of 1800 on The High Price of Provisions gave examples of this. Thus, 'In Lincoln the poorer classes, who (within the memory of the person from whom this testimony was received) had exchanged the use of barley bread for wheaten, returned last year to barley bread.' But the people fought hard for wheat and for fine wheat at that. Arthur Young lamented that ' throughout a great part of the kingdom the general assistance given to the poor is by money, bread or flour, all three being almost equally an encouragement to the consumption of wheat.' [2] The reformers advocated ' soups, rice, potatoes and other substitutes,' but the poor rebelled. The régime of the workhouse was needed to force them into gruel ; they would not even eat the standard wholemeal bread which the *Daily Mail* and the Kaiser forced upon British consumers some years ago. The compulsory sale of standard wholemeal bread was a stock remedy of Parliamentary Committees between 1756 and 1800, but in 1800 the London bakers assured Parliament that ' scarcely any bread is consumed in the Metropolis but that which is made from fine wheaten flour ; that attempts have been made in times of scarcity to introduce a coarser species of bread into use but without success, and that in their opinion the high price of bread would be considered, by the lower classes of people, as a small inconvenience when compared with any measures which would have the effect of compelling them to consume bread to which they have not been accustomed.' [3]

Thanks, however, to the superb response of the soil of Britain, the nation survived the war without starvation or compulsory rationing. When war broke out the Government was nearly scared into public granaries. But Edmund Burke scotched this and the Government confined itself to the encouragement of corn imports by import bounties and licences to import (which in 1800 and 1801 produced large imports owing to the short home crop) and to economies in the use of the existing supply. Hair powder, in which grain was used, was heavily taxed. Distillation of grain was prohibited in particular areas : the Government having an interest in lessening the stocks of Colonial sugar which were piling up in London. It was forbidden to eat new bread ;

---

[1] *Farmers' Magazine*, August 2, 1802.
[2] Commons Committee on the Assize and Making of Bread, 1800, Evidence.
[3] *Ibid.*, Evidence.

and in 1795 and 1800 self-denial was urged upon the people from bench and pulpit.[1]

Between 1815 and 1846 the wealth of the country was certainly increasing faster than its population, but it was being re-invested and two great sections of the people—the textile handworkers and the agricultural labourers—were forced to a lower standard. ' After ten years of absence from England,' said a doctor before the Handloom Weavers' Committee of 1834,[2] ' nothing struck me with more horror than the deterioration in the physical appearance of the people.' The proud weavers starved by thousands. In 1842 their children grubbed in the market places of Lancashire towns for nettles and the rubbish of roots, and the wives of Leicestershire knitters quieted their children with Godfrey's Cordial, a preparation of laudanum. The agricultural poor, when their parish relief was stopped by the Act of 1834, had a way out. They could dig and poach, and by the aid of allotments they dug themselves into a potato standard. However, by 1850 there was a general improvement in both town and country. All were eating wheat and most town workers had some meat as well. The prohibition of foreign cattle was removed in 1842, but the Continent could not compete with the United Kingdom in the supply of live stock. After 1850 such was the prosperity of industry and the improvement in earnings that the demand for a time outran the supply. Prime beef rose from $4\frac{3}{4}d.$ per lb. (1851) to $6\frac{3}{4}d.$ (1861), $8d.$ (1871), $8\frac{1}{4}d.$ (1881). The public was shy of canned meat and concentrated meat stuffs, such as Dr. Liebig's Meat Extract, but refrigeration solved the problem, and in the early 80's the frozen meat trade began its spectacular career.

Major Craigie in his Gilbey Lectures at Cambridge in 1907 estimated that 20,000,000 acres of foreign territory were occupied in growing the imported wheat of the United Kingdom and another 20,000,000 in growing its imported meat and dairy produce. Between 1800 and 1850 the main source of foreign wheat was Russia and north-western Europe. In the 60's the United States of America took the lead. India became important after the opening of the Suez Canal and was followed by the Argentine and Canada, Australia and Roumania. In 1876 the first shipment of wheat was made from Manitoba. It was consigned to a Toronto seed merchant by way of the U.S.A. There is record of a consignment to Glasgow in 1878, but it

[1] For the detail and sequence of these restrictions and economies (1800–1813) see W. F. Galpin, *The Grain Supply of England during the Napoleonic Period,* Chs. II–VI.

[2] *Evidence,* p. 306.

was not until 1884, after the completion of the Canadian Pacific
line between Winnipeg and the head of Lake Superior, that wheat
moved regularly to Eastern Canada and thence to British ports.
Since the war the Canadian West has been the premier source of
supply.

The wheat from the Canadian crop of 1921 billed to the United
Kingdom was equal to 64% of the net wheat imports of the United
Kingdom in 1922 : that from the crop of 1922 to 89·3% of the
net wheat imports of 1923. A considerable part of the Canadian
wheat is re-exported, and the percentage contribution of Canada
to the imported wheat consumed in the United Kingdom—
allowance [1] being made for shipments of Canadian wheat through
American ports and flour mills—may be put at 39% in 1922 and
54% in 1923. In 1924, when the Canadian crop was short and
the American crop heavy, the percentage declined. The Argentine
holds the lead in chilled beef, i.e. beef shipped at slightly under
freezing point, which is not practicable for mutton : New Zealand
and Australia in frozen mutton. All the Dominions look to
Britain as the best market for their dairy produce and fruits.

During the war the activity of enemy submarines necessitated
food control ; and the entry of the Government on to the markets
of the world as a buyer of foodstuffs necessitated price control.
Between the consumer and the Government the British farmer
had an uneasy time, but he responded nobly to the food production
campaign of 1917. 1·2 m. acres of grass in England and Wales
were broken up, and a home supply of 10 weeks in 1914 was raised
to one of 18 weeks in 1918. Had the war continued, this could
have been eked out to 40 weeks' supply by rationing and reduction
of grade. But the war came to a sudden end, and by the end of
1922 the farmer's war-time profits had been lost or transferred to
his landlord in the purchase price of his farm. Peace was almost as
great a catastrophe for him as free trade. The Government was
blamed for running away from its price guarantee at the end of
the war, but the cost of keeping faith was greater than it dared to
incur.

Section 2. The London Corn Market at the Beginning of the 19th Century [2]

If we look only to the Corn Laws, the 18th century seems to
close in an atmosphere of regulation thicker and more aggra-

[1] For method of allowance *cf.* Bureau of Agricultural Economics (Washington), *Foreign Crops and Markets*, July 4, 1924.
[2] Reprinted (with slight alterations) from the *American Economic Review*,
Vol. XV. No. 1, March 1925, by permission of the American Economic
Association.

vating than after or before. Certainly the trade in corn is freer
in England to-day than it was in 1800, because to-day not only
the home trade but also the foreign trade—the major department—is entirely free. But the corn trade was freer in 1800 than
in 1700 ; for in 1800 the home trade, representing nine-tenths of
the total trade, was free, though the other tenth—the foreign
trade—was rigidly regulated. The freedom of the inland trade
in corn was slowly won. From mediaeval times onwards, and
in particular from the fifth and sixth of Edward VI, c. 14 (1552),
there were severe penalties against the statutory offences of
forestalling, regrating and engrossing. The line between these
several offences was not easy to draw, in particular that between
regrating and engrossing.

The statute of 15 Charles II, c. 7 (1663), which Adam Smith
eulogised—he says of it, ' All the freedom which the trade of the
inland corn dealer has ever yet enjoyed, was bestowed upon it
by this statute ' (II. 34)—conceded the liberty to buy corn in
order to sell it again, when it was below a certain limit, provided
that it was not resold for three months within the same market.
In 1772 (12 Geo. III, c. 71) Parliament, zealously incited by
Edmund Burke, repealed the ancient statutes ; and no more was
heard of these offences till in the case of The King v. Rusby
(1800) it was held that under certain circumstances buying to sell
again was an offence still liable to be punished by the Common
Law with fine and imprisonment at least, if not with whipping
and the pillory. The decision, which excited much adverse
criticism in the pamphlets of the day, did not imperil the ordinary
corn dealers, but only certain jobbers who were what we to-day
should call professional bulls.[1] The result was not to abolish
their practices, but to make them for a time more cautious.

In 1795 and the lean years that followed there were murmurs
among the populace—in Cambridge, for example, as may be
read in the *Reminiscences* of Henry Gunning—expressive of a
desire for vengeance on the dealers ; and in 1800 a Committee
of the Lords examined the allegations that were floating about.
They reported that ' they had not been able to trace, in any one
Instance, anything more than such suspicious and vague Reports
as usually prevail in Times of Scarcity ; and they are of opinion
that what have been represented as deep and fraudulent Practices
to raise the market, have been only the common and usual proceedings of Dealers in all articles of commerce where there is a
great demand and where great capitals and great activity are
employed.' And of the dealers in corn they reported that

[1] Committee (H. of C.) on the High Price of Provisions, Seventh Report,
June 24, 1801. Evidence of W. Reynolds, a corn dealer.

' persons engaged in this Branch of trade are highly useful and even necessary for the due and regular supply of the markets and may, therefore, be considered as rendering an important service to the Public at large.' [1]

But the agitation had one good result. It induced the Commons' Committee in the following year (1801) to take evidence from traders with a view to seeing whether defects of machinery were a cause of the high price of provisions. Their recommendations were not revolutionary, but these and the evidence on which they were based exhibit in fullness the structure of the trade in 1800.[2]

Forty to fifty years ago the Corn Exchange had been transferred from Bear Quay to Mark Lane, a freehold property of eighty shares held by the factors and dealers in corn. Fourteen individuals, who were corn factors, held a controlling interest in the shares, and they took care, whenever any person applied to them for a stand, to prevent his obtaining one if he was likely to employ himself as a factor. But to the dealers, whose work was at this time not rival, they had no such objection. Hence the dealers were now almost as numerous as the factors. On the Exchange were sixty-four stands, occupied by some fifty people. Thirty of these were corn factors and twenty were dealers. Eight factors dealt for the Kentish people only and were known as ' Kentish Hoymen.'

Mark Lane was a general market for all the grains, wheat, barley, oats, etc., for home-grown grain and imported foreign grains. The foreign grain and most of the home grain reached London by sea. The amount brought down by river or by inland carriage bore a very small proportion to the total of London's consumption. The supplies from the home counties of Kent, Essex and Suffolk chiefly came from the growers direct, and were sold in ' runs.' One shipload would contain consignments from several growers to several factors ; and the consignment on a particular ship from Farmer A to Factor Z was a ' run.' The supplies from the more distant parts of Essex and from Norfolk and elsewhere came chiefly from the corn merchants, who had bought in the country from the farmers at the farms or on the local markets. Among the several grains a greater part of the wheat came from farmers and a greater part of the barley and oats from merchants. Flour milled in the country and destined for London missed Mark Lane altogether, passing straight from

---

[1] Committee (H. of L.) on the High Price of Provisions, Dec. 22, 1800, Second Report.
[2] Committee (H. of C.) on the High Price of Provisions, Seventh Report. June 24, 1801 ; respecting the Machinery of the Corn Trade.

the country miller, to the town baker by the medium of flour factors. But barley, malted in the country perhaps by the farmers themselves, reached the London brewers through Mark Lane. Very few farmers came up to Mark Lane to sell their own corn; 99 % was in the first instance sold on commission by the factors. Through them the wheat passed to the millers or to shipping factors for reshipment. London millers bought direct for themselves and bought for their own mills only. Distant millers bought through factors. Similarly, through the agency of the factors, the barley passed to the maltsters and the distillers : the malt to the brewers and the distillers : the oats to the dealers or ' jobbers,' as they had been called from old times. The dealer in oats was not a manufacturer, as the others were. He in turn would retail to the public, buy for stable keepers on commission, and perhaps keep horses for himself.

As a seller for his farmer clients the factor was in very much the same position as a modern stockbroker. In the home trade he took his regular commission per quarter and did his best for them. The seller's name was not disclosed except in case of a dispute, and the factor was usually given a free hand as to the price he should take. In the foreign trade there had been a recent change of practice. Here, on account of the extra risk and trouble caused by the outbreak of the French war (1793), factors now received, in addition to the commission per quarter, a percentage on the amount sold. Advices from importing merchants of consignments from abroad were usually accompanied by instructions to sell at specified prices. But whereas according to the practice of the London Stock Exchange the stockbroker deals only with the stock-jobber—buying from him or selling to him according to the client's orders—the corn factor was primarily a seller only and dealt with trade consumers, the millers or their agents. One witness before the Committee of 1801, Nathaniel Brockwood, who was at once a corn factor and buyer for the London Flour Company, was careful to state that he kept his two businesses rigidly separate. ' It is the duty of the Factor,' said another, ' at all Times to do as well as he can for his Correspondents ; it is the interest of the buyer or the miller to buy as cheap as he can. These two operations, the one or the other, will generally give the market its fair value.' [1]

It was complained in these days of rising prices that the factors, selling on sample, exposed only a selection of their samples, so that the buyers had no index of the quantities they represented. What would be the result—this same witness was

[1] Committee (H. of C.). Evidence of the clerk of Messrs. Wilson (corn factors and corn merchants).

asked—of compelling factors to mark on the samples the quantity to which they related ? He replied, ' Great fluctuations would be continually taking place, because it is not infrequent that corn, particularly from abroad, as also from the Coast, particularly the Norfolk Coast, is kept back by contrary winds, and from the Foreign Countries by frost, etc. ; in consequence of large Fleets arriving greater quantities of Corn are for sale on the same Day, the Buyers are timid, and the Corn feels a great depression.' The witness, whose principals were at once factors and dealers, seems to imply that the correction of irregularities of quantity was being better performed by the machinery for equalising prices already at work behind the scenes.

To understand this machinery we must analyse the function of the dealer. A comparatively new personage in the trade of wheat, the dealer was an established institution in that of oats ; and this for two reasons. In the first place, the oats dealer corresponded to the miller and was as indispensable as he, but since the miller in addition to buying the wheat made it into flour, he was called a miller. The buyer of oats contributed no change of form to the product, and so called himself a dealer in oats. In the second place, a great amount of oats was imported from abroad. Between 1697 and 1765 oats comprised more than two-thirds of British imports of grain, and over the whole period from 1697 to 1801 the oats imported into Great Britain were twelvefold those exported : whereas for the other cereals there were in the aggregate big balances of exports. Most of the oats came from Ireland ; for until 1806 Ireland was, for the purposes of the grain trade, a foreign country. Parnell's Corn Committee in 1813 made much of the increase in the food supplies derived from Ireland. But the increases were still mainly in oats, much of which was purchased by Government for the service of troop horses in the Peninsular War.

The growth of this import trade stimulated a class of traders who were objectionable to the old-fashioned dealers, and by common consent called ' jobbers.' ' I mean by jobbers,' said Mr. R. Snell, a *dealer* in oats, ' people who stand between the consumers of this metropolis and the factors, those who buy up the Oats and before the arrival of the fair Buyer or Consumer place them in the Hands of the Factor to sell again the same day or the same market. . . . There is a term at Market when we ask for a sample of Oats, wishing to know whether they are on board ship or in granary, and why we ask is we suppose all oats in granary to belong to those Jobbers, and all People who know the true character of Jobbers will not buy of them.'

With the growing importation of wheat towards the end of

the 18th century, parallel changes occurred in the wheat trade. The dealer dealing in wheat on his own account made his appearance. Dealers, we are told in 1801, ' occur largely in the importing line '; dealing on independent account in British corn ' was not usual but may happen.' Several of the witnesses before the Committee styled themselves dealers. It was a respectable profession. There was doubt, however, about the advisability of factors becoming dealers on their own accounts, a practice which was becoming common, though it is spoken of in 1801 as ' a recent thing.' The factors, it was admitted, ' do at times import on their own account '; and the factors contended it was for the benefit of the country. The Committee thought differently, and recommended that they should be placed ' on the footing of Brokers in other Trades carried on within the City of London.' It was felt that the factor ought not to employ the confidential knowledge he had of the home trade in foreign dealing on his own account, since he then might have an interest in conflict with that of his clients.

But what of the jobbers ? All the witnesses complained of their existence and indeed displayed an inside knowledge of their functions, but nobody admitted to being one or specified any jobber by name. A member of the Committee, giving evidence, said ' I cannot say that any persons make it their chief business.' Who, then, are they ? asked the Committee. ' Persons connected in one way or another with the corn trade, and having property and credit and considering the Prices will go still higher, may make purchases with a view to sell again.' Men of property and credit ! Respectable men did it, but it was not respectable. What then was ' it ' ? In its most refined form it was buying to sell again without handling the produce, with an eye to profit on the rise of price in the interval. It was, as we should put it to-day, the operation of ' bulls ' buying for a rise. A witness describes it thus : ' A person coming to the Corn Market on Friday and finding many Country Buyers, concludes the Market will rise on Monday ; he purchases a quantity of Wheat, 400 or 500 qrs., with a view to selling the same on Monday, and the interval between his buying and selling requires no capital to carry that practice on.' The factors, said the dealers, look up to the jobbers because a sale to them means a second sale later. The dealers, said the factors, are the parents of the jobbers. The decision in The King *v.* Rusby (noted above, p. 226) scared the jobbers for a time ; and the Committee of 1801, relying on the fact that buyers of corn were allowed a month's credit by the custom of the trade, suggested that re-sales within the month should be prohibited with a view to forcing jobbers to take delivery of the stuff and pay for it. But neither the judicial decision nor the suggestion (for a suggestion it remained) offered any real solution of the problem. What the country was suffering from was a prolonged scarcity, with prices mounting ever upwards. Traders themselves recognised that speculation was inevitable ; but in the last few years the movement of prices had been all one way. Jobbers rarely had to resell on a falling market. They seemed to be growing fat on the necessity of the people. As a very level-headed member of the committee put it, ' In times of plenty speculators tend to keep the market more on a level ; in times of scarcity they have it in their power to influence the Market too much.'

Could any device have reduced their influence to its proper proportions ? There was only one device, and that device, from the immaturity of speculative organisation, was precluded. For these Friday to Monday incursionists were embryo dealers in futures. Their service to the country could have been increased and their profits curtailed only by appearance of that other set of animals which we call ' bears.' For then the contest would have been equal. Bulls would have worried and won from bears, and bears would have clipped the tails of bulls. But the bear, the animal who sells what he hasn't and covers his sale at a later date, could not appear so long as wheat was sold in the old way by sample or pitch. America was the first country to grade its wheat, and from America, a generation or two later, the bears came to the port of Liverpool.

Section 3. *Enclosure and Tenant Farming*

The system of agriculture which prevailed over a great part of mediaeval England was brought to an end by the enclosure of open fields, commons and waste. The cultivation of open fields by freeholders and by customary tenants, descendants of villeins, disappeared ; and the cultivation of compact farms by tenant farmers took its place. There were tenant farmers before enclosure, cultivating owners and copyholders after enclosure, but in sum and over the centuries the change was a dual one : from open field to enclosure and from freehold or customary tenure to tenancy at a money rent.

It is, however, wrong to think of enclosure as causing tenant farming, for in general tenant farming came first. The land for tenant farming was derived from many quarters : the lords' demesne, holdings vacated by or taken from villeins, old land purchased and new land reclaimed. After the break-up of the manor there was some stock and land leasing, but it did not develop into the system of *métayage* which is encountered in France. It was only an episode in the transition from manorial farming to renting. Well before the industrial revolution the majority of English land was cultivated by tenants. The industrial revolution did not destroy a yeomanry of cultivating owners, but merely substituted in certain districts one type of landlord for another, the commercial lord for the old-fashioned country squire ; and as the former had money to spend, the change was beneficial to the tenant. An investigation of the Land Tax records in a group of Midland counties shows that in 1780, i.e. in the very early days of the industrial revolution, almost 90 % of the land under review was already in the hands of tenants.[1]

The relation which prevailed in the 19th century between landlord and tenant was the outcome of a long evolution. As from 1600 onwards the value of land rose, so it became customary for the landlord, especially the absentee landlord, to let farms on a beneficial lease, taking a low fixed rent for a period of years and a fine on renewal. The lessees frequently re-let the land to a cultivating tenant, who paid a rack rent, i.e. a rent stretched out to its full annual value. But by 1815 the cultivating farmer usually held directly from the owner. In strong contrast with contemporary Ireland the landlord was normally resident and frequently operated a home farm.

Big resident landlords like Coke of Holkham saw that they could not induce their tenants to follow an improved husbandry unless they were secured in the fruits of their improvement. Therefore they gave long leases of 14 to 21 years accompanied by covenants of cultivation. The long lease was most popular in Scotland, but in England it soon fell out of favour. An effective substitute was found in yearly tenancy plus the custom of tenant right. This body of custom was the foundation of the Agricultural Holdings Acts of 1875, 1883, 1895, and 1908.[2] The outgoing tenant received compensation for the value of unexhausted improvements made by him and also for unreasonable disturbance. Thus the rental relations which in Ireland and America stood for oppression or inefficiency produced in Britain a fruitful partnership ; and the terms of the relationship, whereby the landlord supplied land, buildings, and permanent improvements, and the tenant was his own master, gave to rent an economic significance which is absent in countries where the rental relation

---

[1] *Economic History Review*, Vol. I. No. 1, Jan. 1927, E. Davies, ' The Small Landowner,' p. 112.

[2] 38 & 39 Vict. c. 92 ; 46 & 47 Vict. c. 61 ; 58 & 59 Vict. c. 27 ; 8 Edw. VII, c. 28.

is unusual or unsatisfactory. Hence from England the Ricardian Doctrine of Rent.

Within the elastic framework of tenant farming the change from open field to enclosed farming was gradually accomplished. In statute law enclosure is as old as the Statute of Merton, 1235, and was in progress at varying rates for the next six centuries. It involved the consolidation of scattered strips and their separation from other property, usually by a hedge or wall. It was applied to open field arable, grazing common and waste. Nearly every village had some enclosed land. An enclosure for winter pasture was necessary to the open field economy itself; and orchards had to be protected from damage by beasts. Wholesale enclosure for sheep farming produced an agrarian revolution in the 16th century. In the 17th century, however, enclosure excited less clamour, since it was partly for arable and partly for pasture, following the capacity of the land. Moreover, it was effected silently by private agreement, confirmed sometimes by the Court of Chancery or on Crown Lands by the Crown. After 1688 a Parliamentary title was preferred, and the language of the first Parliamentary Enclosures shows the transition from the old fashion to the new. Thus in 1725 in a bill for the enclosure of a certain parish in Leicestershire the Act is sought ' as neither the Agreements of the said Parties to the said Articles can be made absolutely valid and effectual to answer the purpose thereby intended without the Aid of an Act of Parliament.' [1]

In 1700 there were two great unenclosed areas in England : an unimportant belt in the hilly moorlands of the north and a highly important central belt, which comprised about the half of England and stretched from Yorkshire to Dorset. The latter ' lay almost entirely between two lines, one drawn straight from Lyme Regis to Gloucester and from Gloucester to the Tees Estuary, the second straight from Southampton to Lowestoft passing London a few miles to the west.' [2] The rest of England by 1700 was mainly enclosed. Enclosure was most advanced in counties supplying the metropolitan market, such as Kent and Suffolk, in the industrial, orchard, and cattle-raising counties of the West and in ex-fen or ex-forest, which upon reclamation passed straight into several ownership. It is doubtful whether the open field system ever existed in Cornwall and Wales. For it was only suited to level land fit for the plough.

The northern enclosures displaced no population and caused

---

[1] An Appeal for confirming Articles of Agreement, and an Award, for inclosing and dividing the heaths, wastes, fields and common grounds, in the township of Norton-juxta-Twisscross in the county of Leicestershire.

[2] J. H. Clapham, *The Early Railroad Age*, p. 19 : explaining the map of Parliamentary Enclosures, 1700–1870, after Gonner, facing page 20.

no hardships. Indeed in the Pennine valleys from Rochdale northward to Carlisle open field agriculture was precluded by the lie of the land. Enclosure here meant reclamation from the forest waste. Individual holdings lay in valley nooks or on hill slopes. Wheat growing was difficult and the exposed climate encouraged under-cover industrial occupations. In contrast with what occurred in the Midlands and South the industrial revolution strengthened the numbers and status of the small holders.[1] In the central belt there is little evidence of general displacement of population after enclosure, but the rearrangement worked very hardly on the small man. His rights were uncertain. Even where he could establish them, it was rarely that he could afford the expenses for his share of the bill for quickset hedges and new roads—and the landlords controlled Parliament. But his chief offence was that in an improving age he was conservative. The Act of 1773 (13 Geo. III, c. 81), which might have aided the introduction of turnips into the open field rotation, was a dead letter.

In Wales and Scotland the enclosure movement excited less controversy ; for neither had the open field system of the English plains. Wales was largely pastoral. In place of the English open fields with their more or less regular rotation of crop and fallow, Scottish hamlets had an infield and an outfield, the infield being cropped every year and the outfield irregularly. The hamlets were so small and the system of cultivation so poor that a division of the land by enclosure was at once easier and more advantageous for all concerned ; and the Scottish enclosure legislation of 1695 encouraged the process. Property rights were more clearly defined than in England or Wales, and after 1695 any proprietor having an interest in common could compel the others to divide. Both in Wales and in Scotland land was in comparatively few hands, and it was farmed mainly by tenants before as well as after enclosure.

Many tears have been shed over the disappearance of the open field farmer and commoner ; and certainly the landless labourer of the early 19th century, depending on the parish for his support, was a blot on the rural economy of England. Even Arthur Young, the champion of enclosure, lamented the way in which by 1800 it had worked to the hurt of the small man. He thought that some of his rights might have been preserved, but surely neither legislation nor even political revolution would have altered the essentials. A revolution would have left the working head of the farm in power ; and this by Young's day was the working tenant farmer. Lord Ernle well says : ' The divorce

---

[1] Cf. for an intensive examination of the situation in a part of Lancashire, G. H. Tupling, *The Economic History of Rossendale* (1927).

of the peasantry from the soil, and the extinction of commoners, open field farmers and eventually of small freeholders, were the heavy price which the nation ultimately paid for the supply of bread and meat to its manufacturing population.' [1]

Between 1760 and 1815 the tide of enclosure ran strongly. The war accelerated it and caused some lands to be enclosed for arable which later fell out of use, but their place was more than taken between 1815 and 1830 by the conversion of enclosed grass lands to arable and the further enclosure of waste. In 1801, in the face of opposition from the lawyers and from the clergy, who feared for their tithes, a General Enclosure Act was passed (41 Geo. III, c. 109). By this Act, which was applied mainly to commons, the proceedings of enclosure were simplified and the cost somewhat reduced. In 1836 another Act dealt with the enclosure of the few remaining arable fields. By this time the value of commons as recreation grounds and the lungs of large cities was beginning to be recognised and their use for these purposes was safeguarded in the General Enclosure Act of 1845 (8 & 9 Vict. c. 118).

Section 4. Agricultural Practice, 1700–1875

British agriculture prospered in the 18th century. It is true that in the first three-quarters of the century the average price of wheat was lower than in the century preceding, but the export bounty set a limit to the decline of price in seasons of abundance and the domestic market for all kinds of produce was widened by the improvements in communications. The encouragement of distilling had grave social consequences; but it effected its economic purpose, which was to support the price of cereals, and after 1750 the restrictions on the liquor trade were offset by the expanding demand for wheat as food.

It has been estimated that in the course of the 18th century over 2,000,000 acres of new land were brought into cultivation.[2] Increased yields per acre were obtained in company with the enrichment of the soil and a heavier production of live stock. The notion that the course of improvement was attended by a progressive recourse to inferior soils was the result of observations made during a period of war. The very high prices of the war period were due to the fact that wheat was a necessity. Therefore a comparatively small shortage produced a disproportionate rise in price. Furthermore in many of the war years the weather was bad, and war conditions made imports uncertain and expensive.

[1] R. E. Prothero (Lord Ernle), *English Farming, Past and Present*, p. 149.
[2] *Ibid.* p. 154.

The first of the great agricultural improvers was Jethro Tull (1674–1741), who settled in 1699 at Howberry Farm, Crowmarsh, near Wallingford on the Thames, and moved later to Shalbourn in the south-west corner of Berkshire. He has been rightly termed the greatest individual improver in the annals of agriculture. The new husbandry was called the ' Tullian Husbandry ' —the husbandry of the horse hoe and the drill. The drill sowed the seed in an even line and at a regular depth. Tull had tried in this way to make his labourers sow by hand, but they refused to depart from their old ways and so he was driven to invent a machine. The horse hoe was the complement of the drill. For, as the seed was no longer broadcast, it was possible to work with the hoe between the lines of the growing crop. Thus Tull put agriculture on the way to becoming a continuous course of co-operation with nature instead of two isolated operations— the sowing of the seed and the harvesting of the crop. Thorough pulverisation of the soil utilised soil capacities, hitherto idle, and opened the door of intensive farming to capital and brains. Hitherto it had been confined to specialities like vines and bulbs, where it meant labour by hand and spade. It is not easy to express briefly the magnitude of the change wrought by the Tullian husbandry. It stood for experiment and observation in the place of unreflecting tradition : for soil working to the advantage of the soil in the place of soil scratching to its frequent detriment : for an alert economy in the place of a clumsy routine. The farmers of to-day in the New World as well as in the Old cultivate the growing crop with the horse hoe as part of the nature of things, not knowing that they owe it to Tull or that it took a century and more for the knowledge to reach outlying parts. In the Highland farm of 1769–82 described by I. F. Grant [1] the lay-out was irregular, the crops were sown in patches, the seed was defective, and the yield of weeds was as heavy as that of grain. Arable farming in England in 1700 was certainly in advance of this ; for much of the land was naturally fertile and had long been cleared, and even if the open field system with its third or half in fallow was sluggish and wasteful, it was not unduly exhausting. But, like the gild system, it was inelastic.

From the Restoration onwards the rich were building up landed estates, which their lawyers devised means to perpetuate in the family. Tull therefore found ready imitators in many of the great landlords with whom, as with the highest of them—King George III himself—farming became a hobby. A part of Windsor Park was devoted to model farming. The parsons of the Established Church, neglecting the cure of souls, improved their glebe and

[1] *Everyday Life on an Old Highland Farm, 1769–1782.*

fattened their pigs. It was said of Sir Robert Walpole that
he opened the letters from his steward before his dispatches
of State. In 1730 his brother-in-law, Viscount Townshend,
retired to Raynham in Norfolk and perfected the practice which
he had observed in Holland and elsewhere. He worked out
by experiment the place of turnips and clover in the rotation of
crops and thus founded the famous Norfolk four-course rotation—
wheat, turnips, barley, and clover.

The value of the turnip was threefold. It made a good feed
for cattle. Norfolk therefore became the district in which cattle
were fattened for the London market. Secondly, being a root,
it allowed of cultivation during the whole period of growth and
was therefore a famous cleaning crop. Thirdly, being eaten off
the ground by sheep or fed to the cattle in the stall, it made
manure for the enrichment of the ground, which was specially
needed by the light sandy soil of Norfolk. Later the turnip was
supplemented by the swede—Swedish turnip—and the mangel-
wurzel, a field beet, both of them better frost resisters than the
turnip.

England does not employ the term 'mixed farming.'[1] For
when the Norfolk husbandry became general all arable farming
was mixed. But the 18th-century improvements in grain and
roots were accompanied by improvements no less important in
the preparation and care of temporary and permanent grass
lands. In the North there was much strong natural pasture and
its rural economy rested on cattle. Wheat was imported into
the region. But in the Midlands and South the opposite situation
prevailed. There it was necessary to conserve pasture and to
enclose. Only by enclosure could pasture be protected against
over-stocking. Only on enclosed land was it possible to raise
pedigree stock or fatten store cattle for the market. The old-
time grazier raised sheep for their wool : the new grazier raised
sheep and cattle for their meat more than for their wool and
hides. Improved grass farming and improved arable farming
went hand in hand. For the clover, sainfoin and timothy used
as temporary grasses in the arable rotation were the plants out
of which permanent grass land could be built. There was,
however, need for improved stock which would utilise to the full
the food possibilities of the improved arable and pasture. This
required deliberate breeding ; and the elevation of breeding into
an art was the achievement of Robert Bakewell (1725–1795) of
Dishley Grange in Leicestershire, where his grave was to be seen
in 1913 in a shocking state of damage and neglect.

[1] 'Convertible husbandry' was used in the 18th century to denote the
continuous tillage of improved lands under a succession of grains and grasses.

Before Bakewell's time the attention of breeders was confined to race horses, a luxury and a sport. Bakewell devoted himself to farm horses, cattle and sheep, but he was most successful with sheep. In less than half a century his New Leicesters spread to all quarters of Great Britain. As a breeder Bakewell was less successful than some of his immediate followers : such as the brothers Charles and Robert Colling, who at Ketton, near Darlington on the Yorkshire-Durham border, built up from local stock the world-famous Durham shorthorns—' the most profitable beasts for the dairyman, butcher and grazier, with their wide bags, short horns and large bodies.' [1] But the stock which Bakewell raised was less important than the principles on which he acted. He bred for a purpose and selected his stock accordingly. He found that by breeding in and in he could unite the best qualities in the breed which he selected as best for his purpose. What was impious for man, was sound for live-stock. He kept a record of his results, and pedigree farm cattle took their place beside pedigree race horses. The first herd book, ' The Shorthorn,' was compiled in 1822. Thus Bakewell launched breeders on the course which made the names of British breeds of horses, sheep, cattle and pigs household words the world over. British pedigree stock is the basis of the best herds in the New World.

Thomas William Coke of Holkham, Norfolk (1752–1842), 1st Earl of Leicester but only raised to the peerage in 1837, approved the new methods by his practice and patronage, and made them famous throughout Great Britain. The monuments of his work which abide are, first of all, the estate itself—the rich belt of timber encircling Holkham park, the reclaimed marshland between the park walls and sandhills, and the ridges of wooded sandhills which protect the marshland and were literally won from the sea ; and secondly the memorial column in the park, with figures and inscriptions at its four corners : a drilling machine, ' The improvement of Agriculture ' ; a cow, ' Breeding in all its branches ' ; four sheep and a lamb, ' Small in size but great in value '; a plough, ' Live and let live '—the favourite toast at the Holkham festivals and signifying agriculture before politics. The estate changed under Coke's genius from an exposed rye-growing rabbit warren to a land of heavy wheat crops, rich live-stock, and well-planned protective timber, and was the scene of a princely entertainment every year from 1778 to 1821. At the sheep-shearing festivals, as they were called after one feature in the entertainment, Coke and his tenants gave a display of the latest and best technique. One day the party would ride out to see

[1] W. H. R. Curtler, *Short History of English Agriculture*, p. 233. Chillingham Park, Northumberland, has a pure herd of native Wild Cattle.

soil improvements, perhaps a piece of inoculated pasture land
made by transplantation of sod from a distance ; another day
they would witness the trial of a new machine or implement;
on a third day they would inspect live-stock in the yards. Then
there were competitions in which prizes were given for speed in
sheep shearing and for judging the weight of slaughtered animals.
Good bulls and rams were sold. In 1803 Mr. Burrell of Thetford
exhibited an improved drill, which sowed in one operation a
compound of oil cake and turnip seed. In 1804 Mr. Bevan, a
farmer of the district, won a silver cup for the best conversion of
dry land into water meadow. In 1805 Lord Winchelsea guessed
the weight of Coke's prize Leicester wether to within half a pound.
These are examples of what went on for 43 years ; and the
particular value of the festival lay in the fact that the tests were
practical. The visitors saw the things with their own eyes and
went back to adapt the novelties of Norfolk to their own estates
and soil.

Coke had numerous imitators, many of them fellow Whigs,
like the Duke of Bedford at Woburn Sands, Bedfordshire.[1] What
he and they accomplished by practice and display, the Board of
Agriculture, which Pitt established in 1793 with the Scottish
landlord Sir John Sinclair as its first President, worthily supplemented. Arthur Young was its able Secretary. It was dissolved in 1822 during the agricultural depression of that time,
but while it lasted it stimulated greatly by its prizes and publi-
cations the study and use of improved methods. Its County
Reports issued between 1793 and 1795 constitute, in conjunction
with William Marshall's 12-volume *Survey of the Rural Economy
of England* (1787–98), the chief material for the agricultural
history of this period. The Board was a protagonist of enclosure.

The long war of 1793 to 1815 made a heavy call on the
capacity of the land. Coke, it was truly said, saved England
by the ploughshare when the sword would have availed nothing.
But, though profits were high, the pace was unhealthy, and the
farming community sighed for the old days of steady prices and
a small surplus for export.

There were, however, few years between 1815 and 1837 in
which agriculture was not complaining of distress. The number
of cultivating owners went up during the war owing to the

[1] Francis, 5th Duke of Bedford, 1765–1802, started sheep shearings at
Woburn and in 1798 was elected first President of the Smithfield (Cattle) Club.
John, 6th Duke of Bedford, 1766–1839, was also a patron of agriculture. In
1830 under authority of 9 Geo. IV, c. 113 (local) he rebuilt at a cost of £40,000
Covent Garden Market, a town property of the Russell family. For the history
of the gradual conversion of this public open space into a private market see Sir
John Hunt, *Covent Garden Market* (Report to the City of Westminster).

purchase of land by sitting tenants. After 1815 it declined. Those who had bought land at war prices or contracted new leases towards the end of the war were hit the hardest. Many small farmers sank into the ranks of labourers or emigrated. After 1837 the agricultural sky brightened and remained bright despite Corn Law repeal till the 70's. The funds for land development were abundant. For there were no motor cars, Rivieras or winter sports ; and soil improvement was not a losing game.

Between 1815 and 1875, alike in bad and good times, the progress in technique was continuous. Norfolk gave its name to the half-century which ends with 1820. The next fifty years was the age of Lincolnshire and the Scottish Lowlands ; of tenant right in Lincolnshire and long leases in the Lowlands, of drainage and fertilisers in both. And as in the case of Norfolk, so these districts were the starting-points of practice which was followed elsewhere. Of the Fenland it was reported in 1836 : ' About 10 or 12 years ago, the Fen country grew nothing but oats . . . they are now growing wheat equal to that in any part of England.' Lincolnshire heath land, ' until thirty-five years ago a rabbit warren,' was yielding 32–36 bushels per acre as the result of artificial manure.[1]

In 1848 it was stated that within the last twenty years four-fifths of Cheshire had been drained. In the adjoining county, Lancashire, ' undrained land gives 20 bushels per acre, drained often double,' according to a Lancashire surveyor.[2] The pioneer of the new drainage was a Scottish engineer, James Smith, the manager of a cotton mill in Deanston, Perthshire. In the latter part of the 18th century Joseph Elkington, a Warwickshire farmer, had achieved individual success in the drainage of sloping land ; but he was a farmer and in spite of the advertisement which the Board of Agriculture had given to his methods they were not generally adopted. By the 1830's agricultural engineering was greatly advanced, and Scotland, the home of mechanics, was an ideal trial ground. Smith drained his land ' chiefly with broken stones because I have stones upon the land,'[3] and he invented a subsoil plough for deep ploughing after drainage. His practice was widely followed. In many districts the hollow tile was found to be the most suitable kind of drain, and in the 40's machinery was applied to the making of clay tiles. The cost of drainage was great and the landlords met it, recouping themselves by an increase of rent. The Act of 1846 (9 & 10 Vict. c. 101) authorised Treasury advances repayable in instalments

[1] Lords Committee on the State of Agriculture (1836), Qs. 1140, 496.
[2] Commons Committee on Agricultural Customs (1848), Qs. 2916–2932.
[3] Commons Committee on the State of Agriculture (1836), Q. 14883.

and was supplemented by legislation designed to facilitate private drainage loans and the undertaking of drainage operations by authorised Joint-Stock Companies. Substantial amounts were advanced by the Treasury—£2,500,000 by 1855—but the sum found by landlords from their own pockets was considerably greater.

Well-drained land made it profitable for the farmer to manure his land heavily ; and Great Britain with her extensive foreign trade was easily able to import materials from abroad. Peruvian guano, unknown in 1835, was in such general use by the early 50's that the single firm of Messrs. Gibbs sold over £5,000,000 worth between 1852 and 1854.[1] The epoch-making work of the German chemist Liebig [2] revealed the relation between plant nutrition and the composition of the soil. The chemists analysed the manures into their two great groups, the nitrogenous life givers and the non-nitrogenous body builders. Business firms imported or prepared them ; and thus a great modern industry was born.

John Bennett Lawes, a young landowner trained at Oxford, and his colleague, Joseph Henry Gilbert, a pupil of Liebig, communicated Liebig's discoveries to England and made them available for practical agriculture. In 1843 Lawes opened in London a factory for the making of mineral super-phosphates and began on his estate at Rothamsted, Harpenden (Herts), the field experiments which made Rothamsted the prototype of modern experimental stations, the land itself being used in plots as a laboratory for experiment and observation of results over a period of years. Natural science has been busy with the increase of agricultural production for only three-quarters of a century, but already with results so startling that the economic problem is now the pressure of Food on Population, rather than of Population on Food.

Section 5. Burdens on Agriculture

In distress 1815 to 1837, attacked and driven from its fiscal stronghold 1838 to 1846, the agricultural community found Parliament generally disposed to ease the burdens which pressed upon it other than that of meeting foreign competition without the protection of a tariff. The first burden, the unreformed Poor Law, was lightened by the Poor Law Amendment Act of 1834. The old Poor Law had burdened the agriculturist in three ways. It brought a heavy charge in poor rates, it foisted on him

---

[1] Tooke, *History of Prices*, V. 194.
[2] *Chemistry in its Application to Agriculture and Physiology* (1840).

inefficient labour, and as the possession of the smallest quantity of property debarred a man from relief, it hurt the owner of a cottage or scrap of land as well as the large farmer.

The second burden, Tithes, was adjusted in 1837. Since the Reformation the tithe, or ecclesiastical tenth set apart for the support of the clergy of the Church of England, was partly in clerical and partly in lay lands. Its collection was the occasion of fierce quarrels between the clergy and their flocks in the 17th and 18th centuries. Every new crop was the occasion of a dispute ; for the tithe-payer regarded any increase on this account as an unjust tax on improvements. By 1815 the worst of the evils thus arising had been checked. In some cases upon enclosure the tithe-owner had received a portion of land in lieu of tithe ; and in other cases the payment of tithe in kind had been replaced by a ' modus ' or sum of money calculated upon the value of the annual yield. But any payment, whether in money or kind, which rose as yields rose, was an obstacle to improvement ; and therefore in 1837 tithes were commuted into a fixed grain rent. The basis of commutation was the average annual yield of the previous 7 years, which came to £4 millions net. The future yield was made to vary with the 7-year average price of the various grains, different weights being attached to each. In 1918, in consequence of rising war prices, the upward limit to the index number of 100 was fixed at 109, the point which it had then reached ; and further facilities were given for redemption.[1]

The third burden was the Game Laws. These laws were framed and interpreted in the interests of the land-owners. Poaching was savagely repressed, but the farmer whose crops were damaged by the depredations of his landlord's game had no legal redress. By championing this grievance John Bright won the farmers to his cause in the last days of the Anti-Corn Law campaign. The evidence before the Committee of 1846 over which Bright presided showed that while some landlords kept their game under control, others indulged in their fondness for sport at the expense of agriculture.

'Some years,' said Lord Hatherton, 'after I had been a game preserver I became also an extensive improver of land. . . . I found the two occupations of a rigid preserver of hares and game generally and an improver of land by planting and farming perfectly incompatible. . . . I know that nothing is more common than for large landed pro-

---

[1] The 1918 Tithe Act fixed tithe for the period 1918–1926. The 1925 Tithe Act (15 & 16 Geo. V, c. 87) separated ecclesiastical and lay tithe : vested the former in Queen Anne's Bounty and provided for its extinguishment in 85 years (81½ years in the case of ecclesiastical corporations) by an annual payment of £109 10s. per £100 tithe ; and fixed lay tithe at 105.

prietors who are extensive game preservers to say " My tenants are a capital set of fellows, their fields are covered with,game, they never make the slightest complaint,"—but I have known those same tenants give a very different account of their feelings to others, and there can be no doubt that there is a general repugnance on the part of the tenantry of the country to have their farms largely covered by hares.'[1]

The inquiry brought no immediate legislation, but the farmer's position was improved by the publicity given to the grievance, and in 1880 his right to destroy ground game on the farm was given by the Act of 43 & 44 Vict. c. 47.

The fourth burden was exceptional taxation. In Pitt's time the townsman's income tax was regarded as a set-off to the farmer's war duty on malt. When the income tax was abolished in 1816, the war duty on malt was only reduced. Therefore agriculturists complained with reason that as a class they were over-taxed. But the amendment of the Poor Law in 1834 and the reimposition of income tax in 1842 took the point out of the complaint ; and when this ancient grievance was examined by the Commons Committee on Burdens on Real Property (1846) the issue was shifted from agricultural burdens to a technical point in the law of property, namely the comparative contribution of realty and personalty to local and central taxation. The Committee of 1846 also examined the excessive cost of land transfer and the heavy charges for small mortgages caused by the absence of land registration and organised mortgage credit, but as the majority of farmers were tenants the issue was not a lively one.

The fifth burden was the legal shackles on the development of the great estate. As the country became industrialised, the strict family settlements devised by 17th-century lawyers gravely handicapped the life tenant. For it sometimes happened that he could not grant leases for terms sufficiently long to permit of building or mineral development. The agricultural depression of 1875 prompted the Settled Lands Acts of 1882 to 1890, which removed these handicaps and constitute a good example of the modification of a strongly established rule of law under the influence of new economic conditions.[2]

Section 6. *Foreign Competition and the Long Depression*

In 1875 agricultural depression began to be felt and persisted till the end of the century. It was at its worst around 1880 and in the early 90's, and was the occasion of two Royal Commissions

[1] Commons Committee on Game Laws (1846), Qs. 7265–7275.
[2] Cf. *Economic History Review*, Jan. 1927, W. S. Holdsworth, ' Economic and Legal History,' p. 122.

of Inquiry. 1879 was a terrible year, when heavy rains ruined the home crops and prices nevertheless fell. The cause,[1] not fully realised at first, was the competition of the New World, and therefore the decline was prolonged. In 1875 the estimated capital value of agricultural land in the United Kingdom was £2000 millions, in 1894 £1000 millions. The grain-growing counties of the East and South-East were hit very hard : the heavy clay lands of Essex the hardest of all.

Between 1880 and 1884 the number of farms given up either in despair or for reasons over which the occupiers had no control was stated to have been enormous. On poor estates no attempt was made to bring the land round, it was left alone and gradually 'tumbled down' to such coarse and inferior herbage as nature produced. . . . A regular panic set in ; some tenants who had hitherto weathered the storm refused to renew their leases upon any terms, while others continued from year to year at large reductions. . . . Rents were reduced between 1880 and 1886 from 25 to as much as 80%. [2]

And the next thirty years, 1875–1905, were a lean time for the revenues of Cambridge University. Lucky finds of coprolites (fossil excrement) on college lands were therefore highly welcome. Between 1878 and 1895 the gross rental of the Holkham estate declined from £52,000 to £27,000 : the net rental from £30,000 to £15,000. Specialists raising pedigree stock for export, dairy farmers supplying milk to the towns, and small farmers raising potatoes and market-garden produce came out best. In Essex many farms passed into the hands of Scotsmen, who made ends meet by paring the labour bill and laying down arable to grass. In the Midlands and West, where much of the land was convertible to good pasture, the arable area was severely curtailed. In 1867 the proportion of arable to grass in the United Kingdom was 23 million acres arable to 22 grass, total 45 : in 1907, 19 arable to 27 grass, total 46 (the latter date including an extra million acres obtained in the interval by reclamations). Of the acreage with-

----

[1] I follow sections 21 to 23 of Marshall's *Fiscal Policy of International Trade* 1908 (*Official Papers*, pp. 380–2) : in opposition to the Report of the Committee on Stabilisation of Agricultural Prices 1925 (pp. 1–13). In evidence before the Gold and Silver Commission of 1887 Marshall warned against the danger of applying hastily 'the method of concomitant variations '—' It so happens that free trade came in with the new supplies of gold, and in my opinion the attention which is now given to currency questions is due chiefly to this, that the effects which are caused by the introduction of free trade have been ascribed to the gold mines ' (Q. 9702, *ibid.* p. 58). None will dispute that the violent price declines after the Napoleonic War and the late war were specially injurious to agriculture ; but I hold with Marshall that between 1820 and 1914 the price movements which are traceable to monetary causes were of secondary importance in the determination of agricultural conditions. (For one big cause of high corn prices 1846–75, see above, p. 68.)

[2] *Royal Commission on Agricultural Depression, 1895, Final Report,* p. 8.

drawn from the plough about one-half was in wheat. Even before the depression the receipts from cereals were a minority of the receipts from all land under the plough. After the depression the proportion declined still further. In this way depression was met, though not dispelled. However between 1900 and 1914 there was a slight rise in the price of wheat and a moderate but steady recovery in farming generally. Increased attention was paid to agricultural education and research. Then came the war, the short post-war boom, and the longer post-war depression.

Section 7. The Contrast between British and American Agriculture

Great Britain is an island, America the main and central part of a continent.[1] British agriculture has progressed by intensive methods, American by extension into new areas in which settlement was always ahead of the full use of the older parts. In Britain capital and labour were abundant relatively to land, in America they were scarce ; and therefore in Britain the purpose of farming was maximum yield per acre, while in America it was maximum yield per man or per machine. The American prairies were settled by men who could not afford much hired labour and expensive machinery even less. The settler was so short of capital that he had to pay for his machinery in instalments, as also for his land when he did not get it free. But the British farmer with the landlord at his back could afford both capital and machinery. Even on the basis of cultivated acreage the representative unit of agricultural enterprise is as large in the small island of intensive farming as in the great continent of extensive farming. In the American South, when slave labour was available, the position was different. Labour was docile and cheap, and large plantations were profitable.

The agrarian legislation of Britain falls into two groups, the Enclosure Acts and the Corn Laws. The Enclosure Acts excited a storm for two reasons. They involved disturbance and were therefore offensive to conservatism : and they involved dispossession without the possibility of moving to vacant land elsewhere. They excited less animosity in Scotland because

[1] Great Britain (1926) : Total area under crops and grass , . 30·3 Million acres

	Million acres
Arable land . .	13·7
Permanent grass .	16·6

U.S.A. (1925 Census) : Total area of farms . . . . 924·8

	Million acres
Cropland . .	391·4
Land in pasture .	408·5
Woodland . .	67·6
All other . .	57·2

Scotland was sparsely settled, but in England they broke into the long-established life of fully occupied rural regions. The New England colonists took with them the open field system, and on it built the free community which was so infinitely more valuable to the future of America than the immediately more profitable slave plantation. But there was no landlord and each man cultivated his own portion. The early villagers protected themselves by common effort against enemies without; they could not afford the expense of enclosing each separate allotment. When these conditions passed away, the open field died with them silently. Enclosure hurt nobody because everybody could move to land elsewhere.

The American counterpart of enclosure is the disposal of the public domain. Land laws, always inclining in favour of the small man—especially the squatter, whose presence was such an abomination to the enclosing lawyers of 18th-century Britain—culminated in the great Homestead Act of 1862, under which settlers could acquire farms of 160 acres on the public lands free of charge provided that they lived five years on the homestead. It was a solution which fitted a democracy on a continent. But the prairies were not settled without violent dispossession, for the native Indians stood in the way. Seeing their hunting-grounds slashed by the railways, and their livelihood—the buffalo—destroyed by the white man's rifle, they broke into savage violence and in the ten ruthless years of 1865 to 1875 they were overwhelmed themselves. The Canadian West, being settled later and possessing in advance of settlement a magnificent mounted police, secured order and progress without recourse to extirpation.

When Britain became an importer of wheat, the interest of her farmers shifted from export bounties to protective duties. This protection they lost with the triumph of industrialism in 1846. From 1783 to 1860 the American South had an indirect interest in free trade. Selling nearly the whole of their cotton crop to Great Britain, they stood to gain a greater real price if there were low duties on the manufactures which they imported in return. The Western farmers had less concern in this. They had a growing home market, in the South among the cotton states by way of the Mississippi and in the East among the new manufacturing population. Their interest in the tariff has only been active since 1900. Now they demand protection against the cheaper products of Canada. They were partially appeased by the Fordney Tariff of 1922, but as this did not cure depression they have proposed a more drastic offset to the manufacturers' protective tariff, viz. a reserved home market and the disposal of their surplus abroad in such a way as not to depress the home price. The consumer, it seems, is not consulted. In England the repeal of the Corn Laws was carried by the alliance of industrial producers with wage-earning consumers.

Great Britain became a country of tenant farmers because the ownership of land was an attractive investment for individuals and corporate bodies. It remained a country of tenancy because on the whole the owners did their duty as landlords exceedingly well. Property has the same magic for an Englishman as for a Frenchman or Irishman, but property and undisturbed possession are very nearly the same thing. The desire of the rich to own land and lead the agricultural life forced land values above the ordinary : therefore farmers gained by renting land and reserving their capital for farming operations : and therefore what they sought when depression descended on them in the 1870's was not land purchase but additional security of tenure. It is estimated that in the 1820's 15% to 20% of cultivated England and Wales was worked by its owners ; in 1910 about 10% ; in 1925 perhaps 25%.[1] The increase is the result of purchases made immediately after the war, in some cases to avoid the loss of the farm.

Since 1880 tenancy has been on the increase in America. In that year 74·5% of the farm land was occupied by owners ; in 1910 only 62·1%. The reasons for this are various—the letting of land on a share or money rent to white or coloured persons in the dispersed plantations of the South ; the necessity of men without capital passing through a period of renting before ownership, as soon as free land disappeared ; the strong cityward drift, which puts farms on the rental market when they cannot be sold to advantage. The purpose of recent legislation, such as the Federal Farm Loan (Land Mortgage) Act of 1917 and the Agricultural (Intermediate) Credits Act of 1923, is not to stabilise tenancy but to arrest its growth by lightening the cost of land-owning and rescuing the cropper-tenant of the South from bondage to the middle-man.

British agricultural improvement began with the study and adaptation of continental methods—the Flemish lease, the Dutch turnip, the French vineyard. Very soon Great Britain was learning for herself in every field and teaching to the world the new art of stock-breeding. Such an art was particularly congenial to Englishmen. Their sports centred around animals : horse racing, fox hunting, cock fighting. Country gentlemen having lost the excitement of civil war found an outlet for their

---

[1] Cf., for necessary caution here, *The Agricultural Output of England and Wales*, 1925, Cmd. 2815, pp. 95–6.

energies in field sport and prize farming. Contrast with this the position of the American farmer. He obtained from England his grasses and first live-stock. The potato, though a native of South America, reached North America through Irish immigrants about the year 1718. In general, New World agriculture was backward and, as it seemed to visitors, slovenly. For the American farmer was a pioneer and land winning was more important than good husbandry. He had to be a ' Jack of all trades ' and, when he crossed the Alleghanies, practically self-sufficient. Under such conditions high farming had no chance. Emigrants who brought over the new knowledge could not use it. The native Indian corn, i.e. maize, suited America better than the turnip. It yielded food for both man and beast : eaten it was a second bread, distilled it was a strong drink. Every part of it was excellent for the feeding of cattle and hogs. Though not drilled, it was sufficiently spaced to be cultivated as it grew and was therefore a good cleaning crop. In short, it was a ' Jack of all crops.'

Better cultivation was the purpose behind the new implements used by the 18th-century improvers. As metal was abundant in England and wood relatively scarce, the transfer to iron and steel was made quickly. By 1820 the plough and the harrow were all-iron. The threshing machine, worked by animal or water power, was invented by Andrew Meikle, a Scottish millwright, in 1784. It was a labour-saver as well as a better performer ; but it spread very slowly to the wheat-growing counties of England, where it did not come into general use till about 1830. The large farms of Northumberland and the Scottish Lothians employed steam engines for driving the threshing machine as early as the 1820's, but it was not until about 1850 that the portable steam engine, owned by individual farmers, or a travelling threshing concern, became common on the farm. Messrs. Clayton and Shuttleworth of Lincoln began to supply portable engines in the 40's, and between 1852 and 1855 sold 1390.[1]

In America wheat was still sown by hand in 1840, but the threshing machine was in general use. It had been introduced from Scotland about 1800, and the only obstacle to its use was that the labourers through ignorance spoilt it. When the threshing machine was not available it was customary to tread out the grain by horses. But the threshing machine was not so necessary as a reliable machine which would enable one man and a team to cut, rake and bind in one operation. Here America led Britain. In 1847 Cyrus McCormick moved from the East to Chicago.

[1] Cf. Tooke, *History of Prices*, V. 193.

By 1850 some 3500 reapers were at work on the prairies. The labour shortage in the Civil War gave a great fillip to their use. In the 70's they were made self-binding : first by wire and then by binder-twine. In 1900 McCormick was making about one-third of the binders in the world, but he had keen rivals in America and Canada, and the outcome of their competition was the International Harvester Company of 1902.

In Great Britain even without good inland communications much produce could move readily to market either coastwise or, in the case of cattle, on foot. By 1870 the drover had been replaced by the railway, but there was no reorganisation in the structure of the domestic meat trade. It remained a retail operation, intensified. In America water transportation and railroads revolutionised the meat trade. In 1815 cattle came on foot from the back regions to Boston, Philadelphia and New York, just as they did to London, but between 1815 and 1850 the Mississippi and Ohio Rivers and the Erie Canal supplied a route along which salted pork and lard could be conveyed to distant points. The American meat trade then became whole-sale. Strategic points on inland waters—St. Louis, Cincinnati, Louisville—grew into packing centres. After 1850 the railways challenged the water routes ; and the railroad centres, led by Chicago, erected specialised terminal facilities with which the numerous smaller river ports could not compete. In the 70's the packing houses introduced ice-cooled freight cars, first for meat and then for fruit. In Great Britain refrigeration came from without : being applied first to the shipment of frozen meat from the Antipodes and then to cold-storage plants at the ports of arrival. Meat importers are the packing interest of Great Britain and the steamship companies carry for them.

In British history the friction between landlord and tenant farmer was always less important than that between landlord or farmer and the agricultural labourer. The years of living strife were those in which the labourer came out to assert his rights : in 1830 and in 1874. In 1830 the labourers of the south destroyed cornstacks and threshing machines. Their enemies were their masters and the allies of these, the Government and tithe-owning parsons. In 1874 under the leadership of Joseph Arch they fought a lockout ; but their weapons, the strike and emigra-tion, were double-edged, and the only districts which secured a permanently better wage were those adjacent to industrial areas. The trade unionist of the towns lifted his agricultural brother after him slowly. To this there is no parallel in American history ; for the hired man could always take a farm. In the 70's the American farmers organised themselves into Granges to secure laws which would curb the railroads : next they tried conclusions with the elevator companies and the speculators in the wheat pit. They usually lost, but out of many disappointments, followed in one state—North Dakota—by an orgy of agrarian socialism after the late war, a co-operative movement has arisen which points with pride and hope to the achievements of the Canadian wheat pools and the Californian fruit growers. In Great Britain, as in old Ontario, co-operative marketing has met with greater obstacles. British agriculture on its marketing side is suburban.

CHAPTER XIII

Steam Power and the Engineers

Section 1. Boulton and Watt.   Section 2. Rise of the Machine Tool Industry. Section 3. Coal and the Mining of Tin and Coal.

Section 1. *Boulton and Watt*

JAMES WATT (1736–1819) patented his steam engine in 1769, and the other landmarks in the forty-five years of his working life (1755–1800) can be conveniently remembered by the fives.

1755. In this year Watt went from Glasgow to London to learn his trade of mathematical instrument making, and there abode one year. Having no legal status (for he was a foreigner and too old and did not mean to stay seven years), he was lucky to escape impressment for the Seven Years War. Adam Smith had gone up to Oxford fifteen years earlier and, staying longer in England, was taught less. The two were together in Glasgow from 1756 to 1763, Adam Smith as Professor of Moral Philosophy, and Watt in a workshop adjoining the Department of Natural Philosophy. In 1763 Adam Smith started on the Grand Tour and Watt took a home in the town.

1765. In this year, which was also about the time that Adam Smith began to work on his book, Watt invented the steam engine. They had given him the model of a Newcomen engine to put in working order. On a certain Sunday early in 1765 the crucial idea of a separate condenser flashed upon him. By this he saved heat, and went on to save more by closing the cylinder at the top (so that steam worked on either side of the piston instead of the air above and steam only below) and by enclosing the cylinder itself in a casing packed with steam. ' Thus all Watt's improvements were economical of heat. Economy in heat meant economy in steam, and economy in steam meant economy in working costs, and, above all, in coal.' [1]

1775. In this year he entered into partnership with Matthew Boulton (1728–1809), a hardware manufacturer of Birmingham. He had kept himself going during 1770 and 1771 by following in the footsteps of Brindley, engineering the Monkland Canal which connected Glasgow with the collieries there. He had formed a partnership in 1769 with Dr. Roebuck of Carron, but in 1773 the doctor failed. Boulton, a creditor of the two, then proposed to Watt to take over the patent in satisfaction of his claims and to form the partnership of Boulton and Watt for working it. Accordingly in 1774 Watt came to Soho with his engine Beelzebub, and before the end of 1775 two engines had been delivered from Soho, one to Bloomfield colliery near Birmingham, and one to John Wilkinson at Broseley. The trouble in Scotland was the lack of trained mechanics at that time. For when Watt left the model for the real, he left the clockmaker for the local black-smith. Soho met the need, building on its hardware past. ' We are systematising the business of engine making,' wrote Boulton to Smeaton in 1778, ' as we have done before in the button manufactory ; we are training up workmen and making tools and machines to form the different parts of Mr. Watt's engines with more accuracy, and at a cheaper rate than can possibly be done by the ordinary methods of working.' [2] The installation of the engine was the final labour difficulty. Millwrights were clumsy and they drank. But in 1777 Providence sent to Soho William Murdoch, a big brawny Scot, as loyal as a dog, the genius of fitting tingling at his finger tips, good natured too with the men, and therefore an ideal foreman. It was he who later invented gas lighting, which he installed in Soho in 1803.

1785. In this year the steam engine was first used to drive a cotton mill. It was the unsought crown of five years' effort. First in 1781 came the rotative motion, which Watt patented in the form of a Sun and Planet motion, of his foreman Murdoch's contrivance. Watt substituted this for the simpler crank motion because a rival had stolen the latter from him. Next came the ' double-acting engine,' with a drive to the piston both upwards and downwards. Watt saw his way to this almost from the first, and its presence is assumed in the description under the year 1765 ; but as he knew that such a machine was beyond the intelligence of the average engineer, he did not employ it in the first engines supplied from Soho and he only introduced it in his patented designs in 1782. It was especially suited to rotative

[1] J. Lord, *Capital and Steam Power*, pp. 75–6.
[2] T. H. Marshall, *James Watt*, pp. 123–4.

engines, since its double stroke upwards and downwards solved the problem of continuous motion. Finally, in 1784 he patented the parallel motion. The double-acting engine had to pull as well as push, but the piston-rod moved vertically and the beam attached to it in a curve. How was he to get a rigid communication which would not pull the piston out of the straight ? He solved this by a parallelogram of jointed rods connecting the under side of the beam with the piston rod—hence the name, parallel motion.

The progress of the steam engine was accompanied by progress no less important in the iron industry which supplied the parts. The cylinder was not true as long as it was bored by hand, therefore either it leaked or the piston jammed. John Wilkinson invented a way of boring cylinders which remedied this defect and thereby made the steam engine a commercial possibility. In the first two engines made, one of them for Wilkinson himself, the small parts were made at Soho, the large by Wilkinson ; and Watt superintended the erection of the engine. This was the arrangement followed later in engines supplied from Soho to third parties. Boulton and Watt had a contract with Wilkinson for the work. Furthermore, just at this time, 1780–85, the finishing of iron was revolutionised by Cort and others. Thus was ushered in what may be termed the second stage of the industrial revolution. Isolated progress in the textile, pottery and iron and steel trades now converged on Soho and made Boulton the leader of the new industrialists.

In 1755 Watt went to London to learn instrument making. Three trades supplied the personnel of the new engineering business—clockmakers, with whom instrument makers were associated; the millwrights, who installed and repaired machinery, working generally with wood as their material and water as their power ; and the military engineers now broadening into builders of drainage works and canals. Brindley, the father of canal building, was a millwright, Arkwright was helped in his spinning inventions by a clockmaker of Warrington. From the clockmakers were bred the machine tool makers : to the millwrights succeeded the engine minders and engineering mechanics : from the military engineers of the Continent were descended the civil engineers of England. Among mathematical instruments the most important economically were naval instruments ; for this was the great half-century of British expansion overseas. Her sailors were everywhere, and one of them, Captain Cook, was on the point of discovering a new Continent. Therefore in Glasgow, with its growing trade and shipbuilding industry, such instruments were in brisk demand, and in this vital environment Watt spent his early life. The need of capital took him inland to Birmingham, and technical difficulties denied the high seas to the steam engine until the 30's of the 19th century, but the baby was nursed by Symington in Glasgow a few years before Watt died.

In 1765 Watt invented the steam engine. An invention may be measured either by the gap which it creates between itself and the anticipations of it or by the difference which it makes to economic society ; by either criterion the steam engine is the greatest mechanical invention in human history. Nevertheless, the steam engine too illustrates the law that invention in the last analysis is a social product. There were reasons why it came in the 1760's from the brain of a Scotsman for the service of mines. Science was in the air and had been from the time the Royal Society was founded in 1662. Before 1700 Isaac Newton had elucidated the laws of gravitation and light and Richard Boyle had demonstrated the relation between the pressure of a gas and its volume. Watt was a scientific discoverer as well as a mechanical genius ; and his intellectual stature was equal to that of his colleagues in the Royal Society, to which he was elected in 1785. He associated on level terms with Priestley and Cavendish, who was revolutionising chemistry, and with his Glasgow friend and adviser Professor Joseph Black, the discoverer of the phenomenon of latent heat, which amounts to this. When water is boiling, however much you go on heating it, it will get no hotter : the steam receives the heat and holds it in store. This discovery was central to a powerful steam engine ; and being a master of theory as well as of technique, Watt saw the possibilities of high-pressure steam, although recognising that it was as yet not feasible for technical and economical reasons. Symington and Stephenson by contrast were practical inventors. They adapted to a new use the body of new knowledge crystallised by Watt.

Fire engines had been in action for more than half a century. Thomas Savery, a clockmaker and military engineer of Devonshire, patented an engine in 1698. Thomas Newcomen, a Dartmouth blacksmith, made a successful model engine in 1705 and installed his first working one in Wolverhampton in 1712. Both these inventions utilised the new knowledge relating to the barometer and atmospheric pressure which had reached England from Europe at the end of the 17th century. But neither invented a genuine steam engine. Savery depended solely on air pressure for his lift, which was 34 feet as a theoretical maximum and actually only 15. To pump out a mine by means of such an engine would have necessitated installing them at different levels and pumping the water from level to level. It was thus hardly more than a garden toy. The true line of advance was taken by Newcomen, who in effect mechanised the action of a man working the handle of a pump. The piston which moves up and down in the cylinder was connected by a beam (the pump handle of nature) to work a pump rod. Steam forced the piston up and air pressure forced it down. This allowed of a surface engine and thus of a lift far more than 34 feet, because the area of the steam cylinder could be made much larger than that of the cylinder containing the pump rod. In Newcomen's, as in Savery's, engine steam was used to produce the upward stroke of the piston only. The air when the steam was reduced by condensation into water drove the piston down into the vacuum thus created. Now Watt saw that a cylinder must lose so much heat if a jet of cold water was squirted into it, that some of the next lot of steam would be condensed also. Therefore he added a separate condenser (the revelation of his Sunday walk past the golf house), closed the top of the cylinder and admitted steam alternately above and below the piston. This made the engine a real steam engine. The 'work,' of course, came from the burning of the coal, as in Newcomen's engine, but now the engine did twice as much work in the same time, since two lots of steam instead of one, one below and one above, were used in each stroke of the engine.

In 1775 Boulton and Watt began to manufacture. Boulton brought to his partner Watt not only a skilled labour force, but capital and administrative talent of the highest order. The two seemed made for one another. Three episodes in the partnership will serve in illustration :

1. Before they began Boulton saw that the first thing was to be sure of the patent, which in 1775 was six years old. For Boulton's age was one which resented patents of monopoly. He therefore went to Parliament, and after a fight secured an Act declaring that the sole privilege of making and selling steam engines in Great Britain and her Colonies should be vested in James Watt and his executors for a term of 25 years. This was an improvement on the normal 14 years from the date of patenting.

2. From 1775 to 1785 the biggest customers of Soho were the Cornish tin mines. But their urgency—deep mines suffering from flood—was also their weakness. For they could not pay cash ; and besides there was no precedent for pricing power, the commodity which Boulton had for sale. Boulton therefore devised an experimental system, which in its final form was as follows. The engines were built and erected at the expense of the purchasers, who further undertook to pay annually a sum

equal to one-third of the value of the fuel saved by the engine as compared with a common engine. (The Newcomen engine was well known in Cornwall.) Watt devised a meter, which was kept under lock and key and told him faithfully what the saving was. The arrangement was the cause of much friction, especially later when the memory of the old engines receded and customers were supplied who could have purchased outright.

3. During the financial uncertainties of 1787–9, when London firms were falling fast, even the solid Boulton was involved. Watt's conduct was bad. There had been a foretaste ten years before when Fothergill made a mess of the hardware business and Boulton to the indignation of Watt saved himself by borrowing against the profits of the engine business. In 1787 Watt, already weakened by the strain of invention and commercial worries which he hated but would not leave alone, refused assistance to his partner, and Boulton with difficulty weathered the storm. But he never quarrelled with Watt and the partnership survived to enjoy henceforth prosperity and peace, with nothing more disturbing than an occasional prosecution of pirates.

In 1785 the first engine was supplied to a cotton factory, namely at Papplewick in Nottingham. Hitherto the engine had been confined to pumping mines of tin, copper or coal, tin easily leading, to blowing iron works and pumping water works. Now its range was extended to driving machinery. The first rotative engine was supplied to the Albion Corn Mill of London to the design of the engineer Rennie, and put in action May 1786, but the mill was burned by incendiaries in 1791. By December 31, 1785, there were two in Nottinghamshire cotton mills. By December 31, 1795, there were 47 in cotton mills, the majority in Lancashire, as well as 11 in breweries. By 1800 there were also 9 in woollen mills and several more in other textile mills, but the horse power in the Lancashire cotton mills was much ahead of that in all uses in any other county. Out of 325 produced by Soho between 1795 and 1800, 114 went into the textile industries and 92 into cotton mills. After 1800 the extension of steam power was a matter of comparative cost in competition with water and the adaptation of the productive process to power, whether water or steam. But locomotion offered a new field. In a patent of 1784 Watt had included the specification of an engine to drive a wheel carriage, for the ungracious purpose of blocking the plans of others. He regarded the marine engine made for Symington at Carron as a piracy, but so defective as not to be worth prosecuting. However, in 1807 Soho supplied the engine with which Fulton captured the Hudson River for steam power ; and such were the length and breadth of the

American rivers and lakes that by the middle of the century the steamship tonnage of the U.S.A. was greater than that of Great Britain.

Section 2.   Rise of the Machine Tool Industry

The period 1800–1850 is fundamental to the history of engineering.   1800 serves as a starting point because in that year Boulton and Watt's monopoly came to an end, and 1850 is a finishing point because by that time there had grown to maturity a new industry of machine making by the aid of tools which were themselves machines.   The labour reaction to this growth was the formation in 1851 of the Amalgamated Society of Engineers, replacing the hitherto separate and local societies of smiths, millwrights, pattern makers, steam engine makers, and machinists. It was a centralised society with its headquarters at London, as the situation demanded ; for London was the home of machine making, and the new industry overrode all divisions of handicraft.   London at the beginning of this period was by far the largest centre of skilled population in the country.   Here working under small masters were the best metal workers in the country, goldsmiths, silversmiths, printers, pattern makers, clock and watch makers and makers of scientific instruments.   Labour flowed from the provinces to London because wages there were higher and employment more regular.   Under the leadership of a brilliant group of master engineers, Joseph Bramah, John Martineau, Alexander Galloway and greatest of all Henry Maudslay,[1] London became a nursery of skilled engineers with a general all-round knowledge of engineering, which was not the negation, but the acme, of specialisation to engineering.   The worker from the North might understand spinning machinery from A to Z, but like the old-fashioned worker in a precious metal he knew spinning machinery only.   London turned him into a skilled man by putting him through the general work that constitutes the core of engineering ;   and that general work was provided by the machine tool industry.   The shops were small by comparison with modern standards, having in them one to two hundred workers and less. Practically every worker was a skilled man or on his way to becoming one.   It was these shops which turned out the machinery that made the manufacture of machine parts and of other

[1] The marble bust of Henry Maudslay by Chantrey was left by his grandson, W. H. Maudslay, to the Science Museum, Kensington.   The plate was to have read : ' He invented and made the original lathe with slide rest and in 1800 the screw-cutting lathe—thereby originating the universal thread in screws.   These applied form the groundwork of all mechanical tools and are the parent machines of all mechanical accuracy ' (Times, Dec. 6, 1927).   But owing to legal difficulties the bequest was disclaimed in 1928.

machines a task for common labour. As Galloway said when protesting against the embargo on the export of machinery, ' I can
send a screwing machine into France by which I can make any
French ploughman in a week use and make any quantity of
screws ; but if an English labourer was to generate these screws
here by the same machine, they would not be allowed to be exported.' [1] It was these shops which made for other industries the
exact standardised work that enabled those industries to produce
in mass by power. But power in the engineering shop itself was
comparatively unimportant. The hostility of an old-established
craft like the millwright's is easy to understand, but the skilled
engineer himself was often nervous of the ways which his industry
followed, for he was always taking part in the making of machines
which might one day oust himself, the engineer. Within any given
field of production the consummation of engineering is to shut the
door on manual skill ; and the relentless recoil of the machine on
the hand that makes it is the cause which underlies the diminishing
influence of the engineering trades in the counsels of Trade
Unionism in recent years.

The evolution of machine tool making may be traced through
three generations : Joseph Bramah, 1748–1814, in the first, which
was the generation also of Boulton and Watt ; Henry Maudslay,
1771–1831, in the second ; and James Nasmyth, 1808–1890, and
Joseph Whitworth, 1803–1887, in the third. Bramah trained
Maudslay, and Maudslay, Nasmyth. Bramah and Maudslay
had their shops in London. Whitworth and Nasmyth set up as
machine tool makers in Manchester in 1833 and 1834 respectively,
so that Manchester henceforth was mechanically self-supporting.

A machine tool is a tool operated mechanically in the machine
of which it is a part : for example, the engine lathe in which the
cutting tool has an automatic feed. Other examples are the
mechanical plane, the mechanical slotter, the mechanical drill.
The characteristic of all is that they reduce to precision the
variable action of the human hand and eye. Boulton and Watt
had scarcely any machine tools. All that Boulton could do was
to provide his staff with improved hand tools. Bramah took the
first important step, making machine tools to assist him in the
manufacture of patent locks. Like the elder Brunel he was a
versatile genius, and besides inventing a lock he applied the
principle of the forcing pump to the invention of the hydraulic
press, the publican's pull-over tap, and the water-closet. Safes,
cotton presses, drink, and sanitation : what an exquisite quartet
of gifts to the new 19th century ! Maudslay, his pupil, round
about 1800 made the lathe self-acting. Instead of the worker

[1] Committee on Artisans and Machinery, 1824, Evidence, p. 15.

K

holding the tool against the work, the tool was fixed in a rest and adjusted to the work by delicate screws.   This allowed him to devise a measuring machine, his Lord Chancellor, which measured easily up to a thousandth part of an inch and in its turn led to finer work on the lathe.   These and other machine tools came into common use in the 1820's ;   and Nasmyth, reviewing Maudslay's generation, considered their contribution as important as the steam engine itself.   For, as he said, ' how could we have good steam engines, if we had no means of boring a true cylinder or of turning a true piston rod, or of planing a valve face ? ' Whitworth introduced further precision by working out a series of standard sizes for screws and other machine parts.   Thus came the interchangeable part.   And the standardisation which Whitworth adopted for himself became later the basis of a general standardisation for Great Britain.   An incident in the life of Bessemer, the steel inventor, epitomises the change. Desiring to keep his bronze powder process an absolute secret he gave out the work for the machinery in pieces, ' some in Manchester, some in Glasgow, some in Liverpool, and some in London, so that no engineer could ever guess what these parts of machines were intended to be used for.' [1]   The parts, when assembled by him, fitted and functioned.   This was about 1840. It would have been unthinkable in 1800.   The net result of all these changes was to ensure that any increase in demand by machine users could be met by machine makers.   The London engineers in 1825 urged that they could already.   In words full of significance for the historian of economic theory they affirmed that

men and boys in almost any number may be readily instructed in the making of Machines, and that the great improvement of the Tools used for making machines and for the abridgement of labour in many important parts of the country (which enables them to employ common labourers, who may rapidly become skilled workmen) furnished reasons for believing that the price of machinery is much more likely to be reduced, and that in a short time, than increased by any considerable extension of the business of machine making.[2]

Here is the historical door to the distinction between long and short period normal supply price.   In 1841, when the prohibition of export was again under the notice of Parliament, the position was beyond doubt.   ' Tools have introduced a revolution in machinery and tool making has become a distinct branch of

[1] H. Bessemer, *Autobiography*, 61.
[2] Commons Committee on Export of Tools and Machinery, 1825, *Report*, p. 11.

mechanics and a very important trade, although twenty years
ago it was scarcely known.' [1]

The development of the machine tool industry was accompanied by specialised machine making for the service of particular
trades. So scarce at first was the new textile machinery that
mill owners had to make their machinery before they could begin
to manufacture. Machine making was a normal avenue to mill
owning. But by 1841 not only were some manufacturers making
their own machinery, but also many firms in the textile districts
made nothing but textile machinery; and the pure machine
making firms were dividing up the field by specialisation. ' Of
late years,' said a mule maker, ' the system of classifying the
making of machinery has gone on to a very great extent with us ;
one machine maker often makes one kind his particular study
and another another.' [2] A certain Mexican contract was lost
through the embargo on exports. If England had got it, ' it
would have been sub-divided ; one would have taken the mill
gearing perhaps, and another another kind of machinery.' [3]

It is not easy to say who is an engineer. The driver of a train
is called an engineer in America, a boiler-maker is next door to
an engine builder. But three classes were distinguished in 1841
as engineers proper, namely, (1) makers of heavy machinery—
steam engines, mill gearing, hydraulic presses ; (2) tool makers ;
(3) textile machine makers. In addition engineers were in demand by the shipbuilders for the construction of marine engines
and in railway works for the construction of locomotives. Every
contractor had his engineering staff, every mill its mechanics for
the supervision and repairing of machinery, every mine its
engine-wrights, and the number of Englishmen and Scotsmen on
foreign jobs abroad ran into thousands. ' I was on board twenty
different boats on the Saone, the Rhone, and the Mediterranean,
and I never found one Frenchman as a manager. The stoker was
a Frenchman, but the engineer was invariably an Englishman
taking very high wages, sometimes as much as £1 a day.' [4] So
said an engineer in 1841, who had lived sixteen years in Belgium.

This great and varied class of workmen, well trained, decently
paid, with opportunities at home and abroad of rising to the ranks
of management—the engineer in all his forms—has been neglected
by economic historians. The reason is simple. The personnel
was scattered and as a class it was never the object of those
searching Committees and Commissions of Inquiry in which we
find the clearest statement of contemporary working conditions.
We know most of those who fared worst.

[1] Commons Committee, Exportation of Machinery, 1841, *Second Report*, p. 4.
[2] *Ibid.*, Evidence, Q. 1338.   [3] *Ibid.*, Q. 1396.   [4] *Ibid.*, Q. 556.

Section 3.　Coal and the Mining of Tin and Coal

For various reasons, some of which have been set forth already, Great Britain was the mother country of industrialism. First, she had internal peace and was victorious in the great Napoleonic wars. Secondly, she had a rich Colonial Empire, which served her as a source of raw materials and outlet for finished goods. Thirdly, she had strong institutions of banking, insurance, and stock exchange. Fourthly, she had intelligent workpeople ready for the industrial call, and these were mainly native. Fifthly, and above all, she had one thing further—the coal by which metals could be cheaply worked and power cheaply generated. On the material side coal was the efficient cause of the industrial revolution.

Mediaeval England derived its fuel cheaply and easily from the peat and trees of the waste which surrounded village and town ; and timber being the most valuable thing ' out of doors ' was therefore called a ' forest.' Under the encroachment of cultivation and the demand of the iron industry for charcoal, wood fuel became scarce and pit coal took its place. It was present in great abundance, but, unlike woodland, in certain regions only. Therefore, while Cornwall starved for coal and Cobbett's tradesman boiled his leg of mutton on a neighbour's fire,[1] the Metropolis received full measure from Newcastle, and the outcrops of Staffordshire and Warwickshire coalfields tempted the potters and iron masters into industrialism. Restoration England used coal for domestic and non-power industrial purposes, such as brewing, distilling and soap making. It is estimated that in 1660 the coal produced in the British Isles was only about $2\frac{1}{4}$ million tons, and that forty years later the increase was only 364,000.[2] In 1750 the output was about 5 millions, in 1800 about 10. The advent of canals endowed pit coal with the ubiquity of the forest waste at a price—the heavy price of transport from the pit head to the place of use. Therefore from 1750 onwards coal was the commodity which ruled the economics of transportation. Depicted geographically, the industrialisation of Britain is a laying of population and enterprise upon the areas which had coal underneath. By 1830 the economic kingdom of Britain was a dyarchy of railways and coal.

The mining of coal and tin made a joint demand on the early steam engine, and tin mining was the senior occupation. The Forest of Dean, the oldest coalfield, had fuel above ground in its trees as well as below in its pits ; and the rights of free mining

---

[1] *Rural Rides*, I. 73.
[2] Royal Commission on Coal, 1871, *Report*, p. 13.

belonged of old to every inhabitant of the forest. In Cornwall these rights were elaborated into a body of Stannary Law (Late Latin *stannum* = tin). Tin, though free, was a much prized metal and England in respect of resources and technique dominated Europe ; but by 1700 Holland was importing in serious quantities from Siam, and, though the Cornish output during the 18th century was the chief source of European supply, pewter was gradually displaced by pottery at home and abroad. Therefore Cornish tin mining was highly unstable. In coal mining the ownership of the mines went with that of the surface. Where coal occurred on royal domains, as in the Forest of Dean, it came under some royal control ; but elsewhere the general rule prevailed that the baser minerals became the property of the proprietor of the land. By 1800, as the result of a long evolution, the shares of the old partnerships of tin miners had become a contract wage under capitalist entrepreneurs. This contract or ' tut ' work was akin to the butty system which prevailed in the Midlands throughout the 19th century. The Midland Mining Commission of 1843 defines the butty thus : ' a contractor who engages with the proprietor (or lessee) of the mine to deliver coal or iron stone at so much the ton, himself hiring the labourers requisite, housing his own horses and supplying the tools necessary for working the mine.' [1] The proprietor or lessee was known as the master or owner and the contract price as the charter. This indirect employment was the cause of prolific abuse, leading to exploitation of the men through pressure of the owners on the butty, through irresponsibility for accidents, and, above all, through conversion of the butty into a publican with a tommy shop in the offing. In Northumberland and Durham employment was direct. The mines of coal and iron alike were operated by those who owned the working appliances. Such an operator was either a landowner like Lord Londonderry or a company of royalty paying lessees like the South Hetton (Durham) Coal Co. In the long run this method was better for the men, because responsibility could be attached for accidents, and the Company store was more provocative of a working-men's Co-operative Store than the sidelines of their pal, the butty.

But first the northern miners had to emancipate themselves from bondage. Until the Act of 1775 (15 Geo. III, c. 28) many colliers, coal bearers and salters in Scotland were, as the preamble states, ' in a state of slavery or bondage, bound to the collieries and salt works where they work for life ' ; they were sold with the mines. The Act of 1799 (39 Geo. III, c. 56) completed their legal emancipation, yet the Scottish miner came but

[1] *Report*, p. 43.

slowly into the current of national economic life. The pace was set by his brother across the Border. Just as Scotland taught company banking to Newcastle, so Northumberland taught Scotland and the rest of England the way to corporate life in the minefield. The yearly bond, the voluntary residuum of legal villeinage, was replaced by the monthly agreement in 1844, the year when Thomas Burt and his family lived on the roadside fighting the masters who owned their cottages. It was not abolished in Durham until 1872, and then by agreement between the owners and the newly formed Durham Miners' Association. Northumberland and Durham were peculiar in another way. Their chief market was in London and foreign parts, and their comparatively new home market was provided by the North of England iron and steel industry, which from the first was in a big way and confined itself to iron and steel. In the Midlands and South Wales, on the other hand, small collieries were often attached to particular iron works ; and in Lancashire, as reported in 1873, ' every manufacturer who has had any chance of opening out a piece of coal upon the outcrop has opened it.' [1]

The steam engine began in coal fields. Here Newcomen's engines were to be found. During the first ten years of Boulton and Watt the majority of the orders were for the Cornish tin mines, but this was only because flooding threatened extinction. Tin mining was now all deep mining and concentrated in West Cornwall, having moved from Devon to East Cornwall and from there during the 18th century to the region around Penzance. The coal mines gradually developed the same need. So long as drainage was by gravity only, it was impossible to mine any but outcrop, or valley coal, like that in the Forest of Dean. In other places coal mining was impossible without a pumping engine, and Northumberland was already mining deep when George Stephenson in 1812 was appointed enginewright to the Killingworth Colliery. Except in the Welsh valleys, ' most of the coal which really drove the country came from the deeper and deepest pits. In 1854 the Northumberland and Durham fields were yielding more than a quarter of the English, and nearly a quarter of the British, coal. In the 40's their preponderance must have been greater, and in the 30's greater still.' [2] In 1830, 400 yards was about the limit of profitable operation. Since then the industry has been engaged on three technical problems : deeper workings and thinner seams, mechanical haulage, and ventilation.

(1) The Royal Commission of 1925 revealed the present position

---

[1] Commons Committee on Present Dearness and Scarcity of Coal, 1873, p. 147.
[2] J. H. Clapham, *Early Railway Age*, p. 433.

of the first problem.[1]   The difficulty may be neutralised by machinery, but from the nature of the case cannot be eliminated.

	Extracted	%
1913	from within 500 yards of surface	81
1924	,, ,, ,, ,, ,,	77
1913	from seams 4 ft. thick and upwards	55
1924	,, ,, ,, ,, ,, ,,	51

(2) Metal cages carrying iron coal tubs replaced about 1840 the basket and cable on which the miner came up hanging free with a leg through a rope loop.   The wire rope, first used in Germany, had been fitted to the winding engines of progressive collieries by 1850.   Thus the steam engine at the colliery head had now two functions to perform, the pumping out of water and the winding up of coal.

(3) The coal miner's enemy is explosion.   Sir Humphry Davy's safety lamp of 1815 mitigated the danger, but this could not be reduced to a reasonable minimum until the ventilation was correct.   The Commons Committee on Explosions in Coal Mines (1852) found that ventilation was obtained by one of three methods: either naturally by the rarefaction of the air in the pit, which in some mines was satisfactory in winter time ; or by furnace fires at the bottom of the upcast shaft, assisting natural ventilation ; or by steam jets, whereby mechanical force was applied to propel air through the shaft.   After adjourning to the Royal Polytechnic Institution to observe the demonstrations of Robert Stephenson, the Committee reported that the steam jet was much superior ; and to encourage its general adoption they recommended that increased powers should be given to the mining inspectorate, which had been established in 1850.   In 1855 Parliament compelled the owners to pass rules, but was still shy of interfering with the management.   In 1860 and 1872, having nerved itself to interfere with adults in dangerous trades elsewhere, it compelled the publication and observance of rules under penalty of fine.   This legislation furthermore empowered the miners to station their own checkweighmen at the mine head.

But still the essential process, the extraction of the coal, remained a hand process almost to the end of the 19th century alike in Great Britain and the U.S.A.

Coal mining, despite the tremendous energy it consumes in the mining process, has retained almost unmodified until the very recent past the handicraft characteristics which it manifested one hundred and fifty years ago as it ushered in the Industrial Revolution.   By a curious anomaly that industry which played the premier rôle in the

---

[1]. Royal Commission on Coal Industry, 1925, *Report of 1926*, p. 122.

inauguration of those changes by means of which modern production has been mechanized, has itself resisted tenaciously conquest by the machine, and it has remained to an amazing extent the simple handicraft which gave birth to the coal industry. Coal mining throughout the history of its existence has been in the main a pick and shovel proposition. The resistance of coal to the introduction of machine processes, together with its widespread occurrence, has made it relatively easy for the little business man with a surplus of initiative but with a small capital reserve to enter upon the production of coal. This situation, coupled with the seasonal peak in prices, accounts for the beginning of the problem of over-expansion. Business men in large numbers have entered into the production of coal during those temporary periods when coal mining seemed likely to prove profitable.[1]

In 1890 6% of American coal was undercut by machinery, in 1900 25%, in 1913 51%, in 1924 approximately two-thirds. British progress was slower, in 1901 1·5%, in 1924 19%. But machine cutting is not the whole of mechanisation. A new technique is now available for the machine loading of coal and its transportation to the surface by means of mechanical conveyors. As yet in America and Great Britain only a fraction of the total coal mined is loaded by machinery and transported by conveyors, but it is believed in America that the next few years will see rapid progress towards what one might term the ' Fordisation of coal.'

This presages a grave social problem, comparable with that which faces South Africa when the Rand mines approach exhaustion. For decades the coal beds have been piling population above them. In Great Britain the number of miners has increased continuously for the last half-century :—

Coal and shale mining in Great Britain (figures for 1911 and 1921 include maintenance staff, etc., and are strictly comparable) : 1881, 437,000 ; 1891, 599,000 ; 1901, 752,000 ; 1911, 1,128,000 ; 1921, 1,305,000.[2]

With the immediate aspect of this problem, namely the difficulty of transferring miners from old to new coalfields, we are familiar, but the logical retort to hydro-electric power, which employs a maximum of machinery and a minimum of men, is the complete mechanisation of coal mining. Coal, indeed, is not as regular in its occurrence or as easy to manipulate as water, but even allowing for this we may reasonably apprehend that the future of coal output will be attended by a shrinkage in the labour force required—or if it is not, ought to be. The problem is not peculiar to Great Britain. The bituminous industry in the

[1] G. W. Stocking, ' Labour Problems in the American Bituminous Coal Industry,' *Economic Journal*, June 1927, p. 216.
[2] 18th Abstract of Labour Statistics of the United Kingdom (1927), p. 20.

U.S.A. is subject to acute unemployment in the special form of persistent under-employment, which, being of this nature, does not force itself into public notice and State relief. Fuel began as waste in the countryside. Then it moved to the mine. The farm and the coal field between them produce food (of the white or black variety) and population. Agriculture is still a small-scale occupation and does not produce a greater population than is wanted in the world as a whole. The New World combs Western Europe for land workers ; but it does not, and will not, comb it for miners, because in order of need markets come first, machinery second, and personnel only third.

CHAPTER XIV

THE AGE OF IRON AND STEEL

Section 1. From Charcoal to Pit Coal. Section 2. British Leadership in the Casting of Iron. Section 3. The Puddling and Rolling of Iron. Section 4. The New Steel. Section 5. Pre-War Production of Great Britain, Germany, and the United States.

Section 1. *From Charcoal to Pit Coal*

THE early iron worker reduced his metal by a single operation obtaining iron or steel according to the way he fired his furnace. If in the process he eliminated all the carbon, he secured a soft product, which came to be distinguished by the name of ' wrought ' or ' finished ' or ' malleable ' iron. If, however, a small portion of carbon was left in, he secured a hard product, which was called steel, a word of ancient origin denoting firmness or resistance. At first he could not heat the metal sufficiently to cast it, but when the blast furnace was improved this became possible ; and as far back as the reign of Henry VII guns of cast iron were produced in England. The next advance was the employment of iron cast in a rough oblong as the raw material of the later stages. The oblong was called a ' pig ' from the fact that the molten metal was run into a central channel of sand with side channels at right angles to it. The central channel was the sow and the little side channels were the pigs sucking at the old sow's side. This pig iron became the branching point of the two great departments of the industry, cast iron and wrought iron. In either case the ore was first of all smelted, i.e. reduced to pig in a blast furnace. Then if destined for casting it was reduced again and run into a mould of the shape required. But if destined for wrought iron it was refined and hammered into shape. The casting of iron

K 2

was the work of the foundry and the finishing of iron the work of the forge.

As a result of substituting successive stages in the treatment of the ore for the old direct method, in which there was a large element of chance, the making of steel, which metallurgically lies midway between cast and wrought iron, was improved into a separate art. The steel-maker, who furnished the cutlers and weapon-makers with their raw material, took bars of wrought iron and by re-adding the necessary ingredients converted it back into homogeneous steel. The process, as perfected by Benjamin Huntsman about 1740, involved the melting of the iron bar in a crucible and the casting of the liquid into a bar of steel ; and his product was of such excellent quality that it made Sheffield steel famous in Europe. But the industry was a specialty and its further development was separate from that of the iron industry. It was not the avenue by which the modern technique of steel production was reached.

The iron industry required heat at every stage and therefore its want was cheap fuel, but down to about 1700 charcoal only was employed in ore smelting, the main fuel-consuming process. By this time, however, the forests of England were approaching exhaustion, especially the Sussex Weald, which was the centre of cannon founding in 17th-century England. The industry thus became dependent on imports of pig iron or wrought bar iron from the forest-bearing regions of Scandinavia, and the iron-masters looked anxiously to the American continent for alternative sources of pig iron. But all the while there lay beneath the surface pit coal in inexhaustible abundance. About 1620 Dud Dudley —like Adam Smith a son of Balliol and an author—had experimented with it. It was already in use for heating, baking and boiling, and in the forges of nail-makers and blacksmiths. In the part of Worcestershire where Dudley's works were situated it was so accessible and cheap that he used it for economy's sake. But these were days of civil strife, and owing partly to the upset of the times, and partly (if Dudley's account in *Metallum Martis*, 1665, is to be believed) to the conservatism and opposition of the iron-masters, the process was abandoned, with the result that blast furnace practice remained stationary for another century and the iron trade sank to a low ebb.

Not later than 1709, as Mr. T. S. Ashton shows in his *Iron and Steel in the Industrial Revolution* (1924), the forgotten process was rediscovered and employed by Abraham Darby the First at his works in Coalbrookdale, Shropshire, at the foot of the Wrekin Hill. The pit coal was first coked and then mixed with the ore. Up to about 1760 the new process was confined to Shropshire and Staffordshire, but it was then taken up by iron-masters in South Wales and the North of England, and by 1790 only a fraction of the blast furnaces used charcoal. The reason why pit coal made such slow headway as a fuel was that in 1700 wrought iron was the most important branch of the trade and pig iron when smelted with pit coal was unsuitable for this ; and it remained unsuitable until iron-masters invented a better blast. Therefore ' it was not until after the application of the double-acting blowing cylinder, actuated by the Watt steam-engine, that the victory over charcoal became complete.' [1]

Section 2. British Leadership in the Casting of Iron

In 1700 England was the inferior of Europe in the reduction and working of metals other than tin. Smelting with pit coal was the crucial improvement, but it was only one in a series which by 1800 had placed Britain definitely ahead of Europe in iron smelting and the production of cast-iron goods.

Abraham Darby I (1677–1717) learned in Holland an improved method of casting pots of copper and iron ; and, bringing some skilled workers back with him, he was able to produce in England at a much lower cost than before a range of articles for which there was a popular demand—pots, kettles, firebacks, piping and the like. Most of these had been made formerly of wood or a more expensive metal such as copper. Iron, like cotton, was so abundant as a raw material that when its manufacture was improved it ousted rival materials for mass use.

Abraham Darby II (1711–1763 : in control of the business 1732–62) developed the use of pit coal with such success that he made Coalbrookdale the premier producing centre of cast iron. It is with his name that smelting by pit coal is commonly associated. In developing the process which his father had successfully tried, he took the first step towards the application of steam power to the industry. He depended for his blast on a waterwheel, and water being scarce he erected in 1743 a Newcomen fire-engine, to pump up the water from the lower to the upper mill-pond in order that it might do its work again. ' Just as the Darby process of casting led to improvement and cheapening of the fire-engine, so the latter reacted in benefiting the iron industry.' [2]

Abraham Darby III (1750–1791 : in control of the business 1768–91) introduced no critical improvement in production, but he showed the great field that awaited the new material by building in 1779 the first iron bridge. The bridge spanned the

[1] T. S. Ashton, op. cit. p. 37. [2] Ibid. p. 42.

Severn south of Coalbrookdale, and a small town which sprang up close by was therefore named Ironbridge.

The first iron-master to exploit on a really big scale the improved technique was John Wilkinson (1728–1808). The family works were in the North at Bersham near Chester, but John came down to Broseley, near Coalbrookdale, to manage an iron works, of which in time he became the owner. By 1770 he and his brother were operating plants at Bersham, Broseley and Bradley, which was near Bilston in South Staffordshire. Before the end of his life his interests were far-flung. He controlled collieries and iron works in Shropshire, Staffordshire and South Wales, was interested in tin mines in Cornwall, and had a great warehouse in London and commercial connections on the Continent. By nature very masterful, he enjoyed a distinction denied to a Rockefeller or a Leverhulme, for the coinage in the districts where he was an employer was composed in part of metal tokens inscribed with the legend ' Wilkinson, Iron Master.' The second great captain of industry in the iron trade was Richard Crawshay, the founder of the Cyfarthfa (Merthyr Tydvil) Iron Works, whom people called the Iron King. Four generations of Crawshays managed the business, which in 1840 was spoken of as ' the largest in the kingdom,' [1] but the works were closed as the result of labour trouble and the invention of Bessemer steel.

The districts which after 1760 went ahead with the new technique all possessed the three essentials of coal, iron and access to the sea-board. They were South Wales and Monmouthshire, South Yorkshire, the Newcastle-upon-Tyne district and Scotland. In Scotland the industry was entirely new, but in the other places it was already in being on a small scale.

Scotland's iron industry was founded at Carron near Edinburgh in 1760 by Dr. John Roebuck. It was a striking manifestation of the new industrial era. Chemistry being his hobby, the doctor became a consulting chemist. By discovering how to substitute leaden chambers for glass globes he revolutionised the manufacture of sulphuric acid, which he reduced to a quarter of its former cost. From sulphuric acid he turned to iron : for as a manufacturer of acid he was familiar with the action of coke, which is coal minus its volatile elements, and with the nature of iron ore, from which sulphur is commonly derived. He built his plant on the River Carron a few miles from its mouth at the Firth of Forth, because there he had good water power and access to the sea (the company still operates passenger and freight steamers from Grangemouth to London and other points) and was in the immediate neighbourhood of iron ore, limestone and

---

[1] Dugdale's *Gazetteer*, ' Merthyr Tydvil.'

coal. He obtained from England his engineer John Smeaton and some skilled workmen. Thus launched, the Carron Company, which in 1773 took over the business from Roebuck owing to his financial reverses, grew so rapidly that by 1800 it became the most famous plant in Europe for the manufacture of ordnance. Wilkinson (*cf.* p. 252) had extended his business by devising a new method of boring cannon. The Carron Company specialised in small naval guns, therefore named Carronades. But neither firm was mainly dependent on the manufacture of war material, from which indeed the Carron Company withdrew altogether in the 19th century. For there was a sufficient demand from the civil engineers, now that Great Britain and the rest of Europe were passing to an iron-using basis. The cities, with their growing populations, called for water-pipes, gas-pipes and drain-pipes, the workshops and factories for machinery of iron, the railways for iron rails, iron bridges, iron girders, iron wheels and iron locomotives, the steamships for engines and iron hulls. The engine for Symington's steamboat, of which Watt was so contemptuous that he abstained from prosecution, was made at Carron.[1] In 1801 David Mushet discovered the black-band ironstone on the River Calder near Glasgow in the heart of the Lanarkshire coalfield. It was not developed until railways made their appearance first at home and then abroad, with their insatiable demand for iron in the form of rails and railroad equipment ; but from about 1825 onwards it was mined very rapidly, so that the early railroad age (1825–50) saw Scotland come to the front as a producer of iron. In 1830 Scottish blast furnaces turned out about 37,500 tons of pig, a fraction of the British output ; in 1847, 540,000 tons, more than a quarter of the total. The Scottish iron-masters had the great advantage of using coal and iron on the spot where both were mined. Lanarkshire was flanked by the sea on either side, by the Forth to the east and the Clyde to the west ; and therefore shipment coastwards or for export was easy. When iron replaced wood in shipbuilding the Clyde had the new material at its doors, while Belfast and the north-east coast of England were within a short distance of Scottish supplies.

It is conjectured that Abraham Darby I succeeded in smelting ore by pit coal because he used more powerful bellows. This accords well with the improvements which were made later in the efficiency of the blast in Scotland or by Scotsmen. In 1768 John Smeaton supplied to the Carron works in Scotland a superior blowing cylinder driven by a waterwheel. In 1775 the Scots-

---

[1] See above, pp. 166 and 255.

man, James Watt, furnished Wilkinson with an engine, Soho's first, for the blowing of a large iron furnace. In 1828 a Scotsman in Scotland, James Neilson, the manager of the Glasgow Gas Works, introduced the hot blast. Stanley Jevons pronounced it one of the most surprising instances of economy in the history of the arts. ' Iron-masters,' he says, ' had previously adhered to the mistaken notion that a very *cool* blast was essential to making good iron, and some even tried the use of ice in cooling the air of the blast. But when a blast of air hot enough to melt lead was used instead, the consumption of coal per ton of cast iron made was reduced from 7 tons to 2 or 2½ tons.' [1] The fuel saving in Scotland was exceptionally high owing to the nature of the coal— hard splint, which with the hot blast could be used in the furnace without being coked first. Conceivably, if the technique of cooling had kept pace with that of heating the tropics rather than the temperate zones might have been the seat of civilisation to-day !

The improvements in blast furnace practice applied *mutatis mutandis* to foundry work in the reverberatory or the more modern cupola furnace. In the early part of the 19th century products later made of wrought iron and later still of steel were cast, such as wagon-wheels, cylinders, bridge-girders, ship-plates and rails. But it must not be supposed that the cast-iron product is now obsolete. The casting is the cheapest and most abundant form in which iron occurs in commerce at the present day. A strike of iron moulders brings the engineering industries to a standstill before many weeks have elapsed. As the casting takes clean and exact impressions of a mould, it can be produced cheaply in very intricate forms. Its crushing strength is greater than that of any other material, and being protected by its own skin it resists the atmosphere better than wrought iron or steel. Moreover, under modern methods of treatment the range of the casting has been widened. When castings require the properties of steel, the steel known as mild steel is used. There is also a third variety known as malleable cast iron, in which America has led the way. It is of special value for small castings, and in the light branches of the industry America excels. For example, practically every machine gun has been invented in the U.S.A.

Section 3.   *The Puddling and Rolling of Iron*

The conversion of pig into wrought iron is the second branch of the industry. The record of this branch from 1700 to 1900 is

[1] W. S. Jevons, *The Coal Question*, p. 368.

peculiar—first stagnation : then notable improvement : then extension in the superior form of steel. This steel, mild steel, was the ultimate outcome of the improvements which were made in the finishing of iron by Henry Cort (1740–1800) and his immediate successors. Until Cort's time the practice in iron finishing—the refining of the pig in a finery and the hammering or rolling in a forge or mill—was almost stationary. The trouble was that in the open hearths of the old fineries British pig iron, which had been smelted with pit coal, could only be used if it was subjected to expensive preliminary treatment ; and so unsatisfactory was the domestic product that the British Government in the 18th century went to the length of prohibiting the use of native ores in wrought iron products supplied to it. Moreover the pig, whether native or imported, could only be manipulated in small quantities as long as it was treated in charcoal hearths of the type in use. Bulk production from native ore, the distinctive feature of the cast iron branch, was denied.

From this humiliating case the industry was rescued by the genius of Cort, who was an ex-Admiralty contractor of Fontley near Portsmouth, the great naval depot. He, like so many inventors—Trevethick of the steam locomotive, Symington of the steamboat, Crompton of the spinning mule, John Swindells of the ' Slubbing Billy,' and Heilmann of the machine comb—could not turn his genius to commercial profit. Having expended all his resources in starting the new process he pledged his patents to Adam Jellicoe, a naval paymaster and the father of his partner Samuel Jellicoe. But it transpired that Jellicoe had advanced the money from public funds which had passed to him as Deputy Paymaster of Seamen's Wages ; and the detection of the fraud ruined Cort.

Cort's inventions were two in number, the puddling process and the grooved roller. The puddling process which he patented in 1784 involved the following course of treatment. He laid his pig iron on the sand bottom of a reverberatory furnace, i.e. a furnace in which the metal was heated by the action of the flame in reverberating or striking down from its roof. Such furnaces had hitherto been employed only in foundry work. Cort by keeping the coal and ore separate could use British pig and refine it with the aid of pit coal. This permitted bulk production. Whereas in the old charcoal hearth 1 cwt. was the biggest charge that could be handled at one time, Cort's furnace could handle 2½ cwts., and very soon afterwards twice that amount. The manipulation in the furnace was called puddling because the worker towards the end of his task worked the metal into a ball by the aid of a puddling stick. Puddling was not a new thing.

Cort's novelty was the use of a new reverberatory furnace in which the puddling process was done in a better and larger way.

Cort's second contribution to the finishing of iron was the grooved roller which he patented in 1783, one year ahead of the puddling process. To refine puddled iron and to bring it into usable shape it must be hammered or rolled. The process of pressing metal between rollers was already employed in the tin-plate manufacture of South Wales. This industry originated about 1720 ; and in 1728 the pioneer, Major Hanbury of Ponty-pool, Glamorgan, introduced the process of rolling iron into sheets. Cort carried the technique a stage further. By employing grooved rollers laid in pairs against one another he squeezed out the dross and imparted to the hot metal the shape of the space left between them, for example that of a rail. Therefore by a single operation a long bar could now be quickly and cheaply produced from a mass of iron, while by varying the size and shape of the rolls an infinite number of useful sections could be obtained. Guide rollers, to guide the material, were invented shortly after.

Cort's claim to originality was disputed. Thomas and George Cranage as early as 1766 devised a process for ' rendering iron malleable in a reverberatory furnace ' ; Peter Onions, an iron-founder of Merthyr Tydvil, patented a puddling process a few months before Cort ; and John Purnell, an early contem-porary of Cort, patented grooved rollers. But ' Cort was the first to combine and co-ordinate these fragmentary improvements into a single and new process.' [1] Wrought iron was now within reach of triumphs as great as those of cast iron. It could provide rods, rails, tanks, boilers and ships' plates in bulk. It remained only for the engineers to turn these processes to account by using them in machinery and structural material.

Steam-driven machinery was quickly adapted to the processes of the wrought iron branch. By 1790 steam engines were at work in forges and rolling mills operating trip hammers, tilt hammers and rolls. Fifty years later (c. 1840), when iron bars of unprecedented size had to be wrought for the shafts of the first ocean steamships, James Nasmyth invented the steam hammer. Finally, in the 1860's, when wrought iron was struggling for its life against the new steel, the laborious task of hand puddling was converted into a mechanical process by the employment of ' mechanical stirrers ' i.e. steam-driven puddling sticks. But after 1860 wrought iron had to yield to steel, which replaced it in its different uses one by one.

The economic significance of the improved technique in cast and wrought iron lay in the fact that the greater part of the

[1] T. S. Ashton, *op. cit.* p. 93.

products were capital goods. These capital goods were the out-ward and visible sign of capitalism. To rebel thought the contrast was no longer between rich man and poor man, but between labour and capital, between human beings and material things. The miner who wins coal by pick and shovel means something when he demands the mine for the miners, so does the peasant when he demands the land. But the blast furnace for the iron worker, or the railway for the railwayman, is a folly which answers itself. As the visible stock of iron and steel goods was multiplied, the emphasis of socialism was altered : the Owenite land Utopias yielded to a solid socialism with the State as owner of the instruments of production. No other body than the State was strong enough to control the new impersonal monster. America believes that automobiles are an antidote to socialism, and rightly. For to own and operate capital goods inclines a man to tolerate the system which produces them. A peasant may be a revolutionary, but, if he owns land, he is never a socialist, as Soviet Russia quickly discovered. But for the ownership of co-operative stores British workers might not have traversed so peacefully the interval between the hand loom and the motor cycle.

Section 4. The New Steel

To three Englishmen, one of them a naturalised Englishman of German birth, the world owes the mass production of steel. Bessemer invented the ' converter ' in 1856 ; Siemens the ' open-hearth' process in 1866 ; Gilchrist Thomas the ' basic ' process in 1878. The Crimean War (1853–5) gives the starting-point of the series, because the war directed Bessemer's attention to gun construction and through gun construction he came to iron and steel.

Henry Bessemer (1813–1898) was a self-taught genius and his mind flew from invention to invention till by chance it alighted on steel. He moved, as it were, in an upper atmosphere of discovery above the barriers which separate trade from trade. But he was also a keen business man and he made a fortune, which he valued less for its own sake than for the evidence which it constituted of his epoch-making contributions to industry. As a young man he made all manner of things—cardboard copies of medallions ; a perforated stamp impossible of forgery, which the Government appropriated without acknowledgment (for the rest of his life he hated Government departments) ; an embossed Utrecht (i.e. worsted) velvet, which found its way to the exalted chairs of Windsor Castle and to the lowly seats of London cabs and omnibuses ; a mechanically produced bronze powder, the secret of which he kept during twenty years of manufacture ; a sugar press—the outcome of a casual conversation with a Jamaica planter but which none the less won the Prince Consort's Gold Medal in 1851 ; and finally plate glass, which brought him without knowing it to the verge of his conquest of steel. For he found out the way to roll out glass in a semi-fluid condition in a long continuous sheet, thus telescoping into one operation a long series of laborious hand and mouth processes. This revolutionised the making of plate glass ; and if the plate glass manufacture could be revolutionised, why not also the finishing of iron with its cumbersome puddling process ? That was the question he asked himself in 1855, when he was thinking about gun construction, and forthwith settled down to solve. In the course of experiment he found that two pieces of pig iron, which had accidentally lodged on the edge of a bath containing melted pig, had been converted into shells of decarbonised iron by the action of the hot air from the furnace. In other words, under great heat the iron had automatically finished itself. Here was an idea, and accordingly he constructed a cylindrical vessel in which he converted a charge of seven hundredweights of pig iron at one stroke, without puddling or manipulation of any sort, into fully finished iron. This vessel is the Bessemer converter. He showed the process to George Rennie, the engineer, who at once appreciated its significance. Rennie was President of Section 'A' of the British Association about to meet at Cheltenham in August 1856, and he invited Bessemer to communicate his discovery in a paper. This he did, and at the close James Nasmyth, of steam-hammer fame, jumped up and exclaimed 'Gentlemen, this is a true British nugget.'

So far not a word about steel, but now let us mark the closing paragraph of his paper with its curious title 'The Manufacture of Iron without Fuel' :

Before concluding these remarks, I beg to call your attention to an important fact connected with the new process, which affords peculiar facilities for the manufacture of cast steel. At that stage of the process immediately following the boil, the whole of the crude iron has passed into the condition of cast steel of ordinary quality ; by the continuation of the process the steel so produced gradually loses its small remaining portion of carbon and passes successively from hard to soft steel, and from soft steel to steely iron, and eventually to very soft iron ; hence, at a certain period of the process, any quality of metal may be obtained. There is one in particular which, by way of distinction, I call semi-steel, being in hardness about midway between ordinary cast steel and soft malleable iron. This metal possesses the advantage of much greater tensile strength than soft iron. It is also more elastic

and does not readily take a permanent set ; while it is much harder
and is not worn or indented so easily as soft iron, at the same time it
is not so brittle or hard to work as ordinary cast steel.[1]

This semi-steel, or mild steel, was the famous Bessemer steel,
which set in motion a second industrial revolution.

The Sheffield steel manufacturers scoffed at the process ; it
had nothing to do with real steel ! But the engineers and iron-
masters took it up. At first neither they nor Bessemer realised
that the process was only satisfactory if acid ore, containing little
phosphorus, was used, but Bessemer surmounted this final difficulty by procuring the right type of pig iron from the Workington
Iron Company in Cumberland. To nurse the invention into use
he set up a steel works at Sheffield and persuaded his neighbours, John Brown and Company, to become licensees for the
process in Sheffield. At the end of fourteen years he sold his
works for twenty-four times their original value and in addition
he received from other firms for his patent rights a sum of more
than £1,000,000. His first and best patrons were the railway
companies, the senior of which, the London and North Western,
installed a Bessemer plant in their works at Crewe in 1864. In
1865 the first Bessemer steel plant was opened in America, and
according to the United States census of 1900 there were no fewer
than thirteen towns or villages rejoicing in the name of Bessemer.
All this one self-trained Englishman did, and having done it he
spent his latter days inventing a steamship saloon which would
not rock ; for he was a very bad sailor. But the steamship
crashed into Calais pier ; and Bessemer had to endure the tortures
of sea-sickness until at length in ripe old age he voyaged to that
happy land where there is neither marrying nor *mal-de-mer* !

William Siemens (1823–1883) was a junior member of the
family which founded the famous firm of Siemens and Halske,
the pioneers of electrical engineering in Europe—of the telegraph,
the submarine cable and the dynamo. William came to England
in 1843 to sell a process of electro-plating. He applied first to
an Unternehmer (undertaker), but when the undertaker offered
to bury him on trade terms he betook himself to a more likely
quarter, the firm of Elkington, which accepted his process. A
long and prosperous career of invention followed, concluding
with researches—for he had been trained in science at Göttingen
—into the principle of Regeneration of Heat, from which issued
by steps too complicated to outline the ' Open Hearth ' process of
making steel in 1866. The essential features of the process were
two : (1) The ' regenerative ' furnace, which communicated heat

[1] H. Bessemer, *Autobiography*, p. 161.

to the air supply so that it reached the hearth in a highly heated state. (When our mothers sallied forth on a winter's day they wore on their mouths a regenerative furnace in the form of a pierced metal respirator, from which, as they inhaled the winter's cold, they regenerated some of the stored-up heat which their breath had communicated to it ; but mothers' darlings, treating it as a gag, breathed round the corner !) (2) The use of gas as the source of heat. By using gas fuel any quality of coal could be burned and the converting vessel could be an *open hearth*. Hence the name of ' open hearth,' by which Siemens' process as a whole is known. Thus, from 1866 onwards there were two rival methods of producing steel in mass, Bessemer's and Siemens', and both for a time were confined to the use of non-phosphoric pig. Like Bessemer, Siemens nursed his process into use by establishing a pioneer works at Landore in South Wales. As with Bessemer, his epoch-making contribution to steel was nothing more than an incident in his life as an inventor. In 1879 he followed up his earlier work on electricity by inventing the electric furnace, and in 1883, the year of his death, he applied electric power, for the first time in British history, to a little railway running from Portrush to Giant's Causeway in the North of Ireland. To a mediaeval gildsman a Bessemer or Siemens would have been as abhorrent as a witch.

For a time the manufacturers of the new steel met the demand for acid pig by importations from Sweden and Spain, but, as scientists knew, the ultimate solution would be a process which would eliminate the phosphorus from the more abundant phosphoric ores. In 1878 the solution was found by a young London chemist, Sidney Gilchrist Thomas (1850–1885). He was nothing more than a clerk in a London police court, who attended the science classes at the Birkbeck Institute. His lecturer one day remarked ' The man who eliminates phosphorus by means of the Bessemer converter will make his fortune.' So he went to his little laboratory at home and worked out the theory of it. By 1875 he had found that the essential was a basic lining in the converter which would hinder the phosphorus from entering the metal and deposit it in the slag. The next step was to make the basic lining durable, and this he achieved (with the help of his cousin, P. C. Gilchrist) by adding quicklime during the operation, ' so as to secure a highly basic slag at an early stage of the blow.' In 1878 he announced his result, and for the moment no one took any notice. But the year following he gave a demonstration in Middlesbrough, the centre of the North of England iron trade, which had gravitated thither after 1850 upon the discovery of the adjacent Cleveland iron field. Middlesbrough realised its importance, for its local ore was highly phosphoric. Within a few months the town was besieged by an army of metallurgists from Germany, France, Belgium and America ; and by 1914 the world's production of steel from phosphoric ores, known commercially as basic steel, exceeded that from acid ores. To Germany the discovery was all-important, for the rich iron fields of Lorraine, the loot of 1870, were highly phosphoric. A grateful Germany erected monuments by the score to Bismarck, the man of blood and iron, but to the young Englishman, who unlocked the door to its wealth of coal and steel, its debt was at least as great. The inventor paid a triumphal visit to America in 1881, but his health had been ruined by overwork, and he died in 1885 at the age of 34. A nobler soul never lived. When he was a poor clerk he refused a position as analytical chemist to a Burton brewery from scruples about fostering even indirectly the use of alcohol, and by his will he bequeathed his considerable fortune to the relief of distress among the working classes. He was an inventor and a capitalist, but ' somehow good.'

Section 5.   Pre-War Production of Great Britain, Germany, and the United States

Steel Production in Million Tons [1]

| Country | Bessemer | | Open Hearth | | Total |
	Acid	Basic	Acid	Basic	
Great Britain :					
Average 1901–5 .	1·2	·5	2·7	·5	5·0
1915 . . .	·8	·4	4·0	2·9	8·3
Germany :					
Average 1901–5 .	·3	5·1	·1	2·4	8·1
1913 . . .	·1	10·6	·1	7·3	18·6
U.S.A. :					
Average 1901–5 .	9·0	··	1·0	5·1	15·2
1913 . . .	9·5	··	1·2	20·3	31·3

[1] The years and figures are those given in the *Report on the Iron and Steel Trades* (1918), (Cd. 9071), p. 5, § 7. The total for Great Britain in 1913 was 7·6 million tons. The iron ore raised in Great Britain in 1913 was 15·9 million tons, of which Cleveland supplied 37·6% and Northamptonshire 18·2% : in 1919 and 1920 it was over 12 million tons, but in 1921 slumped violently to 3·4 million tons.

In the decade before the war the steel output of Great Britain increased absolutely, but it was easily exceeded by that of Germany and the U.S.A. with their greater—and in the case of the U.S.A. vastly greater—natural resources.

The circumstances determining the type of steel produced in different countries are (a) the nature of the accessible ore, (b) the purposes for which the steel is employed, and (c) the technical merits of the rival processes within the limits set by (a) and (b).

In Great Britain the majority of native ore was phosphoric, but she had a highly developed import trade in acid ore from Spain. Therefore in this decade she increased in about equal proportions her use of phosphoric and acid ore. But all the increase occurred in the open hearth process, which was technically more suitable for her leading specialities—boilers and ship plates. The Bessemer process did not even hold its own. In Germany the nature of the Lorraine ores confined her to basic steel, and in the pre-war decade, while the output of Bessemer basic doubled, that of open-hearth basic trebled. In the United States of America the ore is derived from the rich region of Lake Superior, the largest iron mining district in the world. The ore is moved by way of the Great Lakes to the smelting furnaces in the region of Pittsburg. In this decade the output of acid Bessemer remained constant, but that of open-hearth basic increased at a prodigious rate. The reason is that at the time when the foundations of the American industry were being laid basic steel was unknown and acid ore was available. Therefore a large number of Bessemer plants were erected. But now she is drawing on phosphoric ores and modern developments in open hearth practice are giving the open hearth an ever increasing lead in all countries.

It seems probable that the open hearth process will supersede the Bessemer process in course of time all along the line; for it gives a larger yield from a given weight of pig iron, and because it lends itself more readily to control it gives also a more reliable product. Engineers, in fact, offer more for Siemens than for Bessemer steel of the same class. The economic historian, a layman in these matters, has to take these statements on faith, but what he can see is that in this industry most clearly science and business march side by side in inseparable strength. The Industrial Revolution began somewhere about 1770, but verily the end is not yet. Some idea of the advance made in the use of iron since that time is conveyed in the following quotation from a recent American work :

At the close of the period 1700–1775 the population of Great Britain was probably in the neighbourhood of 8,000,000. The annual

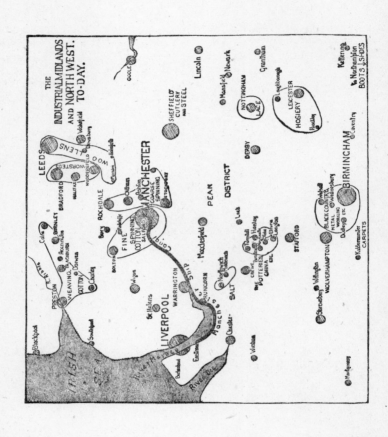

THE
INDUSTRIAL MIDLANDS
AND NORTH WEST.
TO-DAY.

output of pig iron . . . amounted to perhaps 3 to 5 pounds for each person. What this means in the way of general use of iron can only be comprehended if we recall that in the year immediately preceding the world war the outputs of America, Germany and Great Britain ranged from 500 to 1000 pounds *per capita* each year.[1]

We live in an Age of Steel. Steel has revolutionised industry. Will it ever render service to art ? We must hope with Mr. Wells that it will : ' Art has scarcely begun in the world. There have been a few forerunners and that is all. Leonardo, Michelangelo ; how they would have exulted in the liberties of steel.'[2]

CHAPTER XV

THE TEXTILE INDUSTRIES IN TRANSITION

Section 1. Place Names of Textile Products. Section 2. Woollens. Section 3. Silk. Section 4. Linen and Jute. Section 5. Hosiery and Lace. Section 6. Cotton. Section 7. The Great Inventions in the Cotton and Woollen Industries. Section 8. Distinctive Features in the Textile Transition.

Section 1. *Place Names of Textile Products*

WOOL and flax are the products of temperate regions and therefore native to Britain ; silk and cotton are sub-tropical. Many of the textile products bear names which record their original home. Worsted takes its name from Worstead, a Norfolk village, where the fine woollens of the Norwich district were marketed ; the jersey from the island of Jersey ; merino wool from the Spanish word ' merino,' Latin *major*, the royal inspector of sheep walks over which the sheep were driven. Holland is the coarse linen of Holland, which children used to wear as an apron pinned ' afore ' their dress. Cambrics are named after the linens of Cambrai, lawns (perhaps) after those of Laon. Cotton, the Arabic ' qutun ' or cotton plant, discloses its Oriental origin. Calico, which in England came to mean plain white cotton cloth, signified originally the group of products imported from Calicut in India and included many kinds of cloth, plain or dyed or decorated, made of cotton or cotton and silk. Decoration took the form of printing on the fabric a coloured pattern. Chintz (from *chinta*, a spot) signified to the England of 1700 an imported calico printed with flowers or other rich designs. It was used for ladies' dresses and for furniture and bed coverings. ' Bought my wife a chint, that is, a painted East Indian calico for to line

[1] E. C. Eckel, *Coal, Iron, and War*, p. 9.
[2] H. G. Wells, *Modern Utopia*, p. 242.

her new study.'[1] Only the gentlefolk could afford imported chintzes : the common people wore home-printed calico. The stylish miss was a ' Calico Madam.' Muslin, a fine cotton fabric, is derived from Mosul, a town in Mesopotamia : fustian, a coarse fabric of cotton or cotton and linen mixed, from Fustat, the old name of Cairo. The pyjama, a novelty of the 19th century, signifies leg clothing (*pae-jama*), the loose trousers of the East.

When place names became names of products, their meaning often altered, the general rule being that the foreign speciality was supplemented by a cheaper home-made product, which finally replaced it. Damasks, originally the flowered silks of Damascus, became in Europe a linen product with a pattern but without contrast of colour, then by adaptation from linen the woollen stuff used in furniture covering and hangings. Similarly velvet, Latin *villus*, shaggy hair, at first an all-silk fabric, was extended to fabrics with a silk pile on a ground of linen, cotton or wool. The Barcelona napkin which Mordaunt Mertoun wears round his neck in Scott's *Pirate* was an imitation silk made from the fibre of the prickly pear. They were once largely exported from Barcelona. Drugget (French *drogue*) and Shoddy signified originally trashy and cast-off (' shed off ') products, but now they are simply terms for special kinds of rough quality woollen goods.

Section 2. Woollens

As sheep were raised in most parts of England, the spinning and weaving of wool were widely practised arts, but some districts were more favoured than others by natural conditions. By 1700 there were three specialised woollen manufacturing regions in England : the south-western counties of Devon, Gloucester, Somerset and Wilts, which was the senior and at that time the premier woollen district ; East Anglia ; and the West Riding of Yorkshire. By 1800, before machinery had made any visible impression on the industry, the West Riding was as strong as its erstwhile superiors. By 1914 it was far ahead, having 50% of the spindles and 60% of the looms of the British woollen industry ; and its nearest rival was the Lowland counties of Scotland.

The West Riding had many natural advantages. It was a hilly country on the edge of great moors, which carried sheep. When it outgrew its local supply, it was centrally situated for the collection of wool from Scotland, Ireland, Wales and the South. It had much pure water for washing the wool and cleaning the

[1] Pepys, Sept. 5, 1663.

cloth. It had water power for the wheels which drove the old-time fulling mills. In addition its people moved in the free and progressive environment of the North. For an outlet it had Hull, a thriving port with a strong grip on the Baltic trade. North of it was the leading coal district of the country, south of it Sheffield and Birmingham, bounding it on the west was cotton, setting the pace from Manchester. No Coke of Holkham bent its genius to agriculture; no estate builders coveted its moors, as they coveted the exquisite vales of Taunton and the Cotswolds. And so this sturdy northern stock, inhabiting bleak slopes which could never feed a considerable population, found that if they were to increase and excel it must be by industry. When the age of power machines arrived the West Riding followed on the heels of Lancashire, partly because coal lay beneath the county surface, but chiefly because it already possessed social and mechanical aptitude for expansion in company with its neighbour. When steam power ousted water power, the degree of concentration increased and the two districts became an all but continuous factory area, with highly developed trade contacts; and these gave the area an advantage over outlying points in the North as well as in the more distant South. Thus Kendal, Westmorland, famous throughout the ages for the ' Kendal Green ' (which was named from the dyeing material Dyers Broom grown in the locality), lost its woollen industry in the course of the 19th century; and the reason was its isolation in the valley of an otherwise agricultural county.

The worsted [1] industry of Norfolk surpassed that of Yorkshire in 1700. In 1800 it was barely equal to it, and in 1860 it was extinct, having failed to survive the transition to steam power. The absence of coal was a handicap not so much on account of the cost of carrying it from Newcastle as on account of the lack of that mechanical environment which coal and iron engender. But other factors were against Norfolk. It lived in dangerous dependence on Yorkshire merchants for its yarn ; and as power came first in spinning, the power spinners were the first to take up the power loom. Moreover, the Norwich weaving district was an industrial patch in a region of agriculture, and therefore opposition to machinery was more natural and more difficult to overcome. Finally Norwich's excellence lay in luxury goods made of fine wool or of wool and silk ; and the 19th century did not dress in kneebreeches, silk stockings, and flowered waistcoats. It was the West Riding which throve on Army contracts during the Napoleonic war and the West Riding which went on from that to clothe the multitude in Victorian uniformity.

[1] See below, p. 292, for distinction between worsted and woollen.

In the West country, the ancient home of the broadcloth industry, the story of the decline is substantially the same, with the difference that Gloucestershire and Somersetshire retained by excellence of workmanship a share in the manufacture of cloth of the highest quality. Here again the lack of mineral resources is only a partial explanation of the decline ; for it was a short sea trip from South Wales to Gloucestershire. But Bristol in 1800 was a sleepy port, rich and unenterprising and losing foreign trade to Liverpool and Glasgow. In the 30's the citizens of Bristol distinguished themselves by their apathy towards the building of the Great Western Railway ; and perhaps Bristol's manufacturing hinterland failed to hold as much of its old trade as it might have done.

While the mechanical revolution was in progress and the older districts were gradually losing their trade to the West Riding, the woollen industry was relieved of an ancient nightmare, the shortage of raw material. For over a century and a half (1662–1824) the export of wool was prohibited in order that the manufacturers should have an adequate supply. Unhappily Ireland was included in the prohibition. Not only was her woollen industry throttled, but in addition she was forbidden to export her wool to foreign countries. When Parliament in 1739 (12 Geo. II. c. 21) allowed her to export woollen yarn to Great Britain, it was with no thought of fostering an Irish yarn industry, but simply in order to meet the unsatisfied wants of English yarn users. ' Whereas the taking off the Duties upon Woollen or Bay Yarn imported from Ireland, may be of use to prevent the exporting wool and woollen manufactures from Ireland to foreign parts and may be of use to the manufactures of Great Britain,' etc., etc.—an edifying, though callous, preamble ! Enclosure and the art of Bakewell greatly improved the breeds of sheep, but the purpose of the improvers was more mutton and not more wool, for which indeed the grower was not allowed to obtain the natural price. Therefore, while the sheep was being improved as meat, its wool declined in quality. The manufacturers took the home clip at their own price and imported their best wool from abroad—the merino wool of Spain, which entered duty free. On many occasions the manufacturers and the sheep graziers came into fiscal conflict and always the manufacturers prevailed. The ban was not removed until 1824 (cf. p. 57), when with the opening of new sheep raising areas the cloud of shortage was lifting. From 1815 onwards Australia, the Argentine, South Africa and New Zealand gradually displaced Europe as the source of foreign supply. The majority of their flocks were raised from two classes of sheep—the fine wool merino sheep of Spain and the English

the bobbin net machinery, which with the improvements of a century is the basis of Nottingham's lace trade to-day. ' A bobbin net frame,' said Dr. Ure, ' is as much beyond the most curious chronometer as that is beyond a roasting jack.' [1] Felkin, writing in 1867, says ' Heathcote's invention gave to Nottingham a trade which, within fifty years, has mainly assisted to quadruple its population, giving employment year by year at fair wages to probably 150,000 workpeople.' [2] About 1840 steam power was adapted to the process. Up to that date the machinery was in the possession of numerous small owners, who sent their goods by agents on packhorses to London and other big towns. After 1840 the machinery was concentrated in large factories ; and travellers from the large mercantile houses of London waited on the Nottinghamshire lace manufacturers, who in addition had foreign and domestic agents on the look-out for orders. The machine-made lace of Nottinghamshire was fatal to the real hand lace of Buckinghamshire and other counties of the South. No parliamentary candidate, it used to be said, had any chance of election for Aylesbury (Bucks) unless he denounced the machine-made lace of Nottingham. The real hand lace was made by women. It was called pillow or bone lace. The pillow was a hard round cushion in which pins made of bone were fixed ; and among these pins the lace maker moved her bobbins of thread, thus producing the net of thread which is called lace. The general result of mechanical improvement in spinning and weaving was to make the labour of women and children more important than that of men. In lace the reverse happened. The machinery was so complicated that none but men could work it ; and it was instrumental in throwing out of employment the women of the rural counties to the south. The loss of their hand industry was a heavy blow to the village life of these counties ; and attempts to revive it in recent years have been obstructed by the lowness of the earnings which can be made in the face of competition with the machine product.

Section 6. Cotton

The cotton industry is the classical example of territorial centralisation. In 1914, 90% of the industry was localised in Lancashire and the closely adjacent parts of Cheshire and York-shire ; the remaining 10% being in the Paisley district of Glasgow, which climatically and commercially resembles Lancashire. It is not difficult to list the advantages which the cotton industry secured by concentration in Lancashire : a humid climate which

---

[1] Andrew Ure, *Dictionary of Arts*, p. 730.   [2] Felkin, *op. cit.* p. 269.

is peculiarly suitable to fine spinning ; pure water which is
necessary to the bleaching and calico printing processes
proximity to the port of Liverpool ; and abundant coal. But
it is less easy to relate these advantages to the sequence of its
growth.

The cotton industry grew up around Manchester and Bolton
in the 17th century, in attachment to the older woollen industry
on the other side of the Pennine range ; and for the same reasons
The district was empty, the soil was not suitable for arable
farming, there was good water and a very humid climate
Manchester was the commercial centre of the industry and the
products of the district were known generically as Manchester
goods. They consisted of fustians, checks and small wares, such
as tapes. They were rarely all-cotton goods, the warp thread
being of linen or wool, and in the 17th century they were not
a formidable rival to the older textiles.

But the Restoration inaugurated a remarkable change in men's
and women's clothing. Sombre home-made broadcloth—the old
drapery—was discarded for lighter and more elegant material
Supplied at first in the form of linen and silk from the continent
of Europe, the new drapery spread rapidly from the rich down
wards, as soon as it became available in a material not less
beautiful and far cheaper. This material was Indian cotton
The East India Company brought the finished fabrics—calicoes
and chintzes—into England from the East, and by the reign of
William and Mary they were the rage. The older established
woollen manufacturers and the newly established silk manu
facturers had cause for alarm, and in response to their clamour
Parliament in 1700 (11 & 12 Wm. III, c. 10) prohibited the wearing
or use of Indian silks and calicoes painted, dyed, printed or
stained. Thus the protectionist interests represented by the
home manufacturers triumphed (as they had already done in
France in the even more sweeping decree of 1686) over the free
trade interests represented by the East India Company and the
drapers who sold the imported goods. But in order that foreign
trade and shipping should not be discouraged, the Act of 1700
allowed the importation of the prohibited articles for re-export to
the colonies and Europe, and gave facilities for warehousing in bond

However, the hopes of the promoters were frustrated, not
only by smuggling—a risk common to every restriction—but
also by the legal importation of plain calicoes for printing in
England. For England by now knew the Indian art of printing
cotton, having learnt it from Holland, so that by 1720 there
flourished in and around London, chiefly on the Surrey side
a number of calico printing factories, not yet of course of the

power type. Therefore the old established industries returned to the attack ; and the Spitalfields silk weavers, being residents of the capital, brought home to Parliament by demonstration and riot their lament of unemployment with such effect that they secured in 1720 a further Act (7 Geo. I, St. I, c. 7) prohibiting the use or wear of any kind of calicoes. The Surrey calico printers were forced into the printing of linens and fustians or to printing for export ; but the rough cotton manufactures of Lancashire did not come under the ban, and the exemption was formally registered in the Manchester Act of 1735–6 (9 Geo. II, c. 4). Lancashire by this means secured the unique advantage of protection by proxy : complete fiscal prohibition against India with none of the internal restrictions which clogged the woollen industry. And in 1774, when power spinning was developing, the Lancashire manufacturers were strong enough to secure by 14 Geo. III, c. 72, the repeal of the Act of 1720–1, which if now interpreted against them would have prevented their expansion into the finer branches of the industry.

The reason why the cotton industry was the first to be taken over by machinery was partly technical and partly economic. The fibre was uniform and therefore lent itself to machine treatment. But also it was abundant and its product was cheap and in wide demand both at home and in the Tropics. In 1700 raw cotton was obtained from the Levant and Mediterranean : in the 18th century from the West Indies and South America : after 1800 from the North American mainland. The phenomenal increase of raw cotton production, when it was acclimatised on the American mainland, was due to the largeness of the area on which it could be grown and to the cheapness with which it could be produced and made ready for export. The negroes on the plantations grew it and picked it ; and the slow and tedious process of cleaning (i.e. separating the seed from the fibre) was expedited by the invention of Eli Whitney, a mechanic of New England. Whitney's gin (i.e. engine) of 1794 was a hand machine resembling a knife-grinding box, and it was easily enlarged into a machine that could be rotated by a horse. The result was that one man could now clean ten times as much cotton as before and one man with a horse fifty times as much as a man alone. Thus after 1800 both raw material and markets were highly extensible.

Section 7. The Great Inventions in the Cotton and Woollen Industries

Stated simply, the processes of cotton manufacturing are these. The cotton arrives in bales. It is opened and cleansed by ' willowing.' The fibres are then separated by ' carding ' (derived from ' carduus,' a thistle, the oldest form of carding instrument). The hand card was a pair of boards with bent metal teeth between which the cotton was worked. The carded cotton is converted by stages into yarn : first into a roving and then into a yarn. The latter is the spinning process proper. The weaver's work is the crossing of two yarns—the stationary warp by the moving weft—so as to form a cloth. This is the essential ' manufacturing ' process. Before the days of power the weaver was literally a manufacturer. The cloth leaves the loom in a grey state and is then bleached. After bleaching it is dyed, printed or otherwise finished for the market.

The woollen processes differ from these in certain important respects. There is a division into woollen and worsteds. The former consists of short-staple wool, which is carded : the latter of long-staple wool, which is combed. The spinning and weaving processes are in principle the same as those of cotton. But in the finishing processes there are great differences. Instead of being bleached, woollen cloth is pulled, washed and stretched by tentering : then teaseled (so called from the teasel plant originally used to raise the nap) and cropped or faced. Wool is dyed either before manufacture or in the piece. It is necessarily dyed beforehand in fabrics of different colours, and it may be dyed at both stages in fabrics of a single colour.

The epoch of the great inventions opened in 1767 ; and the three inventions which led the way were all concerned with cotton spinning and all the work of Lancashire men. There had, however, as is always the case in the history of invention, been anticipation and preparation. In 1733 John Kay invented the flying shuttle, which consisted of a picking peg contrivance by means of which the weaver could jerk a shuttle through the warp using only one hand. This doubled the work that one man could do ; and thus increased the demand for yarn and the inducement to devise an improved method of spinning. Kay came from Bury (Lancs.), but he was at Colchester (Essex) when he invented the flying shuttle, and the woollen industry was the first to take it up. In 1738 Lewis Paul, the son of a French refugee, assisted by a skilled mechanic, John Wyatt, invented and patented a method of spinning by rollers, but by the time that the patent expired (1752) he had not brought it into successful use. In 1748 he patented a carding machine, which was more successful. This machine too was first employed in the woollen industry. Paul himself was born at Lichfield (Staffs.) and his factory was at Northampton. It was not till about 1760 that the first carding machine was introduced into Lancashire by Robert Peel, the grandfather of the statesman and the founder of the Lancashire calico-printing industry.

James Hargreaves, a Blackburn weaver, who was employed by Peel in his experiments on the carding machine, invented the spinning jenny in or shortly before 1767, but did not patent it till 1770. The jenny (called, it is said, after his wife) was a hand machine, which reproduced mechanically the work of the spinner's hand in attenuating and giving in the yarn. It permitted one man by means of a hand wheel to spin simultaneously more than one cop of yarn (8 in 1767, 16 or more in 1770, 80 in 1784, and ultimately 120).

Richard Arkwright was a Preston barber, who set up as a wig-maker in Bolton, a thriving cotton town. Here in the gossip of his shop he heard talk of a new and wonderful method of spinning cotton between rollers. This of course was Paul's idea. Arkwright, however, was a very able business man. Having constructed with the help of a Warrington clock-maker, also named John Kay, an experimental machine, he looked for business partners. Moving south the year before he took out his patent of 1769, he set up in partnership with Jedediah Strutt, a Nottingham hosier in small premises at Nottingham : built in 1771 a factory at Cromford (Derbyshire), in 1773 a second at Derby, and a third at Belper (Derbyshire). In 1780 he built yet another at Manchester, which was capable of holding 600 workpeople. Arkwright with difficulty upheld the monopoly in his patent till 1785, when it was challenged and annulled. During the period of his monopoly, in addition to operating his own factories, he issued licences to 'adventurers,' among whom was David Dale of New Lanark, the introducer of the cotton industry into Scotland.

Arkwright's machine was driven by water power and therefore called the water frame. The essential mechanical principle was the passing of the thread through pairs of rollers, revolving at different speeds, the spinning and winding being one continuous process. The product was called water twist and was so strong that all-cotton goods, hitherto very rare, could now be made. To-day the great majority of the world's cotton is spun on rollers of the Arkwright type ; and the method, which for a time was known as throstle spinning from the humming noise made by the spindle, is now termed ring spinning from the fact that the cotton is wound on to the spindle through a ring.

Samuel Crompton,[1] the son of a small farmer weaver, improved Hargreaves' jenny by combining a moving carriage with rollers of the Arkwright type. 'In essentials it combined the salient

[1] Cf. *Samuel Crompton*, Centenary Publication by Messrs. Dobson and Barlow Ltd., January 1927, p. 22.

features of Hargreaves' " Jenny " and Arkwright's " Water Frame." From the former, Crompton took the vertical spindles and the travelling carriage, and from the latter the drafting rollers, but he made these essential differences—in the " Jenny " the spindles were stationary and the carriage carried the roving bobbins ; in the mule the carriage carried the spindles, the roving being carried in a fixed creel, exactly as in the mules of to-day.' To this hybrid spinning-wheel the name Mule was given. Crompton did not patent his mule, but by 1779 it was working. On it he spun yarn of such exceptional fineness that his house at Bolton, Hall-i'-th'-Wood, (which in 1900 was presented by Lord Leverhulme to the Corporation of Bolton and furnished by him as a Folk Museum,) was besieged by people anxious to see his machine and buy his yarn. Crompton, however, made little by his invention. He lost the £5000 voted to him by Parliament in 1812 and died in poverty and disappoint- ment in 1827. Mule spinning yields a finer yarn than ring spinning and is the method chiefly used to-day in Lancashire, which is pre-eminent for fine spinning. By the use of mule-spun yarn British manufacturers were able to rival the finest products of the East and to turn to full account the factor of climatic humidity.

The mule being a complicated machine was at first worked by hand, and many minor improvements were added to it by unknown persons. In 1792 William Kelly, Dale's manager at New Lanark, adapted part of the process to water power. Before this date the steam engine had been applied occasionally to the water frame, but it was not in general use here till after 1815. The later invented mule came under steam power first. James Watt stated in 1812 that two-thirds of the engines erected by him for spinning cotton were ' applied to turning spindles upon Mr. Crompton's construction.' [1] In 1825 a Manchester machine maker, Richard Roberts, patented a self-actor mule, and in 1830 his firm, Messrs. Sharp, Roberts and Co., put on the market an improved self-actor, which made the whole operation a genuine power process. But a few hand mules survived in the cotton industry until the cotton famine of 1861-3. It is perhaps no exaggeration to say that Roberts' Quadrant was, as a piece of machinery, even more triumphant than Crompton's mule. It was the most delicate piece of mechanism that had ever been applied as an aid to manufacture, and in principle it has never been altered. Its purpose was to regulate the speed of winding the yarn on the cop according to the amount of yarn already on

[1] Commons Committee on Petition of Samuel Crompton (1812), Evidence— given in G. W. Daniels, *The Early English Cotton Industry*, p. 189.

the cop. This on Crompton's mule had to be judged by the feel of the hand.

While the central process, spinning, was being adapted to machinery, the subsidiary processes were following suit. In 1775, six years after the water frame, Arkwright patented a carding machine, which was an improvement on that of Lewis Paul ; he also adapted the roller mule to the making of rovings, a process previous to spinning. The mule spinners at first depended on hand rovings, then on rovings made by Arkwright's machine ; but in 1782 John Swindells at Stockport invented the Slubbing Billy, a combination of mule and jenny, on which machine rovings could be made to any degree of fineness.

Meanwhile improvements were being introduced at the finishing end. When plain cottons were imported from India, the printing was done in and around London (above, p. 290) and for a time Manchester cottons were sent to London to be printed, but as the Lancashire cotton industry grew it attracted the printing business to itself. In 1784 T. Bell of Preston (Lancs.) patented a method of cylindrical printing, which made the fortunes of the Peel family. Invented for the printing of calico, it was utilised later on the news printing press. The discovery in 1785 by the chemist Berthollet that chlorine could be used to bleach vegetable fibres led to the experimental introduction of chemical bleaching by James Watt in 1786 ; and the process was further developed by Thomas Henry of Manchester. This is an early example of the control of productive operations by applied science. Hitherto Nature had done most of the work. The cloth after treatment by alkaline substances had been left for some months on the grass for the weather to act upon it and finally steeped in sour milk.

The intermediate process of weaving, which was the central manufacturing process, resisted the application of power for a much longer time. In 1787 the Reverend Edmund Cartwright patented a power loom, but lost a small fortune in trying to make it pay. 1806–7 is given [1] as the time when through the efforts of Messrs. Horrocks of Preston, William Radcliffe of Mellor and others the power loom became of commercial use. However in 1834 only one loom out of six in Bolton was a power loom. Then came a rapid change. The spinners attached loom sheds to their mills, and by 1845 in cotton weaving the power loom was supreme.

In the woollen industry machine spinning began in the 1780's. By 1786 Arkwright machines were in operation in Yorkshire, and in 1789 Boulton and Watt reported that they were erecting

[1] *Cf.* G. W. Daniels, *The Early English Cotton Industry*, p. 140 ff.

' two pretty large engines ' [1] for spinning wool at Leeds.   But
the yarn used in the woollen, as distinct from the worsted, branch
was usually mule-spun, and as late as 1850 much mule yarn was
made by hand.   Indeed, in this branch the only power machine
in general use down to 1850 was the carding engine.   Combing,
the preliminary process in worsted spinning, was the most
difficult process of all to adapt to power.   The action of combing
separates the long wool, ' the top,' from the remainder, ' the noil.'
A machine was wanted which would follow the action of the
human hand and give to an obstruction instead of tearing through
it.   The comb patented by Edmund Cartwright in 1789 did not
do this.   An Alsatian, Josue Heilmann, solved the problem in
Germany at about the same time as G. E. Donnisthorpe and
S. C. Lister (Baron Masham) in England.   Heilmann was ruined
by the political troubles of 1848, but Lister, to whom Donnisthorpe
sold his rights, introduced a successful machine comb in 1845.[2]
Improvements in the machine itself and subsidiary processes led
to the square motion machine in 1846 and to the square nip
machine in 1850.   In 1853 Lister acquired the Noble machine, an
improved type invented by James Noble, one of his mechanics.
The Noble comb came into general use in Great Britain.   Its
essential feature is the use of two circles, a revolving comb carrying the wool and a working comb inside the revolving one.   Isaac
(later Sir Isaac) Holden was associated with Lister in the middle
40's.   In 1848 Holden opened a machine-combing factory in
Paris, and concentrating his business at Bradford in 1864 built up
the largest machine-combing concern in the world.

Meanwhile the power loom was slowly conquering the woollen
and worsted industries.   In 1841 the Royal Commission on the
Hand Loom Weavers reported that the power loom was exceptional, but by 1865 it was supreme in worsted, and some years
later in woollen also.

Section 8.   *Distinctive Features in the Textile Transition*

(1) *Continuity of technical progress.*   The transition to power
machinery took a century to accomplish—say, 1770–1870.   Since
1870 there has been constant change in the speed and complexity
of machinery as well as in type and blend of product.   For
example, the old distinction between worsted and woollen has
broken down : and shoddy is an industry in itself.   Artificial

---

[1] Witt Bowden, *Industrial Society in England towards the end of the 18th
century*, p. 85.

[2] To commemorate this and his other inventions S. C. Lister presented to
Bradford the Cartwright Memorial Hall and the Cartwright Statue in Lister Park.

silk is now taking from cotton some of the custom which cotton took from natural silk two centuries ago. Lancashire by using the mule spins finer yarn than any part of the U.S.A., North or South, but because of the variety and fineness of her products she has not yet found it feasible to employ largely the automatic feed which is general on American looms. In January 1925 the writer stood in the upper storey of a North Carolina cotton factory in which three thousand power looms were in action. Each weaver was minding eight to twelve looms, and when the luncheon interval came, about one loom in twenty was left to run un-attended. The' weaver calculates that this pays him if his cloth is running exceptionally well. One thought first of Adam Smith's Invisible Hand and then of the Book of the Machines in *Erewhon*.

(2) *Motive power and concentration.* The transition from hand to steam power *via* water power influenced the localisation of the cotton industry. Down to 1815 the mills using water power were more numerous than those using steam and they were erected in valleys where water power was available. This contributed to a temporary dispersion of the Lancashire cotton industry into rural parts and beyond the borders of Lancashire into Derbyshire and Nottinghamshire. But when steam power replaced water the concentration in Lancashire was resumed. However, the dispersion and return were not violent, being accomplished for the most part within the limits of south-east Lancashire. Many of the early water mills were just outside a small town, and as the industry grew they were absorbed in the area of the growing town. After the introduction of steam, water was still very important for boiler and engine purposes. Steam allowed of urban concentration, but much more important was the increase which it permitted in the size of the factory and the number of spindles per water frame or per mule. One old cotton mill in Bolton, built probably about 1792 and still erect, was not situated on any stream of water, and therefore resorted to the device of Abraham Darby II at Coalbrookdale. A reservoir was built and a steam engine was employed to pump the water from this on to the waterwheel which turned the machinery.

A similar concentration occurred in Scotland, with the difference that the water-power stage was almost coincident with the birth of the industry. Glasgow, with its near neighbour Paisley, was the Manchester and Liverpool of the Scottish cotton industry. Between 1780 and 1815 the cotton mills of Scotland were dis-tributed over the Clyde Valley, Perthshire and the Solway Firth. After 1815 there was a concentration on Glasgow ; and the later eclipse of the Scottish cotton industry, with the one important exception of cotton thread, was due not to any lack of enterprise or of technical advantage, but to the comparatively greater profitableness of shipbuilding and marine engineering. North Carolina, the scene of a 20th-century industrial revolution, is back in the water stage in the new form of hydro-electric power. This combines the advantages of water and steam ; it makes it easy to build factories in a rural district, it avoids the dirt and unsightliness of smoking chimneys, and it maximises the control over natural agents. For at the central generating stations coal is used as an auxiliary to water ; and by the use of high-power transmission the power surplus of one region is transferred to the deficiency of another. This is one of the tactical achievements of what is called giant power.

(3) *Mill owning.* Setting up in the textile business was very different in 1800 from what it is to-day. To-day the problem is to find the capital and the market. Then the problem was to get the machines. Some of Lancashire's most famous cotton firms were founded by men who began life as makers of textile machinery. Such were Adam and George Murray, M'Connel and Kennedy, T. and J. Houldsworth. Robert Owen entered cotton manufacturing through the same door. When he was a clerk in a Manchester drapery establishment, he heard of the ' new and curious ' cotton-spinning machinery. Accordingly in partnership with his informant he started to make mules. ' We had shortly about forty men at work to make machines and we obtained wood, iron, and brass for their construction upon credit.'[1] This was about 1790. By machine making he qualified himself for mill management, and then rose from manager to owner.

The antecedent connexion of machine making with mill owning was replaced, when the two became specialised in separate hands, by an intimate connexion between maker and user ; and this strengthened the tendency to regional concentration. For the textile industries of Great Britain were localised before the days of railways ; and therefore to secure personal contact and economy of carriage the machine makers had to be near the mills. It is no doubt an advantage still, but under modern transport conditions the machine makers of New England through their sales force and service men supply North Carolina as easily as Massachusetts ; and the expense of shipping the machinery—a non-recurring item—is offset by the economy of manufacture in the region where the cotton is grown and the by-products are treated.

(4) *Regional specialisation.* Nothing but local history can explain the very peculiar specialisation in commodity and process

[1] *Life of Robert Owen by Himself,* ed. G. Bell, p. 31.

which has been evolved in Lancashire and the West Riding. Preston and Blackburn weave, Bolton and Manchester spin fine yarns, Oldham and Ashton coarse yarns. And within these general divisions there is a further specialisation in types of goods. In the West Riding by general contrast the division is based on the product, i.e. one district performs all the processes of one product. Thus Bradford, Halifax and Huddersfield specialise in worsteds : Leeds and other towns in woollens : the Dewsbury district in shoddy : and there are further subdivisions, as in the cotton industry. In both counties the specialisation has been achieved without control from above ; nor is it the case of a giant in each district forcing the babes to sit around him. Marshall calls it ' automatic organisation ' ; and it is without doubt the strongest feature in the textile economy of Great Britain to-day. The humidifier, costing a few hundred dollars, will keep the inside of a factory at any degree of humidity, whether it be in Lancashire or North Carolina. But a new district cannot instal in a twinkling those economies external to the four walls of the factory which are the product of a long and peculiar history. North Carolina's strength is her situation with regard to her raw materials and market. She is on top of the raw cotton and she supplies a vast internal market with standard goods produced in mass.

(5) *Dobson and Barlow, Machine Makers.* Messrs. Dobson and Barlow Limited, the doyen of textile engineers, was founded in 1790 to make the mules which had been invented by Samuel Crompton, Bolton's most famous son. Until 1892 the firm was a partnership with varying titles according to the names of the partners : Dobson and Rothwell ; Isaac and Benjamin Dobson ; the Executors of the late Benjamin Dobson ; Messrs. Dobson and Metcalfe ; Messrs. Dobson and Barlow. In 1892 it became a private limited company, in 1907 a public limited company. The founder, Isaac Dobson, came from Patterdale in the Lake District, attracted by the reputation of Bolton, and there he formed a partnership with Peter Rothwell, who owned a timber yard and knew the local spinners. John Metcalfe, a principal from 1839 to 1850, was the brother-in-law of Benjamin Dobson, the nephew of Isaac ; and the two in addition ran a cotton mill at Chorley. The name of Barlow appears in 1850 with Edward Barlow, the son of a Bolton banker. The middle of the century was also a turning point in the firm's career. In 1846 it sold the original works in Blackhorse Street and bought the present Kay Street works, which were then outside the town and overlooked Hall-i'-th'-Wood.

As the firm's records show, the first mules were made

principally of wood, the shafts and spindles being of wrought iron and the pinions and wheels of cast iron and brass, but by 1830 all traces of infancy had disappeared. Indeed the textile machinery of 1830 is far closer to that of 1920 in appearance than to that of 1790. One of the principal improvements in the 20th-century mule was the steel carriage, which was introduced in 1906. The technique of mill construction [1] was also by 1830 modernised up to a point. The Georgian factory—built on the bank of a stream with belfry and gable end and four storeys rising to an attic, which was itself the survival of the days when adjacent householders formed a mill by combining their attics into one workroom—had passed away. From about 1840 to about 1890 there was no marked alteration in structural details. The almost universal type was the cast iron column and the brick arch. In equipment and sanitation the mills were brought more or less into line by the requirements of the effective factory legislation of 1833 onwards. But towards the end of the century mill construction was profoundly modified with a view to securing larger space and a scientific lay out. Thus the opening machinery of the cotton mixing and blowing rooms, which in the older mills was tucked away in the card room, was installed on the ground floor in separate rooms : the spinning rooms were enlarged until they could take anything from 100,000 to 130,000 mule spindles : and the different processes were co-ordinated by a system of internal conveyance. In the last resort the machine maker dictates the size of the factory as well as the individual process.

In the history of Dobson and Barlow the technical landmark in the second half of the 19th century was the purchase about 1885 of the Albert Machine Works from a firm of machine tool makers. Henceforth they were able to manufacture their own machine tools for the production of their increasing range of textile machinery. Thus the partnership of 1790, with a horse gin (i.e. a capstan revolved by a horse) and twenty employees, mostly joiners, became the company of 1892, with over four thousand employees working in metal by the aid of steam power. Since then the firm, in company with other leaders in the textile machine industry, has pioneered technical education and laboratory research. It maintains its support of technical education by the supply of literature, models and lectures to Technical Schools, Textile Societies, and the various organisations connected with the textile industry. This research has two economic objects especially in view. Since Lancashire is confined by fiscal

[1] Cf. *Proceedings of the Textile Institute, Bolton*, 1927. H. Hill, 'Mill Construction.'

circumstances to the finer branches of the world's cotton trade, it is necessary that her machinery should produce a range of 'counts'[1] between wide variations and that it should administer an absolute minimum of harsh treatment to the fine and delicate product which is in course of manufacture. Secondly, the industry must be prepared for expansion into allied lines. Dobson and Barlow were the first British firm to supply machinery for cotton ginning to the British Cotton Growers' Association in 1905 : and about the same time they were the first to produce British-made artificial silk spinning machines for commercial use. In 1927 the Company was engaged in the supply of a complete plant and equipment to three of the most recently established artificial silk companies of Great Britain and Ireland.

The firm, like other firms of old standing, has had its labour troubles. In May 1831, at the time of the general trade union ferment, the employees presented a round-robin, i.e. a petition with the signatures pointing to the middle so that no name should stand first. It was signed by all the 134 workmen and demanded a ten-hour day, restriction of apprentices to one for four men, and a legal five-year apprenticeship. The resulting strike lasted till the end of the year and the strikers collected over £1840 in relief funds. There was trouble again at the close of the Lancashire cotton famine, when one of the demands made and for a time granted was weekly instead of fortnightly pay. But throughout the century the distinctive feature was the general absence of labour friction and the permanence of employment not only through the individual's lifetime but in families. At the centenary of 1890 the Principal, Mr. T. H. Rushton, stated that out of the eleven men employed in 1797 the families of six were still connected with the works and that out of the twelve additional names of 1800 eleven were still on the books.[2]

(6) *Samuel Oldknow, Muslin Manufacturer.* The textile industries supply the clearest examples of a structural transition which was common to all the handicrafts, namely from indirect mercantile control to direct industrial employment. Before the mechanical transition the head of the business was a giver out of work, the transition made him an employer of persons. The

---

[1] A count in the cotton trade is the number of hanks of 840 yards in each pound of weight.

[2] Samuel Crompton, *op. cit.* p. 116. This book contains a history of Messrs. Dobson and Barlow, Ltd., in addition to a monograph on Samuel Crompton. Of 1927 the historian of the firm narrates : ' To-day there are men holding responsible positions in the Works who have been with the Company over 50 years, and it is a point of considerable pride that, with not more than half a dozen exceptions, the Management, Foremen, Representatives, and Heads of the Clerical and Technical Staffs have " served their time " with the Company, and have been promoted from the " bench " or " desk " to a position of trust ' (p. 127).

merchant manufacturer had a warehouse and hunted down the embezzlers of yarn ; the industrial employer had a factory and checked attendance by a factory clock. The progress from one status to the other is well illustrated in the career of Samuel Oldknow of Mellor, near Stockport, the founder of Lancashire's muslin manufacture.[1] At the beginning of his career we find him buying his raw materials, sorting them, giving them out to spinners and weavers with instructions concerning the kind of cloth required. When the cloth is brought in, he gives it out again to be finished. There were no workers on the premises except a few warpers and finishers. After a short while he built bleaching and printing works. Then came spinning mills, first a discarded silk mill, and next a cotton mill, which he built. His warehouse was his head office, and here in time he assembled a number of his most skilled weavers in a loom house under his own eye. He planned to build two spinning mills, one at Stockport for the finest yarns driven by a Boulton and Watt engine, the other at Mellor in the Goyt Valley driven by water power. At Mellor he bought an estate, built there a big house for himself and close by a big mill and houses for the workers, as any Coke of Holkham might have done. But it was the eve of war with France. His capital gave out and he had to part with everything except the Mellor estate and to borrow from his rich neighbour Arkwright (the inventor's son), into whose hands the mill eventually came. He was a good employer and popular with his workers, a patron of agriculture and the promoter and chairman of the Peak Forest Canal, as well as an eminent muslin manufacturer. But he was over-sanguine and the war played havoc with his high-class trade.

How many employers of this type were there ? To how many of these did the war bring financial reverse ? Professor Daniels closes his *History of the Early English Cotton Industry* (p. 148) : ' The social retrogression and evils which mark the industrial revolution period are only in a very secondary sense to be attributed to the economic movement : the primary cause is to be found in the war in which the country was engaged.' This is a useful reminder that Robert Owen as a master was not alone in his generation, but it is unjustifiable as a general statement. For it would be unreasonable to ascribe to the Napoleonic war the disorder arising from the Irish influx or the exploitation of women and children in mines ; and these were major social evils. Moreover, while the war lasted, it stimulated the trades which produced ordnance and Army uniforms, even though it injured pottery and cotton.

[1] Cf. *Samuel Oldknow and the Arkwrights,* by G. Unwin and Others (1924).

CHAPTER XVI

THE INDUSTRIAL REVOLUTION IN RETROSPECT

Section 1. The Birth Decade of the Revolution. Section 2. Copper and Brass. Section 3. The Potteries. Section 4. The Generalisation of Machine Industry. Section 5. Competition and the Unit of Enterprise. Section 6. The State and *Laissez-faire*.

Section 1. *The Birth Decade of the Revolution*

THE French Revolution broke out in 1789 ; that is an historical fact. But it is not possible to assign a political year to an economic revolution : we can only specify a decade—that which opens with the year 1760. In 1760 the Carron Iron Works were erected, and since before this Scotland had no iron industry, 1760 was the year for Scotland. She turned then from the cultivation of a difficult soil to the exploitation of rich resources of coal and iron. This and the foreign trade of Glasgow precipitated Scottish industrialism. In 1761 Brindley's canal from Worsley to Manchester was opened. To the generality this far-reaching wonder was the revolution. Year by year new thousands in all parts of the country beheld this concrete mastery over Nature ; rivers flowed down hill, but canals were taken wherever they were wanted for the service of man. In 1769 Arkwright patented the water frame, and James Watt his steam engine ; 1769 therefore was the birth year of mechanical power in cotton and engineering. In every case, however, the novelties were the fruit of effort which had been in the air for some years previously. In 1754 the Society of Arts was founded at London by William Shipley, in 1760 it was offering rewards for inventions in multiple spinning. Thus both Watt and Arkwright had their atmosphere, the atmosphere of mechanical speculation in the bustling North. The patents issued between 1617 and 1760, a period of nearly 150 years, were fewer than those between 1760 and 1785, a period of only 25 years. Moreover, many of the early patents were mechanical dreams, as wild as the visions of fortunes in the South Seas. Some were not inventions at all but simply importations of foreign methods. After 1760 they were practical and specific, though not at first exact enough to prevent litigation and injustice. Among competing districts Lancashire stood first, partly because of its freedom from restrictions which held back the corporate towns of the South, and partly because the material on which it worked lent itself to mechanical treatment. It chanced that soon after 1760 Great Britain because of her small size became a regular importer of food. Thus early was the stage set for the struggle between Manchester and the landlords.

Section 2.   Copper and Brass

Brass is a mixture of copper and zinc. It was originally made by mixing copper with calamine, the ore of zinc (calamine from the Greek *kadmia*—Theban earth) ; but William Champion's patent of 1738 for making zinc from calamine furnished brass makers with zinc in separated form. Manufactured copper is used in finished copper goods or as the raw material of the brass industry. Bronze, an alloy of copper and tin, is included under the brass industry ; in 1860 it replaced copper in the British copper currency. Battery means hammered goods ; thus in a book of 1802, ' Battery works include pots, saucepans and metals, which tho' cast at first are to be afterwards hammered or battered into form.' [1]

It does not take long for the student of the industrial revolution to realise that it proceeded very unevenly. Cotton and iron were leaders, but some large industries, of which building and coal mining are good examples, can hardly be said to have experienced a technical revolution by 1900. Agriculture, too, occupies a special position. Its technical advance in the 18th century was ahead of that in manufacture, but only in the 20th century, and in countries outside the mother country of industrialism, has the complement of the industrial revolution arrived in the form of scientific marketing by organised farmers. Indeed, the uniformity of the economic world is seen best at points subsequent to the processes of production. Modern methods of office organisation, advertising and accounting are common to all industries to-day ; and the standardisation which is their common factor has invaded the professions, sport, and life generally. But the standardisation of business method was not possible without the aid of exact statistics. In 1834 the Royal Statistical Society was founded ; in 1925 *The Accountant*, the organ of the Chartered Accountants of Great Britain, celebrated its Jubilee of publication, and its age is practically that of accountancy as a profession.

But there is another side to the variety of the industrial revolution which is equally worthy of notice, and that is the relation in which factory industry stood to domestic during the years of technical transition. In the textile industries the relation was one of rivalry. The factory destroyed the domestic system : the machine the handicraft. But even here, it is pertinent to remember, the period from the 1780's to the first

[1] Oxford English Dictionary, *sub* battery.

decade of the 19th century, which was later looked back upon as a golden age of hand-loom weaving, was the rough quarter of a century which elapsed between the cheapening of yarn by the new machine methods and the effective introduction of the power loom. In the metal industries the complementary relation predominated. Here ' domestic industry flourished largely because its materials were provided for it with sufficient cheapness by more highly capitalistic concerns in the previous stages of the productive process.' [1] The heavy industries (and it is these that we mainly think of when we associate iron with cotton in the leadership of the revolution) do not afford so good an example as the more expensive metals, copper and brass, or as iron itself in the expensive form of cutlers' steel.

In the Birmingham brass and copper industries, as in the Sheffield cutlery trade, there were two distinct groups of producers, the makers of brass and steel, and ' the trades ' which used brass and steel as their raw material. Between the twin specialties of Birmingham and Sheffield there were some small differences. Thus Sheffield steel makers depended largely on Swedish iron, therefore they were not interested in the ownership of mines : the cost of their raw materials, like those of textile materials, depended on tariffs and transport charges. Birmingham brass makers used native ore. Matthew Boulton, the leader of the Birmingham industry, was a shareholder in English copper and tin mines, but he overlaid his hardware business with a revolutionary commodity, steam power ; so that the old and the new here were in the same hands. But when in the 19th century mild steel replaced wrought iron, it was under the leadership of inventors dissociated from the traditions of Sheffield. Nevertheless between the industries of Birmingham and Sheffield there was a fundamental similarity of structure. There were two parties, makers and users. The former produced on a comparatively large scale even before the industrial revolution, the latter on a small scale to the end of the 19th century. In respect of diversity in the scale of operations 18th-century Birmingham was close to 18th-century London, where in shop-keeping, wood-working and precious metals great and small flourished side by side. The piecemeal nature of factory legislation reflects the piecemeal progress of textile machinery. But the workshop, which was finally associated with the factory in the Workshop and Factory Acts, was not only piecemeal in the order of arrival but also structurally multiform.

Copper smelting was introduced into England in the reign of

---

[1] H. Hamilton, *The English Brass and Copper Industries to 1800*, Intro. by Sir William Ashley, x.

Elizabeth by German capital and German labour. The first enterprise was at Keswick, Cumberland, where by 1642 there was a colony of 4000 foreign workmen. The Mines Royal, which was a copper mining and smelting company, and the Mineral and Battery Works, which mainly made brass, united in 1668 and had a legal monopoly until 1689, when copper mining was thrown open. But competition did not bring a host of competing producers ; for it was not possible for the brazier to produce his own brass. Since copper and brass making required large amounts of capital, the unit of enterprise was too large to be financed by one individual. Therefore, even though the law was unfavourable to company effort, companies of a sort sprang up in the 18th century. The large concerns did not confine themselves to the supply of semi-raw material to the finishing trades. They were also finishers of certain goods, especially of heavy goods supplied in standard patterns to trade consumers, such as copper pans for distilleries, and sheets and bolts for ship's sheathing, which was introduced about 1760. ' The trades ' covered a large variety of products and processes from cock-founding, an adjunct of plumbing, to coffin furniture. About 1775 the button began to displace the buckle, but the change was within the Birmingham trades and not at their expense. There was no exact division of function between the brass makers and ' the trades ' ; nor uniform relation between the brass makers and the copper-mining companies. Before and during the 18th century certain goods were made both in the factory of the large concern and in the domestic workshop. The rich copper finds in Anglesey (c. 1770) and the rise of Thomas Williams, an Anglesey mine owner, smelter and manufacturer, led to fierce competition between Anglesey and Cornwall and thus to a marketing combine, the Cornish Metal Co., under the control of Williams. Birmingham asserted its independence by forming in 1780 a co-operative concern to make brass for its own trades, and fought the combine by establishing a mining and copper company.

The mediaeval method of wire making is as clear an example of the limitation of human power as could be found in any industry. ' Men sat in swings opposite each other with a thin plate of brass attached to a girdle fastened round their waists and then by stretching forth their feet against a stump they shot their bodies from it, closing with the plate again ; and so on until it was stretched into wire.' [1] In the 18th century this and other processes requiring power were done by the aid of water. In the 19th century the greater development of the heavy iron industry in the Black Country to the west of Birmingham reduced the

[1] H. Hamilton, *op. cit.* p. 344.

brass and copper industries to a subordinate position. The application of steam to the driving of machinery brought most of the Birmingham trades into the factory ; and the last days of handwork were not in Birmingham or the brass industry but among the nail and chain makers of Dudley and neighbouring country towns. The industrial revolution took its mechanical orders from Soho, which was a part of Birmingham ; and when Birmingham was linked on the north with Lancashire and on the south with London by iron rails, its full industrialism had arrived. It was never off the line of progress.

Section 3. *The Potteries*

The industrial revolution in pottery presents many points of similarity with that in cotton. Both were at first domestic industries carried on by hand. The processes occupied the family down to its youngest members, and both were operated on a small scale until the industrial revolution. The pottery of 1700 was a thatched cottage with lean-to working sheds and an oven surrounded by a ' hovel ' of sods to conserve the heat. It employed perhaps six men and three boys, and probably £10,000 covered the value of the whole annual output of Staffordshire. In this peasant workshop the sequence of production was : preparation of clay in a tank and the removal of air holes—a simple process done largely by young boys, as spinning was by girls ; next the essential manufacturing process, the throwing of the ware on the potter's wheel ; finally the finishing of the ware—decoration, baking in clay containers called ' saggars,' and glazing to make the ware hold water and look well. The oven would be fired on a Friday, the ware cooked over the week-end and taken out Monday morning. These stages of production corresponded roughly with the spinning, weaving and finishing of the textile trades.

The cotton industry obtained all its raw materials from abroad, whereas the potteries used none but native clay. But just as the early Lancashire industry progressed from a mixed fabric of cotton and linen to an all-cotton product in the days of Arkwright, so the Staffordshire potters, since from local clays they could obtain only a dirty yellow ware, employed the makeshift of a coat of imported white clay on a local body, and then in Wedgwood's time produced a perfect all-white ware by importing the china clays of Cornwall and Devon. The consumers of drapery forsook woollen goods for French silks and both for Indian chintzes, at once beautiful and cheap. Similarly there was a foreign influence in the use of pottery. China from China was the translucent ware named porcelain, the dinner ware of princes. The East

India Company might possibly use it at a banquet, but as a regular table ware it was beyond the reach even of the rich. Delft produced an imitation porcelain, as Utrecht an imitation velvet ; and from Holland a Delft industry was introduced into England at the ports of London, Liverpool and Bristol. But even as Surrey had a calico printing industry until Lancashire destroyed it by developing its own, so the Staffordshire potteries by native skill improved their own earthenwares until they put other centres out of business. Etruria, as the name would lead us to expect, produced *inter alia* ornamental ware with classical designs, but this part of the business did not pay. It was a hobby of Wedgwood's, valued by him as an advertisement of what English workmanship could do.

The prosperity of Staffordshire rested on the increasing food consumption of the nation. Indirectly it owed much to the art of Bakewell and the tea trade of the East India Company. In 1700 London knew Staffordshire only by the butter pots in which its butter arrived from the North. In 1800 it ate and drank from Staffordshire ware and talked Wedgwood over the table. At an earlier, but not very distant, date, the poor had used utensils of wood and the well-to-do vessels of pewter. Wedgwood supplied his countrymen with a ware which would serve rich and poor alike according to its quality ; and the foreign market was similarly graded, expensive sorts going to the American mainland and the cheap sort to the West Indian islands (above, p. 143). Naturally, therefore, the Cornish tin miners did not love Wedgwood (he feared once that they would lay rough hands on him), but he knew where to seek a market for his Queen's ware, namely in London where Kings and Queens lived, and where he kept a show room, which was a salon. No merchant was more adept than he in introducing new wares under royal or noble patronage. In 1815 the industrial supremacy of Britain was unchallenged. Peace had returned and Europe was prostrate. But in the 1780's, when the American War had terminated badly and trouble with Europe was threatening, the two new industries of pottery and cotton had everything to lose by war and no great history behind them. They opposed Pitt's proposal for Ireland, scenting a new competitor : petitioned the Government to enforce the law against the export of machinery and artisans : resisted the taxation engendered by the American War—the proposed tax on carriage of 1782 and the fustian excise of 1784 : and reiterated their hostility to the Orders-in-Council, which excluded the one of them from its raw material and the other from its best market. Their eagerness for the French Treaty of 1786 was due less to their confidence in the superiority of English manufacture than to the nightmare of an increasing production on a market restricted by wars, transport costs, monopolies and tariffs.

Neither bales of cotton nor piece goods were likely to break in transit, and Manchester even in the days of the Mersey and Irwell navigation did not find it hard to reach Liverpool. But Staffordshire was further inland. Most of its raw material arrived by a roundabout route from a distant corner of England ; and the finished product was exceedingly fragile. It was most unsuited to mule-back transportation. This accounts for the prominent part which Wedgwood and his neighbours played in the construction first of turnpikes and then of the Mersey and Trent Canal. Improved communications led to production on a larger scale. Towards the end of the 18th century the district was producing £300,000 to £400,000 of ware per annum. In place of the six men and three boys of 1700 there were a number of rather small potters, and at their head a few large firms with a personnel of 400 to 500 in each. There was no question of immigrant Huguenots, of imitation of an elder industry or of State aid by bounty or prohibition. The potters did it for themselves. They had the ' experimental bug,' Wedgwood indeed so badly that his extravagance frightened his first partners into dissolution. All through the 18th century every stage in the technique was under constant change and improvement ; and Lancashire, though it had far bigger figures of personnel and output, could claim no more on the technical side. Wedgwood's technique included business technique. We see him promoting sales with one eye on London and the other on the Continent and solving with the help of a brother entrepreneur such new and knotty problems as time-keeping and costing. Etruria in the 1780's was a factory in all but the circumstance that there was hardly any steam power in it.

The weaver's gain from mill-spun yarn was short lived, for it enslaved his children and in time extended its methods to his own handicraft. But none of the inventions of 1759 to 1842, the period of the three Josiah Wedgwoods, hurt the potter. At the end, as at the beginning, his was a skilled trade with a tradition to follow. The skill consisted in the delicacy with which the hand manipulated the clay. There was a scare in the 1840's, but it was not until the 1870's that under the influence of the machine trades automatic aids began to be introduced in the shape of jiggers and profile tools, which reduced the potter's skill by leaving no discretion to him. Wedgwood as early as 1782 used steam power for grinding his materials : his pyrometer measured heat with precision : later the adaptation of the engine lathe to pottery permitted the ware to be ' trued up ' and to receive the design with machine accuracy. But all these means were supplementary to skill and not subversive to it. The lesson of the industrial revolution in pottery is the value of control, of control of physical properties and marketing arrangements : the materials English, the workers craftsmen ; and the product, by reason of its high grade, in international repute.

Section 4. The Generalisation of Machine Industry

For Great Britain as a whole, for its agriculture, industry and wage-earners, the period 1850–1875 was one of steady prosperity. The long aftermath of war had passed away during the critical premiership of Peel. There were no corn laws, and agriculture in spite of free trade boomed. Whereas between 1815 and 1835 the tonnage of the mercantile marine was almost stationary, between 1835 and 1875 it trebled, and because a steam vessel could make several voyages in the time that a sailing vessel made one, entrances and clearances increased sixfold. Britain was well fed. She was also the world's carrier, the world's shipbuilder, and the world's workshop. Amid technical changes about the middle of the century two groups stand out—first the great series which ushered in the age of steel, and secondly the surrender all along the line of handicrafts which had struggled on either without steam power or in competition with it. The steel inventions prolonged Britain's metallurgical pre-eminence despite the slender basis of domestic resources on which it was built. The output of coal in million tons rose from 30 in 1837 to 65 in 1857. In the early 60's it passed 100 and was 200 in 1897. Thus the Victorian age was the great coal age, with Puffing Billys at the portal and steel steamships at the close. At a time when tin mining was in decay and Cornwall was losing its time-honoured skill by migration and emigration, South Wales and the North grew steadily in output and personnel. From the 1860's onwards the coal miners came to the front in the trade union and co-operative worlds.

As late as 1870 there was a considerable body of hand workers in the knitting and woollen industries, but they were always diminishing and their passing was peaceful. The sharpest blow of the period, the Lancashire cotton famine of 1861–3 (once again war was hurting Lancashire), fell on an industry already fully mechanised and partially strengthened against a rainy day by co-operative stores and savings banks. Then for the first time co-operators apprehended the law which has never ceased to surprise them, that in bad times their trade holds up because spending power is concentrated on the necessaries which they in particular supply. But steel and cotton were still in the middle of the century exceptional. A recent analysis [1] of the distribution of industrial occupations in extra-metropolitan England shows that in 1841, the census year selected, the national industries, i.e. the staple industries supplying a national market, were less in personnel than those supplying a local or provincial market. (Agriculture and mining are not classed as industrial occupations.) The characteristic provincial trades of 1841 were ready-made clothing, woodwork, and confectionery ; the characteristic local trades brick-laying, tailoring, smithy work and the trades of the butcher and baker. London contained an immense number of people in industrial occupations, but most of them worked for Londoners : its national services were mercantile, printing being its only considerable national industry. If London were included, the numerical inferiority of national industry in 1841 would be even more pronounced. A comparison of 1861 with 1841 shows the trend of over twenty years, which Professor Day expresses in general terms thus : ' Producers who, in the course of development, were able to extend their market beyond the provincial area found no resting place until they attained a national market . . . the development of market areas was discontinuous.' [2] Among producers on the verge of transition in 1861 were the food trades of different kinds. The miller still ground the meal for the people of his immediate vicinity ; and the distribution of butchers in proportion to population was remarkably regular. Shortly after came the national jump : beginning in luxury goods, such as confectionery and sweetmeats, then reaching to flour milling under the influence of Hungarian roller milling and the concentration of wheat at ports of import. But it is still to come in the butchering of home-grown meat, which as a business presents a comical contrast with the packing plants of North America.

The biscuit and chocolate industries supply examples of the giant business of to-day, their problems of technique and marketing being not unlike those of soap and tobacco. In all four packing is an important factor in the cost of production. The progress from quite small to very large concerns occurred in the latter part of the 19th century. Thus Huntley and Palmers of Reading and Cadburys of Birmingham were established about the same time, 1826 and 1830. The former in 1851 (when it obtained the Bronze Medal, the highest open to the biscuit trade, at the International Exhibition) had 300 workpeople ; in 1900 about 5000. Cadburys were in a small way till 1870. In 1879, when they moved to Bournville outside Birmingham, they had

---

[1] Clive Day, *Distribution of Industrial Occupations in England*, Yale. 1927.
[2] *Ibid.* p. 143.

250 workpeople ; in 1900, 2500 ; in 1926, 10,000. By the reputation of their trade names the leaders secured an international market, which in the chocolate trade became important towards 1900. Recent developments have taken the form of opening branch factories in the Dominions, for example by Fry, Cadbury and Pascall jointly in Australia in 1918 and by Rowntree and Co., Ltd., in Toronto in 1926. The demand for cocoa as a beverage was never very great, but in the 80's the extraction of cocoa essence by hydraulic presses was pioneered by Van Houten of Holland. The cocoa fat, hitherto neutralised by the addition of some product such as starch, was now removed and used in the allied branch of chocolate manufacture. For chocolate and sweetmeats the demand was highly extensible; and the cheapness of sugar in England favoured the growth of the sugarusing industries—sweets, chocolate and jam.

In 1861 transition to machinery was already under way in two important industries hitherto unmentioned—ready-made clothing and boot and shoe. Of these the latter is more important, as it was a skilled man's trade, and not, like the ready-made clothing, ancillary to a main staple.

Shoemakers in extra-metropolitan England

Year	Total	Per 100,000 of population
1841	147,000	112·6
1861	197,000	120·0
1911	175,000	59·3
1921	169,000	54·2

From these figures it is seen that with the change to factory production there was at first an increase in personnel and later, as factory work ousted home work, a decline ; which, when stated as a percentage of the population, was over 50% between 1841 and 1921. The industry is now a factory industry with a national market, but there are still many local shoemakers whose business is shoe repairing.

The technical transition in clothing and in boots and shoes was marked by a very distinctive feature. Here, by contrast with all previous experience, another country, the U.S.A., led the mechanical way. In America [1] skilled labour was dearer than in England ; and the supply of footwear to a frontier population was at once difficult and urgent. Under this stimulus its boot and shoe trade reached a considerable degree of specialisation even while processes were manual. The merchants cut out their

[1] *Cf.* V S. Clark, *History of Manufactures in the United States* (1607–1860), pp. 440–5.

materials at headquarters and marketed the product after it had been made up by local craftsmen. Supplying a demand which was not exacting in matters of individual style and fit, they produced in bulk ; and this opened the way to machinery, first to mechanical devices for cutting the leather, then to pegging machines for fixing the upper to the sole (such as Brunel's father had invented during the Napoleonic war for the mass production of Army boots), and finally to sewing machines. The sewing machine was invented in America about 1850 : 1851 was the date of J. M. Singer's patent. Designed as a hand machine for use in the home, it was speedily applied to the factory production of men's and women's clothing in America and England. After its introduction into clothing, its adaptation to leather stitching was comparatively simple. The dressmakers, being in general a low-paid class of female labour, were not in a position to resist machinery even had they so desired, but shoemakers were radical independent men and averse to change. However, to save their home market British makers had to follow the lead of America, first in the use of machinery, and secondly in the elaborate departmental organisation known as the American or one floor-system. In the 1890's they successfully met a determined American invasion, at the price of using American machines on the royalty basis. Where clothing or footwear is fitted to the individual, the industry is necessarily decentralised. Where it is ready-made, it can be localised in districts where labour is abundant or the raw material is produced. These two factors account for the ready-made clothing industries of London and Yorkshire respectively. The boot and shoe industry, being a separate skilled trade, offers a better field for regional skill than garment making. Long before the days of machinery a great amount of footwear was produced wholesale in a number of centres, of which the two leading were Northampton and Leicester. These two districts were helped by their proximity to raw materials, hides and tanning bark, and by their central position as a distributing centre for a product everywhere in use.

During the last half-century British industry, with the exception perhaps of general farming and the mining of coal and iron, has made absolute progress decade by decade. Old industries have been maintained and supplemented, cotton, for example, by artificial silk. New industries, of which the motor is the premier, have been created. But relatively to some other countries, and in particular to the U.S.A., Britain has lost ground. Her small size, the relative paucity of her natural resources and, of course, the fact that she started first made this inevitable. However, even though the U.S.A. has a financial superiority over all other countries greater by far than that which Great Britain ever had over Europe, there is no longer the same opportunity for persistent superiority in industrial skill.   For this is the age of science and of the application of science to industry, of psychological as well as physical science ; and science is an equaliser. It creates a body of international knowledge, and, though the use of a method may be reserved by law, it cannot long remain unknown or unparalleled.   The service of the laboratory was rendered first to the chemical and iron and steel industries. By-products, which at the beginning of the 19th century were discarded as useless, were utilised at the end of it, because in the interval their use and the means of isolating them had been ascertained.   By-products were not unknown in the pre-laboratory age, but they were utilised only when they presented themselves in usable form.   A good example is the slipper industry of Rossendale, Lancashire.   When the woollen manufacture declined there in the 1850's, one substitute was feltmaking.   The employees in the felt warehouses made slippers for themselves from the spare ends of felt in order to avoid damaging the material over which they had to walk for the purpose of matching the patterns.   Then they made them for their friends, and finally in the 1870's two men of enterprise put the manufacture on a commercial basis, with the result that in 1918 there were some 25 firms engaged in the Rossendale slipper trade, employing about 6000 persons.[1]

To-day the laboratory is constantly extending the range of by-products.   The American packing industry of to-day is the outcome of refrigeration and by-products.   The use of the by-product is only one of the reasons for which the modern business maintains a department of research, but it is a very important one.   Nor is research confined to the giant business ; for the co-operative research association, an outcome of the late war, introduces small-scale industries to large-scale research.

Finally, science in the form of Industrial Psychology is now being applied to the *human* side of industry.   The advance of the mechanical and technical sciences dominated the industrial field in the 19th century.   But since human beings are both the means and the end of economic activity, it is logical to expect that further great progress will result from the application in industry of the sciences of psychology and physiology.   The results already achieved in increases of output and reduction of fatigue and nervous strain and in vocational selection and guidance show promise of a great future.   The study originated in the Scientific Management advocated by F. W. Taylor in America ; but this

[1] G. H. Tupling, *The Economic History of Rossendale*, p. 202 * s*.

system fell largely into disrepute through mishandling, and was never accepted in England : its basis was thought to be too ' mechanistic.' To-day psychologists have entered industry in every great country, but the foremost centre of the movement is probably the National Institute of Industrial Psychology founded at London in 1921.

Section 5. *Competition and the Unit of Enterprise*

The problem here raised bears on three points, which are difficult to separate in narrative : (1) the company *versus* the individual ; (2) competition *versus* legal monopoly ; (3) competition *versus* combination, which may or may not eliminate competition.

1. After the passing of the mediaeval guilds the normal unit of economic enterprise was the individual acting under some degree of corporate control, which weakened as industry grew up outside corporate towns and as the hold of the City Companies over the conduct of their several trades relaxed. In 1700 individuals or private partnerships managed their business as they pleased, with but few restrictions on the labour they employed or the quality of goods they sold. There were, however, certain enterprises where group effort was necessary, in particular foreign trade and domestic undertakings in mining, drainage and water supply. The Joint Stock Company was evolved for these tasks. In the foreign field it proved more efficient and more elastic than the Regulated Company, in which individuals traded with their own capital. In the domestic field its progress was slower. In the copper and brass industries the joint stock form supplied the starting point : only thus could sufficient capital be accumulated for the venture. But in the two copper companies privileged by Queen Elizabeth the joint stock function lapsed from that of entrepreneur to that of rent receiver. For before long they leased their property to individual members or partnerships of members. In general the joint stock company was weak in productive drive, but in spheres outside production its range of enterprise was very considerable and rose to a peak at the beginning of the 18th century. As Professor Scott has shown in his *History of Joint Stock Companies to 1720* it embraced mining, fishing, colonisation, banking, insurance, water supply and a few manufactures. Its strength was in the assembly of capital and spreading of risk and it was not confined to operations of routine. But fraudulent promotion at the time of the South Sea Bubble administered a severe shock to the joint stock method. During the 18th century some unincorporated

companies existed—for instance, in the metal industries. These companies had the power to transfer shares and invest the management in directors, but their legal position was doubtful in view of the Bubble Act of 1719 (6 Geo. I, c. 18), which, after incorporating two companies for marine insurance, proceeded under section 8 to pronounce illegal and void all undertakings acting under obsolete charters or presuming to act as corporate bodies without legal authority.

There was no new joint stock growth until the era of canals. The State might have built these, but State enterprise smacked of royal monopoly and no one petitioned the State to build them. The company organisation with public subscriptions was the alternative ; and docks, railways, gasworks and waterworks were financed by this method. Public utilities and Government funds provided the chief market of the general investor in the century from 1760 to 1860. Public utilities were incorporated by special Acts of Parliament and therefore were Statutory Companies. This was necessary because in order to operate they had to take land and to do things which without parliamentary powers would have been nuisances. As they grew in number, general legislation was passed simplifying the procedure of incorporation, similar to the general legislation for turnpikes and enclosures. There was the Railway Clauses Act of 1845 (8 & 9 Vict. c. 20), the Gas Works Clauses Act of 1847 (10 & 11 Vict. c. 15) and so on—one general Act for each great group. The liability of shareholders in these companies was limited, but so also were their powers. They could devote no part of their funds to objects unauthorised by the terms of incorporation.

For general productive enterprise there was not at first an essential need of the joint stock form. The manufacturer, like the shipowner, could grow from a humble beginning either alone or with partners ; and hundreds of merchants were ready to mount the ladder of industrial undertaking. As the business grew, the owners, by keeping back a part of their profits, provided for its further expansion.

Scotland jumped into industrialism more speedily than England ; and Scottish merchants provided their own start by forming joint stock companies. In these progressive landlords took a share, patriotically ready to develop their district. Scotland was the pioneer of the local banking company. But it was difficult for a group united only by enthusiasm for development and the possession of money to keep pace with a rapidly changing technique of production. Therefore in Scotland, as in the early copper industry of England, the company frequently gave place to the individual. David Dale, the founder of power spinning in Scotland, started as an importer of linen yarn : then with a partner he built spinning mills : later he engaged as his manager Robert Owen, who married his daughter and took over the business with a new set of partners.

The Bubble Act of 1719 was repealed in 1825 by 6 Geo. IV, c. 91. Left to the freedom of the Common Law the tide of company enterprise rose, and the policy of the legislature became more favourable to it. The Act of 1837 (7 Will. IV and 1 Vict. c. 73) allowed Chartered Companies to attach to their shares reserve liability over and above the share itself. The difficulty had been that in the eyes of the law a Chartered Company was a person and as such could not attach individual liability to shareholders, who were but fragments of the person. It was doubtful if insurance companies (and banks in England after 1826), for whom the device of a reserve liability was desirable, could legally enjoy a Charter in which such liability was prescribed. The Act of 1837 found a way round the objection of the Common Law by authorising the grant of liability through letters patent and by empowering Her Majesty in any future Charter of Incorporation to embody the provisions thus authorised. Earlier in the century insurance companies had resorted to special Acts of Parliament in order to secure the necessary powers ; but this was difficult and expensive. The Act of 1844 (7 & 8 Vict. c. 110) provided for the incorporation of companies by simple registration, and by requiring registration from all new companies helped to terminate the unauthorised company ; but it expressly imposed on the members of such companies liability for their debts as though they were private partners. In 1854 a Commission reported against any alteration in the law of partnership, on the ground that the annual increase of wealth in the country was already providing sufficient capital for any mercantile enterprise which had the chance of success ; but in 1855, as a beginning, Parliament by 18 & 19 Vict. c. 133, allowed certain joint stock companies to register with limited liability : viz., companies formed, or to be formed, under the Act of 1844, as well as certain companies formed under private acts. Finally, the comprehensive Act of 25 & 26 Vict. c. 89 (1862), for which the way was well prepared by the Act of 19 & 20 Vict. c. 47 (1856), threw open to all the coveted privilege of carrying on business with limited liability ; all that was needed for registration as a limited company now was seven signatures on a Memorandum of Association, a small registration fee and the addition of the word Limited to the title. With the consequent growth of investment by persons taking no active part in the business the certificate of the auditor (which at first was not compulsory) ' came more and more into prominence, as the safeguard of the absentees—" the watch-dog," as a solemn High Court judgment described him.' [1]

The joint stock company, however, has not eliminated family or private business. For under the Companies Act of 1907 such businesses are able to register as private companies with limited liability, thus enjoying privacy of operation and limitation of liability at the same time. It is frequent for a private company after reaching a certain stage to convert itself into a public company and place its shares on the market. With a private company thus intermediate between the individual or partnership and the public company and the customary progression from one to the other the time-honoured discussion concerning the scope and limitation of joint stock enterprise has lost point. In Adam Smith's day there was body to it, but now the farmer is almost the only operator who does not grow into a company of sorts.

2. The anti-monopoly Act of 1624 (21 James I, c. 3) did not deprive the Crown of the right to regulate foreign trade or to give to trading companies, as a means to that end, exclusive trading privileges. The revolution of 1688 restricted the discretionary powers of the Sovereign ; and Parliament in general favoured an open trade. By 1 Wm. and Mary, c. 89, it altered the definition of Mines Royal to exclude copper mining ; by 9 Wm. III, c. 26, it threw open the African trade to all traders who paid the specified charges for the upkeep of the forts belonging to the African Company ; and in 1694 it resolved that it is the right of all Englishmen to trade to the East Indies or any part of the world *unless prohibited by Act of Parliament*. But there were occasions when Parliament was agreeable to the grant of privileges, and the Government increased the official value of Royal Charters by procuring in advance legislation sanctioning the issue of the Charter. In this way it secured the position of the Bank of England and the South Sea Company.

When a particular company, such as the East India Company or the Hudson's Bay Company, was given exclusive rights in certain areas, the monopoly was absolute against all comers, however constituted. But the grant of a banking monopoly to the Bank of England in 1709 and of an insurance monopoly to the Royal Exchange Assurance and the London Assurance in 1719 was only against joint stock rivals. The London bankers and the members of Lloyd's were unaffected, and benefited by the curtailment of competition. After 1800, in keeping with

---

[1] *Economic Journal*, Sept. 1925, p. 494, ' The First Half-Century of " The Accountant." ' For the position in banking see above, pp. 112 and 116.

the movement towards free trade, exclusive privileges were gradually withdrawn. In 1813 Parliament opened the trade to India. In 1822 it refused to renew the monopoly of the original London Dock Companies. In 1825 it repealed the Bubble Act of 1719 under which the two insurance companies enjoyed their monopoly : in 1826 it legalised joint stock banks outside the London radius : in 1833 it permitted them within the radius and in the same year opened the China trade. Finally, in 1835 Parliament abolished the ancient privileges of municipal corpora-tions, under which, for example, no one not a freeman of the City of London could keep a shop or use a trade there. In this mood it proceeded to the repeal of the corn laws and navigation laws ; and it is not surprising that the upholders of these laws were denounced as monopolists rather than as protectionists. An administrative measure crowned the series. In 1853 the Indian civil service was thrown open to competition, and Whitehall followed by stages. A prospering England believed so utterly in free competition that it was genuinely shocked by Ruskin's denunciation of the political economy to which Competition was the way, the truth, and the life.

3. It was possible to outlaw monopoly, but it was not possible to ensure that competition should prevail either in railways or in productive enterprise. The real threat to competition in the long run was the voluntary combination of former competitors. Business men co-operate for the advancement of trade interests by political action, advertisement or research : for collective bargaining with labour : for the regulation of output or price or both. Co-operation of the first type is constructive, of the second type defensive, of the third type restrictive. All these forms of joint action existed in the late 18th and early 19th centuries, but before the days of limited liability the fusion of large firms by amalgamation was financially impracticable.

The Yorkshire Worsted Committee was constituted to enforce the Act of 1777 (17 Geo. III, c. 56), the main purpose of which was to check embezzlement of materials by the workers. With funds derived from the drawback on soap used in the industry they conducted a campaign against wool smuggling and prosecuted the workers for illegal combination. After the abolition of the soap excise in 1853 they survived for a time as a voluntary body with private funds, but disbanded when the domestic system which gave birth to their main activity passed away. The Cutlers' Company of Sheffield, a Stuart incorporation, seemed destined to a peaceful end after the Acts of 1791 and 1814 had thrown open the trade. One function however remained, the supervision of trade marks ; and an enlarged sphere was opened to the Company when the Act of 1875 for compulsory registration of trade marks [1] made it the official registration authority for Hallamshire. In 1785 the cotton, pottery and iron masters formed the General Chamber of Manufacturers of Great Britain. They brought pressure on Parliament for the rejection of Pitt's Irish Proposals and in support of the Treaty with France ; but soon afterwards they disbanded when conflict of fiscal interest developed between the new industries to which the promoters belonged and the old industries which afterwards joined it. Fifty years later the enemies of the Anti-Corn Law League denounced the League as a manufacturers' association in pious disguise. During the 19th century local Chambers of Commerce at home and abroad have promoted the interests of their members; and the recently established Federation of British Industries has as its purpose the co-ordination of local effort and the promotion of common interests.

Masters have always combined to defeat the combination of their workers. But when combination was legalised in 1824–5 they did not at once establish formal associations, since to do so was to recognise the men's unions and thus to defeat their own purpose. However, when the Trade Unions were strong enough to impose collective bargains, the employers found it expedient to organise in return. In some industries, notably in hosiery, building, coal mining, and iron and steel, the organised representatives of employers and men set up voluntary boards of arbitration and conciliation. These Boards functioned successfully down to the Great War and formed the model for the Whitley Councils set up at its close.

Finally, there is combination for the control of output and prices. Between 1785 and 1792 the Cornish Metal Company and the Anglesey Copper Company divided the English market by agreement, but the agency had no control over supplies. The Cornish mines were small and in a bad way ; and Williams of Anglesey, who was the leading spirit in the arrangement, found that he could not hold them to a limitation of output. In the first quarter of the 19th century there were frequent agreements among the Welsh and the Midland iron-masters for fixing the price of iron. This, however, broke down before the growth of the iron industry in the North ; and during the half-century of expanding trade and technical pre-eminence from 1837 to 1887 the inducement to association was at its minimum. At the beginning of the period the old-established Newcastle coal

---

[1] 38 & 39 Vict. c. 91, s. 9. This was a general Act, short title *Trade Marks Registration Act of 1875*. 31 Geo. III, c. 58 (1791) and 54 Geo III, c. 119 (1814) were local.

trade—a ring which had controlled the sea-borne supply of coal to London since 1771—collapsed. The high prices exacted by it stimulated competition, and railways brought London within reach of supplies from other districts. Therefore by 1845 it had ceased to be effective.

Down to 1887 the general characteristics of the industrial scene were increasing production : an increase in the number and size of individual firms and in the use of fixed capital : keen competition between the manufacturers of rival products : and a high degree of informal automatic co-operation in the textile industries. However, before the end of the century, in spite of free trade, which was believed to guarantee Great Britain against trusts of the American type, amalgamation appeared in certain industries. Among the earliest was the Brunner Mond Salt Union formed in 1889 by an amalgamation of 64 firms. After 1900 the amalgamation movement was rapid and took two main forms. Some were horizontal amalgamations of firms formerly in competition. A frequent characteristic of these was that they enjoyed a conditional immunity from foreign competition, either because of the bulk of their product as in salt and cement, or because of international agreement to abstain from competition, as in tobacco, or because of technical superiority, as in sewing cotton. The second form was the vertical amalgamation of firms operating different stages of the productive process, and these were especially characteristic of the iron and steel trades. But such vertical amalgamation was only one of two routes to the integration of business. For the same result was achieved when a single firm without amalgamation extended backwards to the control of its raw materials and forwards to final manufacture. Finally, between businesses thus integrated there has been a certain amount of combination for the regulation of prices and the mitigation of dumping by foreign countries. The result in British industry as a whole has been (a) to valorise the economies of large-scale production, (b) to shift the plane of competition from many firms of small size to a few firms of giant size, (c) in a few special instances to eliminate domestic competition. Thus Great Britain has fallen into line with the general trend of industrial countries with a protective tariff, such as Germany and the U.S.A.

Section 6. *The State and Laissez-faire*

The individualism of the 18th and 19th centuries was at once a state of mind and an expression of fact. The fact which it expressed was that nearly the whole of the economic services of

M

the country were supplied by individuals pursuing, alone or in association, a profit-yielding occupation. By confining itself to a few simple tasks the State made itself efficient. In public finance it reduced economy to a science and built up a civil service free of corruption. It left foreign trade altogether to its subjects. It supplied the country with a sound currency, but did not embark on banking outside the reception of savings through the Post Office and it surrounded the banks of the country with a minimum of legal restrictions. The one effort of the State as a carrier, the Post Office Steam Packets, was a financial failure. Improvements in the postal services from Ralph Allen to Rowland Hill emanated from private individuals and were introduced under opposition from the regular postal officials. The Government in the 1840's did not seriously entertain the nationalisation of railways. Even Rowland Hill, the lonely supporter of State purchase on the Commission of 1867, considered that the State after buying the railways should lease them to private companies. He proposed competition for the service in place of competition between services. The nationalisation of industry suggested to his generation nothing more hopeful than State monopoly, an evil memory. However, towards the close of the century a revulsion set in. It was due in part to a general awakening to the waste of competition and in part to a class protest from the side of labour against the profit-making basis on which the existing order was based. State ownership, it was urged, would be not only more efficient but more just, because it would retain for society the unearned surplus hitherto appropriated by the capitalist entrepreneur. The practical problem was to make a beginning. Here the working men's co-operative stores supplied the model. For just as the store replaced profit by a consumer's dividend, so also could the municipality by service at cost. Certain services such as gas, water, lighting and tramways are in their nature monopolistic. The municipality, if it does not operate, must at least control. The extension of municipal interprise, being favoured by the new school of Fabian Socialism, received the name of municipal socialism. In this sense Tory Ontario with its provincially owned hydro-electric system is in the Socialist van. From 1890 the field of municipal activity was successfully enlarged ; and the success was claimed as a precedent for the nationalisation of railways and coal mines. In 1868 the Post Office had taken over the telegraphs, and in 1905 it arranged to take over the telephones also. But neither step was inspired by socialism. The public believed that unitary management was essential to efficient service in these fields and that the Post Office, which already transmitted letters, was the best and cheapest body for the transmission of other news. During the War the State operated the railways, handing them back at the close ; and coal was among the industries which were closely controlled. There is no demand for the nationalisation of railways or coal mines on the part of railway users and coal consumers. The pressure comes from organised labour, which is concerned primarily with the protection of its standard of life. If the railway shareholders had been wise they would have supported Labour in its demand for nationalisation, but fortunately for the country and unfortunately for them the Government was not so foolish as to buy them out.

The economic fabric of pre-war Britain was based on her remarkable past. When the world lived on Lancashire cotton, Cardiff coal, and the London money market, the policy of free trade was justified by the facts. But this situation passed away with the War. In the early days of the industrial revolution other countries had to adjust themselves to the fiscal policy of Great Britain in her ambiguous course towards *laissez-faire*. The wars of the 18th century were in part their protest ; but when they acquiesced, as did India under compulsion and France in moments of surrender to philosophy, they lost industrially. To-day it is the task of Great Britain to adjust herself to a world scheme in which the open market is always disappearing over the edge of the fiscal horizon. Therefore the progressive elements in Britain are feeling after a new plan of economic life in finance, production and marketing, as well as in working standards and social insurance. Whether a particular service of production or transport is performed by a department of State, a private firm or a voluntary group of consumers, is altogether secondary to the performing of it well. The general cry against private profit making is as foolish and as suicidal as the fear of State planning ; for the healthy society is one which is balanced. An old unitary State like Great Britain has a difficult area problem. The countries of the New World soon found a working division between federal and provincial authority ; and their economic life has grown up to it. Great Britain has its ' provinces,' but no provincial areas. Some modern services, as for example electric supply, are too big for the single town or county ; and if appropriate areas can be developed, the central government will be free for what it alone can do, the co-ordination of local effort and the arbitration of conflict between class and class.

It is misleading to associate deliberate planning with the death of *laissez-faire*. When our tractarians proclaim its end, they tell us only that economic life must be planned. But the country in which business is least haphazard is the U.S.A. It is also the country which views with the greatest jealousy the curtailment of the field of private enterprise.   In 19th-century Britain there was a riot of *laissez-faire* and social suffering, therefore *laissez-faire* left an evil odour behind it.   In 20th-century America *laissez-faire* and material well-being have flourished side by side, and therefore to America *laissez-faire* has been generally acceptable.   Great Britain has had to compete not only with a Europe which like herself is tired of it, but also with an America which would feel very much at home in Arkwright's Lancashire and furthermore has a Federal Reserve Board and high standards of sanitation.   Such, at any rate, was the atmosphere of America until the end of the 1920's.

PART IV
LIFE AND LABOUR

CHAPTER XVII

REACTIONS OF INDUSTRIALISM

Section 1. Population and Emigration. Section 2. The Poor Law and Apprenticeship. Section 3. The Migration to Industry. Section 4. Precise Reaction of Machinery on Hand Workers. Section 5. Employment of Women and Children. Section 6. The Medical Revolution. Section 7. Sanitation and Housing.

Section 1. *Population and Emigration*

AN important result of man's increasing mastery over nature was the great improvement in the quality and quantity of animal life at his service. The vacant spaces of the New World were populated by choice livestock bred in the Old. It was a monument of human skill. Parallel results were obtained in the increase of crops. Science improved upon art, until to-day the problem of agriculture is to extract from its abundance a living wage for the grower. To these increases of animal and vegetable life man himself reacted by multiplying his species, not deliberately but as a result accruing from the greater ease of winning a livelihood. In the last two centuries there has been a vast transference of population to new lands, under conditions of cruelty as in the slave trade, and with great waste and hardship as in the traffic of emigration from the Motherland. Now at long last we have broken with this gamble in *laissez-aller*. Emigration is controlled both by the sending and by the receiving countries, by the sending country with a view to the protection of the emigrant, by the receiving country with a view to selecting the right type of settler and establishing him in suitable occupations.

Family emigration is generally assisted by friends or organisations, if not by the State. Samuel Gompers, in his *Seventy Years of Life and Labour* (I. 5), tells us how in 1863 his father emigrated the family with the help of £5 10s. from the Emigration Fund of the Cigar Makers' Society of England. To his dying day the boy in him never forgot the narrow streets of Bethnal Green echoing with the tramp of men walking about in groups and wringing their hands over ' no work to do.' But the State's share in the aggregate of emigration was trifling. It used transportation as a means of punishment, sending convicts to New South Wales until 1840, to Tasmania (Van Diemen's Land) till 1853, and to

West Australia till 1867. In the 1820's, when the hand loom weavers were in exceptional distress, it made small grants to assist emigration to Canada ; and between 1836 and 1846 the Poor Law Authorities despatched about 14,000 people abroad, the largest block going from the county of Norfolk. In the third quarter of the century Trade Union Emigration Funds were prominent. But towards the end of it the direction of assisted emigration passed into the hands of philanthropic bodies, which sought in emigration a part solution for the problem of the slum child. Dr. Barnardo (1845–1905), an old Ragged School teacher and a disciple of Shaftesbury, sent his first party of boys to Canada in 1882 ; by 1926 the total was nearly 30,000 (boys 19,500), of whom it is claimed not less than 98% have made good. Down to the War the State, apart from emigrating a few Poor Law children, confined itself to supervision, founding in 1886 an office for the supply of impartial information and steadily stiffening the regulations for ocean transport. Since the War the pace has been set from overseas. In 1917 the U.S.A. began the rationing of immigrants, and changes since then have altered the quota in favour of England and Scotland. The war contacts between the Mother Country and the Dominions, their need of settlers and Great Britain's unemployed have determined the policy which has been carried out under the Empire Settlement Act of 1922. In 1924 and 1925 the number of assisted settlers was over 40,000 each year out of a total emigration of 91,000 and 85,000 respectively. The average cost to the Mother Country was less than £10 per head, but over and above the passage assistance to suitable settlers, male and female, there have been started schemes of selected family settlement, which are much more expensive both in money and supervision. They are based on the belief that quality is more important than quantity. In Canada (April 1, 1923–March 31, 1927) out of 43,449 persons coming forward under the Empire Settlement Scheme, 2630 families, representing 14,529 souls, were migrants under the special scheme of Family Settlement. Their supervision is entrusted to the Dominion Soldier Settlement Board ; and it is the purpose of this expert and experienced authority to prove that with reasonable assistance new comers of British stock can win a decent livelihood from the land in these days when the New World as well as the Old finds it difficult to make agriculture as remunerative as industry or commerce.

During the second half of the 18th century the population of Great Britain grew rapidly. By 1800 the country had awakened to a population question. Earlier statesmen and pamphleteers

had feared a decline. There had indeed been a period in Elizabethan England when colonisation was favoured as a cure for
unemployment, and there was talk of an excess of population.
But the disorder was temporary, and after its last civil war the
country settled down to the development of its industries and
agriculture, with such success that good labour became scarce
and the emigration of artificers to foreign parts was restrained
by law in 1719 (5 Geo. I, c. 27), and again in 1750 (23 Geo. II, c. 13).
There was always a disturbing fringe of poor, but their vagrancy
and improvidence rather than their contribution to numbers was
the object of concern and reform. Josiah Tucker, Dean of
Gloucester (1712–1799), the very liberal contemporary of Adam
Smith, desired to tax luxury and to encourage population by
the admission of industrious foreigners and the endowment of
parenthood. In 1798 Malthus's *Essay on Population* set the ball
rolling in the opposite direction and nerved the country to take
its first census, but he wrote in a period of war when man power
was short and emigration restricted. It was only after 1815
that over-population became an obsession and emigration a
standard remedy. While the memory of war lingered, the
Imperial Government made efforts to direct the flow of emigration to countries still loyal to the British flag, to Canada and
the Cape rather than to the U.S.A., but after 1830 it lost interest
in the Empire and thought only of dispersing the surplus and
preventing the vacuum from being refilled. Providence in the
shape of America solved the Irish problem. In a period of six
years following the famine of 1845 nearly a million souls left
Ireland, and in 1853 (the first year for which separate figures
are available) the Irish emigration was much more than double
that from the rest of the United Kingdom. As the Irish flood
ebbed, a British took its place. No doubt workers out of a
job have always emigrated more readily than others. But the
British outflow was not an emigration of distressed persons from
a country in general distress. It was greater when there were
good times either at home or in the country of destination ; for
then funds were more easily raised for the journey. The New
World was the land of opportunity and the strongest magnet
was gold. The discovery of gold in turn precipitated Australia,
New Zealand and South Africa into economic manhood ; and
after gold came wheat raised on free land by methods which
frequently deserved the name of wheat-mining. In the decade
before the War the demand of the Dominions for settlers and the
enterprise of shipping companies stimulated a flow which in
volume was as great as that from Ireland in the decade after
1845. In the 1900's Scotland discovered Canada afresh.

The growth of population in 18th-century England was due to a variety of causes, of which perhaps the original was the abounding increase in foreign trade and the favourable reaction of this on the technique of production and transport. This made it possible for Great Britain to support a larger population without detriment to the standard of living. The *malaise* of the early 19th century was a growing pain. The reality behind the fear of over-population was the bad distribution of it as it grew. At no time in Great Britain, as contrasted with Ireland, did the population exceed the economic needs of the country.

Population increases by immigration as well as by natural increase. Before 1800 immigration from Europe was important. It came in bulk at certain periods as the result of religious persecution, and also in a trickle at all times on the initiative of capitalists or the individual immigrant. But in 1815 both these sources were dry. France had none to spare : northern Europe now reached America at one leap. However, towards 1900 there was some entry of low grade labour, the backwash of the great outflow from southern and eastern Europe, which is known in America as the New Immigration. The aliens enumerated in England and Wales rose from 0·5 of the population in 1861 to 1% in 1901 ; and the increase excited attention because of its undesirable nature and its concentration at the capital.

In England and Scotland the main source of increase from 1750 was natural increase, reinforced by migration from the sister land of Ireland to both. Dorothy George's *London in the Eighteenth Century* shows that London was struggling then with the Irish problem, which fastened itself upon the North between 1800 and 1850, and on the U.S.A. in the decades following. The natural increase of Britain came in part from greater child-bearing, but mainly from less mortality, in particular less infant mortality. Between 1740 and 1840 the birth-rate rose markedly in the first half of the period and fell slightly after 1820. The death-rate, however, fell strikingly in two great sweeps from 1740 to 1760 and 1780 to 1810. The population of Ireland during the same hundred years increased faster than that of England, perhaps twice as fast, but under circumstances that were very different. The increase was based on the potato, introduced into Ireland about 1600. The potato yields several times as much food per acre as cereal grain, and its cultivation requires little skill. Had it not been for religious and economic oppression, Ireland might have developed as healthily as the North of England or Scotland. But industry and good government were denied to her, and the rural population bred up to the limits of life on a potato standard. The habit of early marriage (and

Ireland is a Catholic country) and the excessive subdivision of land, together with absenteeism and sub-letting, expedited the trend ; and the nearness of Great Britain, with her growing demand for navvy labour, concealed the danger of the general increase. For a population which lives on the potato has no margin between subsistence and starvation. Vengeance descended in 1845 ; and England, the part author of the tragedy, was justly involved in the political and economic troubles which followed.

Estimates based on the census of 1801 and the parish registers of earlier days indicate for England and Wales a population of six millions in 1700, and of about the same figure in 1740 ; and if this is so, the period of rapid and continuous increase, which is revealed retrospectively by the first census, was confined to the years following 1740. In 1801 the population of England and Wales was nine millions. Between 1801 and 1851, a period of 50 years, it doubled to eighteen millions : between 1851 and 1911, a period of 60 years, it doubled again to thirty-six millions. In 1921 it was nearly thirty-eight millions. If the figures are extended to Ireland and Scotland and the year 1921 is compared with 1821, the year of the first Irish census, the result in millions is :

	1821	1921
England and Wales	12	37·8
Scotland	2	4·8
Ireland	6·8	4·4
England, Wales, Scotland and Ireland, formerly the United Kingdom . .	20·9	47·3

In 1821 the population of Ireland was more than three times that of Scotland. County Cork had a population over half that of London, and Limerick a larger population than Warwickshire, which includes such towns as Birmingham and Coventry. For a parallel to such agricultural overcrowding we must go to modern Java. In 1921 Ireland's population was 400,000 less than Scotland's, being passed by Scotland for the first time in the census of 1901.

Malthus taught that population was kept within the limits of subsistence by certain checks—war, pestilence, famine and vice —and that these would operate in the future unless people exercised moral restraint, and in this he taught truly. But by moral restraint he meant celibacy and the postponement of marriage. He allowed no place to birth-control during marriage; indeed, as a clergyman he would have considered it a sin. But the practice of birth-control, perhaps the most remarkable social phenomenon of the 20th century—a practice common both to

Great Britain and to the countries to which British peoples emigrate—has radically altered Great Britain's population problem. New wealth in the hands of people with a rising standard has acted as a deterrent to population instead of provoking an increase, as Malthus assumed it would. Because birth-control proceeds from the rich and educated downwards instead of from the poor upwards, it cannot be exorcised by sermon or law.

Great Britain is now within sight of a stationary population ; and incidentally to this is becoming a nation of older people with females outnumbering males. Down to 1871–5 the average annual birth-rate in England and Wales was increasing. In that quinquennium it was 35·5 per thousand : since then it has declined. But the death-rate, because of improved health, has also declined, though less rapidly. Therefore the population is still increasing, but at a slackening rate. Because old people live longer the increasing births up to 1871–5 have not ceased to have effect. It is seen now in the rapidly increasing number of persons past the working age of 65. But at the other end the increase has stopped. Each year now no more children are reaching 15, the beginning of the working period, than reached it the year before. Between 1903 and 1914 births fell slowly, but infant mortality also diminished ; and consequently the number in the age group 15–20 will be practically the same in 1931 as in 1921. During the war births fell very rapidly, and after the reaction in 1919–20 fell again and are still falling ; and consequently the number in the age groups 15–20 and 20–25 will be considerably smaller in 1941 than in 1931. With regard to females, since one-half of employed women are under 25, the actual diminution in this half will soon be reached. For males of 15–65 the total will grow in millions (all relevant births being known) as follows : 1921, 13·3 ; 1931, 14·9 ; 1941, 15·5. These totals are for Great Britain, and those for 1931 and 1941, being estimates, take no account of emigration.[1]

From 1921 to 1925 inclusive the average net outward migration from Great Britain exceeded 100,000, and 56% was male. If a rate of 100,000 is maintained till 1941 and if 50% is male, then the male labour force in Great Britain will be in 1931 14·4 and in 1941 14·5 millions, i.e. practically stationary. With emigration at a higher rate—and the total net emigration for 1926 was 104,000—it will decline. With a continuing excess of male emigration—and it was still 56% in 1926—it will decline still further.[2]

---

[1] This paragraph is based on figures supplied by Prof. A. L. Bowley, but the writer is responsible for the use made of them.

[2] Figures for 1926 :—To British Empire 84,155 (male 48,227, female 35,928) ; to foreign countries 19,814—total 103,969.

There is one element of uncertainty in the above calculation. Infant mortality may decline at a more rapid rate than has been assumed. In England and Wales the deaths under one year per thousand births fell from 156 (1851–5) to 138 (1901–5) and 110 (1911–15). In 1919 the figure was 89, in 1924 75, in 1925 again 75, in 1926 70. The 1924–5 figures gave some colour to the idea that the decline was reaching its limit, but the further marked improvement of 1926, when analysed regionally, gives promise of yet further reduction.

Per Thousand

Rural South	51
South	60
Midlands	68
London	64
North	80
Average for England and Wales	70

The figures furnish two lessons. First, they approve Britain's courageous expenditure on social insurance since the War. Unemployment was not allowed to smash the standard of family life. Secondly, they summon the North to rid itself of the last taints of industrialism ; for climatically it is at least as healthy as the South. When we recall that less than two hundred years ago (1730–49) three out of every four children born in London died under the age of five, and compare these figures with the present, the contrast is startling.

It was the lack of vital statistics which confused thought in the days of the old Poor Law. There was a consensus of opinion that the bread scale led to improvidence and bastardy and to an increase in the illegitimate birth-rate, but this opinion is not supported by the probable facts. For England as a whole and for selected agricultural districts the birth-rate fell between 1811 and 1821, and the birth-rate for the period 1811–21 was less than that for the decade after 1850, when there was no Speenhamland bread scale and the country was prospering. The larger numbers surviving, and not the larger numbers born, gave colour to the belief that the agricultural labourer deliberately set out to increase his family in order to obtain an allowance for the extra child.[1] Statistics of population and emigration abound to-day. The need is that they should be common, within as short a time as possible, to the whole Empire, and above all that politicians and geographical experts should not enliven their statistics by rash economic statements. Two such are often heard. ' Nearly a

---

[1] Cf. *Economic Journal, Economic History*, No. 2, May 1927, J. S. Blackmore and F. C. Mellonie, ' Family Endowment and the Birthrate in the Early Nineteenth Century ' ; and criticism by T. H. Marshall in No. 4, 1929.

quarter of a million is being added to the working population of Great Britain annually.' This is misleading. It refers presumably to the estimated annual growth of the population between 1921 and 1931 at all ages ; but it is not the old, male or female, whom the Dominions want or will take, and this is the end from which the still continuing growth of population is maintained. Another (frequently heard in the Dominions) is that it would pay Great Britain to divert the dole to passage money.

It is, however, doubtful whether the emigration of a million, on the conditions and from the classes that are insisted upon to-day by the countries of reception, would make any serious reduction in the million of unemployed. And economists themselves are to blame for their loose language on the problem of Population and Food. Some seem to share the delusion that the optimum size of Great Britain is conditioned closely by her paucity of agricultural resources. But it is surely indisputable that for a world trader, except in war time, the 43 millions of Great Britain are no harder to feed than 43 millions of Americans in the north-eastern belt of the U.S.A. Both countries are conconcerned with the fact that the world's population is rising by 15 to 20 millions yearly, and both are interested in the question whether the world's supply of food is increasing more than in proportion to the demand ; but Great Britain is not groaning under diminishing returns or feeling the impact of a world shortage any more than is the U.S.A. The benefit, the only benefit which the Mother Country herself can obtain from the policy of imperial settlement, is better and more reliable markets for her manufactures—markets built up by those who go out as well as by those already there. The Mother Country has good stock which she can ill spare ; and the Dominions have markets which, as fiscal politics go, are hard to share even with the Mother Country.

Section 2. The Poor Law and Apprenticeship

There is always the danger that social or fiscal legislation will fail because it is passed to meet a situation which is just disappearing. The great labour code of 1563, the Statute of Artificers and Apprentices (5 Eliz. c. 4), to which the 43rd of Elizabeth, chapter 2, for the Relief of the Poor, was a supplement, was an attempt to fasten upon an expanding nation the regulations which fitted a municipal economy. It was not barren of good results ; for during the best part of a century the Privy Council and sister bodies, such as the Council of the North, saw that it was enforced. But when Parliament triumphed over

Strafford and King Charles, the poor lost their best friends. They then felt the full force of law untempered by equity or autocracy. Whether the average labouring man was better off in 1800 than in 1600 is a point which for lack of evidence can never be precisely answered ; but it is certain that in 1800 the rich were more strongly rich and the poor more definitely poor. Neither God nor Nature was responsible, but law made by a Parliament of landlords, which ' ordered their estate '—the rich man's enclosure and the poor man's settlement. Till 1800 the problem of poverty was chiefly in the South, where it was a reaction to the industrialism of pre-power days, to the commercial protuberance of the ' Great Wen,' and to the re-shaping of agricultural England by scientific agriculture and improved roads. The fortunate ones of the 20th century live in motor-cars and apartment flats, but the important thing in the 18th century was to have a home, high or lowly ; if high an enclosed estate, if lowly a settlement. On the law of settlement rested the social status of the individual, whether he was a country man or a Londoner.

It is not often that we can say of a law that it was utterly bad even when it was passed, but we may say this of the Poor Law Settlement Act of 1662 (14 Chas. II, c. 12). England was then on the threshold of industrialism ; her mobilisation to industry demanded mobility, and this the law obstructed with numerous injurious reactions. For it was much more than a law affecting the actual poor. It gave power to the parish to remove within 40 days all persons likely to be chargeable. Only those inhabiting a tenement worth more than £10 a year or upwards were exempt ; and inasmuch as down to 1800 the labouring man did not pay more than about £3 for his cottage, the law fixed the stigma of pauper treatment on the generality of the rural population. The confusion between wages and poor relief over which the Commissioners of 1834 wailed was inserted into the fabric of society in 1662. The policeman moves the loafer on, an ungentle act, but at any rate on. The Poor Law moved the worker back to the place where he was last legally settled. The Invisible Hand and the Parish Vestry, the one beckoning the worker forward, and the other hunting him back, between them made a sorry mess of the mobilisation process.

Nevertheless, as we know, people moved, for the law was in a variety of ways circumvented. Workers obtained from their parishes a testimonial acknowledging their settlement there ; and a law of 1697 (8 & 9 Will. III, c. 30) gave legal sanction to the practice, so that henceforth if a worker could obtain the consent of a parish authority it was unlikely that he would be removed before he fell into distress. But if he could not obtain such a certificate his only chance was to take to the road and risk the vagrancy laws. The Friendly Societies Act of 1793 protected members from removal until actually chargeable, and the Settlement and Removal Act of 1795 extended this to all persons. But no simplification was made in the law of settlement itself, which was now very complicated. Two ways in which a new settlement could be obtained were apprenticeship and hiring. The parishes displayed the utmost zeal in apprenticing their poor children to masters outside the parish in order that when the apprenticeship expired they should be free of liability for them. This the receiving parish could not stop, but the grant of a settlement by hiring and service for twelve months led to the artificial ending of contract within the year, and therefore this heading of settlement was abolished by the Act of 1834. In 1817 the House of Lords had proposed a radical simplification, but Parliament would not accept this either in 1817 or in 1834 ; for it knew that parishes would defeat the law's attempt to stabilise the labourer in his new abode by devising new obstacles to his getting there. No solution was possible until the parish was replaced by a larger unit, which was super-parochial financially as well as administratively. In 1846, partly as a sop to the landlords, who were sore over corn law repeal, Parliament made non-removable all persons who had resided in a parish for five years without receiving relief ; and the Act (9 & 10 Vict. c. 66) was so interpreted as to throw on town parishes the cost of non-resident relief for which rural parishes had hitherto paid.[1] In 1862, exactly two centuries after the first settlement Act, the Lancashire cotton famine compelled inter-parochial relief, and this led to the Union Chargeability Act of 1865 (28 & 29 Vict. c. 79), which made the union of parishes the financial as well as the administrative unit. In 1876 three years' residence—the radical proposal of 1817—was adopted, but by this time the question was unimportant ; for outdoor relief had been reduced to a minimum and the old-time chicanery between adjacent parishes was precluded by the Act of 1865.

The Law of Settlement depended for its enforcement on the Vagrancy Laws. Vagrancy was no new thing, but the problem was altered when the parish replaced the central authority of Elizabethan times. Just as the parish overseer was responsible for the poor, so was the parish constable for the vagrants ; and the machinery was inapt and uneconomical. The vagrants were

---

[1] For further detail see A. Redford, *Labour Migration in England*, p. 110.

of various types : unfortunates forced to the road and perhaps kept there by the Law of Settlement ; fortune-telling gipsies ; town beggars ; and sturdy scamps of the type which forced Colquhoun's London into building docks. Laws were passed in 1713, 1740, 1744 [1] defining vagrancy and classifying its penalties. By s. 14 of the Act of 1744 masters of ships bound for Ireland were under penalty to take Irish vagrants at passage rates fixed by the Justices. For, as the Irish had no settlement in England, it was only through the Vagrancy Laws that the Irish problem could be tackled.

Poor relief rested on the 43 Eliz. c. 2 (1601), which remained the framework of the Poor Law system until 1834 ; but before 1800 the framework had collapsed under the impact of economic forces which the age of Elizabeth had not contemplated. The least unsatisfactory part was that which dealt with the impotent and old. For their number did not react to generous treatment by increase ; and if their treatment was often unscientific, yet it was often kindly and reasonable. Just at present one book after another is revealing the life of the 18th century ; and each one shows that the horrors of the 19th century were well represented in the 18th. But the men of the 18th century were not monsters of inhumanity. They simply attacked new problems badly, and their problems to them were at least as new as those of the next century to it. During the 18th century there was a steady growth of social compunction, which reforming radicals of the 19th century mistrusted as sentimental humanity. And when the humanitarians of the 18th century saw the cruelties that were piling up, they too were prone to forget that the 17th century had rocked under throes of war, pestilence and fire, which explain the apparent callousness of an age just freed from these throes to ordinary social ills.

The normal method of relief to the impotent and old, in 1700 as in 1800, was out-of-door. These classes of poor received small weekly pensions, free house room, free clothing. The weak side of it was not the paucity of effort but of results relatively to expenditure. Parish service was underpaid and therefore often bad, but when it was transferred to a contractor it was worse. If the road builder supplies the second chapter in the history of contracting, the Poor Law supplies the first. The parish contracted with the doctor for medical attendance, with the joiner for coffins. It also contracted for the conveyance of vagrants. It was ' usual for one contractor not to take over all the vagrants

---

[1] 12 Anne, Statute II, c. 23 (1713) : 13 Geo. II, c. 24 (1740) : 17 Geo. II. c. 5 (1744).

of the county, but only those who came, or had to be conveyed along a certain route.' [1] By 1815 there was a chain of contractors for passing vagrants to their place of settlement or to Ireland. One contractor had the business of thirteen parishes, another stated that he passed as many as 12,000 to 13,000 a year.[2] These contracts were for definite services, but the practice became an extreme abuse when the parish contracted out its poor either for a lump sum or at so much per head to a workhouse manager, who sometimes supplied the premises and sometimes took over the workhouse belonging to the parish.

The relief of the able-bodied was the main problem of the Poor Law. Long before Speenhamland it was interwoven with that of unemployment. The Act of Elizabeth provided for the giving out of materials to those without maintenance, but by 1720 this method of relief had practically died out. The notion that the poor could be turned into a source of profit was approached in the speculative atmosphere of the South Sea days, but the parishes always lost heavily on their ventures and the workhouse movement of the 18th century took its place. There were two motives behind it : the business motive of assembling the poor under one roof and coping with them as a single problem, replacing as it were domestic by factory relief, and the ethical motive of punishing idleness by compulsory work. The principle of deterrence was present in the workhouse from the first. Bristol led the way, securing a special Act of Parliament for the building of a single workhouse for all the parishes of the town ; and its immediate success was such that it was made the basis of the general Act of 1723 (9 Geo. I, c. 7). This Act *inter alia* gave parishes the power to join together to build a workhouse and authorised any parish or parishes having a workhouse to put ' out of the book ' (i.e. the parish register of poor ordered by 3 Wm. & M. c. 11) all those who refused to be maintained there. East Anglia about the middle of the century built a number of Hundred Houses, but outside the towns the single parish remained the normal workhouse unit, and therefore in 1782 Gilbert obtained a new Act empowering parishes to incorporate themselves into Unions for the whole of their poor relief. It was a voluntary Act, and by 1834 only 924 out of the 16,000 odd parishes in England and Wales were so incorporated. But it was passed at a time of rising prices, when the social conscience had been stirred by the horrors into which drink and neglect had plunged the Metropolis ; and it contained a provision that the able-bodied were

[1] D. Marshall, *The English Poor in the Eighteenth Century*, p. 243.
[2] *Ibid.* p. 244.

to be excluded from the workhouse and have work found for them at or near their place of residence.

The deepening distress of the 1790's forced a further break from the policy of 1723, a policy incorrectly claimed in later days as a wise continuation of the Elizabethan model. The Poor Relief Act of 1795 (36 Geo. III, c. 23) sanctioned the giving of relief in the poor person's home and authorised the Justices in emergency to order relief over the heads of the parish officers. In the same year the Berkshire Justices, assembled at the Pelican Inn, Speenhamland,[1] decided to regulate relief by reference to the price of bread. For this purpose they framed ' the original bread table by which the parish allowance was systematically substituted for the wages of labour.'[2] The decision did not originate the practice of allowance in aid of wages ; it merely systematised a practice which, because it was becoming widespread, needed to be conducted on some regular plan.

Competition did not raise the ordinary wages of the free labourer to a living rate, and therefore the parish found itself the part paymaster of the ratepayers' labour. It intervened between the labourer and his livelihood in different ways. The least objectionable form was one common in small parishes, where the ratepayers bound themselves to provide employment at a given rate for all who were unable to find it. This was called the Labour Rate. The seamy side to it was that these were also the close parishes, which forced on open parishes the burden of part of the labour that they employed. The luckless worker was compelled to travel several miles a day to his place of work for fear he should get a settlement in it. Next there was the roundsman system, prevalent in Oxfordshire, Berks and Bucks, by which the labourers went the round of the parish with a ticket ordering the farmers to employ them. Under this system the parish paid a portion, though not the whole, of the wages from the parish fund. In the vicinity of Bicester, Oxfordshire, the labourers were put up to auction once a year. The farmer whose bid came nearest to the price fixed by the parish got the man he bid for, and the parish made up the difference.

As a last resort there was the parish pit. The labourers loathed it, but now and then they took it philosophically. At Mildenhall in Suffolk ' the paupers form themselves into two gangs, which they denominate the House of Commons and the House of Lords. The House of Commons was engaged at the

---

[1] Speenhamland means the land belonging to the village of Speen, which lies north of Newbury. The land is now within the municipal limits of Newbury, and the Pelican Inn, which was situated about half-way along the present Northbrook Street, has been pulled down.
[2] *First Annual Report of the Poor Law Commissioners* (1835), p. 207.

bottom of the pit, loosening the hard earth, digging the gravel, and throwing it up to the Lords, who were placed above them, and were occupied in sifting the refuse, and throwing what was useful to the top of the pit.' [1]

If the labourers had been without wives and children, the intervention of the Poor Law might have been confined to the provision in exceptional cases of parochial or semi-parochial employment. But the wages that an agricultural labourer could earn, whether in ordinary private employment or in employment in which the parish was in some way concerned, were not sufficient to support a large family. Between 1795 and 1834 the rate of wages varied from 7s. 6d. to 12s. 6d. a week; and when food prices were rising, the price of labour never rose proportionately or as fast. It therefore became customary to assume that a man's normal earnings could not provide for more than five persons, himself, his wife and three children. Labourers with larger families received, as a matter of course, allowances proportionate to the excess. This system of family extras was the allowance system proper, the system which the Berkshire Justices had endeavoured to regulate by a sliding scale varying with the price of bread. It prevailed generally, and it meant for rural England, as a whole, a complete confusion between wages and relief.

Under the double stimulus of national distress and administrative laxity expenditure rose, and the labourer grew to regard the parish allowance as a right. In 1803 the figure for England and Wales was £4·3 m.: in 1815 £5·4 m.: in 1818 £7·9 m. After the war, as conditions somewhat improved, it fell to around £6 m., but in 1831 it was up to £6·8 m. out of a total of £8·2 m. spent on all rates. The population, it must be remembered, was at this time growing fast. The financial burden was not beyond the capacity of the nation; but it offended national sentiment, like the so-called dole of to-day, and the outlay was unequally distributed. Nearly one-half was spent on the agricultural labourer, and mainly in the South. The county of Berkshire, the home of the system, stretches along the south side of the River Thames from Windsor to Oxford. Around Windsor the expenditure was low, for London was within easy reach. In the western section it was high, for example in the vicinity of Farringdon, the great hog market; and the general impression left by the evidence is that much of the unemployment of that time was caused by the system of outdoor relief. In 1834 outdoor relief to the able-bodied was abolished and the expenditure on the poor moved as follows:

[1] *Second Annual Report of the Poor Law Commissioners* (1836), p. 149.

Poor Law Expenditure

Year ending Lady-day	Total Money levied for Poor Rates and County Rates	Expended for Poor Relief	Population	Rate in the £ on Total Amount levied on Annual Value of Real Property		Rate per Head of Expenditure for the Relief of the Poor on the Population	
				s.	d.	s.	d.
1831 [1]	8,279,218	6,798,889	13,897,187	—		9	9
1835 [2]	7,373,807	5,526,418	14,564,000	10	1½	7	7
1836 [2]	6,354,538	4,717,630	14,758,000	8	7½	6	4¾
1841 [2]	6,351,828	4,760,929	15,911,757	8	0½	6	0½
1850 [2]	7,270,493	5,395,022	17,765,000	8	2¼	6	1
1851 [2]	6,778,914	4,962,704	17,927,609	7	9¾	5	6½

The report of the Royal Commission on the administration and practical operation of the Poor Laws in 1834 was followed by immediate legislation, the Poor Law Amendment Act (4 & 5 Will. IV, c. 76) : 'the first piece of genuine radical legislation which this country has enjoyed.'[3] It was radicalism of the Benthamite sort, in that it was aimed at parochial abuses and forced the State-aided pauper into economic self-reliance. The crucial section was section 52, which after reciting the evils of outdoor relief empowered the new Commissioners to issue peremptory orders, after which all relief in contravention thereof, save strictly guarded emergency relief, was illegal. The principles on which the Commissioners acted were two.

1. 'All or nothing.' This was the principle on which the Friendly Societies worked. They would expel a party from benefit if he performed quite simple tasks at home, knowing the abuses to which payment during part work might lead. The Commissioners translated this into the workhouse test. An able-bodied man must be given relief if he demanded it, but he must receive it in the workhouse. He must be altogether dependent or not at all.

2. 'Less eligibility.' This was applied to all classes of pauperism, whether able-bodied or not. Since relief was given, as far as possible, in the workhouse only, the principle found expression in the workhouse regulations. By irksome restrictions and the reduction of social amenities to a minimum, by depressing food and chilly religion, the state of the workhouse inmates was to be made less desirable than that of the most unfavourably placed independent worker.

The Act of 1834 introduced a much needed uniformity into

[1] *Tenth Annual Report of the Poor Law Commissioners* (1844), p. 480. Appendix B, No. 5.
[2] *Ninth Annual Report of the Poor Law Board* (1856), Appendix No. 16.
[3] M. Hovell, *The Chartist Movement*, p. 79.

the administrative scheme. The Gilbert Incorporations being Unions of a sort, lingered until 1845, causing great inconvenience by their salamander-like shape, but with the exception of these all the parishes of England and Wales were incorporated into Poor Law Unions of parishes under the management of unpaid Boards of Guardians, elected from the combined parishes. The increase in the size of the Poor Law unit was an advantage in two ways. It abolished parochial cliques and it created a body on which the central authority could exert its influence. To have dealt with some 16,000 parishes would have been impossible. By the new law the real power was placed in the hands of the three central Commissioners, and to them it was due that the Act was not a dead letter. Their position was parallel with that of the Factory Inspectors created by the Factory Act of 1833.

The Commissioners appointed under the Act—not to be confused with the members of the Royal Commission which drew up the report in favour of the Act—were T. Frankland Lewis, J. G. Shaw-Lefevre, and George Nicholls, with Edwin Chadwick as Secretary. They were known as the three Kings of Somerset House, and their rule was vastly unpopular. They were held responsible for the hated Bastilles (as the workhouses were called), and it was widely believed that they were the authors of an anonymous pamphlet (probably a hoax) entitled *Marcus on the Possibility of Limiting Populousness*, in which the ' painless extinction ' of superfluous babies was solemnly advocated.[1]

The Commissioners were appointed in the first instance for five years, then like Peel's income tax they were renewed periodically, till in 1847 (when it was clear that they had come to stay) their power was transferred to a Poor Law Board. This made their position more constitutional, for it gave the head of the Board official representation in Parliament and took the sting out of the accusation that the Commissioners were a Secret Service directed by their Secretary, Chadwick, a ' monster in human shape.'

Since 1834 there has been no general revision of the Poor Law. For Parliament, though ready to exert its sovereignty in railways, factories and mines, shrank from stirring up the local feeling which any prominent measure of Poor Law reform was certain to excite. It gladly allowed the central authority to introduce reform by executive instructions. The central authority has operated by various devices—advisory circulars, special orders applying to one Union, general orders applying to a group of Unions, and so forth. But from beginning to end the attempt to secure a uniformity of policy has been largely frustrated by the disobedience and neglect of the Guardians. The Royal Commission on the

[1] T. Mackay (Nicholls and Mackay), *History of the English Poor Law*, III. 239.

Poor Laws (1909) recommended sweeping changes. The majority report proposed the abolition of the Unions and the reconstruction of the Poor Law administration under the borough and county authorities, acting in co-operation with voluntary organisations. The minority report proposed the break-up of the Poor Law. Neither report was adopted by the Government.

The effect of the new Poor Law was different in rural and urban districts. In rural districts the new Poor Law achieved its purpose. It was conceived in terms of the agricultural labourer, and after it had been in operation for ten years the evils which it was framed to combat had disappeared. It ended the disastrous confusion between wages and relief, and cleared the way for the re-absorption of labour into agriculture or adjacent industries. The hardships that it caused were temporary, and they were an inevitable part of the price which had to be paid for an escape from the vicious stagnation of the old system. Men who from no original sin had been wasting their lives, gossiping in the parish pit, slacking on the farmer's land, drinking at the beer shop with the parish's money and there concocting schemes for burning their employers' hay-ricks, were squeezed out into the open and made to fend for themselves. The re-absorption is the more remarkable in view of the fact that it was accomplished in the face of acute agricultural depression.

But although the new Poor Law was followed with surprising quickness by local re-absorption or the migration of the surplus elsewhere, it was not the sole cause. Its operation was greatly aided by the concurrent growth of new employments, in particular railway work and coal mining. ' I believe,' said Joseph Sandars, a Liverpool corn merchant, in 1836, ' that there are no less than 20,000 persons employed on the railroad between London and Liverpool. . . . If the manufacturers had been in a state of distress and those railways had not been in course of erection, the condition of the farmers' labourers must have been wretchedly bad indeed.' [1] The railroad conferred a double boon ; for the period of construction, which called for navvy work and indeed sometimes upset the peace and sobriety of the village, was followed by the period of operation, which provided steady work of high grade in all rural districts to which the railway penetrated.

But in urban districts the new Poor Law could not claim the same success, for it had been planned to check abuses which were rare there, and it ignored the needs of the new towns. In the North of England, the ' Gehenna of manufacturing Radicalism,' [2] the new Poor Law met with violent resistance from

---

[1] Lords Committee on the State of Agriculture (1836), Q. 4041.
[2] Carlyle, *Critical and Miscellaneous Essays* (Centenary Ed.). III. 159.

the working classes, and when the manufacturing districts had passed through the morass of semi-capitalism to full factory life, there still remained the chronic maladies of urban destitution— casual employment, under-employment, and the unemployment caused by cyclical depression. The agitation spread rapidly through the North of England, and for a moment it looked as though it would meet with the success which attended the agitation of the Short Time Committees and the Anti-Corn Law League. For a moment it looked as though the agitators had found their Cobden in Feargus O'Connor, the leader of the Chartists. But the agitation failed, and was bound to fail unless it was strong enough to triumph by revolution. For although aimed ostensibly at a single unpopular law, it was really part of a great cry issuing from thousands of desperate and excited men, who knew that they were miserable and struck blindly at the thing which insulted their misery. When the first phase of Chartism came to an end with the imprisonment of the Chartist leaders in 1840, the agitation against the Poor Law burned itself out, and its insults were forgotten in the easier years which followed factory reform and the repeal of the Corn Laws.

Statutory apprenticeship in the trades and areas covered by the Act of 1563 was abolished in 1814 by 54 Geo. III, c. 96 : and the compulsory acceptance of apprentices, an outgrowth of section 5 of the Elizabethan Poor Law, was abolished in 1844 by 7 & 8 Vict. c. 101. In 1842–3, when the Children's Employment Commission reviewed the miscellaneous industries of the country, they found that voluntary apprenticeship, sometimes with un-stamped indentures, was customary in the handicrafts and in small concerns. It was at its best in the skilled trades of London : indeed, social workers to-day know the keenness of the London boy to learn a trade, and of the gulf which exists to his mind between a proper trade and the blind-alley jobs which he sees as the unwelcome alternative.

The repealing Act of 1814 was important, for it administered an official blow to a deep-set instinct, the sort of blow which would be felt by the medical and legal professions if their occupations were thrown open to unqualified persons of any country. Furthermore, it helped the employers, the engineering employers in particular, to defeat the Trade Unions, ' to overwhelm,' as one of them put it, ' the excluding party with new men.' [1] But though in 1814 apprenticeship was valued and tactically valuable, it had long failed of its original purpose, the training of youth for the industries of the nation. ' It had degenerated into a

---

[1] Cf. Clapham, op. cit. p. 207, quoting from Commons Committee on Artisans and Machinery of 1824.

method of preserving close corporations at one end of the scale and a method of social oppression on the other.'[1] Eighteenth-century London was very jealous of its liberties. The evolution of apprenticeship was towards relaxation of the tie, to a three-year learning period with small wages instead of a seven-year with none ; and from indoor to outdoor apprenticeship. The wholesome discipline of the master's home was a cruel farce. The big employer was moving out to suburban residences ; the small master could not afford good treatment. Indeed in the many trades where large and small masters co-existed, the latter were themselves becoming semi-independent journeymen with apprentices. Such a small master could teach his pupil the detail of his trade but nothing more. What the lads lacked was healthy recreation. Having no Y.M.C.A., they indulged in bull-baiting and rowdy sport.

But ordinary apprenticeship was contaminated and over-shadowed by pauper apprenticeship, which was not limited to certain trades and areas ; for every parish had its young whom it bound out—beyond the parish if possible—thus providing industry with a ceaseless stream of cheap juvenile labour. It was thick in the shoemaking trade and domestic services of London, as well as in the new industries of the North. On farms the child had a better time and the environment was healthy, but in the towns the parish children were neglected or maltreated and they were marked off from the ordinary apprentices by the deeply felt stigma of their origin. Parish apprenticeship was just one part of the great problem of waste in juvenile life, and as such was condemned by an age which was outgrowing Defoe's passion for the sight of children at unremitting toil. Laws were passed in 1747, 1767 (London), 1778 (England) for the protection of the parish apprentice, contemporarily with the legislation of 1761 and 1766 on behalf of parish infants put out to nurse. The limit of apprenticeship was reduced from 24 years of age to 21, and a minimum binding rate was prescribed also. The moving spirit was Jonas Hanway, the inventor of the umbrella, Carlyle's ' dull worthy man,' who disputed with Dr. Johnson upon the merits of tea-drinking. Like so many pioneers he had foreign experience. Through the parish apprentice Parliament arrived at the factory child. While thus ordinary apprenticeship was weakening and parish apprenticeship was blackening its name, there was a healthy, if belated, movement for the education of poor children. The charity schools of the 18th century were of religious origin and the precursors of the voluntary schools of the Church of England and Nonconformist bodies, inspired by Bell and Lancaster. But

---

[1] M. C. Buer, *Health, Wealth and Population*, p. 251.

the history of education, except to the extent that industry was involved in it through the operation of the Factory Acts, falls outside the scope of this work.

Section 3. *The Migration to Industry*

Between 1750 and 1850 the centre of industrial gravity shifted painfully from the South to the North—to the North Midlands : to Lancashire and Yorkshire : and to the Lowlands of Scotland. This shifting was accompanied by a considerable redistribution of population. But it is not true to say that the surplus of the rural South moved in any coherent fashion to industrial employment in the North ; still less is it true to say that the specialised industrial workers of the towns and villages south of the Trent so moved. The free movement of families was obstructed by their own reluctance, the operation of the Law of Settlement, and the difficulty of travel (for only at the very end of this period was railway communication in being). Moreover, if the industrial centre shifted to the North, London was in the South, and London continued to grow as rapidly as the new North. London was the absorbent of the surplus population of the counties adjacent to it, as well as of those which, though remote, like Dorsetshire, were nearer to it than to the North. It offered an almost unlimited market for domestic service and general labour ; while for the highest class of mechanical work there was no place so good. However, provided that the expenses of the voyage could be met, the choice was not confined to London or the North. There was the New World, which had for the agriculturist the supreme attraction of land which he could own and cultivate. Emigration was easy for those whose services took them abroad— such as sailors who deserted to the American navy to escape the rigours of the press-gang, or soldiers of the disbanded regiments which helped to people Ontario after 1815 ; and it was made tempting for those who possessed the mechanical knowledge of which Britain for a time had the monopoly. For such mechanics and artisans were eagerly canvassed, and after 1824 there was no legal obstacle to their going. But the tendency in England towards a general northward movement, with some loss from both South and North by emigration, was to some extent offset by a counter-flow from Scotland and Ireland, which filled a great part of the new employment in the North and pushed through to London and the South.

The Scottish influx was altogether healthy ; for the Scotch, though poor, were thrifty and enterprising and gifted with a wonderful power of adaptation, whether to the isolation of a frontier cabin or the scramble of a new industrialism. They did not move under the drag of demoralisation. Their arrival created no problem for the places which received them. A great part of the Scottish emigration was internal to Scotland : a concentration by the Highland and the Lowland villages upon the new industrial belt between the Forth and the Clyde. Another part crossed the Border, leaving a developing country for a country which was more developed and in which therefore the prizes were greater. Scottish mechanics found thousands of unrecorded jobs in England ; and London operatives at times complained of the Scottish lads who were engaged as apprentices and in a few months passed off as men who had served their full time. Meanwhile Scottish drovers were constantly on the road to Norfolk and London, foreshadowing the days when Scottish tenants would pick up bargains among the farms of Essex ; and Scottish harvesters worked their way down the east coast beyond London and through to the agricultural counties of the South. Here they came up against the older stream of Welsh drovers, who blazed the trail for Irish immigrants *via* Bristol and Holyhead.[1]

The Irish influx welled out of Ireland's distress ; and four elements therein may be distinguished.

First of all, there was the harvester who at the end of the season returned to his country and family. Some came by Holyhead and Liverpool, and some by the older route of the Bristol Channel, serving as ballast for the small Welsh collier on its return trip. From Bristol they walked or begged their way into the Midland counties, amassed a few pounds and returned home the way they came. They were the west coast counterpart to the Scottish harvesters ; and the two together filled the gaps left in the rural labour forces by the industrial specialisation of the Midlands and North.

Secondly, there were the Irish who came to stay and to work. The value of one section of this class must not be underrated. For the most expert navvies, who built first the canals (inland navigations, from which the name navvy is taken) and then the railways, were Irish. They worked for contractors, now on one job, now on another ; and they formed the skilled nucleus round which the agricultural labour in the district was trained. The Irish also supplied a large part of the dock labour of Liverpool, of the transport and unskilled building labour of London and other large towns. Where they were congregated, there the worst slums were to be found. They did the work which is done in America to-day by the negro or the newly arrived immigrant.

---

[1] *Cf.* Map F in A. Redford, *Labour Migration in England 1800–1850*, showing the limits of the Scottish and Irish Vagrancy in 1823.

Thirdly, there were those Irish who flocked by families into the industrial districts of Glasgow and Lancashire. The reputed disinclination of eastern Scotland for factory work and coal-hewing was perhaps due to the competition which they had to sustain in these parts from Irish labour. In Lancashire the Irish were unsuccessful as a class in the factories. They rarely reached the spinning room, but both in Glasgow and in Lancashire they abounded in the less skilled branches of hand-loom weaving. By 1840 hand-loom weaving had become the sink of the industrial destitute, and by that time none but the Irish were entering the trade as beginners. Glasgow felt the burden even more than Lancashire : for it was nearer to the Ulster coast from which the main part came, and Scotland had no Law of Settlement to obstruct the inflow. A judicial decision of 1824 to the effect that the Irish had the same immunity from removal in Scotland as natives caused consternation. In England the difficulty of acquiring a settlement offered a crude protection of a sort against the Irish influx. The old Poor Law, it may be, demoralised the English labourer, but it demoralised him in white wheaten bread and it checked in some small degree the deluge which all but reduced Britain to the potato standard of unhappy Ireland.

Fourthly, there were the beggars with the mobility of beggars. The less professional peddled wares and food. In the towns Irish publicans and lodginghouse keepers supplied drink and lodging to their compatriots, resident or casual.

Taken as a whole the mass of migration within England was a short-distance movement, from the countryside to the towns ; and even in the case of Ireland the most part of it only involved a short cross-channel passage. To skilled workers migration or emigration was comparatively easy. When the Shropshire iron industry declined in relative importance its skilled men moved easily to South Wales. The Cornish tin miners and the Derby-shire lead miners moved North in some cases and emigrated in others ; but owing to the clannishness of the older mining districts it was not easy for newcomers to find a footing, especially if imported as blackleg labour. The northward flow was expedited by the action of the Poor Law authorities in shipping children, especially from London, to factories in the North. But in 1816, when the demand for such labour was already declining, it was made illegal to apprentice London children to places more than 40 miles distant (56 Geo. III, c. 139). For several years after the introduction of the new Poor Law the Poor Law Commissioners assisted migration to the North, the largest group coming from Suffolk, but the aided movement was but an insignificant fraction of the whole. By 1850 something like equilibrium was again in sight.

The building of railways in rural districts had brought a new temporary employment. From 1850 to 1875 British industry was prosperous and there was no problem of surplus population and little protracted unemployment.

Section 4. Precise Reaction of Machinery on Hand Workers

Why were the weavers and knitters in continuous distress for about 40 years : and in particular what was the relation of their distress to the introduction of machinery ? Up to about 1805 their position had been an improving one, but from about then to about 1845, while other employments had their good and bad times—good when work was plentiful and bad when it was slack—the weavers and knitters were in continuous distress, literally starving in bad years and all but starving in such good periods as 1823–5 and 1833–6.

One cause of distress peculiar to the weaving population of London, Norwich and the south-west of England was the loss of their industry for technical reasons to the North ; a second reason, prominent in Lancashire and Glasgow, was the Irish influx. But there was an underlying factor which was common not only to the weaving districts but also to the knitting district of Leicestershire, where there was no loss of industry elsewhither and no important Irish immigration. The common factor was the collapse of standards before the impact of industrial *laissez-faire*. During the last ten years of the war the textile markets were highly unstable, and during the period of post-war deflation, 1815–22, employers broke away from the agreed rates which had governed the trades outside London as well as the legally controlled Spitalfields silk trade. The result was a cut-throat competition in which the weak dragged down the strong. The foreigner was not to blame. Prices were smashed by Bolton versus Glasgow on the markets of Europe rather than by England versus France or Germany, and employers were not in a position to refrain from spoiling the market because many of them were financed by merchants, who met the approach of bad times by forcing sales at slaughter prices.

A further factor in the collapse was the influence of bulk production, by machine or hand, on the quality of the product. Novelties gave a brief fillip to prices, but ' the general rule of all fancy goods is that, as they are introduced, they continue to descend until the articles become so bad and the wages so low that they become stale and coarse and badly manufactured and they go out of use and some new article supersedes them.' [1]

[1] Commons Committee on Hand Loom Weavers (1834), *Evidence*, p. 16.

The knitters struggled hard against ' cut up ' work, in which there was no ' fashion,' but the prime offenders, the bag hosiers, who brought their stockings to market in a bag instead of working to the order of a house, were themselves reduced master stockingers. Thus quantity dragged down quality. In the Fieldens of Todmorden the weavers found generous champions. In 1834 John Fielden ' himself, by means of the power loom and hand loom, one of the most extensive manufacturers of the empire,' [1] carried a number of manufacturers with him in support of a Bill by which the average price, as computed from the smallest number of manufacturers who together made half the goods in a town, should be the lowest price payable for the ensuing three or six months. The proposal was germane to the evil, but it had no chance of reaching the Statute Book. For statesmen and employers generally lived in a nightmare of underselling by the foreigner ; and the scattered country weavers and knitters were uncontrollable. The country workers depended mainly on their industrial employment. In Lancashire, according to the evidence given before the Commons Emigration Committee of 1826-7, they were scattered in small hamlets or single houses in various directions throughout the manufacturing country. If they had a farm at all it was a small grass one, on which they placed little reliance. Sometimes, however, it led to their being rated for the support of distressed weavers in the towns. When we read the description of the terrible life endured by the knitters of Nottingham and Leicester—the weekly procession to the pawn shop, the appeasement of hunger by opium and laudanum, the squalor of the abodes—it seems impossible that there could be a worse. And yet there was. In 1843 the historian [2] of the industry tells us that a frame mender tried the country districts as a relief from the towns, but found the conditions still more deplorable and the air of the country cottages so foul that for weeks after he was ill.

In the agony of transition the power loom played a part. It completed the discomfiture of the weavers by forcing them or their children into factory life. They dreaded the confinement of the factory, but if they stayed out and their children went in, the children became the chief bread-winners : which as a proud people they hated. They themselves could hope for work in the power shop only if they were elastic enough to change their habits of life or able to do the mechanical or other heavy work for which male labour was still required. The mechanical operations, as

---

[1] *Hand Loom Weavers Commission* (1840), Pt. IV. p. 257.
[2] Wm. Felkin, *History of the Machine-Wrought Hosiery and Lace Manufacturers*, p. 458.

William Fielden urged in 1827, were numerous. ' There are a great number of persons employed about the power loom in various preparations of the article before it comes into the loom, and so many mechanics are employed in making the machinery and keeping it in order, that I do not imagine from what I have understood, that more than from one-third to one-fourth is saved by the use of the power loom.'[1] The machinery which hurt the weavers was not at first the power loom in their own trade but the machinery introduced into spinning or into branches of weaving other than their own. For the workers thus extruded swelled the ranks of the weavers who still did hand work.

In two finishing industries, cloth weaving in Yorkshire and machine lace-making in Notts, the transition to power production was accompanied by little distress. In 1842 there was a considerable amount of power-driven machinery in Leeds, but outside of Leeds much of the yarn was spun, and most of the cloth was woven, in the cloth-maker's family. ' In the distant townships the scribbling and slubbing of the wool, as well as the scouring and fulling of the cloth after weaving, is done at mills owned in shares by the small clothier.'[2] And the evidence continues : ' In passing through the streets of Manchester at night, intoxication, prostitution and disorder meet you at every step, but in Leeds all was good order and tranquillity.' Doubtless other factors entered in, e.g. the smallness of the Irish element, but there was no mechanical avalanche in Yorkshire and the sturdiness of the small clothier eased the transition from handicraft to steam power. Moreover, the power process in woollen cloth required both strength and skill and was therefore a man's job. Thus this limited section of hand-loom weaving passed through an evolution different from the rest. In the Nottingham lace trade the bobbin net machinery was very complicated and called for skilled adult labour both when it was a hand machine (1825–40) and later when power was adapted to it. Therefore neither the improved hand machine nor the adaptation of steam power displaced male labour. In 1860 the Factory Commissioners reported that in lace factories women and children were employed in the subsidiary processes only. Therefore lace factories were not brought under factory regulations until 1861.

There was no simple correlation between the entry of steam power and the severity of distress. The most acute distress occurred in cotton weaving, where power came first, and in framework knitting, where it came last. In cotton weaving large masses of workers, native and foreign, flooded those sections of the trade

---

[1] Commons Committee on Emigration (1826–7), *Evidence*, p. 181.
[2] *Hand Loom Weavers Commission* (1840), Pt. III. p. 549.

for which power machinery was unsuitable. In framework knitting the native population was confined to a single employment of old establishment and worked on antiquated equipment, which was usually the property of others ; and when steam power at last came it was a blessing without alloy.

During the last years of the French war and the first years of peace (1810–20), there was some rioting and destruction of machinery. The riots were known as Luddite riots, because the workers in smashing machinery invoked the memory of Ned Ludd, a Leicestershire lad who had revenged himself on his master by smashing his knitting frame. But the disorder was not a straight protest against new machinery or factory life. It was perhaps worse in the knitting districts, where there was no new machinery, than in Yorkshire, where the new cloth-finishing machinery was the object of especial dislike. It was at bottom a revolt against hunger and misery and the desperation into which the hand-workers fell in this age of transition. It was a repetition of what had occurred in London before the situation was eased by the Spitalfields Silk Legislation of 1773, and on a par with the revolt of the agricultural labourers in 1830, when they burned hayricks in the name of Captain Swing.

Section 5. The Employment of Women and Children

The Doukhobors of British Columbia—a Russian community which emigrated to Canada on the invitation of the Canadian Government in 1899—make almost everything for themselves. The children learn from their parents. At an early age the boys follow the plough and the girls spin and weave. They sing together, and when in church recite from their scriptures, which they know by heart. The life of the community, and therefore of the children in it, is moral, industrious, and happy except for the conflicts with neighbours and the Government in which their tenets and peculiar psychology have involved them. In Great Britain before the factory age, though the family was an economic unity, it did not function within the shelter of a vital group. It worked to the order of distant masters ; and this encouraged the exploitation of children. The parents assisted in the exploitation, being themselves also subject to it. Thus in the 18th century in Bucks and Beds, a few grammar schools apart, there were no schools except lace schools, and travellers frequently commented upon the pale faces and deformed shape of the girls and women employed in the sedentary and exacting occupation of lace making. Domestic industry was damaging home life, in London as well as the provinces, when factory industry supervened to smash it altogether.

The labour wants of the first factories were supplied in part by the importation of pauper children from the parish workhouses of London, Birmingham and other towns. The children, lacking all family care, were maltreated in the factory and at night herded into 'prentice houses. While the weavers were prosperous they took pride in keeping their children away from factories and paupers ; but as their prosperity faded and as mills were built in centres of population they bowed to the inevitable. It was this or starvation, and their plight was one degree, at any rate, less bad than that of the Spitalfields weavers who, having no factories in their district, took their children to Bethnal Green Road and hired them out by the week or month to anyone who would take them and at any price.

In the factories right down to 1833 the working day was 14 hours, during which, in the good mills, there were intervals for meals. In the busy seasons, when the factory sometimes worked the whole night, the children made odd halfpence. Neither they nor their parents objected to this so much as to the practice of making up lost time without extra pay and to the thievish factory clocks, which were put forward in the morning and back at night. ' In order,' said the Commissioners of 1833, ' to regain the time lost by stoppages, whether from the breakage of machinery, from the want of a due supply of water, or from holidays, it is the custom for the people to work, sometimes half an hour, at other times an hour, and occasionally even as much as two hours daily, until the whole of the lost time is made up.' [1] The Commissioners found that nine was the most usual age of beginning work, seven or eight was frequent, and six not uncommon. Picture the home life of the children ! They came back from work so worn out that they could not eat their supper. Put to bed with food in their hands, they were found clutching it when they were roused next day. At 4 or 5 A.M. the factory bell sounded, and half asleep they stumbled, or were carried, to work to begin again the unending rush. Factory work—said opponents of shorter hours—was light and kept the children out of mischief. The Commissioners indeed produced evidence to show that the conditions of employment were very much better in the new mills than in the old small ones ; that organised cruelty was very rare, having died out along with the parish apprentice system ; and that deformity due to excessive standing was less frequent than formerly. But they found that there were unnecessary accidents owing to the failure to fence machinery

[1] *Factory Commission* (1833) *First Report*, p. 10.

and the practice of cleaning it while in motion, and above all that the hands were over-worked. They were ' sick-tired '— and the children being the weakest suffered most of all.

The Act of 1833, the first to be enforced because it was the first to appoint inspectors, forbade the employment of children under nine at any time and of persons under eighteen at night, and prescribed for those aged nine to thirteen and fourteen to eighteen a maximum of nine and twelve hours a day respectively. The Act was passed during (and indeed partly to counteract) the organised agitation for a shorter working day. Richard Oastler, Steward of the Fixby Estate, Huddersfield, led York- shire, which was the headquarters of the movement. By his letters of 1830 on Yorkshire Slavery he rendered the first of the many services which earned for him the title of the Factory King. John Fielden led Lancashire. Michael Sadler, member for Aldborough, Yorks, presented the case to Parliament, securing a Committee of Inquiry and introducing a Ten Hours Bill in December 1831. When he lost his seat in 1832, Anthony Ashley Cooper (who became 7th Earl of Shaftesbury in 1851) assumed the Parliamentary leadership. To counter the pro- gramme of Sadler and Ashley and to rebut their supposed ex- aggerations, the Commissioners who framed the Act of 1833 were appointed. The workers considered the Act a rebuff. For the Commissioners laboured the distinction between children, who needed protection, and adults, male or female, for whom legal protection was in principle unsound. But the factory inspectors appointed under the Act, by pointing out loopholes, prepared the way for its acceptance ; and the interference with the employment of women in mines by the prohibiting Act of 1842 destroyed the logical objection to their protection in factories. Therefore in 1844 the Government, while still repudiating the ten-hour principle, converted the casual part-time employment of children into regular half-time, included women with young persons, and prohibited children, young persons and women from cleaning machinery while it was in motion. During the next three years Shaftesbury and the factory reformers on the one part, Cobden and Bright and the Anti-Corn Law League on the other, competed for the surrender of Graham and Peel. The Corn Laws fell in 1846 ; the Ten Hours Bill passed in 1847, but by this time Graham and Peel were in exile. None of the terrible consequences foretold by the manufacturers resulted ; for their hysterical forebodings were but the pathology of industrialism. But further laws were needed in 1850 and 1853 to make the ten hours a reality. This was attained by prescribing a normal working day, 6 A.M. to 6 P.M.—first for women and young persons and then for children. The practical effect of this was to grant a ten-hour day to the male workers also, since a factory could not run on their labour alone.

Down to 1853 the Factory Acts were confined to textile factories. That of 1802, the first in the series, applied to parish apprentices in cotton and woollen mills, that of 1819 to cotton factories, that of 1833 to all textiles, excepting lace and partially excepting silk. The lace factories were not regulated until 1861. The generalisation of power automatically extended the range of persons protected. Bleach and dye works were brought under regulation in 1860. The Act of 1864 broke new ground by reaching out to other than textile trades, namely to pottery and certain dangerous trades. Sweeping extensions followed in 1867 ; and in 1878 the Consolidating Act brought under a general definition all factories and workshops. But the makeshift contact with education was deplorable. The Act of 1833, when creating part-time employment for children, ordered the mill owners to make provision for their education in the remainder of the time ; but the factory schools were an educational farce, and Graham's efforts to improve them were thwarted by the struggles between Churchmen and Nonconformists. Of all the shortcomings of the 19th century the failure to provide national education before 1870 was the most unnecessary. Adam Smith advocated it a century earlier and Scotland enjoyed it two centuries earlier. But ' religion,' as Graham said, ' the keystone of education, is in this country the bar to its progress.' [1]

Between 1833 and 1844 the coal mines of South Staffordshire (which were operated on the butty system) and the metal trades of the adjacent Black Country were the stronghold of pauper apprenticeship. So keen was the demand that, as was reported in 1842, there were scarcely any boys in the union workhouses of Walsall, Wolverhampton, Dudley and Stourbridge. ' These lads are made to go where other men will not let their own children go. If they will not do it, they take them to the Magistrates, who commit them to prison.' [2] But this was only a local exaggeration of a more widespread evil, the employment of women and children under brutal conditions, especially in the newer coal fields. The miners themselves objected to their women going underground and kept the practice out of Northumberland and Durham, but it was of old standing in Scotland—in East Lothian in 1842 there was nearly one woman for every three men—and it was on the increase in Lancashire

---

[1] C. S. Parker, *Life and Letters of Sir James Graham*, I. 339, Graham to Brougham, October 1841.
[2] *Children's Employment Commission, First Report, Mines* (1842), p. 41.

and Yorkshire and in South Wales. The advantage of female labour was its cheapness. ' A girl of twenty,' said a Lancashire underlooker, ' will work for 2s. a day or less, and a man of that age would want 3s. 6d.' [1] Scots girls of strength almost super-human carried baskets of coal weighing from three-quarters to three hundredweights up steep ladders. It was as much as a man could do to lift the baskets on to the girls' backs, and some-times they toppled off the ladder into the pit below. ' I have wrought,' said a Scotswoman aged forty, ' in the bowels of the earth 33 years . . . a vast number of women have dead children . . . it is only horse work and ruins the women, it crushes their haunches, bends their ankles and makes them old women at forty.' [2] At last the national conscience was shocked. The Mines Act of 1842 forbade the employment underground of females at any time and of male children under ten. By ordering further that boys under fifteen should not be in charge of important machinery it prepared the way for State control of adult conditions. From 1850 onwards the mine inspectorate did for adult men what the factory inspectorate did for women, young persons and children, and, behind the women's petticoats, for men.

The allotments which decent landlords provided in many counties of the Midlands and South, and which to some extent offset the loss of the parish allowance, had a uniformly favour-able effect on the morale of the agricultural labourer. For they restored a small fraction of the contact between work and pro-duct which is the inspiration of occupying ownership. They provided a way by which the labourers' wives and children could work out of doors without hurt to themselves or their home. Moreover, though the labourers raised potatoes and ate these instead of parish bread, they also raised fresh vegetables. In Dorsetshire there was a poor substitute for the allotment in the shape of the potato patch, which the farmers manured and ploughed for their men, carting the produce to the cottage door. Dorset was one of the Wessex counties in which the Poor Law Commissioners of 1843 found women and girls engaged in rough field labour to the neglect of their homes. In the 60's, in East Anglia, as the consequence perhaps of the decline of the worsted industry, women and children were employed on field work in public gangs under demoralising conditions. Shaftes-bury again fought the good fight. In 1867 it was made illegal to employ any children under eight in a gang, and no women or children in a gang in which men worked. When private gangs

---

[1] *Children's Employment Commission, First Report, Mines* (1842), p. 27.
[2] *Ibid.* p. 30.

threatened to defeat the purpose of the Act, a further Act was passed in 1873 making the employment of children contingent upon a record of school attendance. The Commissioners of 1868–70, however, found that in the North, though young women worked in the fields, no children under twelve and no married women were there, and that wages were better because of the opportunities for industrial employment.

An Englishman would like to indulge the hope that the widespread exploitation of children from 1770 to 1870 was forced upon employers by necessity or at any rate practised without their knowledge. But such a hope is shaken by the record of the cruelty which a small and helpless part of the juvenile population was allowed to suffer in this same period. Among his many philanthropies (cf. p. 345) Jonas Hanway drew attention to the plight of the climbing boys who swept chimneys, but the Act of 1788 mitigating the abuse of apprenticeship to chimney sweeping was a dead letter. Between 1817 and 1819 more than one Bill was thrown out by the Lords, who acted on the advice of Lord Lauderdale, to leave such a question ' entirely to the moral feelings of perhaps the most moral people on the face of the earth.' The Act of 1834 did something—among other things it saved Oliver Twist. Shaftesbury took up their case in 1840 and procured in 1842 an Act which was effective in some districts, notably in London, and disregarded in others. The Lords delayed amending legislation in 1853, the Commons in 1854. In 1861 the Children's Employment Commission found that the old horrors still existed —hardening of knees and elbows through rubbing them in brine, coaxing with the present of a halfpenny, tickling with a brush, and so on. Some towns were notorious—Liverpool, Nottingham, for example ; others had suppressed the abuse by means of local associations. Charles Kingsley's *Water Babies* of 1863 deepened the disquiet caused by the Commissioners' report, and in 1864 it was made illegal for a sweep to employ any child under ten or to allow any child under sixteen to enter a house or be with him while he was sweeping a chimney. This was sufficient if enforced, but it was not thoroughly enforced until master chimney sweeps were compelled by law in 1875 to take out an annual licence from the police and the police were entrusted with the enforcement. The alternative to the climbing boy was a longer brush, which in some houses required the chimneys to be straightened. And who were the most fierce opponents of this new-fangled sweeping machinery ? At first, noble lords speaking in defence of private property, and when their energy flagged, our saintly grandmothers, who were sure that sweeping brushes would spoil the carpets and were so fond of the dear little chaps that they bribed them with sweetmeats to imperil their lives. It is almost unbelievable but literally true. When life is held cheap under the demoralisation of pestilence we can forgive ; but it will not be surprising if some of these apostles of social *laissez-faire* are found on the lowest ledge of Dante's Inferno.

Section 6. *The Medical Revolution*

The medical revolution was coincident in time with the industrial revolution ; and here also Great Britain drew part of her new knowledge from Europe, from Italy as well as from Holland. William Harvey, of Caius College, Cambridge, whose treatise on the circulation of the blood appeared in 1628, had studied at Padua. Influenza and quarantine are Italian words. Influenza= influence = visitation, was applied specifically in 1743 to the ' grip ' which then raged in Italy ; and Italian cities led the way in establishing the detention period of forty days, *quarantana*, for infected ships. The clinical methods and clinical instruction introduced by Hermann Boerhaave (1668–1738) were taken from Holland to Edinburgh, where was founded about 1725 the medical school of the University, the first in Great Britain, followed by the Infirmary in 1736. Intimate contact between the university and the hospital, between theory and practice, thus began in Edinburgh ; and it is the foundation of Toronto's international repute to-day. Wealthy London was later than Scotland ; for professional conservatism showed itself in the 1720's as strongly as in the age of Pasteur and Lister. Whenever we touch on 18th-century education London is no longer first. While Edinburgh was teaching its students in university and infirmary, London contented itself with the private venture schools of individual physicians who took their pupils to walk the hospitals. The late 19th century trained its budding landlords in the offices of land agents in the same bad way. It is therefore not surprising that Scotland came south to conquer London in the person of William Smellie, the founder of scientific midwifery, and John Hunter, the cabinet-maker's assistant and founder of scientific surgery. Smellie began to teach in London in 1739, Hunter in 1773. In 1749 the first of the London lying-in hospitals was founded.

But London was also the capital of the Empire ; and the Army and Navy suffered horribly from disease overseas and on the seas. In times of crisis the Forces were recruited from the sweepings of the country, therefore they had wrecks to cure as well as strong men to protect from gaol fever and tropical disease. How terrible the gaols were John Howard showed in 1774. But the Services had discipline and enforced a regimen. Sir John Pringle,[1] Dr. James Lind,[2] and Sir Gilbert Blane, who added to the lustre of his writings by salvaging the wrecks of the Walcheren Expedition in 1809, supplied the knowledge. Nor were the great sea captains backward in support. They cared for the health of their men. Captain Cook in his voyage of 1772–5 furnished a 100% proof of the value of the new preventive of scurvy. In 1791 the ration of lemon juice was instituted by the Admiralty ; and Nelson, the darling of the Fleet because of his care for the men as well as his personal bravery, built upon the knowledge supplied by the naval doctors. ' I can refuse nothing to this man,' said Napoleon, when a request for the release of some English prisoners was presented in the name of Jenner of vaccination fame.[3]

Great Britain's oversea contacts affected health in a second way. Two great scourges came from the East : the plague, known as Oriental or bubonic plague, which took one-sixth of London's population in 1665, and the cholera, which descended upon London when it was talking Reform Bill in 1831 and the People's Charter in 1848. That there was no recurrence of the plague, not even in 1720–2 when it visited Paris, was due perhaps to the natural decline in its virulence ; but nature was helped by man, for the strict quarantine laws were really enforced. The Turkey Company's ability to enforce them was a valid ground for the postponement of an open trade to the Levant until 1754, when after the passage of 26 Geo. II, c. 18, Dean Tucker's views prevailed.[4] The elimination of plague gave momentum to economic growth and made possible the modern territorial division of labour, which assumes the perpetual action of the industrial machine. But if one of the saving things in war is the hygiene which it teaches, one of the tragedies of peace is the speed with which the lessons are forgotten. The 18th and early 19th centuries are extolled for their individualism. ' There was never perhaps a period when organisation counted for so little and personality for so much.'[5] Therefore Harriet Martineau's England was as unprepared for the Crimea as if there had been no Walcheren or Peninsular war. Shaftesbury as unpaid commissioner and chairman of the General Board of Health had been fighting cholera in London from 1848 to 1854. Florence Nightingale went to him for help, and it was he who improvised the Sanitary Commission which saved the day in the Crimea, when the Army of

[1] *Observations on the Diseases of the Army*, 1752.
[2] *A Treatise of the Scurvy*, 1753.
[3] Quoted in M. C. Buer, *Health, Wealth and Population in the Early Days of the Industrial Revolution*, p. 192.
[4] *Cf.* Josiah Tucker, *Expediency of Opening the Trade to Turkey.*
[5] M. C. Buer, *op. cit.* p. 40.

wealthy industrial Britain was threatened with destruction before the advance of preventible disease. During the Great War the hospital and sanitary arrangements on the French front were perfect, but in Gallipoli, Mesopotamia, and Egypt incompetence sent many to their grave. Shall we again forget?

Industry requires a place of work : the hospital was the factory of the medical revolution. Two sorts of building raised their heads in 18th-century London, the hospital and the dispensary. The mediaeval hospitals of St. Bartholomew and St. Thomas were refuges rather than places of healing. Between 1720 and 1760 old hospitals were re-built and nine new ones founded, including that of Thomas Guy (1724), who devoted his fortune in South Sea stock to its building and endowment. But they were more than places of healing, they were clean and ventilated and they infected their neighbourhood with good habits. Dispensaries were the branch stores of the goddess Hygeia. The first was opened in Red Lion Square in 1769, and by 1800 there were thirteen forerunners of the sixty-nine of to-day. Through the dispensary the doctor learned at first hand how the poor lived ; and in the Parliamentary inquiries of the 19th century the evidence of the doctors again and again carried the day.

Hospitals, dispensaries and medical schools followed in the provinces. There the hospital came first, the dispensary was often attached to a hospital, and medical schools were established in great towns, Bristol 1818, Manchester 1824, Sheffield 1828, Leeds 1831, Newcastle and Liverpool 1832. Manchester's problem was the most acute. She was the nerve centre of an unstable industrialism and weighed down with Irish. Under Dr. Thomas Percival, the pioneer of civilian health, the voluntarily constituted Board of Health tackled the problem of infectious disease which was so disturbing to Manchester's labour supply. The big mill owners responded, improving the sanitation of their mills ; and thus the big unit, hospital and mill, gradually closed down the waste and disease of domestic industry and cellar life. Liverpool followed in 1801 with a fever hospital supported entirely from the rates. For in fever cases voluntary subscription lacked its ordinary reward. The patient had to be hurried in ; he could not wait for the recommendation of a subscriber.

It is hard to resist the conclusion that the Middle Ages were dirty. Perhaps they were too humble to be clean, or like children, too jolly. But dirt was very dangerous to a country whose staple was wool. The cotton lords destroyed the flea by providing the poor with washable clothes. Moreover the doctors soon learned the curative value of fresh air, and therefore the hospitals countered the effects of industrialism by restoring some of the fresh air which the town population lacked. Modern writers are too severe on the lean and roughbred animals of the days before Bakewell ; for as animals they were hardy and fit. But though Bakewell's stock, from the animal's point of view, were unhealthily fat, this fat was vitamin A. Londoners, therefore, no longer needed to wear long boots to conceal their rickets, as Charles I and his Court are said to have done ; and when Bakewell's contemporaries supplied the cities with fresh fruit and green vegetables and the city folk took to suburban gardening, another class of vitamins was assured. Thus healthy diet, which to-day is the central part of a doctor's prescription, rests historically on the 18th-century improvements in agriculture and transport. Medicine has had a strange history. First potions and strange compounds with an element of sorcery in them ; then pills, an outrage of capitalistic advertisement, which defeated for a time the efforts of doctors and agricultural plenty ; and now the regimen of diet, with Abstinence for those who put the welfare of the next generation before present pleasure. Shaftesbury understood the beneficent circle because he had fought so long against the vicious circle of ignorance, intemperance and disease.

To sum up, the medical achievement of 1740 to 1840 was practical and real. By 1800 rickets were no longer common and scurvy had disappeared as a cause of death. Maternity was treated in specialised institutions, to the advantage of mothers and children ; and a beginning had been made with the scientific treatment of infectious disease. Specialisation in medicine was wholly good, as when, for example, in 1837 the distinction between typhus and typhoid was clearly made. Above all, the long reign of smallpox, which is endemic to Great Britain and Europe, came to an end. In the 18th century it was as normal as chickenpox is among children to-day. In the 18th century ' men would not marry until or unless the lady had had smallpox, servants were advertised for who had had it, people who had not had the disease were spoken of as " to have the smallpox," and ladies who had not had it or were not marked were at once regarded as beauties.'[1] Dr. Edward Jenner, of Berkeley, Gloucestershire, signed its death warrant by publishing his discovery of vaccination in 1798. In 1853 it was made compulsory, with exemption for conscientious objectors. The long interval between the two dates was due partly to popular resistance—strongest and still strong in Jenner's native county, partly to the fact that the necessity for periodical re-vaccination was not appreciated at first, and partly to the fact that the public had already adopted from the East a half-way remedy. This was inoculation with the smallpox

[1] G. T. Griffith, *Population Problems of the Age of Malthus*, p. 248.

N 2

itself : which was effective, but spread the disease, since the patient under inoculation communicated the disease in its full strength to others.   Inoculation by cow pox, i.e. vaccination, was confined in the early 19th century to the children of the upper and middle classes.   The lower classes demanded the real thing, and private enterprise was ready in the persons of a farmer, a knife-grinder, a fishmonger, and a whitesmith.   These and others battened on the popular ignorance until in 1840, by 3 & 4 Vict. c. 29, inoculation was made a felony.   Which sort, one wonders, was the 'noculation which Dolly Winthrop advised for Silas Marner's child (Chap. XIII of George Eliot's novel).

But progress sometimes recoils upon itself.   The growing use of hospitals in large industrial centres led to the overcrowding of their wards, with the result that infections, especially those causing suppurations, became very prevalent.   Open wounds and operations such as amputations exacted a fearful toll in human lives because of blood-poisoning and hospital gangrene ; and it became safer to be treated in a cottage than in a hospital.   About 1850 in the General Lying-in Hospital of London the deaths from puerperal fever were alarmingly high.   In 1869 Sir James Y. Simpson, who some twenty years previously had introduced the use of chloroform as an anaesthetic (thereby ridding operations of pain), found that 2 out of 5 operations performed in the hospitals of London, Edinburgh and Glasgow were fatal, as compared with 1 in every 9 operations performed in private houses ; and therefore he advocated the destruction of large hospital buildings and the substitution of huts, in each of which not more than two or three patients should be housed.   But the introduction of the antiseptic method in 1867 by Joseph Lister, then Professor of Surgery at Glasgow, removed the necessity for so drastic and expensive a remedy, though it took several years for its influence in making operations safe to win general recognition. The result of this great English application of the discoveries of Louis Pasteur was that ' hospitalism ' rapidly disappeared and operations formerly considered impossible, e.g. abdominal operations, could be done with safety.   Lord Lister (for so the London Quaker's son was created in 1897) died in 1912 aged 84, two years before a war whose horrors but for him would have been twice what they were.

Section 7.   Sanitation and Housing

Eighteenth-century London was more healthy as a dwelling-place than London before the Fire, though for a period gin palaces cancelled out the gain.   The black rat that carried the flea that carried the plague did not flourish in the new brick and stone with which London was rebuilt. The timbered houses, though beautiful, were liable to fire, and harboured vermin and dirt. The re-building was done by private enterprise, but there were communal wants which individuals could not supply and the corporations of London and other towns because of their deadness did not. Therefore, as in road building, an intermediate instrument was found in the person of Commissioners appointed by special Act of Parliament, beginning with Westminster in 1761 and London in 1766, and followed by Liverpool and Manchester in 1776 and 1786 respectively. It was these variously named Improvement Commissioners, some 300 bodies in all, and not the Mayor, Aldermen and Councils of the old corporations, who were the progenitors of nearly all the activities of the municipalities of to-day.[1] They struggled with the new needs of the growing towns for paving and cleansing. When they began, there were no pipes or gutters. Puddles and garbage lay in the middle of the road. There were no ash pits or privies, the pig was the general scavenger. The towns were three times as unhealthy as the adjacent country. Manchester and Liverpool in 1757 had death-rates of 1 in 25·7 and 1 in 27, against 1 in 68 in Monton Moss, a rural suburb of Manchester, and 1 in 66 in Horwich, a small Lancashire town.[2] Thus the towns lived on the country for their people as well as their food. The weak feature of the statutory authorities was that they worked in isolation. Sometimes the Paving Commissioners were hindered by the continuous tearing up of the streets for the new pipes of the gas and water companies, acting also under statutory power and supplying competing services. Manchester is the solitary instance of a municipality which supplied its own gas, making it at first (1807) for its own offices and later (1817) for the public. Perhaps the most absurd example of municipal abdication was the private fire brigade, which was retained by the fire insurance companies to quench fires on premises insured by them. To buildings not bearing their plate they applied the principle of *laissez-brûler*. In Birmingham it needed the energy of Joseph Chamberlain, when Mayor, to replace private enterprise by a municipal fire brigade in the year of Our Lord 1873.

Frequently the improvements which the Commissioners effected in the main streets were neutralised by overcrowding in the back streets and chaos outside the municipal area. In the Manchester of 1795, outside the main streets which the

---

[1] *Cf.* S. and B. Webb, *English Local Government, Statutory Authorities,* passim.
[2] *Cf.* L. W. Moffitt, *England on the Eve of the Industrial Revolution*, p. 271.

Commissioners were improving, ' unregulated private enterprise had been covering the green fields with mile upon mile of squalid " back to back " cottages, crammed close together in narrow courts and blind alleys ; with underground cellars occupied indifferently by human beings, animals and stores of cinders and filth.'[1] And generally in 1815 the majority of the urban population lived in mean streets springing up in irregular conglomerations for the most part outside the municipal boundary. They did not know each other. According to the census of 1851, the proportion of natives was only just over a quarter in Manchester, Bradford and Glasgow. But the cholera of 1831 and 1848 stung the cities into action. For cholera, though an epidemic from abroad, was carried by the infection of water, which was under civic control. But still the lesson of provision for future growth was unlearned. In Preston in 1844 lines of slums were growing up in the open country. The State of Large Towns Commission of 1845 reported of Merthyr Tydvil, South Wales, that ' during the rapid increase of this town no attention seems to have been paid to its drainage and the streets and houses have been built at random as it suited the views of those who speculated in them.'[2] The result was reflected in the higher death-rate of the country between 1810 and 1840 and the failure till 1870 to effect any improvement on the rate for 1810, namely, 20 per 1000. The campaign of Edwin Chadwick and his medical friends brought the Public Health Act of 1848 (11 & 12 Vict. c. 63), the basis of all later sanitary law. But the Public Health Board of 1848–54—modelled on the Cholera Board of 1832—which was appointed to demonstrate and extend the new Sanitary Law, foundered on local resistance and Parliamentary devotion to *laissez-mourir*. In 1871 the first permanent central authority was established, the Local Government Board, with which the Poor Law Board was now merged. Fruitful legislation followed—the Public Health Acts of 1871–5 and the Acts of 1868–85 dealing with the housing of artisans and the working class.

Shaftesbury built on Chadwick's foundations with a special eye to London's needs. In the common lodging-houses of the 1840's he had found horrors comparable with those in the mines. To eradicate these he obtained philanthropic support for model lodging-houses ; and their immunity from cholera in 1851 wrung from Parliament the Act of 1851 for the registration and inspection of lodging-houses. In the same year the vicious window tax, the enemy of light and health, was abolished (cf. p. 62 n.). But there was still a period of twenty years, 1851–71, during which

---

[1] S. and B. Webb, *op cit.* p. 401.
[2] 2nd Report (1845), Appendix, p. 143.

laissez-faire, now being hunted from factories and mines, ran riot in house building. Everything was sacrificed to cheapness, and cheapness was attained not merely by excluding all conveniences such as the laying on of water, but by restricting the ground space. After 1871 a new chapter in town life opens. The reign of the shopkeepers, builders and publicans, the first to profit by the Municipal Reform Act of 1835 as by the Reform Act of 1832, came to an end. Great industrialists like Joseph Chamberlain gave freely to their cities the genius which had brought them industrial fortunes. The sad thing was that the change came so unnecessarily late.

A large town, it is true, could not be made healthy by a stroke of the pen. The free water that now bubbles up from street corner and public building is the product of high engineering skill. Two problems had to be mastered. The first problem was the delivery of the water in water-tight iron pipes ; for the old pipes of elm wood leaked, the water supply was occasional and very liable to break down in a fire. But iron pipes were introduced in Chelsea in 1746 and were general by 1820, while in 1820 Lambeth and Chelsea obtained adequate water filters. In this there seems to have been an element of luck. For filter beds were installed to remove visible impurities, and themselves becoming dirty obstructed the passage of invisible bacteria more effectively than clean ones would have done. Advocates of temperance may be shocked to read that 18th-century children usually drank small beer. They should not forget that pure water was almost unobtainable. The second problem was the separation of sewage from the water supply. The first closets emptied into drains which had been constructed for the removal of surplus water ; and their contents were taken to the river from which perhaps the inhabitants got their water. This problem was solved by modern systems of sewage disposal and the derivation of water from a long distance. Thus Liverpool went to Lake Vyrnwy in Wales, and Manchester to Thirlmere. It was right, but it is sad that Manchester now needs Mardale, the hidden beauty spot of the English Lakes. In judging the shortcomings of the 19th century it is necessary to distinguish mistakes of avarice or blindness from those which were due to inadequacy of technique. Pure water depended on a new technique, but this cannot be said of dirt removal or provision for fresh air. There was no mechanical difficulty in removing filth as it collected, or in laying bricks with regard for common comfort and health. The trouble was that in the short run slums paid. Shaftesbury found that the vilest houses made the biggest profits. Housing was within the nation's control, and that it was not controlled

is an abiding disgrace to the England that was the workshop of
the world.

CHAPTER XVIII

DOGMA AND REVOLT

**Section 1. Liberalism and Benthamism. Section 2. The Classical Political
Economy. Section 3. The Messages of Cobbett and Owen. Section 4. The
Early English Socialists. Section 5. Carlyle, Ruskin and Marx. Section 6.
The Novel as a Source of Economic History.**

Section 1. Liberalism and Benthamism

FOREIGNERS thought that England's zeal for the abolition of the
slave trade was cant. She had the lion's share of it and ruled
her West Indies worse than France. She converted the heathen
and maltreated Christian children at home. But this was because
they thought of England as a unit. The Quakers who inspired
the crusade were anti-imperial and their own households were in
order. There were very few places where 18th-century England
could see white slavery, for factories were only just beginning
and there were next to none in London. But there were slave
ships and plantations, and 18th-century reformers could hardly be
expected to detect the analogy between slavery and factory work.
The abolition of the trade in 1807 did not end the institution.
Therefore in 1823 an Anti-Slavery Society was formed, with
T. F. Buxton, a Quaker, in Wilberforce's place, and his chief
coadjutors Zachary Macaulay, father of T. B., and the three
Stephens—James, and his two sons, Sir James (Mr. Mother
Country) and Sir George. Their campaign was an exact anticipation of that of the Anti-Corn Law League. They had placards,
lectures, petitions and handsome funds. They faced distractions,
Catholic Emancipation and the Reform Bill, and they made
no solid progress until in 1830 they demanded emancipation,
complete and immediate. They won in 1833 ; and the nation
paid to the slave owners in the Empire £20 millions, of which
15 went to the West Indies. When people are organised in an
earnest movement they see only the need for that ; and if in
the period from 1776 to 1833, from the *Wealth of Nations* to the
first effective factory law, Liberalism seems to us to degenerate
into ruthless pessimism, it is because we forget that during the
war and its aftermath reformers were working for a cause abroad.
It was not selfishness but duty keenly felt, so keenly indeed that
the advent of other ills was minimised. At home they lapsed

into the formulae of Benthamism, exaggerating them as an apology for their inaction.

Benthamism was not a reaction to industrialism but a stage in the history of philosophy, the repudiation of tradition and an appeal to reason and utility. The individual was exalted, yet no more than in the age of Adam Smith. Its teaching was abused by being made to subserve the ends of the rich industrialists ; but it was not meant in this way, and the majority of essential reforms accomplished between 1820 and 1875 had the Benthamite impress upon them. Bentham indeed was most powerful at the time of his death in 1832.

The services of Benthamism were briefly these. First of all, it inspired the logic of political democracy, substituting utility and quantity for abuse and caste. This was the logic of the Reform Act of 1832 and the Municipal Reform Act of 1835. After Bentham's death the political influence of Benthamism bifurcated. One part was taken to Lancashire by his editor and factotum John Bowring, and supplied the cosmopolitan element in the campaign for free trade. The other part remained at London to mix with the views and experiences of the new colonial school—Durham, Grote, Roebuck, Gibbon Wakefield, and Charles Buller, the pupil of Carlyle. Through Durham the views of the radical theorists prevailed over those of the Colonial Office and saved the Empire.

Secondly, it supplied a new measurement for social reform —the maximising of individual happiness. This called for humanitarian legislation, the reform of the savage criminal law and the protection of those who were too weak to protect themselves—children, young persons and women. It also underlay the solicitude of fiscal reformers for the welfare of the masses. When Peel abolished the Corn Laws, when Gladstone reduced the sugar tax, they emphasised the quantitative aspect. Plenty among more people was put before productive power. The ' quality ' in those days, be it remembered, were the undertaxed few, the ' quantity,' the overtaxed many. The Socialist disciples of Bentham carried the measurement a stage further when they based on it schemes of progressive taxation.

Thirdly, Benthamism supplied an argument for the freedom to combine, for such freedom was one of many freedoms and therefore desirable. Place used this with telling effect when asking for the repeal of the Combination Laws in 1824 ; and when Place's work was completed half a century later, the individualist formula of Bentham did duty once again (below, p. 394).

Fourthly, it set a value on individual enlightenment, and

therefore on popular education. This was the side of Bentham most dear to himself. For he was a dreamer of educational Utopias and admired Robert Owen so much that he became a sleeping partner in New Lanark. His *Chrestomathia* of 1814, a series of papers outlining the plan of a utilitarian school, gave an impetus to the Mechanics Institutes, which grew out of the science course given by Professor Birkbeck at Glasgow in 1800. Benthamism and Owenism in conjunction gave to Chartism a distinctive and, from the revolutionary standpoint, a weakening flavour. ' Your Unions,' wrote Henry Vincent the Chartist orator in 1841, ' ought not to assume the character of mere talking clubs . . . the object should be . . . to acquire useful information in the sciences of government and morals and in the laws which regulate the production and distribution of wealth.' [1]

But against all these services must be set the fact that Benthamism by envisaging society as a collection of independent units blinded itself to a fundamental human instinct, namely, for self-help through association. Therefore the school resisted the extension of group life and social control to the industrial sphere. This sphere it was content to reserve to the will of the manufacturers and the abstract laws of political economy.

Section 2. *The Classical Political Economy*

The political economists were Benthamites, but in matters economic the venerable Jeremy was the disciple of Malthus and the elder Mill. The economists drew their laws from the social problems of the day. The new industrialism, the French war, and the life-sustaining properties of the potato gave to these laws form and substance. The law of diminishing returns in agriculture was a heritage from the siege conditions of war time, but it rendered staunch service to the Malthusian law of population, which soon it overlaid. The application of the two laws to social policy was gloomily cruel. In 1825, after ten years of breathing space from war, Malthus had still nothing to offer but deterrents to population—to England the refusal of poor relief after a certain date and to Ireland the demolition of cottages.[2] But he preferred, as less cruel, ' moral restraint,' and he thought that cheap tracts might convince the labouring classes of the truth of this.[3]

A maiden lady, Miss Harriet Martineau, appeared to fill the

---

[1] *English Chartist Circular* (1841), No. 3.
[2] Commons Committee on Emigration, 1826–7, Evidence of the Rev. T. R Malthus, Qs. 3231, 3254.
[3] *Ibid.* Qs. 3377–8.

literary vacuum, and in 34 Numbers of Tales Illustrating Political Economy and Taxation she converted everybody except the poor for whom they were intended. Her method of work was very precise. She furnished herself with the standard works, mapped out a scheme, read as far as was necessary to the number in hand, and allowed the plot to develop as she wrote. The plot was incidental, and in her last numbers she advertised in capitals the heart of the matter.

The condition of labourers may be best improved :
1. By inventions and discoveries which create capital ; and by husbanding instead of wasting capital, for instance, by making savings instead of starting strikes.
2. BY ADJUSTING THE PROPORTION OF POPULATION TO CAPITAL.

Miss Martineau found herself famous. Cabinet Ministers and newspaper editors vied for the privilege of having their proposals supported by her stories. Brougham engaged her for the defence of the New Poor Law, but forgot to pay. The Tales were a fair popularisation of the current political economy. For the text books were dominated by the fixed wages fund, from which it followed that if one worker got more, another got less ; therefore strikes were useless and the only remedy was a smaller population.

The attitude of the political economists to factory reform was ambiguous. The three Factory Commissioners of 1833 were Benthamites, and one of them, Thomas Tooke, a statistician. They favoured factory legislation for minors, but went out of their way to denounce the mischievous agitation of the Short-Time Committees, which ' seem scarcely ever to have considered the law of supply and demand as applicable to the working classes.' [1] Nassau Senior, Professor of Political Economy at Oxford, and one of the four central Commissioners on the Hand-Loom Weavers Commission of 1839–41, opposed the Factory Acts at first, and later supported them. But inasmuch as in the interval the ten hours' day had been fought and won and even employers admitted that they had not been damaged by the restriction, further opposition would have been childish. More-over, Senior retained his animus against the Trade Unions, and Stanley Jevons, in his *State in Relation to Labour* (1882), was almost as bitter and quite as cocksure : ' It is quite impossible for trades unions in general to effect any permanent increase of wages.' [2] Co-operative production appealed to John Stuart Mill, and Henry Sidgwick interested himself in the movement.

---

[1] *First Report of Factory Commissioners* (1833), p. 49.
[2] *Op. cit.* p. 109.

When Messrs. Briggs, the Yorkshire coal owners, inaugurated their scheme of profit-sharing in 1865 the economists were loud in its praise. In fine, in the first half of the 19th century political economy was anti-social. For the next thirty years at least it followed nervously in the wake of facts, reserving its eulogies for such expedients as promised to dispense with the Trade Union.

Section 3. The Messages of Cobbett and Owen

William Cobbett and Robert Owen are among the remarkable men of the century. They were arch rebels who could not be suppressed and they wrote and did positive things. Cobbett, the farmer politician, looked back with longing on the England that was. He loved it and sang its charms in pure and healthy English. He could not abide bullying, and so the Tory Sergeant-Major, who had served in Nova Scotia with jaunty success, came back to England to denounce the cat-o'-nine-tails and to spend two years in gaol. Thenceforward he was a Radical and a terror to the Government. He dabbled shrewdly in the problems of currency and national debt, but he had a greater interest in persons and personalities. We read him for his *Rural Rides*, his generation read him for the *Political Register*, which lashed Churchman and Nonconformist, Tory and Whig with equal glee and exposed one abuse at least per number. In the last great period of his life, the period between the agricultural labourers' revolt of 1830 and the Reform Bill of 1832, he was the giant in the background. In his Tory days he had dodged a court-martial, in 1830 he stood up for his friend, the harried agricultural labourer. A writer in the *Philadelphia National Gazette* of August 18, 1830, trying to explain England to his readers, said, ' The term pauper as used in England, and more particularly in agricultural districts, embraces that numerous class of society who depend for subsistence solely upon the labour of their hands.' The truth of this hurt Cobbett to the quick. ' All of you who are sixty years of age can recollect that bread and meat, and not wretched potatoes, were the food of the labouring people . . . There were always some exceptions to this ; some lazy, some drunken, some improvident young men ; but I appeal to all those of you who are sixty years of age, whether this be not a true description of the state of the labourers of England when they were boys.' [1] Those who paint the scenery of England from the description in the *Rural Rides* are sometimes reluctant to accept his social picture. But if it

---

[1] *Twopenny Trash* (1831), I. 195, given in full in my *Life and Labour*, pp. 84–5.

is dangerous to separate builders from builders' wages,[1] is it not also dangerous to separate what Cobbett says about villages from what he says about those who lived in them ?

Cobbett's life ended in anti-climax. For when he was elected to the Reform Parliament as a member for the industrial constituency of Oldham he was a fish out of water. But the good he did lived after him. Free writing was still penalised ; and the struggle for a free press 1830–6 was quite in the vein of Cobbett and 18th-century London. Some working-men Radicals of London decided to challenge the law. Henry Hetherington published the *Penny Papers for the People*, inscribing on the title-page of July 9, 1831, ' published contrary to " Law " to try the power of " Might against Right." ' Prosecutions followed, and William Lovett, the young co-operator, who later with Francis Place's help was to draft the People's Charter, organised a victim fund. Finally, after a jury in 1834 had decided that the paper in dispute was not an illegal newspaper, the Government in 1836 replaced the 4*d.* stamp, which had been imposed in 1819 to keep down Cobbett's *Register*, by a 1*d.* stamp, which franked the paper through the post. Cobbett died in 1835.

Owen, like Cobbett, spent part of his life in America and looked to it as a land of hope for his community schemes. His instinct was international, the very opposite of the man who wrote in 1817, ' I will die an Englishman in exile or an Englishman in England free.' He was a monotonous writer but a wonderful doer. His thesis, repeated *ad nauseam*, was this : Environment is the cause of differences in character, and environment is under human control. If the care of inanimate machines yields such high profits, how much more will be yielded by the care of animate men and women ? But the adult cannot profit by this care unless as a child he is educated aright.

He had worked his theory out while he was an employer at New Lanark, and during the years of national resettlement 1813–17, when the people's hopes were reviving and the Government was not yet scared into reaction, he was lionised and his views were in general demand. But education, which to him was as important as his mill, brought him into conflict with the Church and he was outlawed. From paternalism he moved to socialism, becoming its literal father. For the first Socialists were Owenite Socialists and he, their ' social father,' beckoned them to villages of mutual unity and co-operation. Owen gave himself to humanity, so fully indeed that he almost lost his own. He was a benevolent autocrat first and last and his system was

[1] *Cf.* J. H. Clapham, *The Early Railway Age*, Preface, p. vii.

everything to him. He led in turn the Co-operative and Trade Union movements of the 1830's, only to leave them for the gospel of Owenism, which became more mystical as the years went by, and he ended life a spiritualist. In 1844–5, when his son, Robert Dale Owen, was a member of the House of Representatives, he paid a triumphant farewell to America. He was now in his 74th year, but far from a dotard. In a letter home at American election time he observed : ' There is more mental slavery in this country in this moment than there is in England.' [1] In his addresses to the American people he pleads as of old ' for the most ample religious freedom,'[2] but he was not class-conscious. He appealed to capitalists to form Joint Stock Companies to solve the ' Great Problem of the Age, that is, how to apply the enormous and ever-growing new scientific powers for producing wealth, beneficially for the entire population.' [3]

An American economist has recently remarked :

There is a growing tendency to treat labour problems neither as matters of abstract justice nor in terms of mass movements, but rather as specific problems arising from the organization and administration of particular industries, as engineering problems of industrial organization. Such an approach to labour problems in the coal industry promises a more complete understanding of the real nature of the problem than has generally been attained.[4]

This was the idea that haunted Owen all his life. He was not a Carnegie and not a Marx. He wanted to be a social engineer, an engineer because engineering was the new power, social because alone in his generation he grasped the full meaning of social responsibility. Mr. Owen had a plan, a grand design. He brought agriculture, manufactures, education and recreation within the limits of a parallelogram. He was too literal, but he touched the general failing of his age, which was not cruelty nor acquisitiveness, but planlessness and a smug resentment of humane control.

Section 4. The Early English Socialists

The classical dogma provoked an intellectual revolt. The fact that the revolt was in the terms of the classical political economy accounts for its practical weakness and dialectical strength. It was proclaimed by a group of writers known as the early English or Ricardian Socialists—Charles Hall, M.D.,

---

[1] *Documentary History of American Industrial Society* (1910), VII. 169.
[2] *Ibid.* p. 157.   [3] *Ibid.* p. 166.
[4] G. W. Stocking, ' Labour Problems in the American Bituminous Coal Industry,' *Economic Journal,* June 1927, p. 214.

William Thompson, John Gray, Thomas Hodgskin and John Francis Bray Most of their work was done in or around the year 1825, when Owenite co-operation absorbed the interest of the working class. They countered theory with theory and therefore lacked the telling historical appeal of Marx. They anticipated his theory of surplus value, but by 1850 they were forgotten. Moreover, their great theory, the right of labour to the whole produce of labour, was individualist (they were not behind the economists in their admiration of Bentham) and their message to the State was ' hands off.' In so far as they had a positive plan, it was co-operative communism and easy money.

However, it is satisfactory to reflect that some Englishmen had the wit to expose the economists—

> McCulloch, Malthus, Mill, a triad famed
> For bold assertions which are soon disclaimed.

They clarified the mystery of the abstraction called Capital by time distinctions quite after the style of Mr. Irving Fisher. ' Capital,' said William Thompson, ' is nothing mysterious : 'tis nothing else but that portion of the products of labour which is not immediately consumed. . . . Ripe fruit is consumed the very day it is produced . . . shoes and other articles of clothes . . . within a few months . . . a chair, a table, a loom . . . in a few years . . . a house in fifty years . . . while statues, the fairest works of art . . . have outlived the immortality of the immortal gods.' [1] And the humbug in the mystery was shown by Thomas Hodgskin : ' To talk of sending away roads, bridges, canals and cultivated fields is a striking absurdity and yet we hear perpetually a sort of cuckoo sound among Members of Parliament who are capitalists themselves, or leagued with capitalists, about the danger of *forcing these things* under the name of capital out of the *country.*' [2] Nor were they afraid of Malthus. ' Insult not,' said William Thompson, ' the suffering, the great majority of men, with the glaring falsehood that by means of limiting population or eating potatoes their own happiness is in their own hands, while the causes are left which render it morally and physically impossible for them to live without potatoes and improvident breeding.' [3] But they were too bold for their generation ; for they recommended birth control and a stationary population. This put them beyond the pale of society. Outraged prelates wrote letters to the Home Office and denounced the rumoured community of sex in the Harmony

[1] W. Thompson, *Distribution of Wealth*, p. 239.
[2] T. Hodgskin, *Popular Political Economy*, p. 253.
[3] W. Thompson, *op. cit.* p. 428.

Community at Queenwood, Hampshire. The will of Thompson—
he died in 1833—which left his body to science and his fortune
to the establishment of a Community, was set aside. ' It is very
unfair,' counsel urged, ' that we married men should be debating
this topic ; it ought really to be tried by a jury of matrons.' [1]

Section 5. *Carlyle, Ruskin and Marx*

Rebels are of two kinds. Carlyle and Ruskin were rebels
within their society, Owen and Marx foretold its overthrow.
Carlyle was the rugged scholar out for a row, and it is hardly
surprising that his *Occasional Discourse on the Nigger Question*
led to a breach with the man whose housemaid had accidentally
destroyed the first volume of the *French Revolution*. For above
all else Mill believed in liberty. At the time of Peterloo Carlyle
was ill and poor, and the misery of the working classes made
a deep impression on a mind similarly attuned, but his economic
writings, *Chartism*, 1839, *Past and Present*, 1843, *Latter Day
Pamphlets*, 1850, were asides. He had no respect for party,
his masterpieces were *Cromwell* and *Frederick the Great*, and he
was poles apart from the democratic aspirations of the British
working class, which is instinctively and immutably peaceable.
Therefore it was his own pugnacious middle class that he enlisted
under his banner. Conventionality for him was the deadly sin
and he did his best to shame the middle class out of it. With his
faith in strong doing he brushed aside the sophistry which held
the individualists back from social reform. ' With two million
industrial soldiers already sitting in Bastilles and five millions
pining on potatoes methinks Westminster cannot begin too soon.' [2]
' It might begin with sanitary regulations, fresh air for towns,
a teaching service and a free bridge for emigrants.' [3] Carlyle
would carry his generation into collectivism, but the machinery
was less important to him than the man. ' Some " Chivalry of
Labour " will yet be realised on this earth,' [4] he hoped in 1843 ;
and he just lived to see a passable representation of it in the
State Socialism of Frederick the Great's successor, Bismarck.
But there are worse bonds than the cash-nexus, as England will
continue to believe, no matter what biographers of Mussolini or
Lenin shall say. If it is not grounded on democracy, industrial
chivalry cannot endure.

John Ruskin was an artist and social reformer. Decently
reared in London and Christ Church, Oxford, he was already

---

[1] Owen's *Crisis*, Vol. IV. p. 35.
[2] *Past and Present*, ' Plugson of Undershot.'
[3] *Ibid.* ' The One Institution.'   [4] *Ibid.* ' The Didactic.'

famous, when he arrived through the political economy of art at the political economists themselves. In 1860 and 1862 he wrote *Unto this Last* and *Munera Pulveris* in article form for the *Cornhill* and *Fraser's Magazine* respectively. We find his arguments and proposals very acceptable. ' A truly valuable or availing thing is that which leads to life with its whole strength.' [1] Again, ' It is, therefore, the manner and issue of consumption which are the real tests of production.' [2] He was certainly not over-bold. Though the artist in him revolted against the classing of man with animals in the Malthusian law, he shirked the issue which William Thompson faced, and wrote feebly : Population ' is limited only by the limits of his courage and his love.' [3] And in the closing section of *Unto this Last* he delivered himself to the enemy. ' Note finally that all effectual advancement towards this true felicity of the human race must be individual, not public effort.' [4] It was disastrous to say this in 1860.

His proposals follow those of his economic master, Carlyle— national education, the organisation of labour, Government training schools, houses for the working classes, and old age pensions. When he was a rich man and a professor at Oxford he tested his theories by practice. The St. George's farms failed. The road-digging produced poor roads but good undergraduates, who in their generation subscribed to Tolstoy ; and the handicrafts which he established at Coniston, his home, and in the Isle of Man had just that measure of success which money and enthusiasm have a right to expect. Why then did *Unto this Last* excite such reprobation that Thackeray, the editor, had to stop the articles ? The answer is simple. Ruskin was a moralist ; and with a great reputation in Art he attacked the enemy in its own stronghold. The early socialists smote shrewdly, but they were poor men to be forgiven and forgotten. Carlyle raged, but he never wrote logic ; he was dyspeptic besides. But Ruskin was an educated gentleman and he spoke without venom or caricature. His hearers might snarl ' *ne sutor*,' but they knew how true it all was, even if they did not themselves feel the joy which he brought into some men's lives. ' To John Ruskin I owe more than I can tell,' says Thomas Burt in his *Autobiography* (p. 144). He read *Unto this Last* with avidity from end to end. Morality, justice, emotion, social affection, the temper—in a word, the soul—of the worker come into effective play as well as the laws of demand and supply : this was Burt's summary of the pamphlet. And that a man such as he, the respected leader of the Northumbrian miners, could not be allowed to read it without a hullabaloo

[1] *Works of Ruskin*, Library Edition, XVII. 84.
[2] *Ibid.* p. 104.   [3] *Ibid.* p. 106.   [4] *Ibid.* p. 111.

means simply that the political economists of the 1860's were petty men in blinkers.

It was left to a German exile living among the Blue-books of the British Museum to supply the real thing. The artist is a simple soul, for he can be coaxed out of revolt by a trial of his schemes. This fate befell Ruskin and his successor in romantic art, William Morris. A new spirit, said Morris to Young Oxford in 1883, ' will abolish all classes and substitute association for competition in all that relates to the production and exchange of the means of life.' [1] But it led only to art guilds and the Kelmscott Press. Karl Marx knew better than this. He had a passable equipment of philosophy. He dug out the parts of history that concerned him, and he hated. Vol. I of *Das Kapital* (1867) appeared in English in 1886, three years after the author's death : in 1894 Engels issued Vol. III. In this interval the New Unionism was born, and however Fabian English Socialism set out to be and however labourish its labour party, Marx was essential to their gospel ; for he was the first rebel since the 1820's who could not be watered down. In hate *per se* there is no social value, but it required bitter words to force mankind to see that the conflict between labour and capital is real and that the workings of competition will drag down the workers unless they combine. The long reign of Samuel Gompers, 1881–1924, was due to the fact that he could not be bought ; and he had many offers. As he saw it in the 70's, the choice for American workers was threefold—Mundella and arbitration ; Lassalle and politics ; Marx and trade unionism. This will read strange to Englishmen, but they must remember that American employers had even less use for the labour union then than now. Therefore for the American Federation of Labour no goody-goody umpiring : no frustration by entanglement in the uncapturable political machine : but straight collective bargaining of a ruthlessly practical order. Thus only would the American workman, immigrant as well as old-timer, dip his pitcher in the bubbling pool of surplus value. Gompers, like Marx, believed in his own country, but his country was big enough to contain him and knew that, other things failing, it had the Injunction up its sleeve.

Section 6. *The Novel as a Source of Economic History*

The economic history of the last two centuries is a novel in one huge volume—the scene Britain, the plot the Industrial

---

[1] Elton, *Survey of English Literature*, 1830–1880, II. 47. Professor Elton was present.

Revolution, ' the lovers' masters and men, the end not yet, perhaps the wedding bells of Mr. Whitley's Councils, perhaps the revolver shots of Communism, but in all probability neither, in all probability just more history with a stationary population, perennial compromise, and landmarks of technique and art. Industrialism, or rather the social regrouping of which it was a part, gave birth in Britain to the prose novel. The age of Smollett and Fielding, the fathers of the English novel, was the gestation period of the Industrial Revolution, and, when the child was born and the Enclosure Movement nearly completed, Jane Austen took up her quiet pen. The value of the novel to the economic historian is least when it is written for him. It is greatest when the economics are incidental, as in Fielding and Scott, George Eliot and Thomas Hardy. From these writers it is not possible to extract a chapter here and there, for the economics are in the setting; and just because they are writing fiction, the setting, when the scene is contemporary, is highly accurate. They left it to us of the 20th century to write documented romance.

Smollett was a doctor, Fielding a magistrate. In *Roderick Random* and *Humphrey Clinker*, in *Joseph Andrews* and *Tom Jones*, as we hurry along at sea or by road, we meet sailors, parsons, wicked London innkeepers, and pregnant women. The things that the Poor Law Commission of 1834 should have said about bastardy are contained in *Tom Jones*. When George Meredith a century later returned to the theme in *Evan Harrington* it was rare enough to make a plot; for England by then was a country of furious cricketers and idle peers, and there was time for a Countess de Saldar to go in and talk.

In Scott the novels that are not historical are packed with economic history:—land improvement from Mr. Mervyn's grasses in *Guy Mannering* (? Mr. Curwen of Belle Isle, Windermere) to Triptolemus Yellowley's drainage and tree-planting in *The Pirate*: smuggling in all its branches—tea, tobacco and lace: gipsy squatting, which provoked the immortal lines by Meg Merrilies beginning ' Ride your ways, Laird of Ellangowan ': ' the debatable land ' of Mustard and Pepper, near by which at Netherby Sir James Graham was to build a model estate: the turnpike road which carried Wandering Willie, blind as his prototype Blind Jack of Knaresborough: the mail cart in which came Auld Reekie's single London letter before the days of ' Mr. Palmer's ingenious invention ': and above all Jeanie Deans' tramp along the Great North Road, as enthralling as Arthur Young's Northern Tour is petulant and ornate. And when we have read the short tale of *The Two Drovers*, what is there to add, save figures, about the cattle trade between Scotland and the South ? Scott lived through the Industrial Revolution to see the ' smoke-pennoned steam boats ' invade the Firth of Clyde, but may we not believe that that other world which he made for himself, and to which we now and always can retire, was the protest of romantic genius against the drabness of industrialism ? To be the citizen of a country in the making is always an exciting thing. David Hume, Adam Smith, James Watt, Walter Scott and Robert Burns, all lived and died within the 121 years from 1711 to 1832. Surely a country never jumped so quickly as Scotland into its full complement of literary riches.

By 1840 England was fairly alive to the Condition of England question. Story-telling had deserted Henry Fielding for Harriet Martineau. Then, as though to rescue the didactic tale from a life of prostitution, Disraeli, Mrs. Gaskell and Kingsley wrote respectable economic novels. Disraeli was the cleverest, for he saw that the best thing was the language of the evidence as actually given ; and if you read the Midland Mining Commission of 1843 you may wonder where you have seen it before. He took the Tommy Shop scene in *Sybil* out of it, now and then sentence for sentence, with Joseph Diggs in place of a certain coal proprietor in the Report named Banks and a sigh for the ' young Queen's picture ' instead of the Commissioner's references to the spread of Chartism.

Mrs. Gaskell writes a real story, but Miss Martineau would have enjoyed it. *North and South* (1855) is too severe on the South. The North of England really cannot claim all the character, whatever Lancashire may say. Canada undervalues the South of England just in this fashion to-day, as though every public schoolboy with an English accent were a weakling. But there are some notable bits in *North and South*. Anent the Ten Hours Act Mr. Thornton puts the men's case, as he sees it and they should. ' I value my own independence so highly that I can fancy no degradation greater than that of having another man perpetually directing and advising and lecturing me, or even planning too closely in any way about my actions.' In other words, ' I want to save my men from being tied to the petticoats of their women.' He had shown the way with his chimneys. ' Mine were altered by my own will, before Parliament meddled with the affair. It was an immediate outlay, but it repays me in the saving of coal. I'm not sure whether I should have done it, if I had waited until the Act was passed. At any rate I should have waited to be informed against and fined, and given all the trouble in yielding that I legally could.' ' Legally ' is excellent ; for on the Common Law of England, administered by judges more orthodox than the classical economists, rested the law of supply and demand. Mr. Thornton, like Gladstone's revenue, was resilient. After the clash, after Margaret, the peacemaker, had stopped a stone and refused the offer of his hand in marriage, he ' went straight and clear into all the interests of the following day. There was a slight demand for finished goods ; and as it affected his branch of the trade he took advantage of it and drove hard bargains.' That is how a world trader is made.

Kingsley dedicated *Alton Locke* to the undergraduates of Cambridge. It was needed ; for Cambridge, and above all the monopolised foundation of King's College, at that time was still frowsty and idle, while Oxford was running the religion and politics of the country. It was the dark before the dawn, which, as it broke in his own College, Christ's, Sir Walter Besant describes in his Autobiography. Alton Locke, poet and tailor, explains why folk turned Chartists. The analysis is good, the remedy, an etherialised profit-sharing, is bad. But as the hero was suffering from consumption, Lilian sent him abroad to die, after first converting him to Christianity. Kingsley could pack a heap of social truth into conversations, which are among the best things in the novel : for example the two pages beginning, ' I say, young 'un, fork out the tin and pay your footing at Conscrumption Hospital.' [1] From these three novelists of industrialism it is refreshing to turn again to the real thing in the country : to Adam Bede and Maggie Tulliver, if we are serious, or if we want a holiday to *Ask Mamma* (1858) and a chilly breakfast at the house of a proprietor ' wot ossed it.' R. S. Surtees being a country sportsman, albeit trained in law, liked the railway ; Dickens, being a Londoner, idolised the coach. Oh ! for a taste of that milk punch which tapped against the window of Mr. Pickwick's chaise.

To laugh with Dickens is to laugh at much that we ourselves are—sentimentalists among cotton bales, hating cruelty yet condoning drink, anxious to hear the worst of America and by corollary very forward in the promotion of international amity. Ruskin says of *Hard Times* (1854), ' The usefulness of that work (to my mind in several respects the greatest he has written) is with many persons seriously diminished because Mr. Bounderby is a dramatic monster instead of a characteristic example of worldly masters.' . . . [2] But here we must call upon the economist's favourite distinction between long and short periods. The short period usefulness of a reasonable Bounderby might have been greater, but the long period worth would certainly have been less. Dickens was always right in his atmosphere, and he allowed himself to be half right in his individuals just because

---

[1] P. 17. edition of 1862.   [2] *Unto this Last*, p. 31.

half wrong was caricature and opened the door of humour. Oliver Twist asked for another helping. Sairey Gamp besought Betsey Prig to drink fair. The boys of Dotheboys Hall were dosed on brimstone and treacle. These scenes, and not the improvement of the poor law, midwifery, and national education, are what Dickens did for England, and they will live for ever.

Another storehouse of humour is Punch, and especially in the earlier years of his life he was a social crusader. Mr. Punch likes travel, but he hates to see signalmen overworked, and because he laughed when he felt like it, he could make England read his sermons.

> Work, work, work,
> From weary chime to chime.
> Work, work, work,
> As prisoners work for crime.
> Band and gusset and seam,
> Seam and gusset and band,
> Till the heart is sick and the brain benumbed,
> As well as the weary hand.

This, the *Song of the Shirt*, by Thomas Hood, appeared in the Christmas number of 1843. When the author was dying of consumption in November 1844, he wrote to thank Peel for his gift of £100 and the offer of a pension. ' Certainly classes at the poles of Society are already too far asunder. It should be the duty of our writers to draw them nearer by kindly attraction, not to aggravate existing repulsions.' It is America's problem : hence Rotary, and hence Sinclair Lewis's *Mr. Babbitt*. It is England's problem also ; and though she is too shy for real Rotary, she can manage quite well the Frothblowers' Anthem.

CHAPTER XIX

THE ORGANISATION OF LABOUR

Section 1. Labour and the State. Section 2. Trade Union Origins. Section 3. National and Sectional Effort, 1830–1890. Section 4. The Labour Trend, 1890–1927. Section 5. Trade Unions and the Law, 1867–1927. Section 6. Wages and Retail Prices, 1800–1900. Section 7. British and American Labour Movements compared.

Section 1. Labour and the State

THE 19th century opened dramatically with the Combination Act of 1800. In 1824, at the effort of Francis Place, it was repealed, but 1800–1824 makes a false period. For the ' Act of

1800 was by itself a negligible instrument of oppression.' [1] And what Place secured in 1824 by 5 Geo. IV, c. 95, was not merely the repeal of the Statute of 1800, but the bigger gain that combination to advance wages or stop work etc. should not be liable to any indictment or prosecution for conspiracy, or to any other criminal information or punishment. But this immunity, exceeding that which was allowed in contemporary Europe or America, only lasted for one year. The House of Commons was speedily roused to a sense of what it had done by the *furore* of combinations and strikes which Place had predicted would not occur, and in 1825 passed a new Act, 6 Geo. IV, c. 129, which, while legalising combination for specified purposes, gave no immunity from prosecution under the common law of conspiracy.

The years 1800 to 1824 must be studied in relation to earlier labour policy and the attitude of the State towards association generally.

The 17th and 18th centuries had a definite labour policy, and that was to keep wages down and suppress combination. The Statute of 1563 prescribed Wage Rates. But, as Professor Heaton shows, in Yorkshire from 1647 onwards the Justices in their assessment were interested only in enforcing a maximum : ' " Shall not take above " is the ever-recurring phrase, the keynote of the proclamation. There was nothing to prevent the master from paying as little as he could succeed in persuading the labourer to accept ; the only business of the Justices was to see that he did not pay too much.' [2]

At the beginning of the 18th century a new argument in favour of low wages was found, which has done good service from those days to these—the danger of foreign competition. Walpole's England was growing rich by foreign trade ; and for increase of riches by foreign trade low wages and a monopoly of skilled labour were judged indispensable. Therefore from time to time upon the petition of Master Manufacturers laws were passed forbidding the combination of journeymen in particular trades : for example, against the London Tailors in 1720 (7 Geo. I, St. 1, c. 13), and Weavers, Combers and Knitters in 1725 (13 Geo. I, c. 34). The Act of 1720, as amended by 8 Geo. III, c. 17, drew down the wrath of Adam Smith. ' Whenever the legislature attempts to regulate the differences between masters and their workmen, its counsellors are always the masters' (I. 143). The complement to this partial legislation was the lengthening list of laws which from about 1700 onwards forbad the export of

---

[1] *Economic Journal*, ' Economic History,' No. 2, May 1927 ; D. George, *The Combination Laws reconsidered*, p. 214.

[2] *Economic Journal*, June 1914, ' Assessment of Wages in Yorkshire,' p. 225.

machinery and the emigration of artisans (*cf.* p. 329). The Act of 1800 arose in the same way as those of 1720 and 1725. The Master Millwrights of London asked for a special law, which at the last moment on the suggestion of Wilberforce was made general by 39 Geo. III, c. 86 (1799). The next year this was replaced by the more famous Act of 1800 (39 & 40 Geo. III, c. 106). The Act, however, seems to have been of little direct value to the masters ; for they dared not, or chose not, to pro-secute under it and convictions were hard to secure. It imposed summary penalties, a maximum of three months' imprisonment on the men and a fine of £200 on the masters ; and summary penalties of any kind were held in disfavour by the Courts. Its chief use was *in terrorem*. It proclaimed positively what other Statutes were proclaiming by repeal, a free trade in labour. The word ' free ' was the razor edge on which Wilberforce's conscience walked, for he too was working to free labour—the black labour of slaves.

The French Revolution was at first a beacon light to English reformers, but when it developed violence and later was captured by Napoleon, it was a nightmare to them ; for it set respectable England against all reform. Therefore the Combination Act of 1800 was in part a police measure in line with the crop of repressive laws which followed the outbreak of war with France in 1793 :

in 1794 the Suspension of Habeas Corpus :
  „ 1796 against Treasonable Practices and Seditious Meetings :
  „ 1797 against Unlawful Oaths (this was the Act under which the Dorchester labourers were convicted in 1834) :
  „ 1799 against Unlawful Societies (this Act was employed against the Chartists, 1839-41).[1]

It cannot be supposed that the Justices in enforcing *maxima* pleased the workers. At any rate the latter were prosecuted from time to time for trying to get more ; and section 13 of the Eliza-bethan Statute, which imposed damages for leaving work unfinished, was freely used against them during the 18th century. But when the Judges advocated the repeal of wage fixing, as tending ' to cramp and tie down that knowledge it was first necessary to obtain by rule,' [2] the workers developed a liking for the ' good old ways,' and at the end of the century held up for imitation the Act which the silk weavers of London had wrung from Parliament in 1773 (13 Geo. III, c. 68).

---

[1] 34 Geo. III, c. 54 (1794) : 36 Geo. III, c. 7 & 8 (1796) : 37 Geo. III, c. 123 (1797) : 39 Geo. III, c. 79 (1799).
[2] Lord Muirhead at the Lancashire Spring Assizes of 1759.

This provided for the revision of Price Lists under the aegis of the Magistrate, and worked well while prices were rising, the revision being effected by mutual consent of masters and men. The cotton weavers in 1800 obtained an Act (39 & 40 Geo. III, c. 90) embodying the principle of wage negotiation under the arbitration of the J.P. But a second Act of 1804 designed to further this was barren, for the workers were forbidden by this time to combine for any purpose whatsoever and the masters were bent on shedding restrictions of every sort. In 1803 the voluminous regulations affecting the woollen industry—compulsory apprenticeship under 5 Eliz. c. 2 : limitation of looms, etc. under 2 & 3 Philip and Mary, c. 11–12 : prohibition of gig mills under 5 & 6 Edw. VI, c. 21 : and others—were suspended.[1] In 1806 a Parliamentary Committee, of which Wilberforce was chairman, recommended their repeal, and this came in 1809. Four years later, again in the face of protest from the workers, followed the repeal of the basic Statute of 5 Elizabeth, c. 4 : the Wages Clauses going in 1813 by 53 Geo. III, c. 40, and the Apprenticeship Clauses in 1814 by 54 Geo. III, c. 96. 'The persons most competent to form regulations with respect to trade were the master manufacturers, whose interest it was to have goods of the best fabric ; and no legislative enactment could ever effect so much in producing that result, as the merely leaving things to their own course and operation,'[2] so a member urged in Parliament in 1814.

The Spitalfields silk manufacturers were now left in the cold, and therefore in 1824, by 5 Geo. IV, c. 66, Huskisson removed the anomaly. In the same year, by c. 97, he repealed the law against the emigration of artisans, but the Committee which proposed it tacked on to it the repeal of the Combination Laws. Thus the manufacturers lost their age-long ally, the Common Law against conspiracy, but the next year they got it back, Huskisson dilating on the tyranny of a militant 'trades unionism,' whose mischievous operations, if not checked, would keep the commercial classes 'in constant anxiety and terror about their interests and property.'[3]

The prosecution of Combinations or Conspiracies (the terms were used indifferently) was as old as the 14th century. When in the early 18th century industry rapidly extended and the enforcement of the Wages Assessment weakened, its place was taken by the prosecution of Combinations under a Statute (if one

---

[1] The northern counties did not come under the statutes of Philip and Mary, but there was Georgian legislation relating to the stamping and sealing of West Riding cloth, and this was not repealed till 1821 (1 & 2 Geo. IV, c. 116, local).

[2] Quoted in A. E. Bland and Others, *English Economic History, Select Documents*, p. 582.

[3] March 29, 1825, *Speeches*, II. 371.

existed) or under the Common Law. Thus in 1706 heavy fines were imposed on six Cloth Dressers of Leeds for the conspiracy of refusing to work for less than 1½d. per hour, and in 1721 a Combination of Cambridge Tailors was prosecuted—in both cases under the Common Law. In the course of the 18th century the doctrine of conspiracy was elaborated in terms of the new faith in a free course of trade. Combination was a restraint on this ; and combination in restraint of trade, by preventing free competition, was the crime of conspiracy.

The savage prosecution of the Journeymen Printers of the Times (1810) was also under the Common Law. The point has been made that between 1800 and 1824 the State was inconsistent in ordering at once no combination by the worker and no regulation by itself. But this is a technical point only. In the 18th century the State repressed Trade Unions by prosecution under the Common Law, and it also did nothing to protect or increase wages save in one or two disquieted industries in the Metropolis. One was the Spitalfields Silk trade, the other the London Coal Heavers, who received spasmodic protection in wage and working conditions by the laws of 1770, 1803 and 1807. In 1831 the Act regulating Coal Whippers' wages lapsed, and between that date and 1909, though many laws were passed forbidding truck, payment at public houses, excessive fines, etc., no law prescribed wage rates, even for women and children. In 1909 the Trade Boards Act was passed : in 1912 the Coal Miners Minimum Wage Act. Thus the issue was shifted from coal-heaving to coal-hewing, from the appeasement of a London nuisance to the part acceptance of a national programme.

The State abandoned the regulation of wage rates in the spirit of one who has seen a new light, and in the same spirit it abandoned the regulation of the rate of interest. The light here was shed by Jeremy Bentham (Letters in Defence of Usury) in 1787, but the old Usury Laws were not abolished till 1854, partly from conservatism and partly because the world of business was usually able to find a way around them. The purpose of Queen Anne's Statute of 1713 (12 Anne, St. II, c. 16)—the prevailing statute for over 100 years—was to give a downward kick to the rate of interest, so that England might be able to borrow as cheaply as foreign Powers. ' No person shall take above £5 per centum interest upon contract.' During the 18th century the market rate was well below this, but the Napoleonic War drove it to the maximum, so that borrowing except on gilt-edged security was penalised. The Stock Exchange evaded the difficulty by ' time ' dealings which technically were barred by Sir John Barnard's Act, and the Bank of England, which had been incommoded by the Usury Laws during the crisis of 1825, was exempted from their operation by s. 7 of the Bank Act of 1833. But after 1815 the mortgage needs of landowners were great, and they found themselves paying to lawyers or insurance companies perhaps as much as 10%. In 1854 (17 & 18 Vict. c. 90) the outworn code was repealed from 37 Hen. VIII, c. 9, downward, saving the statutes relating to pawnbrokers.

The wage rate is the all-important link in the relation between employer and employee. After official assessment had been abolished, the State did its legal best to ensure that the cash wage should be a reality. This was important justice and the only reproach to the State was its inability to enforce its own laws. So too in the relation between creditor and debtor the important thing in the 19th century was not the legal maximum rate of interest, but the treatment of the debtor who for any reason was unable to repay debts legally due. Down to the reign of Queen Anne the law was pitilessly severe towards the defaulting merchant. The Act of 1705 (4 & 5 Anne c. 4) allowed a bankrupt, after paying all he could, to receive a discharge and start again ; and this is the beginning of modern bankruptcy legislation, which was systematised by the Act of 1861 (24 & 25 Vict. c. 134). After 1861 everybody, and not traders only as heretofore, might be declared bankrupt. Adam Smith had spoken of bankruptcy as ' perhaps the greatest and most humiliating calamity which can befal an innocent man ' (I. 324) ; and Mill in a lively and severe chapter denounced the frauds attending insolvency, even after the ' salutary though very insufficient movement in the reverse direction.' [1] (He is referring to the Act of 1861.) It was not till 1883, when the sun of *laissez-faire* was setting, that Joseph Chamberlain sufficiently stiffened the law by giving to the Board of Trade (over which he then presided) the control of bankruptcy proceedings and by imposing severe restrictions on the granting and operation of an order of discharge (46 & 47 Vict. c. 52). But this did not mark a return to the old severity. For one year after the comprehensive Bankruptcy Act of 1861 came the Companies Act of 1862, which permitted what soon became the legal frame of all commercial enterprise— limited liability ; and this is the Magna Charta of Capitalism. The capitalist, sleeping or active, no longer suffers the rupture of his private bench, and still less of his private head, as might have been his lot in the days of Henry VIII ; and if the working man (who enjoys no such limitation in *his* risks) is to compete with him on equal terms, it must be from within a group, defensive or

[1] J. S. Mill, *Principles of Political Economy*, Book V, Ch. IX, 8. 5th Edn., 1862

constructive, which itself is capitalism-proof. The Co-operative Wholesale Society was established in Manchester in 1863—a significant response to the capitalism of 1862. For the Trade Union and the Co-operative Store are the twin pillars of British industrial democracy.

Section 2. *Trade Union Origins*

Trade Unionism had a lusty life among the skilled workers of the 18th century, but owing to the hostility of the law it was secret. By 1800 industries with the strongest organisations were those in which the cleavage between employer and employed was greatest, with the exception of the agricultural labourer, who, though now a wage hand, was too poor and isolated to combine. Among organised trades the shipwrights and workers in wood, the main industrial material then, were prominent. In London some Trade Unions of the 19th century, for example the Hatters and Tailors, can trace a direct descent from the Stuart incorporations of small masters. A few of these small masters rose to the position of merchant employer, but the bulk sank to the level of journeymen, so that the union of small masters became a union of journeymen. Similarly in the 18th century, in Sheffield, the men who had once been independent masters, and to whom the apprentices were bound, formed combinations and engaged in strikes against the Master Cutlers to whose order they worked. On the other hand, there is little evidence of 18th-century combination among the workers in the iron smelting or iron finishing trades. The unit of enterprise here was comparatively large, and this should have favoured combination, but the furnaces were scattered and employers of the Wilkinson type were stern disciplinarians. The miners of the North were directly employed by large coal owners, but in 1800 their bondage was so complete that corporate action only emerged in the desperation of an occasional strike.

Perhaps the strongest 18th-century combinations were in the woollen industry, especially in the south-west of England, where its structure was highly capitalistic. In Yorkshire the persistence of the small clothier delayed their growth, but the woollen combers, who performed a special skilled process to the order of worsted manufacturers in Norfolk and the West Riding, were organised in something like a national union from 1750 onwards. Between 1780 and 1810 they joined with the shearmen and weavers to oppose the introduction of machinery.

The cotton industry, however, was the first to pass over to the factory system, and led the way in 19th-century unionism. Benefit Clubs appeared among the Oldham operatives as early at least as 1792, and during the next thirty years a network of spinners' societies arose in Lancashire and Glasgow, the distinctive features being their continuity and thorough organisation. In the 20's and 30's the cotton spinners dominated the Trade Union world. The hosiery trade was the last of the textile industries to reach steam power. From about 1805 to about 1845 the framework knitters were in almost continuous distress, and between 1811 and 1815 they broke frames as a protest against the cheap work of the bag-hosier. In the Chartist days the grievance of frame rents overshadowed all others. The journeymen of the towns as well as the master stockingers of the country rebelled against frame renting by owners, who were sometimes the hosiery manufacturers themselves and sometimes outsiders, who bought frames as an investment. After the introduction of steam power and therefore of the factory system the structure of the industry became like that of the cotton industry, and in 1866 the United Framework Knitters Society was established.

The worsted and woollen industries of the West Riding were not far behind the cotton industry in turning over to the factory system, yet by 1900 only a small percentage of the workers were Unionists. Possible explanations of this are :

(1) The large number of women and children in the industry ; for all through the century, with the single exception of Lancashire, industries employing women were Trade Union deserts. (2) The variety of products and cleavage of sympathies and interest, not only between worsted and woollen, but also between different towns within this general division. (3) The paternal relations between employers and employed. ' In some of the old family businesses strikes are unknown . . . In the country mills especially, the old relations of employer and employed survive, and the Unions make little headway.' [1] Since then, however, the anomaly has disappeared. The 7000 Unionists of 1904 had risen to over 100,000 in 1920.

Section 3. National and Sectional Effort, 1830–1890

Trades Unionism means the union of a number of trades, and it was distinctive of the years 1829–34, but it was not a federation of trades which were themselves well organised on a national scale. One partial exception to this is provided by the building trades, who about this period were resisting the building contractor. The Operative Stone Masons, built up out of local masons' lodges, claimed a membership of 6000 in 1833. They formed one section of the ' General Union of the

[1] J. H. Clapham, *Woollen and Worsted Industries* (1907), p. 207.

artisans employed in the processes of building ' which the Liverpool painters, among others, had joined in order, as they said, to put down ' that baneful, unjust and ruinous system of monopolising the hard-earned profits of another man's business, called " Contracting." '[1] When the ferment of the early 30's subsided, the separate local societies survived, but in diminished numbers. In the years 1848–52 the Operative Stone Masons, for example, fluctuated between 4700 and 6700 at a period when the Census returned 66,000 ' masons and paviors ' for all England and Wales. But the most active Unionists of the 30's were the cotton operatives, who lived in one county in England or around Glasgow. In 1829 John Doherty, a Manchester Trade Unionist—by birth an Irishman—organised a general Union of the United Kingdom, which really was a federation of local unions of Lancashire cotton spinners and cotton piecers. In 1832 he organised the Potters' Union, also a strictly localised trade. The National Association for the Protection of Labour, 1830, and the Grand National Consolidated Trades Union, 1834, had a nation-wide membership, but they were ephemeral. They were the forerunners of Chartism rather than of the Trade Union Congress of to-day.

Between 1840 and 1870 labour made itself a national force along three parallel lines of endeavour : Chartism, New Model Unionism, and campaigns for the Repression of Truck. Chartism was fed by economic distress and blazed out under the insults of the new Poor Law. The absorption of the workers in political issues, such as factory reform, corn law repeal and the struggle for the Charter, weakened Trade Unionism for a time, but in the end strengthened the labour organisation of which Trade Unionism is a part. For in the Ten Hour Movement and the Anti-Corn Law League the workers learned in the company of their middle and upper class champions how to campaign. In the Chartist movement they learned how to act alone : the Chartists having no friends higher than the rank of Baptists and Primitive Methodists. Therefore the Charter was a unifying force at a time when the unequal progress of industrialism obstructed Trade Union extension. Out of the political experience obtained in the struggle for the Charter the Labour Party fifty years later was born.

The ' New Model ' is the name applied to the Amalgamated Society of Engineers established in 1851 (above, p. 256). Their constitution was distinguished by centralised expert administration and by the size of their funds, a large proportion of which they devoted to friendly benefits—sick pay, unemployment pay,

---

[1] Quoted in Webbs' *History of Trade Unionism*, p. 128.

and pensions. They were prepared to use them on occasion for a strike, but they preferred peaceable methods, and by behaving with moderation they secured the sympathy of the non-wage-earning classes as well as the respect of the employer. The Amalgamated Society of Engineers was followed by other national craft unions, such as the Amalgamated Society of Carpenters and Joiners of 1861. William Allan of the Engineers, Robert Applegarth of the Carpenters and Joiners, Daniel Guile of the Iron Founders, Edwin Coulson of the London Bricklayers, and George Odger of the London Boot and Shoe Workers, a brilliant Radical orator, were all products of the New Model, and they composed the ' Junta ' which, with the help of the London Trades Council established in 1860, fought the battle for legal recognition, 1871–75.

Truck took many forms : payment in the commodity made by the worker, watches, waistcoats, etc. : payment in commodities sold by the employer at his store : payment at public-houses in which the employer or his underling had an interest : and wage nibbling by fines. It was prohibited in general terms by the Act of 1831 (1 & 2 Will. IV, c. 37), but there was no machinery for enforcing this Act, which furthermore applied only to workers engaged in the trades enumerated. It disappeared first in the textile districts, because there the workers lived in towns where there were shops, or where they formed their own Co-operative Stores. It was least objectionable in railway construction, since some form of contractor's shop was inevitable. It was longest lived among the nail makers of Staffordshire, who were swindled over their raw materials as well as over the spending of their paltry wage, and among the miners of South Wales, where it was prevalent as late as 1871. Other mining districts had freed themselves by then. In 1850 the Miners National Association under Alexander Macdonald, supported by local Anti-truck Associations, launched a special campaign. Truck masters were prosecuted and truck was steadily dislodged from the coal fields and adjacent iron works.

After truck had been suppressed the next thing to be fought was ' long pays,' which put the man in debt if not to the employer then to the publican or tradesman. The miners secured weekly pays generally in the 60's and early 70's, coincidently with and largely through the formation of strong County Unions. The Unions, and they alone, made the nominal earnings of the working miner a cash reality.

Between 1860 and 1890, while the engineers and allied skilled trades were concentrating on London and to some extent losing touch with the provinces, the miners, iron and steel workers and cotton operatives were building up strong district organisations and forcing employers to collective bargaining. The Northumberland Miners' Mutual Association was established in 1863, the Durham Miners' Association in 1870. This was the beginning of effective permanent association in these two fields. In both cases it was a conclusion to a long period of intermittent struggle. Before the permanent union there were many strikes and, if the strike failed, the group which had produced it collapsed. When at last a successful strike was fought, the group survived in permanent Union form. Therefore to men like Thomas Burt of Northumberland and William Crawford and John Wilson of Durham, strikes and indiscipline savoured of each other and of the bad old days when the Union was ephemeral. They led their districts through the several stages of collective bargaining. First came the occasional arbitration, to which both parties consented with reluctance : then reference to a sliding scale, a species of mechanical bargaining in which the parties had no grave issue to face so long as the scale itself survived : finally the permanent board, called the 'Wages Board' or 'Board of Arbitration and Conciliation.'

By 1895 there were Wages Boards in all the mining districts ; and in all provision was made at some stage for the action of an independent chairman. But the Federated districts (i.e. those belonging to the Miners Federation formed in 1888, which Northumberland and Durham did not join until 1907) were opposed to arrangements for wage variations, unless a minimum was prescribed. To the doctrine that changes in wages should follow changes in price they opposed the doctrine that wages should be a first charge on production. Perhaps out of conservatism, perhaps from the knowledge that theirs was largely an export trade, Northumberland and Durham were nervous of this claim.

The iron and steel trades were ahead of the coal trade in forming Wages Boards. After a serious strike the great ironmaster, David Dale, procured a Wages Board in the North of England trade, which was followed shortly by a Board in the Midlands and much later by Boards in Scotland and Wales. In both industries the general machinery was the same : Standing Committees for the adjustment of minor differences and a General Board for the determination of general changes. But in the iron and steel trades the sliding scale worked better than in the coal trade, and the workers being more skilled as a body were less apt to indulge in local strikes in defiance of their leaders.

In the Lancashire cotton industry wages have been determined for over half a century by collective bargaining, in which elaborate piece lists are necessary. There are no Wages Boards or Arbitrations, but for many years after 1893 wage changes were made in accordance with the Brooklands Agreement, which laid down that no change in wage was to be sought by either side until at least one year after the last change, and that no single change was to exceed 5%.

Section 4.   The Labour Trend, 1890–1927

In 1887, when Victorian England paused to celebrate its Jubilee, there were few clouds on the horizon of industrial peace. True there had been a serious trade depression, but it was most serious in agriculture; and as the cause in agriculture was the unprecedented inflow of cheap food, real wages were rising. True the Socialist monster was again raising its head, but Karl Marx was a German and his doctrine of increasing misery was obviously false, while the milieu of Henry George—the New-World town, where land values mounted rapidly—was outside the common experience of Britain. The advocates of the single tax, though ' mischievous,' were only cranks. By 1897 there were signs of breakers ahead, but these were not more marked than the apparent capacity of the country to ride them by liberal compromise. In London, indeed, the under-dog had begun to growl. The London dockers in 1889 registered the first durable success of unskilled unionism. But the transference of power from the London Junta to the provincial North did not appear to affect the continuity of trade union tradition. The dockers whom John Burns and Tom Mann led to victory must be an exception—like the trust in free trade Britain; and if socialism meant nothing more than municipal socialism, none but the Lord Aveburys need feel alarm. The miners were growing in strength, but the 90's were the heyday of orderly arbitration and conciliation. Since 1893 there had been an Independent Labour Party. But who could talk of independence when Thomas Burt the veteran Labour leader was proud to inform a Trade Union Congress that the political economists in the person of Professor Alfred Marshall were now on the side of Labour?[1] More disconcerting still for those who feared the toils of capitalism was the easy way in which all parties rubbed shoulders on the Labour Commission of 1891–4. A big strike was a bad thing, but it was also a big opportunity for a Bishop Westcott or a Lord Rosebery.

In this mood the century closed, but by 1910 the feeling was altogether different. The Tariff Reform campaign was a

[1] Aaron Watson, *A Great Labour Leader*, p. 186.

confession of real nerves, quite unlike the Fair Trade heresy of the 80's. The victory of the Liberals at the polls in 1906 was followed by an epidemic of strikes : in 1907 and again in 1911 by strikes of railwaymen on railways in which everybody had shares, in 1908 by a strike of cotton spinners who since 1893 had settled their differences by the Brooklands Agreement. The N.E. coast engineers struck in 1909, the boiler makers in 1910, the London dockers in 1911 and again in 1912 ; 1912 saw a national turn out of miners, 1913 a strike of transport and general workers in Dublin, and 1914, on the eve of the War, a stoppage of the building industry. ' It was as if,' said an American observer, ' the workers had been bitten by some restless microbe and were impatient to make good at one blow what they had failed to achieve in the long years of their stagnation.' [1]

During the War organised labour loyally surrendered its trade union practices in the interest of military victory. In the last year of it the Government inaugurated the scheme of Whitley Councils, so named from the Chairman of the Committee by whom the report in favour of them was presented ; and this report in substance was an invitation to all industry to behave as the coal miners had behaved between 1893 and 1912. But after the War every step towards rehabilitation seemed to be checked by suspicion and fundamental differences of policy. National stoppages in particular trades persisted until they brought other trades to a stop and the private citizen to a state of bewildered irritation—iron moulders, railwaymen, coal miners, and for a night or two in some towns the police. The post-war boom brought high profits and high wages, but the strife between capital and labour constricted the good season. They were as two charioteers whose wheels were locked in their endeavours to race into the promised city. The drone of the Coalition Government—' Produce More '—helped nobody, and feeling went from bad to worse, not indeed in all trades but in those which were most powerful in the strategy of Trade Unionism, until in 1926 the miners rejected the very liberal proposals of the Coal Commission and thus precipitated a General Strike. When it was over everybody was quite sure that it had had no chance ; but there is at least a case for the view that only the radio and a display of overwhelming force at tactical points prevented serious loss of life and property. The unrest of 1900–27 was largely a result of the check to real wages which came about 1900, and which cannot be understood without a reference to the general course of wages and prices from 1800 to 1900.

[1] W. W. Craik, *A Short History of the Modern British Working Class Movement* p. 67, quoting T. Rothstein in the *New Review* (New York), Jan. 1914.

Section 5.   *Trade Unions and the Law, 1867-1927*

Between 1825 and 1871 the law took no cognizance of Trade Unions as such. It allowed combinations for certain purposes, and the uncertainty of the Common Law was reduced by an Act of 1859 (22 Vict. c. 34), which excluded from the definition of molestation or obstruction—terms used in the Act of 1825—agreements for altering wages and hours and peaceful picketing. The long delayed recognition came in 1871. The extension of the franchise had made it inevitable. The London Trades Council by a vigorous agitation from 1863 onwards carried the Master and Servant Act of 1867 (30 & 31 Vict. c. 141), which removed some of the inequalities suffered by workmen in a legal dispute with their masters, and which was supplemented at a later date by the alteration of the rule or doctrine of common employment. This rule, under which, for example, a railway guard or porter, injured by an accident due to the negligence of the driver, received no compensation was modified by the Employer's Liability Act of 1880 and deprived of all application in the Workmen's Compensation Acts of 1897, 1900 and 1906, which gradually introduced into the law the principle that an employer must, subject to certain limitations, insure his workmen against the risks of employment. This was a legal recognition of the employer's duty, supplementing the legal recognition of the employee's right to combine.

In 1867, the year of the franchise extension and the new Master and Servant Act, a Royal Commission of Enquiry into Trade Unions opened its sessions amid the excitement caused by the ' rattening ' (i.e. sabotage) outrages of Sheffield. In 1868 two reports were issued. The Majority Report was cautious. The signatories were prepared to recognise an unwelcome growth, but their plan of dividing the funds of Unions into trade funds and benefit funds showed that they had no sympathy with the corporate life of Trade Unionism or with the means whereby that life could find effective expression. But the Minority Report signed by Lord Lichfield, Thomas Hughes and Frederic Harrison happily prevailed. The legislation comprised the Trade Union Act of 1871 (34 & 35 Vict. c. 31) together with the amending Trade Union Act of 1876 (39 & 40 Vict. c. 22), and the Combination (Conspiracy and Protection of Property) Act of 1875 (38 & 39 Vict. c. 86), which repealed and replaced a makeshift measure of four years previously. The Trade Union Act of 1871 was of less value to Trade Unions than the Combination Act of 1875. In its original Bill of 1871 the Government had grouped Trade Union recognition and the relation of combination to conspiracy in one measure. But the conspiracy clause, which re-enacted in the language of the old Combination Laws heavy penalties against molestation, obstruction, etc., excited such opposition that it was relegated to a separate Act, the Criminal Law Amendment Act of 1871 (34 & 35 Vict. c. 32). This makeshift after four years of trade union protest was repealed by the newly installed Conservative Government of Disraeli.

' The Combination Law of 1875,' says Dicey, ' is, on the face of it, a compromise between the desire of collectivists to promote combined bargaining and the conviction of individualists that every man ought, as long as he does not distinctly invade the rights of his neighbours, to enjoy complete contractual freedom.' [1] The men who fought the legal battle of the Trade Unions were liberal lawyers, with Frederic Harrison at their head, and the Act paid homage to Liberalism by enfranchising the Trade Unions in terms of the individual. They remained voluntary societies, with the freedom—so it was believed for 40 years—of unincorporated bodies ; and they were rescued from the toils of the Common Law by the formula that things done by one or more persons in furtherance of a trade dispute were not to be indictable as a conspiracy, when such acts committed by one person would not be punishable as a crime. This provision was supplemented by section 1 of the Trade Disputes Act of 1906 (6 Edward VII, c. 47), which conferred upon acts which the Statute of 1875 protected from criminal liability a similar immunity from civil liability.

But the Act of 1906 did more than this. It reversed the Taff Vale judgment of 1901 (arising out of the case between the Taff Vale Railway Co. of South Wales and the Amalgamated Society of Railway Servants) and gave to the *funds* of Trade Unions immunity from liability for Torts, i.e. civil wrongs. Moreover it took certain acts, e.g. procuring breach of contract, interference with another's trade, business or employment, which in certain circumstances were actionable civil wrongs, out of that category, if they were committed by any person in contemplation or furtherance of a trade dispute.

In 1906 the Labour Party came into existence, and in 1908 had nearly fifty adherents in Parliament, one group representing the Independent Labour Party and the other the Trade Unions acting in co-operation with the I.L.P. Since Members of Parliament received no salary before 1911, it had become common for the large Unions to establish a fund to provide for the representation of their Union in Parliament and for general assistance to the

[1] A. V. Dicey, *Law and Public Opinion*, p. 269.

Labour Party. In 1907 this right was challenged by Osborne, a member of the Amalgamated Society of Railway Servants and in politics a Liberal ; and in 1909 the House of Lords decided in his favour, ruling that the definition of a Trade Union in the Act of 1871 was an exhaustive description of its activities. This was as though to say that a dog being defined as a quadruped with the functions of catching rabbits and retrieving birds, the act of chasing a cat or killing a rat is *ultra vires* of the dog. The decision created an impossible situation ; for it cast doubt on the legality of the majority of Trade Union activities, educational, municipal, political and friendly, and therefore in 1913 an Act was passed (2 & 3 Geo. V, c. 30) empowering a Union to apply its funds to any lawful objects provided for in its rules, but requiring that, for the support and payment of Parliamentary candidates, it must approve of participation by a majority ballot. · Members not wishing to participate were allowed to contract out without prejudice to their share in its other activities. In 1923 two-thirds of the Trade Unions of the country were affiliated to the Labour Party, the balance belonging to Unions with no political funds or being Unions who had contracted out.

The new Trade Disputes and Trade Unions Act of 1927 (17 & 18 Geo. V, c. 22) is as regrettable as the General Strike which provoked it. For in addition to the suspicion engendered by careless drafting, it brings back the legal uncertainty which the Trades Dispute Act avoided at the price of legal anomaly. Section 1 declares a strike illegal if it has an object beyond the furtherance of a trade dispute in an industry in which the strikers are engaged *and* if it is designed to coerce the Government either directly or by inflicting hardship on the community. It thus puts on statutory record the reproach levelled at the General Strike of 1926. But what serious strike might not be construed now to be illegal ? and by section 1, § 4, once a strike has been declared illegal, the protection conferred on trade union funds by the Act of 1906 disappears. Section 2 protects persons refusing to take part in illegal strikes : section 3 forbids and defines intimidation : section 5 limits the right of civil servants to join a trade union with political affiliations : section 6 forbids public authorities to make trade union membership a condition of employment ; and these sections are not unreasonable. But section 7 authorises the grant of an injunction at the suit of the Attorney General (without prejudice to the right of any person having a sufficient interest) to restrain the application of trade union funds in contravention of section 1. Taken in conjunction, sections 1, 3, and 7 seem to place trade unionists at the mercy of judges and juries, common or special. On juries and particularly on special juries working men are not adequately represented [1] ; and, while it would be improper to accuse British judges or juries of moral unfairness, it is proper to urge that there is such a thing as unfairness of atmosphere. The corporate aspirations of industrial democracy command wide acceptance among thoughtful men, but they frequently run counter to the individualism of shopkeepers and merchants. The memory of injustice dies hard. The monstrous judicial harangues to Chartists and Dorchester Labourers were enough to sicken the working man of the law courts for all time ; and American history shows the length to which the Injunction can be extended in the service of capitalism.

Section 6. *Wages and Retail Prices, 1800–1900*

Owing to truck and wage payment at public-houses figures of money wages in the first half of the 19th century are to some extent fallacious, and there is no means of estimating the totality of the fraud. This reservation should be borne in mind in reading the graph below, which has been constructed to show the broad general movements of money wages and of the prices of those commodities on which wages are in the main expended. The evidence concerning wage rates and retail prices—evidence which nowadays is published in full by the Ministry of Labour—has been collated for the 19th century by statisticians (in particular by Prof. A. L. Bowley and Mr. G. H. Wood) from old price books, parliamentary papers, newspaper reports, Trade Union and Co-operative Society records and the like. Certain index numbers have thus been made available, which, while not claiming accuracy, give a reliable general picture. The graph on p. 397 is sketched from a combination of four such index series. The wages curve is based on the researches of G. H. Wood, published in the *Economic Journal* of 1899 (p. 591) and the *Journal of the Royal Statistical Society* of 1909 (p. 103) ; from 1850 on, agricultural wages are included. The curve of prices is based, up to 1850, on an index number of cost of living constructed by N. J. Silberling and published in the Harvard Economic series in October 1923 [2] ; and after 1850 on the retail price index published by G. H. Wood in the *Journal of the Royal Statistical Society* of 1909 (p. 103). G. H. Wood's series includes house-rent, which is omitted by N. J. Silberling. The halves of the curves which have been fitted together are not therefore strictly

---

[1] *Cf.* W. M. Geldart, *The Present Law of Trades Disputes and Trade Unions* reprinted from the *Political Quarterly*, No. 2, p. 44.
[2] Supplement to the *Review of Economic Statistics*.

comparable ; but the differences are not such as would greatly
influence the shape of the curves.   Every fifth year is recorded,
the intermediate fluctuations being ignored.

Each quarter-century shown on the graph has its own
characteristics, and these may be usefully reviewed.

In the first quarter-century the influence of the continental
wars is clearly marked.   Bad harvests contributed to the rapid
rise of prices during the war ; and until about 1811 wages lagged
behind prices.   From this date, and during the social troubles of
post-war readjustment, prices fell and wages followed, though

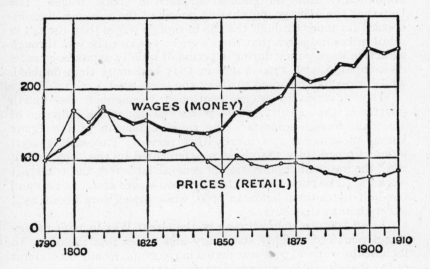

more slowly.   At the time of the repeal of the Combination Act
(1824) wages were 50% higher and prices 10% higher than in 1790.

Between 1825 and 1850 the curves show that both wages and
prices declined, though prices fell more than wages.   In this period
unfettered industry was changing rapidly to full mechanisation,
while the wages of the hand-workers fell away under the competition of machines.   The recorded fall in retail prices may be somewhat deceptive, for towards the middle of the century adulteration
of foodstuffs was flagrant.   Milk was sophisticated, butter well
dosed with water, cheese coloured with harmful chemicals : pepper,
mustard and vinegar were enlivened with brick-dust, starch and
sulphuric acid.   Until the Co-operative Store Movement reached
national dimensions (which did not happen before the 1860's) and
until the tentative measures against adulteration were enlarged
and strengthened by the appointment of inspectors and public

analysts under the Sale of Food and Drugs Act of 1875 (38 & 39 Vict. c. 63), traders treated the working-man's stomach as a sort of wastepaper basket. However, truck and adulteration apart, wages were 40% higher, and prices nearly 20% lower in 1850 than in 1790.

In the third quarter of the century matters took a favourable turn. Rapid transport development by land and sea, backed by coal resources and a Free Trade policy, made England the 'workshop of the world.' The curves show that the workers shared in the general prosperity. In this quarter of the century undoubtedly came the greatest advance in 'real' wages. The fact that the average purchasing power of the working class increased far more through the rise in money wages than the fall in retail prices indicates that there were real gains to be won through an active wage policy during a period of rapidly expanding trade. As compared with 1790 wages in 1875 had more than doubled, while prices had returned to about the same level.

The advance in wages continued throughout the fourth quarter of the century, while prices fell under the influence of abundant foreign imports. The rapid extension of the Trade Union movement also marks this period. The skilled craft unions formed since 1850 were supplemented by the 'new unionism,' the national organisation of general labourers and transport workers. The curves show that by 1900 wages stood at two and one-half times their figure in 1790, while prices were about 25% lower than at that date.

From 1900 to the outbreak of the Great War in 1914 money wages remained roughly stationary and prices rose slightly. To include the war and post-war period in the graph would, on account of the violent rise in prices and wages, nearly treble the scale used, and in brief would show that both prices and wages reached their peak *after* the war, in the winter of 1920-21, from which point they declined together, until a rough stabilisation was reached in 1925, 'real' wages being then about the same as in 1914. In the period of uncertainty which followed the war many wage agreements were made providing for the automatic variation of wages with changes in the official cost-of-living index figures.

A modern judgment of the economic position of the workers must take into account many factors other than money wages and the cost of living, factors which cannot readily be estimated in numerical terms. The eight-hour working day, for instance, and the conditions under which it is worked, compare very favourably with the hours and conditions of fifty or even twenty-five years ago. In ill-health, in old age, and partially in unemployment, the State cares for the worker through insurance schemes. The fall in the cost of living during the latter half of the 19th century hides a considerable increase in house-rents, and part of this increase is attributable to higher rates, for which an improved service has been rendered. The urban worker gets municipal services such as sanitation, better and cleaner streets well lit at night, police protection, and subsidised transport, which blessings were denied to his forebears of a hundred years ago. Better education too is an important asset, especially for the children of the present-day worker. The ' career open to the talents ' is fast becoming a reality, and moreover, in order to secure reasonable mental growth the State through the school medical service protects the physique of the child, even to the extent of assuming the parents' economic burden and feeding the child when necessity or neglect threatens its capacity to derive the normal benefit from school. Thus the State is investing in the coming generation, and protecting the young from the economic evils which may afflict their parents.

On the other hand, there are factors which have had a detrimental effect on the economic position of the worker. The protection of children by the advancement of the age of commencing work has deprived the family of a small but important portion of its earnings ; and this is a reminder that the family rather than the individual is the real unit in wages questions. Against this loss must be set the decline in the number of children per marriage, most marked in recent years. A further and most important consideration is the incidence of unemployment and short-time working in periods of bad trade. Mechanism and standard wage rates, though essential to social progress, have probably decreased the steadiness of employment, and the cyclical fluctuations of trade during the 19th century placed a heavy burden on the working classes during slump periods. This evil is now partly remedied by State Unemployment Insurance, though the scheme has been working under a heavy handicap since the commencement of the severe trade depression in 1921. Lastly, it must be remembered that there has in recent years been a change in the distribution of the ' average ' wage—the unskilled workers have secured much greater proportional advances than the skilled. This tendency, fanned by a militant Trade Union policy, began in the late 1880's : but the most effective period followed the Act of 1909 in protection of ' sweated ' workers. Between 1910 and 1914 membership of the General Labour Union rose from 81,000 to 390,000, and during the War the shortage of skilled men and the relaxation of Trade Union rules resulted in a remarkable advance in the standing and pay of unskilled workers. A further complicating factor is that certain industries containing a large proportion of skilled workers —particularly shipbuilding and engineering—have been subjected to fierce foreign competition since the War and have found it impossible to maintain the wage advances which the ' sheltered ' or home industries—particularly transport—have been able to consolidate. It is, however, doubtful whether this re-distribution can be regarded as permanent. Of special note is the growth of the transport unions since 1900. The figures are taken from the 9th Annual Abstract of Labour Statistics (Labour Dept. of the Board of Trade) and the 18th Annual Abstract of Labour Statistics (Ministry of Labour).

Growth of Trade Unions in the Transport Industry compared with the growth of all Unions (Great Britain and Northern Ireland)

	Railway Service	Shipping	Other (including Road Transport)	Total	Total of all Unions
1892	46,000 [1]	31,000 [1]	77,000 [1]	154,000 [1]	1,576,000
1900	79,000 [1]	14,000 [1]	76,000 [1]	169,000 [1]	2,022,000
1910	116,000	40,000	100,000	256,000	2,565,000
1914	337,000	145,000	219,000	701,000	4,145,000
1920	618,000	177,000	466,000	1,261,000	8,334,000
1923	478,000	92,000	361,000	931,000	5,410,000

Section 7. British and American Labour Movements compared

British labour started the 19th century under legal and political difficulties. Combination was prohibited. The town worker had no vote till 1867, the rural none till 1885. From 1906 to 1927 the status of the Trade Union was privileged. Not only has Labour a vote and a party, but in 1924 that party held office. Indeed in retrospect the remarkable thing is not the rapid growth of the Labour Party in the 20th century but the persistence of the partnership between Labour and middle-class Radicals until the end of the 19th. The American working-man had a vote from the first. Property qualifications were eliminated in the 1820's and after the Civil War racial qualifications also—at least in name. But from the medley of popular excitements at the close of the Civil War no American Labour Party emerged, nor has any appeared since. The division of sovereignty between Washington and the States, and of power between the Executive and two Houses of the Legislature, obstructs speedy legislation ; and the American constitutions, both federal and state, contain Bills of Rights which embody in fullness the 18th century philosophy of economic individualism and governmental *laissez-faire*. The two-party system is much older than the conflict between Labour and Capital, and it is rooted in a strong, yet conservative, democratic device, the ' Electoral Primary.' When Labour grows

[1] Includes all Ireland.

restive, one or other of the parties, usually the Democrats, becomes its friend and weans it from Labour pure and simple. The extremists of Britain are urged to seek their remedy by constitutional action in Parliament ; and with reason, for there is nothing that Parliament cannot do. But when, for example, the cigar-makers of New York after a long struggle carried a law restricting manufacture in tenement houses, it was declared unconstitutional ; and a similar decision upon the eight-hour law of 1899 so disgusted the miners of Colorado with constitutional action that they organised the Industrial Workers of the World (I.W.W.).

There is nothing in American history comparable with the infamous decision of 1834, which brought a sentence of seven years' transportation on six Dorchester labourers guilty of innocent mummery in the course of resisting a reduction in their weekly wage from 7s. to 6s. The early American Labour Unions were exposed to intermittent prosecution for conspiracy. But from 1842, when Chief Justice Shaw held Trade Unions to be legal organisations, down to the early 80's, the Trade Unions felt so secure that they demanded legal incorporation with a view to strengthening their bargaining status and winning public support for their ends.

Their trial came in the 1890's, when they endeavoured to use the weapons of struggle against the great corporations. The big employers had two stand-bys : their own fighting power in a country where little indignation is felt at the employment of physical force against new-comers (thus in the Homestead Strike of 1892 Carnegie's successor hired 300 detectives, and when these were knocked out, was allowed to replace them by militia) : and the Injunction. The first important use of the injunction was in a railway strike of 1888, and it was placed on a firm legal basis in the case of Eugene V. Debs in 1894. Its practical effect was to turn a strike against an employer into a strike against the Government. From that date injunctions followed in rapid succession, both in the State and Federal Courts. In 1897 the ' Blanket ' injunction was allowed, which all notified persons must obey whether mentioned by name or not. Moreover, injunctions have been granted not merely to prevent violence but to protect property, including in property business good-will. The general result has been to make the action of the workers lawful only when the Courts sympathise with their cause.

Except for brief periods following a strike failure, the staple industries of production and transport are now all but blackleg-proof in Great Britain. This has never been true of the U.S.A., and for three reasons : (1) the continuous inflow of immigrant labour, which, though it soon takes to unionism, is, for the time being, a menace to it ; (2) the availability of native labour strongly tinged with frontier independence ; (3) the powers and ramifications of the great corporations. After the breaking of the Homestead Strike, the U.S. Steel Corporation, of which Carnegie's plant was the parent, conducted an open shop campaign in the fields of its new allies. American labour solidarity has been impaired by fundamental facts of history and geography. The South was slave and the North and West were free. The poor white, the forebear of non-unionism in the American South to-day, supported the plantation owners in opposition to the abolitionists, and the Civil War perpetuated the non-class grouping. The labour problem of America or South Africa can never be that of Great Britain and Australia. The ground plan of prairie life was the homesteaded farm of 160 acres, and though there was much hired labour, there was no class of agricultural labour. The immediate result of this, in the days when farms were to be had for nothing, was that the eastern employer had to offer a wage sufficient to restrain his workers from going west. ' Buy yourself a farm ' was therefore a fighting slogan. The further result to-day is that Labour cannot speak for working people as a whole. The State and Federal authorities—in the Federal Authority, the Senate—are weighted in favour of geography against numbers and thus of agriculture against industry ; and the co-operative organisation of agricultural producers has thrown a new gage into the economic arena. This is the real labour movement of the American and Canadian West. Will co-operating farmers and industrial labour produce the seemingly impossible, a new combination against capitalism ? This has been mooted in the Canadian West, which is setting the pace in agricultural co-operation to the rest of the British Empire.

With these differences between America and Britain in mind some parallels in development may be noted. Many of the early 19th-century immigrants were British artisans or German who readily assimilated British ideas. Cobbett and Owen were great figures in American as well as English life. Therefore from 1815 to 1850 the parallel was very close. The Mechanics' Union of Trade Associations (Philadelphia), 1827—a local Union of separate trades—was ' the kind of federal republic ' at which Huskisson took fright in 1825 ; and between 1835 and 1837, when Unionism was engulfed in the general economic collapse, there were State and Inter-state gatherings of local mixed Unions, which borrowed from England the title of Trades Unions. While the short-time Committees of Lancashire and Yorkshire were fighting for a ten-hour day for children, the Unions of the American East were fighting for a ten-hour day for themselves. Already well paid, they desired also a shorter day instead of the farmers' ' sun to sun.'

The hot air of the 30's and early 40's—Reform, Owenism and Chartism—was represented in America by Horace Greeley and others, who founded phalanxes and communities on the model of Fourier and Owen. There was plenty of space for experiment and the element of the bizarre did not offend a people which rejoiced in novelty. Moreover the community seed fell on religious ground, and without religion it has never flourished. Owen bought the land for New Harmony from the Rappites of Harmony, Indiana. An English farmer who visited the Rappites in 1823 wrote : ' These people are never seen in idle groups ; all is moving industry ; no kind of idleness ; no time for it. Religious service takes place three times every day. They must be in the chains of superstition, though Rapp professes to govern them only by the Bible, and they certainly seem the perfection of obedience and morality.' [1] By 1850 the association movement had split into separate enthusiasms for free land, tariff reform and politics. The communities themselves, lacking in most cases a religious bond, either narrowed down into land companies or dissolved after quarrelling. The Mormons, however, being a heterodox body, followed Brigham Young into the desert of Utah in 1847 and held together under a religious autocrat in spite of the persecution which their tenets called down upon them.

In the 50's the industrial structure of America differed from that of Britain more than in 1820 or in 1880 : she was then still smelting iron by charcoal, but she had the railway and the river steamboat and was building up her great internal market. This was the period in which the merchant capitalist was sovereign. Filling distant orders from wholesale stock made by local craftsmen, he instilled into society that respect for the powers of the middleman which is America's counterpart to landlordism. A national Trade Unionism had to await the arrival of large-scale industry after the Civil War. Therefore the way to New Model Unionism was shown by an old-fashioned industry which from its nature enjoyed a national publicity—namely printing—and by the banner industry of American industrialism, the steam railway.

In 1852 the National Typographical Union was founded, and became International in 1869 by the inclusion of Canada ; in 1854 the Locomotive Engineers organised the first Railway Brotherhood. In the 60's and 70's the Brotherhoods developed strength, as the railroad network spread, and therefore American railwaymen were strongly organised at a time when Unionism was non-

[1] W. Faur of Somersham, Hunts., *Memorable Days in America* [1823], p. 265.

existent on English railways. But they did not stand in with the rest of labour. They kept aloof from the American Federation of Labour and were always loth to sacrifice their strong position by sympathetic strikes. The collar-work of American Unionism fell to three industries, which supplied articles of final consumption and were themselves in a process of structural transition —the cigar-makers, the boot and shoe workers, and the garment workers. The cigar-makers furnished the pattern and the man— the first efficient American trade union and a great national labour leader. Samuel Gompers joined the Cigar-makers International Union in 1864, became its President in 1876 and then the first Vice-President and President of the Legislative Committee of the Federation of Trades and Labour Unions of the U.S.A. and Canada (1881–6), out of which issued the American Federation of Labour. Of this he was President from 1886 to 1894 and from 1895 to his death in 1924. Just as cigar-making passed into factory work through the tenement system, so boot and shoe making passed through hand and foot machines into the belting up of machinery to steam. The Knights of St. Crispin (1868–72) were a protest against the conclusion, but their life was short because they resisted what Gompers accepted, the inevitable triumph of large-scale industry.

While the country was yet in the ferment of reaction to the Civil War, the Patrons of Husbandry (1868) and the Knights of Labour (1869) rose and fell. Both favoured secret ritual and both to please their disciples allowed themselves to be diverted to alien purposes. They were swamped by politicians and camp-followers. The co-operative ventures of the Knights of Labour failed, but the organisation itself lingered on, ' a bush-whacking annoyance on the heels of its successor, the American Federation of Labour.' [1]

The American Federation of Labour, following where it can the political structure of the United States, is a Federation with five divisions : Building, Metal, Mines, Railroads, and Union Label trades. Each group has its own Convention, which pursues its own trade purposes. The Federation eschews socialism, or as it is more commonly called radicalism, and frowns on separatism ; therefore it refused membership to the Amalgamated Clothing Workers of Chicago, who established themselves by secession in 1914. American labour leaders are specialists and intensively trained. The Union Label—a method of appeal for public support—originated with the cigar-makers in 1874. The clothing trades of New York and Chicago, where the foreign population is in the majority, have achieved remarkable regional results.

[1] *Documentary History of American Industrial Society*, Vol. 9, Introduction, p. 51.

Since the late war the Amalgamated Clothing Workers of Chicago have won from employers a large measure of joint control, but it required a struggle : which was terminated by arbitration at the hands of professional economists. The Amalgamated Clothing Workers of Chicago operate in conjunction with the employers an elaborate and self-supporting scheme of unemployment insurance. They also have a strong labour bank, which employs an important part of its funds in mortgage loans or house purchase. In their methods they combine genuine democracy with expert direction.

In opposition to the A.F.L. and to these regional developments are the Industrial Workers of the World, who are frankly revolutionary and aim at one big union. They appeared about 1904 ; but suffered eclipse during the War, which the A.F.L. officially supported. They have been termed ' an industrial Klu Klux Klan.' British politicians find themselves at sea when they examine American political democracy, and so also do British labour leaders when they examine American economic democracy. Both are so very different from the English way that at first their genuineness is doubted. But the continental vastness of the United States, the very different views which Americans take of the province of law, and above all the commixture of races and the conditions of material prosperity under which America works should arrest hasty judgment. The American employer had at first no greater belief in high wages than the British, but he has been compelled to pay them because population is scarce relatively to resources ; and he has made money nevertheless through the American genius for mass production and standard methods. The American working man has pondered the philosophy of high wages from the days of Ira Steward, the Boston machinist, onwards. He is practical and will not imperil his stake in the existing order so long as high wages go with it.

CHAPTER XX

FRIENDLY SOCIETIES AND THE CO-OPERATIVE MOVEMENT

Section 1. Friendly Societies and Savings Banks. Section 2. Life Insurance. Section 3. Insurance and the Co-operative Movement. Section 4. Labour Co-partnership and the Co-operative Store. Section 5. Early History of Co-operation. Section 6. The Wholesale Societies. Section 7. The Problems of the 20th Century.

Section 1. *Friendly Societies and Savings Banks*

A FRIENDLY SOCIETY may be defined as a mutual insurance society of the poorer classes for emergencies arising out of sickness, death, and other causes of distress. Dr. Baernreither said that Friendly Societies and Trade Unions ' are only different sides of the same historical process . . . both owe their existence to the same powerful reaction of the working classes against the deterioration of their material condition ; both are among the most conspicuous examples of English self-help ; they mutually supplement each other ; . . . they are twin-children of the same spirit.' [1] This was written in 1889 at the close of a period of fifty years during which the Friendly Societies played a greater part in English life than ever before or after. Before 1840 the movement was in its infancy and the structure of the Societies was often unsound from lack of a central control. After 1889, though the membership increased numerically, the movement was not dynamic. The epoch of English thrift to which it gave group expression gave way to one in which the State did more for the citizen, and voluntary association was directed to other things—trade unionism, co-operation, and labour politics. Friendly Societies have always contained a number of the lower middle class who are above the ranks of manual wage-earners—a valuable element in the national life but not a fighting force. The National Insurance Act of 1911 placed the Friendly Societies not merely under the supervision of the State, but in the position of channels between their members and the State. By strengthening the financial condition of the weaker Societies the Act preserved the contact of the poor with friendly benefits, but it could not preserve the spirit of association by which the early Friendly Societies had grown to corporate strength.

At a time when the legislature was hostile to Trade Unions it permitted and encouraged the Friendly Society as well as its economic complement, the Savings Bank. The first Act was that of 1793, known from its promoter, George Rose, as Rose's Act (33 Geo. III, c. 54). This Act gave to members of Friendly Societies exemption from removal under the Poor Law until destitution actually occurred. The Act of 1793, like Whitbread's abortive Minimum Wage Bill of 1795, was designed to build up a status free from the taint of parish help. Unhappily the design was not realised. Nevertheless, and especially in towns, the Friendly Society Movement made rapid headway, and it was estimated that in 1801 there were 700 clubs in England and Wales with 65,000 members, of which two-thirds were enrolled and submitted their rules to Quarter Sessions. But their financial condition was often weak and all too many were little more than societies of good fellowship, with burial club, annual feast, and

[1] J. M. Baernreither, *English Associations of Working Men*, pp. 157-8.

processions to church, especially for the funeral of a member. Moreover, during the French war and for ten years after 1815 the Government was nervous of association, even for an innocent purpose, when it was accompanied by any of the ritual dear to Friendly Societies. In 1829 their legal status was overhauled, and, as with the Factory Acts and Poor Law, control was transferred from the local Justices to a central authority, known after 1846 as the Registrar of Friendly Societies. J. Tidd Pratt (1797–1870), a barrister of distinction, was the first holder of the office and rendered exceptional services to the movement, bringing the Societies into line with the new actuarial science. In 1875 the law relating to Friendly Societies was consolidated after a voluminous inquiry by a Royal Commission, and again in 1896, when legislation was also passed covering the parallel activities of Collecting Societies and Industrial Assurance Companies.

In the middle of the century the outstanding features of the movement were the growth, usually after reorganisation, of the Working Men's Orders : the connection of these orders with the temperance movement : and the predominance of Lancashire. Thus in the 30's, the Unity of Oddfellows, of which Manchester was the fountain head, became the leader of the movement, followed by the Order of Druids and the Foresters, which were reorganised in 1833 and 1834 respectively. In 1838 came the first of the Railway Friendly Societies, the Great Western : in 1841 the Hearts of Oak, a London Society. All of them, in contrast to the clubs of an earlier day, were advocates of temperance. The Rechabites, a teetotal society, set up their tents, but the strongest of the other Orders were hardly less temperate. Through the Friendly Society the temperance movement took hold both of the Co-operative and the Trade Union movements. Conducting a temperance hotel was one of the original purposes of the Rochdale Pioneers, and the great Trade Union leaders, as well as the Moral Force Chartists, were temperance men.

Sir David Dale in 1871 testified to the importance which unionists like Thomas Burt attached to abstinence from drink. The miners' leaders in particular saw that drink, irregular pay, indiscipline and truck were parts of a vicious economic circle. In Lancashire, the region from which truck first disappeared, two-thirds of the working population were by 1850 in a Friendly Society. The movement was strong also in Middlesex and Yorkshire. The Independent Order of Oddfellows (Manchester Unity) had 46,000 members in 1838, and 617,000 members in 1886. The Ancient Order of Foresters (headquarters, Leeds) had 65,000 members in 1845 and 667,000 members in 1886.

These two Societies took the lead in the compilation of statistics and standardisation of Friendly Society finance.

The contribution of the Friendly Society was of a threefold nature. First of all, it added to the cheer of life at a time when life was exceptionally drab and dirty, alike in the place of work—the factory, and in the place of recreation—the public-house. The Fraternal Orders took fellowship out of the public-house and turned it into enthusiasm for a national temperance movement. Secondly, along with the Savings Bank, it promoted thrift in the important form of provision for misfortune. It was the workers' fine retort to the uncertainties of their life. In the third place, it was, along with the Co-operative Store, a great training in self-government.

But the movement had its weaknesses. Its early weakness was financial. The Fraternal Orders remedied this, but it was the commercial insurance companies which pioneered actuarial science. The Orders learned from them. Furthermore, by the end of the century, though the great Orders were still growing, many Societies were stationary and financially unsound. There was no prospect that the Friendly Societies as a whole would be able to help adequately just those classes which most needed them. As has been well said : ' The class which needs social insurance cannot afford it, and the class that can afford it does not need it.' [1] Finally, although the Friendly Society is a form of group effort, its ultimate purpose, the relief of particular distress, is essentially individual ; and commercial companies, by the development of what is known as industrial insurance, with house-to-house collection of small weekly premiums, cultivated intensively the field of life insurance in which the Fraternal Orders did little. The leader here was the Prudential Assurance Company, which after a slow start in 1848 soon found rapid and unchecked growth. It insured, for example, whole households for burial and offered other small provisions for dependents and old age. On Dec. 31, 1900, it had fourteen million policies with an average premium of twopence a week secured by funds of £17,000,000, which funds by the end of 1925 had risen to £95,000,000. It superseded a host of petty assessment societies (Burial Clubs), many of them managed by committees which squandered their funds and sometimes committed frauds. Although the expenses of industrial insurance are necessarily heavy, complete security is now obtainable.

The Savings Bank was the complement of the Friendly Society, though by no means so important as a form of corporate

[1] International Labour Office, Geneva, *General Problems of Social Insurance*, p. 44.

effort. It was a movement only in the sense that it was zealously promoted at certain times, just as allotments were after the labourers' revolt of 1830. In this respect, whatever its financial achievement, it falls short of rendering a service comparable with that of the People's banks and rural credit banks of the Continent. The idea of a Savings Bank was mooted by Jeremy Bentham under the name of a Frugality Bank. George Rose supported it in Parliament in 1815, and in 1817 secured the necessary legislation. Trustees administered the banks and through the National Debt office found a secure outlet for their funds. At first Friendly Societies, as Societies, were permitted to deposit in them and 4% was allowed as interest. In 1828, when the Savings Bank legislation was consolidated, the rate of interest was reduced to $3\frac{1}{2}\%$. By that time there were 408 banks in operation with £14 millions of deposits and £34 per head, the latter figure indicating that the banks were largely used by smaller tradesmen. In 1835 the legislation was extended to Scotland. This enabling legislation was a natural supplement to the efforts which Parliament was making to secure that the wage-earner should not be defrauded by the payment of wages in ale-houses. Such payment was forbidden in the London coal trade in 1807 and extended to coal mining in 1842. By these means Parliament attempted to mitigate the ravages which intemperance was making in the life of the workers. But Victorian England was more concerned to preach and promote individual thrift than to encourage the Trade Unions to organise against employers who were guilty of malpractice, or to pass liquor licensing laws which would keep the ' trade ' in hand and protect the worker from unreasonable temptation.

From encouragement of thrift in Savings Banks Parliament in 1861 advanced to direct enterprise. In that year, when Mr. Gladstone was Chancellor of the Exchequer, the Act creating Post Office Savings Banks was passed (24 & 25 Vict. c. 14), the State offering its security for the repayment of all moneys deposited through the Post Office. The Act was highly successful from the standpoint of business done, but it was not of distinctive assistance to wage-earners. In the half century from 1850 to 1900, its clientele was largely the lower middle class and the children of the upper middle class. In 1864, encouraged by its success with Savings Banks, the Government passed an Annuities Act (27 & 28 Vict. c. 43) authorising the National Debt Commissioners to insure lives or grant annuities, the Post Office being the channel of contact with the customers; but in 1882 the average of insurance policies issued during the previous 17 years was not 400. In 1882 the scheme was modified by 45 & 46 Vict. c. 51

(effective 1884), but the only important increase was among postal employees, as the result of an appeal to them.   Between 1884 and 1905 the Post Office issued 16,000 policies for £875,000—a paltry figure by comparison with those of any Insurance Company or of the Post Office Savings Bank, which in 1905 had nearly 1½ million new accounts and £42 millions of deposits in the course of the year.   The fatal flaw was the lack of house-to-house canvassing ;   and the possibilities of joint action with the Friendly Societies was excluded by the disinclination of the latter, which feared Government intervention with their management.

Recent Statistics.   The societies registered under the Friendly Societies Act embrace two classes of society, Friendly Societies and Collecting Societies.   Among Friendly Societies the Fraternal Orders and their branches are much the most important.   The Collecting Societies now come under the Industrial Insurance Commissioner in accordance with the Industrial Assurance Act of 1923 (13 & 14 Geo. V, c. 8).   The Chief Registrar of Friendly Societies (Mr. G. Stuart Robertson) is also the Industrial Insurance Commissioner ;   and the Annual Report of the latter includes Companies undertaking industrial insurance (such as the Prudential) as well as Collecting Societies.   The Friendly Society figures are for 1924, the remainder for 1925.

Friendly Societies		No. of Returns	No. of Members	Total Funds £
Orders and their Branches	.	18,254	3·1 m.	40·6 m.
Sickness Benefit Societies	.	1,241	1·0 m.	18·0 m.
Deposit Societies . . .		101	1·0 m.	12·2 m.

There is a variety of other Friendly Societies, which are numerically unimportant beside these three groups.   The Deposit Societies have grown remarkably in funds during the past decade, from under £5 millions in 1913 to £12·2 millions in 1924.   ' The popularity of societies of this class undoubtedly has had an adverse effect on the recruitment of some of the other large classes, and it is probably on this account that the application of deposit principles is receiving the attention of some of the Orders.' [1]

Industrial Assurance		No. of Returns	No. of Policies	Funds at end of year 1925
Companies		18	55·2 m.	151·7 m.
Collecting Societies . .		181	15·4 m.	32·1 m.

[1] *Report of Chief Registrar of Friendly Societies for 1924* : Part 2, ' Friendly Societies ' (1926), p. 1.

Section 2. Life Insurance

Life insurance is not as old as marine or fire insurance. The two companies chartered in 1720 for the business of marine insurance, the Royal Exchange Assurance and the London Assurance, had branches for life and fire, but life insurance was an unimportant part of their business in the 18th century. The earliest of the institutions which survived to the 19th century was the Amicable Society for a Perpetual Assurance Office, 1706, but modern life insurance begins with the foundation of the Equitable Society in 1762. For this Society was the first to procure for itself actuarial tables. Until 1800 life insurance was confined to London, and even thirty years later it was quite unimportant in the provinces. During the operation of Pitt's income tax the allowance on life insurance premiums was a stimulus to insurance, and towards 1830 Scotland began to show the way in life insurance as well as in joint stock banking. In 1815 the Scottish Widows Society was founded, and by 1830 seven Scottish Societies were in operation. After this date progress was rapid, as in the Friendly Society movement.

The fundamental obstacle in the 18th century was the complete absence of mortality tables and of an actuarial science based upon them. The first guesses of the value of a single life took the form of a uniform seven years, regardless of the person's age. In 1661 John Graunt made some initial observations on the statistical material contained in the bills of mortality. In 1692 the Government, as a means of raising money, sold life annuities, giving for £100 a life annuity of £14, without distinction of age. The State, in its need for money and its ignorance, exaggerated the degree of mortality ; and as the purchasers of these annuities were shrewd enough to select healthy lives, it lost heavily. This led to an investigation in 1693 by Dr. Edmund Halley on behalf of the Royal Society. He had to go to Breslau in Germany for his figures of age at death, but with these he was able to show that the value of a life contingency depended on two factors, the rate of interest compounded and the probability of life. Since Halley's time progress has been along three lines : the accumulation of facts, their application to the needs of practical life, and skill in calculation aided latterly by calculating machinery. But throughout the 18th century the business of life annuities remained chaotic. Not until 1789 did the Government distinguish ages in granting annuities. When it did so, it still exaggerated the degree of mortality and between 1808 and 1828 lost two million sterling on them.

Meanwhile, on the lead of the Equitable Society, the problem was being solved from the opposite angle. It employed William Morgan, the nephew of Dr. Price, to construct actuarial tables from figures derived from English sources, beginning with the Northampton table of 1780. At first it over-estimated mortality by one-third, just as the Government had done, but this brought profit to the Equitable and other Societies for the same reason that it brought loss to the Government; for by an annuity the Government received a capital sum and paid out a smaller annual sum as long as the claimant lived, while by a policy the Insurance Company received annual premiums until the insured died, when it paid to his heirs a capital sum. The miscalculation contributed to the boom in insurance, some of it very unsound, in the 1820's. The next name in actuarial progress is that of Joshua Milne, who in 1815 constructed the Carlisle tables of mortality. His book of that year made actuarial science an exact science. Just as from Great Britain, the home of the Friendly Society and the land of its origination, the mutual aid movement spread across the Continent to Europe, so also actuarial science originated in Great Britain and was for long the peculiar and almost exclusive possession of British students. Germany and the U.S.A. borrowed from Great Britain, the first American table appearing in 1868. After Milne's day progress was no longer associated with individual names. The new knowledge was steadily enlarged by the studies of the Institute of Actuaries of Great Britain and Ireland established in 1848. The tables published by this body in 1872, based on experience to 1863, remained to the end of the 19th century the most authoritative information on the mortality of insured lives. The data found by investigation on the part of the Insurance Companies and their servants were supplemented by the information concerning rates of mortality contained in the later censuses. Dr. William Farr was the pioneer here. From 1838 to 1879 he compiled the abstracts in the office of the Registrar-General of Births and Deaths.

At the present day insurance has permeated every class and almost every contingency to which it is applicable. Life insurance is becoming for the average man the normal method of saving; and firms take out endowment policies for their employees, as a provision for retirement in old age. As a business its problems are threefold. First, there is the actuarial problem, the chief factor in which, the expectation of life, is now so exactly known that there is less scope than formerly for one company or society to offer better terms than another. This was originally the main problem. Secondly there is the investment problem, that is to say, the rate of interest that the money received as premiums can earn. The importance of this may be realised by remembering that the value of a payment to be made in thirty years is greater by above a half with interest at 3% than with interest at $4\frac{1}{2}$%, while that of one to be made in thirty-six years is more than twice as great.[1]

The third problem is a social one. Whether the insurance company is one which makes profit for its shareholders or returns the whole of its profits in the form of bonus to its policy holders (i.e. a Mutual Society), is not so important as the high expenditure of energy and money in the solicitation of business ; and this consideration is of special importance in the department of industrial insurance, where the weekly collection of premiums by competing agents involves on the average a ratio of expenses (commission and management) to premiums of more than 40% or 5d. in the shilling. Here, as will be seen in the next section, the Co-operative Movement has broken new ground, using co-operative insurance to gather recruits for the co-operative store and using the device of the store dividend to operate an economical, though limited, form of life insurance. But, of course, the industrial insurance companies are alive to the weakness of the expenses ratio, which is highest among those which operate on a small scale, reaching in one case 79·8 in 1925. In the Co-operative Insurance Society with a premium income of £1 m. (1925) it was 40% : in the Pearl Assurance Company with a premium income of £5·6 m. it was 37·6% : in the Prudential Assurance Company with a premium income of £15·8 m. it was 26·6%. The Prudential's industrial insurance fund is 62% of the total industrial insurance funds of all industrial insurance companies in Great Britain. It reduced its ratio from 36·9 in 1921 to 29·7 in 1923 and 26·6 in 1925, and furthermore gave an increasing share of its profits to industrial branch policy holders ; 1921, £200,000 ; 1923, £906,000 ; 1925, £2,000,000.

Section 3. *Insurance and the Co-operative Movement*

At the time of the passing of the National Health Insurance Act (1911) champions of the Friendly Society movement, such as the late Sir Edward Brabrook, feared the emasculation of the Friendly Society spirit. As provision was made under the Act for the enjoyment of increased benefits by Societies which earned a surplus, scope was left for some group enterprise. But the private companies undertaking industrial assurance were associated

---

[1] Cf. *Encyclopædia Britannica*, 11th Edition, *sub* ' Insurance ' (XIV. 668).

in this scheme, provided that they set up Mutual Insurance branches from which they derived no profit ; and this they did with such vigour that by 1925 nearly half the insured persons were affiliated to 'industrial' Approved Societies. This was not very surprising, for when the law made insurance compulsory, the task was no longer the active one of building up a group with the will to save, but simply the passive one of insuring with one or other of many competing agencies ; and the companies with their insurance experience and machinery of collection were able to go after the business more thoroughly. But the Co-operative Movement (which legally grew up as the foster-child of the Friendly Society under the 'frugal investments' clause of the Friendly Society Act of 1848, 9 & 10 Vict. c. 27) has engaged in national health insurance under the Act of 1911, and at the same time greatly expanded its business and general insurance. Possessing an army of its own employees as well as millions of consumers among the member stores, the federal wholesale society is able to envisage social insurance as a unity ; and possessing an unassailable financial standing as the result of its success in co-operative trading, it is as strong a unit of enterprise as any single company in the world of trade or insurance.

The Health Insurance Section of the Co-operative Wholesale Society Ltd. came into operation on July 15, 1912 ; and in 1926 it had over 220,000 members, organised in some 1300 agencies. The members are individual co-operators in different parts of England and Wales, the Scottish movement having its own organisation. The contact with the C.W.S. as a trading body is represented only by the fact that the personnel in its several establishments constitute strong agencies. In 1927, as the second valuation under the provision of the Insurance Act disclosed a surplus of £742,000, it was able to announce a substantial increase of benefits : a higher rate of insurance benefits for sickness, disablement and maternity, free optical and dental treatment, and an allowance of 85% of the cost of new teeth. The value of a strong central society, which for other reasons commands the loyalty of its members and the respect of outsiders, is seen from such facts as these. It met what it considered to be the un-reasonable demand of the dentists for a 75% increase in the scale of pay, not by reducing the proportion of the free grant, as some Approved Societies were forced to do, but by successful adjust-ments among its widespread agencies. It warned its members of the dangers of unauthorised action, whether in the ordering of dentures or in the acceptance of lump-sum settlements under the Workmen's Compensation Acts. Down to 1927 it had recovered over £350,000 by way of compensation or damages, failures being rare and ' usually owing to some information being withheld or difficulty experienced in securing convincing evidence.' [1] At its 1926 meeting it passed a strong resolution condemning the raiding of the insurance fund through the new Economy (Miscellaneous Provisions) Act. Finally, being a working-class organisation, but not one whose *raison d'être* is insurance, it is able to take a detached view of financial prospects. Press tirades against the General Strike and the annual sermons of bank pundits only irritate the working man. But he pays heed to the Report of his own organisation when it regrets ' the greater number and length of claims owing to the long-continued disastrous [coal] dispute,' [2] and the unfavourable reaction of this on the prospects of a surplus at the next valuation.

But this department of social insurance is less dynamic than the business of life insurance, which the two Wholesales, the English and Scottish, administer jointly as part of their general scheme of co-operative insurance. In 1867, in accordance with the decision of the Co-operative Conference (the predecessor of the Co-operative Union), an institution for the insurance of societies and individual members was organised in company form. Since an Industrial and Provident Society could not at that date undertake insurance and since recent failures among Life Insurance Companies (which led to the protective Life Assurance Companies Act of 1870) had been serious, life insurance was postponed, and the company confined itself to Fire and Fidelity Guarantee. The office work was done at first at Rochdale in the office of the Equitable Pioneers and transferred later to Manchester. In 1886 life insurance was undertaken on the mutual basis, all profits being exclusively divisible with policy holders. Industrial insurance on account of its costliness was discouraged, and was not undertaken until 1899, when, as a preliminary, the company was converted into a society competent ' to carry on the business of insurance in all its branches.' In 1908 the Co-operative Insurance Society (C.I.S.) moved to its present separate premises adjacent to the Wholesale. But still the movement hung fire. It was only from the War period onwards that progress was registered, and then the progress was remarkable. In 1912 the Society was taken over by the English and Scottish Wholesale Societies as a joint property : and at the close of the War, by absorption of the Planet Insurance Co., the C.I.S. entered new fields with machinery and methods similar to those of its company rivals. Its premium income mounted at the following rates :

[1] *Report of Committee of Management for 1927*, p. 4.
[2] *Report*, p. 5.

		Million £
1917		under ½ m.
1920		1·3 m.
1925		2·8 m.
1926 -		3·2 m.

Its business in 1926 was distributed thus :

	Million £
Life	1·1 m.
Industrial	1·2 m.
Fire	0·2 m.
Employers' Liability . . .	0·1 m.
General	0·6 m.
	3·2 m.

'General' business included a notable advance in motor and motor-cycle insurance, thus favouring the policy of co-operators that each new social want shall furnish its quota to co-operation. Let the article be sold through the movement if it is not yet made by it, and insured through it if it is not yet sold or made by it. The assets of the C.I.S. (which rose from £4·9 m. in 1925 to £6·1 m. in 1926) are held, of course, in gilt-edged securities and not in any way compromised by the trading fortunes of the Wholesales.

The chief reason for the increase of business was the more extensive employment of full-time agents, who rose from 60 in 1914 to over 2000 in 1926. The Society has large branch offices in provincial centres and there are 168 district offices in the smaller towns of England and Scotland. The head office at Manchester houses the National Health Insurance Section of the C.W.S. also. The new methods have justified themselves on two grounds. First of all, they have met an insurance need hitherto unsatisfied by a co-operative route. For lack of means prevented many store members from taking out ordinary life insurance with quarterly, half-yearly, or yearly premiums ; and the special device of ' collective ' insurance—to be described in the next paragraph—did not meet the complete insurance wants of co-operators. Insurance is a transaction in which many people insist on privacy, and the ' collective ' insurance which the C.I.S. offers is public and does not grade benefits according to individual wants and individual insurance capacity. Secondly, the new methods have contributed to the progress of co-operation as a trading movement. This answers the old objection that the costliness of industrial insurance is antithetical to the economy of the Co-operative Store. For the field staff of the C.I.S. are co-operative mission-aries, who constantly bring new members to the retail store One C.I.S. agent, for example, introduced no fewer than 500 new members to his local Society in six months, and in one street of twenty houses secured ten new members. In the towns of the South, where the co-operative atmosphere is comparatively weak, there resides just the type of people to whom insurance makes its appeal. They are less solid as a group, but they are thrifty and understand the insurance value of the premiums which the rapid extension of the C.I.S. enables it to offer.

The C.I.S. undertakes two types of insurance termed ' Group ' Life and ' Collective ' Life. ' Group ' Life Insurance is given to members of clubs, trade unions, guilds and bodies of employees ; and entitles the beneficiary to a fixed sum on death. New members are automatically insured on completion of three months' service. This is appropriate to the Co-operative movement, because one working-class organisation naturally gives what business it has to another working-class organisation. ' Collective ' Life Insurance is a device for the simultaneous encouragement of store purchases and insurance. It was along this route that co-operators, feeling after a policy of expansion, first tapped life insurance on a large scale, before reaching the much wider field of house-to-house work. A single policy is taken out by the retail Society, which insures the lives of individual purchasing members. In the most usual form the premium is one penny in the pound on purchases and the sum insured is 5s. in the pound on the purchases of the last year with a limit of £40. Expenses of collection are limited to 3% of the premiums ; and this is possible because the payment can be deducted from credits standing to the member's account in respect of purchases. In 1922, the last year in which this branch of insurance was shown separately, the premium income was £0·5 m. out of a total of £1·3 m. for life insurance, ordinary and industrial.

It has been shown that historically Friendly Societies and Savings Banks were joint endeavours. The successful entry of the Post Office into the latter curtailed its value as a local effort. But the Co-operative Stores are grounded on locality ; for they always encourage their members to let their dividends accumulate and thus they were the most living force in wage-earners' thrift during the second half of the 19th century. But only a small portion of these savings could be safely employed by the Societies or their Wholesales as share or loan capital within the movement. Therefore the C.W.S., after opening a loan and deposit department in 1872, converted this into a bank, which for many years confined itself, *qua* banker, to the provision of banking facilities for Co-operative Societies. Just as the Wholesale Society conducted for its members their wholesale trade, so the C.W.S. Bank became the clearing house for the commercial transactions to which this trade gave rise. In this way the bank built up a commercial banking business, on the top of which in recent years it has elaborated a service for the handling of funds belonging to Trade Unions, Friendly Societies, and other working-class bodies as well as to individual co-operators. It does not, however, accept ordinary trading accounts, as the effect would be to encourage within its fold a rival form of trade, besides calling for special machinery. In its relation to individual co-operators it is primarily a savings bank. It offers a range of deposit rates graded as follows :

Current account, $2\frac{3}{4}$%. (A commission not exceeding 2s. per £100 is charged on withdrawals.)

Accounts for holiday clubs, with weekly deposits and one annual withdrawal, $3\frac{3}{4}$%.

Deposit accounts on notice varying from 7 days to 6 months, $3\frac{3}{4}$–$4\frac{1}{2}$%.

4-year deposit notes in multiples of £1 sterling withdrawable on 3 months' notice, $3\frac{1}{4}$–$4\frac{3}{4}$%, according to the period the deposit is left undisturbed.

The Bank in December 1925 had 20,000 current and 25,000 deposit accounts. It reaches its customers, bodies or individuals, through the Co-operative Store in their locality. The stores act as its agents, paying and receiving from individuals over their counters and submitting to Head Office a record of their daily transactions with the Bank's customers. Each customer is given a registration number, which is stamped on check and credit slips, and under this indicator all transactions pass.

But this is not to say that the Co-operative world is independent of private banks. Each retail Society has its banker, to which it takes its receipts and from which it receives currency. The private bank acts as agent for the C.W.S. Bank, which has accounts with all the leading banks in London and Manchester. But as the Co-operative movement has more than enough funds to finance its development, the services of the private banker are purely exchange services relating to cash transactions. Moreover, the Bank is not a clearing banker, the Westminster Bank acting as its clearing agent and handling also its foreign business. Thus its Danish buyers finance their purchases by selling drafts on the Westminster Bank, London. It would not pay it to belong to the clearing house, as its account would always be one-sided ; for it does not sell to outsiders and therefore no cheques would be coming in. The C.W.S. Bank is thus both a settling house for the Co-operative Movement on its trading side and an investment institution for groups or individuals attached to the movement. At the end of the first quarter in 1872 its total assets were £8000 ;

in June 1925 £31 millions, and its turnover for 1925 was £588 millions.   Its assets have grown since 1900 as follows :

						Million £
1900	.	.	.	.	.	2
1914	.	.	.	.	.	7
1924	.	.	.	.	.	27
1925	.	.	.	.	.	31

As the C.W.S. Bank is a subsidiary of the C.W.S., its depositors have behind it the total assets of the latter, viz. £56 m., with share capital and reserve amounting to £13 m. Within the banking department itself, out of £31 m. of assets, which is also the sum due to depositors, all but £4 m. are held in gilt-edged securities.

The C.W.S. Bank has two distinctive contacts.   The leading Trade Unions bank with it ; and in the General Strike of 1926 the problem that at once arose was, how was their own bank with whom their funds were deposited to supply immediate cash if the taxi-cabs were withdrawn from the streets. Similarly the curtailment of postal services obstructed the routine by which the Co-operative Societies on behalf of the Bank made disbursements to their customers and to Trade Unions among others.   The question whether the C.W.S. should make advances to the Trade Unions in order to tide them over emergencies is not an acute one ; for throughout its long history the C.W.S. has always maintained the position that it is the trustee for its member stores, and that security for the funds lodged with it must take precedence of all else.

Secondly, the C.W.S. Bank has conducted a legitimate business with bodies which, because of their novelty, were distasteful to the non-co-operative world.   Thus in 1925 it financed trade with Russia : the Soviet authorities making shipments of grain and certain Co-operative Societies on the east coast of Britain securing in return a profitable trade in herrings.   The Bank also has had very satisfactory relations with the wheat pools of West and South Australia.   Australian bankers were shy, and the C.W.S. Bank having no prejudices and protecting itself by an adequate margin made the advances necessary to the pool plan.   Moreover, as the Australian harvest occurs in the English winter and the peak of the Australian demand for credit comes in March, this demand dovetailed with the situation at home, where the winter is the saving season when funds are abundant.

When, with the pattern of Germany before it, the British Government embarked on social insurance, the two things most feared were the supposed ineptitude of State administration and the undermining of self-reliance.   To-day it is clearly seen that the State not only need not be inefficient but may be definitely more efficient as its activities multiply. This is especially true of social insurance. For the economy of national provision for the various contingencies of sickness, invalidity, old age, and unemployment depends on each part helping the other and on the avoidance of overlapping. By a unified programme the Government obtains economies comparable with those obtained in the large-scale production of standard goods.

Group effort has always a social value, but unnecessary dispersion may reduce net results—just as at a University the common life of a College may be hurt by an excess of activities of a social or semi-educational nature in College and University. Group effort in social insurance and saving was perhaps more important to the 19th than to the 20th century. In ordinary business saving is as important as ever it was, but with the growth of the large concern an increasing proportion is done by the firm before profits are distributed. So, too, in the co-operative world. The need of producers for credit is shifting from the individual to the body. The appeal to provide and to save had a glamour of its own in Victorian England, but even though done through a group the act was in essence individual. The great part which the co-operative credit bank played in the town and country life of the Continent, and in particular of Germany, led students from other lands to recommend it unreservedly. But it has never succeeded in Great Britain, because such credit was suited only to small independent craftsmen and shopkeepers and to peasant proprietors, of which Britain had few : nor in the New World where, though credit needs were urgent, there were not the savings or the security for operation on Raiffeisen lines.

Since the War, North America has come to realise this. What its farmers need most is cheap credit for the co-operative organisation which handles their products ; and they can command it from independent banks provided their co-operative marketing organisation is sufficiently thorough. It is a question, whether schemes of rural credit for current operations as distinct from land mortgage have not done more harm than good. The leading merit of the Canadian Wheat Pools is that by their system of periodic payment they are bringing the farmers towards a cash basis, as the Rochdale system brought British wage-earners nearly one hundred years ago. The Pool authorities have to dissuade the farmers and their educational organisations from pledging the wheat certificates too freely. They keep the same jealous eye on the earnings they make for their members as the British Wholesale Societies do on the funds deposited with them.

There was a time when the growth of the British Wholesales was supposed to be inimical to the spirit of co-operation. On the contrary, their solidity has allowed them to permeate the movement with new applications of the same fundamental co-operative principle, namely benefit in proportion to patronage. National health insurance, general insurance, banking and saving, have all proved to lend themselves to the scheme of consumers' co-operation, when that scheme is federal ; and as the co-operative world enters one activity after another it works on the magnificent asset of five million members waiting enrolment in the new activity. Thus, to give one final example, the live question of 1926 was pension schemes for employees. Up to March 1926, sixty Societies had introduced schemes and the C.W.S. had one in preparation for its own considerable army. The services of the actuary of the Co-operative Insurance Society were at the disposal of the Societies. The Northern District was planning group schemes for Societies within given areas, carrying transferable pension rights. The Co-operative Union was called upon for model rules, which should secure uniformity and the pooling of experience.

The unity of effort claimed for State insurance is paralleled by the unity which the Co-operative Movement reaches by building harmoniously on its own past. It is fortunate that the headquarters of the movement are in Manchester and Glasgow rather than in London, the political capital. For this preserves the equipoise between State and voluntary effort. The spirit which made Lancashire the pioneer of the great Friendly Societies is still alive and its dynamic outlet to-day is the Co-operative Movement. We can no longer speak of the Trade Union, the Friendly Society, and the Co-operative Society as the three great branches of working-class effort. The trinity, if there is one, is the Co-operative Society, the Trade Union, and the Labour Party.

Section 4. *Labour Co-partnership and the Co-operative Store*

In one sense all business is a form of co-operation. But the co-operation of the Co-operative Movement is a method of business originating and conducted in a safer way. It originates among those who are economically weak, and it is conducted on such terms that all those who are prepared to assume the responsibilities of membership shall have an equal vote in the management of the Association, and share in its rewards in proportion to the degree in which they give their custom to it.

The Co-operative Movement is world-wide and embraces four classes of activity : credit, agricultural supply production and sale, labour co-partnership and the co-operative store. By contrast with the first three the co-operative store is an association of consumers, and here, as well as in the restricted field of labour co-partnership, Great Britain has led the way. For in Great Britain came first that industrial revolution which finally separated most workers from the instruments of production. As wage-earners they formed Trade Unions to safeguard and improve their working conditions, and as wage-spenders they formed co-operative stores to save them from the bondage of debt and truck. The productive society, now commonly termed labour co-partnership, is as old as the store; for in the days of Robert Owen co-operative production and co-operative store keeping were deemed to be starting points towards the greater goal of a co-operative community on the land. Later in the century there was considerable hostility between the two wings. The productive societies or labour co-partnerships in 1925 numbered 105, with share and loan capital of £3·3 m., sales of £5·8 m., employees numbering 11,900, and bonus payments in addition to salaries and wages of £43,000. They are members of the Co-operative Union, but they have their own Co-operative Productive Federation as well. This body was the nucleus of the Labour Co-partnership Association, which was established in 1884 and embraced, in addition to labour co-partnerships founded by workers, firms which had introduced schemes of co-partnership and profit-sharing. The purpose of the Association was twofold: to prevent a repetition of the mistakes which were made in the working man's productive societies promoted in the 1850's by the Christian Socialists, mistakes such as isolation, over-assistance and want of funds which led to their general failure; and to mould schemes of profit-sharing in the fuller form of co-partnership.

The labour co-partnership societies are not in any degree hostile either to the trade union or to the co-operative store. Their members are trade unionists, they have derived much of their capital from the stores and also sell to the stores the greater part of their output. They are strongest in the textile and leather trades, which produce commodities in constant demand by the working class. The Midlands district of Kettering, Desborough and Leicester seems to possess an atmosphere congenial to co-partnership; and this is also a district where enthusiasm for the co-operative store and co-operative interest in politics are strongly developed. The frequency of success in the boot and shoe trade suggests that the technique lends itself to co-partnership. Before the days of machinery the shoemaker was often the independent man of the village and its politician. Some of the societies were founded at a time when the introduction of machinery was forcing the shoemaker into factory life, and co-partnership was a way of escaping from the loss of liberty that factory life threatened. Moreover, a large initial

capital was not necessary, and the difference in grade between
the skilled and unskilled labourer in the trade was not so great
as to prevent the operatives as a body from using with intelligence and effect their constitutional rights. As members they
share in the election of their manager and are represented on
the Committee of Management, and the managers testify to the
loyalty with which their workers work for them as wage-earners
and as committee men support them, especially in the matter
of allowing to the management a free hand in the purchase of
materials. Beside the millions in the co-operative store movement the labour co-partnerships are numerically insignificant,
but they have done a difficult thing very nobly and more than
deserve the support which some stores give them.

The achievement of the Co-operative Stores is very impressive.
In 1919 at the close of the War some 1350 co-operative stores,
with their two Wholesales, controlled an aggregate capital of
£100 millions. Their retail trade totalled £200 m. and they
had about 4½ million members. Despite the long post-war
slump the membership has increased, though the price collapse
of 1921 cost the C.W.S. £5 m. In 1919 the societies varied in
size from 50,000 to 100.000 members, nearly half of the aggregate
membership being supplied by 200 large societies, each of which
had many branches : over one-third of the families of Great
Britain were members of a co-operative store, and from them
they obtained about one-half of their foodstuffs and one-tenth
of all other household purchases. The strongholds of trade
unionism are also the strongholds of co-operation. Though it
has many middle-class members and many rural members, it
is essentially an industrial working-class movement. The well-
to-do, especially London and the South, and the rural population
of the South of England, Scotland and Wales supply few co-
operators. And there is also a class of very poor which, living
on odds and ends of food and second-hand goods, cannot afford
to deal with the co-operative store.

Section 5. Early History of Co-operation

The British Co-operative Movement is now about a century
old. The industrial revolution supplied the necessity and Robert
Owen the inspiration. On the side of consumption the necessity
was an escape from the tyranny of truck, on the side of production
it was the finding of a livelihood by men who were out of employment, perhaps because they had been so wicked as to join a
trade union. Thus the co-operative societies established in the
late 20's and the early 30's were a combination of retail store

and productive society and they were ready to sell their goods to outsiders or to exchange them for those of other societies. The store element predominated at first, when co-operation was the means of raising the funds for a land community. But at the height of the trade union boom (1832–4) the productive side took first place : work in a co-operative society was advocated as an alternative to employment by capitalists and was sought by those who could find none. Though nearly all the early societies were short-lived, they left their mark on the efforts of the next generation. For the Rochdale Pioneers of 1844, with whom the modern movement starts, included among their objects the manufacture of such articles as would give employment to those of their members who were out of work or underpaid, and also the foundation of a self-supporting colony of united interests.

Robert Owen did not found the first co-operative store, nor was his store at New Lanark anything more than a well-run truck shop, but he was a radiator of co-operative ideas. His missionaries carried the new gospel from place to place. One town, one village, would learn what another was doing and thus realise that its little local effort might be built into the foundations of a great national achievement. In the spiritual sense, but in that only, Owen was the parent of British co-operation. About 1850, when the German peasants were in the clutches of the moneylender, F. W. Raiffeisen appeared to rescue them. He was their very father, framing the rules of the first village banks and taking charge of the federal organisation. Such a position the Christian Socialists aspired to occupy in Britain, but here the urge came from below and would not be controlled by patrons. There was indeed one service needed from above, and that service the distinguished lawyers who were the disciples of Maurice and Kingsley fully and gratuitously rendered, securing for co-operative societies the Act of 1852 which gave them a legal personality, the Act of 1862 which conferred the boon of limited liability, and the Acts of 1867 and 1876 which were necessary to federal expansion.[1] Co-operative societies are known to the law as Industrial and Provident Societies and are governed now by the Act of 1893 (56 & 57 Vict. c. 39).

In 1844 the Rochdale Pioneers took down their world-renowned shutters in Toad (T'owd) Lane.[2] This Society has given its

---

[1] 15 & 16 Vict. c. 31 (1852) : 25 & 26 Vict. c. 65 (1862) : 30 & 31 Vict. c. 117 (1867) : 39 & 40 Vict. c. 45 (1876). The Act of 1852 was commonly called Mr. Slaney's Act, after R. A. Slaney, the Cambridge barrister and Chairman of the Commons Committee of 1850 on the savings of the middle and working classes, on the report of which the Act was based. J. M. Ludlow, E. V. Neale, Thomas Hughes and John Stuart Mill gave evidence before it.

[2] It has been conjectured that Toad Lane was originally Tod Lane, from the wool market which used to exist at the end of the lane.

name to the system of sale at market price for cash and distribution of profits in proportion to purchases. But it was by no means the first co-operative store : this honour seems to belong to a society established by some weavers at the village of Fenwick, near Kilmarnock in Scotland, in 1769. Nor is it the oldest store surviving to modern times, being ante-dated by the Lennox Victualling Society, 1812, the Sheerness Economical, 1816, Lockhurst Lane, Coventry, 1832. Nor yet was it the first to adopt the dividend on purchases. The books of the Meltham Mill (Yorkshire) Co-operative Society show that it paid dividends on custom when it was founded in 1827. But the Equitable Pioneers of Rochdale were the first to make a public success of the device, and in the decade after 1844 the few stores of earlier date, as well as those newly established, adopted the dividend on purchases in conscious imitation of Rochdale. The efforts of this society to operate a wholesale branch preceded the establishment of the C.W.S. at Manchester, which thenceforth was the headquarters of the English movement. Many countries have taken the Rochdale rules as their guide after passing through an initial period of isolation and ephemeral success resembling that of the earliest British societies.

An examination of the first lists of societies which later became famous reveals the astonishing contribution made by starving hand-loom weavers. The Rochdale Pioneers were mainly flannel weavers, and in the societies established in Scotland before 1844 it is rare to find one which does not begin as a meeting of poor weavers, sometimes to talk politics, sometimes to promote temperance, and sometimes purposely to open a co-operative store. Regions in which truck was the first to disappear were the regions in which co-operative stores first became general, namely the textile districts of Lancashire and of Yorkshire. In Lancashire the workers lived in towns or close to them and it was unusual for the mill hands to be housed around the mill This condition of things was unfavourable to truck and favourable to the growth of that local spirit for which towns of Lancashire are so famous. In the West Riding of Yorkshire there was more paternalism between master and men, but the Yorkshire employer, faithful to the traditional independence of the Yorkshire freeholder, did not like to see his men ' trucked.' Therefore the promoters of the Leeds Society, flax spinners in the employ of Messrs. Benyon and Co., were able to issue their appeal for the formation of a co-operative mill in 1847 with the approval of their employers, and they received friendly notices in the leading newspaper, the *Leeds Mercury*.

The weavers were generally the first in the field, for three reasons. First of all they were starving and theirs was the greater necessity; secondly they had behind them a tradition of aristocracy; thirdly they were engaged in domestic industry. The weaver worked in his cottage and in his spare time attended to the little co-operative shop, which perhaps was in his own cottage or adjacent to it. On these humble premises was fostered that spirit of unpaid work which alone made it possible for the poorest adults in the country to struggle through the first years of corporate shop-keeping on fractional resources.

The stores of this period generally developed in one of two ways. Either they began with a small flour mill, as did the Leeds Society (most families in the North then made their own bread) and then went on to general groceries; or, like the Rochdale Pioneers, they began with the grocery and later added a bakery or mill. From this they advanced, sometimes rashly, to more speculative lines, drapery, boot and shoe, furniture, butcher's meat, and coal. Not the least of the services rendered by the C.W.S. was the guidance which it gave to the societies in the expansion of their local activities. The difficulties encountered by the early co-operators were much the same everywhere. There was the first great struggle to escape from indebtedness to local traders and the temptation to slip back to easy credit in bad times: the inability of amateur managers to handle the store as it grew: the dishonesty of bad managers who had been imported without care. The hostility of the middle-man was always to be reckoned on, but where the workers were numerous and stood firm, persecution strengthened them. When, however, as at Lincoln, some of the agricultural population tried to embark on co-operation they met with initial difficulties as serious as those which confront farmers' stores in Canada to-day. And similarly in old towns, where the shopkeepers were prominent citizens. The St. Cuthbert's Society was established in Edinburgh in 1859 by joiners and cabinet-makers, but in Perth there was no co-operative store until 1866. Very cautiously in that year five individuals started selling cloth in an attic: in 1870 they came out into the open, but only to sell tobacco and tea; in 1872, meeting with intense hostility from local bakers, they began to make bread.

In the 50's co-operation fell back in Scotland and revealed little sign of a general expansion in England, but after 1860 the growth was remarkable. Beginning with the Cramlington Society in Northumberland, the idea spread like wildfire through the mining districts of Northumberland and Durham. The 60's supplied the birth dates of many of the stronger societies in the lowlands of Scotland and the midlands of England.

There were reasons for the lag and subsequent expansion. Until 1862 the stores ran the risk of unlimited liability, and until 1863 they had no federal wholesale. But the 60's saw a forward sweep in the generalisation of machine industry. The unit of enterprise was growing, and therefore in this period numerous societies were started by the employees of large concerns in the iron and steel and shipbuilding districts of the Clyde and the north-east coast. For a long time the very large towns were relatively backward. Among the great societies of to-day the Royal Arsenal at Woolwich was established only in 1868, the Birmingham in 1881, and the Liverpool in 1886. Even Glasgow and Manchester, the seats of the Wholesales, have not shown the same solidarity in retailing. In the large towns the workers were lost, they did not know each other so intimately, and where they were close to the Wholesales they were sometimes tempted to plunge into big things before they had the strength to carry them. The working man of London, the first to discuss co-operation, was the last to practise it. The heart of London was barely touched by it in 1914. The strongest London Societies are suburban, and it is under their influence that co-operation is at long last spreading inwards. At the centre the competition of private traders is very severe. It has been said of London that it is at once the cheapest as well as the dearest place in the world in which to live ; and in the East End the large Jewish population is an adverse factor, for the Jews love individual trading and give their custom to their own race. The Army and Navy and Civil Service Stores were co-operative only in name. Though founded by salaried consumers, they deal freely with the outside public and distribute profits on the basis of share-holding. These societies, however, supplied the stimulus to parallel societies in Italy, which observed the co-operative essential of the dividend on purchases.

Section 6.   The Wholesale Societies

The outstanding feature of the period between 1860 and 1900 was the growth of the English Co-operative Wholesale Society (C.W.S.), established in 1863, and of the Scottish Wholesale Society (S.C.W.S.), established in 1868. In this generation two great figures occupied the co-operative stage, J. T. W. Mitchell, Chairman of the English Wholesale, 1874–95, and William Maxwell, Chairman of the Scottish Wholesale, 1881–1908. William (later Sir William) Maxwell came from Edinburgh, where he had been Secretary of St. Cuthbert's Society, and, if the greatness of his work is little known, it is because he himself is the historian of the movement in Scotland. Co-operation was the compelling passion of his life, and his sympathy for all forms of co-operation marked him out later for the Chairmanship of the International Co-operative Alliance. The evidence which he gave before the Labour Commission in 1892 reveals a remarkable combination of the old and of the new. He was still inspired by the early ambition of working-men co-operators to break the bondage of the wages system ; and at his initiative the Scottish Wholesale Society and the Glasgow United Bakery Society maintained for many years a scheme of bonus and share participation with their employees, not introducing it in response to remonstrances from without, but pursuing it as one of many ways of evading the friction which he saw might one day arise between the consumers' federations and their employees. But he also realised that the bulk of co-operative production must be undertaken by the Wholesale Societies, and that in Scotland the geographical distribution of co-operators made it possible to centralise the productive establishments of the S.C.W.S. in a single co-operative colony at Shieldhall, Glasgow.

Mitchell had a bigger and a harder rôle to play. The English Wholesale led the way by a few years, and it always worked in perfect friendship with the younger Society, but throughout his life Mitchell was fretted by the opposition of the over-zealous advocates of profit-sharing and independent societies. The magnitude of the business success which the Wholesale Society achieved under his chairmanship caused him to be regarded as something of an absorbing monster. In reality he was the very opposite. He was reared in poverty and lived in austere simplicity. From a day of exhausting business in Manchester, when by his firmness or perhaps by his chaff he had persuaded his Committee to avoid a course which would have lost them many thousands, he would come back to Rochdale to prepare for his Sunday School, of which he was the superintendent. Controlling a business which then had an annual turnover of £10 millions, he died worth £350, working to the very last. Rochdale gave him a funeral such as it had given to no one since the death of John Bright.

The story of the C.W.S. is one of cumulative success. The promoters were Lancashire men. The attempt of the 50's to graft a wholesale department on to the Rochdale Society failed, partly because other stores were jealous of Rochdale's seniority and partly because the amount of co-operative trade was as yet small. But by 1863 there were in Lancashire, Cheshire and Yorkshire some 120 stores with 40,000 members and, after a series of conferences, an agency was opened. In 1864 it was converted into a wholesale house, and in place of selling goods at cost plus commission, the principle of market price and dividend on purchases was applied also to the wholesale transactions, the dividend in this case going to the member stores.   In 1867 the title of North of England Co-operative Wholesale Society was taken.   In 1869 it moved to its present headquarters in Balloon Street, Manchester.   In November 1872 it took its present name of Co-operative Wholesale Society, Ltd.

The Wholesale had to be prepared to supply societies all over England and it also had to meet the legitimate desires of other localities to have a branch of the Wholesale, a warehouse or a factory, in their midst.   Under the double incentive of import facilities and local support, actual or promised, the C.W.S. established branches in Newcastle, 1872, London, 1874, Bristol, 1884, Cardiff, 1891.   The London house was specially occupied with the handling of tea—for London is the world's tea market.   The Bristol depot, for which the Plymouth Society was the most zealous agitator, assisted the spread of co-operation in the west of England, and similarly with Cardiff.   Many were the societies in the south-west of England and in South Wales (the latter only just released from its long nightmare of truck) which the resident officials of the C.W.S. helped with advice and personal labour in the days of their beginning.   But the business of wholesale merchant took the C.W.S. farther afield in quest of supplies : to Ireland and Denmark, Montreal and New York ; to Ceylon, where in 1902, jointly with the S.C.W.S., it purchased tea estates ; to Sydney in Australia, where it established a tallow factory ; and to West Africa, where between 1914 and 1920 the two Wholesales acquired jointly or separately oil and cocoa yielding properties.

The C.W.S. is also a great producer, and it arrived at this function through the opening of a deposit and loan department in 1871.   However, the money of the stores flowed in upon it in such embarrassing quantities that it could not find employment for anything like the whole within its own sphere.   The London Co-operators, G. J. Holyoake, E. O. Greening and the Christian Socialist lawyers, claimed that the funds belonged to the Co-operative Movement as a whole and should be invested in independent productive enterprises, but Mitchell was opposed, realising that success was rarely possible unless the concern was operated by the Wholesale primarily in the interest of the stores. Again and again between 1870 and 1890 the C.W.S. under pressure from without, either from London or from local federations of consumers, gave financial assistance to independent productive ventures.   Again and again they lost money, and the experience of the Scottish Wholesale was not very different.   The crop of failures was especially heavy in the industrial depression of 1879 : and the co-partnership societies which later made good were those which relied for support on local capital and local custom.

The C.W.S. began with the manufacture of biscuits at Crumpsall near Manchester in 1872, and soon afterwards embarked on boots and shoes at Leicester, and soap at Durham. In the 80's and 90's came cloth and ready-made clothing, cabinet-making and fruit-farming. After 1900 'there were notable extensions in two directions. First of all it erected plants for handling imported raw material, such as wheat, on the excellent industrial sites along the Manchester Ship Canal as well as at Dunston and Pelaw on the Tyne. Secondly it took over a number of productive societies (labour co-partnerships), which in some cases were in difficulties and in other cases found it more prudent to accept absorption than to invite the competition of the Wholesale in their midst.

Two considerations influenced the Wholesale in extending the range of its production, the need of its members for the article and the likelihood of commercial success. Thus flour and coal were necessaries of the first order, but the Wholesale in order to avoid competition with local co-operative mills did not enter into flour milling until 1889, nor into the risky business of coal mining until 1917, when in response to strong local demand from a mining region it purchased Shilbottle Colliery, Northumberland. The late entry into flour milling was fortunate for the Wholesale. Flour milling in the 60's and 70's underwent a technical revolution, the most important item in which was roller milling pioneered by Hungary and the U.S.A. England became increasingly dependent on imported wheat, and therefore the old local mills situated inland, which the C.W.S. would have been ready to purchase if it had begun earlier, were no longer suitable. The C.W.S. began at the port of Newcastle in 1891, and to-day possesses large modern flour mills at each of the great ports, at Silvertown (London), Avonmouth (Bristol), Dunston (Newcastle), and Trafford Park (Manchester). The milling development brought to the front a jealousy of old standing. Leeds is the rival of Manchester in things co-operative as well as in business and sport, and Yorkshire co-operators were not disposed to take their orders to Manchester. Therefore, though offers were made by the Wholesale to buy out the local milling federations in Yorkshire, these were for many years rejected. It was not until 1915 that the C.W.S. took over the co-operative flour mills at Halifax, Sowerby Bridge, and Colne Valley. It was not until 1920 that the great Leeds Co-operative Industrial Society became a member of the Wholesale.

The import business brought the C.W.S. into ship owning. In 1876 it began to run boats between Goole and the Continent. In 1906 the service was sold to the Lancashire and Yorkshire Railway. It did not pay for reasons which were fundamental. (1) In order to secure outward cargoes the C.W.S. had to do a general business which was not part of its intention. (2) As the sources of foreign supply shifted, the Wholesale had to shift its business also, but it could not easily transfer its ships. (3) Independent cargo lines fit their business to the seasons and, being on the look-out for traffic in any direction, operate on lines from which a federation of purchasers trading one way only is precluded. The C.W.S. therefore lost some money on its continental service, but its competition helped to reduce freight rates, and the appearance of its ships in Continental ports increased its prestige. How high this prestige is anyone who has visited co-operative organisations in Denmark, Hamburg and Belgium knows.

The shipping venture was the means of bringing the Wholesale into the coal business. It, as well as many retail societies, had abstained from coal distribution owing to the strongly entrenched position of local dealers, many of them members of the stores. But as a ship owner it had to buy coal for export, and from this it came gradually into the wholesale domestic business. While some members were opposed to coal dealing, others, especially the Yorkshire miners, were enthusiastic supporters of coal mining by the Wholesale. But between 1877 and 1882 the C.W.S. had lost £40,000 odd in mining enterprises in the North of England, which had been foisted on them by profit-sharing enthusiasts or groups of stores with a mining membership. When therefore in 1900 some Yorkshire societies promoted a scheme for a West Yorkshire Coal Federation, the C.W.S. held back. It was, however, ready to increase its coal business, which in 1912 amounted to £¾ million. But the Wholesale is not an autocrat : if its members are sufficiently persistent, they can usually secure a trial for a scheme, and so in 1917 the Shilbottle Colliery was bought. Thus the chain from consumer to producer is complete, but it is more likely that expansion in the coal business will take place at the retail end of the chain than that the Wholesale will ever mine an important percentage of its members' coal.

There is also a large margin for expansion in the retail distribution of milk, a necessity of equal importance with coal and one which many societies avoided in order not to compete with members who were milk distributors. Since 1914 there have been considerable developments. In 1925–6 the most notable advance in co-operative trade in Scotland was in the handling and selling of milk and milk products. Though slow to enter the business, the Scottish societies have installed modern hygienic methods of milk retailing and are now in the front rank of the business in Scotland.

The Scottish Wholesale Society, founded in December 1868, has followed closely in the footsteps of the C.W.S., but it has by no means been a slavish imitator. In an ever widening number of activities it is in partnership with the English Wholesale in the tea business, in foreign depots, in certain of the factories that have been taken over from independent productive societies and in co-operative insurance. In the recent development of the milk trade by its member stores it is doing distinctive work. In 1926 it opened a creamery for supplying milk to groups of societies in Ayrshire and it is making similar arrangements for the service of societies in Glasgow. On its Calderwood estate it has established a tuberculosis-free herd of 40 cows for the supply of the highest grade of milk. Finally, the leaders of the S.C.W.S. have always been alive to the labour problem of the co-operative commonwealth. Much has been made of the fact that the Scottish Wholesale had a scheme of profit-sharing with its employees from the beginning, but neither this device nor its abandonment in 1918 is of importance by comparison with the high record of the society as a pioneer in the fuller recognition of the status of workers in the Co-operative Movement.

Section 7. The Problems of the 20th Century

The 20th century opened in a new atmosphere. The bread tax (as co-operators called it) imposed during the Boer War went in 1902, and co-operators assisted at the funeral, but a more evil thing than Protection raised its head. Free-trade England found that it was becoming a country of combines, and to Manchester co-operators Trust was the twin brother of Tariff. Already many times the Co-operative Movement had experienced and benefited from the hostility of private-traders. In the 80's a desultory persecution was instituted by the Traders' Defence Association under feeble leadership. Most employers of labour, when asked to interfere with their men, laughed at the suggestion, but in the 90's Scottish co-operators had to meet a serious boycott by the butchers, who were strong enough to persuade the master fleshers in June 1896 to refuse to sell to co-operative buyers on the Glasgow Corporation Market. The Corporation, however, forbade this discrimination and the farmers did not support the butchers. The latter saved their faces by arranging to sell privately in future, but this did not seriously obstruct the access of co-operative buyers to supplies. The next attack occurred in 1906, when the Associated Owners of Proprietary Medicines declared a boycott on the ground that the co-operative dividend was an act of price cutting. The C.W.S. replied by extending its drug works at Pelaw. Four years later the third and biggest struggle arose. In 1906 Lord Leverhulme had been brought into notoriety by Lord Northcliffe. The controversy cost the proprietors of the *Daily Mail* £50,000 in damages for libel, but neither the denouncers of the Soap Trust nor the public realised at first where Lever Bros. had been most badly hit. The working men and women of England had no reason to complain either of the quality of Sunlight Soap or of the working conditions in Lever's great factory at Port Sunlight, near Liverpool, but good co-operators felt that they ought not to patronise a trust and responded to the invitation of their Wholesale to purchase C.W.S. Soap Flakes and Parrot Brand in place of Lux and Monkey Brand. Accordingly in August 1910 Lever Bros. prosecuted a number of co-operative societies for selling an article different from one which their customers demanded. The action failed, and also the appeal. ' This action was an attempt to establish a new monopoly,' said Lord Justice Buckley. In the old days capitalist entrepreneurs had grown rich by exploiting the inventions of poor mechanics. Now working men co-operators stepped gratis, the law approving, into some of the commercial goodwill of a millionaire soap business.

Friends of co-operation were sometimes afraid that the movement would become by sheer success top-heavy and, as it was charged, materialistic. The record of the new century is sufficient to allay this fear. Because its fundamental principle is sound it is always throwing off new and fruitful efforts. Thus the early co-operators stood for education, and most of the societies divided a small portion of their profits for that purpose. When the State provided education free and when other working-class bodies entered the field of adult education, the educational activities of many co-operative societies languished. Of late years there has been a most successful reorganisation under the expert guidance of an Adviser of Studies, who from Holyoake House, the new home of the Co-operative Union in Manchester, directs the varied educational programme of the Central Education Committee and its allies. This programme includes technical instruction for co-operative employees and officials : general instruction grouped around the history and economics of co-operation : and the training of whole-time students at the co-operative Hostel in Manchester, which is designed as the nucleus of a great Co-operative College.　The missionary of to-day must be a trained enthusiast.　The Co-operative Educational Fellowship bands in a common brotherhood all those who care for cooperative education ; and in the Hostel under their Adviser of Studies a selected few are training for an intensive co-operative life.　The agricultural co-operators of Europe and the New World have approached co-operation from an angle different from that of the industrial co-operators of Europe and Great Britain.　In education the two find common ground.　The first question of the Canadian Wheat Pools is, How does the Old Country organise its co-operative education ?　And similarly industrial England has much to learn from agricultural Denmark.　At Belfast in their 1926 Congress British co-operators met to hear an address on Frederik Grundtvig and the Danish High School, which was the spiritual cradle of Danish co-operation.

In the re-awakening of interest in the non-commercial side of co-operation women have played a great part.　The woman after all is the main wage spender, and therefore it is she who makes or mars the co-operative store.　Up to 1900 her rôle was silent. Since then through the Women's Co-operative Guild she has come to the front, and besides asserting her rightful place in the movement, she has made a healthy invasion of spheres which were formerly considered to belong to men.　In particular the Women's Guild has aroused interest in the wages problem, in so far as it concerns women co-operative employees and women workers generally.　Both locally in filling gaps in co-operative membership and securing the support of co-operators for municipal welfare work, and nationally in the formation of a co-operative opinion in politics, women co-operators have led the way.

The early co-operators by saving their small dividends practised thrift.　There was a poetic justice in the order of the Registrar of Lincoln in 1878 that a certain poor agricultural labourer should make repayment of his debts to local tradesmen at a rate proportional to his probable dividends from the co-operative store.　By co-operation the working classes first cleared themselves of debt and then they accumulated savings.　They literally ate themselves into the possession of capital.　The spirit of thrift for a time found sufficient scope in the friendly society, the savings bank, and the local store.　In due season in response to new needs and greater powers local effort was supplemented by federal developments in banking and insurance, as narrated above (pp. 413-21).

The early co-operators found in the committee-room of the store a school of self-government.　But the machinery which sufficed for a small retail society was quite inadequate to direct a movement which Lord Rosebery fairly described in 1890 as a State within a State. The first store committees did their own buying and selling, their manager being only a shop-keeper. Then the manager was put in charge of the selling, while the committee reserved to itself the delicate tasks of tea tasting and butter sampling. As the society grew the chief business of the general manager became that of buyer for the central store and its branches, the departmental managers being directly responsible to the committee. To-day the stage has been reached in which the biggest retail societies either need or already have a general manager whose primary task is co-ordination. Correspondingly the work and position of the committee have changed. The first committeemen were the pioneers who founded the society. Then in a spirit of democracy service on the committee passed by rotation. But efficiency demanded a board of directors on which previous service should be a recommendation instead of a disqualification. This followed, but for long the members of the board received only nominal attendance fees. To-day in one large society at least there is a salaried full-time directorate.

So much for the executive. What part has the general membership in this democracy of consumers ? In the early days their control was very real, because they were in and about the store every day. As the society grew and branches were established, new machinery was found necessary. This took the form of local committees for the branches ; and to-day in some large societies there are conferences of local committees, which may be regarded as the embryo of a geographical representative legislature. But contact between the individual member and the central management is extremely desirable. Numbers prevent the General Meeting, whether it be the annual or quarterly meeting, from answering this purpose, by itself ; and therefore societies with many branches are following the practice of their federal wholesale and holding simultaneous meetings, with identical agenda for elections and the discussion of educational or business policy. The Wholesale Society holds quarterly meetings of delegates directly elected by its member stores ; and each of the eight divisions into which the territory of the C.W.S. is divided meets to discuss in advance and to vote upon the agenda which is to be taken at Manchester the week following.

Great as the co-operative movement was in the 19th century it remained almost to the end of it in the stage of probation. Only in a few industrial strongholds was the store the leading shop ; while among wholesale merchants the Wholesales were but two new and vigorous competitors. Since 1900, however, the relentless growth of the movement has carried it beyond the possibility of serious collapse ; and its task now is not so much to fight private trade as to accommodate its progress to the parallel efforts of trade unions and agricultural co-operators and to define its relations to municipal and national politics.

The co-operative societies have a labour problem which the structure of the store does nothing to solve. For neither as consumers nor as workers have the army of co-operative employees (which in 1925 were over 200,000 strong—engaged in production 94,000 and in distribution 110,000) found satisfaction in the scheme of the Co-operative Commonwealth. After the abolition of wage bonuses (1891) and of privileged purchases (1895) the employees of the C.W.S. in Manchester built up the Beswick Co-operative Society, which until 1896, contrary to co-operative tradition, had a wine and spirit licence. Presently the society came into conflict with neighbouring co-operative societies and was temporarily excluded from the Co-operative Union for refusing to agree to a boundary with the Manchester and Salford Equitable Co-operative Society. Similarly the Progress Co-operative Society formed by employees of the S.C.W.S. was untrue to type ; for it sold as near to cost as possible and freely to non-members. It was thus in fact a retail business with a limitation on shareholders' dividends.

When the Wholesales went into production they were agreeable that their employees should be members of the local craft unions, but they did not envisage the future status of their distributive employees ; for their consumer philosophy made them cold to the claims of the distributor, whether he were a private shop-keeper or their own servant. In 1891 the Manchester and District Co-operative employees formed an Association, which became in 1895 the Amalgamated Union of Co-operative Employees. This body grew until in 1920 its membership was 100,000, of whom 90,000 were co-operative employees, the remaining 10,000 belonging either to the National Union of Shop Assistants or to the unions in whose trade they worked. But as a special union for distributive employees in co-operative employment conflicts with the trade union principle of national organisation by trade or product, the present distribution of membership is between one of three bodies : the National Union of Co-operative Officials ; the National Union of Distributive and Allied Workers ; and the National Amalgamated Union of Assistant Warehousemen and Clerks. The productive employees remain members of their trade organisation as before. After 1900 the Amalgamated Union of Co-operative Employees conducted an agitation for better wages, which secured a minimum wage for adult males in the C.W.S. in 1907. In 1912 the principle was extended to women employees of the C.W.S. in response to pressure from the Women's Co-operative Guild. In 1911 the A.U.C.E. encouraged strikes against individual societies and between 1918 and 1924 engineered more than one disconcerting stoppage. The C.W.S. saw the storm coming and at one point organised a war chest with a guarantee fund from its store members of £427,000. But this development was very distressing to co-operators. The Co-operative Congress of 1916, considering that the existing joint committee of the Co-operative Union and Parliamentary Committee of the Trade Union Congress was not sufficient, set up a system of National and District Conciliation and Wages Boards. Through this machinery post-war breaches, though not averted, were softened, most of the employees' demands being conceded.

The co-operative stores have also an agricultural problem. At the end of the War the Retail Societies and Wholesales in Great Britain occupied and for the most part owned some 38,000 acres of land, which was used mainly for the raising of market garden produce, the fattening of store cattle and other purposes in which the stores had a direct interest. By the end of 1924, 157 societies in all occupied 72,000 acres, but they did not escape the results of new purchases at fancy prices and the general post-war depreciation in agriculture. In 1921–2–3 they incurred losses on their farms averaging £¼ million in each year, and the loss was thus substantially higher than the £100,000 odd charged as interest by the societies to themselves. Accordingly the Report submitted to Congress in 1926 urged that societies should abstain from general farming and concentrate on the supply of produce which their own departments can sell to their members.

However, while co-operative societies have been no more successful than individual farmers as producers, certain of them have for many years successfully adapted their structure to a rural membership. Thus Lincoln is an industrial town in a rural region, agricultural machinery being its staple manufacture. The Lincoln Society cultivates 600 acres of land and has furthermore a number of village branches. Most of these were established to supply a wage-earning population of agricultural labourers, navvies and railway men, but some of the members are small farmers. Under the inspiring leadership of Duncan McInnes, Chairman of the Lincoln Society, 1882–1903, a scheme was developed under which members supply the Society with butter, eggs, fruit and vegetables, and spend the proceeds if they so desire at the store. The Society has numerous shops in the town ; and the vans and motor-lorries which deliver bread and groceries to the branches collect farm produce in return.

In the 1880's both Wholesales went to Ireland in quest of butter, first establishing depots and then operating creameries. This brought them into conflict with the Irish farmer ; for though they acquired their first creameries in response to the requests of local farmers, they soon found themselves in rivalry with the co-operative creameries established by the Irish Agricultural Organisation Society from 1894 on. After a long controversy the C.W.S. parted with most of its creameries, 1908–12, but it retained that at Tralee, where it had also a bacon-curing establishment. If the ultimate test of co-operation be the enrichment of life by corporate effort the C.W.S. was going beyond its sphere in establishing creameries in Ireland. To the Irish farmers it was simply a proprietary concern, with a suspicious record of absorbing weaker brethren. Further the Irish creameries export most of their produce to Great Britain and much of this to co-operative stores ; and Irish agriculturists, farmers and labourers alike, have needs as consumers which are only partially met by the Agricultural Supply Societies. The Irish Agricultural Organisation Society is strong on the productive side. In 1925 it had a membership of 150,000 farmers and 325 creameries with a turnover of £5 millions, but its wholesale trading department is weak, having shown losses from 1921 to 1925. Arrangements were proceeding in 1927 for the re-organisation of the trading department and the association of the two British Wholesales in its management.

In 1906 the S.C.W.S. opened an agency at Winnipeg and later bought land in Saskatchewan, in order that Scottish co-operators might eat their own bread as they drank their own tea. This, of course, was technically impossible ; for in the process of shipment and storage the grain from a particular farm loses its identity. The S.C.W.S. therefore was nothing more than an absentee landlord in a country where absenteeism is fatal. In 1925 it sold its Hughton (Sask.) farm to a Community of Mennonites, who were unable to complete the transaction, and then to a land company for re-sale to individual farmers. Pushing back to the source here was an excess of literalism. The truer line of development is that which has followed upon the institution of the Wheat Pools in Canada and Australia : liaison with the Pool officials ; financial accommodation, as in the case of Australia ; and the institution of a central wheat-purchasing office in Liverpool. For if the Pools should succeed in what is their ideal, namely to eliminate the last remaining capitalist middleman, the consumers of Great Britain will find themselves

confronted by the agricultural producers of the New World
organised in the panoply of co-operation ; and Canadian co-
operators can talk the gospel of the producer as convincingly
as British co-operators talk that of the consumer.

Finally, the stores come into contact with the local and central
authorities of the State.   Between the co-operative store and the
municipality the relation is one of similar structure for different
purposes ;   for both are associations of consumers.   To the
municipality belongs the operation of monopolistic services, in
addition to the provision of social amenities which are not bought
or sold.   One task of the municipal authority and of the co-
operative store is to ensure that the life of the rural community
in their neighbourhood shall not be maimed by their industrialism.
For though peculiar reasons have hitherto retarded the growth
of agricultural co-operation in England and Scotland, it is hard
to resist the lesson of other countries that rural life demands
for its health an organisation of producers.   Membership in a
consumers' association is not enough.

The contact with the central authority covers law, finance
and politics.   After overcoming an early suspicion of association
in any form, the State readily granted to the Co-operative Movement what alone was asked of it—a legal framework within which
co-operators might work out their own salvation.   In the lawsuit
with the soap combine the judges were strongly on the side of
the co-operators against monopoly.   But the State is also a tax-
gatherer.   The co-operative stores do not pay income tax on their
dividends, not because of any statutory exemption but because
of its nature.   Successive Chancellors of the Exchequer and
the Departmental Committee on the Income Tax of 1905 have
decided that the purchase dividend was not profit in any sense in
which liability to income tax arose.   In 1915 co-operative societies
were subjected to Excess Profits duty, but this was repaid to them
in 1918.   In 1920 they were made liable to the Corporation
Profits tax to the extent of their undivided surplus, but in 1921
Parliament exempted them.   The proposal of the 1920 Royal
Commission on Income Tax to tax them on that part of their surplus
which was employed in increasing reserves and extending plant
fell through.[1]   Yet it is clear that if the Co-operative Movement
expands to the degree anticipated by its champions, a considerable
inroad will be made on the yield of the income tax.   When the
War necessitated the rationing of supplies the Government
had at its elbow a wonderful consumers' organisation in full
working order, of which it was singularly slow to make use.

---

[1] But it was adopted in principle in the Finance Act of 1933—see C. R. Fay,
' Co-operators and the State,' *Economic Journal*, Sept. 1933.

In the recruitment for the Forces the one-man business—the most wasteful form of distribution—enjoyed the greatest consideration, and the co-operative stores the least. Until Mr. Clynes was appointed Food Controller in 1918, the authorities showed themselves above the average in blindness to the economic evolution in their midst.

Born in the days when the feuds among Chartists were distracting working-class effort, the Co-operative Movement eschewed party politics ; indeed, political neutrality was almost as fundamental a part of the Rochdale system as the dividend on purchases. In 1917 the movement broke from its long past by deciding to seek direct representation in Parliament. Of this there was need in view of the expansion of the State into social affairs and the special problems of the War. The small group of five members who sat in Parliament as Co-operators in 1926 exerted an influence which harmonised not only with the traditions of co-operation but also with present national interests. They spoke for the consumer and free trade. Furthermore in a year when the community had to face a general conflict between the Government and organised wage-earners, they brought the solvent of the working-class wage-spender—of public opinion, as it is *not* expressed in the popular press. But the major problem is the relation of the Co-operative Movement to the Labour Party, and this is the object of anxious effort to-day. Once elected, the co-operative members work with the Labour Party. But should a co-operator run against a Labour candidate, as he might against a Conservative or Liberal ? Further, although no doubt the majority of active co-operators belong to the Labour Party, yet there are many Conservatives and Liberals in the Co-operative Movement. Are these to be exposed to the dilemma of a divided loyalty ? The easy solution would be neutrality, except where a candidate is co-operative. But this would be to purchase static fairness at the expense of dynamic service. For the future of the Labour Party depends on its power to develop a policy which is at once constructive and practical ; and this is precisely the strength of working-class consumers' co-operation. Tactful compromise will play a more important part in the solution than the strict logic which commends itself to some other lands.

Statistics have their uses, but for better or for worse Great Britain has parted from the days when her statisticians could unfold their array of world primacy and incessant increase. Quantity of product dominated in the 19th century. When quantity abates, must we revert to the nightmare of decline ? Should we not rather associate quantity with quality and prize it only when it is an index of qualitative social advance ? It so happens that figures of consumers' co-operation show ceaseless advance even through the racking decade which followed the Great War. Let co-operators not forget that this has been accomplished on the sterling foundations of that industry and commerce which they call capitalist, but which in fact provides them with the earnings they spend at their stores. Conversely let Industry and Commerce not forget that in the Co-operative Movement the nation possesses an engine, potent and reliable, as well for the maintenance of internal social peace as for the striking of a just bargain with the Continents which possess the foodstuffs and raw materials of the 20th century.

STATISTICS OF CONSUMERS' CO-OPERATION
MONEY IN MILLIONS STERLING

		1908		1925
Retail Societies in Great Britain and North of Ireland	Number	1,428	..	1,289
	Membership	2·4 m.	..	4·9 m.
	Share and Loan Capital	34·5 m.	..	100·6 m.
	Sales	69·7 m.	..	183·5 m.
	Surplus	10·7 m.	..	20·4 m.
English Wholesale Society	Share and Loan Capital	3·4 m.	..	6·9 m.
	Wholesale Trade	24·9 m.	..	57·7 m.
	Value of Production	5·7 m.	..	26·4 m.
Scottish Wholesale Society	Share and Loan Capital	2·7 m.	..	7·7 m.
	Wholesale Trade	7·5 m.	..	17·7 m.
	Value of Production	2·2 m	..	8·7 m.

SUPPLEMENT

A DECADE OF RATIONALISATION (1922–1932)

SOME years before the war Max Weber, the German historian, gave currency to the term, rationalisation. He applied it to the economic life which emerged in Europe in the age of the Renaissance, the Reformation and the Discoveries. This life was both rational and national : rational and experimental in opposition to the traditionalism and routine of the Middle Ages, national and protestant (or rather puritan) in opposition to the regimen of Empire and Papacy. To-day the world is again using the term to describe the efforts made to recover from, and learn from, the upheaval created by the Great War. It seems to have been employed first in Germany with reference to the reorganisation of German industry under the conditions imposed by the Peace Treaty. Owing to the contact with Reparations control from above was large, but when the world adopted the term, it had no close reference to the extension of the sphere of the state, i.e. to 'nationalisation,' the traditional policy of socialism. It signified rather a concerted departure from pre-war routine, however accomplished ; and in general organised labour looked with suspicion on a policy which laid emphasis on efficiency, mechanisation, scientific method, standardisation and the avoidance of waste. The war had accustomed the world to one kind of rationing, the apportionment of resources under the menace of scarcity ; and the peace compelled it to another kind, the control of markets under the menace of profit-killing excess. Immediately after the war there was a lust for ' decontrol,' but when the short post-war boom collapsed there arose a feeling that recovery must be planned. Thus the rationalisation of which we talk to-day stands in complete contrast with the process at work in 16th-century Europe. Then it manifested itself in the emergence of the individual and the relaxation of corporate control. It accepted without question the dictation of market price, competitively determined ; and it fortified itself by a philosophy first of natural liberty and then of utilitarian hedonism. Bentham was its eventual God. To-day *laissez-faire* is dead. All along the economic line we are striving to replace automatic adjustment by conscious control, extending to things hitherto believed unamenable to regulation, such as the direction of investment and the control of the price level. Each state, each industry, each great business has, or is feeling after, a plan. And just as the advent of modern arithmetic and double book-keeping favoured the genesis of competitive capitalism, so statistical science, with its index charts, trade barometers and business forecasting, is aiding the planned capitalism of our time. In Russia there is no god but Statistics. The change in attitude towards combination and monopoly within the last twenty years is truly remarkable. We welcome and urge combination where we used to dread and obstruct it. The deadly efficacy of substitution has robbed monopoly of its claws : for with modern science there is no commodity which cannot be imitated, no want which cannot be satisfied by an alternative route.

The old dread has vanished most completely in the case of the railway, which to mid-Victorian England was the monopolistic danger *par excellence*. In July 1932 the Railway Pool Committee invites the Ministry of Transport to bless the pooling arrangements of the L.M. and S. and L. and N.E. Railways, although the two control 70% of the general railway business. It sees on the one hand 'a vital national industry stricken during a period of unexampled depression to a point which threatens exhaustion,' and on the other hand a plan which promises relief. Similarly in August 1932 the Road and Rail Transport Conference presents an agreed report for ending the war between motor and rail. It recommends no forcing back of established traffic to the railway, but greatly increased taxation of heavy lorries, the stoppage in future of the diversion of unsuitable traffic to the roads and a licensing system which will terminate the present unrestricted entry into the haulage industry.

Free trade was formerly regarded as the greatest protection against trusts and other restraints upon trade. To-day some of those who still oppose a protective tariff are prepared to move to the more extreme restraint of import boards and quotas. The quota system already in operation for coal mining was applied by the Wheat Act of 1932 to domestic wheat growing, not to prevent excess of output, but to arrest decline, and to secure a market at a standard price (fixed at 10s. per cwt. till 1935). The operation of the Act is in the hands of a Wheat Commission. Thus under the voluntary Wheat Pool in Canada, the Federal Farm Board in America and the Wheat Commission in England the grain trade has been subjected to new controls in the interest of the producer. The legislation was not favoured by traders either in the coal or the grain trade ; and many question the wisdom of giving assistance to domestic wheat growers by a device which adds to the burden of a food tax the further burden of an elaborate and expensive control. The peculiar position of England, however, must be borne in mind. For from 1929 onwards, as each European nation stiffened its barriers against the cheap wheat of the New World, this country became the market for the world's distress surplus. The complement in the New World is the complete closing down of its labour market to European immigration. Birth control made its appearance before the sweeping restrictions on immigration : and where it was necessary before, it is doubly necessary now.

Changes in the technique of production are ceaseless. Now one science and now another is to the front. Coal is close to the point where it will be available in liquid form on terms that can challenge petroleum. We now have creaseless cotton. Instantaneous freezing permits the retention of the qualities of freshly caught fish—and so on. Business in general has not yet reached the point at which it can with advantage grow no larger ; and ever new lessons are being taught by the achievements of great consolidations, such as Unilever and Imperial Chemicals. Theorists are studying the structure of competitive industry in the light of an optimum and showing how there may be one optimum for technique, another for management and another for finance. In the view of Lord Melchett, the problem of big business is to combine central control with sufficient elasticity lower down, so that action may be neither arrested nor delayed, at the same time keeping a grip on essential features of policy such as finance, expenditure, sale and relations with other great groups of industrialists throughout the world. The last item is the distinctive one in rationalisation. And we come even closer to the new atmosphere if we look at the problem through the eyes of those who sell to the final consumer. With them demand comes first—except indeed in Russia where consumption is rationed and there is a chronic shortage of supply. ' The unit must be planned as a marketing entity before it is planned as a producing one.' ' The pre-requisite for all planning is a careful estimate of market conditions.'

Post-war London has grown remarkably in population and metropolitan grip. Here in their fullness can be seen those changes which are revolutionising the retail trade of the country : the great departmental store, with its mail-order department, the chain store, which sells to the million at low fixed prices with self-service and no advertisement : the chains of speciality shops—cafés, provisions, tailoring, boot and shoe. The central element common to all is mass buying. They have overturned the old-time wholesale house and commercial traveller, the old-fashioned display of white ' Manchester ' goods, bought twice a year and left to sell themselves. They buy in such mass that they can offer a ceaseless variety of colours and styles. Instead of fearing a change of fashion, they welcome and provoke it.

Since the depression there has been a marked change in the type of purchasing. Rich purchasers of a few big articles are over-shadowed by the numerous small purchases of all classes. Spending power has declined since 1929, but not seriously. It is sustained not only by the higher real wages of those in employ-ment, but also by the existence of the Social Services. The bottom, therefore, never falls out of the market, as happens sometimes in a community of farmers. The big retailers are studying, as never before, the behaviour of demand. They are in lively competition with one another and with the Co-operative Societies, whose happy combination of retail and wholesale society admits them to a full share of London's growing trade ; and their buying range reduces to a minimum the danger of exploitation at the hands of those who may try to obtain a partial monopoly of production or transport.

The figure of insured males unemployed (Great Britain and Ireland) was 941,000 in 1924 and remained around the million mark until the onset of depression at the end of 1929. It then rose rapidly, passing the 2 million in February 1931, and in June 1932 it was 2,358,000. The period of aggravated unemployment was also the period of steadily declining wholesale prices, and the phenomenon is world-wide. This country, therefore, in common with others, officially desires some rise of these prices to the neighbourhood, say, of the average for 1929. But it is at least possible that the progress of rationalisation is itself adding to unemployment. There is little warrant for the view that the economies of rationalisation will cause such an increase in the demand for the product as to reabsorb the labour which in the first instance it displaces.

The International Labour Office in *The Social Aspects of Rationalisation* (1931) puts it thus:

The effect of constant new progress being made is that new workers are constantly being dismissed, even before the others have been able to find a new job. The consequent unemployment should be con-sidered to an increasing extent as a sort of physiological unemployment. By this we mean a sort of unemployment that must be accepted as normal, since its causes cannot be abolished without injuring general progress. This idea affords an additional argument in favour of developing unemployment insurance for granting fair compensation to the victims of an evil for which society as a whole is responsible and which to some extent is inherent in progress itself.

The Chancellor of the Exchequer is concerned with ration-alisation to the extent that, when the revenue permits, he may be able to find money for the reorganisation of industry. This was the distinctive feature in the budget of 1928, which made preliminary provision for the Rating Relief Act of 1929. Local rates, in the opinion of the Government, were ruining industry and dragging down local government by drying up the sources of local revenue. Some part of the burden, therefore, was transferred to central shoulders, and special favour was shown to distressed industries, including agriculture. In 1930 and in 1931 (with its supplementary budget) the Chancellor was fighting hard, in the teeth of an economic blizzard, to balance his budget. The standard rate of income tax was raised first to 4s. 6d. and then to 5s., at which rate it was continued in 1932. In 1930 and 1931 Mr. Snowden was Chancellor of the Exchequer. He evinced his loyalty to fiscal orthodoxy in 1930 by refusing to renew certain safeguarding duties (though the McKenna duties were retained from necessities of revenue) ; and in 1931 he indulged his life-long radicalism by introducing a land tax of 1d. in the pound on capital values, to take effect after the necessary valuation of the land. His declared purpose was to abolish the scandal of the private appropriation of land values created by the community. But it soon became clear that the financial situation was worsening rapidly and that no bearable increase of taxation would bridge the gap. The May Committee on National Expenditure, appointed in March and reporting in July 1931, proposed drastic economies of £96 million in all in unemployment relief, educational salaries and the pay of the Services. The reluctance of the Labour Government to accept a cut in Social Services was a factor in precipitating the political crisis which resulted in the formation of the National Government at the end of 1931. By economies on the one hand and a successful appeal to income taxpayers for the punctual payment of the three-quarters instalment due in January Mr. Neville Chamberlain, the new Chancellor of the Exchequer, balanced the budget of 1932 (and incidentally repealed the new land tax). Whatever the disadvantages of economy and high taxation, it may be stated with confidence that without a balanced budget the great conversion of July 1932, which put British credit on a 3½% basis, would have been impossible. The Treasury announced on August 15, 1932, that out of £2,086 million of 5% War Loan, £1,850 million had been converted. The final total of Dissented Stock was £165 million, or 8%, just as in Goschen's conversion of 1888.

Fiscal policy, too, has been brought within the compass of rationalisation. Without commerce the colonial empire of the 18th century would have had no substance. It foundered not because commerce was the essence of the pact, but because there was no constitutional equality among the parties to it. This equality, however, is complete both in law and fact since the Statute of Westminster, 1931. After the war imperial preference became a lively and also a party issue. It made some progress when the Conservatives were in power and halted when they were in opposition. However, the spirit of imperial cooperation, without which imperial preference is an irritant, advanced throughout. At the Imperial Conference of 1930 Great Britain declared that while her interest precluded an economic policy which would injure her foreign trade or add to the burdens of her people, this interest did not preclude cooperation or market propaganda. She agreed to reconstitute the Empire Marketing Board and to retain for three years the existing preferences. Since it began active work in 1925, the Board has achieved notable results in stimulating the demand for home-grown and empire-grown produce. In stimulating demand it reacted favourably on the quality of production and packing : witness its investigations into the consumption of canned fruits and vegetables and the remarkable increase of home canning in 1931 and 1932. The increased consumption of empire tobacco from a trifle in 1913 to about 30 million out of about 200 million lbs. in 1929–31 reflects not only the stimulus of preference (which in 1926 was stabilised for 10 years at a 25% rebate of the general duty), but also the results of judicious advertisement, supported by improving quality. In its various tasks the Empire Marketing Board was assisted by three things:

(1) It touched patriotic feeling. It received from the trade, the Press and the public authorities, local and central, a large amount of virtually free advertisement. It makes the same appeal as the National Mark, which is in process of introduction, product by product, under the Agricultural Produce (Grading and Marketing) Act, 1928. (2) It was moving with the trend of trade. The Imperial Economic Committee (13th Report) compared the trade of 1903 with that of 1925–28. It found : ' In 1927 Great Britain and North Ireland utilised round about 40% more produce from the Empire Overseas and only about 15% more of foreign produce. Meanwhile the export trade declined in volume, but that to the Empire Overseas about 9% as compared with a fall of nearly 30% in that to foreign countries. As a whole, trade with the Empire Overseas increased by some 10% or 12%, while that with foreign countries was stationary and declined to some extent.' (3) Its work was supported by imperial liaison in other fields : e.g. the Merchandise Marks Act of 1926 : the Cinema Films Act of 1927, prescribing an increasing quota of empire-produced films for British use : the uniform standards of the British Engineering Association : trade arrange-

ments between the British Steel Export Association and the Canadian Iron and Steel Industry : co-ordinated research in such problems as the diminution of damage in transport.

Great Britain, therefore, went to Ottawa in July 1932 not merely with something to offer in the shape of preference (for the Import Duties Act of 1932,[1] which prescribed, with exceptions, a 10% tariff, provided for preference to the Dominions at a rate to be determined by November 1932) ; but also with a tradition of recent co-operation and an awareness to possibilities. She and they are searching after a programme of complementary activities in types and ranges of goods, which it may be necessary to revise from time to time as local industry grows in the newer countries of the Empire. If a tradition can be established against the sudden and arbitrary raising of duties in deference to the wishes of particular industries, that of itself will be a great boon. The Government went to Ottawa, with the full support of British industrialists, to work out an imperial plan ; and the results, as announced on August 22, 1932, are in brief as follows :

Great Britain and the Dominions have signed agreements, which will last at least five years. Great Britain continues the preferences in the Tariff Act of 1932, and in addition imposes new or increased duties on foreign imports ; in particular, wheat 2s. per bushel, butter 15s. per cwt., raw fruit, dried fruits, milk products, various rates ; linseed (of special importance to Indian agriculture) 15% ad val., copper 2d. per lb. The new duties on wheat and raw metals are conditional upon supply to Britain at not over world prices. Correspondingly, foreign dumping is precluded by a general agreement to prohibit imports which through State action will frustrate the effect of the preferences. Meat imports are to be governed by a programme of quantitative regulation designed first to encourage home production and then to give to the Dominions an expanding share of Britain's import trade. The restrictions on live cattle from Canada are relaxed.

The Dominions grant Great Britain increased preferences by the removal or lowering of existing duties and agree, through the machinery of their Tariff Boards, to give to British producers ' full opportunity of reasonable competition on the basis of the relative cost of economical and efficient production.'

There are those who condemn the new fiscal policy as an aggravation of economic nationalism. The World Economic

[1] 22 Geo. V, c. 8. The First Schedule exempts from the 10% ad valorem duty wheat, meat, books, and numerous raw materials. Section 2 sets up an Import Duties Advisory Committee, with power (s. 3) to impose an additional rate on ' articles of luxury or articles of a kind which are being produced or are likely within a reasonable time to be produced in the United Kingdom in quantities which are substantial in relation to United Kingdom consumption.'

Conference summoned in 1927 tried in vain for freer trade : then for a tariff truce among the countries of Europe, which lapsed through failure to ratify. Great Britain has so valuable a trade of import and export with countries like Denmark and the Argentine and such heavy investments in South America and other foreign parts that she cannot acquiesce in a programme which aims at the erection of new barriers. We must visualise for the future a British tariff scheme of this type : a general tariff ; above that a discriminating tariff reserved for retaliation ; below that a conventional tariff with countries with whom she has tariff conventions ; finally, below the conventional tariff the imperial tariff. Such a scheme strikes, of course, at the root of the policy of free trade and most favoured nation treatment bequeathed by Cobden. But if negotiation for better terms takes the form of saying to foreign countries, ' This is the limit of our concession, grant us a similar rate and you too shall have it,' Great Britain would retain tariff autonomy here, apart from her commitments to the Empire ; and in view of the importance of her market to certain countries, an impetus might be given to a general reduction of tariffs. In that event the new imperial tariff will be in retrospect a stepping-stone to those freer economic relations which Geneva sought in vain.

The return of Great Britain to the gold standard at the old parity in 1925 involved a process of deflation which reacted injuriously on the export trade. Coal exporters, for example, received some 10% less in sterling than they had done a short while before ; and the attempt to bring wages into line with receipts was in part responsible for the paralysing coal strike of 1926. The final step in the return to pre-war tradition was taken in 1928 when the Treasury and Bank notes were amalgamated as one issue under the Bank of England, and the new fiduciary issue was fixed at £260 million (the amount of the actual maximum of Treasury and Bank of England notes in 1927). Some elasticity, however, was introduced by the power given to the Treasury to authorise a temporary fiduciary increase.

The Macmillan Report on Finance and Industry (June 1931) set out with authority the sequence of events since 1925. It emphasised the dominating position of America, the boom and consequent drain of gold to America, the superimposed drain of gold to France in the process of the stabilisation of the franc, and the serious consequences of the sudden cessation of foreign lending by creditor countries as the boom drew to a close. The gold standard was not working as it did before the war. In the 19th century international trade was not so much on a gold basis, as on a sterling basis, which in fact was gold. With London as the centre, free gold, free trade and continuous foreign lending went hand in hand ; and the economic fabric was such that changes in the stock of gold affected speedily the prices and costs of the countries concerned, lowering them when it went out and raising them when it came in. But by the policy of the Federal Reserve Board the new gold was sterilised (dare we say ' rationalised ' ?) : and by the operation of the flexible tariff a barrier was automatically opposed to the inflow of just those extra imports which in the absence of new lending were required to secure an equilibrium in the balance of payments. Hence at a time when there was no new Rand coming into production, the existing stock of gold in the world was most unequally distributed. By the end of 1931 three-quarters of the whole was in two countries, the United States and France, the extra gold taken by France in the last five years being about equal to the new gold mined. The Macmillan Committee drew special attention to the slender basis of liquid resources on which the Bank of England operated, particularly in view of the short-term balances held by foreign countries in sterling ; and their fear was soon justified.

In June 1931 the international crisis began in Austria upon the failure of the Credit Anstalt. From Austria the crisis spread to Germany ; and the Bank of England gave assistance to both. The Hoover moratorium on inter-government debts eased the situation, but as the crisis widened, the drain on London continued. Momentary relief was secured by the issue of extra notes under the emergency clause of the Act of 1928 and by the credits secured from the Bank of France and the Federal Reserve Bank of New York (£25 million from each). But meanwhile England was involved in a political crisis over the balancing of the budget, which the Government considered indispensable to the restoration of confidence ; and the last straw was added by the report of mutiny in the fleet at Invergordon over the cuts in pay. On September 21, 1931, the Act to suspend the operation of the gold standard was hurriedly passed, the Treasury being authorised to take measures for meeting difficulties arising in connection therewith. Pursuant to this the Finance Act of 1932, Part IV, created an exchange equalisation account with funds not exceeding £150 million ' to be invested in securities or in the purchase of gold in such manner as they think best adapted for checking undue fluctuations in the exchange value of sterling.' In terms of the New York dollar sterling moved from around the old parity of $4·86 to 3·37 (average of December 1931) : which was followed by a slow improvement to 3·75 (average of April 1932), and then by another fall.

The departure from sterling, because it was resisted to the

uttermost, did not impair confidence.   It brought relief to British finance and industry, though causing loss to foreign holders of sterling.   While there seems to be no desire for, or intention of, a return to gold at the old parity, the future of sterling is as yet (August 1932) unknown.   Some desire the speedy stabilisation of the pound at a workable parity somewhat lower than the old : others favour the continuation of what is for the time being a managed currency.   It would be misleading to say that the dividing line is between those who desire a return to the impersonal tyranny of gold and those who would ' rationalise ' it by management.   For both are agreed that the gold standard cannot work unless the conditions are deliberately created in which this is possible.   The difference concerns the point at which management is to occur.   Meanwhile the Lausanne Agreement of 1932, by reducing reparations to a shadow of their original astronomical size, has taken the first step towards the abolition of the international unreason which causes kegs of gold to move from country to country in the place of genuine trade.   If western capitalism founders in our time, posterity surely will give as its verdict, ' Suicide, whilst of unsound mind.'

Note.—The *Economist* of October 22, 1932, contains an Ottawa Supplement in three parts : I. The British Concessions ; II. The Dominion Concessions ; III. General Considerations.   Part III is controversial, and hostile to the Ottawa Agreements.   The constitutional objection was effectively met by Sir John Simon (House of Commons, October 20).   But I agree with the *Economist* in its strong condemnation of ' quotas and other quantitative import restrictions.'

NEW LITERATURE—1928–1932 (JULY)

INTRODUCTION

The Wealth of Nations

SCHOLARS are always at work directly or indirectly upon Adam Smith. For he revealed not merely the *principia* of a new science, but the flowering of a new order of society, resting on capital, competition and laissez-faire. The reprinting of Richard Cantillon's *Essay on the Nature of Trade* of 1755 (edited by Henry Higgs for the Royal Economic Society, 1931) does not diminish his stature. Consistently acute and pursuing with imagination lines of abstract thought, Cantillon is the father of Ricardo and Cournot rather than of Adam Smith. All three lack the catholic appeal of the *Wealth of Nations*. In the University of Chicago Commemoration Lectures, *Adam Smith 1776–1926* (1928), Melchior Palyi, discoursing on the *Introduction of Adam Smith on the Continent*, proves this in detail. The Continent devoured Adam Smith because he spoke to it from the mother country of industrialism in persuasive terms of applicable things. He reached Germany *via* Göttingen in Hanover, which then belonged to the King of England. His free trade was welcome to Hamburg, an emporium of commerce, and to Prussia, an exporter of grain. Stein was to emancipate the peasants, and Adam Smith stood for liberty ; Hardenberg was to dissolve the gilds, institutions to which Adam Smith also was utterly opposed. In France he speedily displaced the Physiocrats, whose contempt for commerce was fatal to them in an industrial age. Simonde de Sismondi and J. B. Say incorporated him into their books ; and through these two France, though never too sincerely, learned the economic philosophy of shopkeeping England.

James Bonar, *The Tables Turned* (1930), gives to perfection the classical atmosphere—*Adam Smith among his Books* (and here we should have by our side *The Catalogue of the Library of Adam Smith*, prepared for the Royal Economic Society by Dr. Bonar, 1932) ; *The Malthusiad : David Ricardo* (which we may take as introduction to Mr. Sraffa's forthcoming edition of his works) ; and finally, *John Stuart Mill, the Reformer*. Dr. Bonar imagines these great ones in Elysium, awakened to speech by our memory of them. It would be good to talk also with Nassau Senior, as we now might do through S. Leon Levy's masterly reconstruction of Nassau Senior's Oxford lectures of 1847–52, under the title *Industrial Efficiency and Social Economy* (2 vols., 1928). Senior in his lectures drew fully on his experience as a commissioner for the Poor Laws and the Hand-loom Weavers. To the historian he is more illuminating than his contemporary, Mill.

Will anyone ever write a new Wealth of Nations ? Virtually

H. G. Wells has essayed the task in *The Work, Wealth and Happiness of Mankind* (1932). Mr. Wells is at once a scientist and social novelist. He writes brilliantly on the evolution of technique, on the conquest of substance, distance, hunger and climate. This new effort at a Wealth of Nations is compared with the great original in a review article in the *Economic Journal* (Sept. 1932).

PART I

FISCAL POLICY AND FINANCE

C. I. *From Walpole to Pitt*

The *Cambridge History of the British Empire* (Vol. I, 1929) surveys colonial origins ; and in C. 20, *Mercantilism and the Colonies*, J. F. Rees deals thoroughly with this side of trade policy. Mercantilism he defines as the economic expression of militant nationalism—which is good, provided that ' militant ' suggests ' naval ' in the case of England. Most refreshingly, he does not wallow in the details of the Navigation Laws. He emphasises the growth to predominance of sugar and the West India interest, the new value given to the northern colonies of America, as they grew in population and had need of manufactures from England, and the persistence of debt and financial embarrassment among colonists lacking a sufficiency of stable money and depending on one or two fluctuating crops. G. S. Graham's *British Policy and Canada 1774–1791* (1930) shows mercantilism dying hard. Having lost the American colonies, England tried to erect a new triangle of trade : Great Britain, Canada and the West Indies. But economic forces were too powerful. What the loyal colonies wanted and what they finally achieved was a direct trade of Canadian flour and lumber in exchange for West Indian molasses and rum.

Although, as yet, there is no full study of Pitt's economic policy as a whole, first as peace and then as war minister, one side of his work has been analysed anew in E. L. Hargreaves' *The National Debt* (1930), Cs. 6–9. This book is, further, of importance in that it fills the gaps between the landmarks of famous sinking funds and examines alternative methods of relieving the burden of debt—for example, terminable annuities and conversions. Goschen's conversion, described in full in C. 12, is pronounced to be ' undoubtedly the most successful operation of its kind that has ever been performed on the National Debt.' The principal involved was some £600,000,000 ; and the reduction of interest from 3 per cent. to 2½ per cent. brought a saving of £3,000,000 ; a trifle, indeed, when compared with the saving of £23,000,000 arising from the conversion of War Fives in 1932.

C. III. *Peel, 1788–1850*

Three recent books, written from different angles, exalt the statesmanship of Peel : A. A. W. Ramsay, *Sir Robert Peel* (1928) ;

G. Kitson Clark, *Peel and the Conservative Party 1832–41* (1929);
D. G. Barnes, *History of the English Corn Laws 1660–1846* (1930).
Mr. Barnes rises to unqualified admiration when he reaches Peel. If
the part of Cobden was decisive, it was because he converted Peel.
' The repeal of the Corn Laws, without the active support of Peel, was
impossible *at this time.*' Mr. Kitson Clark does not go beyond 1841,
but all that he says prepares the way most luminously for the great
ministry of 1841–6. Peel was as truly and ' abusedly ' a national
minister in 1846 as was England's Prime Minister of 1931. He put
the needs of his country above the advantage of his party and of
himself. He had always done so. In opposition he had refused to
promise the repeal of the malt tax or to oppose the new Poor Law
because he knew that both were necessary. He was always having to
restrain or oppose his friends—a crazy King, reactionary lords, violent
Orangemen. But he was a conservative in that he conserved the
State. Dr. Ramsay's work exhibits the many-sidedness of Peel,
especially when he was in office. In foreign affairs he pursued peace,
regaining the confidence of France whom Palmerston had estranged.
In Ireland, while ready to fight for the Union, he tried to continue the
moderation of the Whigs, but O'Connell declined a Tory alliance. In
fiscal reform and factory reform, as well as in corn law repeal, he had
to fight the ' malice domestic ' of Disraeli and others. He carried
repeal, but could not survive it, because 1846, unlike 1829 or 1867,
involved for Tories a sacrifice of material interest as well as of principle.
Moderate in his approach to every problem, Peel towered above his
fellows in a crisis. The portraits in these books suggest the man.

C. IV.   *Gladstone 1809–1898*

Gladstone's generation worshipped him, and in this mood Morley
and Buxton wrote. Free trade, however, is passing away, and it is
therefore desirable for those who still believe in him to emphasise the
other side of his system, his genius for economy and sound finance.
F. W. Hirst, an old disciple, does this in *Gladstone as Financier and
Economist* (1931). Not only did Gladstone delight in economy, but he
converted the nation to his delight. The fear that an income tax
would encourage public extravagance is probably the reason for his
hostility to this best of all taxes. It has been customary to think of
Gladstone as indifferent to Empire, but as Mr. Hirst shows, referring to
Dr. Paul Knaplund's *Gladstone and Britain's Imperial Policy* (1926),
Gladstone passed from a rather pedantic classicism, based on his
study of Greece and Rome, to a large sympathy with the ideal of a
British Commonwealth of Nations, such as inspired the radical Lord
Durham (see Chester New, *Lord Durham* (1929) and, in particular, his
valuable note on the Theorists of 1830, p. 374). Indeed, we owe the
preservation of the Empire in the nineteenth century to Radicals and
Liberals, as surely as we owe free trade to the Tories from Pitt to the
youthful Gladstone himself.

That the Anglo-French Treaty of 1786 originated with the

Physiocrat, Dupont de Nemours, and was pressed from the side of France, has long been known. Now, it appears, we must think similarly of the Treaty of 1860, which we call Cobden's Treaty. This is the burden of A. L. Dunham's *Anglo-French Treaty of Commerce of 1860 and the Progress of the Industrial Revolution in France* (1930). The French archives contain the Basis of a Plan, the work of Michel Chevalier, on which the Treaty is clearly based. The crucial meeting was between Cobden, Chevalier and the Emperor Napoleon at St. Cloud in 1859. But Chevalier's part has been forgotten, perhaps because of the unpopularity of the treaty in France. While Cobden became a national hero, Chevalier earned little praise and much abuse. Napoleon's readiness was determined by considerations of foreign policy and a solicitude for the welfare of the working-class. Did France, in concluding this treaty, blunder a second time? This book suggests a cautious ' no.' The manufacturers made good use of the imperial loan granted to them to sustain the new competition; and the textile districts advanced notably in technique and scale of operation. But the pace was not revolutionary. France never had, in England's sense, an Industrial Revolution.

C. VI. *Currency and Banking*

It would seem almost that economic historians are gifted with prescience, so timely are the recent additions to the history of currency and credit. In the *Economic History Review*, Vol. I, No. 2 (1928), *Credit in Medieval Trade*, M. Postan shows how sale on credit was the financial basis of medieval trade, permeating every economic relation. Out of this developed naturally organised dealings in the instruments of credit, the buying and selling of bills of exchange, and the like. For this we turn to the articles of R. D. Richards in the *Economic Journal* (*Economic History*) and the *Harvard Journal of Economic and Business History*, and to his *Early History of Banking in England* (1929), which makes brilliant use of original documents belonging to the Exchequer, the Treasury and the Bank of England. The origin of the goldsmith's cheque, we learn, was the note drawn on the Exchequer by pensioners, annuitants, and holders of ripened debentures. Previous to the goldsmith bankers were the ' exchanging merchants ' (as we should say, merchant bankers); the exchange brokers dealing in bullion; the scriveners, whose original business was the writing of bonds; the corn bodger and the wool brogger, the latter the banker of the country weaver and thus a precursor of the country bank. C. 3 of *Early History* analyses the extent and significance of the so-called Stop of the Exchequer in 1672; while C. 4 passes in review the various predecessors, projected or actual, of the Bank of England (the nation's public bank)—the Orphans' Fund of the City of London, the Million Bank, Chamberlen's Land Bank and others. Finally, in *Economic Journal* (*Economic History*), Jan. 1928, he gives a full-dress picture of *Edward Bakewell, a Pre-Bank of England English Banker*. Students of banking history are greatly in Mr. Richards' debt.

W. Marston Acres' *The Bank of England from Within 1694–1900* (2 vols., 1921) provides a fund of entertainment. It does not tell us as much as we should like to know about the growth of banking policy, the use of the discount rate, the relations with the Government and other banks, but we see how the staff lived and worked, the wages paid (and the perquisites), the measures taken to enforce discipline, the extension and layout of the Bank's premises ; and there are many good stories of forgeries, alarums and the solemn conservatism of the Direction.

A. E. Feavearyear, *The Pound Sterling* (1931), is the most apposite of all. He gives us the history of England's money of account from the earliest time to 1928. The word 'sterling,' he rules, comes from 'star' or 'starling,' an emblem on the coin, and not from the money of the Easterlings. The early centuries were afflicted by debasement, which stopped as far as the rulers were concerned in the reign of Elizabeth. Mr. Blondeau's mill of 1663 put the clipper out of business. The work of Lowndes and Newton is carefully appraised in Cs. 6 and 7, which explain the obscure course by which England arrived at a gold standard. As to the origin of domestic banking, it would seem that we are justified in thinking still that about 1640 the goldsmiths came into sudden and decisive prominence. They were the creators of that which is of the essence of banking as we know it, a fiduciary currency within the nation. At this time they displaced the scriveners as keepers of merchants' cash, and they made then great profits from melting the new silver which the Spanish Treaty of 1630 brought to London for coining. The second half of the book is occupied with the evolution of central banking, with emphasis on the bank's jealous guardianship of the standard of value. The author does less than justice, perhaps, to the part played by Ricardo in inspiring the Bullion Committee ; and he writes of modern developments with more confidence than his material seems to warrant.

To appreciate the international standing of London as a financial centre, it is necessary to go outside England, as, for example, in A. S. J. Baster, *The Imperial Banks* (1929), where the evolution of banking in India and other parts of the Empire in contact with, and often under management from, London is portrayed.

Finally, we have the historical chapters in J. M. Keynes, *Treatise on Money* (1930). The influence of Spanish silver on the economy of Europe has always excited the interest of theorists ; and here, it seems, there is between Mr. Keynes and Adam Smith a great opposition. Mr. Keynes would like to believe that the mines of Mexico and Potosi and the treasure ship of Mr. Phipps precipitated Europe into progress and industrialism. Whereas Adam Smith says scornfully : ' It is not by the importation of gold and silver, that the discovery of America has enriched Europe ' . . . Rather ' by opening a new and inexhaustible market to all the commodities of Europe, it gave occasion to new divisions of labour and improvements of art, which, in the narrow circle of the ancient commerce, could never have taken place for want of a market to take off the greater part of their produce ' (I. 413–14).

PART II

TRADE AND TRANSPORT

C. **VII.**   *The Course of Foreign Trade*

The key to Part II is the evolution of Great Britain from merchant carrier to industrial producer. Only if we understand this transition is the momentum of eighteenth-century England comprehensible. Carrying was overseas carrying. The importance of foreign commerce is well brought out in the two new volumes of E. Lipson's *Economic History of England, The Age of Mercantilism* (2 vols., 1931). Vol. II, C. II, contains a weighty account, company by company, from the Merchant Adventurers to the South Sea Company, of the various companies by which the foreign trade of England was conducted. Vol. III, C. IV, The Mercantile System, describes the growth of colonial trade, *i.e.* with the West Indies and American mainland. Mr. Lipson follows Schmoller in interpreting mercantilism in the broad sense of economic nationalism. He shows in one field of activity after another the advance from a municipal to a national view ; and illustrates by quotation and résumé the progress of mercantile thought. Mr. Lipson is equally thorough in his sketch of industrial evolution, industry by industry ; and it is of great advantage to be able now to follow each of the leading industries through their evolution from, say, 1500 to the eve of the Industrial Revolution.

The concept of a metropolitan market, advanced in C. VII, section 3 of the text was taken from N. S. B. Gras. In his *Stages in Economic History* (*Journal of Economic and Business History*, May 1930) Mr. Gras discusses the value and limitation of ' stages.' We have stages based on the type of society, as in Adam Smith (hunting, pastoral, agricultural, commercial), and in Karl Marx (feudalism, capitalism, socialism) ; stages based on exchange, as in Hildebrand (barter, money, economy, credit economy) ; or on industrial organisation, as in Bücher (production for home consumption, retail handicraft, wholesale handicraft, centralised machine industry). Finally, we may take the range of the market : village, town, nation, world. Mr. Gras argues that the stage method may be of genetic value in explaining how one stage grows out of another, but he warns us against hasty correlations of different types of stage ; and he conceives of the metropolitan market as the stage beyond the town market. This concept certainly avoids one pitfall. England was not a national trader before she was a world trader. Within the shell of commercial empire and overseas trade she grew to be a great national producer. There was in her history no evolution from town to national and then to world market.

C. **VIII.**   *Ports and Merchant Shipping*

C. Wright and C. E. Fayle, *History of Lloyd's from the founding of Lloyd's Coffee House to the present day* (1928), is authoritative, and displaces, of course, the slender account given in the text.   Mr. Wright signs as Chairman of Lloyd's Brokers' Association.   The book is lavishly illustrated with plates and facsimiles ; and as it would be presumptuous to summarise a long and intricate story in a few sentences, the student is referred to the review by C. R. V. Coutts in the *Economic Journal* of March 1929.

C. IX.   *Roads and Canals*

It is always dangerous to study the evolution of modern technique with one country alone in mind.   This danger is altogether absent from C. E. R. Sherrington's *Economics of Rail Transport in Great Britain* (1928) ;   for the author writes with full knowledge and personal experience of American transportation.   This is not a history, so much as a treatise with a historical background.   But the background is often in great detail.   Thus Vol. I, Cs. 2 to 6 contain a detailed history of each of the main systems of to-day.   Four chapters are of general historical interest : Vol. I, C. 11, Growth of Government Regulation, 1830–1900 ;   C. 12, Government Regulation, 1921–5 ;   Vol. II, C. 13, Road Competition ;   C. 14, State Ownership.

PART III

AGRICULTURE AND INDUSTRY

C. XII.   *Agriculture*

In the decade before the war there was hardly a year in which some important work did not appear upon enclosure, tenancy or the condition of the agricultural population, and it is symptomatic, perhaps, of the lessening importance of agriculture that the output since then has been very small.   For a general view R. E. Prothero (Lord Ernle), *English Farming, past and present* (1st edition 1912), in company with H. L. Gray, *English Field Systems* (1915), still holds the field.   We have, however, two re-issues of standard works : Mr. and Mrs. G. D. H. Cole's fully annotated edition of *Cobbett's Rural Rides* (1930) ;   and T. E. Gregory's reprint in facsimile, with introduction, of *Tooke and Newmarch's History of Prices* (1928).   A reference to Agricultural, Farming, Drainage, Harvests in Tooke's superb index will indicate its value to students of nineteenth-century agriculture.   For the eighteenth century there is a challenging article by T. H. Marshall (*Economic History Review*, Vol. II, No. 1, 1929), *Jethro Tull and the* '*New Husbandry*' *of the Eighteenth Century*, which constrains us to ask, Was Jethro Tull a fraud ?   His points are : (1) Though a good practical farmer and a national force in introducing the drill and the horse-hoe, Tull was a bad scientist, publishing false theories at a time when others were exploring a better way.   (2) His principles of continuous wheat and no manure for wheat were bad.   By insisting on the horse-hoe for wheat, he forced himself to misuse his drill and sow wide.   (3) While his disciples in the 1760's were advertising these erroneous principles, other reformers were busy with numerous practical suggestions of great value and effectively exposed Tull's errors.

C. XIII. *Steam Power and the Engineers*

Erich Roll's *An Early Experiment in Industrial Organisation, A History of the Firm of Boulton and Watt, 1775–1805* (1930), enhances the significance of this great firm in the genesis of modern industrialism. In 1795 (again a five !) the control of the firm passes to the second generation, James Watt Junior and Matthew Robinson Boulton ; and they complete the transition from a firm of engineers drawing income from royalties to a great engineering factory drawing profits from manufacture. Soho Foundry was erected ; and new methods were introduced in costing, salesmanship, division of labour, assembly and routing of materials, payment of wages and welfare schemes. We are impressed by the high degree of the planning. We seem to be listening to the things that a twentieth-century American efficiency expert would have recommended, if he had been called into life in 1795.

It is the distinction of the school of economic historians whose father was the late George Unwin that they release and synthesise a mass of local business records hitherto unknown or barely known. This virtue is very clear in T. S. Ashton and J. Sykes, *The Coal Industry in the Eighteenth Century* (1929). Geography, technique, structure, labour conditions, Scottish collier serfdom and the Northumberland bond are analysed. The general impression is that of an industry which, though causing crucial change elsewhere, was itself a rude and loosely organised handicraft. The interpenetration of coal with the iron and steel industries belongs, we are reminded, to the nineteenth century. Another general conclusion relates to that hotly debated question, Was the worker better off, say, in 1837 than before the Industrial Revolution ? As regards coal, the authors reply, the conditions and wages of the adult collier improved, ' but only a very determined meliorist, blinded by a preconceived theory, could assert with confidence that it was better to be a collier's child in the opening years of Victoria than in those of George II.'

C. XIV. *The Age of Iron and Steel*

The most difficult part of economic history to teach or write is always that of the last generation. If we stop our story at 1870 we convey the impression that the crucial changes associated with industrialism had worked themselves out by then. This, of course, is overwhelmingly untrue of the engineering industry. Hence the importance of a book relating to the evolution of an engineering centre in recent times, such as G. C. Allen, *The Industrial Development of Birmingham and the Black Country 1860–1927* (1929). After a brief sketch of economic development before 1860 we are given : Birmingham and District in 1860 ; Prosperity and Decline, 1860–1886 ; the New Era,

1887–1914. Birmingham and District contrasts notably with Lancashire. Before 1860 there was 'no rapid transition from small- to large-scale industry and no general introduction of machinery such as occurred in the textile trades.' The old industrialism of iron production and hardware manufacture culminated around 1875 and the region fell upon hard times. But without any advantage of location or raw material it recovered brilliantly by switching to the new industries of which engineering was the core, to cycles, automobiles, modern machine tools and the like. It is a notable example of the power of skilled labour and established business to draw new activities to its neighbourhood ; and of the way in which one new industry gathers around itself a variety of accessories, *e.g.* the motor called for electrical apparatus, woodwork, leatherwork, etc. And in such a region industries grow for which there is no natural advantage other than the existence of labour and a consuming market. One may cite Cadburys at Bournville and the rise of a large sausage-making trade in the heart of the old iron district at Tipton, as examples of this.

In C. XIV, section 5 of the text, the pre-war production of iron and steel is compared with that of the United States. There is a long story behind these figures ; and D. L. Burn has written the first instalment of it in *Economic Journal (Economic History)*, Jan. 1931, *The Genesis of American Engineering Competition 1850–70.*

C. XV.   *The Textile Industries in Transition*

We do well to remember that the Industrial Revolution cannot be written in. terms of the textiles only. Nevertheless, cotton is the great exemplar, because here occurred within sixty years, 1760–1820, fundamental changes not only in the technique and organisation of production, but also and at the same time in the manner of life and economic balance of the family. Of course, 1760 is not the beginning of industrial capitalism, but it is about then that England strides ahead of Western Europe towards the industrialism of the modern world. It would hardly seem possible, after the researches of Unwin, Daniels and general historians, that much crucial new material could, at this time, be brought to light concerning the early growth of this single industry ; yet such is the achievement of A. P. Wadsworth and J. de L. Mann in *The Cotton Trade and Industrial Lancashire 1600–1780* (1931). Lancashire before the Revolution and in the opening stage of it has been re-written from unquestionable sources. For the first time we have solid living portraits of John Kay, Lewis Paul and John Wyatt. Modern research emphasises the changes in manufacturing organisation and business method which accompanied the new machinery ; and in this work we have the letters of Henry Escricke, dealer in cotton and yarn (1738–41) ; extracts from the records of the still active firm of J. and N. Philips and Company for 1753–69 ; and a full portrait of Samuel Touchet, M.P., a great financier and merchant of eighteenth-century Manchester. Most arresting of all is Miss Mann's C. 10, The French Cotton Industry and its Relations with England.

The French Government encouraged invention, and John Holker, of Lancashire, all but had the distinction of launching a textile revolution in eighteenth-century France. A section by Mr. Wadsworth describes the problem of labour and wages, as it should be described, in careful co-ordination with the changing organisation of the industry. However, to a native of Liverpool the most satisfying part is that which relates the commercial expansion of Liverpool with the manufacturing expansion of Manchester. Chapters upon Indian influences on the Cotton Trade, The Export Trade in Cotton Goods, The Organisation of the Overseas and Inland Trade, lead up to the internal transition ; and show the new national production arising within the frame of commercial empire.

But we cannot know more of Lancashire without desiring more of Yorkshire also ; and this we have from W. B. Crump, *The Leeds Woollen Industry 1780–1820*, which is written around the papers of Benjamin Gott, Yorkshire's Samuel Oldknow and the builder in 1792 of Bean Ing factory on the outskirts of Leeds. Here again the revolutionary element is less the individual machine than the central organisation. Many of the processes of 1820 were closer to those of 1770 than to those of 1870, but the organising enterprise is altogether modern. We see the new influence filtering through the Pennines from Arkwright's Lancashire towards Halifax and Huddersfield. We locate the Luddite riots of 1812—Huddersfield the centre of them and Leeds exempt, because Leeds then had neither the gig mill nor shearing frame, the unpopular cloth-finishing machines against which the Yorkshire workers struggled with characteristic stubbornness. Finally, we have plates and explanations of the new machines, and extracts from a record of mill practice ; and we are introduced to the subtle distinction between mill and factory. The mill is an outfit in a building —a fulling mill, a scribbling mill, a gig mill, driven by hand, horse or water ; it is, at first, complementary to the domestic system. But the factory is the new unit of enterprise, embracing mills, workshops, gas-house, warehouse and the rest. The centralising force in the factory is the great engine from Soho, which Gott daringly installed in 1792, to drive the fulling and scribbling plant.

C. XVI.   *The Industrial Revolution in Retrospect*

America, whose economic story is more recent than our own, has for some time appreciated the value of industrial biography. At first it was largely a story of fortune building without the law, but now the gallery is more representative. Recent additions are Cyrus Adler's *Jacob H. Schiff*—the head of the banking firm of Kuhn Loeb (1928) ; S. M. Vauclain, *Steaming Up*—an autobiography by the president of Baldwin Locomotives (1930) ; C. W. Ackerman's *George Eastman*— of Eastman Kodak (1930). These we can match with Count Corti's *Rise of the House of Rothschild* (1928) ; *Viscount Leverhulme*, by his Son (1927) ; J. A. Spender's *Weetman Pearson, first Viscount Cowdray 1856–1927* (1930) ; and Iolo A. Williams, *The Firm of Cadbury 1831–*

1931 (1931).   Mr. Wells in *Work, Wealth, etc.*, by imposing American extravagances on a background that is primarily English, produces a picture of the capitalist entrepreneur that fits into his notion of the robber ' persona,' but is repugnant to historical sense.   Judiciously employed, industrial biography illumines the history of the industry to which it relates—in the examples given, the history of international financing, of soap, of overseas contracting, and of cocoa and chocolate.

At this point we may draw attention to two articles by H. A. Shannon, *Economic Journal* (*Economic History*), 1931 and 1932, on the Coming of General Limited Liability.   Mr. Shannon examines the nature and duration of the first 5000 limited companies and shows decisively that the new era begins not in 1862 but in 1856 with the Joint Stock Companies Act of that year.

PART IV

LIFE AND LABOUR

C. XVII.   *Reactions of Industrialism*

Section 1 of C. XVII (Population and Emigration) was written with Canada chiefly in mind, and here the outstanding feature was the absence of state control.   The other side is now given in F. H. Hitchins' *The Colonial Land and Emigration Commission* (1931).   The Commission operated from 1840 to 1873 and was concerned mainly with the advertisement and organisation of emigration to Australia, which, by reason of its distance from England, its uninhabited vastness and its early use for convict settlement, compelled governmental action even in an age of *laissez-faire*.   W. A. Carrothers, *Emigration from the British Isles* (1929), tells the story as a whole.   It is especially strong on Wakefield's work in Australia, and on the transatlantic flow to the United States and Canada after the Irish famine of 1845.   Both works emphasise the importance of emigration to English shipping.   The early abuses in this traffic compelled government intervention, and the Passengers Act of 1855, the last of a long series (18 & 19 Vict. c. 119), stands out as the Magna Charta of the emigrant.   See also the present writer's *Youth and Power* (1931), C. 6, The Peopling of a New Land. Another critical article by T. H. Marshall is in *Economic Journal* (*Economic History*), 1929, *The Population Problem during the Industrial Revolution*.

For a general view of the reactions of industrialism through a single pair of spectacles it would be hard to find a work more fundamental and more satisfying than Ivy Pinchbeck's *Women Workers and the Industrial Revolution* (1930).   To the woman and to the family the Industrial Revolution in its long course brought changes of a radical order.   If the tearing away of an occupation once so ubiquitous as spinning, and the replacement of the father, the skilled hand-weaver working at home, by daughters working in a power-driven weaving-shop, be not economic revolution, then nothing is. But we are not committed thereby to the view that pre-1760 was paradise. As the pace quickened towards the machine age, woman became increasingly a beast of burden. With hand and foot she had to work harder, and she suffered also by extrusion into employments for which she was unfitted, such as coal-mining and rough labour on the land. When machinery at last came, it brought nearly always a balance of advantage to the family. For the intensification of domestic industry was destroying the home; but when home and work-place were separated, it was possible to recreate the home. Coal-mining has its own peculiar history. In 1842 women's labour was abolished underground. Their employment was not universal, but in certain districts it was of old standing and it became grossly inhuman, as the depth of mines and pace of exploitation increased, as well as unnecessary, since machinery could be used instead. At every turn this study of women warns us against hasty generalisation. If the industrial revolution widened the field of women's employment here, it narrowed it there. In the dairy and in retail trade the women of the eighteenth century often led a more satisfying life than their emancipated sisters of a later day. For each great section of her study, agriculture, the textile trades, the metal trades, mining, millinery, etc., the author gives wage rates in so far as they are available.

There has hardly been time for students to digest the three new volumes of S. and B. Webb, 1500 pages in all, on the Poor Law. *English Poor Law History: Part I, The Old Poor Law; Part II* (2 vols.), *The Last Hundred Years* (1932), completes their thirty years of research into the structure and functions of English local government. Unemployment, the minimum wage, and public health are studied in their relation to poverty; and the story runs through to the present with compelling authority in view of the leading part played by one of the authors on the Royal Commission of 1905–10.

C. XVIII. *Dogma and Revolt*

The best life of Karl Marx in English is now Otto Rühle's *Karl Marx, his Life and Work*, translated by E. and C. Paul (1929). In *Youth and Power* (*op. cit.*), C. 7, 'The Psychology of Social Revolt,' the present writer has drawn on Rühle's book in an attempt to place Karl Marx in relation to his predecessors, the early English Socialists, and his successors the rulers of Soviet Russia.

J. L. and Barbara Hammond in *The Age of the Chartists: A Study of Discontent 1832–54* (1930) do not offer another history of Chartism. Indeed, after the comparatively recent work of Hovell, Beer and Julius West there is little new to say here. They seek rather to throw up the general bleakness of those years; and they show how justifiable was the workers' discontent with the blessings of statistical progress. If we may say so, the book is part payment for the attention bestowed upon their earlier work in the text and footnotes of Dr. Clapham's *Railway Age*.

C. XIX.   *The Organisation of Labour*

The best supplement to the Webbs' general history of Trade Unionism is the study of the aspirations and achievements of organised labour within a particular industry. Such a study will normally embrace the last hundred years ; and we are given exactly what we want in W. H. Warburton's *The History of Trade Union Organisation in the North Staffordshire Potteries* (1931), to which Mr. Tawney contributes a preface. We escape here from the dead level of class rage on which Marx dramatised the relations of masters and men. We see why the Potters' Unions were caught up for a time in the militant Unionism of the 1830's and then fell back into prosaic routine ; why arbitration worked, though only for a time ; the wrong turns taken by Unionism—emigration, co-operative production, failure to organise the women—as well as the final achievement in 1919 of a single National Association, embracing both sexes. Our eye is directed to the self-contained isolation of the Potteries, with their conservatism (*e.g.* the yearly hiring and the custom of payment on the basis of ' good from oven '), with their great variety of product, which was inimical to a standard wage, and with the fierce competition of the master potters among themselves. In the second half of the nineteenth century machinery arrived, but in spurts ; and the potters grudgingly acquiesced. Throughout the workers are very close to their product. In pottery, as in coal, and certain other industries, there was close contact between selling price and wages, especially as selling price fell ; and to break or at any rate modify this contact was the main purpose of Unionism.

C. XX.   *Friendly Societies and the Co-operative Movement*

The *People's Year Book* of the English and Scottish Co-operative Wholesale Societies, and the *Year Book of Agricultural Co-operation*, issued by the Horace Plunkett Foundation, record annually the progress of consumers' co-operation and agricultural co-operation at home and abroad. The C.W.S. bank is England's leading contribution to co-operative credit in recent years ; and it is examined in its place in the general treatise of N. Barou on *Co-operative Banking* (1932).

With this wealth of new literature before us it is important to ask ourselves again the old question, What is the relation of economic history to economic theory ? E. F. Heckscher, *Economic Journal* (*Economic History*), Jan. 1929, *A Plea for Theory in Economic History* ; Werner Sombart, *Economic History Review*, Vol. II, No. 1, *Economic Theory and Economic History* ; and L. Robbins, *Essay on the Nature and Significance of Economic Science*, C. 2 (1932), give different answers. The first would write economic history around the history of prices, the second finds history, as he writes it, to be economic theory, the third is quite clear that it is ' the explanation of the historical manifestations of scarcity.' But economic historians can hardly leave it at that.

THE LITERATURE OF 1928–1932 (JULY)

C. W. Ackerman, *George Eastman.*
W. Marston Acres, *The Bank of England from Within, 1695–1900* (2 vols.).
C. Adler, *Jacob H. Schiff* (2 vols.).
G. C. Allen, *Industrial Development of Birmingham and the Black Country, 1860–1927.*
T. S. Ashton and J. Sykes, *Coal Industry in the Eighteenth Century.*
D. G. Barnes, *History of the British Corn Laws, 1660–1846.*
N. Barou, *Co-operative Banking.*
A. S. J. Baster, *The Imperial Banks.*
James Bonar, *The Tables Turned.*
Cambridge History of the British Empire (Vol. I, *The Old Empire*; Vol. VI, *Canada*).
R. Cantillon, *Essay on the Nature of Trade* (ed. Higgs).
W. A. Carrothers, *Emigration from the British Isles.*
G. Kitson Clark, *Peel and the Conservative Party, 1832–41.*
Chicago, University of, Commemoration Lectures : *Adam Smith, 1776–1926.*
Cobbett's *Rural Rides* (ed. Cole).
W. B. Crump, *Leeds Woollen Industry, 1780–1820.*
A. L. Dunham, *Anglo-French Treaty of Commerce of 1860 and the Progress of the Industrial Revolution in France.*
Economic History Review.
Economic Journal (Economic History).
C. R. Fay, *Youth and Power.*
A. E. Feavearyear, *The Pound Sterling.*
G. S. Graham, *British Policy and Canada 1774–1791.*
J. L. and B. Hammond, *The Age of the Chartists.*
E. L. Hargreaves, *The National Debt.*
F. W. Hirst, *Gladstone as Financier and Economist.*
F. H. Hitchins, *Colonial Land and Emigration Commission.*
Journal of Economic and Business History (Harvard).
J. M. Keynes, *Treatise on Money* (2 vols.).
Viscount Leverhulme, by his Son.
E. Lipson, *Economic History of England, The Age of Mercantilism* (2 vols.).
Macmillan Committee *On Finance and Industry.*
Chester New, *Lord Durham.*
People's Year Book (E. & S. C.W.S.).
I. Pinchbeck, *Women Workers and the Industrial Revolution, 1750–1850.*
A. A. W. Ramsay, *Sir Robert Peel.*
R. D. Richards, *Early History of Banking in England.*
E. Roll, *An Early Experiment in Industrial Organisation, Boulton and Watt, 1775–1805.*
O. Rühle, *Karl Marx.*
Nassau Senior, *Industrial Efficiency and Social Economy,* 2 vols. (ed. S. Leon Levy).
C. E. R. Sherrington, *Economics of Rail Transport in Great Britain* (2 vols.).
J. A. Spender, *Weetman Pearson.*
Tooke and Newmarch, *History of Prices* (ed. Gregory).
S. M. Vauclain, *Steaming Up.*
A. P. Wadsworth and J. de L. Mann, *The Cotton Trade and Industrial Lancashire, 1600–1780.*
W. H. Warburton, *History of Trade Union Organisation in the North Staffordshire Potteries.*
S. and B. Webb, *English Poor Law History* (3 vols.).
H. G. Wells, *The Work, Wealth and Happiness of Mankind.*
Iolo A. Williams, *The Firm of Cadbury, 1831–1931.*
C. Wright and C. E. Fayle, *History of Lloyd's.*
Year Book of Agricultural Co-operation.
(August 1932, J. H. Clapham, *Economic History of Modern Britain, Free Trade and Steel, 1850–1886.*)

SELECTED READING

INTRODUCTION

W. R. Scott, ' Adam Smith, Master Mind Lecture ' (*Proceedings of the British Academy*, vol. xi.) ; J. B. Hollander, ' Adam Smith, 1776–1926 ' (*Journal of Political Economy*, April 1927).

PART I

CHAPTER

I. N. A. Briscoe, *Economic Policy of Robert Walpole* ; E. F. Heckscher, *The Continental System* (Carnegie Endowment).

II. Huskisson's Speeches : ii. 465, *Effects of the Free Trade System on the Silk Manufacture*, Feb. 24, 1826 ; iii. 253, *Civil Government of Canada*, May 2, 1828 ; A. Brady, *William Huskisson and Liberal Reform*.

III. G. M. Trevelyan, *The Life of John Bright* ; Disraeli's *Coningsby*.

IV. Sydney Buxton, *Mr. Gladstone, A Study* (alternatively, *ibid.*, *Finance and Politics*, 2 vols.).

V. L. C. A. Knowles, *The Industrial and Commercial Revolutions in Great Britain during the Nineteenth Century* (Part vi.) ; J. M. Keynes, *The End of Laissez-Faire* ; E. M. H. Lloyd, *Experiments in State Control* (Carnegie Endowment).

VI. R. H. Tawney, Introduction to *Discourse upon Usury* (by Thomas Wilson) ; J. Sykes, *The Amalgamation Movement in English Banking, 1825–1924* ; H. S. Foxwell, ' A History of Barclays Bank ' (review article, *Economic Journal*, Sept. 1927).

PART II

VII. N. S. B. Gras, *Introduction to Economic History* ; H. R. Fox Bourne, *English Merchants* ; L. H. Jenks, *Migration of British Capital, to 1875*.

VIII. D. J. Owen, *The Port of London Yesterday and To-day* ; A. W. Kirkaldy, *British Shipping*.

IX. S. and B. Webb, *English Local Government, The Story of the King's Highway* ; W. T. Jackman, *Transportation in Modern England* (2 vols.).

X. H. G. Lewin, *Early British Railways, 1801–1844* ; E. Cleveland-Stevens, *English Railways, their Development and their Relation to the State.*

XI. Evelyn Murray, *The Post Office* (Whitehall Series) ; Encyclopædia Britannica, *sub* ' Telegraph ' and ' Telephone.'

PART III

XII. R. E. Prothero, *English Farming Past and Present* ; J. L. and B. Hammond, *The Village Labourer.*

XIII. T. H. Marshall, *James Watt* ; J. Lord, *Capital and Steam Power.*

XIV. T. S. Ashton, *Iron and Steel in the Industrial Revolution* ; H. Bessemer, *An Autobiography* (out of print but used fully in A. P. Usher, *The Industrial History of England*, c. 13).

CHAPTER

XV. H. Heaton, *The Yorkshire Woollen and Worsted Industries*; G. W Daniels, *The Early English Cotton Industry*; Dobson and Barlow, Ltd., *Samuel Crompton*.

XVI. H. Hamilton, *The English Brass and Copper Industries*; V. W. Bladen, 'The Potteries in the Industrial Revolution' (*Economic Journal, Econ. Hist.* No. 1, Jan. 1926); Clive Day, *Distribution of Industrial Occupations in England*.

PART IV

XVII. M. D. George, *London Life in the Eighteenth Century*; D. Marshall, *The English Poor in the Eighteenth Century*; A. Redford, *Labour Migration in England, 1800–1850*; M. C. Buer, *Health, Wealth and Population*.

XVIII. F. J. Klingberg, *The Anti-Slavery Movement in England*; G. D. H. Cole, (1) *Robert Owen*, (2) *William Cobbett*; Disraeli's *Sybil*.

XIX. A. V. Dicey, *Law and Public Opinion in England*; S. and B. Webb, *History of Trade Unionism*.

XX. Encyclopædia Britannica, *sub* 'Insurance' and 'Friendly Societies'; S. and B. Webb, *The Consumers' Co-operative Movement*; C. R. Fay, *Co-partnership in Industry*.

For general reference :
(1) Pre-1800 : G. Unwin, *Studies in Economic History*.
(2) Post-1800 : J. H. Clapham, *An Economic History of Modern Britain* (*The Early Railway Age, 1820–1850*).

Students should have ready access to three books :
(1) *Dictionary of National Biography. Epitome.*
(2) *Chronological Table of the Statutes* (By Authority, 1917–18).
(3) *Parliamentary Papers, 1801–1900* (P. S. King. Index).

NEW LITERATURE

G. C. Allen, *Industrial Development of Birmingham and the Black Country, 1860–1927*.

A. E. Feavearyear, *The Pound Sterling*.

I. Pinchbeck, *Women Workers and the Industrial Revolution*.

A. P. Wadsworth and J. de L. Mann, *Cotton Trade and Industrial Lancashire, 1600–1780*.

For general reference :

J. H. Clapham, *An Economic History of Modern Britain* (*Free Trade and Steel, 1850–1886*), espec. c. ix, on Money, Prices, etc.

Economic History of Europe since the Reformation (Oxford, 1937), under the direction of E. Eyre—especially Parts I and II. The chapter on 'British Banking and Finance, 1793–1931,' by R. G. Hawtrey, is of fundamental importance.

BISHOP GROSSETESTE COLLEGE
SIBTHORP LIBRARY
LINCOLN

INDEX